STOP CRUEL

OPPORTUNITY

HOMOPHILE
ACTION LEAGUE
-
PHILADELPHIA

LONG ROAD TO FREEDOM

San Buenaventura
"Friends of the
Library"

LONG ROAD TO FREEDOM

THE ADVOCATE HISTORY OF THE GAY AND LESBIAN MOVEMENT

Edited by
Mark Thompson

Foreword by Randy Shilts

Design by Deborah Daly

ASSISTANT EDITOR
Don Alan Romesburg

CONTRIBUTING EDITOR
Masha Gessen

PHOTO EDITOR
Suzanne K. Benson

RESEARCHER
Jennifer M. Finlay

PRODUCTION ASSISTANT
David Paul Nelson

Stonewall Inn Editions

ST. MARTIN'S PRESS
New York

*Dedicated to the following editors,
writers, and other contributors to* The Advocate
who have died from AIDS.

Steve Abbott, journalist

Dan Allen, correspondent

Crawford Barton, staff photographer

Steve Beery, writer

Stuart Byron, media columnist

Matthew Daniels, news editor

Douglas W. Edwards, Los Angeles editor

Nathan Fain, health columnist

Peter G. Frisch, publisher

Alan Grant, chief financial officer

Richard Hall, book editor

Brent Harris, associate editor

Larry J. Kaufman, advertising manager

Barry Laine, arts writer

Ray Larson, art director

Rafael Llanes, advertising manager

Michael McMahon, advertising manager

Robert I. McQueen, editor-in-chief

Philip Minges III, regional editor

Robert Pruzan, photographer

Darrell Yates Rist, writer

Craig Rowland, journalist

Vito Russo, film critic and writer

Randy Shilts, staff writer

Robert S. Silver, managing editor

Rusty Smith, subscription manager

George Stambolian, book critic

Daniel Tarango, classifieds manager

G. Luther Whitington, senior editor

George Whitmore, journalist

NOTE TO THE READER

The articles from *The Advocate* included in this book have been, for the most part, greatly condensed or reedited. Occasionally, when suitable original material was not available, new text has been written. Similarly, not all of the photographs used in this book were first published in *The Advocate*. Other material has been collected from the following individuals and institutions, which are gratefully acknowledged: Jim Kepner and the International Gay and Lesbian Archives in Los Angeles; Bill Walker and the Gay and Lesbian Historical Society in San Francisco; Robin White and the Walter Blumoff Collection; Rich Wandel and the Bettmann Archive. The editors of this book are also appreciative of the many gay and lesbian photographers who researched their personal archives to locate the images included in this book.

For information about *The Advocate* or to subscribe, write:

The Advocate
6922 Hollywood Blvd., 10th floor
Los Angeles, CA 90028
(213) 871-1225

Toll-Free Subscription Line: (800) 827-0561

Design by Deborah Daly

LONG ROAD TO FREEDOM: THE ADVOCATE HISTORY OF THE GAY AND LESBIAN MOVEMENT. Copyright © 1994 by Liberation Publications, Inc. All rights reserved.Printed in the Unites States of America. No part of this book may be used or reproduced in any manner whatsoever without written permission except in the case of brief quotations embodied in critical articles or reviews. For information, address St. Martin's Press, 175 Fifth Avenue, New York, N.Y. 10010.

Library of Congress Cataloging-in-Publication Data

Long road to freedom: the Advocate history of the gay and lesbian movement / Mark Thompson, editor; foreword by Randy Shilts.
   p. cm.
A collection of articles, photographs, essays, interviews, and cartoons from *The Advocate*.
   ISBN 0-312-09536-8
   1. Gay liberation movement—United States—History. 2. *Advocate* (Los Angeles, Calif.)—History. I. Thompson, Mark.
II. *Advocate* (Los Angeles, Calif.)
HQ76.8.U5L65 1994
306.76'6—dc20   94-1925
                                                        CIP

First Edition: June 1994

10 9 8 7 6 5 4 3 2 1

CONTENTS

LIST OF ILLUSTRATIONS

Images are listed in the order that they appear in the book by description, photographer/artist, and source.

Front Endpaper
Homophile protestors in front of the White House, Washington, D.C. (1965): photographer unknown/International Gay and Lesbian Archives (IGLA)

List of Illustrations
Gay Pride rally, Golden Gate Park, San Francisco (circa 1974): Crawford Barton

Introduction
Advocate tenth-anniversary illustration: Dennis Forbes
Jim Kepner: photographer unknown
Toby Boy cartoon (1973): Toby/*Advocate* archives
David B. Goodstein: Don Bachardy
Robert I. McQueen: Victor Arimondi/Michael Shively Collection
"Touches Your Lifestyle": Crawford Barton
Niles Merton: Wayne Shimabukuro
Richard Rouilard: photographer unknown

1967–68
Black Cat Protest (1967): photographer unknown/IGLA

PRIDE front page (1967): *Advocate* archives
Jerry Joachim, PRIDE president: photographer unknown/*Advocate* archives
Black Cat protest (1967): photographer unknown/Jim Kepner Collection
Sir Lady Java (1967): photographer unknown/*Advocate* archives
Ronald Reagan: publicity still/*Advocate* archives
Lee Glaze: Townsend Studios/Jim Kepner Collection
Dick Michaels: Jack Monroe/IGLA
Danny Combs: Pat Rocco/IGLA
Gay man, Miami (1972): photographer unknown/Jim Kepner Collection
Handcuffs: photographer unknown/ Jim Kepner Collection
The Queen: publicity still/ *Advocate* archives
"Pat Rocco Presents": Pat Rocco/*Advocate* archives
Pat Rocco: publicity still/IGLA
The Killing of Sister George: publicity still/Bettmann Archives

Yukio Mishima: publicity still/ *Advocate* archives

1969
Fairy princess (1972): photographer unknown/IGLA
Barbara Gittings (1973): Bettye Lane
Lesbian bar (1942): publicity still/*Last Call at Maud's*
Troy Perry (1969): photographer unknown/Metropolitan Community Church, Los Angeles
Military cartoon (1969): Buck shot/*Advocate* archives
Gail Whittington in the *Berkeley Barb:* photographer unknown/ *Advocate* archives
Rev. Ray Broshears: George Mendenhall/*Advocate* archives
Pat Brown burning SIR card: photographer unknown/ *Advocate* archives
Ramon Navarro: publicity still/ *Advocate* archives
Paul Ferguson: Kris Studios/ *Advocate* archives
Troy Perry at the Dover (1970): photographer unknown/Jim Kepner Collection

Al Gordon mock-up bathroom entrapment (1974): Walter Blumoff/San Francisco Gay and Lesbian Historical Society (SFGLHS)
Bathhouse raid cartoon (1969): artist unknown/*Advocate* archives
Roger Garrett and Don Johnson (1969): publicity still/*Advocate* archives
Jon Voight in *Midnight Cowboy:* publicity still/*Advocate* archives
Joe Dallesandro in *Flesh:* publicity still/Bettmann Archives
William F. Buckley and Gore Vidal caricatures: artist unknown/*Advocate* archives

1970
Gay Pride Day, New York City (1970): Rich Wandel/ Bettmann Archives
Troy Perry and Carol Shepard at vigil, Los Angeles (1970): photographer unknown/ Jim Kepner Collection
"I am a friend of Troy Perry" button: The John O'Brien Collection/IGLA
Furies collective (1970): Joan E. Biren (JEB)

ACKNOWLEDGMENTS

The editor would like to thank the following individuals for helping to make this book possible. At St. Martin's Press: Michael Denneny, senior editor; Keith Kahla, associate editor; John Clark, assistant editor; Amelie Littell, managing editor; Meg Drislane, associate managing editor; Jolanta Benal, copy editor; Twisne Fan and Karen Gillis, production supervisors; and Doric Wilson, indexer. At *The Advocate:* Sam Watters, publisher; Susan Turpin, senior vice president; John Knoebel, vice president; and Todd Ruston, computer services. At large: Richard Rouilard, for proposing the creation of this book; Robert Dawidoff, for his support in its making; Malcolm Boyd, for always believing it was possible.

FOREWORD

by Randy Shilts

Behind the huge cherrywood desk, Minnie, the obstreperous miniature schnauzer, yapped at no one in particular, while her equally obstreperous owner, publisher David B. Goodstein, barked at an advertising salesman. Down the hall, the marketing manager was conducting his own preview of all-male "art films," while in the next room an associate editor was musing about the cybernetic relationships between the work of William S. Burroughs and Dr. Timothy Leary. It was May 1975, and those were my first moments at the offices of *The Advocate,* even then the nation's largest gay newsmagazine and soon to be my employer.

It was a new era for all things homosexual, and we were passionately engaged in defining and creating what a national gay newsmagazine should be—for there had never been one before *The Advocate. After Dark,* with its endless profiles of handsome, scantily clad ballet dancers, models, and actors, came close, but with nary a mention of the word "homosexual." To a twenty-three-year-old fresh from journalism school in Eugene, Oregon, the prospect of helping to create a new type of publication for our new movement was electrifying. We were writing about issues that had never been discussed before and about events that had never transpired before.

By then, *The Advocate* was eight years old, having grown from a small newsletter in Los Angeles into the most important gay magazine in the early seventies. Vestiges of the old days persisted, however. Gone, but not forgotten, were "Groovy Guy" contests and cartoons featuring a silk-shirted, limp-wristed, and bouffanted gay stereotype called

"Miss Thing." The classified advertising was still entitled "Trader Dick's," however. (The publication's identity was so caught up in its classified ads during my early days at the paper that a major marketing campaign included distribution of the Trader Dick Peter Meter—plastic rulers annotated according to size.)

On the more serious side, as the fledgling lesbian and gay movement burst forth in every corner of America, it was our mission to become the closest thing to a newspaper of record that the early gay movement could have. In retrospect, what we considered great breakthroughs would now be greeted with a yawn. Today we take for granted that we have gay and lesbian members of Congress, judges, and city councilors. In those days, we featured as a great watershed gays being elected to positions in college student governments. In 1976, I counted myself lucky for corraling an interview with a fairly obscure runner-up to a Mr. America bodybuilding title. Today, Martina Navratilova, one of the world's greatest female tennis players, routinely chats about her homosexuality in *Sports Illustrated.* Just getting a source to allow us to use his or her genuine name represented a huge challenge in those early years; today you cannot get sources to *stop* talking about themselves. Times, like *The Advocate* itself, have changed.

My personal tenure at the paper lasted from 1975 until 1978. By 1975, the new publisher, millionaire ex-stockbroker David B. Goodstein, had instituted measures considered radical in the realm of gay newspaper publishing. He insisted that his reporters be paid a decent wage and that no check from his business should ever bounce, demands that gay publishers have a difficult time meeting even today. Rather than enlisting the usual array of frustrated gay activists and female impersonators as writers, he actually hired people who had degrees in journalism. Slowly, the paper's quality improved.

Its timing could not have been more propitious. The late 1970s witnessed a dramatic sweep of events heralding the new gay movement: Anita Bryant pontificated in Florida and brought national headlines to the gay cause for the first time. Harvey Milk was elected in San Francisco. Harvey Milk was murdered in San Francisco. Protests routinely drew crowds of hundreds or thousands. Members of Congress were starting to talk about us in Washington.

The magazine's response to all this varied as *The Advocate* struggled for an identity, torn between being an unbiased news source, a movement cheerleader, or a seat of aggressive (and sometimes strident) advocacy journalism. For all the talk of providing balanced news, publisher Goodstein, for example, was loath to quote anyone against whom he held a personal grudge—a problem given the fact that he cultivated grudges against a good number of the nation's gay and lesbian leaders. In the early 1980s, when a strange new disease was beginning its prowl through major cities, *The Advocate* was not sure what to say about it, and so wrote virtually nothing at all about AIDS until after the subject was picked up by the mainstream press. The journal has also had more recent lapses. In the early 1990s, after repeatedly railing against the practice of outing, one editor launched what still stands as the highest-profile outing in American journalism, exposing a high-ranking Defense Department official as gay.

None of this, however, should obscure the fact that *The Advocate* has been and remains the single most important publication in the history of the American lesbian and gay movement. In fact, no other periodical even comes close. Since late 1992, when the magazine went glossy, it has made quantum leaps in content, quality, and style and provided some of the most earnestly competent journalism relative to the gay movement to be found anywhere.

The pages that follow chronicle the growth of *The Advocate* from its earliest, amateurish efforts to its most recent well-polished pages. The excerpts do not trace the growth of a publication as much as they outline the growth of a new movement in the throes of self-creation. Few other books offer such a sweeping insight into the social dynamics that brought the lesbian and gay movement to the place it is in today. In its quarter-century struggle to define itself, *The Advocate* has had a key role in defining our cause and our community.

Gay movement luminaries, friends, and foes (circa 1977) as assembled from the pages of *The Advocate* by artist Dennis Forbes on the occasion of the publication's tenth anniversary: (*top third, left to right*) Calvin Culver, Johnny Mathis, Elton John, Divine, Charles Pierce, Gore Vidal, William S. Burroughs, Rex Reed, Armistead Maupin, Morris Kight, a former Mr. America, Anita Bryant, S.I. Hayakawa, John Briggs, Ed Davis, Tom Waddell, Willie Brown; (*middle third, left to right*) Bette Midler, Mae West, Christopher Isherwood, David Hockney, Don Bachardy, Paul Cadmus, Rod McKuen, Patricia Nell Warren, Cycle Slut, Alan Spear, Elaine Noble, David Kopay, Leonard Matlovich, Jack Campbell, Betty Berzon, Jean O'Leary; (*bottom third, left to right*) Ray Broshears, Malcolm Boyd, Troy Perry, *Advocate* staff member, Bill Rand, Rob Cole, Robert I. McQueen, David B. Goodstein, John Preston, Sasha Gregory-Lewis, Dick Michaels, Bruce Voeller, Bella Abzug, Franklin Kameny.

INTRODUCTION

by Mark Thompson

Few publications in American life have had a more intimate relationship with their readers than *The Advocate*. From its modest, homespun beginnings twenty-six years ago to its preeminence today as the largest gay and lesbian newsmagazine in the world, *The Advocate* has recorded the story of a remarkable community-in-the-making with proximity, verve, and a dedication not often found in the nation's press.

The swift growth of the gay and lesbian movement in the latter half of the twentieth century can arguably be counted as among the most significant social events of our time. Yet few outside the movement's ranks have contributed impartial witness to the emergence of this new, previously unrecognized class of people. Our rise to visibility, then to community, and, finally, to a full-fledged identity has remained to most of society a frightening, incomprehensible development of postmodern life, just one more rift in an increasingly anxious age. *The Advocate* has done its best to stand on both sides of this great divide; fueling the birth of a shame-free consciousness for the homosexual minority by offering principled reportage and positive imagery, while at the same time justifying the love that dare not speak its name to a prejudiced majority, which the novelist Christopher Isherwood sharply referred to as "the heterosexual dictatorship."

Like any intimate union, the relationship between *The Advocate* and its readers is richly complex. The publication initially came into existence to bolster confidence and instill pride where before there had been precious little. In short

order, as this overview of *The Advocate*'s evolution will show, it grew from being primarily a catalyst for social change to a critical voice within its own community. The pitch could range from sage to shrill, and later, some claimed, to curmudgeonly and somber, out of touch and asleep even to the sound of its own noise.

But over the years the publication has displayed a rare capacity for self-reinvention, much like the people it serves. It has been almost a case where the news—the facts of the day, the truth to be told—was simply *too* much, too much for *The Advocate* not to go a tad somnambulistic from time to time. From a period when homosexuals were regarded as second-class citizens, if regarded humanistically at all, to countless brutal assaults and numbing assassinations, to the mounting horrors of the plague, *The Advocate* has had to make sense of the senseless, take stock of outrageous injustices unfamiliar to the mainstream.

At its most awake, the tiny newsletter now grown to sleek newsmagazine stands as a hopeful beacon, holistic in its concern for a people previously broken, adamant in its conviction that the pieces stay mended together. "*The Advocate* was for many of us the first exposure we'd had to the idea that what we are is not bad," says one longtime reader, speaking for many. "It was a light in the dark by which we could navigate."

Not surprisingly, the publication itself germinated and took root in the darkness that so much of gay life inhabited a quarter of a century ago. The first issue, dated September 1967, was clandestinely printed in the basement of ABC

Television's Los Angeles headquarters by gay men working there. Five hundred copies of the crudely composed twelve-page paper were quietly passed out for twenty-five cents each, mainly from behind the counters of the city's gay bars. In retrospect, from a basement duplicating machine to a half-lit bar was not an inappropriate route for the paper; in 1967, most of gay life, if it was lived at all, was carried out underground, hidden and disguised by any means available.

Unrest and Uprising

Before *The Advocate* came secretly rolling out of the Silver Lake mailroom of one of America's largest media conglomerates, it had existed in an even more humble form as the newsletter of PRIDE, a local homophile organization whose acronym stood for Personal Rights in Defense and Education. The group was started in May 1966 by Steve Ginsberg, a local activist, and others concerned over mounting police harassment of Los Angeles homosexuals. As in most urban centers, fear and loathing ruled the day; anxiety over the capricious nature of law enforcement agencies when it came to homosexuality—bar raids, illegal entrapment, and a widespread application of "lewd conduct" laws made just about anybody open for arrest at any time—was further

Gay activist and historian Jim Kepner.

entrenched by the low self-esteem and apathy most gays then felt. PRIDE dealt with the problem outright, holding regular meetings and social events for its members and guests as well as staging public demonstrations protesting oppressive police tactics.

Jim Kepner, a writer who had been active in gay and progessive circles on the West Coast since coming out in San Francisco in 1942, remembers Ginsberg's reasoning for creating the militant group. "He said we needed to start an organization that would instill pride and draw in the bar crowd—the leather and lace crowds," Kepner recalls. "It was the leathermen and queens who were getting hit by police, so they had a natural inclination for militancy." While PRIDE was not the first group for homosexuals to be formed in Southern California, its birth came during a period when local activism was at a particular lull.

The nation's first ongoing gay political organization, the Mattachine Society, had in fact been started in Los Angeles

over fifteen years before—in December 1950. The society's founder, Harry Hay, built the small discussion group gradually, but theoretical differences within the expanding organization resulted in its fracture by spring of 1953. By then, however, other branches of the society had begun to put down strong roots in a number of other American cities, inspiring the first wave of the gay (then known as "homophile") rights movement in the United States.

Kepner was a regular at Los Angeles Mattachine meetings, where up to one hundred people would attend. The discussion often revolved around "the queens and the bulldykes who, many felt, were giving the rest of us a bad name," he says. During one especially rancorous meeting Kepner lost his patience with this conservative line of thought and lectured the group, arguing: "They are the ones that make a gay life for us—establish places to go and a sense of community."

In early 1953, as tensions within Mattachine grew to a boiling point, local activist Dorr Legg appeared on the scene with *ONE,* the nation's first publicly sold, avowedly gay publication. The magazine established a foothold, taking downtown offices in Los Angeles's historic Goodwill building, and invited Kepner aboard as a volunteer. His debut article, "The Importance of Being Different," was published in the March 1956 issue of *ONE,* and soon Kepner was contributing reams of material to the handsomely produced journal, his work appearing under several different bylines. *ONE* and its parent organization, ONE, Inc., expanded throughout the decade, the magazine becoming one of the most eloquent and widely heard voices for the burgeoning homophile cause before its demise in 1968.

As influential as the Mattachine Society and *ONE* had been, by the late sixties both institutions had lost steam; dwindling membership and readers clearly left space for a new kind of organization and publication. The time was also ripe for a whole new style of dealing with the problems homosexuals in society had long faced; the polite, assimilationist approach taken by the homophile generation seemed out of sync with the confrontational, rapidly evolving mores brought on by the radical politics and sexual revolution of the sixties. If the stage was set, it was the particularly brutal

Los Angeles Police Department raid on the Black Cat bar in the first hour of 1967 that put the players in motion. Police swept into the Black Cat shortly into the New Year, severely beating an employee and arresting others there and at another nearby Silver Lake gay bar. A few weeks later, PRIDE organized its largest public protest ever in response to the attack, two and a half years before another police raid on the Stonewall Inn in New York City would similarly ignite gay men and lesbians on the East Coast.

The Los Angeles gay community was galvanized, and PRIDE swelled with new members. Among the recruits was Dick Michaels, a professional writer who had attended several meetings and PRIDE-sponsored dances the previous fall with his lover, Bill Rand, but who had nevertheless kept a reserved distance. The Black Cat raid and subsequent demonstration changed all that. The group needed every volunteer it could attract, and Michaels seized upon the task of revitalizing the group's struggling newsletter. "It soon became apparent that the gay community needed something more," he would later comment. "It needed something that had a chance to grow into a real newspaper; it needed a publication with widespread circulation, some way to get the word out about what was happening."

The almost nonexistent coverage of gay news by the *Los Angeles Times* and the blatant homophobia of the *Hollywood Citizen-News* made the need for a regular gay newspaper all the more urgent. Michaels spent the summer of 1967 mulling over his idea for expanding the PRIDE newsletter, enlisting the help of Rand and their friend Sam Winston, a talented artist and cartoonist with an offbeat sense of humor who chaired PRIDE's publications committee. "We formulated a crude plan, which depended more on guts than sense," recalled Michaels, yet the trio persisted. They settled on a name, the *Los Angeles Advocate,* and decided to fill the new publication with as many features of a regular newspaper as they could: news, editorials, cartoons, letters, reviews, and classified ads. Their only investment was a used IBM

This playful character by the artist Toby was *The Advocate*'s unofficial mascot during its early years.

typewriter bought for $175, which they used to laboriously type out each column with justified margins. Headlines were rubbed down one letter at a time from sheets of transfer type. The whole thing was composed at Michaels and Rand's small Wilshire district apartment and then reproduced in the mailroom where Rand and another PRIDE member worked.

By Michaels's own admission, the contents of the first issue were "hardly breathtaking." The incendiary front-page banner, U.S. CAPITAL TURNS ON TO GAY POWER, was actually the heading for a rather plodding piece about the Third National Planning Conference of Homophile Organizations (NACHO) held in Washington, D.C. Elsewhere in the eight-and-a-half-by-eleven sheet was a notice about *ONE*'s fifteenth anniversary, an editorial promising not "to be dull," news about the Black Cat court case, travel tips, and a review of *Queer Path* ("To say that this book emphasizes the darker, sadder side of homosexual life is putting it mildly"). Still, a claim had been staked.

The paper grew rapidly in content during the following months even though PRIDE disintegrated, a victim of internal squabbling and piled-up legal bills. Undaunted, *The Advocate*'s founding trio bought the rights to the publication from the organization for one dollar and kept meeting their deadlines. By July 1968 the newspaper had a telephone and its first paid employee; the next month saw a completely typeset issue. On the first anniversary of its creation, fifty-five hundred copies of a professionally printed thirty-two-page *Advocate* were circulated throughout California's southland.

The local gay community seemed ready to embrace its new mouthpiece. In October, the Rev. Troy Perry placed a paid ad announcing the formation of the Metropolitan Community Church. Gay bars, restaurants, and other area businesses decided it was also time to take the wraps off gay life and be publicly affirmative. The paper was now tabloid size and sold openly in coin machines around the city. By

June of 1969, the month the Stonewall Riots took place, the newspaper had acquired a national distributor and dropped the words "Los Angeles" from its name.

The Advocate had moved from a cramped apartment to a second-story suite of offices over a bar on Western Avenue. In due time, it would expand again to a roomy bungalow nearby. One thing that didn't seem to change was the long hours involved. Although Michaels and Rand were able to quit their well-paying jobs to work full-time on the newspaper by the summer of its second year, the workload did not ease. "We invented the eighty-four-hour work week," Michaels lamented. Kepner, who by then had joined the fledgling staff as an all-round reporter, remembers not only the grueling pace but the responsibility of seriously covering such a far-ranging field. "We were very concerned about staying in touch and giving representation to the various factions of the community," he says. "We knew the gay community was diverse, but we had no idea *how* diverse. We were also militant, which scared a lot of people."

There were other problems to attend to beside deadlines, payrolls, advertisers' demands, and the host of dilemmas any struggling publication must face—there was the matter of editorial control. Under Michaels's firm hand, there was little allowance for journalistic leeway. The paper was filled with news—all the minutiae one could possibly want to read about a movement then taking hold of a new generation of activists across the nation. Gay Liberation Fronts were springing up in city after city like exotic blooms after a rare desert rain. A new leadership was taking charge, too, spouting radical slogans of militancy that made older activists pale. Still, the journalism in *The Advocate* was seldom colorful, interpretive, or wide in scope. "He was strait-laced and not inclined toward the 'new journalism' of the underground press," says Kepner. "Michaels often rewrote things and argued with staff members who wanted a more free style."

The paper's regular editorial pages were filled with opinion, but often it seemed a case of one voice trying to out-shout the other. Women's issues and the progress of other burgeoning liberation movements were given scant coverage. *The Advocate* was an important achievement—all the more so considering how far it had gone in such a short time—but it seemed insular, oddly cut off from the rest of the world. Given society's horrendous attitudes about homosexuality and the mainstream media's virtual blackout of gay concerns, Michaels's tact is understandable. Still, *The Advocate*'s first editor-in-chief covered his one neighborhood to the exclusion of others. But soon, all of that was to change.

Great Expectations

By 1974, *The Advocate* had grown in stature and size to the point where it could justify its claim of being the "newspaper of America's homophile community." Even though the bulk of its coverage and readers were still based in Southern California, the periodical's print run had steadily increased to forty thousand copies per issue, and its pages included news accounts and columnists from other large cities, where *The Advocate* was available for purchase at select locations.

The movement's ambitions had grown dramatically as well; the social and political agenda set forth by gay and lesbian leaders, while not always precisely delineated, was at least well vocalized. The American Psychiatric Association's classification of homosexuality as a mental disorder had just come crashing down, thanks to the persistent efforts of activists, and municipal gay-rights ordinances were being proposed and state sodomy laws were being challenged nationwide. Job discrimination in government and private sectors, child custody, and legal reform were all on the front lines. Most important, men and women in previously unimagined numbers were coming out in small towns and big cities everywhere.

Among the swelling tide of immigrants to gay liberation was David B. Goodstein, a millionaire investment banker from New York who had moved to San Francisco in the early seventies at the behest of his firm. Goodstein had barely arrived, however, when he learned that the bank was letting him go because it had discovered he was homosexual. Rather than sue for damages, Goodstein decided to stay in the Bay Area and become involved in gay liberation. He explored the current terrain and decided that what the movement needed was a well-financed, professional organization. Reaching into his own pocket for ten thousand dollars, Goodstein founded the Whitman-Radclyffe Foundation in 1972 and installed activist Jim Foster as executive secretary. Goodstein's motives were immediately suspected by some of the movement's more radical elements, however, and were put to the test when radicals tried and failed to take control of the fledgling foundation. But Goodstein stubbornly persisted on his own track, raising additional large sums of money for Whitman-Radclyffe projects that over the next few years ranged from a halfway house for gay convicts to a massive public information and education campaign.

Goodstein had learned firsthand the complicated dynamics of the nascent liberation movement, but rather than be discouraged by "the bickering, infighting, pettiness, and unrivaled stupidity and incompetence" he railed against, the well-off newcomer to gay politics decided to forge on. He wanted a publication he could call his own, a bully pulpit from which he could advance his views uncontested. He explored the possibility of purchasing *After*

Dark, a slick if somewhat superficial New York entertainment magazine with a predominately gay appeal, but the idea never worked out. It was at the urging of a recent acquaintance, artist-editor Dennis Forbes, that Goodstein turned an eye toward *The Advocate.* The two men had met and become friends when Goodstein contributed an article to *Vector* magazine, the monthly organ of the Society of Individual Rights (SIR), a gay advocacy organization begun in San Francisco in the mid-sixties at which Forbes volunteered his services as a part-time art director.

Like Goodstein and countless others, Forbes had migrated to the tolerant city in the early seventies looking for a more permissive lifestyle than the one he could find at home, which in his case was Des Moines, Iowa. Nothing seemed to spring from his suggestion, though, until one day early in December 1974 when Forbes received a call. It was Goodstein, who excitedly announced that he had just purchased *The Advocate* with the intention of turning it into a truly national biweekly gay newsmagazine. He offered Forbes any job he wanted on the soon-to-be reconfigured staff except for the position of editor, which he had filled with John Preston, a young journalist based in New York.

As Goodstein not only wanted the content of the new *Advocate* to read "more professionally" but its layout to be upgraded as well, Forbes signed aboard as the publication's designer. At the beginning of the new year, Forbes, Preston, and Goodstein's business manager traveled to Los Angeles, where they spent a month as "flies on the wall," says Forbes, observing the staff at work. Their presence was met with coolness and clear disapproval, as the old regime of reporters and editors nervously wondered what the outsiders had in mind. They had little time to ponder, however, since in short order the newly hired trio set about remaking *The Advocate* to Goodstein's mandate.

THIS ISSUE BEGINS NEW ERA FOR GAY PEOPLE, the cover banner on the January 29, 1975, edition grandiosely proclaimed beneath a full-page photograph of openly gay actor

Controversial gay businessman David B. Goodstein was publisher-owner of *The Advocate* from 1975 to 1985.

Cal Culver. Gone was the jumbled newspaper format with its endless columns of dull type; readers now held a graphically sophisticated tabloid-style magazine on newsprint. Gone, too, were many of the bylines and features of the old *Advocate.* Local gay activists were furious. Goodstein was sweeping *The Advocate* clean not only of previous journalistic ways, but of a whole school of Los Angeles activists who had once had unlimited access to the publication's pages.

"He wanted to work from within the power structure and work for change inside, rather than storming the barricades," explains Forbes about Goodstein's motives. "He saw *The Advocate* as the only serious voice in the gay movement, and as a result of that attitude there was a lot of negative reaction from people who were closed out." The new publisher had other changes in mind, too. To further shift emphasis from Southern California, he moved the paper's offices to a suburban office complex in San Mateo, about twenty-five miles south of San Francisco. Most of the old staff was let go or chose not to make the trek north. Those few contributors who did decide to weather the upheaval, like Jim Kepner, who remained in Southern California filing news reports for another year, found they frequently clashed with the policies of the opinionated new owner.

Goodstein was determined to make his $350,000 investment pay off, and he set out to make over not just *The Advocate* but the face of the gay movement as well. A. J. Liebling's acerbic line "The freedom of the press belongs to him who owns one" had never been truer. Some movement spokespeople, especially adversaries of the powerful businessman, now simply ceased to exist in print, consigned to a gulag of unmentionable names. New personalities and voices were actively promoted and recruited. I was part of this fresh infusion, invited to contribute to the recast newsmagazine by Goodstein himself.

Lesson of a Lifetime

We had made contact some months before, when I

asked Goodstein to write an article about gays and the political process for a gay student newspaper I was putting together at San Francisco State University. I had also asked camera-store owner and political hopeful Harvey Milk to contribute similar remarks, knowing the two men's ideologies would be different, but not having a clue that their clashing views would ignite a long-festering feud. I was doing what I thought every good editor was supposed to do: stir controversy and, maybe, raise a little hell.

Gay and lesbian students on campus, where I was enrolled in the journalism department, had been doing exactly that during the previous two years. We formed a Bay Area–wide coalition, which included young scholars from as far away as Berkeley and Stanford, and pursued an active schedule of meetings, public presentations, and on-campus socials. Like Michaels, I had been an editor of my high school and college papers, and so it seemed natural to propose creating a journal of our own, appropriately titled *The Voice*. I made sure the tabloid-sized paper was professionally typeset and printed, with a polish unusual for student productions. It must have caught Goodstein's eye. In April 1975, just as I was putting finishing touches on the third and final edition of *The Voice* and preparing to celebrate graduation with a summer trip to Europe, Goodstein wrote, summoning me to his office.

I had been aware of *The Advocate*, occasionally plunking quarters into one of its coin machines on Polk Street, but the paper felt oddly remote to my interests as a young person just coming out. The gay world it reflected seemed, at best, narrowly circumscribed and ingrown, and at its worst, predatory and hardscrabble. Nothing of the intrigue and enmity then circulating around its new owner was known by me the afternoon I stepped into Goodstein's plush San Mateo quarters, done up with bright paisley fabrics and expensive artwork on the walls, including Paul Cadmus's impressive allegorical canvas *A Study for David and Goliath*. The publisher wanted to know if I'd like to write for *The Advocate*, and, aware of my upcoming tour, proposed that I

Editor Robert I. McQueen brought a sophisticated sensibility to the publication's pages during the late seventies and early eighties.

interview artist David Hockney in Paris. I allowed that community-oriented journalism was exactly my interest, having been fascinated while growing up with stories of my grandfather's work on a small regional paper in Nebraska, but then I had to admit that I had never heard of Hockney. Goodstein sputtered in shocked disbelief, but I received the assignment nevertheless.

I spent an afternoon with the artist in his Left Bank studio and then moved on to Amsterdam, where I researched more pieces about gay people and places of interest. What concerned me most, however, was a phone call I was waiting to receive—a call that would forever alter my outlook on being gay. Before leaving for Europe, John Preston had taken me aside and shown me a file of clippings the paper was collecting about the growing gay movements in other countries. Among the accounts was an item about Spain's gay uprising and how it had been brutally suppressed under Franco's totalitarian authority. There were even rumors circulating about special prisons and work camps for gays. Preston wanted me to go to Spain and see what I could find.

On my third day in Amsterdam, the anticipated call came through. "Come at once," the voice on the raspy line said. I was given a time and a place to meet— a park bench on Las Ramblas in Barcelona—and then the caller hung up. I left immediately that night, camping on the floor of a crowded train until I arrived in the Catalonian capital two days later. I found the park bench and waited. Several hours passed before my informant made his presence known; he was a distinguished-looking professor from the local university, one of the few members of MELH (Spanish Movement for Gay Liberation) who had not been arrested or forced completely into hiding. Only six members of the once-thriving group remained active, and even they were fearful of arrest.

I spent the next twenty-four hours with the resilient half dozen men and women of MELH, their struggle and courage in the grip of fascism a lesson indelibly impressed upon my consciousness. When I returned to the United

States that fall and filed my stories, I felt certain as never before that *The Advocate* and the just cause it represented would be forever worthy of my attention. I joined the staff in early 1976, dividing my time between assisting Forbes and writing feature articles, and soon discovered others who came to their work with similar dedication, if for various reasons.

By then, Preston had left the publication and in his place was Robert I. McQueen, a darkly handsome and discerning man who had previously worked with the *Salt Lake Tribune* and the University of Utah. Key to McQueen's spirit of activism was his thorny relationship with the Mormon Church, which regarded his prominent role as the new editor of *The Advocate* with considerable dismay. Try as they might, they could not convince McQueen to return to the fold, so church elders, armed with an impressive document, showed up at *Advocate* headquarters one day and excommunicated their wayward son on the spot. McQueen was not afraid to write about his troubles with the Mormons, nor to publish articles about the struggles of other gay men and lesbians with organized religion. In fact, he was fearless about most matters of importance to his readers, and ushered in a new era of incisive journalism and lively coverage on a wide range of topics.

McQueen was a composer and poet during his off-hours, and so put a high emphasis on cultural reporting. Articles on opera appeared as frequently as pieces on disco, and believing above all else that reading mattered, he devoted numerous pages to the coverage of authors and their books. Famous names from all areas of the arts consented to be interviewed: Gore Vidal and Christopher Isherwood (in the first of their many *Advocate* profiles), Bette Midler and Lily Tomlin (both interviewed by Vito Russo near the beginning of their—and his—enterprising careers), and a surprising parade of others, from Beverly Sills to Timothy Leary. Political analysis and news writing were also greatly improved; Randy Shilts began a series of groundbreaking pieces about health problems then troubling the gay community, and Sasha Gregory-Lewis expanded coverage of women's issues and zealously delved into investigating the New Right's homophobic agenda.

The mainstream media began to take notice at last. HOMOSEXUAL PERIODICALS ARE PROLIFERATING, *The New York Times* announced in an August 1978 piece about *The Advocate* and other gay magazines such as *Christopher Street* and *Blueboy*. Articles in the *Chicago Tribune, The Wall Street Journal, Los Angeles Times, Time,* and *Newsweek* similarly reported on the expanding gay press, usually concentrating on the high-profile *Advocate,* and more often than not dwelling on readers' mobile lifestyles and expendable incomes rather than on their struggle for civil rights.

The mass coming-out and sudden ascendancy of the gay Boomers—the post-Stonewall generation who had come of age in the late sixties and early seventies—had infused fresh vitality into the movement, but not, it seemed, to *The Advocate*'s subscription list. Many former readers had dropped away with Goodstein's dramatic retooling, and it was argued that young urban readers had less need of a strictly gay publication than might have been foreseen. "I must honestly say that none of my friends read it," says Forbes, who retired from his post in June 1976 with the sense that his duty had been done. "It was an odd situation. Even many of the people who worked on the magazine would probably not have participated in gay activism otherwise. It was a professional job for them, and that was it. They seemed curiously distant from what they were writing about."

The main strength of the magazine seemed to be in those areas of the United States where gays were isolated and felt inhibited, due to employment or family ties, from living fully open lives. Advertising was problematic as well, with very few national accounts, aside from an occasional liquor or record company willing to take the plunge. Many used the excuse of *The Advocate*'s sexually explicit pull-out classifieds section (dubbed the "Pink Pages" after the color of the paper it was printed on) to keep from committing their advertising dollars. But Goodstein, like McQueen, remained adamantly sex-positive, and refused to let thinly veiled prejudice sway his conviction that the classifieds—many gay men's only sexual outlet—not be sacrificed for ready cash.

In truth, it was Goodstein's deep pockets that kept the publication going through the next several years, a period of rising backlash fueled by the antigay campaigns of Anita Bryant and John Briggs and the assassination of Harvey Milk, who had finally achieved public office as a San Francisco city supervisor. With McQueen's astute hand on editorial content, Goodstein continued slowly to build the publication; a new generation of readers eventually replaced the old, and improvements such as better paper stock and four-color covers were incrementally added. Fresh talent, like associate editor Brent Harris and art director Ray Larson (who had been friends of McQueen from his Salt Lake City days), were also brought on staff, adding their keen abilities to producing an ambitious publication with limited resources every two weeks.

Pat Califia was another addition to the staff during this time, contributing insightful essays about the nation's rising tide of "new puritanism" and stemming the flood the best she could with her widely read "Advisor" column in which readers' intimate queries about sex and relationship were candidly answered. Califia is one of the many writers and editors over the years for whom *The Advocate* has served as a springboard to a larger career.

The Advocate Experience

As dedicated as he was to making *The Advocate* a success, Goodstein began to tire of his acquisition before long, and turned his sights on other areas of gay life he thought needed reform. Being a Jew and overweight, Goodstein was always sharply reminded of the rejection brought on by not fitting into standard categories. And being homosexual no doubt fostered an even greater sensitivity to the pain nonconforming individuals often experience in society. Whatever personal discomfort Goodstein felt on account of these three conditions, he sought to transform angst into awareness about the rich potential present in every human life.

He sought out the help of Rob Eichberg, a psychologist with a long history of grassroots activism. Eichberg, who had been committed to counseling people of color since coming out in 1970, discovered that many of the same psychological issues applied to gays as to other oppressed groups. He started a consciousness-raising group for gay men in Los Angeles, out of which sprang the idea for a political action committee. "We needed a project and decided to change the face of gay rights in Los Angeles by passing a municipal gay-rights resolution," remembers Eichberg. David Mixner, a political consultant then handling Tom Bradley's mayoral campaign, and businessman Tom Scott were among those recruited in the formation of the Municipal Elections Committee of Los Angeles (MECLA), which by 1976 was holding hundred-dollar black-tie dinners and other upscale fund-raising events. "We raised more money in a shorter time than any other gay group," explains Eichberg, and by the following year MECLA was able to effectively lobby the City Council into passing a gay-rights resolution.

MECLA's dramatic coup was Goodstein's kind of success, so he invited Eichberg to come north and inspire gay men in the Bay Area to similar achievement. The psychologist created a training seminar to which sixteen prominent community leaders, including McQueen, Foster, and attorney Jerry Berg, were invited. The weekend conference, held in a retreat center near Monterey, was well received, and Goodstein immediately asked Eichberg to consider taking

The newsmagazine's mid-seventies slogan, "Touching Your Lifestyle," was emblazoned on its cover, billboards, and even T-shirts.

the workshop "on the road." He proposed forming an organization—to be known as "The Advocate Experience"—which would help gay people overcome low self-esteem, addictive behavior, and other problems brought about by society's intolerance.

Backed with Goodstein's money and Eichberg's know-how, The Advocate Experience was launched one cold evening in March 1978 at the Jack Tarr Hotel in San Francisco. Among the local gay luminaries invited to attend were writers Armistead Maupin and Randy Shilts, who had recently left *The Advocate* to pursue his journalism career elsewhere. Antagonistic rumors about the pilot event being of an est-like bent had been circulating around town for weeks, and suspicions were not allayed when Goodstein regally commandeered the assembled movers and shakers. At one point, the entire evening ground to a halt when participants were asked to rate one another according to looks. "David was often very controlling, and that triggered off people's resistance to authority," Eichberg observes. But changes were made by the time the first paid workshop was put to the test in May, and soon the consciousness-raising Experience was attracting hundreds of gay men and lesbians and their families and friends to weekend retreats around the country.

"We were doing pioneering work, dealing with fundamental issues about shame and coming out, and helping people to integrate their sexuality into the rest of their lives," says Eichberg. But as more often than not in his life, Goodstein was misunderstood. "People reacted to his being aggressive and were put off by that, rather than acknowledging his passion and commitment. He was a fighter—fighting for his own self-respect and dignity as well as for our community's," concludes his former partner.

Among the Experience graduates to attract Goodstein's notice was marketing consultant Peter G. Frisch. Eager to spend more time expanding his new interest, Goodstein appointed Frisch to act as publisher of *The Advocate* in his stead during the next five years. Frisch immediately got to work and, with the clear-eyed zeal that seemed to characterize many an Experience alumni, hired a trained sales staff and aggressively pursued advertising from the burgeoning gay businesses and mainstream firms alike. The first national advertisers in *The Advocate,* such as Absolut Vodka and a handful of others, wondered whether they might experience a backlash from nongay consumers. But Frisch considered each new national account a victory for the magazine and its readers.

Other graduates of The Advocate Experience went on to establish some of the gay community's leading organizations—the Human Rights Campaign Fund, the Stop AIDS Project, the Public Awareness Project, and National Coming Out Day, among others—a record Eichberg proudly lists. Still, The Advocate Experience continued to be met with objection in certain quarters, especially from many staff members of its namesake publication. Goodstein had insisted that *The Advocate* publish a regular column promoting Experience activities; this amounted to an infringement of the journalistic boundary between press and capital, an inviolable divide.

Taking potshots at Goodstein, and by extension *The Advocate,* had by the early eighties become a favorite sport of wags and critics within the community. The magazine seemed like a slow-moving target, the old "gray lady" of gay media, which by then had exploded into dozens of local publications; some large cities even had more than one gay newspaper, and the National Gay Press Association could count hundreds of attendees at its annual conventions. Upstart papers like the *New York Native* seemed feisty and daring when compared to *The Advocate*'s more cautious and reserved tone, especially when it came to reporting news about the spread of a mysterious new disease called GRID. But if *Advocate* editors did not exactly leap on every new theory-of-the-week, neither did they shirk their considerable job of providing a comprehensive national picture on what was shaping gay and lesbian lives—for better or worse. And all on a budget that would make others in the profession blush.

Maintaining a balance between editorial objectivity and impassioned advocacy has not always been an easy task for the nation's gay journal of record. That the publication has appeared less than sure of itself over the years is evident; its reach exceeded its grasp at times, and it seems unfocused on

Niles Merton served as *Advocate* publisher from 1985 through 1992.

certain issues. Perhaps it is enough to say that *The Advocate* has always been there; a fresh edition without fail every two weeks. Certainly, that is accomplishment enough during a time when every survival is worthy of note. But, of course, there are reasons beyond longevity alone to commemorate the ground-breaking trail—however vertiginous—*The Advocate* has blazed through our lives.

Transitions

By spring of 1984, Goodstein had grown demonstrably weary of the internecine climate of the Bay Area's tightly knit gay world. He decided to consolidate his financial resources in Southern California, packed up *The Advocate* and those staff members willing to make the change, and reestablished the newsmagazine in cramped offices in downtown Hollywood. Goodstein wanted to once again turn his attentions elsewhere and began casting about for a capable successor. A bright, recently elected director on the board of the National Gay Task Force caught the publisher's attention and was duly invited to his palatial home, situated high atop a Malibu ridge overlooking the Pacific Ocean.

"I was twenty-eight years old, very self assured, and quite arrogant," recalls Niles Merton. "Goodstein, I decided, was not going to intimidate me." Undaunted, Merton met "the most influential man in the gay community," spending an afternoon with Goodstein and his lover, David Russell. At the conclusion of the day, Goodstein abruptly announced that Merton should assume *The Advocate*'s helm. "I was amazed," says Merton. "*The Advocate* was the pinnacle of gay power. I accepted the offer on the spot."

Merton got busy at once, acquiring larger quarters in Hollywood—the entire tenth floor of a well-known office building there—and began expanding the business into mail order and video production. In addition, the publication, now circulating 65,000 copies per issue, was shrunk to standard newsmagazine size and given a glossy cover. Merton's activities were brought to a temporary halt, however, when Goodstein was stricken with bowel cancer. He died on June 22, 1985, leaving the publication's future seemingly secure. It was the legacy of a contentious but deeply caring man, a man who, it would be observed, never found the liberation he sought for others.

Death had by then become a frequent enough visitor in and around the corridors of *The Advocate* that Goodstein's unexpected passing registered less of a shock than it ordinarily might have. The gay community was being decimated by AIDS, the anguish of grief and loss a palpable current in the air. McQueen, tired after ten years of leadership and feeling the onslaught of HIV disease himself, stepped slightly to one side and filled his vacated post with Lenny Giteck. The former *Advocate* correspondent carried out his new duties with a steady, if somewhat stolid hand, and brought a carefully calibrated pitch to the publication during a time when speculative, reactionary journalism was more the norm in the gay press. When Giteck's tenure came to an end in the fall of 1987, Stuart Kellogg, who had worked as *The Advocate*'s managing editor in San Mateo and more recently as the editor of its erotic companion publication, *Advocate Men*, stepped in.

With Goodstein no longer in control, "*The Advocate* ceased to be primarily a civil rights effort, but rather became a profit-making venture," explains Kellogg. "There was an ambivalence at the administrative top, a pressure toward sex and a nervousness about it, a push toward *People* magazine–like commercialism, and every now and then a revulsion from it. The direction was scattered—and it showed. We were carrying out a wobbly mandate." Kellogg graciously maintained order and balance during the next couple of years, through McQueen's death from complications due to AIDS and the loss of other longtime contributors and readers to the plague. He resigned, emotionally spent, but with the feeling that it was "a privilege to have worked there. To be able to earn your keep while working for gay lib was inconceivable to me as a teenager in Connecticut. I could experiment with thoughts of freedom while not abandoning the other values I already had and treasured."

The Advocate's next editor, Richard Rouilard, brought a flamboyant and hard-driving presence to a publication that had become shell-shocked, even moribund. He awoke the old staff with a tireless energy for the basic principles of ad-

Richard Rouilard brought an energetic, daring style to *The Advocate* in the early nineties during his two-year tenure as editor-in-chief.

vocacy journalism, and enthusiastically recruited literate new writers and women editors, reaching out to the community in bold strokes. One of Rouilard's first acts was to significantly increase international reporting and the coverage of issues pertinent to lesbians and gay people of color. He restimulated circulation with outrageous celebrity interviews and stirred national controversy by outing closeted public officials. Above all else, the colorful editor-in-chief plunged the *The Advocate* back into its own community, a place from which it had been estranged for some time. Under his leadership, the magazine achieved a new standard of excellence for gay journalism, a quality not seen since McQueen's early days as editor.

Rouilard had a genius for making the world take notice. But after two daring, frenetic years the publication teetered on the edge of burnout, its resources taxed beyond what, apparently, its league of paying readers could allow. Near the conclusion of 1992, new managers were sought and soon found; ownership and editorship changed guard once again. With Sam Watters becoming publisher and Jeff Yarbrough assuming duties as editor-in-chief, the principal voice of America's gay and lesbian community was carried off to yet another chapter.

Any publication of conscience has a reason for being—a fact made evident by this short history of one of the world's most important gay institutions. *The Advocate* has been a witness to courage—the stamina, outrage, bravery, and love that have propelled the gay and lesbian struggle for civil rights on its course. No single book can fully tell that story; many volumes are now required. This compilation of writings and photographs excerpted from *The Advocate*'s past twenty-five years serves as a testament to the countless individuals who have staked their hopes and dreams on the freedom the newsmagazine has upheld. As shown here, that road has been long. And, as *The Advocate* continues to remind, the journey is far from over.

—MARK THOMPSON,
SENIOR EDITOR
January 1994

LONG ROAD TO FREEDOM

NO MORE ABUSE OF OUR RIGHTS AND DIGNITY

abolish arbitrary arrests

PEACE OFFICERS — NOT STORM TROOPER

BLUE FASCISM MUST GO!

STOP ILLEGAL SEARCH AND SEIZURE

The Los Angeles ADVOCATE 25¢
VOL 2 NO 2   Copyright 1968 Los Angeles ADVOCATE   March 1968

IT'S THE HEAT, BABY

SPECIAL INSIDE

MEN'S fashion

I gave at the Office!!!

The Los Angeles ADVOCATE 25¢ Ⓐ
VOL 2 NO 3   Copyright 1968 Los Angeles ADVOCATE   MAY 1968

THE FINE ART OF ENTRAPMENT

INSIDE:

Law Reform:
The First Step   2

Golden Baskets
Uncover the 'Dirt'   4

Lick 'em, but
Don't Join   5

That's No Lady;
That's Rod Steiger

Victim Tells How Hollywood Vice Fracture the Law
BY JIM W.

The Los Angeles ADVOCATE 25¢ Ⓐ
VOL 2 NO 6   Copyright 1968 Los Angeles ADVOCATE   June 1968

The STARS

The FABULOUS DIETRICH

The INCOMPARABLE CHARLES PIERCE

The EYE-BULGING ZERO MOSTEL

Gays & the Draft   Page 3

The Infamous 647   Page 9

Merry Christmas

Pat Rocco's Latest

The Los Angeles ADVOCATE 25¢
VOL 2 NO 12   Copyright 1968 Los Angeles ADVOCATE   DECEMBER 1968

"WE ARE BORN"

1967/68

The first issue of *The Advocate* appeared in September 1967. Twelve pages long, with primitive graphics and crowded typeface, and devoid of any literary (or even journalistic) distinction, the publication had more the look of a mimeo throwaway than a professional magazine. Nor were matters helped by the addition in the second issue of a Foodstuff column that attempted to explain to the neophyte cook "the secrets of an excellent salad," and, later, offered tips for converting cabbage into "the tastiest" of vegetables. The tips, however, were for gay white men only; *The Advocate* wholly ignored people of color and almost never referred to lesbians, addressed their issues, or did anything to cultivate their participation.

Things improved little throughout the first year of publication. The addition of theater, book, and film reviews succeeded only in introducing writing interchangeable with that of mass-market fan magazines (Marlene Dietrich: "We know the legend, but to find the legend true and alive, staggers the heart and mind"). And the occasional poem in the early *Advocate* reads today like inadvertent satire: "Come, Love, drench quick my unquenchable fire."

Yet amateurish and bland as these initial issues were, they were not devoid of political content. One front-page headline read, L.A. COPS, GAY GROUPS SEEK PEACE—a peace, it turned out, based largely on police denials of entrapment and on the willingness of gay representatives to enter into a loaded discussion of what "proper" behavior on the street and in bars entailed. This was, after all, 1967. And given the self-hatred and apologetics endemic in the lesbian and gay world in that pre-Stonewall year, it was downright militant for *The Advocate* editorial writer in the second issue to write ringingly, "Will the day come when law officers will not be allowed to vent their hatred of homosexuals...? That day will come. We do not ask for our rights on bended knee. We demand them, standing tall, as dignified human beings. We will not go away."

The first days of 1967 saw demonstrators staked outside Los Angeles's Black Cat bar protesting police entrapment of gays.

Those proud-spirited words, however strangely they rang when placed alongside recipes for salad dressing and reports of "fabulous" Halloween plans, were decidedly in advance of what most gay people were saying (or even thinking) at the time. I myself, for one, was engaged in 1967 in the more typical pursuits of burying my feelings in fourteen-hour workdays and lamenting my "sick" existence in thrice-weekly psychotherapeutic sessions with an analyst who had smugly announced his certainty that I could "win the good fight" and emerge as a functioning heterosexual.

This view of homosexuality as pathology was still the hegemonic one in the psychiatric profession in 1967 and it still wrecked widespread havoc with gay and lesbian self-esteem. When the psychiatrist Charles Socarides published his influential *The Overt Homosexual* the following year, he was merely codifying the common psychiatric view that homosexuality represented a destructive disruption of the "normal" developmental process. And in those years, the psychiatric profession served as the putative cultural police, the prime arbiter of health, morality, and truth, its views everywhere parroted. *Time* magazine in 1966 characterized homosexuality as "a pathetic little second-rate substitute for reality, a pitiable flight from life. It deserves no encouragement...and, above all, no pretense that it is anything but a pernicious sickness."

Hollywood, of course, peddled the same line. A rare, nonstereotypical lesbian or gay character might now and then appear in a film, but the school-teacher who commits suicide in *The Children's Hour* represented the far more typical view of what was a fitting end for such a sinister, depraved creature. It surprised no one when the New York State legislature voted overwhelmingly in the mid-sixties to keep on the books the sodomy law criminalizing homosexual behavior; or when the *liberal* Mayor John Lindsay authorized a "cleanup" campaign to rid Washington Square Park in Greenwich Village of its "undesirables"; or when the Supreme Court in 1967 sustained the constitutionality of an immigration law that barred homosexual aliens from entry or, if they were already in residence, from citizenship.

Yet by 1967 the seeds of change *were* in the air. Only a few months before the initial issue of *The Advocate* appeared, the country's first student homophile league had been formed at Columbia University, and by the following year, the North American Conference of Homophile Organizations (NACHO)—the fledgling attempt to create a national political force—adopted the slogan "Gay Is Good." That same year, at the American Medical Association's annual convention, a small, brave group of activists noisily protested the continuing adherence to the pathology model of homosexuality.

The general climate had shifted in a direction that would soon allow many more gay men and lesbians to think of ourselves as merely *different* (rather than deficient), and therefore entitled to all the rights and privileges of first-class citizenship. This new perspective owed much to the African-American struggle for equality, and particularly to the growing militancy among young blacks who insisted that "black is beautiful," that being different, far from being a deficit, was a blessedly preferred state when compared to the deadening conformities of mainstream white America.

And the youthful white radicals of S.D.S. (Students for a Democratic Society) added their own liberating voices. They insisted that the powers-that-be and the "experts" were precisely those elements in our national life that had gotten us into the immoral war in Vietnam, had turned the United States into

The newsletter of the Los Angeles homophile group PRIDE (Personal Rights in Defense and Education) was the precursor to *The Advocate*.

We are born. And like all infants, we are and will for a time be clumsy, awkward, full of innocence, and perhaps even a little ugly—except, of course, to our parents. Any new newspaper faces a precarious existence. With few staff members and even fewer dollars, The Los Angeles Advocate's chances of survival would be rated by experienced journalists as somewhere around zero. Yet, we've decided to stumble ahead with this venture because, we feel, The Advocate can perform a very important service as the newspaper of the homophile community—a service that should be delayed no longer. Homosexuals, more than ever before, are out to win their legal rights, to end the injustices against them, to experience their share of happiness in their own way. If The Advocate can help in achieving these goals, all the time, sweat, and money that goes into it will be well spent.

—From First Editorial

Homosexual Bill of Rights

BASIC RIGHTS

1. Private consensual sex acts between persons over the age of consent shall not be an offense.

2. Solicitation for any sexual acts shall not be an offense except upon the filing of a complaint by the aggrieved party, not a police officer or agent.

3. A person's sexual orientation or practice shall not be a factor in the granting or renewing of federal security clearances or visas, or in the granting of citizenship.

4. Service in and discharge from the Armed Forces and eligibility for veteran's benefits shall be without reference to homosexuality.

5. A person's sexual orientation or practice shall not affect his eligibility for employment with federal, state, or local governments, or private employers.

AREAS FOR IMMEDIATE REFORM

1. Police and other government agents shall cease the practice of enticement and entrapment of homosexuals.

2. Police shall desist from notifying the employers of those arrested for homosexual offenses.

3. Neither the police department nor any other government agency shall keep files solely for the purpose of identifying homosexuals.

4. The practice of harassing bars and other establishments and of revoking their licenses because they cater to homosexuals shall cease.

5. The practice of reviewing less-than-honorable military discharges, granted for homosexual orientation or practice, shall be established, with the goal of upgrading them into fully honorable discharges.

6. The registration of sex offenders shall not be required.

7. City ordinances involving sexual matters shall be rescinded and these matters left to state legislatures.

8. Conviction for homosexual offenses shall not be the basis for prohibiting issuance of professional or any other licenses nor for the revocation of these licenses.

9. No questions regarding sexual orientation or practice shall appear on application forms, personnel data sheets, or in personal interviews.

10. No government agency shall use the classification of homosexuality as an alleged illness to limit the freedom, rights, or privileges of any homosexual.

—*Adopted by the North American Conference of Homophile Organizations, August 17, 1968*

"**C**hances are excellent that during your life you will be questioned, or perhaps even arrested, in connection with sex laws or lewd conduct laws. 'Be Prepared' becomes much more than the Boy Scout motto—it is essential."

—FROM AN ARTICLE ENTITLED "IF YOU'RE ARRESTED"

---

a predatory imperialist power, and had at home perpetuated class and racial inequalities in order to preserve their own privileges. In making such an indictment, the eloquent radicals of S.D.S. went a long way toward undermining the legitimacy of authority in general—including, by implication, those medical and cultural authorities that had done so much to keep lesbians and gay men in cowed subjection.

Many of us sensed at the time that these sixties rebels were exploring and articulating views central to our liberation as gay people. But it was quite another matter to be able to mobilize ourselves quickly in behalf of our own issues. Too many of us had been taught for too long that we were second-rate and second-class to discard those notions overnight; indeed, many of us had to undergo a protracted struggle against our own ingrained previous assumptions before we could begin to activate ourselves politically. I myself wrote a series of passionate articles in defense of the countercultural rebels, yet could not quite—not yet—fully articulate the relevance of their views to my own plight.

Indeed, *The Advocate* in its first year of publication was to some extent ahead of where many of us (us middle-class gay white men, that is) were. Along with calling for basic civil rights, it discussed whether our cooperation with health authorities in regard to venereal disease was in our best interest, printed cautionary articles on entrapment, bar raids, and arrest, demanded (yes, in 1968!) an end to the military's antigay policies, and declared that *of course* many homosexuals felt they were "sick"—who wouldn't, given the negative social pressures on them?

In its first year *The Advocate* also lamented the fact that none of the Los Angeles homophile organizations had responded to its suggestion of a cosponsored monthly dance to build a war chest for fighting against legal discrimination. And it printed a challenging letter from pioneer activist Jim Kepner deploring the long-standing notion that homosexuals should leave it to the "experts" to plead our case.

It's debatable how "characteristic" such assertions were during *The Advocate*'s first year of existence. For every call to arms, there were two or three calls to regression (not a bad ratio, perhaps, in these proto-political years)—calls against cruising in public parks or behaving in "poor taste" on the streets; calls to be "above reproach," to "get our own house in order" before asking heterosexuals for acceptance. And yes, there were yet more recipes for zucchini salad and Sirloin Tips Umbriago—to say nothing of prominent announcements of "marriage classes" designed to "help prepare for and preserve lasting relationships between homosexuals" (to shape them up, in other words, so they would be deemed acceptable to middle-class America).

The first sixteen months of *The Advocate*, in short, can be said to represent accurately a subculture that in 1967–68 was trailing at its back a host of camp clichés and garden-party stereotypes—even as it peered gingerly into a far more militant future. *The Advocate*'s sticky journalistic melange proved, in any case, to be precisely what its readers wanted. From a print run of five hundred copies for the first issues of September 1967, *The Advocate* had grown by December 1968 to a printing of seven thousand copies an issue. And it proudly announced to its readership that it would soon "take another major step in its program to give the homosexual community a full-fledged newspaper."

—MARTIN DUBERMAN

T I M E L I N E

AUGUST 1967 The newsletter of PRIDE (Personal Rights in Defense and Education) became *The Los Angeles Advocate*. ❏ The third national North American Conference of Homophile Organizations (NACHO) met in Washington, D.C., with friction between East Coast and West Coast representatives. ❏ A federal court in Minneapolis ruled that it is not illegal to produce and mail materials depicting the male nude. ❏ The national board of directors of the American Civil Liberties Union called for decriminalization of consensual sex practices. ❏ Ten patrons were arrested in a gay bar raid in the Silver Lake area of Los Angeles.

SEPTEMBER Vernon Mitchell of the Committee to Eradicate Syphilis opened a clinic in West Hollywood, creating dissent among activists who worried that cooperation with the Health Department would encourage police abuse.

OCTOBER ONE, Inc., the nation's oldest homophile group, celebrated its fifteenth anniversary with founder Dorr Legg.

NOVEMBER Gay activist Craig Rodwell opened the world's first gay bookstore, the Oscar Wilde Memorial Bookshop in New York City. ❏ At Project H, a New York City conference sponsored by the Episcopalian Dioceses of New York, Connecticut, Long Island, and Newark, ninety priests agreed that the church should classify homosexual acts between consenting adults as "morally neutral." ❏ California Governor Ronald Reagan defended himself against accusations by *New York Times* Washington-watcher Drew Pearson that he harbored a "homosexual ring" in his administration.

DECEMBER Dozens of gays from three western states and Canada met at a Seattle conference hosted by the Dorian Society, the Association for Social Knowledge of Vancouver, and F.E.M. (Female Education Movement).

JANUARY 1968 Police arrested a go-go dancer for showing his pubic hair at a West Hollywood gay bar. ❏ Under pressure to abandon its militant roots, PRIDE was dissolved by its founders, who sold *The Advocate* to Dick Michaels, Sam Winston, and Bill Rand for one dollar. ❏ Der Kreis, the world's oldest known homophile organization, headquartered in Zurich, Switzerland, closed its doors after thirty-five years.

FEBRUARY The Mattachine Society of Washington, D.C., provided legal support for an electrician whose security clearance was denied after accusations of homosexuality; two years later, he lost in the U.S. Court of Appeals.

MARCH *The Advocate* reported the October suicide of Jack McQuoid, a sixty-year-old Pasadena man awaiting trial on vice charges; Pasadena papers did not report the story. ❏ An Orange County man lost his home and auto insurance after a neighbor saw him kiss a man in his backyard. The neighbor reported the incident to the police, who contacted the man's insurance company.

At the instigation of PRIDE president Jerry Joachim, leaders of Los Angeles's homophile organizations met for the first time in June with Captain Charles Crumly, head of Hollywood's vice detail. Members of ONE, the Council on Religion and the Homosexual, and Daughters of Bilitis were among participants discussing entrapment, bar raids, and crimes against homosexuals.

THE BLACK CAT CASE
The first hours of 1967 saw Los Angeles police officers raid New Year's parties at the Black Cat and New Faces. Both bars, located in the Silver Lake district adjacent to Hollywood, were vandalized and patrons were seriously injured; one suffered a ruptured spleen and fractured skull. Sixteen men were arrested and found guilty of lewd conduct. The issue of the unconstitutionality of police raids on homosexual bars galvanized gay militants and, with the help of Los Angeles attorney Herbert Selwyn, was appealed up to the Supreme Court, where gays lost when the high court refused to hear the case in October of the following year.

Sir Lady Java, a Los Angeles female impersonator, headed an October picket line in front of the Redd Foxx Club to protest the Los Angeles Police Commission's Rule 9, which prohibited full drag performances on stage. Java alleged that the rule prevented her from making a living; by January 1969, the rule was officially revoked.

REAGAN STANDS FIRM
During 1967 and 1968, California Governor Ronald Reagan issued two conflicting statements, one of which called homosexuality a "tragic disease," and another proclaiming that homosexuality should be illegal. When Kevin Macre, president of the Society for Individual Rights (SIR), wrote a letter demanding that the governor explain his desire to outlaw illnesses, he received a reply from a Reagan assistant stating only that "the governor will stand by the statements he has made on homosexuals."

APRIL The Society for Individual Rights (SIR), San Francisco's gay political-cultural organization, announced that it was near bankruptcy.

MAY Mike Hannon, a former policeman who was running for Los Angeles District Attorney, told *The Advocate* that sexual acts committed in private by consenting adults should not be prosecuted; he lost the election. ❑ American Civil Liberties Union lawyer Joan Martin told a meeting of the National League for Social Understanding that some police officers routinely misrepresented facts in order to convict homosexuals. The Los Angeles city attorney's office, she said, preferred to try defendants from the same arrest on different dates, further encouraging misrepresentation of the truth. ❑ San Diego's newest gay group, the Sons and Daughters of Society, held its first meeting.

JUNE The California State Supreme Court ruled unconstitutional a Los Angeles ordinance the police department had employed to close male erotic movie theaters and arrest their owners. ❑ According to the Mattachine Society of New York, arrests of homosexuals by police decoys dropped from over a hundred per week to nearly zero. The organization had successfully lobbied Mayor John Lindsay to issue an executive order forbidding city police from making arrests for "homosexual solicitation" without a signed citizen complaint. ❑ PRIDE, the homophile organization that spawned *The Advocate,* shut down after less than two years of activism.

JULY Calling for "completion of the American Revolution," two dozen San Francisco gays picketed that city's Federal Building. Their demands included equal federal employment opportunities, an end to discrimination against homosexuals in the armed services, and federal legalization of consensual sex practiced in private. ❑ Justice John Merrick of Los Angeles County Court voided a Los Angeles ordinance against nudity on private property.

AUGUST A dedication to militant law reform and a formalization in structure swept through the North American Conference of Homophile Organizations (NACHO), which met in Chicago.

SEPTEMBER Demanding equal access to the Yellow Pages, San Francisco homophile groups lodged a complaint with the California Public Utilities Commission asking for a separate listing of "Homophile Groups"; the phone company acceded in August 1971, after several years of court struggles.

OCTOBER The Rev. Troy Perry held the first planning meeting in Los Angeles for what would become the Metropolitan Community Church.

NOVEMBER Seventy-five San Diego men were arrested in connection with homosexual activities in a three-week sweep of Balboa Park and beach areas.

DECEMBER After reports that homosexuality was on the rise in South Africa, the parliament considered passing laws banning gay sex; such laws were later passed. ❑ The New Jersey Supreme Court ruled that homosexuals have the right to assemble in public, overturning the revocation of three New Jersey bars' licenses for "permitting apparent homosexuals to congregate."

PATCH RAIDS POLICE STATION

A year before the Stonewall Riots shook New York, Los Angeles felt a similar temblor when the Patch, a popular gay nightclub located near the city's harbor, was raided. Co-owner Lee Glaze, who billed himself as "the Blond Darling," turned his sharp tongue against the police with great effectiveness. Advocate *editor Dick Michaels and his lover, Bill Rand, happened to witness the crowd's flower-power reaction to the raid and provided the following account.*

By midnight the club was packed with about 250 customers, some drinking, some milling around, and some gyrating wildly on the dance floor. Bill and I were leaning against the jukebox near the bar when we saw five or six uniformed police come through the door. They were led by the vice cops.

A few minutes later we saw them taking two guys out. Those were the only arrests made out of the large throng there. Contrary to rumors that spread the next day, it was not a raid in the usual sense. The main purpose seemed to be to harass and to intimidate the gays. After the two arrests, the cops stuck around for about fifteen minutes more, checking ID's here and there.

As soon as Lee found out what was going on, he went to the stage. As the cops looked on, he exhorted the gay audience not to be intimidated by the tactics of the straight society and to stand up for their rights. "It's not against the law to be a homosexual," he said, "and it's not a crime to be in a gay bar." Everyone, he urged, must band together to fight for their rights.

In what took on the air of a political rally, Lee was interrupted several times by applause and cheers. "We're Americans, too!" one boy shouted. At one point, I saw a uniformed cop applauding.

After announcing that the Patch would furnish a bail bondsman and a lawyer for the two arrested, Lee offered a wild idea. "Anyone here own a flower shop?" he asked. Someone did. "Go clean it out. I want to buy all your flowers," he shouted, and then invited everyone to go down to the station with him after the club closed to welcome out the two hapless victims. There were more cheers. Everyone was enthusiastic about the prospect of a hundred or more queens descending on the Harbor Division station.

A hard core of about twenty-five took off for the police department's modern Bastille in a small caravan, arriving there before three A.M. They marched into the waiting room carrying bouquets of gladioli, mums, daisies, carnations, and roses (but no pansies). The stone-faced desk sergeant looked confused for a moment, then told everyone that they would have to be quiet if they wanted to stay there. From time to time, some cops wandered out to view the weird assemblage, shook their heads, smiled, then disappeared.

The bondsman finished his business quickly and left, telling Lee that the two arrested would be released shortly. The police, however, had other ideas. The minutes dragged on into hours. The flowers began to wilt and the patience of the group began to wear thin, but the hardy band hung on. It was about five A.M. when one of the prisoners was released. He was immediately covered with the bouquets, and pandemonium reigned. The same thing happened when victim number two was released a half-hour later. Having finally fulfilled their mission, the tired group drifted off home.

Popular Patch bartender and activist Lee Glaze was an early champion of homosexual rights in Southern California. He was often the master of ceremonies at fund-raisers and other gay social events.

THE WORLD IS MY ASHTRAY

DICK MICHAELS

The Advocate's original editor/publisher had an unlikely background for founding the first effective national gay newspaper: He edited a chemical trade journal.

One night in 1966, Dick Michaels, a Ph.D. in chemistry, went out with his lover, Bill Rand, to the Red Raven on Melrose Avenue. Though they had entered the bar only moments before the police did, they were caught in a raid and Rand was charged with giving blow jobs on the dance floor. That night, Michaels became a gay-rights activist.

In other matters, Michaels remained conservative and unsympathetic to the "back of the paper," where reviews and interviews ran. One writer recalled that the editor hated the new musical *Hair,* since it was about hippies who refused to go in the Army. Still, Michaels's newspaper was a devoted vehicle for activists; if anyone took a photo of any demonstration, chances were it would run in *The Advocate.*

Both used pseudonyms: Michaels was really named Richard Mitch, and Rand was Bill Rau. Rand, a former callboy, was younger than Michaels. Colleagues say he was as inefficient as Michaels was efficient, and because Rand was *The Advocate*'s first business manager, it's a wonder the paper stayed afloat.

Michaels ran a tight ship. When a reporter was on a long-distance call, he had Rand stand nearby holding an egg timer; when two minutes were up, he cut off the interview, finished or not.

"He had the drive and competence that could get the paper out on time, even if the staff walked out the night before it was due," recalled historian Jim Kepner, an early staff member. "He worked us seven days a week, long hours. But we were thrilled to be in at the beginning."

Dick Michaels wrote a regular column, commenting on the events of the world around him. From syphilis to sex in the park, nothing was above—or below—his commentary.

The August 18 issue of *Time* magazine carried a review of Judy Garland's recent stint at New York's Palace Theater. We imagined a senior editor shouting across the room, "Get a couple of headshrinkers to find out why queers like Judy so much." We gravitate toward superstars, one doc says, because "these are people they can idolize without getting close to. In Judy's case, the attraction might be made considerably stronger by the fact that she has survived so many problems; homosexuals identify with that kind of hysteria." Says another Manhattan psychiatrist, "Judy was beaten up by life, embattled, and ultimately had to become more masculine. She has the power homosexuals would like to have, and they attempt to attain it by idolizing her."…

Boys with long hair are barred from Disneyland. What of such Disney breadwinners as Davy Crockett, Daniel Boone, and Cinderella's lover?…

Dr. Charles W. Socarides called for a national center for sexual rehabilitation to study and treat homosexuals. He thinks the problem calls for a program like those for mental retardation, epilepsy, and alcoholism….

A story making the rounds has it that a young man was at a cocktail party when the hostess swooped down and gushed, "You're the man from Alcoholics Anonymous, aren't you?" "No," he replied, "I'm from the Committee for the Eradication of Syphilis." "Oh yes," she burbled, "I knew there was something I'm not supposed to offer you."…

The Los Angeles County Commission Against Indecent Literature doesn't seem to be able to decide what its own name is. One of the pieces of material it sent *The Advocate* bears the letterhead LOS ANGELES COUNTY COMMISSION AGAINST INDECENT LITERATURE. Perhaps the Commission thought that the original ON OBSCENITY AND PORNOGRAPHY didn't clearly state what side of the question it is on. A copy of a speech included in the bundle proclaims, "The widespread publication and sale of pornography is an assault on fundamental decency. 'WHAT WE GAZE UPON, WE BECOME.' "Ah, if only it were so!…

Some friends of mine were in San Diego recently, driving along a stretch called "the milk run." That's where a lot of sailors hitch rides to Los Angeles. They picked up a lad and started toward L.A. The conversation took a predictable trend, and the boy quickly said, "Now don't start that, fellas! I've already had six blow jobs, and this is as far as I've gotten."…

Ralph Ginsburg, publisher of the now defunct *Eros,* is still fighting the postal authorities. This time they claim that one of their own postmarks—from Intercourse, Pennsylvania—was obscene when Ginsburg mailed out ads for his magazine from that point. I wonder how they feel about Queen City, Texas….

You can't join the Los Angeles Police Department if you've ever had syphilis….

All this talk about sex in the park, with the mud below and the sky above, leaves me cold. I've never been one for the nameless sex of the park, which lacks the delicacy of even the well-run whorehouse. I've long since gotten over my guilt feelings about being homosexual and don't have the slightest secret desire to be caught and punished.

—DICK MICHAELS

THE BEAD READER

Of the many people who wrote for The Advocate *during its early years, Sam Winston seemed, more than anyone else, to be the publication's popular voice. Following are excerpts from his column, "The Bead Reader," which covered everything from one-night stands to coming out.*

San Francisco Impressions

The people there don't have to travel any great distances to be with people of their own sympathies. They are more closely knit, more ready to accept than the uptight Los Angeles fragmentaries. Even in the gay places, different types mix more easily than in Los Angeles. There is little suspicion at seeing a hippie in a leather bar or a leather queen in an elegant restaurant.

Folsom Street...four bars...so packed. It's shocking because I'm not used to hearing propositions so idly dropped...to feeling hands *there.* But mad fun. So many to choose from, and me, a new face in town. "Do you dig three-ways?" (Not tonight.) Blushing? Me? That guy has good vibrations; that one, no. Wow! God, what a beautiful human being. I make sure I touch his body as I squeeze past. (I'll take it, and don't wrap it; I'll eat it here.)

"You've won what we're still fighting for," I tell him above the clamor of a Folsom bar at one A.M., his legs clamped around mine, his hand between my legs. "But I guess that's why I like Los Angeles. It's a challenge...well, like I've noticed that here you assume everyone knows the scene. You don't run around asking, 'Do you smoke grass?' That seems like an unimportant question. San Francisco is beyond such banalities. Whereas in Los Angeles they're still fascinated with the childish. You people are beyond that."

Sex in the Park

Griffith Park, stretching through the hills above Hollywood, is a refuge, a place for people to gather, to protest, to sing and feel free. Freedom, however, goes hand-in-hand with responsibility.

Homosexuals say they "cruise" the park because there aren't enough places to make contact in the city. I find this reason a crutch, a rationalization. Homosexuals find it easy to hike through the underbrush of the winding trails; they feel semi-secure in their sex-hunt. And by now a section of the park known as Horseshoe Bend has become a hunting ground for a small percentage of hungry homosexuals and a headache for the Hollywood vice squad. The situation is a stalemate of forces and philosophies.

I asked one homosexual who frequents the park for sex, "Why must they have sex there? Why can't they make contact there and go home—to privacy?" His answer: "Sometimes they do. But interest is lost if they do that. And besides, it's easier and less involved there."

Another park-hunter warned me against writing this. "You'll ruin a good thing. They're gonna do it somewhere, and they're not hurting anyone. You'll just stir up trouble and get the police down on us."

But the park police are well aware of what goes on. The rangers inform the vice squad of situations they can't cope with. Any homosexual who thinks he can pull the fuzz over their eyes has a rude awakening in store. Griffith Park is one of the most closely surveilled areas of Hollywood.

Some things are clear. Homosexuals are a minority. Like all citizens, they

Who's the grooviest guy in L.A.? Starting in 1968, *The Advocate* sponsored the Groovy Guy contest in which seven contestants backed by local bars were judged on physique, facial features, and grooming. Twenty-three-year-old Danny Combs took the winner's crown—a daisy chain.

Why won't the bars of Los Angeles stand up and support the right of the homosexual to sit quietly sipping a beer without fearing for his personal physical safety and financial security? Are they too hungry for the gay dollar to recognize his rights to ordinary citizenship? Some are interested, and to Lee Glaze, [owner] of The Patch, I am sincerely grateful for his stand. I hope that many others will join together to fight for the lowly social animal…the homosexual.

—L.T.H., Los Angeles

If all gay bars had customers such as mine, there would be no further harassment from various agencies such as the police and the so-called "straight" public. Throughout these problems their attitude has been "We're doing nothing wrong. We're hurting no one. There's nothing illegal about a bar being gay. And we're staying. Period."

These people have finally had it. They're standing up for their rights as individuals.

—Lee Glaze, Proud Homosexual, Los Angeles

I read with interest your article on "Entrapment" by Jim W. While I was delighted to see that Mr. W. won his case, I must ask why he stopped there. He has answered his own lament by not immediately bringing suit for false arrest, for conspiracy to deprive him of his liberties and rights…for malfeasance, and for any number of other offenses I am sure a good lawyer would know.

Why, oh why, do people, having won an immediate personal victory, always stop there, instead of nailing the thing down, and doing much greater good for many more people? Otherwise, it is extremely understandable just "how they can get away with it and still be within the law." The many Mr. Ws don't invoke the law against them, and thereby *let* them get away with it. I presume there is still ample time for the bringing of suit against the police and other involved municipal officials. You will be doing a service to everyone, if you encourage Mr. W. to do so….

I feel I have earned the right to say if you truly believe in a principle it is well worth it, as miserable as it may be at the time. When you're done, the world will accept you on *your* terms rather than theirs, and you can stop worrying about "exposure." I have.

The closet is getting stuffy; it's time we began to enjoy the fresh air, the freedom, and the exposure. It really isn't that bad. Take the plunge. The water's fine.

—Franklin E. Kameny, Washington, D.C.

Homosexuals have not rioted even once, and yet they are forbidden to serve in the U.S. Armed Forces, and the majority of business establishments will not employ a homosexual. Therefore, the time has come for all homosexuals to establish clubs throughout the nations, with the "father" club in Washington, D.C. Surely then the accounts of our peaceful way of life will be a most refreshing change of pace from the daily reports of violence, riots, and the like.

—George L. Jacks, Berkeley

For many years, I gave a great deal of my time and energy to the homophile movement. Then I just got exhausted, and decided it was time for me to save myself and a single homosexual individual instead. Today, my lover and I own a mail-order protest-button business which gives us an annual income of $30,000.

You can best serve the homosexual community by being a success yourself. The homophile movement has done nothing to develop a more civilized society for gay couples. The movement should cover individual success stories that hold up what others have succeeded in doing in life. It would go a long way toward correcting the warped public stereotype of homosexuals as mindless, miserable swishes wasting their lives away parodying women. Nobody ever fired their bosses for being gay.

—Randolphe Wicker and Peter Ogren, New York

If being "unsuccessful" means that I care about other homosexuals and about the only groups that care about them and me, then I wish to remain unsuccessful, gentlemen, and I hope never to have enough money to keep me from caring.

—Stephen Abramowitz, Brooklyn

have the responsibility to keep freedom alive, provided they receive equal treatment under the law. Heterosexual society cannot expect homosexuals to respect laws that are applied unevenly and unjustly against them. But in the chain-link of responsibility, *both* parties must live up to the contract.

In a sense, Horseshoe Bend is a moral question—not publicly, but individually. Each homosexual who chooses to have sex in the park—to loiter or solicit—harms his rights and the rights of *every* homosexual.

A sex-hunter of the park recently told me: "You won't change fairies. They'll always cruise the park and have sex there. And if you close the park to them, they'll go someplace else."

All right. If we can't change these people, we will have to prevent them from harming themselves, heterosexuals, and law-abiding homosexuals. If they believe the law is wrong, we should get together to change the law. I certainly am not going to give up my rights, my chance to gain equality, because he wants to suck cock in public.

A Letter Home

Dear Mom and Dad,

You asked me in your last letter what I want for Christmas this year. Well, I thought and thought…of all the banal gifts we pester one another with…gifts of apology, gifts that try to buy what is not buyable, gifts of gratitude, gifts of guilt. But not for this year…no, not for this year. If Christmas is to mean what it's supposed to mean, then let's exchange gifts that *are* meaningful. The most important gift you could give me would be my freedom.

Free me from my guilt, from all those intricate lessons which were suddenly held meaningless against my thundering need. Talk to me of compassion and understanding, and talk to me as a person, not unlike any other. Talk to me as your son. I know I should not feel guilty for who and what I am, and yet your voices from my childhood sit upon my conscience like schoolroom misdemeanors.

Free me from my fear. Do not slap back at me with quotes from cellars of accountable wisdom. I have my wise-way sayings, too, for ammunition. But such armaments are for children who are afraid. Reply in an attempt to collide with the truth and be better for the intercourse. I am afraid of losing…what? Your respect? Your love? Your regard? Do I have any of these while living a lie in your presence? Or in my presence either? I have been afraid to admit to myself or to the world that I am different, and I *must* admit it to *you* first before its awesome weight will slip from my shoulders and I can stand erect.

Free me from this unjust sense of failure which I harbor. So I have not lived the life you'd have me live…because I *am* different. Had I one leg, or no eyes, or no hands, the world would have had pity on me. But pity for either circumstance would be a terrible burden. But an unseen difference is somehow loathsome to many, and so I have lived in terror and self-pity all these years, afraid to stand proud and thankful as a man should stand. I used to point the terrorized finger of blame at everyone (even you), but a few confrontations with blame have taught me better.

Let the truth be said, so we may at last approach each other as human beings, not as self-inflicted cripples. Neither of us can afford regret. There aren't enough years left…and there is too little love in the world for regrets. Let's love now, this Christmas, and keep on growing, and learning, and loving.

—YOUR HOMOSEXUAL SON

Ultra High Camp at First Gay-In

While making my regular Sunday run through Griffith Park last St. Patrick's Day, I happened upon one of the maddest scenes of the year. Scattered along the park's main road (as opposed to the trails leading into the bushes) were signs reading, "This Way Girls," directing the traveler higher into the hills. There at the famous Horseshoe Bend (a familiar spot to local park fanciers), I discovered a throng of about two hundred wild fairies having a festive affair.

The area was aflutter with activity and queens buzzing about. A net had been strung and a heated game of volleyball was in progress between the Nells and the Butches. Limp wrists were flying everywhere, frantically fanning the air in search of the ball. Boys in tight pants were careening on skateboards down the hairpin curves of the park like Olympic skiers. Such a group of delightfully outrageous queens I wouldn't have believed—some in rags, some in tags, and some in velvet gowns! There were lavish pants, fluffy sweaters, fur hats, beads, earrings, and flowers everywhere—not to mention a bevy of beautiful numbers. This was surely Los Angeles's first major Homosexual Love-In.

Leading the flamboyant festivities was a truly mad, mad woman called "The Duchess." Wearing finger curls, broad-brimmed bonnet, Audrey Hepburn sunglasses, and semi-psychedelic pantaloons which looked like Mama Cass's bedspread, the Duchess was every bit the dedicated hostess—the Perle Mesta of Griffith Park. Each fascinated new arrival succumbed to the gaiety of the gathering and quickly joined in the fun and celebrating. All the little domestically inclined ladies of the group had baked cakes and made punch to ply the eager guests who dropped in on their way to the woods.

In charge of serving the goodies was "The Princess," a convincing young boy in a long apricot-colored gown and matching high heels. (High heels in the park, *really*, my *dear!*) A sexy young number in a yellow jacket offered her a ride on his motorcycle, but the poor Princess could not risk having her wig blown off. Alas, the sacrifices of a femme fatale!

During an interview with the Duchess, she informed me that she had sent several queens ahead of the entourage to spray the whole area fuchsia pink, and had hired a plane to fly over during the activities and drop tons of sequins on the gathering. Somehow, the elaborate plans failed to materialize.

But aside from the sheer enjoyment and mass camp of the festivities, it was encouraging to see all these people asserting their right to gather in public for a family outing, to come out of their dark shadows of fear and paranoia, and to establish themselves as free American citizens engaged in "the pursuit of happiness." Passing heterosexuals should have been no more offended by boys in tight pants or fuzzy sweaters than I should be by straight girls in their ever-rising miniskirts and bulging blouses. The Duchess and her young crowd stir us with hope of a new generation of homosexuals, ready to disrobe themselves of the usual society-oriented fears of being "different" and to fight for their place in a hypocritical world which preaches, but seldom practices, equality for all. We hope to see more of the Duchess and her court teaching Los Angeles how to enjoy life.

At sundown the festivities were still going at a mad pace. The Duchess was untiringly slicing cakes, pouring punch, and searching the sky for her sequin-loaded plane.

—P. Nutz

THE NATIONAL HOMOSEXUALITY TEST

A recent television special, *The National Smoking Test*, tested how much we know about the disputed cancer-stick. Due to the popularity of this presentation and our interest in public enlightenment, we present for your self-examination this pertinent probe of a topic relevant to most of us: The National Homosexuality Test.

1. What is a homosexual?
  A. A fruit.
  B. A fairy.
  C. A queen.

2. How can you recognize a homosexual?
  A. By his lisping speech.
  B. By his willowy movements.
  C. By his skirt and blouse.

3. What is a coming-out party?
  A. When a homosexual discovers he swings.
  B. When a debutante makes her entrance into society.
  C. When a homosexual debutante makes her entrance into society.

4. What is a closet queen?
  A. A latent homosexual.
  B. A semi-latent homosexual.
  C. I can't remember back that far!

5. What causes homosexuality?
  A. A domineering mother.
  B. A homoerotic experience.
  C. Sunspots.

6. Is homosexuality a crime against nature?
  A. In all instances.
  B. Only in the United States and Disneyland.
  C. Not unless you get caught.

7. What do homosexuals do in bed?
  A. Sleep.
  B. Each other.
  C. The Bugaloo.

8. What is sadomasochism?
  A. Two sinful cities of the Bible.
  B. Erotic decorating style.
  C. Crab ointment.

9. What is a drag queen?
  A. A trick with moral hang-ups.
  B. A titless princess.
  C. A dyke with Platforatte.

10. What is a gay marriage?
  A. A loud Polish wedding.
  B. A union between two homosexuals.
  C. A union between two or more homosexuals.

ANSWERS: (1) A, B, C, and then some... (2) They are generally found in gay bars groping around in the dark. (3) A broken zipper and a dozen lecherous old men. (4) A weirdo who gets her kicks in closets. (5) At present there is no single known cause of homosexuality, but man has developed numerous techniques for making the duration pleasurable. (6) Only when including both animal and plant life. (7) What comes naturally (or unnaturally, depending upon personal preference of participants). (8) A love affair between a hammer and an anvil. (9) Ten yards of chiffon with a queen inside. (10) The art of having your cake and eating it, too. —P. Nutz

A Night at the Hollywood Jail

Sitting at a friend's house a little after midnight on a Tuesday, I became a part of a typical night in the police-vs.-homosexuals story. My friend got one of those frantic calls from the Hollywood Police Station. A friend of his (whom I'll call Bob) had just been arrested in Barnsdall Park. Since his friend's car was still at the park, we drove there to get it, then went to the police station. My friend said, "It might be a good experience for you." At the police station, we waited almost three hours for our buddy's release. Then we learned what had happened:

Yes, Bob had been in the park that night. While there, this not-young man walked up to him without speaking. Since the guy's looks turned him off, my friend walked away. The man followed him, and walked up to him again. Bob has been suffering from an acute rash all around his abdomen and genitals, and has been under a doctor's care for it. It itches a lot. And when you itch, you scratch. Bob picked this inopportune moment to itch, and so he scratched— "down there." The silent man then spoke his first words to him: "This is the heat, baby, you're under arrest."

That sounded pretty silly to Bob, so he sort of grunted a laugh and walked away. Immediately two other guys leaped out of the darkness, and all three jumped him and handcuffed him. It was all that simple and fast.

Waiting in the station was quite an experience, as my other friend had promised. We walked in and asked the sweet old lady at the desk (who was hired to protect and to serve) what the charge against Bob was. She didn't know, since she hadn't received any information yet. Just then they brought the Barnsdall haul in—Bob and another kid, who was shaking in terror. She looked up at the officer in charge of these dangerous prisoners and asked him what the charge was. "Would you believe 647-A [lewd conduct]?" he said. She looked them up and down, nodded her head, and said, "I'd believe it."

She explained that their booking department was understaffed that night and that there would be a delay. We sat down. The bail was set at $625, which meant going through the hassle of getting a bondsman. Plainclothesmen, about six or seven of them, wandered in and out. One officer in uniform came in and laid his club and sawed-off something-or-other on the desk. "Where have you been?" someone asked him. "On a robbery." "Did you catch the robber?" "No. I wouldn't know what I'd have done with him if I had." My friend and I looked at each other and winced.

They hadn't taken the terrified arrestee from Barnsdall into the back room yet. The officer kept asking him for information, but the kid was so scared that all he could say through his shaking was that he wanted to see a lawyer. The officer's voice rose as he told the boy that there were no lawyers in the station. If the kid didn't tell them his name, and so forth, they would lock him in a cell, and he wouldn't get any food or be able to call anyone, and there he'd rot.

A gorgeous vice officer in white Levi's and showing quite a basket came through and broke the tension....And so it went, the sweet smell of success permeating the atmosphere, queens, punks, drunks, lost and found, good, bad, and indifferent trotting through. I started adding up in my head: $625 for this one, $625 for that one, but the sum got beyond me.

Bob says that he and his doctor are going to fight the case. Already the police have their timing confused. Perhaps they set their watches by bar-time.

—Corbet Grenshire

Scenes from an Entrapment

The following conversation is excerpted from an account by Jim W., who was driving home late one night through Hollywood when a Volkswagen pulled up next to him at a signal light. The driver caught his attention with "weird and peculiar" gestures, and then parked around the corner when the light changed. Curious, Jim parked across the street from the insistent driver and waited until he approached the window.

OFFICER: Where are you going? Just driving around?

ME: Just about to go home. I have to get up at six.

OFFICER: I was hoping to find some action. How about you?

ME: That all depends. Right now I'm heading for bed.

OFFICER: That sounds good, too. What do you like?

ME: Satisfaction, usually.

OFFICER: Just satisfaction? Sounds pretty one-sided....

ME: How do I know you're not a cop?

OFFICER: That why you won't say what you like?

ME: Is that why *you* won't? Somebody told me recently that it is the law now that if you asked a cop if he was one, he had to tell you.

OFFICER: Yeah, I heard that, too. I think it's true.

ME: Well, are you a cop?

OFFICER: No, I'm not. Are you?

ME: No, of course not. You know I'm not. Don't you?

OFFICER: I don't know. Why won't you tell me what you like to do? It's getting late...maybe I'd better go and look for someone else. It's getting late.

ME: Yes, I guess you'd better. I'm awfully tired and I've got to get some sleep.

OFFICER: It's too bad. Probably could have had a ball. What do you like best? [*I wondered how I could find out about him without implicating myself. A question was the best way, I decided, noncommittal on my part and requiring only an answer from him.*]

ME: Do you like to "sixty-nine"?

OFFICER: Yeah, I dig that. Say, it's getting cold out here. Can I sit down for a minute? [*He opened my car door. The interior light wasn't working and didn't go on.*]

ME: Well, I've got to go, but I suppose I should have been more hospitable earlier and asked you to sit down.

OFFICER [*leaning into the car on one knee*]: Sure you wouldn't want to come with us? [*He looked up past me, and I heard a second voice.*]

2nd OFFICER [*at my window*]: Everything all set?

1st OFFICER: Yeah. Okay, just relax. We're police officers. [*He and the other officer showed their badges.*] You're under arrest.

ME: Oh, no! What for?

1st OFFICER: You know what for.

ME: But I didn't do anything. How can you? [*They started forcing my arms behind my back and forced handcuffs on me. Then they made me get out of the car. They proceeded to "frisk" me.*]

2nd OFFICER: What did you get?

1st OFFICER: He said he liked to "sixty-nine."

THE PLIGHT OF THE SEX OFFENDER

Written in a California state prison by a gay man using the pen name Michael Selber, the following excerpt is taken from a three-part article, "View from a Garbage Heap," which appeared in The Advocate *in late 1968. The manuscript was smuggled out of prison and kept by a friend until its author was released on a technicality after spending nineteen months in Atascadero.*

"Atascadero" is a Spanish word which may be loosely translated as "garbage heap." There is a grim humor in this definition, as well as a frightening reality, for several hundred Californians who regard Atascadero State Hospital as their introduction to a human garbage heap.

These men are "mentally disordered sex offenders." They are sane, competent, and legally responsible, often intelligent and talented, and sometimes outstanding in their business and professional lives....A fraction of them will spend twelve to thirty-six months in treatment at Atascadero, a "maximum-security" hospital, then return to court to be sentenced for their crimes. But a substantial number will get neither treatment nor sentence. They may simply be locked up for years.

No one would be surprised if an enterprising journalist arranged a fake commitment as a mentally disordered sex offender in order to write an "inside story." Involved in the business of news for more than twenty years—as a reporter, writer, editor, and publisher—I have every qualification to cover the assignment except one: objectivity. I *am* a sex offender.

But the axe I have to grind is not just my own. I am one of hundreds of men who are, in an age of enlightenment, imprisoned for sickness. Though found to be "mentally disordered," we are confined in prisons, not hospitals. We are handled as criminals. Yet we cannot look forward, as criminals do, to the possibility of parole or discharge. We are committed for an indeterminate period. It is not impossible that many of us will spend the rest of our lives in prison.

In my case—and I am more representative than unusual—the punishment in no sense fits the crime. I was convicted of a misdemeanor, "contributing to the delinquency of a minor," punishable by a term of no more than six months in jail. I have already spent more than twice that time behind bars. I would be free now if I had been sentenced as a criminal. Because I am considered a sick person—a mentally disordered sex offender—I am locked up. Yet as a sick person, I have no access to treatment that would relieve my disorder.

It is impossible to be "objective" about the details of the crime without seeming to minimize my guilt. I have no desire to do that, and I think the details are largely unimportant. In brief, the case involved a fifteen-year-old boy who came to my apartment at his own invitation. He was fully aware that I was a homosexual, and he assured me of his similar tendencies. The fact that his was the initiative in no way altered my responsibility as the adult involved. And if I was more stupid than guilty, I was no less guilty.

Eventually my case came to trial....The judge ordered me placed in custody and delivered to Atascadero State Hospital. Pile a storage bin high enough with material that you never remove, and you have a garbage heap. With much to offer society, we look forward to its recognition that the idea of garbage heaps for human beings is obsolete.

FILM: *THE QUEEN* AND KING OF GAY EROTICA

The Queen, an unusually frank documentary about a drag beauty pageant, enjoyed a successful mainstream commercial run. Released by Grove Press, the avant-garde publishers, this Evergreen film was directed tastefully by Frank Simon. The narrator, Jack Dorosow, is also Flawless Sabrina, organizer and Mistress of Ceremonies. Among the difficulties encountered in arranging for the show is finding twenty-eight rooms in a hip hotel that will keep this gathering of queens. If there is a central character, it is Richard Finochio as Miss Harlow, a willowy youth who seems even more girlish out of drag with the blonde hair and soft, delicate features of a Madeleine Carroll.

Although most of the action is humorous, there are some surprisingly touching moments. Regarding a sex change, one states she wouldn't think of it. How horrible it would be to have it "whacked off"! One of the Negro sisters expresses her sincere disappointment at being rejected by the Army. Another talks about her "husband in the service." When the big night arrives, New York's Town Hall is crowded, and we spy among the judges such celebrities as Andy Warhol and Terry Southern. The suspense is surprisingly real, and as the contestants are narrowed down to the final three, a close-up of Miss Harlow's nervous fingers reveals her bitten fingernails. She is the winner!

The festivities over, we see Miss Harlow wafting her willowy self to the bus station. The pathos of the situation is graphically depicted in the final shot of our "Queen." She is sitting in a phone booth of the crowded station, crown in hand, gazing wistfully down at her prize.... You might even shed a tear.

—BART CODY

PAT ROCCO

Gay filmmaker/photographer Pat Rocco's simply made erotic shorts were praised with almost blind enthusiasm by a gay press eager to find its own heroes. Overlooking the amateur acting and low-budget look of his movies, one *Advocate* writer called Rocco "the Beatles of the male film genre." Because of restrictive laws then in force, Rocco could not show hardcore sex, just nude men fraternizing in romantic settings, often outdoors. There was no dialogue. As critic Sam Winston noted, "None is needed." In an era before cable television and video cassettes, films like Rocco's offered one of the few sexual outlets then publicly available to gay men. Movies like *When the Cat's Away, The Sailor and the Leather Stud,* and *Autumn Nocturne* were screened in adult theaters, sometimes in male-themed festivals, such as the 1968 Pat Rocco Film Festival at the Park Theater in Los Angeles.

Rocco began his professional career working as a singer, dancer, actor, and producer in Hollywood during the early sixties. In January of 1969, SPREE (The Society of Enlightened Pat Rocco Enthusiasts) was started by Dick Winters, Jim Kepner, and Chuck Robinson in honor of Rocco's work. "We had not seen films before with gays as lovers or gays simply enjoying themselves," recalls Kepner. The gay social club met the second Tuesday of every month for the next ten years.

Rocco continued to make his short films and documentaries—almost forty in all—but withdrew them from distribution in the early seventies when gay theaters went hard-core. He remained a galvanizing political force in Los Angeles gay life, however, helping to organize Christopher Street West, which produced the city's Gay Pride parade, and sat on the board of the Gay Community Services Center and other local groups. The plight of homeless gay youth was of particular concern to Rocco, who, after his filmmaking days were over, went on to create social agencies throughout California to tend to their needs.

> "**M**art Crowley's *The Boys in the Band* may be one of two or three strictly gay plays to win rave notices from major theater critics. But in one way or another, the critics usually say the play depicts the true world of the homosexual. And by 'true world,' they mean the 'sad,' 'tragic,' or 'miserable' world of the homosexual. The critics may know about the theater, but as for knowing about homosexuals, we're afraid they've been cruising in the wrong places."
>
> —DICK MICHAELS, commenting in an *Advocate* editorial

Tribadist trio *(left to right)*: Susannah York, Beryl Reid, and Coral Browne in the film version of *The Killing of Sister George,* a dark melodrama about London's lesbian underworld during the sixties. Of the play, which ran in Los Angeles simultaneously with the film, Dick Michaels wrote: "Highly successful in London and New York, it came to Los Angeles billed as a 'hilarious' comedy. It is not. It is one of those curious mixtures of comedy and drama. Maybe I'm misreading it because I see more in the characters than does a straight audience who finds them 'hilarious.'"

BOOKS: *NUMBERS* AND *MASK*

Two well-known authors, on opposite sides of the Pacific, published new "homophile literature" in 1968. Following the tremendous success of his first novel, *City of Night,* John Rechy explored one gay man's struggle for sexual conquest and adoration in *Numbers. Advocate* critic Corbet Grenshire described antihero Johnny Rio's surreal saga through Los Angeles's Griffith Park and downtown tearooms as "a nightmarish journey into the square root of sexual infinity. Rechy's talent to conceive, however, outshines his ability to transfer his dreams to print. It is like the feeling one gets when he sees an artwork of great scope and imagination, but whose execution is a bit immature and sloppy."

American editions of Japanese author Yukio Mishima's *Confessions of a Mask* and *Forbidden Colors* were also published during the year. Reviewer Mel Holt described *Confessions* as "an adolescent's first discovery of his homosexuality. Mishima sensitively describes what it was like to live in pre-war Japan and to find one's sexual drive in opposition to a rigid Japanese culture. [The protagonist] faces the fact that to survive in a polite Japanese culture he must live behind a mask of propriety." In an article about the author, *The Advocate* quoted Christopher Isherwood: "One might say, 'Here is a Japanese Gide,' but no, Mishima is himself—a very Japanese Mishima; lucid in the midst of emotional confusion, funny in the midst of despair, quite without pomposity, sentimentality, or self-pity."

Los Angeles **ADVOCATE**
VOL. 3 NO. 1   25¢   JANUARY 1969

WHAT'S GOING ON HERE?

REGISTER   VOTE!!

Los Angeles **ADVOCATE**
VOL. 3 NO. 2   25¢   FEBRUARY 1969

Sal Mineo's
Big New Hit: **Brutal, Exciting!**

Los Angeles **ADVOCATE**
VOL. 3 NO. 3   25¢   MARCH 1969

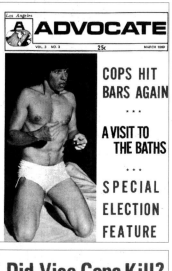

COPS HIT
BARS AGAIN

* * *

A VISIT TO
THE BATHS

* * *

SPECIAL
ELECTION
FEATURE

Did Vice Cops Kill?
STORY, PAGE 1

Los Angeles **ADVOCATE**   25¢   APRIL 1969

Prison Rules
NOT BY GAYS!

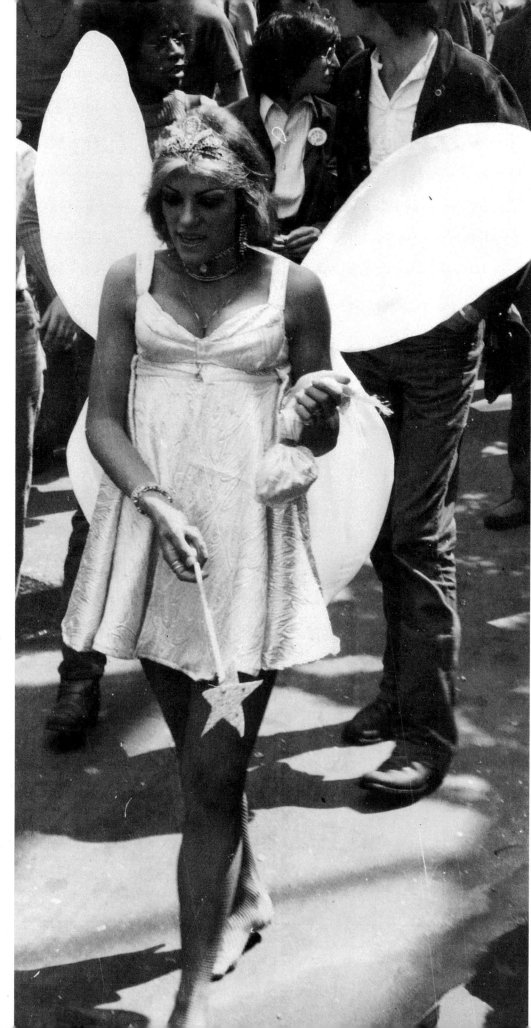

THE BIG BANG

1969 For most of us who were gay or lesbian before the Stonewall Riots, the year 1969 came and went without our realizing that events of that early summer would soon change our lives forever, that the rebellion at a little gay bar in Greenwich Village was the start of a movement to decriminalize, demedicalize, and devillainize us. Since for many of us our main source of news was the "establishment" press such as *The New York Times*, it was no wonder that we missed the significance of the riots: "Four Policemen Hurt in Village Raid," the *Times* ho-hummed on page thirty-three the day after.

It was probably hard for many of us to believe that the energy of anger and the unity that was mustered by the hundreds of gays and lesbians who took part in the riots could be sustained and channeled into a powerful national movement. Our incredulity was well founded on our recent history of victimization and intimidation. Gays and lesbians who came out in the fifties, as I did, often felt that their best chance for survival was in stealth and hiding.

The Open Door, a lesbian bar in Los Angeles, was my favorite haunt in 1956, but there was nothing open about us "gay girls" who frequented it. The friend who first took me there suggested that if I talked to someone in the bar I might not want to give my real name. You were cagey about saying where you lived and worked until you really knew a person. One woman told me that on her first night in a gay bar she had been instructed by a stranger in the restroom that she had better be careful of "police plants." In such a climate of fear, how could we have trusted one another enough to plan a movement together?

Our fear was not paranoid. This was still the McCarthy era. If your employer found out that you were homosexual, you could lose your job. The police could, and often did, come into a gay bar and haul everyone off to jail in a paddy wagon, where they would be booked and held overnight, their arrests announced in the newspaper for neighbors and relatives to see.

Even walking to or from a gay bar exposed us to danger, not just from

A gender-bending ambassador of gay spirit during an early march for civil rights.

young males who felt threatened by the units we created together but from the police. One night, dressed in high heels and capris, I walked with my butch lover across the street from the Open Door to another lesbian bar, the If Club. A policeman, no doubt lying in wait for just such a couple as we were, picked us up—we were jaywalking, he said—and made us get into his car. He drove to a dark side street and questioned us graphically and with obvious great relish about our relationship. Then he made her get out of the car, lectured me about the terrible path I was taking, and told me he would let us off this time but he'd better not see me in the neighborhood again. Jan and I walked back to the If Club. The women there to whom we told our stories said we were lucky to have gotten off so easily. One of them had been raped by a cop in similar circumstances. How could it have occurred to us to protest against the policeman's behavior, to file a complaint?

By the mid-fifties there were several homophile organizations in California: the Mattachine Society, Daughters of Bilitis, ONE, Inc. But when Daughters of Bilitis was formed in San Francisco in 1955 not even the organizers knew of the existence of Mattachine, which had been started in Los Angeles in 1950. The straight media did not carry news of homophile organizations in the fifties, and those organizations had little effective means of spreading word to potential members.

If gays and lesbians in the fifties were generally so oppressed by homophobia, so unaware of their human right to dignity and respect, so apolitical, what made the explosion of Stonewall possible in the next decade? The rebellion at the Stonewall Inn probably could not have happened at any other time in American history.

The sixties, a decade of liberalization and liberation, first witnessed the growth of a militant movement of African-Americans for civil rights. The model of that movement ushered in other civil rights movements by Chicanos, Native Americans, and Asian-Americans. The women's rights movement was reborn with the call to consciousness issued in Betty Friedan's 1963 book, *The Feminine Mystique*, and the subsequent formation of the National Organization for Women. Throughout the decade, minorities and the oppressed of America were demanding changes. They slowly provided a model for gays and lesbians to see themselves as a minority group, to understand the ways in which they too were oppressed, and to demand change in a language and tone as militant as those used by the other groups.

But it is doubtful that gays and lesbians would have been able to define their status as an unjustly oppressed minority and to communicate their message if many other factors had not affected the social climate of the decade. For example, the sixties saw the wide dissemination of the Pill, which ushered in a "sexual revolution" among heterosexuals that destroyed the pretense that heterosexuality was superior to homosexuality because the purpose of heterosexual intercourse was procreation. The hippie phenomenon of the sixties also altered the tenor of American life by its challenges to mindless convention. There was often little to distinguish the popular "unisex" style of the day from gay or lesbian style. Homosexuals were thus rendered a bit less alien.

The antiwar movement affected the gay and lesbian movement in a more subtle way. The protest against American participation in Vietnam, led by the New Left, helped to destabilize the notion of the infallibility of authority. If authorities in public office could not be trusted to keep us out of an unjust, absurd, and wasteful war, why should Americans believe that authority in general, which had been held sacrosanct in the fifties, could be trusted? The pronouncements of medical authority, for example, that defined "mental health" could now be questioned: Were homosexuals sick just because psychiatrists said they were?

BARBARA GITTINGS

In 1958, Barbara Gittings founded the New York chapter of Daughters of Bilitis; in 1966 she split from the pioneering lesbian group, whose magazine *The Ladder* she had edited, to join the new, more radical Homophile Action League. A participant, with her life partner, Kay Lahusen, in all the first gay protests—at the White House, the Pentagon, and Independence Hall in Philadelphia in 1965—Gittings was an early gay media activist as well, hosting a weekly gay news show on New York public radio in 1970.

By the time Gittings organized a "Hug a Homosexual" booth at the American Library Association convention in Dallas in June of 1971, she had been working for the rights of lesbians and gay men for thirteen years. When gay participants were given the opportunity to set up a booth at the convention, Gittings and her cohorts decided to seek maximum impact by offering kisses instead of speeches. Though the booth caused a sensation, none of the convention participants actually dared enter it—leaving Gittings to kiss lesbian author Alma Routsong (Isabel Miller) for two hours.

Nightclubbing at a Los Angeles women's bar circa 1942.

TROY PERRY

One of the West Coast's most active—and charismatic—gay leaders was Troy Perry, the twenty-eight-year-old founder of what *The Advocate* called "a bold new church." The tall, dark, and handsome native of Tallahassee, Florida, was a Pentecostal minister and father of two sons. After moving to Los Angeles and witnessing police repression, he became a gay activist.

In October 1968, he conducted his first service of the Metropolitan Community Church in his living room. Twelve people attended, but by the following year Perry was renting a chapel whose 150 seats were regularly full. It was a congregation on the move: Twice the Reverend Perry's flock was asked to leave its rented premises. In what amounted to a gay miracle, Perry launched a drive to raise funds for a new church, and within three months had the needed $16,000 down payment.

"We organized with the hopes of reaching those people who cannot or will not attend church because of the attitudes of other religions concerning homosexuality," the outspoken young preacher said. "Most gays believe very strongly in God, but most churches simply refuse to let them worship Him. ...God made all of us. He loves homosexuals as much as any of His children."

The homophile organizations that were formed in the fifties and sixties became aware of the ways in which the country was changing, and their numbers grew, albeit slowly. By 1969, there were already dozens of homophile groups in America savvy enough to present homosexuals as a minority, whose stuggle for civil rights was not unlike those of other ethnic minorities. In conservative dress, they picketed the White House and the Pentagon, demanding an end to discrimination against homosexuals. But the imagination of large numbers of gays and lesbians still was not captured.

The times required drama. Early in the year, the Homophile Action League of New York declared, "We live in an age of revolution, and one of the by-words of revolution in this country is 'confrontation.'" The League complained that the more subtle, less risky approaches of the old homophile organizations were getting gays and lesbians nowhere. By June, almost as though they realized that a decade of social upheaval would end in another six months and homosexual progress would have been minimal, gay and lesbian activists stood poised, waiting for the shot to be fired that could begin our revolution.

The Stonewall Riots, one gay wit observed, was "the hairpin drop heard 'round the world." As the pages of *The Advocate* (far more astute about such things in 1969 than *The New York Times*) showed, the Stonewall Riots happened quite spontaneously, on the night after Judy Garland's funeral, when, with their heightened emotions, the drag queens, along with a handful of butch dykes at the Stonewall Inn, came to the end of their patience with the police raids on Greenwich Village gay bars that had been harassing the patrons for the past weeks. However, at any other time, the unrest at the Stonewall might have been just that and, as *The New York Times* had believed, nothing more significant.

But the historical moment was right: It was precisely time for the Big Bang. Stonewall was an icon that provided the drama that had been lacking to capture the gay and lesbian imagination. In the months that followed, the alternate press and homophile organizations spread the story of the riots to people who understood their significance.

But the riots had perhaps an even greater significance for young gays and lesbians who had not been members of homophile organizations, who had had no experience of the repressive fifties and the timidity and self-doubt that era had created in older gays. Primed by a decade of militant movements, they brought an unprecedented vitality and conviction to the struggle for our rights. With Stonewall as a symbol, young gays and lesbians developed their own rhetoric of revolution and the tools with which to disseminate it.

The Gay Revolution, as it was then called, immediately helped pave the way for a lesbian-feminist revolution that sometimes acted side-by-side with the gay movement and sometimes in opposition to it. Unlike the "gay girls" of the fifties, lesbian-feminists complained that "gay" was a male term. "I'm angry, not gay," lesbian-feminists said. Their first priorities were building a "women's culture," by which they meant a lesbian-feminist culture. Gay men were as suspect to them as heterosexual men.

The Advocate provided an inadvertent illustration of what made many women dissatisfied with the emergent gay movement. Even though the publication billed itself as "The Newspaper of America's Homophile Community," lesbians were rarely mentioned in its pages. While 1969 saw the birth of both the gay movement and the lesbian-feminist movement, it would take almost two more decades before the "lesbian and gay movement" could be born.

—LILLIAN FADERMAN

T I M E L I N E

JANUARY   A reader informed *The Advocate* that during nighttime arrests of gays in Hollywood's Barnsdall Park, handcuffed arrestees were held in view as lures until apparent quotas were filled. ❏ The publishers of *Girlfriend* magazine, a heterosexual pictorial, were denied the right to receive funds through the mail by the U.S. Post Office. ❏ Five specialists at the University of Washington Medical School, including a urologist, a gynecologist, and a plastic surgeon, formed a team to perform sex-change surgery on qualified transsexuals. ❏ The Danish parliament considered a bill to legalize marriages between homosexuals; the bill would be continually rejected until 1989.

FEBRUARY   The Correctional Association of New York called for an end to that state's criminal statutes against abortion, prostitution, and homosexuality. ❏ Two Los Angeles bars were raided and ten patrons arrested. ❏ More than a hundred homosexuals demonstrated outside the Dutch parliament against a law criminalizing homosexual acts between an adult and a minor.

MARCH   A federal judge ruled that a Yugoslav man with admitted "homosexual tendencies" could become an American citizen. ❏ In answer to an *Advocate* inquiry, the Internal Revenue Service said it had never ruled on whether the government would accept a joint tax return from a homosexual couple. ❏ A twenty-year-old man was found naked by police in Irwindale, California; he complained that assailants had stolen his clothes, including girdle, sandals, platinum wig, and yellow sunglasses. ❏ The government of New Zealand refused to recommend changes in its antigay laws.

"The Department of Defense announced today that it has eliminated another threat to the security of the United States..."

> "*I* really don't see any wrong in what I'm doing, and I'm not ashamed for the ones I've loved. But the Army doesn't care how honest you are, how hard you've worked, how your fellow soldires look up at you as a loyal friend. If you're queer, you're dirt, a waste, a bitch, you name it....I just wish the society today would give us a better chance in life."
>
> —EXCERPT FROM A LETTER BY A TWENTY-YEAR-OLD SOLDIER facing discharge because he is gay after serving fourteen months in Vietnam

APRIL   A study released by the American Civil Liberties Union examining forty-eight Los Angeles County law enforcement agencies reported that one in ten officers was cited in complaints for unprofessional conduct. ❏ Ten members of the off-Broadway production *Che,* including an usher, were jailed for "consensual sodomy and public lewdness" onstage. ❏ Unmarried septuagenarian Vivien Kellems of Washington, D.C., refused to pay taxes until the IRS refunded $73,000 she said she'd had to pay over the last twenty years because she remained single.

MAY   New York City authorities confirmed that homosexuality would no longer bar placement in civil service jobs. ❏ Poet Allen Ginsberg was punched in the mouth by a reporter from the *Arizona Republic* during an argument about homosexuality. ❏ Homophobic Los Angeles City Councilman Paul Lamport lost his bid for reelection and blamed *The Advocate* in part for his defeat. ❏ Pat Rocco's nude ballet film, *A Breath of Love,* was accepted for screening at the San Francisco Film Festival. ❏ Canada repealed its sodomy laws. ❏ For the first time since 1871, West Germany decriminalized male homosexual sex acts between men over twenty-one. East Germany had repealed its antigay law a year earlier.

JUNE   Several days of gay rioting followed a raid on the Stonewall Inn on Sheridan Square in Greenwich Village. ❏ Connecticut became the second state, after Illinois, to repeal its sodomy laws. ❏ While police looked the other way, a group of neighborhood vigilantes chopped down fifteen dogwood trees, eleven London pines, and numerous cherry trees in a New York City park that had allegedly become a meeting place for homosexuals. ❏ Ian Phillips, avowed heterosexual and interior decorator, told UPI that he was "fighting the control homosexuals have" over his profession. ❏ Seven undercover San Francisco policemen were issued wigs and dresses to combat a wave of purse-snatchings and rapes. ❏ After thirty-two years, the statue of David at Forest Lawn Cemetery in Cypress, California, had its fig leaf removed.

JULY   Calling itself part of the "gay youth rebellion," the Gay Liberation Front formed in New York City. ❏ The Mattachine Society and Daughters of Bilitis held their last of four annual demonstrations at Independence Hall in Philadelphia. ❏ Clifford Norton, a budget analyst for NASA, was reinstated by court order after having been fired for being homosexual. ❏ Kansas reduced consensual homosexual sex from felony to misdemeanor status. ❏ Atlanta police were armed with flash cameras in order to "clean up" that city's parks of "undesirables." ❏ Tower Records in San Francisco acceded to gay protests and rehired an employee fired for acknowledging his bisexuality. ❏ An economics professor at Northeastern State College in Oklahoma charged that students and faculty conducted homosexual orgies on campus.

AUGUST   The fifth North American Conference of Homophile Organizations (NACHO), meeting in Kansas City, saw the formation of a radical caucus. ❏ Alaska's Supreme Court ruled the term "crime against nature" unconstitutional. ❏ After twice being asked to move its worship site, the Metropolitan Community Church launched a drive to raise funds for a permanent home. ❏ Eighteen of the "grooviest guys in California" vied for the second Groovy Guy contest in Los Angeles before nearly nine hundred spectators.

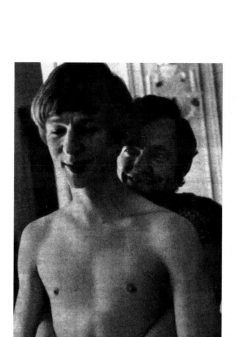

In April, when twenty-one-year-old Gail Whittington (*left*) lost his accounting job with States Steamship Company in San Francisco after this picture of him was published in the *Berkeley Barb,* it provoked a loud gay response. Protests spread as far south as Los Angeles, where gays picketed the company's offices.

SEPTEMBER After a two-year review, Oregon officials recommended liberalizing state sex laws. ❏ Ed Davis became the new chief of the Los Angeles Police Department, unleashing an era of even greater homophobia.

OCTOBER "Suicide squadrons" of the Gay Liberation Front in New York disrupted a meeting of mayoral candidates after waiting almost two hours for replies to questions they had submitted. ❏ A fourteen-member task force, sponsored by the government's National Institute of Mental Health, headed by Dr. Evelyn Hooker, and consisting of psychologists, sociologists, lawyers, and a theologian, released a report highly critical of antigay laws. ❏ Dianne Feinstein, running for the San Francisco Board of Supervisors, told a gay audience she supported getting police out of restrooms and onto the streets. ❏ A Seattle minister serving a ten-year sentence for sodomy was granted a hearing in a federal appeals court. ❏ On Halloween, the *San Francisco Examiner* dropped purple ink on lesbians and gays who were outside the paper's offices protesting an article calling homosexuals "queers"; gays labeled the event "The Day of the Purple Hand." ❏ The University of Minnesota recognized a club for gays and sympathizers called FREE (Fight Repression of Erotic Expression). ❏ Gay students at the University of California, Berkeley, staged "gay power" demonstrations and guerrilla theater skits during Cal's orientation week. ❏ The Congress considered a tax reform package that included relief for unmarried taxpayers; the package later failed.

NOVEMBER The *Los Angeles Times* was the target of a boycott called by the Homosexual Information Center over the paper's refusal to print the word "homosexual" in any of its advertising. ❏ Mattachine Midwest planned legal action to protest a sweep of Chicago gay-bar raids that had netted twenty-three arrests. ❏ Arguing that a state law against oral copulation violated First Amendment rights, a Los Angeles attorney petitioned the California courts to overturn it.

DECEMBER In a landmark decision, the California Supreme Court ruled that the state cannot revoke a teacher's credential over charges of homosexual conduct; the plaintiff chose to remain anonymous. ❏ Police arrested twelve gays protesting the *San Francisco Examiner* over an article that called homosexuals "queers" and "semi-males with flexible wrists and hips." ❏ The Gay Activists Alliance formed in New York as a less radical alternative to GLF and a more progressive option than the Mattachine Society. ❏ Ministry student Richard Daller surprised worshipers at San Francisco's Grace Cathedral by reading a diatribe against gay oppression instead of the assigned liturgy. ❏ Morris Flores, a Los Angeles transvestite known as the Little Flower, was stabbed to death in a gay barroom brawl, and his friend Gregorio Garcia, known as the Model, was left in critical condition. ❏ Hawaii's state Penal Revision Project recommended that private homosexual activity be legalized. ❏ Tom Mauer, representing the Kinsey Institute for Sex Research, told a San Francisco gay group that "the time is right for homosexuals to act."

Controversial San Francisco gay activist the Rev. Raymond Broshears announced in November plans to challenge the California penal code's section 290, which required that so-called sex offenders be registered with local police.

BURNING DIFFERENCES
In November, Pat Brown of the militant Committee for Homosexual Freedom, burned his membership card for SIR (Society for Individual Rights), charging San Francisco's largest gay organization with being too conservative.

THE RAMON NOVARRO MURDER

One of the longest pieces ever run in The Advocate *detailed the trial of Paul and Tom Ferguson, charged with the sex-linked murder of silent matinee idol Ramon Novarro. The Ferguson brothers, Chicago natives, were burly, handsome, and young. Paul Ferguson, twenty-two, had worked as a hustler, in which capacity he went to Novarro's Laurel Canyon mansion on October 30, 1968. That night, Paul took his seventeen-year-old brother along.*

The trial was held the following August. Sensational bits of evidence peppered news accounts and goaded both prosecution and defense to rehash every lurid detail. The Mexican-born actor, once a rival of Rudolph Valentino, was found nude, his hands tied behind him, and covered with more than two dozen lacerations and other injuries. Two bathrooms were blood-smeared, and a mirror bore the greasepaint inscription US GIRLS ARE BETTER THAN FAGGITS.

Each brother claimed innocence and blamed the other. Tom said he was on the phone at the time of the murder (verified by the girlfriend he called) and Paul protested that he was passed out drunk. Both were convicted and given life sentences.

NOVARRO STAR WAS LONG TIME FALLING, *headlined one of* The Advocate's *many stories on the case. The dashing lead of* Ben-Hur, The Prisoner of Zenda, *and* Scaramouche *played his last starring role in 1940. But the actor invested well and lived graciously. Generously, too: For years he helped maintain many members of his family. But his discretion and good reputation were forever lost. The trial, we observed, "threw on his life an unhappy light it never had in fact."*

Jim Kepner, The Advocate's *reporter for the entire trial, found that the case raised more mysteries and questions than it solved. "I do not feel justice was done," Kepner wrote. "An elaborate game has been played that covered up pertinent evidence....The jury acted with flagrant irresponsibility to bring a shotgun verdict, inconsistent with the evidence and the law." Prevailing homophobia proved an accessory. Newspapers were in a frenzy detailing this queer Norma Desmond and his dirty secrets. Kepner noted that "the alternately lurid and tedious trial often seemed less concerned with the Chicago brothers than with convicting the semi-retired screen star of homosexuality." Here, as reported by Kepner, Paul Ferguson answers the prosecution.*

Paul Ferguson had gotten Novarro's number that week from a realtor and phoned Novarro from where he was staying in Gardena. "I heard about you, and I'd like to come up."

Novarro asked about his age and looks, then agreed. "Come on up. We'll have a few drinks, and we'll see." The brothers hitchhiked to Hollywood and a friend drove them over.

Paul hadn't seen even a photo of Novarro before the aging actor let them in. They sat in the den and drank—more than a fifth of vodka for Paul, and as much for Novarro.

The actor read their fortunes, saying that Paul had a long life-line and a long money-line and could become a superstar like Burt Lancaster. He called his publicity agent to set up a Friday meeting for Paul. "I said I didn't have anything to wear and he said from now on he'd take care of everything."

"You visualized yourself as an actor? Felt he could open doors for you?"

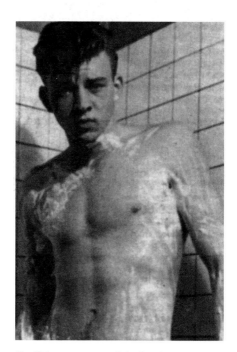

The deceased: Novarro in his prime.

Paul Ferguson, one of the brothers convicted in the killing of Novarro.

"You get carried away sometimes. Novarro definitely was serious. Kind of overwhelmed me...While he was phoning the agent about making me a star, he said Tommy could do his gardening.

"I played 'Swanee River'—some shit like that—on the piano, and Mr. Novarro tried to teach me a song he'd wrote. Tommy was on the phone....I didn't pay attention. I called him over to sing a ballad. We horsed around with the castanets. I was real drunk. He asked who was going to stay. I asked could we both stay and I lay down awhile. He said okay. I kept drinking till I went to sleep. They were going out in the garden....I passed out. Don't know how long.

"Tommy woke me and said, 'This guy is dead.' I told him to just get away. Didn't know what he was talking about. Then, I was *really* moving! I got up and followed Tommy into the bedroom. No lights. He said, 'See, this guy is dead.' He said it as if he'd say, 'Hand me a pencil.' I saw the body....No clothes. Didn't recognize the blood, except it was dark. I was trying to see if he'd turned blue, then it dawned on me that it was stupid to see if somebody was blue. Touched him. Starchy...I just about went to pieces. I seemed to get drunk again. I think I was crying.

"I said, 'Help me lift Mr. Novarro up on the bed.' Then I noticed he was tied. It just looked like a dark line.

"I listened to his heart. Dead. I told Tom we should call the police, and he called me a fink. And that's what I was, a fink. Hey! What I did next don't make no sense without the conversation me and Tom had."

Most of that conversation was never admitted.

"Then he said, 'Let's make it look like a robbery,' and 'I didn't mean to do it.' I went out and knocked over chairs, took glasses in the kitchen and started washing dishes. I was confused—like I was three different people.

"Found Tommy writing on the mirror—he told me, I didn't see it....Didn't ransack the drawers....I never saw no wallet, no prophylactic—and no cane, till the D.A. brought that cane out. I never struck Mr. Novarro—with anything.

"I used T-shirts and shorts to mop up the blood....The stain it was going to leave bothered me. When you look at somebody and you're drunk, you get confused—like I look at Tommy's shirt and it was bloody, and I thought it was mine.

"I saw Tommy on Mr. Novarro's chest, cutting marks on Mr. Novarro's cheek. I said, 'What the fuck are you *doing*?' He said, 'I'm making it like scratches, like a girl.'

"Didn't look for anything of value....Took a white shirt, and threw the mop-up garments away when we went out the window."

"Why try to make it look like a robbery?"

"Stupidness, I guess....I didn't think I was still drunk. Seeing Mr. Novarro made me sober up—and that knife business, scratching his face.

"Went out the window and hitched a ride down to Sunset. I told him Tommy Vic would know what to do. Called Victor and said I had to talk to him. Tommy went to sleep on his leopardskin couch."

He spoke intensely, doggedly. I grew less certain of his guilt. He stuck to points that could not hope to win jury sympathy. Counsel and court were castigating Novarro's sex habits. Only Paul defended the man he allegedly killed. It would have been easy to say the old creep wouldn't keep his hands off.

"Heard of his death on the radio next morning. Took a bus to Venice Beach. Walked all the way to San Pedro, then to Stew's house, where we was when arrested."

TELL IT TO TULLULAH

In April, *The Advocate* launched an advice column by Gary Donovan. His gimmick was to spin cross-chat between himself and a fictional counterpart named Tullulah, attempting to channel the legendary backstage wisdom of Tallulah Bankhead. Gay men and the occasional lesbian told Tullulah (and Gary) everything from dating woes to self-esteem troubles.

Dear Tullulah: I've met a guy who is almost just my type. He's sweet and intelligent and we get along very, very well. One problem, though. He's so nelly in public that it is getting embarrassing.
—Butchie, Los Angeles

"Okay. Solution, Tullulah?"
"Well, Gary, I find that many times people who tend to be a little nelly in private sort of go onstage when they get in public. It's sort of an I'll-show-them-I-don't-give-a-damn attitude. Of course, it shows that the person doing it doesn't give a damn but it does give the rest of us a bad name. Try to help him butch it up in public, or else don't go out in public with him. There's a time and a place for everything and the present time and public places are not appropriate to proclaim that one is gay."
"You don't approve of drag queens and such?"
"If our final goal is for the homophile world to integrate with the straight world, we have to behave as if we were responsible people to be accepted as such."

Dear Tullulah: My girlfriend and I are both so butch that when it comes to cooking, sewing, and housekeeping, nothing is getting done. We both like neatness, but we can't afford a maid, and we just don't know anything about housekeeping. What is a girl to do?
—Messed Up, Chicago

"The two should get divorced and each marry a femme who is more domesticated. Hopefully, they'll live happily ever after."
"But, Tullu, you don't break up a partnership just over housekeeping."
"True, Gary. I think the best way of handling the situation is for each of the two girls to start assuming a portion of the housework. They may not like it, but it might strengthen their relationship as a whole. It might help each to realize that love is doing some of the things we may not want to do for another."

Dear Tullulah: I have been "married" for two and a half years—and to the same boy. We love each other and get along well both in and out of bed. What's the problem, then? My lover and I haven't had sex with anyone but each other all the time we've been together and don't want to. I've read in gay publications that a faithful gay relationship just won't work.
—Worried in Advance, Los Angeles

"There aren't any laws or traditions to pressure two men into staying faithful. In fact, the traditions are all in the other direction—so much so that some people seem to measure success by the number of tricks they have."
"Who makes the rules then, no one?"
"They both make the rules and it's their business what they are. After two and a half years, I think they are well on their way to succeeding."

"Tullulah, you're looking ill. Why don't you tell me *your* problem while I make a pot of coffee?"
"I heard about six different suicide attempts across the country. Five were successful. In these last few days, I have done some study that amazes me."
"One of the commonest things I hear associated with suicide threats or suicides is the unbearable loneliness that goes along with having no one who cares. What are your thoughts, Tullulah?"
"All of us need other people. At times, we think that we can get along alone. We may begin to discourage our friends from helping us. We may even attempt to close God out of our lives. When we do these things, we may all be leaving ourselves open to the loneliness that may lead to suicide attempts."
"Tullulah, what thoughts would you like to close with?"
"Well, Gary, two thoughts run through my mind. They are: *There but for the grace of God go I* and *'Am I my brother's keeper?'* "

DEATH AT THE DOVER

In the early spring, the gay community in Los Angeles was outraged by several vice officers' brutal attack on a man named Howard Efland. This police beating was fatal, and the alternative press, especially *The Advocate,* offered its sole media coverage.

Details of the case are still uncertain. Following the custom of the times, Efland was identified in articles only as J. McCann, his pseudonym when frequenting the Dover, a skid-row hotel commonly used for gay assignations.

At 12:55 on the morning of March 9, Efland, a male nurse described as a slightly built, timid man, was dragged from a second-floor room. Witnesses, summoned by the commotion, said he was handcuffed and bleeding from the mouth. Two men dragged him down the hall, his feet barely touching the floor.

In March of 1970, the Rev. Troy Perry led 120 marchers to a rally behind the Dover Hotel to commemorate the fatal beating of Howard Efland by Los Angeles vice officers.

The witnesses stopped retreating when another man, tears streaming down his face, ran in crying, "They're killing him! They're stomping him!" Efland, thinking that the plainclothesmen were trying to rob and kill him, screamed for help.

The following Monday, the ACLU told Efland's friends they could do nothing without a complaint from his family. The coroner's office failed to confirm to Dover residents that Efland was even dead.

On April 4, however, a seven-man jury presided over a coroner's inquest in the matter. Efland's parents believed police statements that their son died of a heart attack, and neither hired a lawyer to represent him nor even attended the inquest themselves. Doctors testified that Efland in fact died from a massive hemorrhage resulting from a ruptured pancreas. Numerous other contusions were found on the body.

The arresting vice officers, Lemuel Chauncey and Richard Halligan, were quick to introduce Efland's past lewd-conduct arrests, and testified that Efland had groped Chauncey. Efland kicked him in the groin, Chauncey also testified, which caused him to black out and fall on the victim's stomach knee-first. A third officer testified that when he arrived at the Dover, Chauncey and Halligan were exhausted and Efland lay motionless.

A hotel patron testified that he saw two men holding the handcuffed Efland while a third man kicked and beat the prisoner, kneed him in the stomach, and, after he fell, jumped up and down on him.

But despite testimony from more than one eyewitness contradicting police accounts, the jury ruled "excusable homicide," and that Efland had been resisting arrest.

The Advocate blasted the "psychotics" of the Los Angeles Police Department and advised homosexuals to attend future inquests. "Frequent attendance at such whitewash parties," one columnist urged, "might even make the homosexual community less passive in the face of the shit the cops dish out in the name of law and order."

"GET THE PIGS OUT OF THE PISSOIRS"

The volatile issue of police entrapment continued to heat up gay protest. Some of the dozens of cases hit the press, but even more did not. Victims of so-called lewd-conduct arrests risked losing their jobs, their apartments, even their insurance. Many of those arrested had not even responded to the sexual advances of under-cover officers—being in the wrong park or restroom at the wrong time could get you arrested, and it was always your word against the vice cop's.

Far from responding strictly to public complaints, these arrests were frequently made during hours in which the public was nowhere near these areas, and via surveillance mirrors and screens that even monitored private toilet stalls.

The gay community began to fight back in court. What follows are excerpts from a complaint filed in Alameda County Superior Court in July 1969 by San Francisco's Society for Individual Rights (SIR) and from The Advocate's *reporting on the breakthrough legal action.*

Attorney Al Gordon, a longtime supporter of gay rights, poses for *The Advocate* in a mock-up of an entrapment scene.

"When a member of the public enters [a public] restroom, the officer…will approach a urinal and often expose his penis in such a manner that it will be in full view of the suspect if he should look in the officer's direction.

"The officer's stance and conduct are calculated to, and frequently do, excite the sexual drive of the suspect if he is at all homosexual or ambisexual. Frequently, the officer will massage his penis so as to have an erection. That is, to all outward appearances (regardless of his possible contrary but concealed mental intent) he masturbates. While he is engaging in this conduct, he will fix his gaze on the penis of the suspect, and if the suspect looks in his direction, the officer will raise his eyes to focus on those of the suspect in an attempt to convey the message that the officer is sexually aroused and…desirous of sexual relations with the suspect."

SIR president Larry Littlejohn further charges that plainclothes police officers are themselves creating a social evil and violating the spirit of the law by loitering in public restrooms, and that vice officers, in their eagerness to make arrests, often arrest totally innocent persons.

Homosexuals have the right and need to use public restroom facilities, Littlejohn pointed out. Those homosexuals who would not otherwise be involved should not be exposed to the enticing blandishments of plainclothesmen any more than heterosexuals should be exposed to the antics of these officers. "We are not taking issue with the need for law enforcement, but only with the method of enforcement," he said.

SIR's complaint offers an explanation for frequent charges by police that suspects facing "lewd conduct" arrests "resist" the arrest: "Such resistance may be and frequently is the direct result of the arrestee's doubt as to the officer's status as an officer. This doubt is generated by the officer's own unofficerlike and criminal behavior in the restroom…."

The officer then calls for assistance from a fellow officer stationed nearby, and together they attack the suspect. "The primary purpose of the beating is not, as contended by the officers, to overcome the alleged resistance to an arrest, but—in view of such beatings' severity—to appease the perverted and sadistic needs of the officers themselves," SIR charges.

As a result of these police practices, SIR's complaint states, homosexuals are being deprived of substantive due process under law, and of equal protection of the laws. —ED JACKSON

> "It's likely that many of us will want to turn up our noses at these cases. 'These T-room queens give us a bad reputation and deserve what they get when they're arrested,' we may think. However, it's really the cops' bad manners that cause a lot of the public trouble."
>
> —REPORTER ED JACKSON

TERROR IN THE TUBS

It was just one of those days when nothing went right. I didn't really want to go to the baths this particular night, but Pat and I had been out celebrating his sixth annual twenty-first birthday, and we decided to stop by the tubs for a little while on our way home.

Midnight on a Monday night isn't the best time to go to the baths, we found out. There didn't seem to be anyone around except a few expired numbers asleep in the TV room. We were just about to give up in despair and leave, when Pat (greedy queen that he is) made a new friend. So off they went to a room to talk and get acquainted, leaving me to find something to do until he was ready to go home.

Finding no live action anywhere, I was on my way to the TV room, hoping there might be a good horror movie on the "Late Late Show." Suddenly, I heard people running and screaming, "Get into your rooms and lock the door, quickly!"

I couldn't figure what all the commotion was about. All too soon I found out. With a splitting crash, the entrance door came smashing down, and cops began pouring in like storm troopers. Queens were dashing everywhere like frightened jackrabbits, smashing into each other in their frenzy.

In a flash, I dashed into the nearest room and locked the door. As I sat there disbelieving that all this was really happening to me, I could hear the blue-uniformed troopers rushing about, pounding on doors trying to catch two people together, and obviously disappointed at finding everyone alone in their rooms.

Outside I could hear voices (supposed they were police voices, 'cause they were deep) snarling with animosity. "Something in here stinks," snarled one. "I smell faggots!" "Is this the fruit playroom?" "There's a whole nest of them over here." "For a health club, they sure don't look very healthy."

Just then there was that ominous knock on my door and "Open up in there." I opened the door and faced my antagonist. I was then taken into the main room, where a dozen queens were already dressed and clustered on the floor. I looked up just in time to see Scotty, the manager, being dragged out handcuffed and solemn. Someone informed us that he had shot his partner, and we were all being held as accomplices.

Everyone was wondering what was going to happen to us. Queens were moaning about losing their jobs, the money they had saved for some project, whom to call to bail them out. All I could think of was how to explain this to my lover, who thought I was visiting an old friend for his birthday. I made promises to give all my money to the poor, even to join the Reverend Perry's church, if the Lord would just get me out of this mess.

One queen wanted to know how they could break doors down to get into a place. "First of all," replied the cop, "they teach it to us in school. But we don't break doors down—we knock, and if there's no answer, we lean our ears against them to hear if anyone is at home, and sometimes the door just falls in."

Finally, about four A.M., after arresting one number for outstanding traffic tickets, they had checked on the last one of us. To our surprise, they bade us all a fond good night and left just as quickly as they had come (if a lot less dramatically). As soon as the last uniform disappeared out the door, there was the maddest rush for an exit since the *Titanic*.

Once outside, I took a deep breath of fresh air, started my heart pumping again, and began work on the story I would have to tell my lover.

I may never take another bath.

—P. NUTZ

Acting Up at the Stonewall Riots

The first gay riots in history took place during the predawn hours of Saturday and Sunday, June 28–29, in New York's Greenwich Village. The demonstrations were touched off by a police raid on the popular Stonewall Inn, located at 53 Christopher Street. This was the last (to date) in a series of harassments that have plagued the Village area for the last several weeks.

Plainclothes officers entered the club at about two A.M., armed with a warrant, and closed the place on grounds of illegal selling of alcohol. Employees were arrested and the customers told to leave. The patrons gathered on the street outside and were joined by other Village residents and visitors to the area.

The police behaved, as is usually the case when they deal with homosexuals, with bad grace, and were reproached by "straight" onlookers. Pennies were thrown at the cops by the crowd, then beer cans, rocks, and even parking meters. The cops retreated inside the bar, which was set afire by the crowd.

A hose from the bar was employed by the trapped cops to douse the flames, and reinforcements were summoned. A melee ensued, with nearly a thousand persons participating, as well as several hundred cops. Nearly two hours later, the cops had "secured" the area.

The next day, the Stonewall management sent in a crew to repair the premises and found that the cops had taken all the money from the cigarette machine, the jukebox, the cash register, and the safe, and had even stolen the waiters' tips!

Since it had been charged with selling liquor without a license, the club reopened as a "free store," open to all and with everything being given away, rather than sold. A crowd filled the place and the street in front. Singing and chanting filled Sheridan Square Park, and the crowds grew quickly.

At first, the crowd was all gay, but as the weekend tourists poured into the area, they joined in. They'd begin by asking what was happening. When they were told that homosexuals were protesting the closing of a gay club, they'd become very sympathetic and stay to watch or to participate.

The crowds were orderly and limited themselves to singing and shouting slogans such as "Gay Power," "We Want Freedom Now," and "Equality for Homosexuals." As the mob grew, it spilled off the sidewalk, overflowed Sheridan Square Park, and began to fill the roadway. One of the six cops who were there to keep order began to get smart and cause hostility.

A bus driver blew his horn at the meeting, and someone shouted, "Stop the bus!" The crowd surged out into the street and blocked the progress of the bus. As the driver inched ahead, someone ripped off an advertising card and blocked the windshield with it. The crowd beat on the sides of the empty bus and shouted, "Christopher Street belongs to the queens!" and "Liberate the street!"

Christopher Street, from Greenwich to Seventh Avenue, had become an almost solid mass of people—most of them gay. No traffic could pass, and even walking the few blocks on foot was next to impossible. One little old lady tried to get through, and many members of the crowd tried to help her. She brushed them away and continued her determined walk, trembling with fear and murmuring, "It must be the full moon; it must be the full moon."

Squad cars from the Fourth, Fifth, Sixth, and Ninth precincts had brought in a hundred or so cops who had no hope of controlling the crowd of nearly

NEW YORK NOTES

The Sheridan Square revolt has had some amusing, baffling, and disturbing aftermaths. With our ears to the ground, we've been able to feel some of the vibrations, and in a few cases, we've been present when new social experiments were taking place.

Local newspapers picked up the uprising and played it to the hilt. The *Daily News,* as usual, made fun of the gay community, referring to the rioters as "queen bees," and so forth. The *New York Post,* on the other hand, was somewhat more sympathetic, and *The Village Voice* carried two front-page photographs and two articles describing the events that led to the outbreak.

After the young people rioted, the prophet of the new age, Allen Ginsberg, walked amid the rubble, inspecting the Stonewall and commenting on the changed appearance of the gay clientele as contrasted with those of ten years ago. "They no longer have that 'wounded' look," he said. Ginsberg took to the concept of "gay power" and identified himself as a homosexual. "It's time we did something to assert ourselves," he mused.

"After all, we do comprise ten percent of the population."

As a result of the Stonewall revolt last month, the gay youth rebellion is continuing to grow in strength and momentum. Under lavender banners, a large contingent of the newly formed Gay Liberation Front marched from Washington Square to Sheridan Square, chanting and shouting the slogans of the new militants: "Gay Power. Gay Power to the Gay People."

Martha Shelley of Daughters of Bilitis and Marty Robinson of New York Mattachine spoke to the assembled revolutionaries, galvanizing them with denunciations of the prejudice and harassment that have been endured by homosexuals for so long. "We're tired of being harassed and persecuted," shrieked Shelley to the crowds. "If a straight couple can hold hands in Washington Square, why can't we?" Many of those assembled clasped one another's hands. There were shouts of approval.

Banners waved in the air with interlocking male symbols on one side and female symbols on the other. As the crowds marched through Manhattan streets, they sang "We Shall Overcome," which, even *The Village Voice* admitted, was "curiously moving."

The Village Voice was the object of the Gay Liberation Front's first picketing demonstration, a protest that was triggered by that paper's refusal to print the word "gay" in its advertising columns. The liberation group, incensed by the paper's easygoing use of such words as "fag" and "faggot" in its regular columns, met after the picket with Howard Smith and other *Voice* officials, who are said to have agreed to a liberalization of the advertising department's policies. The columnists, however, are not subject to censorship by the *Voice,* and it would seem that words such as "faggot" may continue to appear in random articles about homosexuals.

A few New York stages are heartily enjoying a newfound freedom: nudity. Off-Broadway is buzzing with gay-ety. At least six theaters are featuring plays whose theme is homosexuality.

The Players Theater is host to *Geese,* a two-part drama with glimpses into the love and sex lives of two lesbians and a male couple. The males strip to their birthday suits, and in a butchy, back-slapping, college-hero spirit they proceed to kiss, fondle, hug, hump, sigh, and vow eternal love in front of a curious audience that has never seen such goings-on before.

Theatre de Lys features *Spitting Image,* a lighthearted account of the trials endured by a male couple who give birth to their own biological freak: a baby! Their paternal instincts are rallied to protect the little monster from distraught heterosexual authorities. The resulting comedy is equal to an episode of "Petticoat Junction."

Two articles, both written by homosexuals, have appeared in *The New York Times* bitterly attacking *The Boys in the Band* as a hymn to heterosexuality and a homosexual put-down. Homosexuals who praise this play, say the authors, are catering to a concept of homosexuality that makes it seem like an inferior type of sexual expression.

One of New York's newest Turkish baths was raided recently and twenty-two persons (including employees) were arrested. The owners of the bath (who were not paying their dues to the police) were not present when the raid took place. Reports indicate that the police vented their wrath by leaving the premises in a mess.

Forty Gay Liberation Front members stormed out of a hot-tempered meeting recently to join Women's Liberation Front activities. Bitter floor fights had erupted over the question of homosexual involvement in radical front groups, including the Black Panthers, SDS, and Women's Liberation. Some felt that such involvement was a dissipation of homophile efforts, and that such activities might reflect badly on the homosexual community in general. Others, supported by a number of professional revolutionaries, hope to swing GLF into activities that will aid causes other than those of homosexual civil liberties. Whether SDS and the Black Panthers will come to the aid of the homosexual community remains to be seen.

History's first college-level homosexual dance was a smashing success. Hundreds of young people attended, crowding the upper and lower floors of the parish hall at the Church of the Holy Apostles, a large metropolitan house of worship. Father Weeks, rector of the church and a member of the newly formed New York Council on Religion and the Homosexual, greeted the students, and so did the Rev. Robert Wood, author of the ice-breaking book *Christ and the Homosexual*.

The students represented a vast cross section of the community and were as healthy and happy-looking as any large group of today's students. Not only were they well-behaved, but they evinced an obvious joy at being able to meet for fun under such favorable circumstances. "It's much better than dancing in a Mafia-operated bar," said one youngster.

—Lige Clarke and Jack Nichols

two thousand people in the streets. Until this point, the crowd had been, for the most part, pleasant and in a jovial mood. Some of the cops began to become very nasty and started trouble. The focus of the demonstration shifted from the Stonewall to "The Corner"—Greenwich Avenue and Christopher Street. The intersection, and the street behind it, were a solid mass of humanity. The tactical police force arrived in city buses. One hundred of them disembarked at The Corner, and fifty more at Seventh Avenue and Christopher.

They huddled with some of the top brass who had already arrived, and isolated beer cans, thrown by the crowd, hit their van and cars now and again. Suddenly, two cops darted into the crowd and dragged out a boy who had done absolutely nothing. As they carried him to a waiting van, brought to take off prisoners, four more cops joined them and began pounding the boy in the face, belly, and groin with nightsticks. A high shrill voice called out, "Save our sister!" and there was a general pause, during which the "butch"-looking "numbers" looked distracted.

Momentarily, fifty or more homosexuals who would have to be described as "nelly" rushed the cops and took the boy back into the crowd. They then formed a solid front and refused to let the cops into the crowd to regain their prisoner, letting the cops hit them with their sticks, rather than let them through.

The cops gave up on the idea of taking prisoners and concentrated on clearing the area. They rushed both ways on Greenwich, forcing the crowds into Tenth Street and Sixth Avenue, where the people circled the blocks and reentered Christopher. Then the cops formed a flying wedge and, with arms linked, headed down Greenwich, forcing everyone in front of them into side streets. Cops on the ends of the wedge broke off and chased demonstrators down the side streets and away from the center of the action.

They made full use of their nightsticks, brandishing them like swords. At one point a cop grabbed a wild Puerto Rican queen and lifted his arm to bring a club down on "her." In his best Maria Montez voice, the queen challenged, "How'd you like a big Spanish dick up your little Irish ass?" The cop was so shocked he hesitated in his swing, and the queen escaped.

The police action did eventually disperse the crowds. Nearly two hours after the bus had been delayed, the area was again peaceful. Apart from the two to three hundred cops standing around the area, it looked like an unusually dull Saturday night.

Then, at three A.M. the bars closed, and the patrons of the many gay bars in the area arrived to see what was happening. They were organized and another attempt was made to liberate Christopher Street. The police, still there in great numbers, managed to break up the demonstrations. One small group did break off and attempt to liberate the IND subway station at Sixth Avenue and Waverly Place, but the police went in and chased everyone out.

Sunday night saw a lot of action in the Christopher Street area. Hundreds of people were on the streets, including for the first time a large "leather" contingent. However, there were never enough people to outnumber the large squads of cops milling about, trying desperately to head off any trouble.

One of the most frightening comments overheard during the fracas was made by one cop to another. "Them queers have a good sense of humor and really had a good time," he said. His "buddy" protested: "Aw, they're sick. I like nigger riots better because there's more action, but you can't beat up a fairy. They ain't mean like blacks; they're sick. But you can't hit a sick man."

—Dick Leitsch

THEATER: *FORTUNE AND MEN'S EYES*

Sal Mineo's previously unproven directorial skill is exhibited in *Fortune and Men's Eyes*—his pacing is lightning swift, his stage movement interestingly yet unobtrusively flowing. Since much of the dramatic action in John Herbert's play takes place offstage, Mineo was wise to put more of the play before the audience.

The added rape in the shower room is staged so effectively that the brutality knocks you breathless. And the addition of a couple of short scenes involving new prison arrivals being made to strip and shower breaks the tedium of the one-cell bickering.

Don Johnson plays Smitty, the young and innocent newcomer who believes that if he is a model prisoner, jail will be bearable. Mineo takes the role of Rocky, the pimp who tells Smitty he will be his protector if Smitty will put out for him. Otherwise, Rocky will ensure his being gang-raped by at least fifty guys in the storeroom.

An interesting point answers those who think one experience, or even a series of homosexual experiences, "makes" a man gay for life. When, after several months of being Rocky's "punk," Smitty declares his love for Mona, another cellmate, Mona wisely realizes Smitty will go back to girls on release.

Roger Garrett is excellent as the soft, sensitive Mona, who tries to attract attention to himself, but ends up being the target of the fifty-man Sodom Roulette in the storeroom.

Johnson, after a weak start, builds up steam in his portrayal of the pivotal character, Smitty. This is his first professional role, and the young actor deserves high praise for such a memorable debut.

But much of the production's success is due to Michael Greer as Queenie, the domineering "queen mother." His high camp and low comedy are hilarious, coupled with a cutting edge of self-defense. —JAY ROSS

"*In a role in which he must purposely act a godawful yahoo-ing Texan, Jon Voight explores the nuances and explodes with more facets than a geodesic dome. He is beautiful in face and physique, although the latter is visible only in glimpses. Hollywood is still being coy.*"
—CRITIC JAY ROSS, reviewing gay-themed *Midnight Cowboy*, which went on to win an Oscar for Best Picture

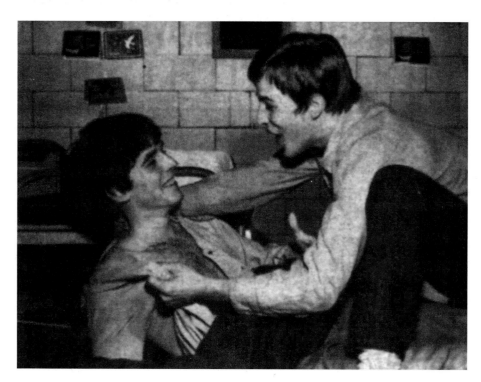

Roger Garrett as Mona (*left*) and Don Johnson as Smitty (*right*) in one of the lighter moments of *Fortune and Men's Eyes.*

BUCKLEY VS. VIDAL: BITCH FIGHT OF THE YEAR

After ABC teamed William F. Buckley, Jr., with Gore Vidal to cover the 1968 national political conventions, the anticipated fireworks were not long in coming. While arguing about the Chicago police riot, Vidal called Buckley a "crypto-Nazi." Buckley blew his cool in front of ten million viewers, responding, "Now listen, you queer...I'll sock you in the goddamn face and you'll stay plastered!" A year later, *The Advocate* reported that in the August and September issues of *Esquire,* the scrapping continued:

"PLEASE INFORM GORE VIDAL NEITHER I NOR MY FAMILY IS DISPOSED TO RECEIVE LESSONS IN MORALITY FROM A PINK QUEER."
—A telegram Buckley intended to send Vidal, as revealed in the August *Esquire*

"I am not an evangelist of anything in sexual matters except a decent withdrawal of the state from the bedroom. There will always be morbid twisted men like Buckley, sniggering and giggling and speculating on the sexual lives of others."
—From Vidal's response to Buckley in the September *Esquire*

FILM: JOE D'ALLESANDRO IN THE *FLESH*

At last a perfect film has emerged from the Warhol Factory—*Flesh,* in Eastman color. Andy's components are here—a wild assortment of way-out personalities allowed to act on, and react to, each other.

But while Andy was in the hospital recovering from a bout of Valerie Solanisitis, his right-hand (or, more descriptively, his right-testicle) man, Paul Morrissey, has added a strong directorial touch and superb camera artistry, along with judicious editing.

This is made more apparent after the Warholesque opening shot of nineteen-year-old star Joe D'Allesandro sleeping. It must have been three minutes long and seemed like twenty, but never again does the film stop or even slow down.

Joe's wife (Geraldine Smith) wakes him and asks him to go out and earn $200 for her new girlfriend's abortion. "Earning" means hustling men. Morrissey avoids judgment of the hustler's life, either by implication or by omission. He shows it as it is, from the most ordinary to the far-out.

The transvestites are great. Candy Darling acts and looks almost like a real girl, wearing the totally artificial look of the thirties (platinum-blond hair, carmined bee-stung lips, pasty white makeup, and pencil-line eyebrows). Jackie Curtis does the overly delicate bit, but is laboring under a gross misapprehension from his ten o'clock shadow on down.

Louis Walden plays Joe's former workout buddy, whom Joe hits up for a never-repaid "loan" each time he pays a "social call." Louis wants Joe to move in as his lover, as in the midst of a clinch, he delivers the cliché: "We're not queers." D'Allesandro profers his hustlerian credo: "What's straight? Nobody's straight! All you're doing is letting somebody suck your peter!"

Arriving home, Joe meets his wife's new girlfriend, Patti D'Arbanville, and is then told to go fuck off. The girls strip him when the wife brags about his body, and the girlfriend helps the wife humiliate him as they embrace and caress each other while lying alongside his nude body.

Near the beginning of *Flesh* is a sequence of the naked Joe playing with his baby daughter. So much a total part of the film, it shows Joe lavishing all his love on the one creature who will accept it. D'Allesandro is a man of shifting appearance and nuances, and expresses a world of emotion within the framework of his low-key characterization. Prediction: Within two years, Joe will be a top American film star. Hopefully, Morrissey will be directing him.   —JAY ROSS

TEXAS SEX LAW VOID
See Page 1
Newspaper of America's Homophile Community
So. Calif.
35¢
The ADVOCATE
50¢
Elsewhere

NUDES CAUSE FUROR

Stories on Pages 3, 5

PERRY STARTS FAST
So. Calif.
35¢
Newspaper of America's Homophile Community
Issue No. 39
The ADVOCATE
50¢
Elsewhere

THE BIG GAY PARADES

New York
Los Angeles
Chicago

Resting in Central Park after New York's long march

SEX LAW TEST
Page 1
Newspaper of America's Homophile Community
The ADVOCATE
So. Calif.
35¢
Issue No. 40
50¢
Elsewhere
Trailblazing Company Theatre

GAY RIOT IN NEW YORK
Newspaper of America's Homophile Community
So. Calif.
35¢
The ADVOCATE
Issue No. 43
50¢
Elsewhere

Gay-In III

GAY LIB NOW!

Rich Wandel, who photographed for *The Advocate* and the New York paper *Gay,* was one of a gay and lesbian multitude celebrating Gay Pride Day, 1970, in New York City's Central Park. Of his photographs, Wandel said, "The camera provided a barrier, a needed insulation for me from the justifiable anger that was very much a part of the early post-Stonewall movement. I could act as the observer and deny the emotion at the same time all the excitement was there."

1970 Stonewall capped a five-year rise in gay militancy, yet few outside New York recognized what a deep change it had made. Los Angeles's Gay Liberation Front didn't start until December 14, 1969. I attended its first meetings as an aloof *Advocate* reporter, then went on to the electric, chaotic, and inspiring National Gay Liberation Conference in Berkeley. It upset ideas about our goals and community which I'd evolved since coming out in San Francisco in 1943 and joining the homophile movement in 1953. Although never quite accepted as a gay hippie-counterculture-radical, I joined the "Revolution," remaining skeptical of its apocalyptic manifestos and zany tactics.

In 1970, *The Los Angeles Advocate* became biweekly and nonlocal. Our news was unlike today's: so many raids and arrests that bar owners who sold the paper complained, "Lay off the cops and raids won't happen." Yet they *had* happened, often, since long before *The Advocate* or *ONE* magazine was around to report them. Los Angeles police (like many other law enforcement agencies) busted three thousand gay men each year on sex charges, and many more for "vagrancy" or "disorderly conduct." It took us years of protests to lower the statistics. But by 1970, we had begun to protest—in unforeseen new ways.

Our polite earlier movement had sought straight authorities to represent us, to define us, defend us, and perhaps cure us. But suddenly, our movement was transformed—no longer cap-in-hand, no longer suit-and-tie. Where we had quietly discussed "the problem," we began to confront the world. Where we'd begged for understanding, we demanded equality. Where we'd sought acceptance by the establishment, we told the establishment to bug off. Where we had dressed to "look straight," we dressed for the fun of it, or "to blow people's minds." We traced persecution of gays to oppression of women, saying that neither could end without reconstituting society, banishing gender roles, capitalism, religion, and the military-industrial complex. We hoped to remake the world.

In early 1970, when many lesbian-feminists and a few blacks began to call the rest of us white, male chauvinist pigs, we began to watch the words we used. At the same time, we grew from forty organizations in the United States and Canada to two hundred by the end of the year.

Many other changes were taking place. Gay books were increasing in number—and becoming more positive. Gay lib nurtured a flowering of gay art. Independent filmmaker Pat Rocco's gay shorts and documentaries inspired us. Guerrilla theater hit the streets, enacting campy fairy tales with political punch. Exuberant "Gay-Ins" were held in Los Angeles's Griffith Park and attacked by police, who said homosexuals only came there to have sex in the bushes. But everything was up for debate: gay marriages, gay communes, even gays in Cuba.

The Rev. Troy Perry's militant gay actions frightened Metropolitan Community Church (MCC) parishioners who wanted a cozy closet to worship in. From various backgrounds they brought clashing ideas about worship: Should services be stately and liturgical, or pentecostally emotional? Ought words like "gay" or "our community" be uttered in church? Was MCC saying that "God loves us in spite of our being gay"? Did Perry and two women disgrace the church by getting arrested in a gay-rights demonstration? Perry's fast on the Federal Building steps looked to conservative parishioners like a filthy hippie encampment.

Gay Liberation Fronts around the country picketed randomly, rowdily, campily. We joined other causes and, in an *Advocate* column, I argued that no human rights issues were foreign to us, that it was time for gays to join the human race. Not everyone agreed. Some gay demonstrators treated anyone on the streets as an enemy. We vented our anger on older homophile groups and gay bars. It was easier to attack our own—to subject Rocco, Christopher Isherwood, Tennessee Williams, Paul Goodman, and other well-known gays to star chamber proceedings—than to effectively hit the enemy.

In turn, some older leaders scorned the new militants. A few, like Franklin Kameny in Washington, D.C., Craig Hanson in Los Angeles, and Larry Littlejohn in San Francisco, tried to bridge the new and old. But liberationists could be as dogmatic and intolerant as the old-liners. In August, radicals and San Francisco street people broke up the final North American Conference of Homophile Organizations (NACHO). The group was already torn between the bossy East and the pluralist West, over litigation strategy, and over whether to bar organizations that "damaged our image" or involved themselves in "extraneous issues." "It's time for the old groups to leave the field," Morris Kight said. Anarchy faced off with arrogant conservatism, and anarchy won.

To hold Los Angeles's first Gay Pride parade we fought the Police Commission for the right to assemble without posting a $1.25 million bond. Police Chief Ed Davis said it would be like permitting thieves and burglars to discommode the citizens, and predicted hardhats would mob us. We started marching (emboldened by news of New York and Chicago parades) fearing that might happen. A week before, some of us had asked Hollywood hustlers if they felt a gay community center would be helpful. Many who'd said no later joined the parade, and some staged an all-night sit-in to protest Perry's arrest.

We had a glowing vision: of rapidly creating a new world, freed of sexism, racism, ageism, looksism, exploitation, monogamy, and possessiveness. With gay liberation groups springing up all over, and New York's Gay Activists Alliance introducing militant but focused confrontational zaps, 1970 launched a decade in which our newly national movement marched from victory to victory—seeing no clouds on the horizon. —JIM KEPNER

I AM A FRIEND OF TROY PERRY

The Rev. Troy Perry (*right*) sits next to Carol Shepard, head of the Los Angeles chapter of Daughters of Bilitis, and lesbian activist Kelly Longman (*left*) on the corner of Las Palmas Avenue and Hollywood Boulevard as the 1970 Los Angeles Gay Pride parade passes by. Perry had publicly declared at the onset of the parade that he would continue his curbside vigil "until someone from the city of Los Angeles came and talked about gay rights." Two hours later, police arrived and arrested the trio for creating a public disturbance. They spent the night in jail and were released the next day on their own recognizance. Perry, however, marched to the front steps of the Federal Building, where he continued his protest, sitting for the next eleven days without food. Finally, Los Angeles city councilman Robert Stevenson came and spoke with the courageous clergyman about gay and lesbian concerns.

The Furies, a lesbian/feminist collective active in the early seventies, had several group houses where women could live cooperatively putting feminist separatism into practice. The Furies published a feminist newsletter, and created a great deal of the feminist theory of the day.

T I M E L I N E

In January, California Assemblyman Willie Brown announced that he would again introduce a bill to decriminalize consensual sex between adults. Brown modeled his bill, AB 701, on legislation adopted in Illinois. The reform, which made Brown a hero in the gay community, got stuck in committee and never made it to the governor's desk.

"HEY, BARTENDER, DO YOU HAVE A SAFETY PIN?"

An ongoing furor in the gay press followed arrests of male go-go dancers from such Los Angeles bars as the Meat Market and the Off-Broadway. The Police Commission considered allowing nude entertainers under a "look but don't touch" law, but settled on a "fig leaf ordinance," requiring local dancers to wear G-strings.

JANUARY   More than 250 homosexuals, led by the Rev. Troy Perry, marched for police reform on Hollywood Boulevard. ❑ A year after a Society for Individual Rights (SIR) member was shot dead by an Oakland, California, vice officer, the police department shifted several of its vice officers to other departments and told them to "refrain from enticing homosexuals in public places." ❑ The University of Minnesota recognized a club for gays and sympathizers called FREE (Fight Repression of Erotic Expression). ❑ Customs officials seized and sought permission to destroy ten artworks from an international erotic exhibit scheduled to show in New York City; permission was denied by a New York court citing the First Amendment.

FEBRUARY   Sixty protesters demanded the removal of a sign warning FAGOTS STAY OUT from Barney's Beanery, a West Hollywood eatery that had borne the plaque for more than twenty years; the sign continued to be a symbol of discrimination for over a decade, being removed only to be replaced at least three times. ❑ Two California college instructors were suspended after displaying nude models before a sociology class in order to demonstrate that there is nothing obscene about sex organs. ❑ NBC television showed a six-part series on homosexuality as part of its newscast "Close Up." ❑ A California appeals court ruled that a private room in a massage parlor is still open to the public, upholding "lewd conduct" charges against a masseuse.

MARCH   A resolution asking the Episcopal Church to "open her eyes and ears" to the suffering of homosexuals was passed by a convention of several hundred clergymen. ❑ A gay San Francisco postal worker fought an attempt by the Civil Service Commission to terminate him for "moral incompetency," recovering his job in November, and paving the road for future Civil Service Commission reforms. ❑ A New York youth arrested in a raid of the Snake Pit, a gay bar, barely escaped death after he leaped from the second story of a police station and was impaled on an iron fence; he later confessed he was an Argentine national afraid of deportation. ❑ A Los Angeles police officer fatally shot Larry Turner, a twenty-year-old black transvestite. ❑ A Buenos Aires court freed a surgeon who had been sentenced to three years' imprisonment for performing sex-change operations. ❑ Italian scientists announced the discovery of a drug that elevated sexual excitement in humans and animals and made male rats mount one another.

APRIL   Sandra Hagen of Brooklyn, New York, and Antoinetta Garland of Nashville, Tennessee, who fell in love during basic training for the Women's Army Corps, sought and were later granted honorable discharges after harassment drove them to go AWOL. ❑ The *Los Angeles Times* rescinded its ban on the word "homosexual" in advertisements. ❑ Dr. Otto Butz, acting president of Sacramento State College, refused to recognize the Society for Homosexual Freedom, a student group. ❑ Gay Liberation Front of Southern California threw a picket line around the Spanish consulate to protest a bill pending in the Spanish parliament that would penalize suspected homosexuals and associates of homosexuals.

MAY   Chanting "Suck cock, beat the draft," and "Bring our boys home," members of the Gay Liberation Front joined a Washington, D.C., war protest and initiated a "nude-in" in the Lincoln Memorial reflecting pool. ❏ David Stienecker, editor of the Mattachine Midwest newsletter, went to trial for defaming a Chicago vice officer who the publication claimed had made as many as a dozen "public indecency" arrests per day. ❏ Honolulu police reported that a blackmailer extorted payments of up to $1,800 at a time from at least three homosexuals. ❏ Sixteen men were arrested, one on an outstanding traffic warrant, during a raid on the Regency Baths in Los Angeles. ❏ A U.S. District Court in Sacramento ruled it legal to mail so-called obscene material upon request. ❏ The Denver Police Department was ordered by a county court to stop harassing employees and patrons of that city's Club Steam Baths.

JUNE Lesbians and gay men commemorated the Stonewall Riots with marches in New York, Los Angeles, San Francisco, and Chicago. ❏ The Los Angeles county clerk requested the California legislature tighten its laws against same-sex marriages after he received a flood of inquiries from gay couples wanting marriage licenses. ❏ Novelist Christopher Isherwood showed up at Los Angeles's Griffith Park for the second Gay-In, which included a body-painting booth dispensing the slogans "Super Fag" and "Fuck Forever." ❏ Tom Eckler of Los Angeles was arrested after telling the police officer who confiscated his "Gay Power" button, "Wear it in good health, dear." ❏ CBS was accused of antigay discrimination by the New York Mattachine Society for not hiring a gay man.

JULY Daughters of Bilitis convened in New York City and dissolved its national structure into a federation of autonomous chapters. ❏ San Francisco gay activists picketed Macy's over the department store's refusal to work with gay organizations and to stop arrests in its restrooms. ❏ The Rev. Troy Perry ended a ten-day fast for homosexual rights and sex law reform after "meaningful discussion" had begun with Los Angeles officials. ❏ The clubhouse of ONE in Phoenix was damaged in a fire thought to have been caused by arson. ❏ The University of Nebraska approved Professor Louis Crompton's proposal for a course in homophile studies. ❏ A Cincinnati judge dismissed charges of "aiding and abetting liquor law violation" against forty-nine persons arrested at a private gay party.

AUGUST Black Panther leader Huey Newton called on blacks to view the Gay Liberation Front and the Women's Liberation Front as "friends and potential allies," and said that gays "might be the most oppressed people in our

The "Rockefeller Five," arrested during the first Gay Activist Alliance demonstration in front of Rockefeller Center in August, stand outside of court in New York City with their supporters. In front, from left to right, are Tom Dorr, Marty Robinson, Phil Raia, Jim Owles, Arthur Evans, and lawyer Irwin Strauss.

Menacing Feminists

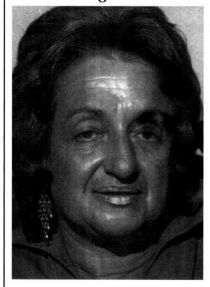

A year after National Organization for Women (NOW) founder Betty Friedan called lesbians a threat to the women's movement, a resolution supporting lesbian rights was withdrawn during NOW's convention because the national committee judged it too controversial. On the opening night of the national Congress to Unite Women, twenty-five women wearing T-shirts emblazoned with the words LAVENDER MENACE—Friedan's slur of choice—took over the stage.

Meanwhile, at Columbia University, Kate Millett, an intellectual leader of the feminist movement, was exposed as a lesbian by radical lesbian and gay activists in October, sending shock waves through feminist ranks.

A year later, the lesbian rights resolution was approved by the NOW membership.

society." ❑ After New York University gay students who were denied the space to have a dance peacefully protested and were attacked by police, nearly 2,500 gays rioted in New York City; there were eighteen arrests and a dozen injuries, half of which involved police. ❑ President Nixon "doesn't think people of the same sex should marry," White House press secretary Ron Ziegler announced in a letter to the *Advocate*. ❑ United Nations Secretary General U Thant agreed that the U.N. would consider a request to study the question of gay rights; over two decades would pass before the United Nations granted a gay group nonorganizational membership status.

SEPTEMBER   Unidos, a Los Angeles organization for gay Chicanas/Chicanos, held its first meeting. ❑ A federal judge enjoined the University of Minnesota from refusing to hire twenty-eight-year-old librarian James McConnell solely because he was homosexual. ❑ San Francisco police chief Al Nelder talked with gay community leaders in a meeting Jim Foster of SIR called "pleasant and cordial." ❑ A militant faction of the New York group Homosexuals Intransigent campaigned for a gay takeover of parts of Manhattan. ❑ James Agnew, son of the vice president, denied published reports that he was living with the male owner of a Baltimore beauty salon. ❑ The Teachers Advisory Council of Minneapolis approved a Guthrie Theater production about homosexuality to be shown to more than a thousand high school students, with a discussion to follow.

OCTOBER   Three demonstrations capped a week-long sit-in protest of New York University's antigay hiring policies. ❑ Police sweeps of Balboa Park, a popular cruising area in San Diego, resulted in 135 arrests. ❑ Detroit's newest gay bar was shut down during its peak hours for a late-night fire inspection; its owners charged harassment. ❑ Producers of the "Dick Cavett Show" agreed to host two spokesmen from the Gay Activists Alliance on a November show. ❑ Putting his job on the line, Professor Mike Silverstein of California State Univesity, Hayward, came out to a crowd of three hundred students in an attempt to start a gay students' union on campus.

NOVEMBER   A San Francisco psychiatrist wrote in *Today's Education* that gay teens establish their sexual identity before reaching high school and should be left alone. ❑ Los Angeles gays protested Mensa, an international high-I.Q. club, for censoring a gay ad from its newsletter. ❑ The Rev. Troy Perry ran as a write-in candidate for California lieutenant governor. ❑ KRLA, a Southern California radio station, placed a full-page ad in the magazine supplement of the *Los Angeles Times,* calling for tolerance of homosexuals. ❑ Yukio Mishima, Japanese author of the gay classic *Confessions of a Mask,* committed ceremonial suicide inside his country's military headquarters.

DECEMBER   KNBC-TV in Los Angeles won the Best Documentary award from the Southern California Radio and Television Broadcasters for "Out of the Shadows," a special program about homosexuals. ❑ The Vineyard, a religious organization working with the homophile community in New Mexico, celebrated its first anniversary. ❑ The Gay Activists Alliance of Long Island claimed victory by establishing dialogue with the Nassau County Human Rights Commission. ❑ The lesbian Minerva Club formed in Geneva, Switzerland.

ZAP! BOFF! POW!
GLF PULLS THE PLUG ON SHOCK THERAPY

They never knew what hit them. Politicians, writers, and other arbiters of the status quo found themselves confronted by gay activists, sometimes in drag, always with bullhorns. Disrupting and demanding, all in the name of dialogue. This zap targeted psychologists.

A film about shock therapy for homosexuals, which was being shown to a group of 140 mental health professionals, was suddenly interrupted when members of the Los Angeles Gay Liberation Front (GLF) raised shouts of "Barbarism!" "Medieval torture!" and "This is disgusting!"

Lights were turned up and nearly a third of the audience, led by activists Tony DeRosa, Don Kilhefner, Morris Kight, and Steve Beckwith, marched to the stage of the Music Room in the Biltmore Hotel. "I had hoped we could get through with Dr. Feldman's film and presentation and open some dialogue and discussion," Dr. Albert Marston of the University of Southern California's psychology department told the audience.

In the first part of his presentation British psychologist Dr. M. Phillip Feldman had stressed the ethical responsibility involved in using the behavior modification techniques pictured in the film. He said that they were used only on homosexuals who had sought help and who the researchers had been convinced genuinely wanted to change.

In oversimplified form, the technique worked out by Dr. Feldman—and since tried with varying degrees of success by other researchers—consists of showing the subject a photo of an attractive male and giving him a weak electric shock if he does not reject it within a specified time—initially eight seconds. As the treatment progresses, more and more attractive photos are used and the "safe-viewing" period randomly varied. Interspersed with the photos of males, the subject is allowed to view, if he chooses, photos of females without shock.

Dr. Feldman said he did not think anyone had any moral right to use such techniques on unwilling homosexuals or anyone else "who doesn't ask for them. I do not serve as the agent of society. I'm not here, either in America or in England, to do society's bidding. I'm here to help people who ask for this.

"This means we didn't keep in treatment any patients who were referred by the law or by the courts," Feldman continued. "I thought this was totally wrong. If it became clear early in treatment that they didn't want to change, we let them out through the back door. I can say this here, I couldn't say it in England."

Kight, however, took the tack that the very existence of such techniques was a threat. "You are a party to this," he told the group. "You must be responsible. With this kind of treatment you could make a Nazi."

Dr. Feldman replied that in the interrupted film, "I make just this point."

Kilhefner took over the microphone. "I'm a firm believer in free speech," he said. "But what you people out there call free speech in fact has been a monologue for over a half century. And we would like to start a dialogue." He claimed that GLF would print Dr. Feldman's speech at its own expense for those who wanted to read it later, "but right now the GLF is suggesting that this morning be reconstituted. If a dialogue is to begin, let it begin now. You

GAA HITS *HARPER'S*

Manhattan's Gay Activists Alliance (GAA) staged an all-day sit-in October 22 at the New York offices of Harper's *magazine. At issue was a recent article describing homosexuals as "condemned to a state of permanent niggerdom among men."*

The GAA handed out literature asking for "equal time for the gay community in the form of an article of rebuttal...which could alleviate the damage Harper's *had done." William S. Blair, the magazine's publisher, refused to print such an article by GAA or to commission an unprejudiced article from other sources. "However, we are willing to write a letter to GAA saying that we are not personally against the civil rights of homosexuals, or fail to recognize that they are treated harshly and should not be," he said.*

Joseph Epstein stated in his piece that homosexuals are "cursed, and I'm afraid I mean this literally, in the medieval sense of having been struck by an unexplained injury, an extreme piece of evil luck....There is much that my four sons can do in their lives that might cause me anguish, that might outrage me, that might make me ashamed of them and of myself as their father. But nothing they could ever do would make me sadder than if any of them were to become homosexual."

Both GAA and the magazine's editors agreed that the sit-in had been productive. "There was an exchange, and those things are always valuable," said managing editor Robert Kotlowitz. GAA president Jim Owles said he thought the demonstration would make the magazine think twice about running similar articles. The magazine provided coffee and doughnuts to the demonstrators.

Gay liberationists take over the rostrum at the Behavioral Modification Conference in Los Angeles. Dell Reed is in the foreground, and (*from left*): an unidentified man, Tony De Rosa (*barely visible behind*), Don Kilhefner, Dr. Marston, meeting moderator, and another unidentified man.

The oppressive dogma of "sin and sickness" put forth by church and state was targeted by Gay Liberation Front members, some of whom demonstrated their views before New York's St. Patrick's Cathedral in October.

have been our oppressor for too long, and we will take this no longer.

"We are going to reconstitute this session into small groups," he continued, "with equal numbers of GLF members and members of your profession. We're going to be talking about what you as psychologists are going to do to clear up your own fucked minds."

"I'm not a psychologist," a young black man in the audience protested.

"This is what we're going to be doing, baby," Kilhefner kept on. "Anybody who can't dig it, we ask you to leave."

"We ask *you* to leave," one man said loudly. "Yeah," a woman shouted, triggering applause.

"Sorry, buddy…" said Kilhefner, who was nearly drowned out in a rising storm of boos, protests, and hand-clapping. He kept shouting, "No more, baby, no more, baby!"

Added GLF member Ralph Shafer, "Ever since I was five years old, I've been reading books about homosexuality written by psychologists and psychiatrists and I've been seeing films…and we're sick and tired of it. Now we want to be treated like human beings."

A young woman who later identified herself as Cheryl A. Bartlett, a therapist at Fairview State Hospital in Costa Mesa, California, yelled, "Listen, buddy, when Dr. Feldman came in here, he said we're going to be dealing with a situation on a voluntary basis. We want to deal with people who come to us and say, 'I feel anxiety, I feel hostility, I feel tensions, because I am what I am, and I want to change.' You people are happy, go your way. God be with you."

Beckwith objected that if there were any homosexuals who felt anxiety, it was because of what society had done to them.

Despite the apparent hostility of many in the audience to the GLF invasion, most seemed interested in talking with the demonstrators face to face. Fewer than twenty persons actually left, and about a dozen discussion groups formed.

The discussions—which went on for about an hour—were far-ranging, with one of the most heated topics being the tactics the GLF had used, rather than homosexuality. But some GLF members did manage to get across the idea of a valid gay lifestyle to many conference participants to whom it was obviously a novel concept.　　　　　　　　　　　—STAFF REPORT

The Brief Life of Stonewall Nation

GLF's fantasy of possessing California's Alpine County became a centerpiece of gay lib's wild and media-wise tactics. Equal parts revolution and sit-in, it was the quintessential zap, playing on heterosexual fears of a queer nation.

It started in the state supreme court, which ruled to eliminate a one-year residency law, requiring only ninety days before residents could vote. The West Coast GLF saw an opportunity and leaped at it, targeting Alpine County, a mountainous area just south of Lake Tahoe, for political takeover.

Just before buses were to begin rolling lavender hordes into Alpine County, however, the story hit major newspapers and network television. The public and the politicians were in an uproar. GLF, which had agitated for the takeover, said that their goal from the beginning was to get the words "gay" and "lesbian" into the national media. "Stonewall Nation," as they had named their utopia, was revealed to be only a hoax.

"I imagine a place where gay people can be free," declared activist Don Jackson. "A place where there is no job discrimination, no police harassment or prejudice. A place where love rules instead of hate. A place where a gay government can build the base for a flourishing gay counterculture and city."

Alpine has 367 registered voters out of a total population of 450 people. A voting bloc of 200 to 300 gays would have a very good chance of seizing the county's government, explained GLF leaders.

"At this point, we have 479 signed up," community organizer Don Kilhefner said at a news conference October 20. "We project the first group of 250 to 300 people going up as of January 1. By April, we should be able to initiate the procedure to recall all the elected officials of Alpine County, and immediately have a new election in which homosexuals will be elected to all county offices."

The state attorney general's office in Sacramento said the requirements for a recall election are complex, but generally a petition signed by a modest number of eligible voters would be sufficient.

State law requires professional qualifications for many of the county offices. There would have to be two attorneys to serve as district attorney and Superior Court judge, a registered civil engineer to serve as road commissioner, four credentialed teachers to serve as the school board, and a doctor to serve as health officer. Two doctors, two lawyers, and several teachers have already signed up.

Herbert Bruns, a rancher who is chairman of the Alpine County Board of Supervisors, is not laughing about the proposed gay takeover. "We have a real nice county here. Naturally, we'll do everything we can to prevent anyone from taking it over. They will receive a hostile reception when they come. Apples and peaches don't grow very well in Alpine's cold climate," he said. "No fruit is very welcome up in our particular county."

"We hope there will be no violence," said Lee Heflin, another GLF organizer. "We plan to do this as peacefully as possible. But we're ready."

"Make no mistake," said Kilhefner, "we aren't just fooling around." If the Alpine project succeeds, he expects to see similar communities established elsewhere in the nation. "Almost any state in the union has an Alpine," Kilhefner said.

"We're ready to sell our house and move," one longtime lesbian couple told *The Advocate*. "We'd like to have a little country store in Alpine. Long Beach is for the birds."

Gay Lib Spreads Across the Nation

WASHINGTON, D.C. / Washington's Gay Liberation Front, organized in late June to "overcome the oppression and repression that has [sic] been shoved down our throats for so many years," is currently meeting weekly. The Tuesday-night sessions now see anywhere from one hundred to two hundred gays gathered at Grace Episcopal Church. Unlike the situation in other major cities, Washington's homophile organizations, now numbering three, appear to be cooperating well.

CHICAGO / Two hundred men and women rallied at Chicago's Bug House Square on June 27 to protest discrimination against homosexuals. The rally, held to commemorate the Christopher Street gay riots in New York City last year, was only the second such event in the city's history and climaxed the events of Gay Pride Week.

BALTIMORE / The growing gay liberation movement has added another chapter here, its first in Baltimore, and what one member called the first homosexual civil rights group in this city. Like many of the new gay freedom groups all over the country, Gay Liberation Front Baltimore was formed to combat an increase in police harassment, or, as its official statement of purpose puts it, "to counteract intensified political oppression from the Establishment."

SEATTLE / Members of the Gay Liberation Front marched through the city on Memorial Day and handed out free oranges stamped "Gay Is Good." Chairman Earl Corse said, "We are new in Seattle, but you damn well better believe you'll be hearing from us."

LOUISVILLE / The first action of the city's newly formed Gay Liberation Front was to throw a picket line around the Queen Bee Club. Activists charged the club with exploitation of homosexuals.

PITTSBURGH / The newly formed Homophile Organization of Pittsburgh has changed its name to Mattachine of Pittsburgh, acquired some one hundred members, filed a complaint with the local police and human rights commission in an arrest case, held a productive meeting with the city's top police officials, laid plans for a picnic and Gay-In, arranged with some of its members to start a soda bar for teenagers, and is working on plans for a fashion show—all in less than a month of existence.

"Good-bye, My Alienated Brothers"

Del Martin's Farewell

In 1955, Del Martin and her lover, Phyllis Lyon, founded Daughters of Bilitis, the nation's first lesbian organization. Martin's activism continued throughout the fifties and sixties, and included a stint on the board of directors of San Francisco's Council on Religion and the Homosexual, one of the first efforts to establish dialogue between gays and straights. In autumn of 1970, however, she parted ways with the burgeoning gay movement, citing significant philosophical and moral differences. Her biting criticisms of the predominately male movement foreshadowed those soon to be articulated by many other lesbians who, like Martin, turned their efforts toward women's liberation instead. Following are excerpts from Martin's statement published in The Advocate.

Longtime lesbian activists **Del Martin** (*left*) and **Phyllis Lyon,** under the watchful eye of **Eleanor Roosevelt.**

After fifteen years of working for the homophile movement—of mediating, counseling, appeasing, of working for coalition and unity—I am facing a very real identity crisis. I have been torn apart. I am bereft. For I have been forced to the realization that I have no brothers in the homophile movement....Like my sister Robin Morgan, I have come to the conclusion that I must say, "Good-bye to all that."

Good-bye to the wasteful, meaningless verbiage of empty resolutions made by hollow men of self-proclaimed privilege. They speak neither for us nor to us. They acknowledge us, and then dish us in their "male only" sanctuaries. It's the system, and there is not one among them with guts enough to put a stop to it. And, too late, they shall find that the joke is really on them.

Good-bye, my alienated brothers. Good-bye to the male chauvinists of the homophile movement who are so wrapped up in the "cause" they espouse that they have lost sight of the people for whom the cause came into being.

Good-bye to the bulwark of the Mattachine grandfathers, self-styled monarchs of a youth cult which is no longer theirs. As they cling to their old ideas and their old values in a time that calls for radical change, I must bid them farewell. There is so much to be done, and I have neither the stomach nor the inclination to stand by and watch them self-destruct.

Good-bye to all those homophile organizations across the country with an open-door policy for women. It's only window-dressing for the public, and for mutual protection in the small towns of suburbia. It doesn't really mean anything and smacks of paternalism.

Good-bye, too (temporarily, I trust), to my sisters who demean themselves by accepting "women's status" in these groups—making and serving the coffee, doing the secretarial work, soothing the brows of the policy-makers who tell them, "We're doing it all for you, too." Don't believe it, sisters, for you are only an afterthought that never took place.

Good-bye to the "Police Beat"—the defense of washroom sex and pornographic movies. That was never my bag anyway.

Good-bye to all the "representative" homophile publications that look more like magazines for male nudist colonies. Good-bye to the biased male point of view. The editors say they have encouraged women to contribute, but that they don't. Nor will they until the format is changed, policy broadened, and their material taken seriously.

Good-bye to the gay bars that discriminate against women. Good-bye to those that "allow" them in only if they dress up in skirts, while the men slop around in their "queer" costumes. Gay liberationists are right when they observe that gay bars ghettoize the homophile community.

Good-bye to the Halloween Balls, the drag shows and parties. It was fun while it lasted. But the humor has gone out of the game. The exaggeration of the switching (or swishing) of sex roles has become the norm in the public eye. While we were laughing at ourselves we became the laughingstock and lost the personhood we were seeking. It is time to stop mimicking the heterosexual society we've been trying to escape. It is time to get our heads together to find out *who we really are.*

Good-bye to the male homophile community. "Gay is good," but not good enough—so long as it is limited to white males only. Lesbians joined with you in what we mistakenly thought was a common cause. A few of you tried, we admit. But you are still too few, and even you fall short of the mark. You, too, are victims of our culture. Fifteen years of masochism is enough. None of us is getting any younger or any closer to where it's really at. So, regretfully, I must say good-bye to you, too. It's been nice and all that, but I have work to do. My friends neither look up to me nor down at me. They face me as equals, and we interact reciprocally with respect and love.

There is no hate in this good-bye—only the bitter sting of disappointment. Momentarily I am pregnant with rage at your blindness and your deafness—the psychosomatic symptoms of narcissism and egocentricity. But my rage will pass, for I realize you were programmed by society for your role of supremacy.

But somehow I expected more of you. I had hoped that you were my brothers and would grow up to recognize that freedom is not self-contained. You cannot be free until you free me—*and all women*—until you become aware that in all the roles and games you play, *you* are always "IT."

I must go where the action is—where there is still hope, where there is possibility for personal and collective growth. It is a revelation to find acceptance, equality, love, and friendship—everything we sought in the homophile community—not there, but in the women's movement.

I will not be your "nigger" any longer. Nor was I ever your mother. Those were stultifying roles you laid on me, and I shall no longer concern myself with your toilet training. You're in the big leagues now, and we're both playing for big stakes. They didn't turn out to be the same.

As I bid you adieu, I leave each of you to your own device. Take care of it, stroke it gently, mouth it, fondle it. As the center of your consciousness, it's really all you have.

Fault Lines

"An old French saying expresses the fear that the Revolution, like Saturn, will in turn devour its own children. And too often, when a minority group begins to rise up from its oppression, it behaves in a Saturnine fashion, as some of its unhinged members rush screaming to the fore, demanding vengeance for its sufferings. Lacking any sense of reason, strategy, or decency, they land their blows almost invariably on friend instead of foe, with the frequent result that most of the gains are wiped out just at the moment of victory."
—COLUMNIST JIM KEPNER, commenting on the rising discord between the new generation of gay liberationists and longtime homophile movement leaders

"Gaydom seems divided into two camps lately: the 'integrationists' and the 'segregationists.' The integrationists' main idea is that places that are exclusively gay are 'ghettos'—bad places to live or play....Exploitation in the ghetto? Sorry, I can't buy that. Let me worship, dance, drink, and live where I feel most comfortable. Don't 'force' me to 'integrate.'"
—COMMENTATOR ED JACKSON

"Gay men refer to 'homosexuality' and 'lesbianism' as if they were two different things. We are all homosexuals. Gay women need their own organizations until they can deal with men."
—GLF MEMBER CHERI MATISSE, reflecting on increasing lesbian dissatisfaction with the gay movement

"Violence is a means of oppression used on us, and we are told we must accept that. Bullshit. As violence shall oppress us, so shall it liberate us....Our leadership would do well to remember that Mao says that leaders must march ahead of the movement, not behind it."
—STUDENT MILITANT CHARLES THORPE

MISS THING   by Joe Johnson

THROW ANOTHER FAG IN THE FIRE

Journalist Reed Severin investigated historical sources of common epithets for gay men. Criticizing such words as "gay," "faggot," and "sissy" as based in "the heterosexual society's enforcement of sexual conformity," Severin tried unsuccessfully to promote the term "homoerotic," or "HE," in their place.

— In 1870, the term "to turn gay" is recorded as meaning to become a prostitute. In 1825 the phrase "to lead a gay life" meant to live immorally, especially by prostitution. Another expression of the times was "gay in the arse." The "gaying instrument" isn't too hard to guess. It was the earlier offspring of the Old German *gahi*, meaning fast or impetuous. The *Oxford English Dictionary* even claims it came from the German *wahi*—pretty, beautiful, or good.

— "Faggot," also spelled "fagot," comes from the French word meaning a bundle of sticks used for fuel. The word "fag" was used to designate younger boys doing menial tasks for older boys in British public schools, but this usage comes from "fatigue"—not "fagot." By 1555, in England, "faggot" referred to burning heretics alive, as "to fry a faggot." As early as 1591, the word also appeared as a term of abuse or contempt for whores.

— "Sissy" came to refer to homosexuals in the late nineteenth century. Originally it meant a "passive" homosexual. The slang began in the United States as a variation on "sister." But it doesn't come from "sister" meaning a sibling, but rather from its use as a term of address for "low" women ("Now look here, sister!").

A "RESEARCH VOYEUR" UNCOVERS THE WORLD OF TEAROOM SEX

Around five o'clock on a weekday evening a man enters a public restroom in a city park. He pauses briefly at the urinal, then approaches a man seated in one of the stalls. The man in the stall grasps the other man's penis and pulls it to his waiting mouth....

This scene is typical of hundreds performed in restrooms throughout the country. The "instant sex" is impersonal, devoid of involvement, a furtively shared encounter without commitment. It is, in a sense, the lifestyle of a large number of homosexuals.

Sociologist Laud Humphreys spent two years researching the phenomenon of this type of impersonal sex. In a recently issued study, *Tearoom Trade: Impersonal Sex in Public Places,* he has outlined his findings. Ironically, this activity, although widespread, has rarely been studied.

What type of people frequent "tearooms"? And why are public restrooms chosen for sexual activities? Surprising, to Humphreys anyway, is the diversity of people found in such places—married men with children, single straight types, doctors, teachers, salesmen, and even gas station attendants. Quick sex can be had in other places, such as in theaters, in cars, and behind bushes; yet public restrooms are still the predominant meeting place for those in search of "instant sex."

The number of persons participating in tearoom activity is enormous. Humphreys said that one summer afternoon he witnessed twenty acts of fellatio in the course of an hour while waiting out a thunderstorm in a tearoom. Participants assured Humphreys that it was not uncommon for one man to fellate as many as ten others in a day.

Many men frequent the same facility repeatedly, thus becoming known as regulars, some stopping off on their way to or from work. A physician in his fifties was so punctual that he appeared at almost the same time each day for a blow job. Another man, a salesman, usually visited his favorite men's room at least twice a day, and he claimed to have had as many as four orgasms in a twenty-four-hour period. He was married and the father of two children. Of Humphreys's research subjects, 54 percent were married and living with their wives.

In order to definitively research his subject, Humphreys became, for all intents and purposes, a voyeur. "Fortunately, the very fear and suspicion of tearoom participants produces a mechanism that makes such observation possible," he explains. "A third person—generally one who obtains voyeuristic pleasure from his duties—serves as a lookout, moving back and forth from door to window. Such a 'watchqueen,' as he is labeled in the homosexual argot, coughs when a police car stops nearby or when a stranger approaches. Having been taught the role of watchqueen, I played that part faithfully while observing hundreds of acts of fellatio.

"It is difficult to interview these people without becoming depressed over the hopelessness of their situation," Humphreys concludes. "They are almost uniformly lonely and isolated; en route from the din of factories to the clamor of children, they slip off the freeways for a few moments of impersonal sex in a toilet stall."

—MEL HOLT

HUSTLERS: DIRGE FOR A DYING BREED

He slouches against a window of the Gold Cup on Hollywood Boulevard, a Naugahyde Navaho with a cassette player clamped to his ear—hair down to his shoulders, his lanky calves cased in buckskin. Mick Jagger? Peter Fonda?

"Fonda Peter" would be more to the point—because, my friend, you're looking at a hustler, Model 1970.

You have a different image of the hustler? You've read *City of Night,* so you know that one can always spot a member of the trade by the pout, the T-shirt, the thumb in a belt loop? Poor old dear, you're living in the past.

The youthquake has shaken the knights of the street no less than the other segments of Young America. The shake-up affects not only the hustler's dress and grooming, but his whole self-image…and consequently his performance in the sheets. Those addicted to the company of hustlers know that the overall picture has changed markedly in the last half-decade—not with the disappearance of those hustlers rooted in the working classes, but with the entry into the trade of the new breed of middle-class dropout.

Note the changes resulting from this new arrival. First and most obvious is the change in looks. Costumes aside, the new breed tends to be tall, willowy, endomorphic, somewhat slight of chest. One remembers the eyes.

By contrast, his counterpart in the old school was short to medium in height, chunky in build, with pectorals and biceps that he liked to show off. One remembered the cock.

The old-schooler got his build playing sandlot football, helping his uncle dig postholes, then doing six months of reform school. In contrast, the new hustler got that trim body by surfing, running cross-country at Burbank High School, then doing six months of intensive frugging at a Hollywood discotheque.

I've mentioned that an altered self-image has led to the new hustler's new performance in the sheets. I refer specifically to the loss of that old defensiveness about masculinity. Well-hung and gifted with the knack of erection on command, the old-school rent-a-stud had a sexual range from A to A-prime. He took a passive role in fellatio. Period.

The new hustler is apt to have few if any illusions about his sexuality. Not only will he kiss, but he'll do so without prompting. The new hustler regards nothing this side of Kafka as off-limits. At the same time (sad to report) he's apt to have difficulty getting and keeping an erection, in sharp contrast to his old-style counterpart. The client may have to resort to the sexually bizarre to excite the new-schooler totally.

The old-schooler's inner conflict about his masculinity set up a tension, a dynamic of the libido that gave his sex acts the desperate passion of the forbidden. The new-schooler, for whom nothing is forbidden, has substituted affection for passion.

Perhaps the much-heralded "open society" will soon bring us such a plenitude of sexual outlets that we won't need to resort to paid professionals. If so, we should all welcome this new openness.

But a few of us old diehards will continue to feel nostalgic for hustling as it was. At the passing of the old-style laddie-of-the-night, let the mature homosexual doff his hat and observe a moment's silence. Then let him replace his hat, adjust his wallet, and go forth, determined to make the best of a new world.

—LEONARD RIEFENSTAHL

FILM: BOX-OFFICE CHIC

"My parents are running scared with the roles I've played. First Queenie in Fortune and Men's Eyes, *then that landlord in* The Gay Deceivers....Well, finally I've had a change of pace in* Stanley Sweetheart. *I play a lesbian."*
—PERFORMER MICHAEL GREER

"I've no intention of making a change to playing with an acid-rock band. It would be like Bette Davis trying to be a go-go girl!"
—LIBERACE

In 1970 homosexuality became box-office chic. But in typical Hollywood fashion, most of the movies depicted gays as disturbed, ranging from the depressed and tragic characters in *The Boys in the Band* to the psychopathic pederast son in *The Damned*.

A remake of Oscar Wilde's *The Picture of Dorian Gray* showed Helmut Berger cruising a waterfront tearoom, and at the supposed height of his decadence, picking up a black sailor to swollen orchestrations of funk. In *The Vampire Lovers*, vampire Mircilla Kornstein draws blood not from sucking necks but from performing cunnilingus on her unsuspecting victims. Reviewer Harold Fairbanks commented, "If we are to draw any conclusions from this picture, it's that being a vampire, or even a lesbian, in those times was not all you could wish it to be, but being Jewish didn't help any either."

Comedy accompanied horror. *Myra Breckinridge*, the film adaptation of Gore Vidal's scathing transsexual spoof, starred Rex Reed and Raquel Welch as the male and female versions of the title role. Director John Huston starred, and even Mae West broke her twenty-six-year self-imposed absence from the screen, as talent agent Leticia Van Allen. Her entrance showed West sizing up a row of handsome men, including a young actor named Tom Selleck. When he told her he was six feet seven inches, she retorted, "Let's forget about the six feet and concentrate on the seven inches." The film's most infamous scene, however, involved Raquel Welch, actor Roger Herren, and a dildo.

"The audience cannot fail to get the point, nor does Rusty, as Myra straps on the dildo and plunges into the void," said *The Advocate*.

Another comedy with mixed messages was *The Private Life of Sherlock Holmes*. The plot revolved on the assumption that Holmes, a lifelong bachelor, is homosexual. But by story's end, the world-famous sleuth becomes romantically involved with a woman. It seemed gay and lesbian themes in comedy were permissible only if homosexuality itself was the butt of the joke.

A handful of films did present positive images of gays and lesbians. Larry Kramer's screenplay adaptation of D. H. Lawrence's *Women in Love* won high praise for director Ken Russell's nude-male wrestling scene and the acceptance, or at least recognition, of same-sex love. In *Something for Everyone*, Anthony Corlan, as Angela Lansbury's gay son who is seduced by the amoral, pansexual Michael York, brought such sensitivity to his role that Fairbanks noted, "It is a pleasure to report that, for once, homosexuality is treated honestly in a movie, instead of the pandering gratuitous examples we have had of late."

In *Monique*, a heterosexual marriage on the rocks is saved by the free-spirited title character, who has an openly loving sexual relationship with both husband and wife. Said critic Jeanne Barney, "The characters suffer neither pain nor punishment for supposed transgressions, nor does the film proffer any messages or morals. Indeed, if there were a moral in the film, it would be that sex between people who love each other is a good, constructive activity."

Bob Mizer: Cinema's Poet of "Ass Capades"

For longer than many care to admit, the Athletic Model Guild (AMG) has been cranking out flicks that straddle porn and pretense, coming dangerously close to bona fide gay erotic art.

A typical AMG "Ass Capade" takes two or three sinewy drifters, costumed to suit whatever fetish Mizer is featuring at that moment. The boys wander into a slapped-together setting: a locker room, a reformatory, a college dorm, a classroom, a construction site, Marine barracks, the North Woods, Old Laredo, Hustler's Row.

Within the first two minutes, the kids have found a pretext to shuck their costumes; within four, to shed their inhibitions. By the end of ten minutes, their "relationship" has spanned a wide range. And somehow, despite the X-rated story line, the whole production manages to convey the innocent glee of a towel fight.

Bob Mizer, the mastermind behind AMG, is cameraman, casting agent, and director extraordinaire. His greatest talent, however, may be for recruiting endless hunky models, most of whom have never before experienced an overtly homoerotic act. Yet, by the quiet confidence of his manner—by appealing to the sexual exhibitionist, the narcissist in every well-built boy—Mizer induces these young straights to play passionate sodomites.

Starting in the 1940s, Mizer began recruiting models, filming them in the semi-raw, and selling the results openly to mail-order customers—all at a time when homosexuality tippytoed through America's closets and back alleys, terrified of the light.

Mizer the Bold, stubborn and realistic, single-handedly took on a brigade of vice cops, city attorneys, and bluenoses—and won. His victory freed the options of all those photographers who have entered the field subsequently. Long before *Mattachine Review* and *ONE* magazine had taken up the pen to educate the public, Mizer was filling the margins of his publication, *Physique Pictorial,* with eloquent exposés of entrapment and with defenses of the untrammeled pursuit of happiness.

In person, Mizer hardly looks the part of the movie mogul. At AMG, his combination home and studio in downtown Los Angeles, you'll find him behind stacks of glossy photos and film cans. (Even to get that far you'll have to brave AMG's chain-link fences, alarm systems, watchdogs, and caged monkeys.) There sits a graying man in his forties, resembling a suntanned Raymond Burr—his face a record of good times and bad. Mizer's choice of clothing is casual to the point of vagrancy—typically a sweatshirt (too small) and a pair of cotton slacks (too wrinkled).

His first movies often languished on a level of phony Roman low camp, with toga-clad hustlers stumbling through plaster-of-Paris parodies of slave auctions. This phase gave way to the Sweet Leilani period, with Hawaii consisting of a couple of dead palm fronds, a blanket of plastic grass draped over the tiles of the famous AMG swimming pool, and two Texans bumping their flower-print crotches to the melodies of Henry Owen.

A prediction: When the gay filmgoer tires of soporific pseudo-poetics and plotless, witless zigzag, only then will AMG return to vogue. With his stable of new-to-the-scene studs, his fine eye for truth, and—above all—his respect for the viewer's time, Bob Mizer truly deserves to have that vogue once more.

—Leonard Riefenstahl

THE DEMISE OF A DRAG LEGEND

Ray Bourbon changed his name to Rae when he had a sex-change operation in the fifties, a change of gender not recognized by the author of the article below. For thirty years before that, he was known as the world's foremost female impersonator, coming up through vaudeville, starring on Broadway with his friend Mae West, and entertaining Hollywood royalty at his own Sunset Strip nightclub. Miss Rae Bourbon also cut albums of her outrageous comedy songs such as "Queen of the YMCA," "She's Only a Link in a Daisy Chain," and "Let Me Tell You About My Operation." They were the last recorded traces of an entertainment legend before her tragic fall. She died the year after her arrest in a badly lit jail cell.

He once performed before a packed house at Carnegie Hall. His last performance was before a few of the local citizenry in District Court at Brownwood, Texas. The jury said, "Life." Rae Bourbon was seventy-eight on August 11. He marked the occasion in his cell, a forgotten relic of another age. He was arrested the previous December, along with protégé Randall "Bobbie" Crain. A pistol allegedly owned by Bourbon and identified as the weapon used to kill pet shop owner A. D. Blount had been found beside a Texas highway.

Bourbon was a sucker for small animals. He had seventy-one—dogs, cats, and a couple of pet skunks—when he set out for Ciudad Juárez, across the Texas border from El Paso, in September 1967, to fulfill a nightclub engagement.

Bookings were no longer so easy to get, and funds were low. He started the long trip from Kansas City, where he had last appeared, in an old car crammed with everything he owned and towing his pets behind in a special trailer. Thirty-five miles from El Paso, the car caught fire. Everything was burned but the trailer, which was saved by a man with a tank truck full of tree spray.

His wardrobe gone, Bourbon could not keep his Juárez date. He was stranded. Somehow, he scraped together enough money to buy another old car, and started out again for another booking in the Midwest, towing the trailer with his pets.

Two weeks and three hundred miles later, the car broke down for good. Bourbon was forced to board his animals at Blount's kennels and go on alone on the bus. "When he found out I was an entertainer, the price went to fifty dollars a day," Bourbon said. "I didn't know this until I called him from Kansas City."

Finally, Bourbon managed to get enough money ahead to redeem his pets. He rented a truck and called Blount from a phone booth to tell him he was coming. "He told me not to come. He had already disposed of the pets. Had it not been for the station attendant and some man and his wife, I'd have died in the phone booth," Bourbon recalled.

For the next several months, he obsessed over finding and recovering his pets. Enter Bobbie Crane, who headed for Juárez to search for the missing animals.

Bourbon related: "Several days later, at the club, I'd just gotten my makeup on when a waiter came and told me that the boss wanted to see me in the office. It was full of police and two Texas Rangers with warrants from Texas for my arrest, as well as warrants for Crain.

"That was when I found out the man that had had my pets had been shot, supposedly with my gun," said a stunned Bourbon, who had bought the gun after a recent robbery attempt. "I thought I was going to die at that moment."

Now Bourbon waits in Brown County Jail. Eventually, he will be moved to the state penitentiary or to a prison hospital. "I know I can't last much longer," said Bourbon, who had a massive heart attack while awaiting trial. "I'm just praying that I'll be able to die on the outside."
— ROB COLE

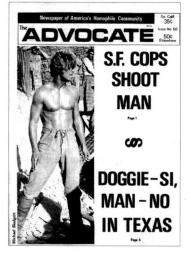

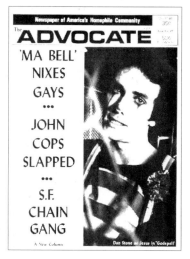

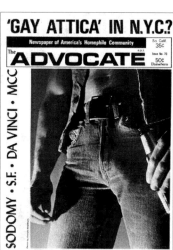

SPEEDING UP

1971 In June of 1971 I could feel the hot breath of a mounted policeman's horse on the back of my neck, just before I was arrested for protesting over a gay-rights bill outside of New York's City Hall. The cop was cute. His name was Frank. He was all business, though. He kept me handcuffed for seven hours before he finally let me go. I was guilty, but at the trial I was acquitted.

This was the year we began to make ourselves real. For decades, homophiles had spoken in polite whispers. In 1969 a gay battle cry had been sounded at Stonewall. In 1970 we got organized and began to argue over our goals. Nineteen seventy-one was the year we grew loud enough to be heard, and like us or not, America could no longer deny that we were there.

The shadowy world inhabited by homosexuals was being exposed to the public spotlight. Although most TV shows still hid gay men and lesbians with potted palms and silhouettes, gay representatives were invited to show their faces on "The David Susskind Show." Though news photos still showed the backs of two men or women holding hands, the first male-male kiss appeared on screen in *Sunday, Bloody Sunday*, the story of a gay man hopelessly in love with a bisexual. Most films dealing with homosexuals were unhappy. In *Fortune and Men's Eyes*, the world of prison abuse and rape was explored. In *The Music Lovers*, a distraught Tchaikovsky teetered near the border of hysteria. In *Some of My Best Friends Are...*, a sodden Christmas Eve was spent by the self-hating denizens of a gay bar. And in *Death in Venice*, an aging homosexual gentleman, his hair-dye dripping down his fevered cheek, died on the beach, painfully yearning for a beautiful young boy who frolicked unaware in the surf.

But we were beginning to speak for ourselves. The title of Rosa von Praunheim's German documentary delivered his whole message: *It Is Not the Homosexual Who Is Perverse, but the Society in Which He Lives.* While arguments still raged over Dr. David Reuben's ludicrous accusation that we used light bulbs as dildoes, books like Dennis Altman's *Homosexual: Oppression and Liberation* clearly defined our problems and outlined the solutions. E. M. Forster's *Maurice,* an interclass gay love story, hidden since 1914, finally saw the light. Arthur Bell's *Dancing the Gay Lib Blues* and Donn Teal's *The Gay Militants* described the first year and a half of the post-Stonewall movement.

I saw it all from New York City. The Mattachine Society's pleas for tolerance had been outshone. The Gay Liberation Front, which had tried to support many causes with its revolutionary Marxist ideals, was on the wane. The Gay Activists Alliance (GAA), with its focus on reforming the system to include gays and lesbians, was the leading light, and I was its vice president. Nineteen seventy-one was the year that GAA opened the Firehouse, a four-story extravaganza of gay liberation, whose first floor was lined with a huge mural that contained pictures of everyone from Walt Whitman to the drag queens at the Stonewall. There, Vito Russo presented all-night film festivals where we could react as lewdly as we pleased. And there, we inaugurated gay disco with huge weekly fund-raising dances. Once, we took a whole dance with us at two A.M. to hold a loud protest outside a City Council member's apartment house, to embarrass him into holding a meeting to consider our civil rights bill.

We were wildly ambitious. Our meetings drew hundreds of energized activists into a score of committees. It got so complicated that we needed a Committee on Committees to untangle the jumble. We were, as the slogan said, everywhere. Most of our "zaps" were in town: at Clancy's straight bar protesting homophobia, picketing at the Board of Education to protest firings, registering for a double room and announcing intent of sodomy at the YMCA to protest discrimination, bursting into several branch offices of the Household Finance Corporation so Arthur Evans could scream about refusals of loans to gays.

We traveled to Hauppauge, Long Island, to protest police brutality; to Bridgeport, Connecticut, to protest antigay violence; and thousands of us went to Albany, where we listened to Jim Owles demand a statewide civil rights bill on the steps of the State House. Homosexuality was becoming legal, if not protected, in states like Idaho, Oregon, and Colorado that year. Nineteen seventy had seen Gay Pride marches in New York and Los Angeles. In 1971 their size doubled, and parades were spreading everywhere: Philadelphia, Detroit, San Francisco, Washington, D.C.

When we weren't working on politics, we were revolutionizing our personal lives. I moved from a solitary apartment into a gay commune. On weekends I dropped a tab of acid and went to the fabled Continental Baths, where I could dance, swim, eat, get massaged, have lots of sex, and listen to Bette Midler sing and throw poppers into the audience, composed of gay men in towels and straight couples in evening dress. We had become chic. I spent my first summer on Fire Island, where gays lived as they wanted to and straight people came to stare. Emboldened by all this freedom, it's small wonder that I chose that year to come out to the president of the college where I teach and I drew up plans to be the adviser to a gay club at school. In 1971 all things seemed possible.

We were drunk with our own sense of new power. We truly believed that once we had presented our case to the nation, our rights would be granted immediately. It took a lot of battering before we realized we were in for the long haul. It took fifteen years for New York's gay civil rights bill to pass. The gay club at the college lasted two years and wasn't resurrected until two decades later. Becoming real, it turned out, was only the beginning of our struggle. But we had opened our door wide in 1971, and we were determined that it would stay open.   —ARNIE KANTROWITZ

Arnie Kantrowitz (*center*) during a Gay Activists Alliance zap of the Fidelifacts investigation agency in New York City. The January 18 action was organized to protest the company's selling of information speculating about the sex lives of gay employees.

The indomitable Vito Russo selling "gay balloons" at a Gay Activists Alliance Street Fair held June 26 in New York City.

T I M E L I N E

What a Drag

A star-studded New York premiere of the San Francisco drag performance troupe the Cockettes, fueled by rave reviews of the West Coast show by Truman Capote and Rex Reed, was met with high expectations of camp, kicks, and political satire. Marlene Dietrich lent the group her limo when they arrived on Halloween night; just over a week later, a packed house of over a thousand people at the Anderson Theater witnessed the opening of "Tinsel Tarts in a Hot Coma."

Unfortunately, the show flopped. Sally Quinn wrote a review for *The New York Times* entitled "The Cockettes: The Show Was a Drag." Over half of the house left after the first two hours of the four-hour fiasco. Beating a hasty retreat, Rex Reed was overheard moaning, "My God! This is worse than Hiroshima."

JANUARY   Proposed changes in the Texas penal code would have made it legal for a man to have sex with a dog, but not with another man; the proposal failed. ❑ Washington State's Judicial Committee proposed reform of antigay state laws; four years later, sodomy laws would be repealed. ❑ The Family Service Agency of San Francisco, a nonprofit organization for the welfare of families, voted to name a gay man and a lesbian to its board of directors. ❑ Two Los Angeles men were arrested by officers who burst into their Silver Lake district home and charged them with lewd conduct; charges were later dropped after a protest led by the Rev. Troy Perry. ❑ In a controversial letter, columnist Ann Landers advised a distraught gay teenager to seek therapy—not to convert to heterosexuality, but to find self-acceptance.

FEBRUARY   Eminent psychologist Evelyn Hooker, in a speech at ONE Institute in Los Angeles, blamed President Nixon's attitudes about homosexuality for the lack of federal gay law reform. ❑ San Francisco gay activists urged homosexuals to tear up their Macy's charge cards in protest of thirty-eight felony vice arrests in the store's restrooms. ❑ New Orleans gay activists warned gay tourists about potential entrapment during Mardi Gras. ❑ Washington, D.C., gays picketed the Plus One, a gay bar, alleging discrimination against women, blacks, and drag queens. ❑ Arguments over the the "new" issue of sexism split the Milwaukee Gay Liberation Front into the Radicalesbians and Gay Male Liberation.

MARCH   In one of the largest gay demonstrations to date, upwards of three thousand lesbians and gays marched on the New York State capitol building in Albany to demand civil rights for homosexuals. ❑ Two hundred and fifty people attended the first Gay Liberation National Conference in Austin, Texas, though some delegates walked out, protesting the presence of heterosexuals. ❑ A witch and a warlock led hundreds of gays and lesbians in prayer to exorcise antigay forces from a Los Angeles police station. ❑ Members of Daughters of Bilitis picketed St. Patrick's Cathedral in New York to protest the church's treatment of women. ❑ More than a thousand attended the dedication service of MCC's first permanent home in downtown Los Angeles. ❑ Despite a blinding snowstorm, more than 250 Canadians attended a homophile forum and dance in Downsview, Ontario.

APRIL   An estimated ten thousand lesbians and gays joined the largest-ever antiwar march in Washington, D.C., while gays swelled a similar march in San Francisco. ❑ The New York GAA asked the state court to intervene after its certification as a nonprofit group was denied by a state official; a year later, the court granted the group the right to incorporate. ❑ Sixty-five people turned up at the first gay liberation meeting held in the state of Missouri. ❑ A so-called panel discussion on homosexuality published in *Playboy* was exposed by *The Advocate* as a composite of two-year-old interviews. ❑ The city clerk of New York threatened a minister who had performed more than twenty holy union ceremonies for gay couples with arrest, but never made good on the threat.

MAY   A gay hairdresser from Cuba won a federal court order granting him U.S. citizenship despite an Immigration and Naturalization Service policy banning immigration of known homosexuals. ❏ A psychologist monitored an encounter session between sixteen police officers and sixteen homosexuals at a Howard Johnson's hotel in San Jose, California. ❏ Oregon repealed its sodomy laws.

JUNE Gay students at Columbia University occupied a dormitory lounge to protest the college president's and a black student group's claim that gays were not a legitimate minority. ❏ Three hundred and fifty lesbians from across the country met in Los Angeles for the Gay Women's West Coast Conference. ❏ A longtime Methodist minister who had recently come out was suspended by church officials in San Antonio, Texas. ❏ The San Francisco Association for Mental Health issued a policy statement saying "homosexuality can no longer be equated only with sickness." ❏ In a move described by some as a resignation and by others as an ouster, Dick Leitsch left as executive director of the Mattachine Society of New York. ❏ God and meteorology were praised when a rainbow ring formed around the sun during a gay-rights rally in Sacramento.

Arthur Evans of the Gay Activists Alliance confronts New York City Board of Education officer Murray Rockowitz during an April fifty-person sit-in protesting antigay discrimination by the city school system. Five activists were arrested.

"Anyone who finds a penis obscene is forgetting where he came from," said Stan Williams when the fire department seized his thirty-five-foot "cockapillar" from Hollywood's Gay Pride parade in June. Further controversy broke out over a banner declaring, SUCKING IS BETTER THAN WAR.

JULY The University of Maryland Students for a Democratic Society (SDS), a radical leftist organization, officially recognized gays as an oppressed minority and equated discrimination of homosexuals with racism. ❏ Famed civil rights lawyer William Kunstler agreed to represent gay students at the University of Kansas in their fight for official recognition; the appeal lost when the Supreme Court refused to hear the case three years later. ❏ A new chapter of the Gay Activists Alliance in Cleveland vowed to repeal Ohio's sodomy laws; a year later, they succeeded. ❏ Indecency charges against two Chicago men for kissing on a Loop streetcorner were dismissed after gay community protests. ❏ Nearly two hundred Connecticut gays marched from police headquarters to the City Hall of Bridgeport protesting a wave of police harassment. ❏ Scottish doctors hailed a drug reported to curb sex urges in men, including those who had "a need for sex daily."

AUGUST A hundred balloon-bearing gay Texans paraded through Dallas proclaiming "Love Day." ❏ A petition to remove homosexuality from the

A lesbian marching at the Christopher Street Gay Pride Parade in June.

FRANKLIN KAMENY

It was said of him that he never wasted time being nice. From the late fifties, when he organized the Washington, D.C., Mattachine Society after the Civil Service Commission (CSC) discovered his homosexuality and fired him from his job as a government astronomer, Franklin Kameny was known as an adamant, effective fighter.

Though he had no legal training, he represented himself in his case against the CSC, appealing all the way to the Supreme Court, which declined to hear his suit. Though he did not win, his determination led him to handle dozens of other cases involving federal discrimination against gays.

Through most of the sixties, Kameny stood out as one of the most militant figures of the homophile movement and was its vital link to Stonewall-era activism.

He never gave up. In 1971, Kameny made headlines as the first open homosexual to run for Congress, though he only garnered 1.6 percent of the vote.

American Psychiatric Association's 1974 edition of its *Diagnostic and Statistical Manual* of mental illnesses and character disorders was started by the lesbian newspaper *Mother.* ❑ By a sweeping majority, the National Student Congress endorsed the creation and funding of a "gay desk" to help campus gay groups function effectively. ❑ Cleveland's GAA countered recent police sweeps of Edgewater Park by holding an all-gay rubbish pickup. ❑ Underage gays staged a kiss-in in Trafalgar Square, London, to protest a section of Britain's Sexual Offences Act, which permitted homosexual lovemaking only when both partners are over twenty-one.

SEPTEMBER A *Playboy* survey concluded that homosexuality among men is declining. ❑ Ten activists picketing what they called the antiwoman dress code of a Tennessee gay bar were arrested on charges of loitering and held for $300 bail. ❑ *San Francisco Chronicle* charges of "gay take-over" arose when an openly gay man was elected chair of a community relations unit for an area including the Castro district. ❑ Editorials in *The Washington Post* urged an honorable discharge for a gay Navy man outed by his disgruntled lover; one month later, the man was honorably discharged. ❑ New York's GAA launched a letter-writing campaign against talk-show host Johnny Carson because of his antigay humor and continuing use of the word "fag."

OCTOBER CALIFORNIA SAYS "NO SEX," headlined *The Advocate* after legislator Willie Brown's liberal sex law reform bill was defeated by a vote of 41 to 25. ❑ Florida Circuit Court Judge Thomas Testa ruled a Miami city ordinance against cross-dressing unconstitutional. ❑ The California penal code's castration provision for repeated sex offenders was revoked, though eleven assemblymen voted to retain it. ❑ A mixed crowd of five hundred gay and straight students flocked to a fund-raising dance for the Kansas Gay Liberation Front in Lawrence. ❑ The U.S. Court of Appeals ruled explicit portrayal of lesbian sexual activity obscene. ❑ Mike "Michelle" Tidwell was chosen Miss Arkansas 1971–72 during Love a Homosexual Weekend in Hot Springs. ❑ Pacific Telephone stated that it would not hire a known homosexual.

NOVEMBER Gay leaders condemned as "disastrous" a Nixon Administration proposal to automatically fire federal employees belonging to any group the government listed as "subversive"; the proposal went nowhere. ❑ San Francisco gays claimed partial credit for electing gay-friendly candidate Richard Hongisto as the city's sheriff. ❑ Indiana gay activist Charles Avery was named executive secretary of the newly formed People's Party. ❑ St. Sebastian's Church in Chicago hosted a monthly mass for gays but tried to prevent it from being announced publicly. ❑ The support of two Dutch Catholic teachers' groups helped win a nondiscrimination policy for gay teachers in Holland.

DECEMBER Two new murders of gay men in the Washington, D.C., area brought the toll of mysterious gay deaths to fourteen in a three-year period. ❑ Two bars in Rochester, New York, were closed and three patrons arrested in that city's first gay-bar raid in over thirty years. ❑ Bert Chapman of Howell, Michigan, was released from prison; Chapman, arrested in 1940 for an alleged homosexual offense, had been confined as a "criminal homosexual psychopath" for thirty-one years.

A Campus Crusader in High Heels

"He may be student body president, but he still has to do the dishes around here," Jack Baker's lover told *The Advocate*. James Michael McConnell was talking about the first gay activist ever elected student body president at a major university—a remarkable illustration that, to the 43,000 students at the University of Minnesota, sexual preference doesn't make any difference.

It is Baker himself who has done much to create that kind of tolerant climate. During the past eighteen months the twenty-nine-year-old law student has spoken to nearly a hundred different church, campus, and community groups. He has appeared numerous times on local TV and radio talk shows, and lengthy, sympathetic profiles of him have been published in the area's two daily newspapers.

Baker's election has drawn national media attention as well. *The New York Times, The Washington Post, Time,* and national wire services all carried articles. Earlier, the Associated Press had distributed a wire photo of the candidate's most popular campaign poster—Baker wearing Levi's, a sport shirt, and high-heeled shoes.

Baker first attracted widespread notoriety when he and McConnell applied for a marriage license in May 1970. The couple invited reporters to interview them, but the publicity cost McConnell the librarian's job he had been promised at the university. The incident created a wave of sympathy among their fellow students, however, an attitude probably reflected in Baker's election.

The university's Board of Regents—which unanimously denied McConnell the library job last July—has apparently taken Baker's new appointment in stride. When Baker dropped in on the regents during a recent meeting, Albert V. Hartl—one of the crustiest conservatives on the board—glad-handed the new student body president and told him to be sure to stop by the house, if he ever gets up to Fergus Falls. A nice gesture, but what Hartl doesn't know is that Baker really plans to visit Fergus Falls this summer, just to drop in on Hartl. And he'll bring along McConnell—the man Hartl voted to deny a job.

Not everyone on campus has been so welcoming of Baker. One antagonist's letter came to the *Minnesota Daily,* the campus newspaper, which had heartily endorsed Baker as "the most qualified and capable candidate." A member of the right-wing Young Americans for Freedom wrote to demand that the university "not permit a filthy queer to become president of the student body....Keep America beautiful by stamping out queers."

A few days later the *Daily* printed three letters in rebuttal. "Why don't you judge Mr. Baker on what he does for the university rather than on his love life?" wrote one student. "These 'un-Americans' have been a useful part of humanity as long as any other people."

Ask him how long he's been out, and Baker's eyes look skyward. "Well, if you mean in terms of socializing and going to bars, it would be since 1963, in Arizona," he says. "That was just before I enlisted in the Air Force."

It was in 1966, at a party in Oklahoma City, that Baker met McConnell. "It was a friend who introduced us," recalls McConnell. "I think he was trying to play matchmaker. Jack and I went together for nine months before we became lovers—on his birthday in 1967." "Yes, that was the day when God shined His love upon us, and we were joined forever," says Baker, smiling. "Besides, I was horny." "You're always horny," replies McConnell with a laugh.

—Lars Bjornson

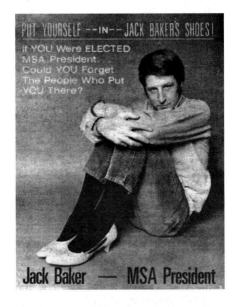

WELL-HEELED FIGHTER
Though Jack Baker was successful in politics, the student activist and his lover, Mike McConnell, lost their battle to be legally married. A marriage license was issued t them at one point, but a few months later the Minnesota Supreme Court revoked it.

MORRIS KIGHT

SCREAM AND SUCK YOUR THUMB!
In activist gay apparel, Kight presides over a Gay Liberation Front "scream-in" and "suck-in" at the West Hollywood office of so-called Primal Scream Therapy. Its proponent, Dr. Arthur Janov, called homosexuality "unreal love made by unreal people," and claimed that all such "neuroses" could be cured by screaming. In May of 1971, gays screamed back.

Though he'd only become a gay activist two years earlier, by 1971 Morris Kight was omnipresent in Los Angeles's Gay Liberation Front. A political wheeler-dealer par excellence, Kight was best known for his Dow Action Committee, protesting the manufacturers of napalm during the Vietnam War. Kight had a genius for publicity. His rhythmic Texas cadence and gracious manner masked a sharp, creative intellect, and while some denounced him as a "media freak," he became an often-quoted and much-photographed spokesperson for gay liberation.

Kight's announcement in this September interview that the GLF was suspending public meetings for a "breathing spell" and assessment came as a bitter shock to many of its members. But his departure from direct-action militance did not end his activity. In fact, it left him free to become a principal architect of the Gay Community Services Center in Los Angeles, soon a prototype for similar institutions across the country.

You say that many of your goals have been achieved.

Well, we said to be gay and proud you had to say it, act it, believe it, and live it. We call that self-realization. You say: Here I am—I'm gay. So what? Beyond that self-realization comes affirmation—you affirm your gayness and your pride in it, and that makes you a stronger person. I guess over in the Christian church they call it "salvation." I can't think of a better word: becoming conscious that you are not disconnected from your brothers and sisters, that you have a duty to them, and you fulfill it.

So where does that leave the Gay Liberation Front?

Many of the goals that the Gay Liberation Front of Los Angeles started out to achieve have been achieved, and to some extent we have passed our usefulness. Perhaps it's time for us to take stock of ourselves, to see where we are.

I think almost every group in the country has been moved by us. The programs that we created or invented, ideas that we espoused, have become the programs and ideas of other groups. Certainly we have made mistakes, and we are sorry for that. But any group that attempts as much as we've attempted in the past two and a half years is bound to make mistakes.

What is left for us to do are political things that no other group might do as effectively—draft counseling, help for gays now in military service, and help in a number of other ways which haven't yet been channeled.

Frankly, I'm sure we are going to get our freedom. I see it everywhere: in the marketplace, in the stores, in the homes, in dealings with families, in the kind of attention we get from radio, television, and the newspapers. While we don't get the coverage we deserve, the quality of it has changed.

Still, I realize we're not home yet. We have a long way to go. There are 1,750 arrests in Los Angeles each month. I weep for each of them. Everyone who's denied a job, I weep for. Everyone who is driven from their homes by a misunderstanding family, I have to offer my love to.

But, believe me, it's changing. Take *The Advocate*, for instance. It couldn't possibly have been done ten years ago. There would have been nobody to have written it. There wouldn't have been news to write about in the first place, and, in the second place, the police would have come and carried the staff away. Now it can be published.

Gay Life in Vietnam

The following questions and answers are excerpted from a year-long correspondence between an Advocate *reader ("Statesider") and a gay soldier ("Sarge") stationed in Vietnam. Letters from the serviceman abruptly ceased in early 1971.*

STATESIDER: Is there a notable, or should I say observable, gay life in Vietnam?

SARGE: I find that wherever I am stationed in Vietnam, there are people of the gay persuasion. This includes military personnel, civilians, U.S. business firms' personnel, and the Vietnamese themselves. However, gay life is not nearly as open as it is stateside. The expression "It takes one to know one" is surely applicable here. Of course, there are a few recognizable gay bars in Saigon, but in general, things go along on a more private and individual basis.

Is it true that many service couples go on R&R together, as if on a honeymoon? Is this practice well known?

Yes, many service couples do go on R&R together, especially the girl-type of the species. My special friend and I went to Sydney last month, and it was absolutely great. Gay GIs are made to feel very welcome by the Aussie homophile community. And Aussie men are big and lusty!

Is the incidence of gays in the service taken casually? Is it considered personally dangerous to associate with such a group?

I would *not* say that when a guy is found out to be gay in the service, it is ever taken casually. To be gay and in the military is definitely a no-no, though many do get away with it (they beat their meat a lot). Of course, there are a few noncareer types who couldn't care less if they associated with known gays or if they are caught and branded as same. But for the man who is making the service a career, it is just not worth the risk—better be a loner.

When two service personnel are caught at it, what is actually done?

When soldiers are actually caught, well, life becomes a bit hairy, to say the very least. At present, it is standard in all branches of the service to "board" [convene a hearing] the person or persons out of the service—and with a dishonorable discharge. He may be jailed during this brief or lengthy procedure, or he may be confined to quarters (if commissioned). This may or may not also involve a court-martial.

One nice little kicker, though, is that the "action" is always hard as hell to really prove, in that one must actually be caught in the act, and by more than one witness.

But, even if nothing was proved, your remaining time in the service could be highly unpleasant.

Have there not been several—or many—hushed-up suicides among service personnel in Vietnam? Wasn't one recent group suicide because of revealed homosexual actions?

In no former military action by U.S forces has there been such a high suicide rate. However, no other action has lasted this long, involved so many people, and been so palpably purposeless and impossible to win. The number of actual, true suicides is probably double that admitted; the circumstances of this fruitless war are solely to blame. Of forty thousand dead, possibly six thousand were deliberate suicides. These are figures known to the Pentagon and to the Administration, but [they] will never be given out publicly.

Gays? In the Military?

By its third year of publication, The Advocate *had run scores of articles on the problems gays faced in the armed services. Some were features, like a 1970 report headlined* MILITARY POLICIES ON GAYS MAKE NO SENSE. *Most, however, covered court-martials, dishonorable discharges, and ruined lives. The Advocate would still run these stories more than twenty years later.*

During this peacenik era, avoiding the draft was often a greater priority for gays than trying to get into or stay in the military. Even gays who "checked the box"—declared that they had homosexual tendencies—were sometimes sent to 'Nam.

Gay Liberation brought help. GLF radicals in New York suggested that Advocate *readers write in the truth after the question about homosexual tendencies was officially dropped. (Even straight men were beating the draft by using that option.) More conservative organizations, like the Homosexual Information Center (HIC) in Los Angeles, counseled a loud refusal to offer proof on whether or not one was gay. That worked too, according to HIC head Don Slater, who told* The Advocate: *"We haven't lost a man to the service since 1967."*

It's really sad…always some of the nicest guys.…

Is it not a popular belief that certain units of the commandolike Green Berets are entirely "self-contained," including sex acts and personal practices?

Ummm…yes, my dear! Our own rough, tough Green Beret types are often certainly "self-contained," meaty little groups. After all, think of all those long, lonely patrols and the very isolated base camps. There is much talk!

Probably in their super-duper physical prowess lay the reasons for their known S&M preferences in sexual activity. This is not my particular bag, and except for a couple of personal friends here, who *are* Green Beret types, I give that sort of action a wide berth.

My friends tell me, however, that they have some absolutely *wild* orgies and parties, frequently, "out back" where no gals are handy. And these affairs include *all hands,* from the commanding officer to the lowest private!

I was told, in one instance, of a live grenade being shoved up someone's you-know-where, and the little trick was to remove it before it decided to go off! *Not* my cup of tea, but it shows what some groups will do for kicks.

Very frequently "husband teams" (these are pairs in which one is in charge, loosely named the "husband") will go out on patrol together, and they always seem to be much "closer" when (and if) they return. Bonds of love, or something like that.

According to my sources, raping captured Vietcong (before more definitely disposing of them) is also quite usual. Maybe they've learned to "love Charlie's brown"? A proposed affair with a Green Beret should suggest anything can happen—and probably will! These are all too rugged for an old bat like me.

Seriously, while it seems to have been broadcast stateside that the Green Beret units are being broken up, it is rumored that the thinking behind such an action is at least partly because of the acknowledged "homo" implications that have gotten around.

More truthfully, the Green Beret units are simply going further underground, are still doing the mad things they are known for, publicly and otherwise.

As a final question, and in consideration of your on-the-spot experiences of many years, what would you advise that young draftees and new servicemen who realize they are gay should do about it? Should they at once scream for the shrink, to tell all and hope for a discharge? Or should they decide to tough it out?

If the young man has the ability to always be discreet in his actions, I might say, "Stay in and tough it out." This will require considerable willpower, partly because of the things flaunted in his face daily. Also, the immature boy, who believes that he is "not too committed" at seventeen or eighteen, may unconsciously become an obvious flaming faggot at twenty-one. If he is already committed to being a blatant—not a latent—then I would say, by all means, see the shrink and get out of service before tragedy strikes. He would have nothing but problems if he stayed in.

For the *very* discreet, mature gay, especially if he is a simple voyeur type, the military service is a mental (only occasionally physical) smorgasbord, featuring thousands of healthy, beautiful, young male bodies, all somewhat "ready." But for the guy who is in doubt about himself, or who is in any way just a little obvious, or one who doesn't really know where he's going or how he'll develop, the road in the military is a hard one (no pun intended). He may end up with a court-martial, with a dishonorable discharge, or even in prison.

"It's Hell Being Gay and Handicapped"

I can almost hear the outcries from readers who will be positive that I set out to pry into the private life of a handicapped gay vet. However, nothing could be further from the truth. The following interview resulted when Serge, a nineteen-year-old, well-built amputee, came up to me in a Seattle bar one Friday afternoon. Like most gays, I'd had little actual contact with this one aspect of homosexuality, except for occasional references spotted in the personal ads of various homophile publications.

You said you weren't born this way. How, then? The war?

The conflict. You know [Vietnam] is not really considered a war. Not yet. Probably never.

You want to talk about it?

I sure do. I've made some big mistakes in my life, but my biggest one was in not checking that little box marked "homosexual" at the induction station. I must have been crazy not to. But you know, I had this funny idea that it was really clever of me to pull the wool over Uncle Sam's eyes. Well, let me tell you, old Uncle really put the shaft to me. He put it to me real good.

Did you have sex in the service?

Nope, believe that or not. I was too damn tired to do much of anything. After basic training, it was Vietnam. I wasn't there but a month before I stepped on the land mine. So, I came back to the States a very bitter young man. It was just like one of those sob-story movies. I didn't want to see or talk to anyone. But after a while I just got this sex urge. I don't know really how to explain it. It was something that I couldn't get over anymore by jacking off. And I did masturbate. Quite a lot, as a matter of fact. I might have come back an amputee, but not a sexual cripple. I could still get just as hard as before.

You seem to have adjusted fairly well.

To the leg, yes. To my new gay life—never. When I was in one piece, I was actually glad to be gay. I mean, it was really a blast. Two guys in bed can have one hell of a good time. But now I see that it's only fun when you've got a good face, good body, and a healthy cock. Take away any of those three vital ingredients, and your soup suddenly sours.

There are handicapped homosexuals who have overcome their misfortune and still manage within the homophile community.

How many do you know personally? That's the point I'm trying to make. They're there, all right. But you don't know any. Do you know why? Because you're not one of them. Like seeks out like. That's especially true in the gay life.

I don't want people going home with me just because I'm a cripple. And that's what's happening to me. I've become an object. I'm beginning to attract this strange type of people who have this hang-up for the maimed.

What's more, I get all sick inside when I realize that I'm going home with these people more and more. Because I can't do without sex. As many times as I tell myself that I can, I can't. I get to a point where I have to have it—really have to have it. It's even worse when I remember how it was before. That's what really makes it hard. I mean if I'd been born without a leg, it might have been different. I might not have known what gay life *could* be like. But I marched off to battle for God and my country. You tell your readers that. You tell them that it's hell being handicapped, but it's really hell being gay and handicapped.

—WILLIAM J. LAMBERT III

Letters to the Editor

Fight for Gay Lib Becomes a Battle of the Sexes

Response to my piece about the need for lesbians to part company with gay men has been varied. With few exceptions, lesbians have reacted promptly and simply with "Right on, sister!" Many male homosexuals have been either surprised, puzzled, angered, or hurt. Others (mostly the younger men) have said, "Okay, you have stated the problem. But you didn't carry it through to the next logical step. What do we do about it?" First of all, I would suggest that you get together in "men only" sessions and find out where your heads are really at. How serious are you about "togetherness" of males and females in the homophile movement? Be honest about it and stop camouflaging your organizations with "open" membership policies where lesbians can contribute their dollars, but not their minds. Male homosexuals seem to have tunnel (penis) vision.

Secondly, to those of you who still claim you wish to work cooperatively with your lesbian sisters, I would offer the warning that the going will be rough, that the burden which the lesbian previously carried (being transitional, exercising patience and understanding, mediating disputes, reinforcing crushed egos) will be yours. It will be up to you to renew contact and sustain communication once it is reestablished. For the lesbian's first priority now is to the women's movement.

Thirdly, and hardest of all, you will have to change your reading, speech, and thought patterns. How many of you read lesbian publications, lesbian articles in your own male-oriented newspapers and magazines? Have you read any of the literature that has come out of the women's movement? Do you still speak of lesbians as dykes, "the girls," as butches and femmes? If you do, then you're certainly out of touch.

If you are truly concerned—as many of you have indicated—then it would behoove you to do a little research on your own. But first there has to be some indication that you really mean it, that you are seriously concerned about the alienation of your lesbian sisters.

The question is not "What can we do?" It is "What are you willing to do?"

—Del Martin, San Francisco

I am disappointed by such stands against cooperation with male homosexuals as have been expressed by Del Martin and others. Such stands are replete with anti-male hostility, and should be abandoned for more factual statement of problems. On the question of gay women's lib, I feel that they are quite guilty of misjudging most gay men. They do everyone an injustice when they say that we "show a great deal of hostility toward our gay sisters and even more… toward our nongay sisters."

Whatever their motivation, be it fear or hatred of men, or a childish desire to emote rather than communicate, let them be reminded that if there is a male "chauvinism," there is also a female "chauvinism," as they themselves have so adeptly shown us.

Rather than exchange insults with the loudest segment of them, let us seek out rational members of their group to see what the problem is and how it may be solved. Let's get on with it.

—Jim Bradford, Chicago

I'm as aware as anyone of the problems incurred, the inequities experienced by those of the female sex. These things concern me as a female—but I'm not "just a female"—I'm a female homosexual!

I read with dismay, and have known those locally, who have allowed their desire for the ideal—in "our world" at least—to alienate them from the homophile cause.

Most disturbing is the loss of able and informed leadership and workers from a movement that has limited resources in this area, to pour

I Was a Recruiter for the Kinsey Sex Survey

themselves and their talents into an already well-filled and free-flowing river of effort. Women's lib has *all* women to draw from in its just and necessary battles—the heterosexual, the bisexual, and even the homosexual. Gay groups have only themselves to turn to.

There are many to fight for women's lib; our own army is limited and small by comparison. We must not decimate the ranks that cannot be refilled, espouse causes that need us less. No group is perfect, but if we all sail the ship safely together, it can be brought safely to port.

—Rob Willis, Dallas

Gay women may be making a serious tactical error by aligning themselves with the women's liberation movement. Del Martin's complaint that gay men's organizations have pushed women into a secondary role is justified, but that does not mean that lesbians have more in common with heterosexual women than with gay men.

If women's lib succeeds, heterosexual women will enjoy the same status as heterosexual men. But the lesbian will find herself in the unenviable position of the male homosexual. She will still be discriminated against and restricted to low-paying jobs.

Working together has problems, but they must be overcome in the interest of unity. Many gay men have difficulty relating to women. They have been conditioned to be protective, assertive, and paternalistic toward women. And they have been beaten down for so long, that when they finally get in a position of authority, they become too aggressive, too domineering.

Women share some of the blame. Because of their conditioning, they have not asserted themselves enough, they have not spoken loudly enough, they have permitted themselves to be pushed into playing the stereotyped "woman's" role.

—Don Jackson, San Francisco

The famed Kinsey sex researchers were about to conduct a massive survey on homosexuality in the Bay Area, announced the article in the *San Francisco Examiner*. The survey was to take a year, and recruiters were needed to sign up all types and ages of gay men and lesbians. New in town and desperate for work, I decided to apply for the job.

I was hired and given an official ID card from Indiana University with my picture on it, smartly laminated, with my title as research assistant for the Institute for Sex Research. My boss explained that I should carry the card with me at all times because we had complete police cooperation, and I would not be arrested for approaching anyone or if there was a raid in a bar.

My first day on the job was a swinging Sunday afternoon. I entered a bar in a gay part of town known as the Miracle Mile and immediately felt all eyes in the place look me over. I figured that I would seek out the friendly faces first. The younger ones thought it was amusing when I showed them my card as a sexologist—a few even thought I was putting them on before I gave my speech.

Some said they were happy and there was no need for a survey as they already felt liberated within themselves. I finally got together a rebuttal speech which I memorized: "Sure, you're happy in San Francisco, Los Angeles, and New York, but what about our gay friends in Gary, Indiana, Mt. Clemens, Michigan, and such places, who can't always flee a small town and come to one of the gay meccas? They live in constant fear within themselves. You will be helping others and, in turn, will be helping yourselves." This, plus my sincerity and belief in the survey, usually worked.

One day, Hilda, the project's field director, explained that the survey needed to expand its range of subjects. "So now we want you to go out and recruit gay men over forty," she said. "Do they exist?" I replied. All I had seen in the bars were the stereotypical dirty old men, and they were few and far between. Hilda gave me a list of dinner bars that were elegantly decorated and had background music. "You will find them there," she said.

As before, I would wait until one man played a game with my eyes and then approach the individual or group. Usually, one of the super-feminine bitches would scream out, "Miss Kinsey is here," and the others would giggle about it. Many of the drunk ones would sign up, but when called back for the interview they would either have given a phony phone number or they would change their minds in the reality of daylight.

One time I went to a dinner bar and approached a fifty-year-old-looking man who was sipping a martini while Peggy Lee torched out "Is That All There Is?" I gave my usual pitch. "I don't give a damn about your sex survey," he responded, screaming out for everyone to hear. "I have lived my life. My life is finished. I have been harassed and picked on by society all of my life, and now you want me to go and help this goddamn social cause of yours. Well, go straight to hell."

He then turned around on his stool and faced the bar. All of the other customers stared at me intensely. Hating awkward exits, I held my head high, looked back at the laughing crowd, and thought lovely Barbra Streisand thoughts. The man then turned back to me and said in a soft voice, "You're very young to be doing something like this. I didn't mean to insult you. I'm very drunk." I hesitated purposely for a second, then smilingly whispered, "I can't be insulted. That's why I do this." He laughed. "Let me see the card," he replied. "I'll fill it out." Soon the whole bar was eagerly asking what the scene was about and, as I explained it from table to table, they all signed up.

I was next instructed to sign up lesbians. Why couldn't the lesbian recruiters get lesbians? I wondered. But I did need the work, so that Saturday night I took a bus to the outskirts of town to a bar I had been told about.

As I very timidly walked into the bar, a hefty, masculine-looking bartender asked for my ID card. I told her that I was from the Kinsey survey and that they had previously called. She nodded an unhappy approval. "What'll ya have, buster?" she said with a scowl.

The drinks were a staggering $1.10, so I figured I better get there fast. "A straight martini up, drip dry and hold the olive," I ordered, sensing the hostility toward me in the room. After two drinks, I started my approach toward two girls.

One was quite hostile, but the feminine one of the couple wanted to sign up. The more masculine one, however, voiced a big "No" as she tore up the card into shreds before my very eyes. The bartender served me my third martini as she said with a wicked laugh, "Just make sure you don't get hit in the head by any beer bottles, honey."

As I turned away from the bar and faced the crowd on my stool, I found myself unintentionally cruising them. They looked so much like guys. Not the rough, heavy stereotypes I thought of as lesbians, but more like gorgeous young surfers with long hair. Suddenly, a drunken, tall girl with closely cropped hair came over. "Honey, I'd know you anywhere!" she exclaimed. I told her I was a guy and showed her my ID card. "Bull! You're the girl I met that wonderful weekend in San Diego," she continued. I did have a good build—I mean chest-wise—and noticed I was wearing a navy blue surfer shirt with a large yellow stripe across the front.

We kept chatting, and she played my little game, as she called it, and signed up. Then some of her friends came over and signed up. She kept buying me martinis and introducing me as "Honey from San Diego."

The drinks were hitting fast, and I suddenly had to go to the bathroom. As I walked toward the johns, I noticed that girls were lined up in front of both the men's and women's rooms! *I can't cause a scene, or I'll lose them,* I thought. *What the hell, I'll be Honey.* We filed into the men's room two at a time, and I explained to the girls in the head that I was really a guy. They assured me that they knew I was. "Well, what'll we do about the bathroom situation?" I pondered. One of the girls answered, "We'll make it easy on you, man. You stand up by the urinal, and I'll sit down over here." In no time at all, I signed up my partner in the bathroom and she helped me sign up others when we left. The ice was broken. Finally, at one A.M., two girls gave me a ride to the corner of Market and Castro streets, near my apartment. As I waved good-bye, I spotted three drunks. "Look at the dykes and the faggot," they yelled out.

I ignored them, but one lunged right at me and kicked me from behind. I turned around and slugged him square in the mouth, so hard that I had a tooth in my fist and it was bleeding. Another rushed up and jumped on my back as still another came forward. They got me on the ground, but for just a second.

Suddenly, my assailants were pulled away. My two girlfriends from the car had jumped out to aid me, and together we clobbered them all.

—JAMIE JORDAN

"There is a fantastic amount of alcoholism and people with alcoholic problems in the gay world. Since, for the most part, the gay is forced to live a schizophrenic existence, one could see where alcoholism could be brought about by psychological problems. These are the facts, and they have been ignored far too long."
—WRITER SANDY PHILLIPS, reporting on the growing number of support groups for gay and lesbian alcoholics

MISS THING   by Joe Johnson

"What kind of survey did you say this was?"

THE VIEW FROM THE VICE

After dozens of Advocate *articles recounting sordid tales of police harassment, news editor Rob Cole sought an unlikely interview with Dr. John B. Williams, the author of a police manual entitled* Vice Control in California. *Williams, a gruff eighteen-year veteran of the Los Angeles Police Department, had served as lieutenant in charge of the Administrative Vice Division and gone on to teach police science at both the University of Southern California and California State College, Los Angeles. Williams spoke candidly, apparently unaware of the nature of the publication.*

EFFEMINIST MEN
By 1971, New York's Gay Liberation Front splintered into several smaller groups. One of the newly formed factions was the Effeminists, a group of gay men who believed that gay men's oppression and women's oppression were caused by male supremacy and that both issues needed to be addressed together. The group visibly presented its views on the streets of New York throughout the early seventies.

In your book you state: "Homosexuals are constantly seeking recruits and prefer young boys to older men or older queers. The contaminating influence they exert can be reduced to a minimum by tough, relentless law enforcement." Now, I would like to find out if, with gay liberation these days, you have changed your views.

The reason for the statement is, when the guys are young, they call themselves queens and belles. Now, when they get older, they switch to what homosexuals call "aunties." These aunties are thirty-five, forty, and older. They cannot attract other homosexuals. So these people prey on young, good-looking guys, or, when they can't get them, attack small children, as one guy did the other day and raped a one-and-a-half-year-old and killed her

Now, the danger with these guys—you can prove it to yourself by going in any bar where any of them hang out—they will approach you and usually start with, "It's bad to go with women because they can become pregnant, they'll double-cross you, and you can get V.D. It's better to try it just this once." They are constantly recruiting young guys.

I see. Do you base your opinions on personal research?

I worked homosexuals and narcotics for fifteen years, and I worked every bar in L.A. and every fruit bar, and I came to know these people quite well. If you watch them operate, and they are approaching another homosexual, you can tell whether they are or not by listening to what they call "gay talk." In the book, there's a whole list of all the gay talk.

To my way of thinking, the homosexuals can be very devastating, particularly when they get older and start preying on small children. With every one of these guys, when you find them slaying a small child, you'll find perversion in their background, without exception.

This recent case that you mentioned. Was the child a girl or a boy?

It was a girl.

Why would you say this was a homosexual, then?

According to the student [who told Williams the story], the guy was a homosexual. I didn't read the article. Are you with the *Times?*

No, I'm with *The Advocate.*

Oh. My argument against [homosexuals] is that, number one, these people recruit, and, number two, the older ones attack small children. That's why I don't like anything public. Private, there's no problem.

My part is this.…I'm not espousing anything, just how you catch 'em and what I learned working [as a policeman] for eighteen years. Like I said, there isn't a bar I haven't been in, and although they tend to congregate around a few of them, they *are* spread out. They're what they call recruiting—they're looking. That help you any?

MUSIC: SYLVESTER SIZZLES

The crème de la crème of the underground, and even a few of the overground, were taking off their hats to Sylvester and His Hot New Band on October 16 at San Francisco's Palace Theatre. It was his last local show before he left for a nine-week engagement in New York.

At the pre-show party, the likes of Grace Slick, Marty Balin, and people from United Artists, Capitol, and Electra were upstaged by ten camera-hungry Cockettes who decided to crash their old friend's party. The star of the evening arrived late, however, because of having to send out for more rose petals and champagne to fill his evening bath.

At midnight, a crowd bulging out a block in each direction of the Palace Theatre was close to a state of riot. Tickets were being scalped, and doormen had already succumbed to a mob of gate-crashers when Sylvester stepped out of his limousine.

Camera flashes, tinsel headdresses, fainting old ladies, and a chorus of "Oooh's" topped any previous thirties nostalgia or rock happening. It was, as a glamour queen in front of me said while passing around a rhinestone-studded snuffbox, "Nothing but the best, honey!" I was thankful that I'm not allergic to fur.

Once inside, it took half an hour for the *Satyricon* mob to settle, with transsexuals molesting straights in the aisles, people climbing over seats or tripping on long, jeweled robes, shrieking, cheesecaking, and getting stoned. The show before the show ended with screaming, whistling, and applause as Pristine Condition announced Sylvester and His Hot New Band. Sylvester danced out onstage singing "I Don't Know What You've Come to Do."

Crotches were wet as he belted out a gospel blues number, "One-Way Ticket to Love." It's about the heartbreak and disappointment of one-night tricks. "Hello Sunshine" came out over the house like a sheet of blue satin.

But he still wasn't peaking until he crooned "God Bless the Child That's Got His Own." The song also hints mild support to the rumor that his family is sitting shivah because of his "drag act," which is actually not a drag act, but rather a trip advocating confusion of sex roles. He carries the subtleties of a heavy man behind his glamour-queen facade.

Singing half his own material and half old songs, Sylvester seems to be unlimited in his range of style and music. From hard rock to gospel blues to the blueblackest Harlem moan, he simultaneously has the style nuances and command of Nina Simone, Bessie Smith, Billie Holiday, James Brown, and Tina Turner.

He looks down his nose and summons all the pride and dignity of ten thousand years of blackness. He wants to sing the way his cousin Holiday and his grandmother Julia Morgan did when they sang at the Apollo in Harlem. And he does. Sylvester pees a holy light of blues all over his audience, bows his head, and walks off stage as if he hadn't done a thing.

This is the first big act to break nationally with an up-front gay theme. Sylvester and a few others are making America beg for our cultural revolution. Consider the impact. —CHRISTOPHER LILLY

COOKING WITH BAD TASTE

One popular column during the early seventies was Lou Rand's "Auntie Lou Cooks." Dispensing kitchen tips with an earlier era's queenlike tone, the column had a campy sense of humor that often lacked racial and cultural sensitivity. Despite his chatty lightness of tone, Rand often resorted to ethnic slurs when presenting non-Anglo-American recipes in his column. Unfortunately, The Advocate's editors were slow to recognize their own insensitivity—some of its readers, however, were very offended.

Nothing could sound much gayer than a Baked Indian Pudding, but our spies say it's an old New England favorite. So we baked us an Indian! And why not? Frankly, we never knew of any Indian being of much "personal" use. Aside from those fantasies of *Song of the Loon*, it seems they just "won't," usually.

Two issues later, a letter to the editor read:

Although we encounter racism in many forms, seldom is it as blatant and unexpected as your Auntie Lou column, "Bake an Indian for Lunch Today." Surely your readers are sensitive enough to the exploitation of other minority groups to feel as offended as we were.
—RARIHOKWATS, MOHAWK NATION

Books: *The Gay Militants*

Only a few years ago, the worm turned, and water flowed uphill: Homosexuals began *demanding* their rights. And the world would never again be the same. The gay militant was here.

These recent years have seen such a burgeoning of gay progress and gay pride that the gay organizers of old (like 1950) must be astounded by it all. The new activists are probably also somewhat astounded, for it is really an astounding and exciting story.

In *The Gay Militants,* Donn Teal records every exciting chapter in this awakening, concentrating on the year and a half that started with the Stonewall Riots in June 1969. He has produced a valuable history book of the new gay movement—a volume that is must reading for every gay activist, psychologist, and legislator, and certainly for every homosexual who is "queer" no more.

By and large, Teal lets the story unfold in the words of participants, observers, and reporters. He quotes at great length from press reports—establishment, underground, and gay. He quotes from flyers, manifestos, and from crucial meetings held in the midst of the turmoil of a sudden event. And he has obviously taken the pains to contact everyone who might have material pertinent to the story.

Teal rarely intrudes on a narrative being told by others. When he does, it's only to fill in the story or to tie some of the accounts together. If *The Gay Militants* can be faulted at all, it's on this point. One wishes, from time to time, that Teal would step in and evaluate events or people or groups—to put them in perspective and help readers assess their relative importance.

This hands-off approach does have its advantages. Teal has produced a book without a trace of bitchery on the author's part. And this is a refreshing rarity in gay writing. He tries to be eminently fair to everyone—and succeeds in doing so.

Teal opens his book with the Stonewall Riots and their immediate aftermath. The first two chapters are filled with fascinating details of that momentous week, colorfully told by the varied participants.

In the third chapter, however, Teal dips back into preceding years. Without actually saying so, he reveals that the new era of militancy actually had its beginning on the West Coast: PRIDE and its demonstration protesting the Black Cat Raid in Los Angeles (early 1967); Leo Lawrence and his very militant Committee for Homosexual Freedom in San Francisco (spring 1969).

The bulk of the book, however, deals with those events since June 1969—both within and outside the movement: the growth of the Gay Liberation Front and its spread to every major city and college campus across the country; the West Coast Gay Lib conference; the Snake Pit raid in New York City; gays putting the pressure on New York politicos; different factions of the movement, their philosophies and their stands; the Lindsay zaps; the *Harper's* zap; Barney's Beanery in Los Angeles; election year; the "reform" of NACHO; Alpine County; and many other happenings.

There is also a chapter on the women's movement, written by several unnamed lesbians who are active in gay and women's liberation. —Derek Martin

By June, the rowdy spirit of gay and lesbian activism had swept across the nation. Demonstrators assembled in previously unimaginable numbers from Los Angeles's Hollywood Boulevard (*above*) to New York's Central Park (*below*), leaving nothing hidden from public view.

GAYS BLOODIED IN N.Y.

Newspaper of America's Homophile Community

The **ADVOCATE**

So. Calif 35¢
Issue No. 86
50¢ Elsewhere

Fred Halsted
His S&M Flicks
Stir Up New York

PRISON DOCS LIE

GAA BUILDS WAR CHEST

Newspaper of America's Homophile Community

The **ADVOCATE**

So. Calif 35¢
Issue No. 88
50¢ Elsewhere

DOES PORN REALLY OFFEND?

CANDIDATE TOURS GAY BARS

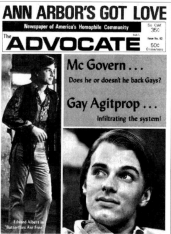

ANN ARBOR'S GOT LOVE

Newspaper of America's Homophile Community

So. Calif 35¢

The **ADVOCATE**

Issue No. 92
50¢ Elsewhere

Mc Govern...
Does he or doesn't he back Gays?

Gay Agitprop...
Infiltrating the system!

Edward Albert in "Butterflies Are Free"

McGOVERN'S FOOT-IN-MOUTH

Newspaper of America's Homophile Community

So. Calif 35¢

The **ADVOCATE**

Issue No. 98
50¢ Elsewhere

Mass Murderer
A Gay Masochist ??

BIG
48
PAGE
ISSUE

•BAR BUSTS
•ZAPS
•POLITICS
•'HEAT'
•ABC MOVIE
•SEXPERT
•VD on TV
•SUICIDE

SHIFTING GEARS

1972 Middle Americans had only begun to open their eyes after closing them tightly against powerful explosions caused in a hopeful countercultural revolution. What they saw in 1972, no matter their sexual orientation, confused them. Arguments broke out between those who would integrate gays into mainstream political culture and those who believed that culture to be rotten to the core. Even so, these two wings of the movement marched together in gay parades.

Neither group had yet heard faint hints of the arrival of the "Me Generation," the coming ascendancy of greedy yuppies over sharing hippies. "None of us are free till all of us are free," Bakunin's anarchist slogan, reverberated wherever there was disagreement about gay rights treated as an isolated issue. Some hoped to link the gay and lesbian cause to gender and racial inequalities, the exploitation of the Third World, war resistance, and ecological imbalance. Scorn for Republican and Democratic "solutions" found the principal political parties characterized as "Tweedle-Dee and Tweedle-Dum." Social revolutionaries in urban centers bathed smugly in the colorful waters of rushing change, and laughed away cynical prophecies that rightly predicted widespread decay.

Indeed, some of the most telling signs of the times were the patches sewn over the holes in worn-out jeans: butterflies, peace signs, hearts, smiles, and other idealistic symbols, usually fixed prominently on a wearer's rear end. Not surprisingly, a Gallup poll revealed that half of all college students had tried marijuana at least once. And John Waters's cult film *Pink Flamingos* introduced transvestite superstar Divine, playing "the filthiest person alive," to an unsuspecting nation.

Much of the year centered on electoral politics. While Democrats gave some evidence of their sympathies for gay rights, the party self-destructed long before Election Day, rumors being rife about the mental health of its first vice-presidential nominee. Senator Edmund Muskie's candidacy came to an abrupt halt after Republicans smeared his wife and he scandalized macho pundits by weeping in public. Representative Shirley Chisholm, another early runner armed with good

Photographer Crawford Barton had an eye for celebrations of San Francisco gay life. The brakes were off as these Dykes on Bikes made their presence known during Gay Pride Day.

intentions, stood up for gay rights. But a passionate defense of the love that dare not speak its name ended with a blooper: "Every time you see one of these people," she counseled the media, "just say to yourself, 'There but for the grace of God go I.'" Though Democrats disavowed gay-friendly ads for their candidate a week before the election, the campaign season ended with gay delegates appearing on the floor of the National Democratic Convention for the very first time.

Among those who died in 1972 was Paul Goodman, popular father figure of the New Left and a gay man of letters who called himself an anarchist. Goodman had been present at earlier gay conferences in the sixties and had come out at the height of his fame in an article published in the antiwar magazine *Win*. Critic Murray Kempton called Goodman "America's most creative social thinker." There were other deaths, too. Gossip columnist Louella Parsons, film star Maurice Chevalier, and muscle man Charles Atlas all passed from the scene. As a journalist, I think I celebrated only the timely passing of FBI director J. Edgar Hoover—publishing a headline in the newspaper *Gay* that read "Ding! Dong! The Wicked Witch Is Dead."

The East Coast's gay movement knew one of its best years before experiencing a period of disarray and slumber. Zaps aimed at the recalcitrant establishment were numerous. During the spring, activist Rich Wandel led a 155-mile march from Manhattan to Albany, stopping to celebrate gay liberation in small towns along the way. And the force of gay sensibility in popular music and dance surfaced with the onset of disco played at full tilt in the Ice Palace on Fire Island. Celebrating the vibrant new counterculture, I danced there with my lover of ten years, Lige Clarke, the most beautiful man I'd ever seen.

Clarke had lettered most of the signs used in the historic first march for gay rights, which I'd organized at the White House in 1965, and had worked with me in 1969 as coauthor of *The Advocate*'s first New York column. That same year we appeared in Al Goldstein's groundbreaking newsstand photos of nude males making love, published in the popular Manhattan sex review, *Screw*.

Clarke and I also coedited *Gay*, the country's first gay newsweekly. When we later resigned from *Gay* to travel and to write books, an *Advocate* headline called our four-year-old newspaper the nation's second-largest gay periodical. We called it, merely, "a sweet song." But *Gay Sunshine* and *The Advocate* remained after our editorial departure, as national chroniclers of the burgeoning movement, aided and abetted by local publications then starting up.

For me, a high point of 1972 was the publication by St. Martin's Press of my first book coauthored with Lige. Titled *I Have More Fun with You Than Anybody*, it was the first dual autobiography by a male couple reflecting philosophies of life and relationship. Lige and I made countless television and radio appearances, and in mid-year a lavish party was thrown for us as well as for the authors of *The Gay Crusaders*, Kay Tobin and Randy Wicker, at the home of Dr. George Weinberg, author and coiner of the word "homophobia."

John Francis Hunter, in his 1972 book, *The Gay Insider: U.S.A.*, called us "the most celebrated and recognizable homosexuals in America." Hunter's tome became the first chronicling of an author's cross-country travels, hoping to show, as he put it, where male homosexuals "can find love, companionship, truth, beauty, sex, God, liberation, good gay food, a crash pad, tools of torture, V.D. treatment, therapy, group therapy, tonsorial attention to poodles, codpieces, poppers, danger, a fix—or all of these—anywhere in Gay America."

It was a tall order, but one that seemed entirely feasible in a time filled with the heady sense of gay triumph. —JACK NICHOLS

"I believe that each one of us has his own responsibilities before Almighty God. Each one of us will stand and answer for the way he has lived. The homosexual and the person who is not homosexual must answer equally. I know that God loves each one of us....Being homosexual should not be any reason for discrimination."
—DALE EVANS, PARTNER OF SINGING COWBOY ROY ROGERS

The word "homophobia" entered the popular lexicon when psychologist George Weinberg published *Society and the Healthy Homosexual*. "He digs deeply into the causes—and effects—of homophobia," said *Advocate* critic Patrick Doyle, "reminding us that, of all living species, the human race is the only one to condemn the fact and practice of homosexuality."

T I M E L I N E

In what was perhaps the first successful attempt to have a legal gay "marriage" in Canada, TV personality Michel Girouard wed his accompanist, Rejean Tremblay, in February at a Toronto discotheque. The two drew up a long business contract that bound each to the other financially and also included their pledges of emotional devotion. As thirty-five reporters looked on, Girouard, wearing a red silk Nehru jacket with rhinestone collar, exchanged vows with Tremblay, dressed in a blue velvet tuxedo.

Robert Martin, petty officer third class, served as communications controller on a NATO base in Naples, Italy. His record was unblemished until the Navy accused him of anal intercourse with another sailor, who confessed under interrogation to "playing the female role" in the act. Government treatment of Martin, nicknamed "Radioman" or "the Ram," drew international protest; New York Congresswoman Bella Abzug labeled the case a witch-hunt and interceded on Martin's behalf. He was released with a general discharge at the time. Four years later, the Navy upgraded him to an honorable discharge.

JANUARY   A New York City Council committee voted against Intro 475, the gay civil rights bill, prompting a GAA call for "total war" against Mayor John Lindsay; activists characterized his support as insufficient. ❏ The Gay Switchboard, an information and referral service, opened in New York City, logging four hundred calls per week. ❏ Six Washington, D.C., activists were arrested at the Iwo Jima Memorial for protesting entrapment and brutality against gays cruising there. ❏ The Southern California Psychiatrists Society endorsed a call to legalize homosexual activity in private. ❏ The pro-Castro American group Venceremos Brigade called gays "parasites in the revolution."

FEBRUARY   At the invitation of Radicalesbians, Midwest lesbians met for three days in Yellow Springs, Ohio. ❏ New York City Mayor Lindsay issued an antibias order protecting city employees from antigay discrimination. ❏ Two Rhode Island mayors reacted to Lindsay's order by refusing to hire homosexuals in city government and vowed to fire anyone found to be gay. ❏ *The New Republic* noted lesbian and gay organization and increasing political clout in an article entitled "The Gay Vote."

MARCH   The Equal Rights Amendment, passed by the Senate and sent to the states for ratification, was hailed as a possible keystone for gay rights. Twelve years later, still not ratified, the measure would be seen as dead. ❏ The California Democratic Council adopted a sweeping gay plank, endorsing the legalization of consensual sex; honorable discharges from the military; and a ban on discrimination based on sexual orientation. ❏ The Society for Individual Rights backed the legalization of marijuana. ❏ An American Bar Association committee urged the repeal of laws forbidding consensual homosexual sex. ❏ Two Seattle men were charged with disorderly conduct for holding hands during "couples night" at a local skating rink.

APRIL   Hawaii decriminalized consensual homosexual sex acts between adults. ❏ Dozens of gays picketed the Academy Awards ceremony, protesting Hollywood's distortions of gay life. ❏ San Francisco supervisors banned discrimination based on gender and sexual orientation in the Administrative Code regarding city business; the move brought gay-rights clauses into the policies of dozens of firms. ❏ Openly gay Jack Baker was reelected student body president at the University of Minnesota. ❏ Boston police admitted that one of their patrol cars got stuck in the Fenway, a wetland park notorious for gay cruising. ❏ William Johnson of the Church of Christ became the first open homosexual permitted ordination in a major denomination.

MAY   Pediatrician and presidential hopeful Benjamin Spock put in a brief appearance at the Los Angeles Gay Community Services Center. ❏ Lesbians led the gay contingent of a major antiwar march in Los Angeles. ❏ FBI chief J. Edgar Hoover died. A longtime enemy of lesbians and gays, he was rumored to be a closeted homosexual and cross-dressing aficionado. ❏ The Denver Hilton Hotel evicted two men for dancing together. ❏ Services of Hollywood's Radical Gay Christians were disrupted by four intruders shouting, "You can't be queer and Christian." ❏ "There is nothing sick or unnatural about homosexuality," said Dr. Judd Marmor, vice president–elect of the American Psychiatric Association, at a meeting in Dallas. ❏ Italian gays, hoping to start a gay

political party, filed papers with the Ministry of the Interior; later, they joined forces with radical leftists to form a short-lived party sensitive to gay rights.

JUNE   An estimated 2,500 homosexuals marched in Philadelphia in the city's first Gay Pride parade; other cities around the country reported record turnouts. ❑ A San Jose woman won custody of her three children in what was believed to be the first such victory for an acknowledged lesbian. ❑ Los Angeles lesbian-feminists led a Father's Day demonstration against the "Daddy

Tank," where lesbians at Sybil Brand Women's Prison were placed for special punishment. ❑ The Gay Community Counseling Center opened in Chicago. ❑ Police pulled the liquor license of a straight Rhode Island nightclub over its female impersonator cabaret show, "Guys Will Be Dolls." ❑ Syndicated columnist Jack Anderson revealed that the Gay Liberation Front appeared on a list of organizations monitored by the Secret Service in an effort "to prevent political assassination." ❑ The California Supreme Court ruled nude sunbathing legal under certain conditions. ❑ Gay teachers organized a caucus within the National Education Association. ❑ Two seminars on rectal health care for men had to be moved from a New York City Democratic Club meeting hall to a church basement after officials objected to the word "rectal" in advertising.

JULY   Sacramento State University launched what is believed to be the nation's first college-affiliated gay studies program. ❑ The Lesbian Switchboard started in New York City. ❑ Discrimination against gays in housing, public accommodations, and employment was made illegal in Ann Arbor, Michigan. ❑ Arsonists caused $10,000 in damages to San Francisco's MCC, the second such attack in two weeks. ❑ Forty-three men were arrested at a Galveston, Texas, bathhouse; four of them were bound over to a grand jury on sodomy charges.

AUGUST   John Wojtowicz robbed a Manhattan bank to fund sex-change surgery for his lover, Ernest Aron (a.k.a. Liz Eden), only to be caught later by police; the story was made into *Dog Day Afternoon*, a feature film starring Al Pacino. ❑ The arrests of twenty-two men at the Black Pipe, a Hollywood beer bar, prompted a surge in gay activism. ❑ San Francisco's GAA disbanded and reformed as the Gay Voters League, endorsing the reelection of Richard Nixon. ❑ Time, Inc., was hit with a $2.7 million invasion-of-privacy suit over a photo of a gay wedding that accompanied a *Life* magazine article titled "Homosexuals in Revolt." ❑ A forty-year-old civilian Navy employee hanged himself in his Pentagon-adjacent apartment five days after his arrest on a sodomy charge. ❑ The House of Lords, Britain's supreme judicial body, ruled that gay personal ads constitute a conspiracy to corrupt public morals.

MEDIA BASHING

In April, eight members of New York's GAA were beaten and kicked by employees and guests of the New York Hilton Hotel while attempting to leaflet a dinner held there. Former GAA president Jim Owles (*far left*) required seven stitches. Recent incidents of biased journalism and antigay editorials caused the GAA to target the banquet for the Inner Circle, an organization of political writers. The incident was not reported in *The New York Times* or the New York *Daily News*, and none of the attackers were arrested.

New York Post columnist Pete Hamill wrote that "six grown men stood over one of the gays, kicking and punching him; the wives in the balcony must have sighed in relief, knowing that one Saturday night, at least, *they* wouldn't get it."

Michael Maye, a former boxing champion and head of New York City's Uniformed Firefighters Association, was eventually brought before a grand jury for assaulting Morty Manfred, a gay activist and Columbia University student. After a five-day trial, Maye was acquitted.

Terry Morone, Jim Devinny, and Mike Leuthe were three of the fourteen Buffalo gays who demonstrated against the New York State Association of City Councils at the group's winter meeting.

DR. EVELYN HOOKER

Psychologist Evelyn Hooker, while teaching at the University of California, Los Angeles, in the early fifties, began a radical course of research disproving the theory that homosexuality was a mental illness. In 1957, her ground-breaking study, "The Adjustment of the Male Overt Homosexual," concluded that homosexuality was a "deviation in sexual pattern which is within the normal psychological range." She also attacked previous studies, because they had focused only on homosexuals who had sought medical or psychological help, rather than examining the vast majority of homosexual men and women who considered themselves psychologically healthy.

Ten years later, President Johnson appointed Dr. Hooker to head a Task Force on Homosexuality for the National Institute of Mental Health. In October of 1969, the task force submitted its report, recommending the repeal of sodomy laws and better public education about homosexuality. The report was largely ignored at the time, but was later used by gay activists in the fight to remove homosexuality from the American Psychiatric Association's list of disorders.

Throughout the early seventies, Dr. Hooker continued to fight tirelessly for gay and lesbian rights, and it was in part due to her lifetime of achievements that the APA removed homosexuality from its list of mental illnesses in 1973. Her courageous stand for gays and lesbians against both an unsympathetic society and her own psychiatric peers was integral to the advancement of gay rights. In her own words: "Are homosexuals social outcasts? My God. Christopher Isherwood, Howard Brown, Merle Miller, Sidney Abbott, John Maynard Keynes. Are these people social outcasts? Some of the most moral men I know are homosexuals."

SEPTEMBER A Superior Court judge ruled unconstitutional a California law that made oral sex a felony. ❑ San Diego police arrested fifty-nine men in local parks over Labor Day weekend; gays claimed entrapment. ❑ The California Committee for Sexual Law Reform joined with SIR of San Francisco to organize and raise funds to fight antigay sex statutes. ❑ The Long Beach, California, gay bar owners association, FROGS (Friendly Relations of Gay Society), held a two-week "Frog Festival," a public relations stunt that included frog races and frog food products, all in an attempt to win the approval of the straight community. ❑ Disneyland guards prevented a man from entering the theme park wearing a T-shirt with the words GROOVY GUY on it until he turned the shirt inside-out. ❑ A New York City policy requiring known homosexual cab drivers to undergo regular psychiatric checks was scrapped after GAA demonstrations and sit-ins. ❑ English Quakers urged that the age of consent be lowered to fourteen.

OCTOBER The lesbian *Ladder*, America's oldest existing gay publication, folded after sixteen years. ❑ The operator of a Coral Gables, Florida, "modeling agency" was quoted in *The Advocate* as saying that the demand for male hustlers was higher during the Republican convention than during the Democratic. ❑ The Homophile League of Holyoke, Massachusetts, convened a New England gay coalition. ❑ A gay couple joined the bridal registry of a downtown Denver department store. ❑ A University of California study showed that California prison sentences for sodomy averaged nearly the same as sentences for manslaughter. ❑ The Pennsylvania House awarded $133,000 to a man who spent nineteen years in prison on charges of sodomy and corrupting a minor, of which he was later cleared. ❑ The sensational trial of Juan Corona began; he was convicted of the sex-related slayings of twenty-five men near Yuba City, California, and received twenty-five consecutive life sentences.

NOVEMBER A special televised "V.D. Call-In" hosted by Dick Cavett and Geraldo Rivera attracted fifteen thousand calls. ❑ Detroit voters turned down a new city charter that would have prohibited discrimination against gays. ❑ Manhattan's Lesbian Liberation Committee staged dance-ins at three popular singles bars. ❑ Joe Acanfora, a gay man who had won a battle for teaching certification in Pennsylvania, filed suit in federal court after being shifted to a non-classroom job by his district; he eventually lost his case when the Supreme Court refused to hear his appeal. ❑ A Louisiana district judge ruled that the state may ban sex acts when practiced by gay couples, but not when practiced by heterosexual couples. ❑ The Satyrs, a Los Angeles–based gay motorcycle club, marked its eighteenth anniversary.

DECEMBER The Mississippi Supreme Court ruled that Peeping Tom laws apply to men only. ❑ The Whitman-Radclyffe Foundation, a San Francisco gay political group, was granted federal tax-exempt status. ❑ The penalty for "deviate sexual intercourse" in Pennsylvania was reduced from ten years to two. ❑ New York activists zapped a straight bar where a lesbian was assaulted in an argument over using the phone. ❑ A Seattle judge allowed two lesbian lovers to keep their children but insisted they maintain separate residences. ❑ Dozens of vacationers were arrested for lewd conduct when Arturo's, a popular gay resort in Puerto Rico, was raided for the first time in twenty-five years; all charges were later dropped, and officials scolded the police for the bust.

Infighting Mars Pride Week Planning

On June 25, gays will be parading through the streets of nearly every major American city and in several foreign countries to mark the anniversary of the Stonewall Riots. Tens of thousands are expected to march.

For many less-liberated homosexuals, however, the events of the day will bring shame and dismay. Already, in Los Angeles, New York, and San Francisco, bitter controversies are brewing between those who want either a "respectable" observance or none, and those who want a joyous celebration of pride in their homosexuality.

Bitter wrangling in Los Angeles on this and other issues is threatening to result in a Hollywood Boulevard parade substantially diminished from the parades of last year and the year before, according to the convenors of Christopher Street West. A large part of the community, generally the more radical part, has insisted that there should be no "censorship" of entries. As one result, the parade for two years in a row has included elements variously denounced as "obscene," tasteless," and "reinforcing the fag stereotype."

New York's Christopher Street Liberation Day Committee is having its own troubles, marked by the resurgence of a long-standing controversy over whether the parade should be simply a mass protest march or more traditional in form, like Hollywood's. As usual, the nation's largest gay parade will probably be in New York, where up to twenty thousand people marched last year.

The most spectacular parade this year may be in San Francisco, but that city's parade has also run into dissension, with radical groups accusing their old nemesis, the Tavern Guild, of trying to take over. Unpredictable activist the Rev. Ray Broshears sent out leaflets detailing parade rules and regulations. Among other things, the leaflet specifies, "All people on your entry and marching must be properly clothed. The determination of what is or is not proper will be made by the parade marshal…and his detail man from the San Francisco Police Department vice squad. Anyone violating the code will be asked to leave the line of parade, and should there be any hassle, you shall be arrested."

—Staff Report

Controversy over whether Gay Pride marches should be centered around protest instead of celebration erupted in major cities. At issue were naked boys and drag queens as representative images of the gay and lesbian community.

A GRANDDADDY OF GAY LIBERATION

The huge antiwar rally on Boston Common had everything, even a large gay contingent. An old man, slightly stooped and bearded, was seen slowly working his way toward the gay crowd. His clothes were baggy and worn. One young rallier, in sequined pantyhose and ochre eye shadow, gave the old man the once-over and, turning to his friends, asked, "Who's *that* old fart?"

That old fart just happened to be Prescott Townsend, one of Boston's few living legends. If anyone were to be designated Granddaddy of Gay Liberation in Boston, Townsend must cop that honor. For years—decades—he has been actively part of the gay scene. He was the driving force behind the original homophile groups in this prim and repressed city. Prescott was breaking open closets in the face of Boston's entrenched hypocrisy long before any of the current gay groups were ever formed.

P.T. (as he is known) was born on June 24, 1894, a child of Boston's tight-lipped elite. He claims that twenty-three of his direct ancestors came over on the *Mayflower* and that his family has been concerned with Boston ever since. Townsend grew up in the rigid social structure of the time and enrolled in Harvard College in 1914. This was about the same time he came out. "Everything was very much undercover," he recalls. "Homosexuality was unmentionable. They avoided saying the word." But how are you going to keep them in the Social Register after they've discovered boys? "I was thrown out the same year as Barbara Hutton," Townsend boasts, "and for the same reason!"

In 1944, P.T. was arrested and charged on a morals offense with a youth. Before sentencing, the judge asked the prisoner what he had to say for himself. Townsend responded: "So, what's wrong with a little cocksucking on the Hill?"

In the mid-fifties, he organized biweekly meetings at the Parker House Hotel for what has been called by one friend "the first social discussion of homosexuality in Boston." Townsend led this core group of twelve to fifteen people as they became the Boston chapter of the Mattachine Society. But that association was short-lived. Townsend went on to establish his own homophile organization in the early sixties, the Boston Demophile Society. Some of the regulars—to the extent that there were any regulars other than Townsend—included a middle-aged Boston banker, a contemporary friend or two, young screamers who had no idea what a homophile group was all about, and perhaps some prototype groupies who just dropped by for the action.

Though a thorough eccentric, Townsend must be honored for his early work in the homophile movement. Whether it was the independence fostered by his Boston Brahmin background, or whether it was the lingering rebellion against society instilled through the Bohemian life of the twenties, P.T. stepped forward when the field was wide open, and in his totally unorthodox way, he began to shake things up.

—JON C. MITZEL

CAMPAIGNING AT THE BARS

Los Angeles District Attorney candidate Vincent Bugliosi speaks out at a Silver Lake leather bar.

It was a night nobody, a few years ago, would have believed could happen. Los Angeles district attorney candidate Vincent Bugliosi, seeking one of the most powerful posts of its kind in the nation, went campaigning in the gay bars.

He visited sixteen of them one night in late April, from a little neighborhood watering place where old friends drop in for a beer, to a hustler hangout where he couldn't believe the painted "women" were men, to the leather places where there's no doubt about who's a man (and you better believe it, Mary), to the huge, crowded Bitter End West, where kids gyrate to the frantic strains of acid rock and nobody much cares what sex you are.

Along the way, the thirty-seven-year-old Bugliosi learned a lot about the gay community, and the gay community learned something about him.

The tour was arranged by Citizens for Bugliosi, a gay-dominated volunteer committee. It became clear almost immediately that the candidate was uneasy about the tour and its possible effect on the WASP bedroom communities whose support he so desperately needs. He was badly shaken at one point by

Bella at the Baths

In her trademark big hat with her trademark big voice, New York Congresswoman Bella Abzug stepped past the sea of towel-wrapped bodies onto the stage at the Continental Baths. She looked down at her floor-length, polka-dot gown as the thunderous applause subsided, then quipped, "I'm not sure I'm dressed for the occasion."

Bette Midler and Tiny Tim have performed at this New York pleasure dome, where Abzug courted not the gay audience but the gay vote. "Those shut out are urged to come in," she exhorted. "The young, the fifty-three percent of this country who are women, gay people, racial minorities...can participate in the total life of America. We need to move this country away from poverty, away from a war that most people are against, and away from sexism of all kinds. People have got to have the freedom to live their lives as they please!"

the comment of a man in one of the leather bars that "You've got a lot of guts to come into a gay bar like this." Bugliosi didn't understand that the guy was referring to the pathological fear most straight males have of gay hangouts. In fact, it developed that he didn't understand the fear, either. What he thought the guy meant was that he was risking a heavy political backlash by campaigning in gay bars. But he went on with the tour.

Bugliosi got a generally good reception. There were also a lot of people who obviously *didn't* know who he was, and cared less. And there were some like the painted drag at the Speak 39 who commented after the candidate walked away, "I think he's full of bullshit. I think he's queer as a three-dollar bill; that's the only way he's talking this bullshit. No straight person sticks up for a homosexual."

Bugliosi, who made the name that will really elect him, if anything does, by his determined prosecution of counterculture antihero Charlie Manson, is about as straight as they come, in more ways than one. The youngest of five children of Italian immigrants, the deputy district attorney is a Catholic family man with a pretty wife, two children, and a tract home in the upper-middle-class suburbs. He is also a professor of criminal law at Beverly College.

So what was such a man doing campaigning among the perverts, risking his political neck? It would be hard to answer the question for the drag in the bar. But he was utterly at ease. A quick handshake, sometimes just the name, "Vince Bugliosi," sometimes the explanation, "running for district attorney." Down the line of faces, some puzzled, some friendly, some impressed. Here and there an enthusiastic supporter who did, indeed, know who he was.

Occasionally, Bugliosi would put his hand lightly on a guy's shoulder and lean forward to listen very intently to a question, then bend down to reply in the guy's ear, to make himself heard above the noise and the din. He did it with elderly Jewish ladies at a street rally on Fairfax Avenue a while back, too. But this wasn't Fairfax Avenue, and uneasy expressions would appear on the faces of the people in Bugliosi's entourage, or perhaps the hovering bar manager, remembering the times in years past when less physical contact than that would be excuse enough for the vice.

The pitch, everywhere, was basically the same. After a while, it began to sound like a broken record to those in his party. "You can vote, you can tell your friends to vote," the candidate told patrons over and over again in the crowded bars. "You've got to get me in. We've got to get out people like [longtime incumbent Joseph] Busch, who has the same intellect as someone like [police chief Ed] Davis, same type of SS intellect....Busch, like Davis, thinks that homosexuals are criminals."

"Baby, you've got my vote," a slightly tipsy customer named Joe shouted out during one stop.

Bugliosi pressed on. "You're going to have to tell your friends to vote, okay? Not just your gay friends, but your nongay friends...." "What's wrong with being a homosexual?" Joe cut in.

"There's nothing wrong with being a homosexual," Bugliosi replied earnestly. "If you guys can get on the phone...you could start right now, calling up friends. Because people, not money, are going to elect the next district attorney. We've got to prove to people that the D.A.'s office is not for sale. That's all there is to it. Busch has all the big wealth behind him, all the Birchers, all the people with these warped, twisted minds, puritanical views...."

Somebody interrupted with a loud "Amen!"   —ROB COLE

"WE WERE THERE!"
HISTORIC GAY BROADCAST
FROM DEMOCRATIC CONVENTION

An era ended in the wee small hours of July 12, and a new, brighter one began.

It began when an acknowledged homosexual woman and man took their places at the rostrum of one of the world's great political forums—the Democratic National Convention—as accredited delegates and spoke seriously for nearly half an hour about gay rights.

Their audience may have been small, but they were heard. For the first time in nearly two thousand years, homosexuals are back in the mainstream of the political process, stating their case before a national audience that has finally begun to listen.

The hour of the morning took off some of the bloom. Although the unblinking eye of one television network, CBS, remained focused on the podium throughout the ten-minute speech by Jim Foster, chairman of the political committee of the Society for Individual Rights in San Francisco, and through most of the slightly shorter speech by Madeline Davis, of Buffalo's Mattachine Society of the Niagara Frontier, few were awake to hear them.

However, Foster was interviewed by NBC for nearly two minutes at about six P.M., and the minority plank and the topic of gay liberation were referred to by television newsmen numerous times throughout the evening in the context of other serious issues.

Asked if he thought the American people were ready to accept the gay liberation movement, Foster told NBC that he thought "they certainly are ready to accept it, once they understand precisely what it is, and once they understand that the principles involved in gay liberation are very basically civil rights issues, and that the time really has come to end the kinds of discrimination and the kinds of arbitrary and discriminatory law enforcement practices that are practiced against gay people in this country."

There were a total of five gay delegates and alternates seated at the Miami convention. The alternates—Renee Cafiero and Danece Covello of New York and Lowell Williams of Minnesota—were not as much in the limelight, but other delegates were aware of their presence.

The whole country was aware of Foster and Davis. "We do not come to you pleading for your 'understanding' or begging your 'tolerance,' " Foster said in his rostrum speech. "We come to you affirming our pride in our lifestyle, affirming the validity of our right to seek and to maintain meaningful emotional relationships, and affirming our rights to participate in the life of this country on an equal basis with every other citizen...."

Davis said the "twenty million" gay Americans are "the 'untouchables' in American society. We have suffered the gamut of oppression, from being totally ignored to having our heads smashed and our blood spilled in the streets. Now we are coming out of our closets and onto the convention floor to tell you, the delegates, and to tell all gay people throughout America, that we are here to put an end to our fears."

Well-known gay activist Dr. Bruce Voeller (*above*) made headlines when he chained himself to phones at George McGovern's campaign headquarters in New York protesting the candidate's backtracking on gay issues. Voeller was previously active on the Gay Citizens for McGovern Committee, which had worked tirelessly for the candidate.

McGovern had run numerous ads in *The Advocate* promising reform in federal employment, housing, and military policies. Still, on July 25, he issued a statement backing off his pro-gay positions through his press secretary.

Phone calls up and down the campaign chain of command got *The Advocate* to hold its presses and produced a statement from McGovern that he was not withdrawing his earlier promises.

But that was not enough for Voeller and other members of Gay Activists Alliance. They occupied the Democratic candidate's New York headquarters for five hours on August 21, demanding that McGovern publicly reaffirm his position on gay rights.

FEAR AND LOATHING ON THE CAMPAIGN TRAIL

While jockeying for position, Democratic Presidential hopefuls George McGovern, Hubert H. Humphrey, and Eugene McCarthy rode the political line between gay appeasement and mainstream acceptance. Responses to gay rights varied widely, swinging from warm endorsement to coy apathy, and, closer to the Democratic National Convention, outright rejection:

McGovern: *"I have spoken out on [gay] issues many times, and I feel they are pertinent and viable."*
—*at a January press conference*

"I'm not going to take responsibility for those [pro-gay civil rights] statements. But I don't believe in discrimination against people on the grounds of sex, and that's as far as I'm going to carry the issue."
—*denouncing his national headquarters' proposals in October*

Humphrey: *"I'm not an expert on homosexuality, and I'm not going to get involved in a detailed description of what we'll do."*
—*to* The Advocate *in January*

"I see no reason why homosexuals should be excluded from equal protection under the law. Homosexuals are citizens; let us treat them as such."
—*in a May letter to a gay activist*

"The government has the right to lay down certain criteria for sensitive employment, because there are a number of people that feel homosexuality can be used as a way of blackmail."
—*speaking on a Los Angeles TV talk show in June*

McCarthy: *"I am for abolishing all discrimination in housing on the basis of age, sex, race, and sexual orientation.... All discrimination in the Armed Forces should end."*
—*in a February conversation with California gay leaders*

MIAMI BEACH DIARY: PEOPLE LIB AT THE REPUBLICAN CONVENTION

Gay liberation and "people liberation" couldn't be separated in Miami Beach during the Republican Convention in late August. As I arrive Monday, the city appears in the most beautiful light I've ever seen; but the tone is not beautiful (the best of times, the worst of times). At a grassy spot in front of the convention center I come across a speaker addressing a group of about two hundred, almost all young, nearly all long-haired. "There's going to be a lot of shit coming down here," he says.

I head for Flamingo Park, where many gays have pitched tents along with members of other groups. Within half an hour of my arrival at the park's gay area, I feel I've known some forty or fifty people for all of my life. There, we talk about the direction our continuing liberation should take. Also debated is the rally scheduled for later in the week. Some of us feel that the demonstraton should have an antiwar, anti-Nixon focus. Others hold out for concentrating on gay issues. Several move back and forth, unwilling to stick rigidly in one position.

Ann Woytow came down to Miami from her home, the address of which is the Sidewalk in Front of the White House. Through friends, Ann has managed to get the bare requirements of life while she has stayed in front of the house Nixon temporarily occupies. Her instinct for survival has enabled her to endure difficulties that would cripple the average person.

Calling all gays "my boys and girls," Ann tentatively begins to explore the politics of the situation at Flamingo Park. "We can fight like cats and dogs with each other, but we can get together on a fight, too," she says. "Just let anybody attack any one of us, and every one of us is going to fight back."

On Wednesday, while approximately twelve hundred people were being arrested, Ann stayed overnight in the park guarding the clothes and belongings in the gay area. When tear gas drove her to leave the park on Thursday, she managed the hauling of loads and loads of the scanty but valuable property of the gays to Miami's new Metropolitan Community Church.

Like Ann, Severin of Atlanta has a feeling of responsibility to gay individuals and groups. I interview Severin, who took his name from a song, as we sit under a tree at the edge of the park. "Even at a conference like this, underneath the rhetoric there's a lot of confusion," Severin observes. "Many of the people here don't have a full sense of [gay] identity. If we're going to be politically effective, we have to get our own consciousness together."

As Severin speaks, two gay men walk up in black costumes, one in a maxi-dress and the other in a jumpsuit. The man in the long black dress wears a red handkerchief on his head, while the jumpsuited man has on a silver fool's cap. They are prepared to lead Tuesday's parade from the park to the street in front of the convention hall.

Severin gives them hell, tells them they are just playing into the hands of a hostile straight public. "The people who see you won't allow you to be free when you're wearing costumes like that," he says.

The two men look confused. The chances of Severin's complimenting them on their costumes had, they thought, been at least as probable as the result they got. Then the man in the maxi-dress smiles a small, ironic smile. "You don't like my dress," he says in a teasing, meek voice. Everyone laughs, and the tense moment passes.

Flamingo Park officials, who would detest being called "officials," decide to let the gay group lead Tuesday night's parade from the park, an interesting political move. This is the last night that Flamingo Park people are clearly separated into such groups as women, YIPs, gays, and VVAWs (Vietnam Veterans Against the War).

By Wednesday, everyone agrees either to join the demonstration against Nixon or to go his own way. Since I choose to be in an immobile group—those who would try to prevent Nixon from reaching the convention hall by passive resistance techniques—I know little of what the five other large groups plan. At the beginning of the immobile group meeting, I observe that, of those assembled, over 10 percent are definitely gay.

Later "people liberation" becomes the key. All of us march out of Flamingo Park Wednesday afternoon without identifying buttons and banners, with individual differences temporarily held in abeyance.

My group sits in the intersection at 30th and Collins surrounded by at least thirty Florida state patrolmen. There must be at least eighty of us, about thirty women and fifty men sitting in a circle, immobile and passively resistant, intent on blocking Nixon and the delegates as they begin to go to the convention center. The patrolmen, holding long clubs, have mace, tear gas, and pepper gas canisters hanging from their belts. The tear gas is used right away.

We had brought white cloths and water-filled plastic bottles with us. So we wet the square white cloths and put them around our faces. Since we have been doing Allen Ginsberg's "Ahhh" Om (which had become personal spiritual-and-emotional property of all of us) and since there's nowhere to look except to whatever gods might exist, we continue our "Ahhh" as we go limp and are loaded onto two trucks.

The men are taken first, with the most important men—including Ginsberg and his friend Peter Orlovsky—being the very first ones grabbed. Loading us into the first truck takes a great deal of time, about an hour it seemes to me. But, like almost everybody else, I am not wearing a watch. I'm about tenth from the last one thrown up. As a consequence, I'm able to lean forward and encourage our sisters and a few brothers who are the last of the men.

In the first truck, Ginsberg is inventing chants while Orlovsky and others offer their ideas. I suggest, "Nixon Brought Us Together." If there is one man responsible for our being where we are, it's Richard Nixon. That slogan feels right as we chant it.

The trip takes twenty or thirty minutes. The lack of oxygen in the truck, the whispered "Be quiet, save the air," and the intense heat make this a very frightening journey. Some of the men silently pass around oranges, canteens of water, and peanuts. We're sweating so much that the liquid and the salt from the peanuts serve as survival fare.

The ride delivers us to Dade County Jail, where we're lined up, frisked, marched to appear before judges, and kept waiting in large enclosures and small cells. Each of us handles being busted differently. At first I feel excitement and gratitude for the camaraderie. Later, I feel depressed, dirty, and awfully isolated.

After a few terrible hours, I'm among the men taken to Dade County Stockade up near the freeway into Miami. The word "bust" has a quite literal as well as metaphorical meaning. In the last dark hours of Thursday morning, I lie on the floor of the stockade like a balloon with all the air let out of it.

—Dan Allen

Gay men and lesbians united in protest at the Republican National Convention.

THE SUBMERGED LESBIAN

The lesbian with a heterosexual marriage is a paradox. No one will believe she is a lesbian, not even her lesbian sisters. Therefore, she finds herself on the outskirts of both worlds.

She does not dare enter too enthusiastically into the activities of the heterosexual society, for fear some partially hidden desire may destroy her and those who love her.

By the same token, she is not allowed full membership into the lesbian community, because her sisters fear impossible involvements.

If, by some extraordinary stroke of luck, she has married a man who knows and understands her needs, she may find some measure of contentment. This sort of relationship will, at least, permit her to look (however surreptitiously) for fulfillment with less fear than her not-so-fortunate sisters.

Difficult as it may be for the average lesbian to make contacts, imagine the frustration of the housewife and mother who is also a lesbian.

Married men move about in homophile society with amazing acceptance—amazing, that is, to his homophile sister who doesn't have this freedom. Homophile males seem to see nothing sinister in the marital status and fatherhood of his associates.

Why, then, do lesbians assume that marriage and motherhood disprove any and all claims to lesbianism? Parenthood is so much easier, biologically, for a female. It does not even require her active participation.

If the plight of the married lesbian is tenacious, how much more so is that of the bisexual female? She is ridiculed by her sisters with terms of derision—or worse, she is ignored, which can be the greater heartache.

Today, there is hope for young girls who suspect their own "difference." The censure is no longer so strong. She may accept herself as she is and arrange her lifestyle accordingly.

Things are not so simple for those whose lifestyle has already been established along lines that must be continued whether they fit the individual or not. Whatever her frustration, the married lesbian cannot reinstate her life along different patterns without causing undue heartache to many people.

Her only hope is that somehow, through some miracle, she may find a compatible soulmate whose commitments (and thus her demands) are similar to her own. There is little likelihood of this, unfortunately, because she must live in a shadow world beneath a shadow world where she will continue to survive on dreams of a tomorrow that, quite probably, will never come.

Is there no way to reach her? In this age of all-encompassing communications, there must be one medium that can hold out a discreet hand to the many lonely lesbians living amid the nonunderstanding crowds of suburbia.

—PEGGY JAYLEEN BELL

Now It's S&M Liberation

It was bound to happen: sadomasochistic liberation! Over the past eighteen months the Eulenspiegel Society, originally a masochist liberation group, has held weekly meetings, consciousness-raising groups, and campaigns to correct erroneous concepts of sadomasochistic sexual orientation.

The group's name is taken from Richard Strauss's tone poem *Till Eulenspiegel's Merry Pranks,* based on an old folk tale about a practical jokester. "We're the only aboveground S&M group in the world," declares Pat Bond, founder of the New York group. "And although we're small, we're just the tip of an iceberg."

Sitting in on a Sunday-night meeting is an enthralling and eye-opening experience. Most of those involved in S&M lib tell of years of guilt and frustration before meeting others who shared their inclinations.

Almost universally, they disavow the popular misconception that they want to inflict pain and domination on unwilling partners or have themselves brutalized in a fashion not to their liking. Their relationships, they insist, are filled with love and concern for their partners, as much as or more than conventional straight or gay affairs.

Here is a sample of personal testimonials at a single meeting:

—"I'm a homosexual S. Not a sadist, a master—I distinguish between the two," one thin, middle-aged man wearing a black cap said.
—"I'm a homosexual, a faggot," the next man commenced. "I don't like the words 'gay person.' I've been having relations with women the past two years and have found my fantasies are becoming increasingly masochistic. In 1968 I had an affair with a girl who had just been a member of a motorcycle gang. But another person came around, and she dropped me. Now she's a radical lesbian. She said I used my bisexuality and was the worst type of male chauvinist."
—"I'm a homosexual, a masochist. I'm into being used and abused with imagination and wit," another man chimed in. The crowd exploded with laughter.
—"People think there's no love in an S&M relationship," added a gay S. "But there is a lot of love. When I'm with an M, no matter how violent I'm being, causing him pain and tears, there's concern there for him, for his delight in the pain I'm giving him." On cross-examination, he said he would stop if, in his judgment, the person really wanted him to do so.
—"I spend most of my time being dominant in the outside world," a rugged man in his late twenties related. "I'm a masochist, sexually. I'm a heterosexual, but I have homosexual fantasies in relation to S&M. I like to be dominated by a master who puts me into a position where I have no choice over what happens to me. It's not the homosexual sex I like, it's being forced to do things I don't like to do.

"Fortunately, my wife digs the scene, and I am very happily married. By becoming a sexual masochist, I found I became a better person. Most people sublimate their sexual sadism and masochism in nonsexual ways, like getting into a fight in a bar or provoking conflicts at work. I have a very good job in advertising, and I function better because of sublimating my destructive urges into sexuality," he concluded to hearty applause.
—Randy Wicker

MISS THING   by Joe Johnson

"Well, it's leather, isn't it?"

TELEVISION: *THAT CERTAIN SUMMER*

British rock star David Bowie, described by *The New York Times* as "the first acknowledged bisexual superstar," got a standing ovation at his American premiere before a capacity crowd in Carnegie Hall September 28. Reviewers were less enthusiastic, however, criticizing Bowie's use of open homoeroticism in his performance.

New York magazine critic Alan Rich, who flew to England to preview Bowie's show, titled his review "I've Been to London to See the Queen." The *Times* critic remarked, "David Bowie? Ugh! Call it freak rock, transvestite rock, or decadent rock, the uglies are the latest giggle on the pop music scene."

What other reviewers referred to as his "fag come-on" consisted of a few instances when Bowie engaged in overtly homosexual conduct. At one point during the Carnegie concert the singer kissed his handsome lead guitarist. Later, he sank to his knees before the musician and moved his head back and forth as if giving him a blow job. Wearing a Day-Glo green and pink jumpsuit, Bowie in one song declared, "I've been waiting for a man, waiting for a man to come along for so long, just waiting for a man."

I admit to having approached the screening room at Universal Studios with misgivings the night they showed the press their new television movie, *That Certain Summer.* Theater screens had exploited the negative aspects of homosexuality until the still-more-lucrative black market beckoned, and now it was television's turn, I thought, to recycle the same thoughts for the titillation of the stay-at-homes.

Well, I was wrong. What unfolded in the next seventy-seven minutes was the most tasteful, accurate, and compelling story on homosexuality to reach the screens thus far, with perhaps the exception of the film *Sunday, Bloody Sunday.* While *Sunday* was more explicit because of the market for which it was made, *That Certain Summer* makes its points no less forcefully, but without nudity, bed scenes, or passionate embraces.

The story is contemporary: Hal Holbrook and his wife, Hope Lange, were married for eleven years and are the parents of a boy. Then, no longer able to resist his homosexual inclinations, Holbrook confessed them to his wife, gave her a divorce and custody of the child, moved to San Francisco, and began his life anew.

This background information is given the audience during the course of the film, which begins as Holbrook is viewing home movies of his past life just before the arrival of his son, now fourteen, for a visit. Since last seeing the boy, Holbrook has acquired a lover, Martin Sheen, and the two have been having a relationship for nine months in Sausalito.

Holbrook wants his son to meet Sheen and accept him as a good friend of his father's, without having to explain the relationship in great detail. The son is not all that naive and senses right away something is not as it seems. He resents

and rebuffs Sheen's attempts to become friends, then provokes a situation which forces Holbrook to finally tell him the truth and hope the boy is sophisticated enough to understand.

The filmmakers have fashioned a picture of homosexuals as solid, upstanding citizens, who hold responsible employment, and don't swish or giggle or conform to any of the other gay stereotypes—in other words, real people who just happen to be homosexual. They have caught the quiet, not-overly-demonstrative love the two men have for each other without having to belabor the point, and also the attitudes of surrounding characters, most of whom accept them without questioning their sexuality.

That Certain Summer is a sensitive film gays will probably appreciate. Even more important, ABC's telecast of this movie will reach many more people than even the most successful theatrical film, and either correct erroneous impressions of gays they already had or introduce them to what the majority of gay people are really like.

—HAROLD FAIRBANKS

ATTACKS ON N.Y. GAYS

Newspaper of America's Homophile Community

The **ADVOCATE**

So. Cal 35¢
50¢ Elsewhere

Dallas Attorney Murdered

New Orleans: After the Tragedy

David Stephenson

GAY CENTER BURNS

Newspaper of America's Homophile Community

The **ADVOCATE**

So. Cal 35¢
50¢ Elsewhere

FBI enters weird bus caper

St. Francis in the buff: Graham Faulkner

ARRESTS AT GAY SIT-IN

Newspaper of America's Homophile Community

The **ADVOCATE**

So. Cal 35¢
50¢ Elsewhere

Cops who are gay and proud

Peter Burian

NEW ORLEANS TRAGEDY

Newspaper of America's Homophile Community

The **ADVOCATE**

So. Cal 35¢
50¢ Elsewhere

GAY PRIDE ISSUE

BIG GAY PARADES

COMING OUT!

'GAY'S AS GOOD'

NEW ORLEANS MEMORIAL

Nick Nolte in *The Last Pad*

TRIALS BY FIRE

1973 The gay liberation movement had proven that it was not just another fad; in fact, it was clearly on the verge of becoming professionalized. But our successes triggered antigay violence in general and a backlash from the police in particular, both of which threatened gay communities throughout much of North America.

Police departments across the nation continued efforts to arrest gay men for "loitering," or having sex in public places. The most curious story of the year involved a forty-foot bus that appeared in Denver, Indianapolis, and eventually Miami. Its sole occupant, the driver, would lure gay male bar patrons into the vehicle, only to drive them to a waiting police car. The entrapment was particularly irksome in Denver, where acts of "deviate intercourse" had become legal the previous year.

In a most novel effort in Los Angeles, thirty-nine men were nabbed by the police in Griffith Park as "fire hazards." In Indianapolis, fifty-four men were arrested at a Club Steambaths, and fifty-one were charged with "frequenting a dive." Occasionally, local communities sided with the police. In Boston, residents of the Bay Village neighborhood tried to close two gay bars.

But bathhouse raids seemed minor compared to the violence against gays that year. Arson, a crime that can be committed facelessly in the dark, was clearly the fastest-growing assault on our communities. Metropolitan Community Church buildings in Los Angeles and San Francisco were burned down. But the greatest tragedy of the year was the torching of a gay bar in New Orleans, in which thirty-two men died as they tried to claw their way to fresh air.

The enemy, alas, was not always outside the gates. After Wayne Henley killed Dean Corll in Houston, he accused Corll of torturing and killing twenty-seven boys, aged thirteen to twenty years old. Not wishing to see that at least some of Corll's victims were gay, homophobes were quick to blame gay liberation for one of the largest series of murders in United States history: We had presumably made it easier for Corll to pick up young men. Fearing a political

A defiant Troy Perry stands in the rubble of his burned-down church.

81

backlash, many activists in the community redoubled their efforts.

After former New York City Health Administrator Howard Brown came out publicly, he joined others—including Dr. Bruce Voeller, Professor Martin Duberman, publicist Ronald Gold, and longtime activist Franklin Kameny—to form the National Gay Task Force. Their goal was to "focus on broad national issues" and bring "gay liberation into the mainstream of American civil rights." Lambda Legal Defense and Education Fund was also incorporated before the end of the year. Even MCC's Rev. Troy Perry went national, leaving the Los Angeles "Mother Church" to inspire the formation of congregations elsewhere. On more local fronts, Jim Foster became treasurer of the California Democratic Committee; Harvey Milk ran for the Board of Supervisors in San Francisco; Jim Owles tried for a City Council seat in New York; and Jack Baker made a similar bid in Minneapolis. While their efforts were not successful, they paved the way for other openly gay candidates to win public acceptance.

I spent most of the year spreading the word about *Out of the Closets: Voices of Gay Liberation,* the first anthology of essays by and for gay people. Coeditor Allen Young and I hit the road, speaking at universities like Ohio State in Columbus and Cornell in Ithaca, New York, where gay student organizations were underfunded but operating anyway. Forget hotels! We were housed in dorm rooms and sometimes slept on floors.

While Allen and I were on the road trumpeting the benefits of coming out, we were often billed with other nationally known figures like Perry and Phyllis Lyon and Del Martin, whose *Lesbian/Woman* had also just been published. Since we had a reputation as radicals, we tended to attract a hip crowd that was still optimistic about an overthrow of the patriarchy and that supported causes like the Cuban revolution. The young men and women had come out, often fiercely and defiantly, but they weren't sure where they were going. "What do we do now that we're out?" asked one bearded man whose denim jacket was covered with political buttons. Allen and I didn't know the answer, so we began to assemble our next collection of essays around that topic.

In 1973, there weren't all that many gay and lesbian books (aside from marginally gay titles like Carson McCullers's *Member of the Wedding*). Several women's presses, including Diana Press, Naiad, and Daughters, Inc., started up to fill the void. Local gay liberation newspapers were beginning to flourish, too. Positive plays about us, like Jonathan Ned Katz's *Coming Out!* and Al Carmine's *The Faggot,* opened in New York City. Gay and lesbian music was also emerging, mostly in the form of gutsy anthems like "Angry Atthis" by Maxine Feldman and "Stonewall Nation" by Madeline Davis.

It's not clear what the average gay person in the street thought of all these events—good and bad. But if head counts matter, they probably listened to the good news only and concluded that the struggle was over. A proposal to march on Washington, D.C., was opposed by gays living there. And according to newspaper and police tallies, the number of gay-rights marchers in New York, San Francisco, and other major cities was actually decreasing. Many lesbian-feminists, discouraged by drag queens and men calling themselves "male lesbians," withdrew their active support of gay liberation. They increased efforts to form separate organizations and agendas. Other gay men and lesbians turned in their walking shoes and wrote checks for lobbying groups instead. Aside from a brief flurry of activity in response to Anita Bryant and John Briggs, it wasn't until the advent of AIDS that the movement would regain a fervent level of personal commitment by everyday gay men and lesbians. —KARLA JAY

"Try It … You'll Like It" spoofed a popular ad slogan. Poster producer Stephen Wholey posed models Bill Dykeman and Dick Dawson as wholesome gay recruiters.

Gay glee over the troubles of President Nixon is reflected in this cartoon. Deeper concerns were covered in a late-spring story headlined WATERGATE: WERE GAYS "USED" IN GOP PLOT?

Activists turned out at ABC Television offices on both coasts in February to protest against "objectionable dialogue" in an episode of "Marcus Welby, M.D." In the segment, a diabetic father called his homosexual tendencies "degrading and loathsome" and his life "a cheap, hollow fraud." Dr. Welby termed the gay urges "a serious illness."

In April, a dozen New Yorkers were arrested while protesting the defeat of Intro 475, the latest incarnation of the city's proposed gay-rights bill.

---

and Councilman Robert Stevenson, three Los Angeles candidates who had courted the gay vote, were swept into office in an early show of gay voting power. ❑ Compulsives Anonymous, a support group for men addicted to tearooms, began in Los Angeles. ❑ In Nashville, Tennessee, a Puerto Rican female impersonator was crowned Miss Gay America, receiving $1,000 and a new Pontiac. ❑ Canadian gay groups meeting in Ottawa formed the National Gay Election Coalition.

JUNE   *Gay,* the nation's second-largest gay newspaper, folded in New York City after three years. ❑ The Rev. William Alberts, who married a gay couple in a Boston United Methodist church in April, lost his job and was expelled from the ministry as a result. ❑ The Lesbian Liberation Committee of New York's Gay Activists Alliance broke away to form a separate organization, Lesbian Feminist Liberation. ❑ Connie "Mac" McConnohie, lesbian activist, prison reform worker, and ex-con, filed her candidacy for the Detroit City Council with the slogan "Put a Real Man in Common Council"; she was not elected. ❑ Lesbian activist Mina Robinson announced the formation of a lesbian culture center in Los Angeles; soon after, it closed. ❑ British sports celebrity Tim Brand-Crombie came out in London's *Gay News,* becoming the world's first openly gay powerboat racer.

JULY   A "Lavender Patrol" in San Francisco drew criticism from gays when its founder, the controversial Rev. Ray Broshears, suggested carrying rifles. ❑ Lesbians picketed the *Atlanta Journal* over that newspaper's failure to cover Gay Pride events. ❑ The head of Portland's gay Second Foundation and its $3,000 treasury disappeared, but the organization did not file a complaint with the police; the incident was never investigated. ❑ Manhattan gay leaders charged that police refused to investigate a series of sometimes fatal attacks on patrons of local leather bars.

AUGUST   The American Bar Association adopted a resolution urging states to repeal all anti-gay-sex laws. ❑ GAA New York voted to seek historic landmark designation for the Stonewall Inn; the designation would not be granted for over twenty more years. ❑ Jo Daly of San Francisco became the first openly gay person appointed to a city position when she took a post on the Cablevision Task Force. ❑ Protesting male supremacist exhibits, Lesbian Feminist Liberation paraded an eighteen-foot lavender dinosaur, identified as female, in front of New York City's American Museum of Natural History. ❑ Dallas police seized an estimated 100,000 names while raiding a callboy service. ❑ The New York Matts, a gay softball team sponsored by the Mattachine Society, played police from the Sixth Precinct in a charity game umpired by local reporter Geraldo Rivera; the police won, 16–0.

SEPTEMBER   Seattle passed an ordinance forbidding employment discrimina-

Gay activist and leader Bruce Voeller (*above, center*) and friends celebrated during the New York Gay Pride Parade in June.

When Voeller gave up his career as a professor of biology at Rockefeller University to cofound the National Gay Task Force in 1973 and become its first executive director at a $200 a week salary, he had experienced antigay discrimination first-hand. Married for eleven years before he came out, Voeller had to go to court to retain visiting rights with his children. A New Jersey judge ordered in 1974 that Voeller not have his lover present when his children visit and not introduce his children to any of the gay programs of which he was a part.

The Black Lesbian Caucus (*below*) also marched in New York's Gay Pride Parade.

tion against gays. ❏ Camera shop owner and newcomer to electoral politics Harvey Milk announced his first campaign for the San Francisco Board of Supervisors; he lost. ❏ Opposing the sex-law reforms of new City Attorney Burt Pines, Los Angeles Police Chief Ed Davis lashed out at gays, calling them "predatory creatures." ❏ Pulitzer Prize–winning poet W. H. Auden, who once said, "I had no trouble after I learned that I was queer," died. ❏ The American Baptist Association, the American Lutheran Association, the United Presbyterians, the United Methodists, and the Society of Friends (Quakers) launched the National Task Force on Gay People in the Church to press for reforms in the National Council of Churches of Christ. ❏ A Chicago judge declared a thirty-year-old ordinance against cross-dressing unconstitutional. ❏ A London psychiatrist suggested that homosexuals make the best and safest teachers for small children.

OCTOBER   The National Gay Task Force formed in New York; its stated goal was "to bring gay liberation into the mainstream of American civil rights." ❏ Indianapolis vice cops raided a meeting of the fledgling Metropolitan Community Church there. ❏ Lambda Legal Defense and Education Fund, a gay advocacy group, was incorporated in Albany, New York. ❏ Following a similar action by his New York City counterpart, San Francisco's police chief signed an order prohibiting his two thousand officers from using the words "fruit," "queer," "faggot" and "fairy." ❏ A black Alabama teacher fired over alleged homosexuality denied that he was gay and sued the local school district. ❏ Fourteen men, including Christopher Paul Lewis, the son of actress Loretta Young, were indicted in an investigation of so-called "chicken porn" and charged with ninety counts of oral copulation, sodomy, and lewd acts with children under fourteen; nine, including Lewis, were fined $500 and given five years' probation. ❏ Gay Australian novelist Patrick White won the Nobel Prize for Literature.

NOVEMBER   A Michigan judge ended a three-year custody battle by returning eight children to their mothers, who were lovers. ❏ The Berkeley, California City Council prohibited companies doing business with the city from discriminating against gays. ❏ Over fifty Midwestern lesbians and gays, attending a conference in Champaign, Illinois, sponsored by the National Gay Mobilizing Committee, discussed and rejected the idea of a national gay-rights march on Washington, D.C. ❏ One hundred persons gathered in Breda, Netherlands, to attend the Second Congress on Pedophilia.

DECEMBER   The American Psychiatric Association's board of trustees voted to remove homosexuality from its list of psychiatric disorders. ❏ Activists met in Sacramento and San Francisco to demand that sexual orientation be eliminated as a factor in parole decisions, that gay literature be made available to prisoners, and that gay inmates be segregated in California prisons. ❏ A Los Angeles woman picketed the Donut Chalet, a doughnut shop and teen hangout, claiming that her fifteen-year-old son turned homosexual after spending time there. ❏ The U.S. Civil Service Commission proposed that new regulations keyed to job performance replace the ban on hiring or retaining homosexuals in federal agencies. ❏ In what the National Gay Task Force hailed as a major gain, NBC rejected a script for its "Police Story" series because it might offend the gay community. ❏ Two inmates at Leavenworth Penitentiary filed a lawsuit challenging the Federal Bureau of Prison ban on homosexual sex; they lost their case. ❏ A nationwide campus fad—running nude, or "streaking"—was reported by both *Time* and *The Advocate*.

Destined to become a leader in the lesbian and gay movement, ex-nun Jean O'Leary (*above*) made her public debut in June 1973, when she mounted the Washington Square stage of the Gay Pride rally to proclaim, on behalf of Lesbian Feminist Liberation, that transvestite entertainment was an insult to women. All hell broke loose in the audience, and Bette Midler (*below*) was drafted to sing a soothing rendition of "You Got to Have Friends."

RISING FROM THE ASHES

Two separate fires destroyed the "mother church" of the Los Angeles Metropolitan Community Church. Seventeen firefighting units converged late on the night of January 27, as fire destroyed all furnishings and seriously damaged records. Then, on April 6, a second blaze left only crumbling walls. Damages were estimated to be in excess of $150,000.

Using the picture shown above, the Rev. Troy Perry made a grimly effective appeal for funds to build a "bigger, better" church. But replacing the first building owned, as Morris Kight observed, "by the forces of gay liberation" would not be easy. The building housed a gay seminary, food and clothing banks, rap groups, counseling, and other services. The fire damaged the Torah of the Lesbian and Gay Metropolitan Community Temple, which also held services there.

Arson investigators concluded that the first blaze was accidental. "If that's true, I'm thrilled," commented Perry. "But I'm still not sure."

TRIUMPH AND TRAGEDY, headlined *The Advocate*'s coverage of a fearsome blaze that destroyed a New Orleans gay bar on June 24. While New York and other cities saw their largest Gay Pride turnout yet, in the French Quarter dive known as the Up Stairs Lounge, twenty-nine people died.

The fire, one of the worst in New Orleans history, was suspected to have been caused by a firebomb. Local and national televison reports, *The Advocate* noticed, "struggled visibly to reconcile natural human shock and dismay with the dislike of homosexuals so deeply ingrained in American society." Most broadcasters appeared reluctant to say the word "homosexual" on the air.

Troy Perry flew to the scene, and memorials held in five cities mourned the individual lives lost and the vulnerability of all lesbians and gays to hate crimes. Three burn victims later died, bringing fatalities to thirty-two. One man had escaped the building, only to go back inside to retrieve his trapped lover. Their bodies were found together.

More than words and tears poured forth. With *The Advocate* as its center point, a national board of trustees for the New Orleans Memorial Fund swiftly raised more than $15,000.

Aside from the fiery disasters at MCC Los Angeles and in New Orleans, a series of gay buildings went up in flames this year, causing grief and worry:

—The recently opened Gay Services Center in Buffalo was destroyed March 23, in a fire blamed on faulty wiring.

—Two San Francisco bars, Toad Hall and the Exit, burned on Gay Pride Weekend.

—The building leased by the San Francisco MCC was gutted July 27, in a three-alarm fire described by fire department spokesmen as "definitely" arson.

—The Arch Café, a gay bar in Springfield, Massachusetts, was destroyed September 12 by a bomb blast. There were no casualties.

GAY IS GOOD TELEVISION

Los Angeles's Gay Community Services Center, the nation's largest institution of its kind, grew rapidly in its second year. It increased the number of clients served, the types of services provided, and—most important—the amount of money it acquired through grants. Following its million-dollar federal grant the previous year, the center was awarded an additional $15,000 through the Department of Health, Education, and Welfare to fund a drug abuse counseling program. A volunteer-staffed V.D. clinic, also at the center, would soon win government funding as well.

The media turned up its coverage accordingly. After a year of trying, the center obtained permission to broadcast public service announcements. Dozens were aired, yielding hundreds of calls. Two venerable reporters from the Los Angeles Times *even hosted a TV tour. Here,* The Advocate *reports on the reporting.*

Following the visionary lead of Morris Kight (*left*), Don Kilhefner (*standing*) and John Vincent Platania help found Los Angeles's Gay Community Services Center.

Reporters Art Seidenbaum and Charles Champlin led the audience of "City Watchers," a program on public television station KCET, on a twenty-four-minute whirlwind tour of the center.

Don Kilhefner, the center's executive director, initiated the dialogue by explaining that one of the center's main functions is to be a group of gay people helping other gay people to find out "what it means to be gay...encouraging people to explore, experiment, develop a sense of gay consciousness...the joys and ecstasies of being gay."

The point was evidently missed by the interviewers, who asked, "Aren't you in service to help the oppressed? I didn't think you were a social service to help the joyous." One of the center's staff members, the Rev. Richard Nash, took up the point and explained that being gay is often "a source of trouble, of hostility, of resentment, of oppression. To provide an alternative to that, so that people can have a positive experience of their gayness, is why we have such a program."

The interviewers repeatedly brought out the so-called threat gay persons pose to nongay society, asking if being gay was different from being homosexual. "Yes," Nash said, "we make a distinction in that term. Homosexual refers more particularly to a kind of behavior, a sexual behavior at that. We think we're a lot more than sexual beings, and we'd rather concentrate on who we are rather than what we do."

"You don't believe that the nongay world is afraid of you?" one of the *Times* reporters asked.

"I think that people are afraid of anybody in this society who takes their own life into their own hands," Kilhefner answered. "What we're dealing with here is a very powerful question: people defining themselves, a question of personal freedom. And sure, this society finds that a threat."

In explaining the purpose of the center, Kilhefner noted that there are at least 750,000 people "who recognize themselves as gay in Los Angeles County, and not a single social service agency was directed toward their needs. The center represents the gay community saying: 'No longer will we wait for you to recognize our community, we're going to start providing those social services for ourselves.'" —MARTIN ST. JOHN

"HERE I AM—I'M GAY"

On October 3, a forty-nine-year-old physician and former chief health officer of New York City told six hundred of his colleagues attending a symposium on sexuality that he was gay. The announcement by Howard J. Brown created a sensation and gave the cause of gay liberation perhaps its biggest single boost since a similar revelation by novelist Merle Miller three years before. Brown went on to play a prominent role in the movement until his death from a heart attack in early 1975. Here are excerpts from an article he wrote for The Advocate *explaining his decision to come out.*

The people who basically led me to my decision were the brave men and women of the Gay Activists Alliance who have fought so magnificently for gay rights in New York City. Though I had helped them behind the scenes, really I was like the other successful homosexuals I know. I stayed hidden and let these gallant boys and girls work hours and days and even be beaten up in a fight that really I should have joined. Whenever I hear criticism of these magnificent fighters for human rights from pompous, closeted, successful gays, I get so enraged I can hardly continue my friendship with them.

My professional life has been spent working for better medical care for the poor. In this, I have gotten to know crusading labor leaders in the forties, crusading health leaders in the fifties, and crusading civil rights leaders in the sixties. In qualities of concern and leadership, the leaders of the gay movement clearly rank with the leaders of these other fights against human oppression. Jim Owles, Marty Robinson, Dr. Franklin Kameny, Nathalie Rockhill, Dr. Bruce Voeller, and Morty Manford are among the gay heroes of New York who will rank in history with leaders in the fights against economic and racial oppression. These gay leaders moved me, just as leaders of other fights had earlier.

It is one measure of how society has really oppressed me, that though I had been active in the fight for the poor and for civil rights, it never occurred to me that I could fight for the rights of homosexuals. The gay freedom fighters redefined my previous feelings of shame at being a homosexual into a sense of rage that society could do this to me and so many of the people I loved.

Now it seemed that I could help the cause by saying, "Here I am. I'm gay, a queer, a fairy, a faggot, and there are so many like me that you can't shame or hurt us any longer."

Though I expected some publicity, what has happened is, to me, still astonishing. A front-page story in *The New York Times* was followed by similar stories in newspapers across the country. I have been interviewed by every television station in New York. I have received over two hundred letters, and five publishing houses want me to write a book. That my announcement would attract so much attention is a measure of how much more needs to be done.

My position is not that I am to be tolerated as a homosexual because I am successful and rather square. Rather, [straight society] must not deprive any of us homosexuals of our basic human dignity. This right to dignity has nothing to do with success or an acceptable image.

Am I glad I made the announcement? You bet I am.

A Psychiatric Revolution Behind Bars

"Something incredible is happening at Atascadero State Hospital: A psychiatrist is trying to teach homosexual inmates how to be gay." So reported The Advocate's *Rob Cole about an experiment at the California prison hospital. The innovative project was the work of psychiatrist Michael Serber, who believed "psychiatry shouldn't be used to oppress." Instead, the program retrained what Serber called "inadequate homosexuals" in the social skills found most acceptable in the gay community while at the same time minimizing their problems getting along in a homophobic society. Serber's gay-affirmative approach was controversial, to say the least.*

Excerpted here is the personal view of one man in the program, Tom Close, who was nearing release. A former teacher in his late thirties, Close had been incarcerated in Atascadero for two years following a conviction on child molestation charges.

I had been in the closet all my life, and never knew the gay world—a world both new and rather strange to me. It is sad that this world would never have been opened up to me until I left the hospital, but that was the old system. The policy was, It's okay to be homosexual and we will help you with your problems, but we will not help you to become homosexual.

Things are different now. A concerted effort is being made to give us the skills we need to be successful homosexuals.

The first phase of the program is homosexual social skills. With gay students from Cal Poly, San Luis Obispo, serving as models, we were taught cruising from eye contact to wrap-up, and given the opportunity to practice our dancing. Although I personally prefer to avoid the artificial role-playing of the bar scene, it made me comfortable with another alternative of making contacts.

For me, the best part was the dancing. I would have been very uncomfortable dancing with another man had it not been for this group. My confidence and skill increased so that I felt totally unashamed dancing with another man at one of our ward parties—and our ward is 80 percent straight.

For many of us, this was the first contact we had with successful homosexuals. Sure, we live with other gay guys here, and we have many opportunities to relate with them. But we were all unsuccessful homosexuals, and without the constant feedback from our models, we might never have been quite as successful as we wanted.

This group was a big turning point. The Cal Poly guys helped me change my attitude about sex. I think the statement that sums up things best was when one student said, "Why, I wouldn't think of having sex with my best friend. Good friends are much more hard to find than sex partners, so why take a chance on ruining friendship, the greatest thing a gay can have?" We also explored the age-old problem of making permanent relationships and concluded that there is no easy way, and failure is common. But the rewards, when found, are great enough to keep trying.

The consciousness-raising phase was strictly a channeled rap session. Each meeting we selected a topic of discussion and explored each other's ideas and feelings on a wide range of topics. Our opening topic was "Gay is ____." We ranged from homosexual problems, to family, to women, to sexual and life roles, and many more [issues].

"They weren't into sex that much. They wanted a lot of thrills, pools and things like that. They wanted to sit around and have tea. But women do not want a bath as we know it. They were on a whole different trip."
—Steve Ostrow, owner of New York's Continental Baths, on why the experiment to open his lavish bathhouse to gay women failed

I found myself really torn inside. I began the group by saying, "Gay is good, and gay is hell, but for me, gay is reality." My group took a somewhat liberal gay lib stand, and I found myself becoming more conservative than I really liked to help neutralize their position. For me, this group posed a lot more questions than it gave answers.

These questions were quite pertinent, for we all must face them at some time in our lives. Each of us must decide where he stands and be willing to stand up and be counted to the extent with which he is comfortable. Part of me says, "Stand on a soapbox and shout," while another says, "You have got to be crazy. Keep your mouth shut." I wonder where I will stand when I leave here?

These sessions, as well as the patient's regular therapy group, tackle the serious underlying problems that made us sex offenders. We work very hard with men who feel so insecure with adults and fearful of close relationships that they allow themselves to take only one alternative: a child with whom they feel comfortable and safe. Along the same line, we help men overcome their fear of inadequacy which forces them to have to buy their love rather than risk a seemingly terrible rejection inherent in any relationship.

We help men by encouraging them to accept their strong homosexual feelings by showing them that the only things telling them to go straight are parents and society.

Things are always changing, even now.

THE NAKED TRUTH

During 1973, Robert Opel made a name for himself as a contributing photographer to *The Advocate* known for his whimsical gay sensibility. The following year, he became notorious for streaking the Academy Awards, and appearing in the buff before the Los Angeles City Council during a hearing to consider a ban on public nudity. Most council members grinned while Opel bared it, but Ed Davis, the city's notoriously homophobic chief of police, could barely contain his disgust. Shortly after Opel was carried away, the council voted in favor of the ban.

HARVEST OF HORROR

In a year of loss for the gay community, no event created more of a sense of dread than the case of Dean Corll, a thirty-four-year-old Houston man found to have sadistically killed at least twenty-seven teenage boys. It was the nation's "highest known toll of indisputably homosexual sex killings," reported The Advocate. *Corll was shot to death in August by one of his intended victims, who then led police to mass grave sites.* (photo, right). *The gruesome discovery, shortly following a similar incident in Miami in which a youth was tortured and then dismembered, sent shock waves through the nation. Gay leaders, fearing political and social backlash, immediately responded in indignation over the news media's emphasis on the homosexual aspects of the killings. "Why is it that the chain of mass killers from Jack the Ripper to the Boston Strangler have never been called 'heterosexual murderers'?" asked one spokesman.*

The sadomasochism-tinged slayings also stirred controversy within the gay community around its underground, but visibly growing, leather subculture. At The Advocate's *request, Larry Townsend, a counselor and widely known authority on the leather lifestyle, commented on the killings in Texas and Florida and a series of unsolved mutilation murders in Long Beach, California.*

"Don't Play with S&M"

I cannot let Larry Townsend's lies and rationalizations about S&M as related to murder go unanswered. For years, S&M advocates have propagandized homosexuals not merely to tolerate but actively defend sadomasochism, even experiment with this grave perversion. Now we can see S&M for what it is: a distortion of the psychosexual personality which has as its ultimate result the freeing of the primeval, murderous animal which all societies have battled to restrain for thousands of years.

In this one year, which is not even over yet, we have had the following S&M murders come to light: four knife slayings and perhaps one drowning (this organization's vice president) of adults in New York City; four molestation murders of little boys, also in New York City; four increasingly ferocious murders in Los Angeles County; thirteen murders in Miami; two murders in upstate New York; twenty-seven undeniably sadistic murders of boys in Houston by three killers working in concert; and twenty-eight gay men (and four hangers-on) in the New Orleans gay bar fire, for *arson is a form of sadism* (according to the *Encyclopaedia Britannica,* no less); total, eighty-two, possibly eighty-three men murdered by sadists.

No, we are not dealing with an isolated deviation but rather with the necessary end result of the indulgence of sadomasochism.

Townsend says that "the S&M exchange is just that—an exchange—basically seeking the same sensual experience as any other sexual interaction" and that sadists act "only" with the "express or implied consent" of their victims. That is a baldfaced lie. Let him tell that to a friend of mine who, when a cab driver, was hailed by two men in full leather drag, told to drive to an uninhabited warehouse area of Manhattan, robbed, and then systematically beaten for a half-hour by men "who knew what they were doing, so that they caused no permanent injury and no obvious marks to substantiate a police complaint."

Let Townsend tell his lie to the graves of the boys in Houston, or to the men in California, Florida, and New York. Don't buy it, folks. And don't play with S&M—it's a force you don't understand.

—L. Craig Schoonmaker,
New York City

When we read about these gruesome mutilation murders, it seems only natural to ask ourselves, "Could this creep really be gay?" The answer, I think, is much more complex than a simple "yes" or "no."

Just as most human beings possess the emotional potential to be either homosexual or heterosexual, so do most of us retain the residual elements of a more primitive sexuality. Because the sex drive is the only component of our personalities to be seriously restricted by society, it is the one most likely to emerge in a strange or distorted form. And even this is a subjective statement, based upon the arbitrary standards established by our social conditioning.

When a crime of unusual and bizarre circumstances takes place, it is viewed with horror but also with a strongly morbid fascination—as witnessed by the flocks of curious onlookers who gathered outside the home of Albert Brust in Miami. Why this fascination?

Dean Corll, following the classic pattern of heterosexual child molesters, utilized a younger fellow to lure his victims into his web and physically used or abused them; then, probably motivated more by fear of discovery than anything else, he murdered them. As yet, we have seen no indication of Corll's having had any gay social aspects in his life; that is, he is not characterized as having been involved in any adult activities with other gays.

This would seem to point up the basic inadequacy within his ego structure, a typical inability to relate to a peer group. Like the dirty old man who seduces little girls, Corll sought release by using kids. His behavior pattern relates about as closely to a gay S&M person's as does that of a heterosexual murderer-rapist to the style of the het "family man."

As gays, we are easily embarrassed by sensationalized bizarre behavior on the part of any homosexual. But in neither Corll's nor Brust's case should we feel a kindred humiliation. Without being able to interview either of them, and having only the sensationalized news stories to go on, I am loath to attempt any sort of in-depth analysis. I can, however, point up the gross inconsistencies between the apparent behavior of these two men and that of the normal S&M or "gay leather" people within our own community. For most who are actively involved in the scene, it is a game to be played on the weekend, with the largest percentage being interested in the role of bottom man, or M. This is just as true of the het S&Mers as it is with us.

In the true S&M relationship, there is a good deal more involved than the physical abuse of one person by another. As I have been at some pains (no pun intended) to explain in my own writings, the S, or topman, is never going to derive the full pleasure he is seeking unless he provokes an appropriate response from his subject.

In other words, the S&M exchange is just that—an exchange, basically seeking the same sensual experience as any other sexual interaction. If the M is to be subjected to pain, or whatever, it is only with his express or implied consent. If the scene is carried beyond the limits of the M, it becomes quite a different matter. Those outside the "leather circle" may not understand why or how such a relationship can come into being, or how it can be enjoyable; but they should realize that it is in no way lethal.

Another victim!

Adding to this concern is the apparent factor of misconception on the part of investigating officers. I understand that they have been questioning patrons of gay leather bars, and have been looking into the lives and habits of people who are active in the S&M scene. In my opinion, this is an extremely infertile line of inquiry. People who are able to express their sexuality … to act out their desires in a nondestructive exchange are the least likely to commit this sort of crime. Even if the components for violence lie within them, the very act of sex play tends to become the "safety valve," permitting the steam of passion to escape before it causes an explosion. The most appropriate place to seek this murderer is deep within some dark and hidden closet.

In summary, then, it would be my opinion that these dreadful, violent crimes have come into being as the result of individuals who were unable to find socially acceptable outlets for their sexual urgings. With society's cap screwed down so tightly, we can expect that the weakest will sometimes explode.

The Politics of Feeling
By Arthur Evans

One of the powers behind Manhattan's Gay Activists Alliance was a fiery writer named Arthur Evans. His radical research into gay culture later filled several books. In the early seventies he moved to San Francisco, where he became a regular commentator for The Advocate.

Anthropologists have discovered an astonishing fact: Only a minority of the world's different societies have ever been hostile to gay people. And of that minority, only a few (mainly the huge industrialized countries of the present era) have been hostile enough to treat us like sickies or criminals.

Why are we oppressed in modern times? What has caused so many societies of the past few hundred years to depart from the norm of history and treat us so badly? Unfortunately, I think there are a lot of muddled beliefs now being circulated in the gay community as to why we are oppressed. Admittedly, some of these beliefs seem coherent from a distance, but when you look at them up close, they evaporate like cigarette smoke. They don't really *explain* things.

For example, a lot of gay activists blame our problems on the Judaeo-Christian religious tradition. They think that our oppression is simply a lingering aftermath of the days when Christianity ruled Europe like so many fiefdoms.

These activists think that the road to liberation is through education. They say, "Show people how old-fashioned their prejudices are, and things will change for the better."

Another popular explanation of why we are oppressed lays the blame at the couch of the psychiatrists. Gay critics are quick to point out how psychiatrists, both Freudian and behavioristic, simply *assume* as a matter of faith that homosexuality is a sickness. And once they make this assumption, the psychiatrists lose no time in having us committed to asylums, giving us electric shock "therapy," cutting out parts of our brains, or castrating us.

A large number of gays attribute our oppression to what they call "sexism." Nobody can doubt that gay people fly right in the face of sexist values. Gay women make a virtue of being strong in mind and body, and independent of male domination. Gay men are not ashamed to show feelings, to wear colorful dress, to show warmth and tenderness to other men.

But sexism, like Christianity and psychiatry, turns out to be just another symptom, not the cause. We still haven't reached the "why" of the matter.

Maybe we can't see this "why" because it's too close to us. Sometimes things get to be so much a part of our lives that we forget they're even there. We become like fish who don't see the water in the tank at all—unless it goes bad.

BETTY FRIEDAN CALLED "DYKE BAITER"

The "water" in our particular tank came into being just a few hundred years ago. It was around the beginning of the sixteenth century, when something very strange began to happen in Europe—the rise of what came to be called the industrial economic system. This system is based on massive regimentation of the work force, with the bulk of the population being forced to labor eight hours or more a day on a job most of them hate. It requires unquestioned obedience to economic and political hierarchies, with the constant threat of imprisonment or death for those who rebel.

What happens to the sensual life of *a whole society* when the majority of its members have to "earn their living" this way? What is it that makes people act like a well-orchestrated band of automatons? Are people like that naturally? Or do you have to rip out their emotional guts?

The industrial economic system is built upon the death of feeling. It requires that people constantly repress their fantasies and desires, discipline their souls into bureaucratic routines, cut themselves off from nature, and deny the excitement of the moment for the security of the future. The industrial system is like one great night of the living dead, where the whole populace is reduced emotionally to the level of zombies.

What do you think would happen to "the system" if everybody suddenly came alive? Imagine people having sex with each other when they want, the way they want, for kindness and love, for fun, for the thrill of being alive.

The system can co-opt most anything, but it cannot co-opt people honestly expressing their deepest feelings. A population in touch with its feelings would refuse to be regimented as a machine—even for the sake of the Gross National Product. It would rebel, and the technocrats and bureaucrats in charge of the industrial system know this quite well.

We gays are oppressed because we are in touch with feelings that serve no "useful" purpose to the industrial system. In fact, the system perceives these feelings as a threat because the systematic repression of feeling is the very source of its power.

The Gay Revolution is a revolution in feeling. Tactics that simply rehash standard methods of political protest do not do justice to this fact. That's why just sending letters to members of Congress or lobbying in back rooms quickly loses the sense of color and excitement that make our movement move. That's why good zaps are so exciting, almost magical, and why they are so potent politically.

"Nothing great is ever accomplished without passion," said the German philosopher Hegel. That statement is especially true in politics, and above all in the politics of feeling.

Let us rise up and pour forth our love and our anger.

Attacks on lesbians and other feminists by Betty Friedan, founder of the second wave of feminism, have produced a backlash.

Under the name "The Feminist Community," women representing a wide spectrum of the women's movement held a press conference in New York on March 7, to show solidarity with lesbians and denounce Friedan's remarks about lesbians as "irresponsible," "unrepresentative," "vicious," "sensational," and "unsisterly."

Many at the conference indicated that Friedan must be highly regarded for what she had done in the past. Still, Friedan was called "the Joe McCarthy of the women's movement" by Ti-Grace Atkinson; a "lesbian-phobe" and a "dyke-baiter" by Jill Johnston; "myopic" and "a conjurer of phantoms" by Toni Carabillo; and a "narcissistic and self-congratulatory polemicist who has reached new heights of paranoia and egotism" by Brenda Fasteau of the National Women's Political Caucus.

Although Friedan has continually made derogatory comments about lesbians (notably in *McCall's* and *Newsweek*), the hostility toward lesbians expressed in her article "Up from the Kitchen Floor," published in *The New York Times*, was the most obvious to date.

In the article, intended to be a ten-year history of the women's movement, Friedan said she was told that lesbians were organizing to take over the National Organization for Women (NOW) and the women's movement, had used her for respectability and contacts, and furthermore had plotted to seduce and blackmail her.

Friedan said in the *Times* that "it was both hurting and exploiting the women's movement to try and use it to proselytize for lesbianism because of the sexual preferences of a few."

A source at the *Times* informed the New York Gay Activists Alliance of the article a week before publication, in time for seven lesbian-feminists (six of them members of NOW) to try to change the article. It was learned that NOW officers had already advised Friedan to tone down her comments about lesbians, but to no avail.

The article followed on the heels of NOW resolutions passed without opposition in Washington, D.C., to initiate and support civil rights for lesbians, and thus put NOW officers in a difficult position. Although NOW national officers were anguished by Friedan's statements, they felt they could not officially participate in the press conference.

Statements supporting lesbians and criticizing Friedan were issued from several leading feminist organizations and numerous individuals, including Gloria Steinem and Kate Millett. Steinem did not attend the press conference because of fears that the press would pit her against Friedan in a personality fight and disregard the issues. (In *McCall's*, Friedan has characterized Steinem as a man-hater.)

Millett, another movement leader dismissed by Friedan (who implied in her article that Millett's support is from radicals and man-haters) sent a message: "It is my belief that lesbians are the vanguard of the women's movement, both as the group of women independent of men and in their role as activists working for the cause during the last several years. I am convinced that we have contributed significantly to the progress and success of our collective struggle."

—BARBARA LOVE

TELEVISION: "AN AMERICAN FAMILY"

Public television's much-discussed "An American Family," a twelve-part nonfiction series similar to "Margaret Mead's New Guinea Journal," focuses on the Loud family of Santa Barbara, California. The series' aim in filming these particular American "natives" was to illuminate and reflect facets of behavior, feelings, and attitudes common, in various degrees, to all American families.

By the second installment, the oldest son, Lance, has moved to New York and set up in the Chelsea Hotel with his friend Sorin. Transvestite actor Holly Woodlawn is a friend and neighbor. After a month, his mother comes for a visit. Lance is only nineteen, and she wants to give him both support and direction.

The mother and son go out to a show together. He tells his mother how exciting New York is: "Everyone is famous and interesting, and they know exactly what they want to do." He camps a little, shows off a little, and complains a little. ("There was so much you guys could have done with me.")

An American son: Lance Loud.

His mother is affectionate but firm. He shouldn't depend too much on Sorin. He should get a job. He should take care of his health. But she encourages him. "I don't want you to give up without a fight. This is the sort of thing you've been interested in all your life." By "sort of thing," she means the life of New York and the theater. Returning home, she is seen telling her husband that she is happy that Lance was doing things.

But when the series was viewed and written about, the Louds found themselves less happy. *Time* magazine talked about Lance's trip to New York in terms of a family's "anguish" and "troubles," informing its readers that "eldest son Lance has migrated to New York to join the gay community."

In the Sunday drama section of *The New York Times*, critic Stephanie Harrington complained that mother and son had failed to let it all hang out at the Chelsea. "You wonder at the fact that not once do they utter the word 'homosexual,'" wrote Harrington. "Of course, this might be admirable if it represented a sophisticated and understanding acceptance of reality by Lance's parents. But it doesn't. They simply refuse to acknowledge the reality. In the end, the silence is shattering."

The Advocate contacted Lance, who felt that it was Harrington who had not represented the reality of the situation. "I can tell my father everything and do," said Lance. "I'm proud to be an American homosexual. Like, my mother really understands me, and my father does, too." Future installments will show Lance camping it up in Paris with painted nails and later, back home in Santa Barbara, getting into face makeup while his sisters watch and comment approvingly. In his father's office, he puts on bracelets and tells his father he hopes he won't get the wrong idea. "I won't get the wrong idea, sweetie," his father says with a grin. It is quite plain that the entire family accepts Lance.

The "anguish" and the "trouble" which Lance brings to "An American Family" according to *Time,* was not noticeable to this reporter viewing the series. Their easy acceptance of his lifestyle is certainly not average. But is it an acceptance based on self-delusion, as *The New York Times* has asserted?

Lance says it is not. And he has seen his family in more than twelve one-hour installments.

—LEO SKIR

BARBARA GRIER

With an investment of two thousand dollars and a small list of potential readers, the Naiad Press opened its doors in January. It took a year before all the copies of its first book, Sarah Aldridge's The Latecomer, *sold, but the press was off and running. Other titles soon followed—coming-out novels, historical romances, mysteries, poetry, and diverse nonfiction works—all aimed at the lesbian reader. Over time, Naiad would become the largest lesbian-feminist publishing house in the world.*

Naiad's roots date back to The Ladder, *the first national lesbian periodical. Started in 1956 under the auspices of the pioneering lesbian group Daughters of Bilitis, the newsletter became a glossy magazine read by women around the world before its demise in 1972. The Ladder's editor, Barbara Grier, and her life partner, Donna McBride, were then approached by two other women who asked them to join in the founding of a lesbian press.*

"I wanted a woman to be able to walk into any bookstore and find the material she needed to make her feel good about herself," Grier would say twenty years later, with the press still going strong with hundreds of books—from reprints of lesbian classics to works by new writers—to its credit. "I have spent my entire life determined to bring people to books and books to people."

BOOKS: *THE PERSIAN BOY*

Mary Renault has long been to the gay novel what Ray Bradbury has been to the equally ghettoized genre of science fiction. Her best-selling novels without exception deal primarily with characters who are clearly homosexual.

She portrays their relationships with depth and intimacy that astonishes many gays ("How could a woman possibly know so well what it feels like to be a gay man?"). Yet so easily does she introduce her homosexual themes into stories that are panoramically conceived and masterfully told that she finds access to a wide readership denied to those writers who stick closer to the purview of the gay world.

She is a superb storyteller. With a richness of texture and an amazing economy of narrative style she re-creates an entire epoch in all its complexity without ever seeming labored or complicated. The author seems to disappear and we see ancient Greece and the neighboring lands as they must have been seen at the time.

Having just gone excitedly through *Fire from Heaven*, which took up the early life of Alexander, as well as *The Last of the Wine* (beautifully recounting the friendship of two of Socrates' disciples) and *The Middle Mist* (her lone lesbian novel), I feel that *The Persian Boy* is Renault's masterpiece.

The Persian Boy is about Bagoas, a young eunuch who was bed partner first of Darius of Persia, then of Alexander the Great. Bagoas is mentioned in several ancient accounts of Alexander's life. Quintus Curtius tells us that after the Persian defeat at Gaugamela, the Persian general Nabarzanes (involved in Darius's murder) brought Alexander "great gifts. Among these was Bagoas, a eunuch of remarkable beauty and in the very flower of boyhood, who had been loved by Darius and was afterwards to be loved by Alexander." From such scant historical accounts, Renault has resurrected a character so overpowering, so sadly appealing, that it is hard to concede that this is not the actual Bagoas of 2,300 years ago.

Renault's Bagoas was born in a hill fortress west of Susa and had expectations of growing into a tall, handsome Persian warrior until his parents were slain bloodily before the boy's eyes. Young Bagoas was captured, and then castrated and sold into sexual slavery. He eventually came to Alexander's bed and frequently shared it, surprising Alexander with evidence that a eunuch is not necessarily fully incapacitated.

The boy never gave up longing to ride as a soldier with his king. His sharing of the hardships of the amazing campaign through lands that are now Afghanistan, Turkestan, Kashmir, and the Punjab won for him the grudging respect of the Macedonian troops. But the campaign was seemingly endless (in eight years Alexander conquered two-thirds of the known world), and his men refused to go on. Alexander gave up bitterly and returned over almost impassable desert to Susa and Babylon to reorganize his army, but contracted a fever and died after refusing medical attention.

Renault describes the unfamiliar as if it were familiar. By projecting Alexander's conquests entirely through the eyes of the eunuch, she has created an appealing, chillingly realistic character who will not soon be forgotten. For all the panorama of characters who leap amazingly to life, she has created in the damaged boy a figure whom many gays will find too real for comfort.

—JIM KEPNER

Firebug foiled at the altar

Newspaper of America's Homophile Community

The **ADVOCATE**

So. Calif 35¢

50¢ Elsewhere

Navy torpedoes Gays

Fuzz beach nudes

Lesbians blast sexism

Gay pride is everywhere!

Newspaper of America's Homophile Community

The **ADVOCATE**

So. Calif 35¢

50¢ Elsewhere

SPECIAL 24 pages of gay travel

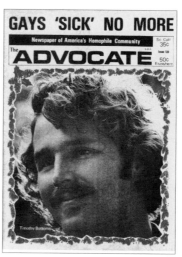

GAYS 'SICK' NO MORE

Newspaper of America's Homophile Community

The **ADVOCATE**

So. Calif 35¢

50¢ Elsewhere

Timothy Bottoms

Newspaper of America's Homophile Community

The **ADVOCATE**

50¢

Lesbian legislator elected

Bomb scare in Chicago

Rob Roy in Boy! Leek

SICK NO MORE

1974 The year of the Symbionese Liberation Army shoot-out in Los Angeles and the resignation of President Nixon was a mix of news of oppression and sporadic civil rights victories, victories that were the product of years of political work in places as different as Lincoln, Nebraska, and New York City. Each victory, to those of us who were paying attention, seemed monumental.

Just before the first of the year, the American Psychiatric Association's board of trustees declared we were no longer sick. This was the lead story of the year's first issue. Five cities passed gay-rights ordinances. Honeywell, Northwestern Bell, and even AT&T banned discrimination in employment. The National Education Association voted to support gay people's right to teach.

There were causes for concern, too. The U.S. Centers for Disease Control reported that between 21 and 31 percent of venereal disease in the United States was carried by gay or bisexual men. And lesbians and gay men began to address another problem long closeted in the community: alcoholism. By February, there were sixteen gay Alcoholics Anonymous groups in the United States and by year's end the gay AAs had won the right to be listed in the AA directory of groups.

Gay-rights activists and *Advocate* investigative reporters in Portland, Oregon, and Los Angeles found police keeping files on people suspected of being gay. The files, the police claimed, could provide sources of information on subversive and terrorist groups. A few years later, we were able to prove that women's and gay organizations were targets of the FBI's notorious Cointelpro program which was designed to defeat the efforts of African-American, women's, and gay-rights organizations' struggles for equal rights.

In many ways 1974 was a bellwether year for gay politics. U.S. Representatives Bella Abzug and Edward Koch sponsored the first gay-rights legislation in Congress. Their bill would become a litmus test for every Congressional candidate in the country. And in Boston, Elaine Noble, a multiple-issue Democrat,

Elaine Noble became the first up-front lesbian state representative in the history of the United States. Running in a precinct near downtown Boston, Noble beat the owner of a swinging singles bar to gain a seat on the Massachusetts legislature. Telegrams bore messages of elation, including "Congratulations. At last I now feel free."

97

became the first out-of-the-closet gay person in the U.S. to win a seat in a state legislature.

Equally portentous were signs of increasing participation by up-front lesbians and gay men in the Democratic Party. While much activity was publicized in Los Angeles and San Francisco, gay and lesbian mobilization in the mainstream political system seemed to occur in any community with an out-front gay person.

However, revisiting 1974 in the pages of *The Advocate* showed me I had a severe case of tunnel vision while working for the publication, first for two years as a stringer and then as a staff member. I remember only the victories.

I have no memory of the stories of police brutality against hustlers and cruisers, of pornography cases, or of issues concerning relations between adults and young men. In fact, as a woman, I don't think I ever read those articles. Although always aware that the publication's advertising revenue was derived from establishments catering to the sexual lifestyles of gay men, I ignored the ads, most of which were offensive to me.

In my mind, the paper was always the publication of record for the gay movement, an important vehicle for liberation. Most other women did not share my view, and my association with *The Advocate* was filled with painful attacks from many lesbians.

A well-off Chicago attorney told me I should go on welfare and write for the struggling lesbian press. A lesbian author who would later gain national attention among mainstream publishers refused to be interviewed in the publication, telling me I shouldn't be working for a sexist organization that supported the male patriarchy. When national fame reached the author, however, her agent called and asked me to interview her. Capitalism has a way of mending some political differences.

Personally, I felt more oppression as a lesbian than as a woman. (Evidence of that oppression became clear when I left the publication—I was unable to find a job in journalism for several years because *The Advocate* was on my résumé.) Gender-related issues didn't exist in a struggling business whose task was to put out a paper every two weeks. There was a tremendous sense of camaraderie on the *Advocate* staff. Exigencies of business and excitement about what we were creating removed many barriers.

Over time, three movements—the "gay" movement, which included lesbians, the lesbian separatist movement, and the women's rights movement—all contributed substantially to the progress of lesbian and gay rights, despite the frictions among them.

Author and activist Rita Mae Brown summed up the sentiments of many at the first anniversary of the founding of the National Gay Task Force near the end of the year: "The goal of gay liberation for the next five years, ten years, fifteen years, for however long it takes, is political power."

The same issue of *The Advocate* quoting Brown's seminal comment also reported the publication's sale to David B. Goodstein's Liberation Publications. Goodstein, an establishment millionaire dedicated to gay rights, brought a practical understanding of the relationship between money and politics and an intuitive knowledge of the power of the press with him to *The Advocate*. The publication gave him an important platform and brought to the rest of us a deep understanding of realpolitik. Under Goodstein's tutelage, the publication would not only be a source of information for its readers, but a force to be reckoned with, studied even in the corridors of the White House.

—SASHA LEWIS

OUR CRISIS: LEADERSHIP

Gay communities everywhere generally have more shortages than a tribe of pygmies. The shortage of money is chronic and felt by everyone. It's the problem mentioned most by those working to better the lives of gays. But there is another shortage that is also chronic and, in the long run, much more damaging to the gay movement: the shortage of good, effective leadership.

Unfortunately, our movement seems to attract more than its share of petty rip-off artists and professional failures, that is, people who have failed at everything they have ever tried to do so far in their lives, who have no known record of accomplishment in anything, and who wouldn't know how to accomplish anything if their lives depended on it. They try to cover up all this with a big mouth and a smattering of Roberts Rules of Order. It doesn't work. In time, they move on to infect some other gay group or to start a new one themselves (this automatically makes them "leaders").

We think the problem is a serious one. We think that true leaders in the various gay communities must give sober thought to this problem. Some way must be found to cope with the destructive element and the phonies; some way must be found to attract competent people to help us and to make an atmosphere that will nurture accomplishment rather than chaos.

—FROM AN *ADVOCATE* EDITORIAL

T I M E L I N E

COURT ASKS FOR PENIS INSPECTION

As part of his defense of a man charged with lewd conduct, attorney Al Gordon sought a court order to have a physician examine the penis of a Los Angeles police officer. "In the case at hand, the officer's penis is real evidence," said Gordon in his pretrial discovery motion. "In the arrest report, he states that the defendant touched said penis."

In asking for the measurement, Gordon was trying to dispute the officer's claim that the defendant touched his penis while the officer was holding it. If the penis was a small one, Gordon asserted, he would not have to seek other proof.

In April, protesters charged the Los Angeles bar After Dark with discrimination against women and blacks. One placard read, AFTER DARK IS AFTER DARKIES.

JANUARY Three police officers in Albuquerque were fired after brutally beating two gay men. ❏ The entire Hollywood vice detail (sixteen officers) seized records and properties of Los Angeles filmmaker-activist Pat Rocco, arresting him on charges of conspiracy to commit sodomy and oral copulation; in December, he was cleared of all charges. ❏ An Oklahoma county court handed down a fifteen-year prison term to a twenty-seven-year-old bookstore clerk for selling an adult magazine to an eighteen-year-old college student. ❏ Del Martin founded a second chapter of NOW in San Francisco called the Golden Gate chapter, laughing off accusations from members of the old NOW chapter that she was rallying "lesbians and dingbats." ❏ Arsonists destroyed a gay café in San Francisco. ❏ The Frente de Liberacion Homosexual, a new gay organization in Mexico, announced its intention not to apply for legal organization status until sex laws in that country changed.

FEBRUARY Missouri lawmakers proposed legislation branding homosexuality a disease and requiring gays to report themselves for listing to the state health department; it did not pass. ❏ Gay students in Mississippi lost a lawsuit against a university newspaper that refused to print their ad. ❏ Republican senators in Maine threatened to attack state funding for the University of Maine at Orono if a scheduled statewide gay conference was held; the conference went ahead as planned, and the senators backed down. ❏ Gay fundamentalists left the MCC of Portland, Oregon, to establish a new evangelical church. ❏ The University of Manitoba newspaper reported on the rural Canadian group Gays for Equality, which hailed the slow but steady growth of "prairie lib" and celebrated its two-year anniversary. ❏ Two Swedish lesbian mothers were married by a Copenhagen priest.

MARCH New York City officials approved the use of gay Big Brothers, then reversed their decision. ❏ A group of gay professors in San Francisco launched a pioneering lesbian and gay "free university" known as Lavender U; it closed after a year. ❏ *Chicago Daily News* writer Mike Royko angered gays by comparing homosexuality and bestiality in a column about "Banana Lib," in which "men in love with monkeys" achieve acceptance by "coming out of the cage." ❏ The Department of Defense restored the security clearance of an openly gay man after suspending it for a year. ❏ The Minneapolis City Council unanimously passed a gay-rights ordinance. ❏ *The New York Times* surprised readers with its unprecedented six-part series entitled "Homosexuals in New York: The Gay World." ❏ The Israeli Knesset voted down a bill to decriminalize gay sex.

APRIL Kathy Kozachenko became the first openly gay person to be elected to public office in the United States, taking a seat on the Ann Arbor City Council. ❏ Pennsylvania Governor Milton Shapp issued the first state executive order banning employment discrimination on the basis of sexual preference. ❏ The U.S. Supreme Court refused to hear a challenge to a Texas law banning transvestism. ❏ The Rhode Island State Council of Churches voted to recognize the Metropolitan Community Church as a member of the association. ❏ An Atlanta man and twenty-five accomplices robbed a grocery store in drag. ❏ After arduous debate, the World Services of Alcoholics Anonymous agreed to list gay AA groups in its directory. ❏ Phoenix gays restored The Hiding Place, a gay bar badly damaged by arson, enabling it to reopen within two days. ❏ April was V.D. Awareness Month in California. ❏ A British gay-basher got a life sentence for murdering a gay man in a park.

MAY In Congress, Bella Abzug and Ed Koch, both Democrats from New York, introduced the first federal civil rights bill for gays. ❏ *Male Homosexuals,* a book by sexologists Williams and Weinberg, declared that being out of the closet is mentally and financially healthier than being closeted; their study was of over five thousand men in the United States and Europe. ❏ Voters in Boulder, Colorado, overturned a local gay-rights ordinance; a month later, a U.S. District Court judge voided the reversal. ❏ More than four hundred gay demonstrators held hands to form a ring around the base of the Statue of Liberty. ❏ A majority of 205 respondents to an *Advocate* poll strongly backed zaps, rallies, and other militant tactics. ❏ A Philadelphia judge awarded a lesbian couple custody of a transvestite teenage boy who was not biologically related to either of them. ❏ Chile's right-wing junta began a terror campaign against homosexuals, including castration, rape, torture, and the public display of gays' dead bodies. ❏ London squatters claimed a storefront as Britain's first gay center.

JUNE A supporter of New Hampshire Governor Meldrim Thomson paid $1,075 to prevent gay students from winning an auction bid for a pancake breakfast with the governor. ❏ Firefighters extinguished three small fires set by an arsonist in the new home of the Los Angeles MCC. ❏ On its second birthday, the National Bisexual Liberation movement claimed sixteen hundred members in five cities. ❏ The American Nurses Association denied appeals to set up an official gay task force within its ranks. ❏ Hawaii held its first Gay Pride parade.

JULY Detroit enacted major gay-rights legislation, banning all discrimination on the basis of sexual orientation. ❏ Activists picketed a Seattle pizzeria that had expelled two women for kissing and hugging. ❏ The American Library Association awarded the third annual Gay Book Award to Jeanette Foster, the seventy-nine-year-old author of the 1956 study *Sex Variant Women in Literature.* ❏ Bearing a banner that said, GOD LOVES GAY PEOPLE, DO YOU?, Phoenix activists held a six-day, 130-mile march through the Arizona desert. ❏ Gay-themed books held for years in the closed shelves of the Hollywood Public Library were released to general circulation. ❏ A heterosexual fireman in Illinois lost his job because he admitted to one youthful gay experience.

AUGUST AT&T, employer of more than one million, announced a new policy of nondiscrimination against gays; a year before, the Minnesota chapter of the American Civil Liberties Union had threatened to sue the corporation for

After the New York City Council defeated Intro 2, a gay-rights bill, in May, the Pride Parade in June (*above and below*) included messages appealing for gay liberation and equality.

LAVENDER AND HORNY
Citing the animal as maligned and gentle, a Boston group distributed posters of a lavender rhinoceros with a red heart (*left*) as a gay symbol. The gentle animal took gay Boston by storm, rearing its head on buttons and even on city-approved subway placards.

Things are changing.
Gay people are not invisible anymore;

But then again,
We never really were.

2

MOST-WANTED LESBIANS

Two lesbians topped the FBI's most-wanted list in the notorious kidnapping of Patricia Hearst. The newspaper heiress was the second victim of San Francisco revolutionaries who called themselves the Symbionese Liberation Army (SLA); earlier they had assassinated a local school official.

SLA members Patricia Soltysik, aka Mizmoon, and Camilla Hall were lovers. The SLA surprised some radicals by accepting their comrades' homosexuality. FBI agents used the lead, and grilled patrons and employees of Bay Area gay bars about Soltysik and Hall.

The pair met in Berkeley, where twenty-three-year-old Soltysik worked as a janitor and raised guide-dogs for the blind. Hall, a social worker five years older, wrote her love poems, one of which was published in the *San Francisco Chronical*:

*I will cradle you
In my woman hips
Kiss you,
With my woman lips
Fold you to my heart and sing:
Sister woman
You are a joy to me.*

Relatives were puzzled that these "sweet young women" joined a terrorist group. Their reasons died with them when they perished with other SLA members in a fiery May 17 shoot-out in Los Angeles.

antigay hiring practices. ❏ The American Psychiatric Association joined the American Bar Association in opposing the federal ban on gay immigrants and visitors. ❏ The National Teachers Association voted to add the words "sexual orientation" to the antidiscrimination provisions of its membership policy. ❏ At the annual Friends General Conference in Ithaca, New York, George Leaky, a prominent Quaker leader, declared he was bisexual. ❏ A group of lesbians and other women painted the word "sexist" in large purple letters on bridal and porno shops in downtown Philadelphia; two were arrested. ❏ *Encyclopaedia Britannica* editors agreed to add an entry on the gay liberation movement and the struggle for civil rights for homosexuals. ❏ The Soviet Foreign Ministry accused two British journalists of homosexual acts with Soviet citizens, prompting Reuters to recall them from their assignments. ❏ A study by the Mexican government concluded that gays are less prone to suicide than straights.

SEPTEMBER   Boston activists filed incorporation papers for a Gay United Fund, the nation's first gay fund-raising and disbursement project. ❏ A *National Observer* article headlined THE YMCA: IT'S ALSO YMC GAY brought denials from the Young Men's Christian Association. ❏ Two teenage boys, committed to an Illinois mental hospital for having consensual sex, won damages against the hospital for mistreatment that included being tied to their beds. ❏ Six Orange County gay bars fought local authorities for arresting a large number of their patrons in an apparent campaign to shut down the bars; *The Advocate* reported over two hundred arrests, while mainstream sources claimed closer to fifty. ❏ As a result of gay protests over homophobic segments of "Marcus Welby, M.D.," Listerine withdrew its sponsorship of the popular TV show. ❏ Dr. Gaylord Parkinson, a former California Republican Party chairman, was arrested for oral copulation in a San Diego men's room.

OCTOBER   More than a million dollars in federal grants was awarded to the Gay and Lesbian Services Center of Los Angeles—more grant money than was received by all other gay organizations in the nation combined. ❏ The headquarters of New York's Gay Activists Alliance was burned by thieves who stole its office equipment. ❏ Gays held an overnight vigil to protest a shutout of gay news in the *Los Angeles Times.* ❏ Security guards of the Rev. Billy Graham quickly quashed a gay protest featuring a banner that read, GOD LOVES GAYS—DO YOU?, at Graham's Hollywood Bowl appearance. ❏ A nineteen-year-old Florida youth described by his high school counselor as a "red-blooded, fun-seeking American boy" got ten years' probation after he pleaded guilty to murdering a man he said made homosexual advances on him.

NOVEMBER   Dick Michaels sold *The Advocate* to lawyer and businessman David Goodstein for $1 million. ❏ Two Seattle women launched the Lesbian Mothers Defense Fund.

DECEMBER   In *The Minneapolis Star,* Minnesota State Senator Allan Spear declared that he was homosexual. ❏ Two Dayton, Ohio, African-American lesbian mothers living on public assistance sued for the right to marry, although they lacked both legal representation and support from local gays; they lost. ❏ The Portland, Oregon City Council voted 3–2 to ban antigay discrimination in municipal employment. ❏ The world's first international gay congress was held in Edinburgh, Scotland, drawing two hundred delegates from ten countries.

New Kinsey Study Scraps More Myths

Alfred Kinsey is familiar to a great many people as the man behind America's most comprehensive survey of sexual behavior and attitudes. To gay people, Kinsey's work is especially meaningful, because it marked the virtual beginning of sympathetic and scientifically accurate study of homosexuality.

Kinsey died in 1956, but the research group he founded (the Institute of Sex Research, in Bloomington, Indiana) continues to investigate homosexuality (and heterosexuality) in a scientific and humanistically positive way. Now in preparation is another study of homosexuals in San Francisco, which should be published soon.

This San Francisco study will be the first truly in-depth, large-sample study of homosexuals ever made. The institute interviewed 1,500 people in person, three to five hours each, using a 175-page questionnaire; some were heterosexual (for comparison purposes), but most were gay. Men outnumbered women two to one, but even so, the researchers interviewed three hundred white lesbians and seventy black ones, which is the largest lesbian sample ever for a scientific study.

One can get an order-of-magnitude view of several statistics of interest to gay people by looking at the overall sample totals:

About 37 percent of the gay white males thought "quite a bit" about sexual things during the course of the day; 18 percent hardly thought about them at all. Only 12 percent preferred sexual partners with large penises.

About 17 percent consider a permanent relationship to be the most important part of their lives; 20 percent don't consider it important at all. In the year before interviewing, 28 percent had had sex with over fifty partners, 31 percent with six partners or less. Two-fifths were living with a roommate who was gay, but only two-thirds of these were having a sexual relationship with him. Among women, a gay roommate was much more likely to be a lover.

About 18 percent of the men had attempted suicide at least once—usually very early in their gay careers, when they were coming out.

There seemed to be some indication that gay women had more *male* sexual partners after adolescence than straight women; this tended to indicate that (probably only some) gay women chose homosexuality because of dissatisfaction with heterosexual relationships, and that some straight women chose heterosexuality because they were unhappy with their gay relationships.

This is evidence against the psychiatric notion that homosexuality is merely an "arrested" stage of development on the path to heterosexuality; the gay women in question had tried both and preferred the gay.

Gay people already know much that will be "discovered" in the study, since they've been doing the field work (so to speak) ever since they came out. But the framework established by the institute's study will be used by behavioral scientists for years to come.

—Charles Bonnel

LINES IN THE SAND
Gays on both coasts fought battles for turf and the right to bare all. In New York, the arrests of several gay men at Riis Park for nude sunbathing focused media and public attention on the thriving gay scene at the beach. The expected result was a showdown on the constitutionality of laws prohibiting public nudity. At Southern California's popular Venice Beach (*below*), gays and other proponents of sunning in the buff turned the other cheek on the newly enacted Los Angeles County nudity ban. The police issued citations to those who refused to cover up.

RITA MAE BROWN

Rita Mae Brown is chic and earthy. Her brains blaze. She recently wrote a novel about a poor Florida girl named Molly who grows up to be a lesbian and goes to New York. Gloria Steinem says *Rubyfruit Jungle* is "a good and true account of growing up un-American in America." Jill Johnston, a lesbian writer for *The Village Voice,* says *Rubyfruit Jungle* is "an authentic reckoning." Brown says it's her.

"It isn't the traditional woman's life, but it *is* a woman's life," she explains. "I hope a lot of gay men read it. If gay men can identify with Molly, they're going to find out that lesbians are not 'the other,' that we're not so fucking different, that we're all pretty much the same underneath the phony externals."

Rubyfruit Jungle—direct, gutsy, funny, human—could well make Brown a gay legend at age twenty-nine. Certainly, she will be famous now among gay women. But she's no newcomer to gay community affairs, and she is as much an organizer as a writer.

In 1966, she was one of the first members of the Homophile Students League at Columbia University. Later, she helped found Radicalesbians in New York. "The Homophile Students League was very exciting," Brown recalls. "But it was a battle even then. There were only two women in the whole thing. We were just ignored and rolled over. It took me about six months to figure out that, boy, these guys didn't give a shit whether I lived or died. They didn't see that my issues are their issues.

"So I left and went to the women's movement. Which was *worse.* I got beaten up. I got harassed. I got bomb threats. I got thrown out of NOW because I was lesbian. Then I went to Redstockings, the radical women's group. They told me I was unnatural and threw me out, too. So I decided to fuck this shit, as Little Lulu says, and started Radicalesbians with a few other people."

The hostility between gay men and women is largely due to mutual ignorance, Brown feels. "Most men, whether they're gay or straight, know nothing about women's lives. They don't identify with women. I can identify with a man, because I was trained to from the time I was tiny. When I went to the movies, Burt Lancaster was much more exciting to me than the drip in the crinolines waiting for him.

"Gay men are much less shallow than straight men, but we're so unimportant to them; we're so removed from their lives," she continues. "The average gay man has no real bloodline to another human being who is a woman. So, in a way, gay men are really more insensitive to us than straight men are, even though they have traits that make them more lovable as people."

All this can make women hostile. "Once a woman becomes clued in on how she is made an object to be pushed around in this culture, those little differences you notice become infuriating. They become intolerable." Brown believes gay women should come out of the closet, but not because things are getting better. The new openness about homosexuality has only exposed lesbians as the first victims of backlash against the women's movement, she says. "What we get is our own self-respect. Which is the reason so many women are willing to take such bad treatment. What I would tell a gay woman to do is, first, understand yourself. Rid yourself of those parts of your identity where you were trained to be passive and subservient and think you're worthless. Once you get over that hump, you'll be in shape to fight what's going to happen to you."

—STAFF WRITER

THE VOTE THAT "CURED" TWENTY MILLION

Gay Liberation got its biggest boost since Stonewall on December 15, 1973, when the American Psychiatric Association (APA) removed homosexuality from its list of psychiatric disorders. The APA's board of trustees approved the change by a vote of 13-0 while meeting at its Washington, D.C., headquarters.

An old gay nemesis flew promptly into action. Dr. Charles Socarides, an anti-gay activist who had advocated detention camps for homosexuals and was the media's favorite expert on matters gay, demanded a popular referendum. Four months later he got it, and the 17,905 members of the APA voted by secret ballot, again in Washington, D.C.

This first account chronicles the December vote. The second follows the private thoughts of Bruce Voeller, executive director of the National Gay Task Force (NGTF), on the final removal of a cornerstone of homophobia.

Dr. Robert L. Spitzer, of the APA's Task Force on Nomenclature, said homosexuality was removed the list of psychiatric disorders because it did not "regularly cause emotional distress" or generally create "impairment of social functioning."

Although several other professional organizations have in recent years adopted policies stating that homosexuality is not sick, the psychiatrists' association was the most important nut to crack. The APA nomenclature is generally regarded as the official definition of mental disorders.

Gay leaders, holding their own press conference in APA headquarters immediately after the APA officials ended theirs, generally agreed that the psychiatrists were simply recognizing what many have known all along—that gays can be as happy and healthy as anybody else.

Frank Kameny, head of the Mattachine Society of Washington, D.C., who has long battled psychiatrists over their nomenclature, termed the decision "one of the major bulwarks for support of the patterns of discrimination" in such fields as criminal law, civil service employment and private employment, the armed forces, and security clearance systems.

APA President Dr. Alfred M. Freedman said that in place of it's previous stand on homosexuality, the APA has created a newly defined disorder, labelled "sexual orientation disturbance." An APA resolution stated that the new category "is for individuals whose sexual interests are directed primarily toward people of the same sex and who are either disturbed by, in conflict with, or wish to change their sexual orientation. This diagnostic category is distinguished from homosexuality, which by itself does not necessarily constitute a psychiatric disorder."

Gay leaders noted the limitations of the APA move but nonetheless hailed it as a historic step. "We have won the ball game," announced Ronald Gold of New York, who helped spur the APA to action by cornering Spitzer and convincing him to reconsider his own attitude toward homosexuality. "No longer can gay people grow up thinking they're sick."

Activist Barbara Gittings noted the necessity of organized gay pressure in making the change. "If we had left it up to the APA to come up with something like this, it would have taken at least another thirty or forty years," she commented.

HAPPY AND HEALTHY
"I don't feel any healthier today than I did yesterday," said Jean O'Leary of New York's Lesbian Feminist Liberation regarding the American Psychiatric Association's ruling removing homosexuality from its list of mental disorders. "This historic decision will have many implications, especially for lesbian mothers who will no longer be judged unfit on the basis of their sexuality."

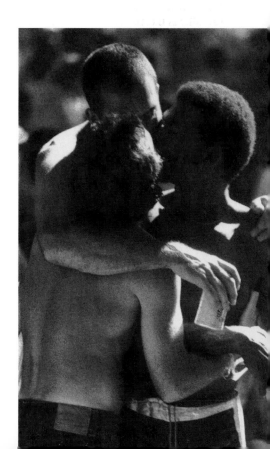

FOR WHOM THE BALLOT TOLLS

It's nine-thirty in the morning, April 9, and Frank Kameny and I are again sitting in the board room at the headquarters of the APA in Washington, D.C. It's a gray Monday, toned in shades of uncertainty. Have they voted for or against us? We don't know, and if the APA does, no one tells us.

For Frank this means an answer to a dozen years of intensive effort in the movment. For me, it's fewer years, but ones of similar commitment. For the millions of isolated gays across the country who have little or no contact with other gays who have learned to like each other and themselves, it's whether or not they're going to have last December's boost to self-esteem cut out from under them.

The network camera crews turn on their lights, and APA President Alfred M. Freedman begins to speak, outlining the board's agenda. He introduces the head teller, in charge of voting. We learn that our item, the Socarides referendum, will be the last item reported from a long ballot.

The teller announces the number of ballots returned (10,555). He details the number of faulty ballots, the percent response for each of the various

Gay activists who helped cure the American Psychiatric Association of its homophobic attitude included (*left to right*) Frank Kameny of the Mattachine Society of Washington; Ron Gold, communications director of the National Gay Task Force; Barbara Gittings, head of the Task Force on Homosexuality of the American Library Association; and Bruce Voeller, executive director of the National Gay Task Force.

regions, the number of responses to each item on the ballot. It sounds like a college course in sociological statistics.

Meanwhile, Frank and I sit waiting, repeatedly photographed by cameras searching for hints of our feelings, observing us like some sort of parlor-broken zoo animals brought in to hear our fate. I turn to Frank and tell him I'm nervous for the first time in over a year, and he smiles and says he's not.

The teller drones on about numbers, while I flash back to the train trip down to Washington last night. What to say to the press if we lose, what to say if we win. I fussed for four hours over rhetoric and wordings, only to decide finally that if we win, I will simply say that the way has now been cleared to get on with the real issue, from which our attention and energies have been so irritatingly pulled.

All gay women and men call on their fellow citizens and the APA to address the real issue—injustice to one's fellow human beings. These are the abuses the century-old categorization of homosexuality as a mental disorder served to bulwark.

My attention is pulled back to the board room. The teller finally comes to some votes after a seemingly endless preamble. He announces results of the election to the 1975 presidency of the APA: Judd Marmor, professor of psychiatry at the University of Southern California, has won! Marmor and his two opponents strongly supported gay rights and opposed the Socarides referendum. All three signed a letter the National Gay Task Force had sent (at a cost of some three thousand dollars) to eighteen thousand members of the APA, urging defeat of the Socarides referendum. But Marmor was particularly known for his opposition to the sickness model.

Frank and I sit, anxiously hopeful that the Marmor victory augurs success on our issue. The tension in the room grows as others see the same potential meaning. Dr. Freedman catches my eye, and from the president's chair gives me a friendly grin as I mock-bite my nails. He, too, has yet to hear the vote on the referendum.

If you want to know about risks in wearing contact lenses, you don't consult a heart surgeon even though he's a doctor. Similarly, no one *should* want eighteen thousand psychiatrists to vote on whether or not homosexuality is a mental disorder. Some psychiatrists claim to be experts on how to help children involved in parental divorces, some in helping suicidal persons, others in drug abuse, alcoholism, or aging. Almost none has carefully studied homosexuality or read current research about it, but all were asked to vote on it.

9:50: A proposal to reduce the number of APA members needed to call a referendum from two hundred to fifty is defeated. Hurrah!

9:55, 10:00, 10:10: The teller drones on about votes on this and that, issues only a loving member of the APA could care about.

10:15: A resolution passes increasing the term of office of the president from one year to two. Gay-friendly Spiegel and Marmor will have double-length terms. Hurray! A bit of light is beginning to shine through the gloom.

10:20: The teller finally comes to our lives. A stereotypical hush falls on the room. The teller reads the referendum, in which a yes vote is a vote *for* us. Frank and I lean forward to hear as cameras click away.

"Yes, 4,854 votes, or 58 percent." We've done it! "No, 3,810 (37.8 percent), abstaining, 367 (3.6 percent)." We've won!

Moreover, we've won by 1,200 more votes than the new president-elect (unfair as the comparison is). Our costly letter has perhaps made the difference. Throw away the defeat speech and tell the world to cut the sickness crap and start helping us get our rights—start teaching that the *real* struggle is for recognition that gays love and care for each other; that to be gay is to have a life-permeating affection for one's fellow beings. If you can't stand or understand affection and caring, you're a homophobe.

I must make it my first job to send the news and my thanks to the many people who helped get out the letter to APA members. Gay people come through when much is at risk and a photo finish looks imminent.

People who'd never contributed before sent in fives and tens. Several non-gay psychiatrists contributed, including Marmor and Bob Spitzer.

Whatever else, all gays, not just those few of us lucky enough to be in the movement, can now view themselves with pride—pride they should have had all along, but that's easy for us to say.

We're a day nearer the time when young gays will look at us with incomprehension and some embarrassment when we reminisce about such things as being in the closet and being told we're sick.

—BRUCE VOELLER

OLIVIA RECORDS

When Judy Dlugacz and nine other partners borrowed four thousand dollars in 1972 to form their own record label featuring women musicians, employing women engineers and producers, and being distributed by a grass-roots organization of women entrepreneurs, people said they were throwing their money away. "We took their doubts as a personal challenge," said Dlugacz. Two years later the women of Olivia Records celebrated the success of their daring venture.

With popular albums like Cris Williamson's *The Changer and the Changed* and Meg Christian's *Scrapbook*, the young company took off beyond anyone's expectations. These and other Olivia-produced works provided the inspirational soundtrack for a new generation of lesbian and feminist listeners, who, by 1974, were turning to the burgeoning women's music scene of concerts and outdoor festivals in ever-increasing numbers. "What we have been able to do is find an audience that was looking for us and interconnect with a network of producers, distributors, and musicians that have been the envy of many other independent record companies," Dlugacz proudly noted.

LESBIANS TAKE OVER APA PANEL

"Homosexuality: Where Do We Go From Here?" was a program of APA's convention, held in May in Detroit, intended to help direct the psychiatric profession after its historic vote.

A delegation of radical lesbian-feminists mounted the stage mid-program, took over the microphones, and halted the exercise with protests against what they identified as sexism on the part of the panel.

The demonstrators challenged the five-member panel of gay activists and pro-gay psychiatrists for having only one woman, Barbara Gittings. They also charged that Gittings and the other gay panelists, Frank Kameny and Bruce Voeller, represented the professional gay establishment in somewhat formalized relationships with the APA, while the protesters represented grass-roots gay militance—especially on behalf of women, who, they argued, were being ignored in the convention program.

Many of the psychiatrists attending the panel discussion walked out when the lesbian takeover began.

The protesters were participants in a gay mental health counter-convention held in Ann Arbor, Michigan, the same week and sponsored by the Gay Awareness Women's Kollective (GAWK) and the Gay Liberation Front of Ann Arbor. More than 120 participants in the Ann Arbor conference, both men and women, had agreed to let the group of lesbians speak for them, on the grounds that men had traditionally assumed the role of spekespeople in the gay movement while women had often been rendered invisible.

Hours before the start of the scheduled APA panel, delegates from the counter-conference met with the panel members and demanded that the men withdraw, leaving the panel with Gittings and four Ann Arbor women.

Two of the men, Voeller and Richard Pillard, a pro-gay psychiatrist from Boston, agreed to withdraw, but the others declined. Panel moderator Dr. Kent Robinson asked the Ann Arbor representatives to accept a compromise, permitting women to have three of the five seats on the panel.

The protesters explained that their motivation was not mere statistical juggling. "Our experience is that if men have an option, they will not listen to us. We can no longer afford to give people the option of ignoring us," they said.

As part of the "compromise," it was agreed that Spitzer and Robinson would contact the APA convention office and attempt to secure a room so that an all-lesbian panel could be presented two nights later.

The originally scheduled gay panel began on time, with Spitzer, Kameny, and Gittings presenting their prepared remarks. Then Rachel Kamel of Ann Arbor and Joan Nixon of Bloomington, Indiana, presented a speech prepared cooperatively by women who had attended the Ann Arbor session.

As they ended their speech, Kamel said, "We've been pretty nice so far. Starting from now, we're defining what happens in this workshop. I want to see all the lesbian sisters up on the stage, right now." About two dozen lesbians came and stood in a line on the stage.

"And as our next move, I want to see these men off the stage," she said. Confronted with demands that he step down, Kameny sat firmly in his place and replied, "I was chosen to be here, I was invited to be here, and I'm going to remain here." As he spoke, one of the women took the microphone Kameny was using off the table. —STAFF REPORT

"Women don't want to be nags or shrews, but we're tired of playing the traditional role of being subservient to men. We've been forced into separatism."
—PHYLLIS LYON, LESBIAN ACTIVIST

GAY LIFE IN A RURAL TOWN

Late at night, in a dark room and a warm bed, the sound of a strong, male voice is heard. "Shippensburg? What's that?"

Of course, it's an understandable question, Shippensburg being what it is, a rural town of about five thousand in the south-central part of Pennsylvania. It's the stereotype of one of those little, nondescript towns that one sees on the map and laughs about; naturally, no one's heard of it.

Whenever I return to the Philadelphia area (where I lived for several years before moving here), my gay friends express their sympathy for me and for my plight in rural America. They also question my sanity.

Well, I'm no crazier than most people, so one shouldn't feel sorry for rural gays, because there *is* gay life in those small towns.

One of the main differences I've often run into is that the rural situation lacks many of the often-thought-of ways to meet fellow gays. There are no gay bars, nothing even close to a bath, and no cruising places. As a result, one is forced to improvise.

Although it's more difficult finding gays in a small town that has no meeting places, the rural town doesn't have many of the blocks to friend-making that one finds in the city. While I'm walking down the street in Shippensburg, it's not uncommon for me to find myself saying hello to total strangers and even starting conversations with them. This almost never happens to me in Philadephia.

I'm not putting down the urban scene; I enjoy it, and it serves a much-needed purpose. However, in a rural situation in which few people publicly announce their sexual orientation, I find myself getting to know *people* first. If someone happens to be gay, it comes out as the friendship builds and may become part of our relationship. It feels good to know that the man I'm making love to knows me.

Which brings me to the point that it's a lot easier to get into and maintain a relationship here. The slower pace of life allows one to become friends first, then lovers, and to come to know each other on less of a sex-oriented basis.

With less competition, temptation isn't so great; the absence of continuous outside pressures on the relationship gives the people within it a chance to settle down. Sure, a gay relationship here has all the strains and stresses of any relationship, but at times, I think of it as a honeymoon away from the push and pull of the urban scene.

Now that I've made rural America sound like a gay paradise, I must admit that there are definitely negative aspects, the main one being fear of discovery. In a small town, everyone can know what is going on with everyone else, whereas it's possible in the city to hide away and to be known only to the people one wishes to know.

There are a number of gay couples living here with a great fear of being discovered, simply because a small town, with a small mind, can make much unpleasantness. Our community could almost blackball a person out of existence if it wanted to. However, even this lack of "coming out" can be a benefit. I don't come out until I can trust the people who know me, which prevents the majority of people from stereotyping me as a gay or a queen.

I'm seen as a unique individual to them, incapable of definition, which paradoxically gives me greater freedom to be myself.

—JACK GOLDMAN

RFD, a publication by and for gay men living in rural settings, was launched in 1974. According to a notice sent to potential subscribers in rural gay households coast to coast, the magazine's Iowa publishers hoped that *RFD* "will provide a means of sharing with your country brothers your thoughts, feelings, hopes, fears, joys, drawings, poems, and advice on being gay in rural America." Stapled to each cover of the first issue was a package of pansy seeds.

THE HOLLYWOOD MARRIAGE IS SUCH A GAY AFFAIR

"I was at a party in Malibu—my first big Hollywood let's-all-get-slowly-smashed-on-Sunday-type party—and there were all these famous faces...there were a lot of actors there that the word on them was they were queer. But this was a boy-girl party: Everyone was paired off...all those beautiful men and gorgeous broads...I realized Judy Garland was in the room...and the guy she's with, one of her husbands, he sort of supports her across the patio...

"And then this crazy thing started to happen: Every homosexual in the place—every guy you'd heard whispered about, all those stars, they left the girls they were with and started a mass move toward Garland...I'll never forget all those famous secret gays moving across this gorgeous patio without a sound..."

The words are those of a screenwriter, dutifully recorded in William Goldman's *The Season,* a factual and candid look at some aspects of the entertainment megalopolis. The scene is not uncommon to the Hollywood milieu. A gay party that really isn't or really is—depending on how you look at it. What the screenwriter failed to mention was the reaction of the girls and wives left stranded by the male exodus to La Garland.

Did they object? Did they share the enthusiasm? Did they give a damn? It's all mixed up in a crazy California institution called "the Hollywood marriage," a euphemism meaning that the husband is gay and the wife may or may not be. Observers from F. Scott Fitzgerald to Joan Didion have had a crack at writing about it, although they've usually concentrated on a single couple or a small corner of the scene. The whole canvas is something else.

There is no figure, probably never will be, on the exact number of homosexual producers, directors, writers, cinematographers, and assorted production personnel represented in the Hollywood dream factory, but the figure, even thinking conservatively, has to be substantial.

In private, many are open about their sex preferences and secretly resent the covering up they must do. Others are outrageous camps who would cut a person dead if he asked for a dollar donation to the Gay Community Services Center.

Still others insist their sexual adventures constitute only a tiny part of their lives, and therefore, all this talk about gay liberation is so much dead air to them. Many are such confirmed closet cases that they refuse to work with associates who are well-known gays.

However, they all have one thing in common. They are married. To women. The "Hollywood marriage," they believe, rightly or wrongly, protects them from any *real* exposure.

To get closer to the Southern California phenomenon, I interviewed, on a casual basis, several famous, financially secure, and talented craftsmen. Each is gay or admitted to being gay to some extent. For the most part, their social lives include their wives, and socializing is largely restricted to the Malibu beach party type of affair described by Goldman's screenwriter, dinners at "in" places, and an almost compulsive preoccupation with film fetes.

The director is a study in perpetual motion. Never long in one place, never allowing himself a spare moment when nothing is happening. He is the classic "busy man." His wife is a well-known actress from another film era, old enough to be his mother. She is forever opening and closing boutiques that never make any money. In their home above the Sunset Strip, where every table is laden down with silver-framed photos of the wife, there is a continual procession of "houseboys," who, like the boutiques, never last long.

"We have the ideal marriage," he tells me. "We each have freedom. She has her weaknesses, and I have mine. I've always thought a man should be allowed a weakness or two."

"How does your wife feel about the houseboys?"

"Oh, she loves them, really. And they love her. I must tell you my wife's not in good health. I've been very protective with her. She was such a great actress on the screen."

"Would you ever announce to your working associates that you were gay?"

"But I'm not, I told you. I'm bi."

"Well, would you tell them you're bi?"

"What would be the point?"

The comedian, a grandfather, is articulate as all get out. And he's a great host and a genuinely funny man, although his screen and television roles give him little more to do than look outraged or befuddled. He has the ability to cut through most of the self-justification bullshit, and his theory on the endurance of the "Hollywood marriage" is apt.

"I'm not exactly buying your 'Hollywood marriage' hook," he starts. "I know what you're saying, and I think you're partially right. But in my case, I think it's a little different, and I don't think that I'm unique. See, I was married a long time before I discovered what I really liked in bed, that I was gay.

"The whole thing goes back to that damn Production Code, Will Hays, the Breen office. You ever read that code? Read it sometime. Unbelievable. There was such a morality backlash about Hollywood. According to the Bible-beaters, it was 'Sin City, U.S.A.'

"The studio heads decided they were going to come down hard on anyone who didn't keep clean. This was in the days when studio heads were gods. It was murder for straights, so you can imagine what it was like for gays, or 'pansies,' as they used to call gays in the executive offices. Every contract had a clause that said if the actor or director was into anything that could, in any way, be construed as 'immoral,' he could be booted out on his ass.

"First thing the old studios did when they had a hot property who was gay was marry him off fast, to a secretary, a starlet, a second-unit director. The divorce could come later. The studio thinking was it's not what you know but what you can make people believe. And in the eyes of the old-timers, the public would never believe that a man who was married could be a homosexual.

"The public is a hell of a lot smarter than that today, and frankly, I don't think it gives a hoot, anyway. The studios and the moguls and the code are gone, but this old way of covering up hangs on. I think that's why your 'Hollywood marriage' hangs on. The boys just haven't gotten the word that their lifestyle is all nostalgia. Could be they believe Hollywood's yesterday is all that's left that's glamorous or interesting.

"Silly, isn't it? Besides I'm getting to the point where a hot shower is more exciting than a piece of ass, and my wife was always a great cook. I feel like old Eddie Robinson in *The Cincinnati Kid* when he said to Steve McQueen, 'At my age, it's all academic.' "

—J. MORIARTY

"Finally, I am a fucking movie star, and I got pickets in front of my theater. For Christ's sake! Can't they leave me alone for once?"
—BRUCE DERN, on gay rage over his playing a homophobe in *The Laughing Policeman*

"**W**e have been working to combat the problems of lesbian invisibility for a long time. Now NBC has made us visible to millions of prime-time viewers as the most evil of all creatures."
—A PARTICIPANT IN THE ZAP OF NBC OVER ITS ANTILESBIAN PROGRAMS

BOOKS: *THE FRONT RUNNER*

Patricia Nell Warren's stunning new novel, *The Front Runner,* is a modern love story about gay people, yet it cannot be called a gay novel. It can stand on its own literary merits and will not have to depend on any special target group of readers to be appreciated.

Set during the years 1974–1978, it tells the story of Billy Sive, a very gifted young collegiate runner with Olympic aspirations, and his relationship with Harlan Brown, the tough thirty-nine-year-old ex-Marine track coach who helps him prepare for the 1976 games in Montreal.

That the two are gay and living together doesn't cause undue concern among students or faculty at small Prescott College in upstate New York, but as the news spreads throughout sports officialdom, rampant homophobia surfaces. Not only is Billy and Harlan's affair seen as a threat to the cherished traditions of masculinity in sports, but it also challenges the authoritative distinctions between coaches and their athletes.

The men become reluctant celebrities, constantly in the public eye. Their newly acquired status as symbols of gay liberation, and the reaction by both friends and enemies, leads the novel to a devastating, emotion-packed conclusion.

"I wondered a little bit: Am I going to be able to hack the fact that I have no personal experience of cruising in male bars?" said Patricia Nell Warren about the writing of her gay male classic. "I would think that even a lesbian might possibly pause a bit before she started to write something about gay males. Then, I reassured myself. Well, gee, they're human beings and feelings are feelings."

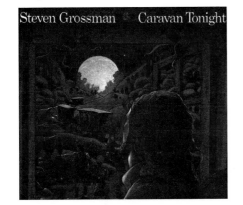

Steven Grossman's album for Mercury Records, *Caravan Tonight,* was the first album by a forthrightly gay singer-songwriter to be released by a major record company. "A satisfying blend of melody and message," according to *Advocate* critic Christopher Stone, Grossman's album astonished gay listeners with its candid reflection of the problems that gays face in straight society. "For the first time I could write what I felt and not what I thought other people wanted to hear," Grossman said about his songs, which dealt with topics as varied as coming out to one's family, cruising in gay bars, and the religious ramifications of being gay.

Any work of literature, no matter how great, doesn't cause revolutions in attitudes or behavioral patterns. But very gifted, perceptive writers accurately reflect and portray social changes taking place during their time. *The Front Runner* is not a manifesto, but it is one more sign that the emerging force in gay life today is the young, masculine, athletic homosexual.

As the book's characters demonstrate, true masculinity doesn't rule out such virtues as gentleness and sensitivity. In fact, the man (gay or straight) who is secure in his masculinity is more likely to be gentle and kind than the one whose masculinity is suspect, and *The Front Runner* has the unmistakable feel of this truth on every page.

—SCOTT LANGDON

January 29, 1975   Issue 156/50 cents

THE **ADVOCATE**

THIS ISSUE BEGINS A NEW ERA FOR GAY PEOPLE

THE **ADVOCATE**

TOUCHING YOUR LIFESTYLE   NO.169, JULY 30, 1975, 50 CENTS

CIVIL SERVICE DROPS BAN/ S.F. TACKLES MA BELL
PRIDE MARCHES ON . . . AND ON

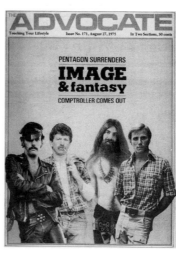

THE **ADVOCATE**

Touching Your Lifestyle   Issue No. 171, August 27, 1975   In Two Sections, 50 cents

PENTAGON SURRENDERS

IMAGE & fantasy

COMPTROLLER COMES OUT

THE **ADVOCATE**

Touching Your Lifestyle   Issue No. 176, November 5, 1975   In Two Sections, 75 cents

IN THIS ISSUE READ WHAT DEMO PREXY HOPEFULS ARE SAY-ING ABOUT GAY RIGHTS, PLUS FOUR EXPERT OPINIONS ON THE SUBJECT OF

SEX

UALITY AND GAY SENSUALITY. AND CHECK IN ON THE HOUSTON SCENE AND GET UPDATED ON THE LATEST WINS OF BIG CHIEF DAVIS IN HIS EFFORTS TO KEEP GAY COPS OFF THE L.A. FORCE . . .

Family Matters

Advocate staff photographer Crawford Barton, known for his sensitive documentation of San Francisco's gay scene, caught this intimate exchange off the coast north of the city.

1975

The Advocate itself was the big story of 1975. It had begun as a local paper in Los Angeles. Using that strong base of advertising support and a piecemeal distribution system, it had become the dominant gay voice in the country by default.

But the editorial vision had never caught up with the reality of circulation. Even though it carried news from elsewhere, *The Advocate* was still essentially a Los Angeles gay paper that happened to be circulated outside of Southern California. David Goodstein, the new owner, wanted more. He certainly wanted a stronger power base for himself, and he had every intention of using *The Advocate* as his way into national gay leadership. He wanted something that reflected a more sophisticated audience and that would attract more upscale advertisers. I was to be his vehicle for the changes. One of my most appealing attributes, so far as Goodstein was concerned, was that I was a "New York editor," one of the few who was "out" at his job.

My name appears on the masthead of all but the first and last issues of the year, though I was on staff as a shadow editor for a number of months before. My original job was to observe the publication, look at possible changes, and create a new vision for it. Trying to separate *The Advocate* from its Southern California roots, Goodstein moved our offices to San Mateo, twenty miles south of San Francisco. The look began to be more slick. The graphics were dramatically improved. Circulation increased.

All our new ideas created an identity crisis: Was this a magazine or a newspaper? Goodstein and I clearly wanted it to be a magazine, but we were stuck with a newsprint format for financial reasons. We tried to follow the lead of other alternative publications—*Rolling Stone,* et al.—by forcing a magazine design into a tabloid format. We also wanted something that spoke to our readers in a more complete way, not just a source for news information. May I burn in hell for approving a new advertising and promotional theme: "Touching Your Lifestyle." It came complete with T-shirts and posters.

113

The whole issue of "lifestyle" was an incendiary device in arguments within the gay world. Was *The Advocate* really talking to people about their way of life, or were we trying to convince them to be good consumers? Or were we trying to create a political force? Or a cultural one?

What's most interesting to me now is the persistence of the concerns that we covered, and that we experienced. We had themed issues on "Gay People in the Military," "Gay People as Parents," "The Parents of Gay People,"—all of them questions that would still dog the gay movement two decades later.

There were battles for civil rights bills; there were questions about how lesbians and gay men would get together; we had feature articles on spirituality and on the developing gay literature. An editorial I had written complaining about the national advertisers who wouldn't support *The Advocate* was no different from one that an editor would write today. It's amazing how persistent the issues of gay activism are. It forces us all to wonder if there are some things that will never change.

Gender was one of the most persistent problems for the community, and for *The Advocate*. We were at least beginning to address some of the same problems then that exist today over how a publication like *The Advocate* could speak to both men and women. The essential problem, especially since the big national advertisers wouldn't come into our pages, was the tenor of the advertisers we did have, most of whom used overtly sexual images of gay men—even insurance agencies used nude or nearly nude models to appeal to gay clients. No matter what we did with the editorial content, the tone of the magazine would be biased by all those beefcake pictures.

The beefcake presented one special problem: the classifieds. One of the first things that we tried to do with the publication was to separate out the personal ads. Our original vision, which was eventually realized years later, was to create a separate publication. There was a problem with that part in 1975. We did some market surveys which told us that, rather than being a distinct market that might support a second publication, the readers of the classified section were the most loyal, and they were the largest group of subscribers we had. To remove the personals would be to kill off the paper. We chose a middle ground—we created a separate section that could be pulled out of the center of the paper. The result wasn't perfect, but without the personals we were closer to a publication that could be given to your parents and politicians—a surprisingly pressing point in 1975.

The most lasting change in *The Advocate* came with the appearance of new bylines. One of the claims to fame I will always have was my hiring of Randy Shilts in the middle of the year. Shilts had been a stringer for the paper as a student journalist; when he graduated, we gave him the first full-time reporter position. One measure of the quality of a publication is supposed to be the number of writers who go on to write books. The roster of *Advocate* writers who joined up in 1975 who did just that is more than impressive: Sasha Gregory-Lewis, George Whitmore, Arnie Kantrowitz, and Shelly Singer are among those who, like Shilts, became successful authors.

Nineteen seventy-five was a building year for the paper, and for many of us who would go on to create the next step in gay culture. We began to get the big interviews, we laid the foundation for national advertising, we began to recruit a cadre of professional writers while continuing to address the persistent issues of how we as lesbians and gay men could live together and with the rest of society.

—JOHN PRESTON

A NEW ERA?

Letters to the editor reflected not only readers' attitudes toward the new format, but the diversity of their views toward one another:

"You have screwed up a lively gay paper. Now we get 'sedate' covers and Rex Reed-y writers. Why the hell are you doing this? Shouldn't be called Advocate *at all—call it* The Closets' Town and Country.*"*
—Los Angeles

"I doubt you people are even gay. You certainly have made a mess of things. It is another classic case of Jews taking over something and ruining it for everyone else."
—San Francisco

"Too sexist!" —New York City

"Head for the hills, queers, the cunt-lovers have taken over The Advocate.*"*
—Jacksonville, Florida

"More lesbians regularly read your paper than you might have thought—and we appreciate the new stuff being done by and about women." —Whittier, California

"Your publication spurns blacks like the plague, except when they can be used to further your sales. We're not just music makers for the mere release of your tensions and anxiety, we're people, loving, warm, and OH! so real." —Goleta, California

"Please shove your 'respected news journal' up your faggy Jewish ass. I don't know which I hate more, Jews or queers, but the combination of both has got to be the lowest shit on earth. God bless Adolf Hitler."
—Unsigned

"Gay is pride, awareness, and love. The Advocate *puts all this across."*
—Atlanta

T I M E L I N E

JANUARY   A national gay civil rights bill, HR 166, was introduced in the House of Representatives. ❑ Two men in Phoenix were granted a marriage license by the county clerk. ❑ The University of Montana offered the state's first gay studies course. ❑ The American Psychological Association and the American Association for the Advancement of Science echoed the American Psychiatric Association in deeming homosexuality not an illness. ❑ In New York, NBC held a "summit conference" with representatives of the gay community. ❑ The New York sodomy law was declared unconstitutional by the New York State Court of Appeals. ❑ In Montreal, over 350 Canadian and American lesbians participated in the second annual North American Lesbian Conference

FEBRUARY   Howard Brown, M.D., chairman of the National Gay Task Force and the first head of the New York City Health Services Administration, died at age fifty. ❑ "The Secret," a Lutheran-sponsored television program about a guilt-ridden, unhappy gay high school wrestling coach who accepts his homosexuality as sinful, aired on 370 independent stations nationally.

MARCH   On recommendation of the Boulder, Colorado, city district attorney, county clerk Cela Rorex issued Dave Zamora and Ave McCord a marriage license; the move caused a month-long rush on the clerk's office, until the state attorney general voided the D.A.'s recommendation. A court later revoked all of the licenses. ❑ A National Council of Churches of Christ Conference in Chicago concluded that antigay discrimination is immoral. ❑ The week after her show premiered, Cher received 212 fan letters proposing marriage—seventy-seven of them from women. ❑ Pledging to "fight on" as a "lesbian, feminist, and Amazon," Susan Saxe was arrested by the FBI for her involvement in the robbery of two banks and a National Guard armory in 1970 and jailed for seven years.

APRIL   The Arizona Superior Court deemed unconstitutional a recent gay marriage attempt, paving the way for the state legislature to pass an emergency bill defining marriage as possible only between a man and a woman. ❑ Fires gutted Boston gay bars Twelve Carver and Herbie's Ramrod Room. ❑ In Iowa City, four hundred people attended the Second Annual Midwest Gay Pride Conference. ❑ Following the previous year's first in gay political coverage, *The New York Times* printed an article entitled "The All-Gay Cruise: Prejudice and Pride," breaking an unwritten editorial rule of silence on gay features at the newspaper. ❑ Dozens of gays wore lavender armbands to services at a Sydney, Australia, cathedral, protesting antigay statements made by the Right Rev. Lance Shilton, the city's Anglican dean.

MAY   The California sex bill, approving of all consensual sexual acts between adults, passed the state Senate by a narrow margin, becoming the first law in the United States specifically decriminalizing consensual sex acts to clear both houses of a state legislature; it was soon after signed into law by Governor Jerry Brown. ❑ In an appeal brought by Tacoma educator James Gaylord, the Washington State Supreme Court ruled that a public school teacher could not be dismissed solely on the grounds of homosexuality. ❑ Boston NBC affiliate WBZ–TV hired lesbian Ellen B. Davis as an adviser and commentator. ❑ The president of Mormon-owned-and-operated Brigham Young University, Dallin

Protesters marched on FBI headquarters in Washington, D.C., after the FBI's hunt for two reportedly lesbian fugitives left a trail of jailed gay activists across the eastern United States. Federal officials had claimed that a "lesbian underground" was hiding Susan Saxe and Katherine Ann Power, who took part in the murder of a policeman during a 1970 Boston bank robbery.

Oaks, proclaimed at a press conference that drug users and active homosexuals were "two influences we wish to exclude from the BYU community." ❏ The keynote speaker at the Coalition of Christian Citizens meeting to kick off a campaign against the California sex bill was Commander Matt Koehl from the American Nazi Party headquarters in Arlington, Virginia; two months later, the campaign ended in whimpering defeat when the group failed to even come close to acquiring enough signatures to call a repeal vote.

JUNE The San Francisco Board of Education voted to include gay people in its new affirmative action resolution. ❏ Seattle ex–Salvation Army bell-ringer, Sam Deadrick, who had been fired for being gay, was awarded back pay and damages by a city hearing panel. ❏ The American Theological Society's Committee on Sexuality, a committee of Roman Catholic theologians, released a report condoning homosexuality as a "natural and irreversible state" and charging that the Church's stigmatization of homosexuality was partially at fault for the oppression of homosexuals by society. ❏ Canada's National Gay Rights Coalition was formed at the third annual Canadian Gay Rights Conference in Ottawa.

JULY The United States Civil Service Commission dropped its ban on lesbians and gays in civilian federal government jobs. ❏ The State of Washington's sodomy law was repealed. ❏ In New York, two hundred demonstrators marched on St. Patrick's Cathedral in opposition to a campaign against gay civil rights by the Roman Catholic Archdiocese. ❏ Santa Cruz County, California, became the first county government to ban antigay employment discrimination. ❏ The Sun Ray Beams Motorcycle Club, claiming to be the first lesbian biking organization, was founded in Miami.

"*Baldy Hanson [a fellow legislator] was running around the Senate making all kinds of snide remarks. At various committee meetings he was threatening that he was going to introduce a resolution appropriating three hundred dollars for any homosexual Senator in order to go to a psychiatrist and get cured. My reaction was, 'You goddamn cheapskate. You can barely get into a psychiatrist's front door for three hundred dollars—let alone be cured, even if there were a cure.'*"

—MINNESOTA STATE SENATOR ALLAN SPEAR, speaking of one incident he had faced since coming out a year earlier

GAY PRIDE NATIONWIDE
Drag queens and studs (*left*) hose down onlookers during the San Francisco Pride Parade while buttons from around the country (*right*) reveal a diversity of gay voices.

HERO SUES PRESS
Ex-Marine Oliver "Bill" Sipple faced an unwanted spotlight when he pushed down the barrel of Sarah Jane Moore's gun outside the St. Francis Hotel in San Francisco, preventing an assassination attempt on President Gerald Ford. Tipped off by gay activists, the national press disclosed Sipple's homosexuality and ran headlines dubbing him a "Homosexual Hero" and "Gay Vet." After his family read of his being gay, they stopped speaking with Sipple. He launched a multimillion-dollar suit against seven newspapers, charging invasion of privacy. The suit was quickly thrown out of court.

AUGUST The First National Conference of Integrity, a group of gay Episcopalians, convened in Chicago. ❏ Seattle's Gay Community Center opened a twenty-four-hour hotline for male victims of sexual assault. ❏ The Gay Media Coalition called for a boycott of *The Village Voice,* long criticized for its negative coverage of gay and lesbian issues. ❏ The Moscow, Idaho, City Council appointed openly gay Gilbert E. Preston to the city's Fair Housing Commission. ❏ A purge of lesbians at the Boca Chica Naval Air Base in Florida brought out Pat Veldon, who filed legal action against the Navy; she was eventually given an honorable discharge. ❏ Over two weeks in Tyler, Texas, six gay men were beaten and two were shot by teenage males while local police arrested twenty-five men for loitering in a city park.

SEPTEMBER The words I AM A HOMOSEXUAL stretched across the chest of Sgt. Leonard Matlovich on the cover of *Time* magazine after he came out; a month later he was dismissed from the Air Force, and after a lengthy court struggle, accepted a $160,000 settlement in 1980. ❏ The New York City Council voted down a gay civil rights bill for the fifth year in a row. ❏ The Los Angeles city Civil Service Commission voted unanimously to adopt hiring standards allowing openly gay women and men into the police force. ❏ In an episode of "All in the Family," Archie Bunker inadvertently saved a drag queen's life through mouth-to-mouth resuscitation after mistaking him for a woman. ❏ In Orange, Massachusetts, the Rev. Edward T. Hougen came out to the parishioners of the Central Congregational Church in his usual Sunday sermon, simultaneously announcing his resignation. ❏ South Australia became the first Australian state to repeal laws against sex acts between consenting adult males.

OCTOBER Governor Milton Shapp of Pennsylvania vetoed an antigay bill passed by unanimous vote in the state senate. ❏ Four hundred lesbians and gay men in Washington, D.C., attended a GAA-sponsored three-day conference called "The Federal Government and Gays." ❏ In Oregon, a U. S. District Court ruled that gay New Zealand native Paul Brodie could not be denied naturalization as an American citizen merely because of his sexual orientation. ❏ Bloomington, Indiana, Mayor Frank McCloskey recommended the expansion of municipal civil rights ordinances to include gays.

NOVEMBER Robert I. McQueen became the new editor of *The Advocate,* replacing John Preston. ❏ Big Brothers of Washington, D.C., adopted a policy requiring employees and volunteers to sign a statement that "I am not and have not been a homosexual." ❏ At the University of New Mexico, openly lesbian P. M. Duffey-Ingrassia was elected homecoming queen, prompting Governor Gerry Apodaca to bow out of the parade at the last minute. ❏ The Mississippi Gay Alliance held the first gay and lesbian convention in the state.

DECEMBER Pro-gay liberal George Moscone won a run-off election to become San Francisco's mayor. ❏ The Arizona Court of Appeals struck down the state's sodomy law. ❏ In Philadelphia, sixty gay activists held a sit-in at a City Council meeting to protest alleged stalling on a gay-rights bill. ❏ Anchorage's city assembly unanimously passed a gay-rights ordinance despite protests by Mayor George Sullivan. ❏ A survey of 1,930 English adults by London's *Gay News* revealed that 45 percent believed "there are certain occupations that homosexuals should never be allowed to have, like being teachers or doctors," while 30 percent disagreed.

BETTE MIDLER

Don't let all the recession-obsessed soothsayers fool you. People are still lining up to see a good show. At around midnight of the evening before tickets went on sale at the Minskoff Theatre for Bette Midler's *Clams on the Half Shell Revue,* the line began to form for what turned out to be the largest single-day ticket sale in Broadway history.

It wasn't always so easy to sell tickets to a Midler concert. There was a time when you could take your pick of any one of fifty empty folding chairs in the basement of the Continental Baths on 74th Street. All you had to do was take a breather from the upstairs activity. The rest of the patrons were one hundred feet away, splashing in the pool, oblivious to the fact that the little woman with the red hair would someday command the attention of the entire entertainment industry. Midler would complain weekly that the pool activity and "that goddamn waterfall" were cramping her act.

She was singing in showcase bars and gypsy hangouts in the theater district when she heard about the Continental Baths and its owner, Steve Ostrow, who would give her fifty dollars a night to sing for gay men in towels. It proved to be the turning point in her career, garnering her the attention of the New York press and eventually an audition for "The Tonight Show." The publicity she got at the time was due as much to the fact that she was singing in a gay bathhouse as the fact that she was shaping up as the hottest thing in music since Barbra Streisand. Critics waxed ecstatic about the Jewish girl from a Samoan neighborhood in Hawaii who grew up to be the darling of the beautiful people in a decadent New York bathhouse.

It also provided Midler with enough comedy material to last her entire career. She went through it in a weekend. The Rev. Troy Perry of the Metropolitan Community Church came one Saturday night to make a speech about the advent of Gay Pride Week. Bette rushed into her dressing room and shouted, "Quick! Gay priest jokes!" Onstage she feigned incredulity. "Whh-haaat is this? Bingo on Friday, Bango on Saturday? They oughtta call this dump 'Our Lady of the Vapors.' Tonight he'll walk on the water in the pool, and tomorrow night he'll be walking the third floor. Puhleeese."

It was a happy family in spite of the chic invaders who grew in number each week. Midler, now appearing occasionally on late-night television, would remain fiercely loyal to the Continental and the gay men in her audience. "Lissen, they gave me a big push and that'll always be part of me even after I've moved on. Me and those guys just went somewhere else." Move on she did, to pack Carnegie Hall on a late June night in 1972 and to draw almost a hundred thousand people to Central Park for a concert. She began to work on her first album and embarked on a cross-country tour.

Once again the following year, Midler reminded us that she was loyal and grateful to her gay following by appearing before seventeen thousand gay men and women in New York's Washington Square Park to help celebrate Gay Pride Week. In jeans and a red workshirt, knotted at the waist, she burst upon the stage and drawled, "Listen, I heard a little bit of this on the radio and it sounded like you people were beating each other up out here so I came to sing a song." She did two choruses of "Friends" and was carried over the barricades to a waiting car.

A few months ago plans were completed for her return to Broadway. The show opens in Philadelphia, and Midler can see me for a brief session on the day she is preparing to leave. When I arrive at her house in Greenwich Village she is in the kitchen in a green velvet bathrobe, making scrambled eggs. She's just gotten up.

"So how does it feel to be back on Broadway?" "Well, I'm not there yet, but I'm excited and looking forward to it." Then a quick change. "Vito, what is the meaning of that earring you wear in your right ear as opposed to the left?"

I tell her that it means absolutely nothing, and that it's only jewelry, which I am getting tired of because it attracts more attention than it's worth. I also tell her that in case she's wondering, it's not an S&M thing with me.

"Yeah, Vito, that's what they all say." I point out that the world is changing rapidly and that some people can't cope with it.

"But it's the way of the world, though, Vito. We're not the first people to have to go through traumas or crises. You wouldn't have wanted to be around during the Black Plague now, Vito, would you? There are always the best of times and the worst of times all the time. It's part of being on the planet. We haven't learned everything yet."

I think about her comments in *Gay* magazine two years ago when asked what she thought of gay liberation. "For Christ's sake, open your mouths," she said, "don't you people get tired of being stepped on?"

"You know, I'm sort of involved in the gay issue," I announce.

"Involved, Vito? *Involved?*" Her eyes are wide in disbelief of my understatement. Then she smiles and says: "Really, it's nice. I absolutely think you should be."

I ask if she thinks there's a gay audience any more than there's a straight audience.

"I don't know about that, Vito, I really don't. I know that there are individuals, but I don't know if there's a group of people who call each other up and say, 'Let's all meet tonight and we'll go to see, uh, Shirley Bassey.' I just don't think it happens. It's *not* the way it is."

I feel obligated to point out that the issue is that performers should let their gay fans know that it's all right to be whoever you are. I do *not* point out to her that after a recent screening of *Sunday, Bloody Sunday* Shirley Bassey said that she had to leave the theater because seeing two men kiss made her sick to her stomach.

"Oh, hell, Vito, listen, It's all right for *anybody* to be who they are. Just as long as they don't let their dogs shit on the street. Just so they don't make your life miserable. I don't think there's enough time to fritter your life away thinking bad things or venomous thoughts about other people and how they live."

She is tired from sitting and has to go to Philadelphia in a few hours. My final question is, How does she want to end up? A slow and famous smile creeps across her face. It's evident she's thought all these things before. "Retirement is the pathway to an early grave. When you lose your work and what interests you, you lose your will to live, and I'm not that kind of person....I think there are so many paths to take, so many things to learn in this world."

—VITO RUSSO

"I was fighting for gay rights before it became fashionable. Way back in the twenties, in New York, I got hold of the police and started explaining to them that gay boys are females in male bodies. I said, 'Now look, fellas, when you're hitting one of them, just remember, you're hitting a woman.' That straightened them out."

—SCREEN SIREN MAE WEST

CHRISTOPHER ISHERWOOD

All who attended the recent Gaythink at California State University, Long Beach, agreed that it was a great success, the most stimulating conference of its kind yet seen on a West Coast campus. One reason for that was a lively appearance, one humid evening, by one of our greatest living writers, Christopher Isherwood.

Isherwood was born in England, but has been an American citizen for thirty years now. He is the author of ten novels (*A Single Man,* he says, is the best; *Berlin Stories,* on which *Cabaret* was based, is the most popular), plus plays, film scripts, essays, biographies, poems. After spending the first half of his life wandering the world, he settled in California, where he and Don Bachardy, the artist with whom he has lived for twenty-two years, have a home in Santa Monica Canyon, not far from the ocean.

His entrance on campus is undramatic, but subtly calculated to surprise (he hasn't written a dozen or so movie scripts for nothing). Refusing a seat, Isherwood spins a lounge chair around neatly, turning it into a mini-rostrum, and, placing both hands on the back, looks about with birdlike expectancy.

At seventy-one, he wears his years very lightly indeed, looking almost boyish and oddly "foreign." The natty corduroy jacket, the open yellow shirt, the hair cropped to Prussian shortness, the alert blue eyes, the precise British voice deploying a steady flow of American vernacular, don't quite belong. But his vitality is striking, and he often seems far ahead of his radical questioners in his thinking about gayness. Startled guffaws punctuating the two-hour-long exchange suggest that some of his ideas are almost shocking.

Someone asks about promiscuity. Is it true what they say about gay people? If it is, does it matter? Does he believe in monogamy in gay relationships?

"Oh, no—*that* I'll say right off." He seems so surprised that the audience laughs. "I have the greatest respect for lust. I don't believe in simulating bourgeois marriage. In fact, I don't think a long-term relationship exists, it hasn't been tested, until it's been exposed to—what's a polite word—screwing around?"

Someone else is worried about his remarks concerning casual sex versus long-term relationships.

"There's nothing greater in terms of our life on earth than an enduring relationship if it's truly loving. But we are brainwashed into accepting the standards of the hetero majority, and we need to keep reminding ourselves that we needn't—shouldn't—conform to straight standards that long-lasting love isn't compatible with promiscuity. That love can enter into one-night stands, too. Such love *could* be higher in its nature than domestic love, because it verges on that thing we all talk about so much but rarely meet—love for mankind."

Wasn't it difficult for Bachardy, a young blond student wonders, before he became a recognized artist? Wasn't he always being put down, referred to as Mr. Isherwood II, and so forth?

A FATEFUL MEETING

"We first met at a party," recalled Don Bachardy, pictured above (*left*) with his longtime companion Christopher Isherwood in 1953. "And at the end of it Chris and I kissed and hugged each other and lost our balance and fell right through a window we were standing next to…

"I looked very young for my age; I was eighteen and he was forty-eight. In fact, when we went to New York the rumor went around town that Chris had brought a twelve-year-old boy with him!

"But we never put up any pretense. If you don't know about the guilt which people think you ought to feel, then you don't feel it. It never occurred to me that we were doing anything out of the ordinary. Looking back on it, though, I realize it must have been pretty shocking to a lot of people in those days."

"That question is slightly complicated by the fact that he's sitting about two feet away from you. Don, would you like to speak?"

Bachardy, a lean man in his early forties with a shock of silver hair, responds: "Yes, it was tough for a while. It wasn't Mr. Isherwood, though; *Mrs.* Isherwood was more like it. But in the long run, it had a good effect because it just made me work harder to establish myself as Mr. Bachardy."

Isherwood says he doesn't altogether care for the word *gay*. "To my old-fashioned ears it sounds coy. But 'homosexual' is so cumbersome. 'Gay' is fine as a slogan, a watchword, a term to describe our philosophy, our attitude toward life. But not, I think, as a title for the movement. I prefer the words used by our enemies. I used to call myself a bugger when I was young. Now I feel at home with 'queer,' or 'fag,' when I'm feeling hostile. It makes heterosexuals wince when you refer to yourself by those words if they've been using them behind your back, as they generally have." Some other answers from a long session:

On friends: "Throughout my life, at least eighty percent of my friends have been gay, and I feel strangely ill at ease when I'm away from gay people for long periods, almost as if I was being deprived of oxygen."

On closetry: "I do wish more of our brothers and sisters, especially prominent people, could bring themselves to come out of their closets. Nearly always the world knows who they are already, however hard they try to fool it. Coming out would actually make their lives less isolated and troubled; it would give them faith and courage in themselves. And isn't that worth far more than the notoriety they already enjoy?"

On minorities: "We are the only minority which isn't tied to any one race, so we can claim to be supremely natural since we occur in all races. For the same reason, we are the only minority that can never be wiped out. They may kill the Jews, wipe out the blacks, but homosexuals will go on reproducing themselves in every race and in every generation."

Of the "decadent" Berlin of *Cabaret*: "It really wasn't that way. Actually, Berlin's gay bars in the thirties were very cozy, like parlors where everyone came to relax around a nice warm stove while the snow fell outside." The word "decadence," pronounced with a thrilling Edith Evans tremolo of distaste, sends him off on another tack.

"Of course, people take this attitude that Germany went to pieces between the wars because of its 'decadence.' By which they always mean homosexuality. At least, I've never been able to discover that they have anything else in mind. It's such rubbish, sheer Nazi propaganda. Germany went to pieces because of a war started by greedy old men who sent out all the best young people of a generation to die…."

The meeting ends with a loud burst of applause. Isherwood has wooed and won. He applauds right back: "I've always liked that Russian custom."

Half an hour after the meeting's end, Isherwood and Bachardy extract themselves. "How did it go?" Isherwood asks. "I never feel we've really gotten below the surface until someone gets hostile." He seems a trifle disappointed.

They pass by the Gay Pride exhibit, which consists of two glass cases, one containing a toilet roll on a roller, on which is inscribed the words: SO YOU THINK GAYS ARE REVOLTING? Isherwood suddenly seems a lot older, but placid and perfectly content with whatever it is that is happening. He is humming to himself in a peculiar way, like a small mobile beehive, as he heads off toward the darkened parking lot.

—W. I. SCOBIE

GAY PARENTHOOD

"Ordinary" is the first word that hits you when you meet the six children of the Schuster-Isaacson family. The eleven-year-old boy wants to be an Air Force pilot. Another son hasn't decided whether he wants to be a professional football player or a preacher. One of the six-year-old twins wants to open a candy store when he grows up, while his double wants to be a first-grade teacher.

The eight-member clan is as wholesome as your mom's apple pie, as ordinary as a hot dog, and as American as your Chevrolet. Except for one thing. The family has two moms, Sandra Schuster and Madeline Isaacson. And the two moms are out-front lesbians who have become the *cause célèbre* of gay parenthood because of their long and well-publicized battle to keep custody of their children.

The sprawling five-bedroom-and-rec-room house, nestled in a typically American suburban setting, shows no signs of the family's three years of highly volatile legal battles. A painting of an anglicized Jesus smiles benevolently on the religious magazines, coloring books, and football shoulder-pads which dot the living room floor. Instead of carrying flaming, antisexist political slogans, wall posters espouse messages like "God Is Love."

The kids don't show any signs of particular anxiety despite the fact that a late October court hearing might break apart their contented family scene as Sandy and Madeline's ex-husbands again plead for child custody. The kids seem more concerned with tomorrow's football game and paper-route collection. They barrage the reporter with questions about his parents, brothers, and sisters while they again drag Jacob, the friendly basset hound, off the couch. The are apt to ask visitors if they are gay with the same casual air with which they would offer a glass of water.

Neither do thirty-four-year-old Madeline and thirty-seven-year-old Sandy show signs of strain from the legal entanglements which have brought them to national prominence. The cheerful pair talk more of the hopeful "miracles" that have kept them together than of the avenging ex-husbands who have tried to drive them apart. They tell their story with a dash of this hope and a large dose of polish, a polish that comes from a lot of practice in telling it to the college campuses around the nation and professional groups as prestigious as this year's national convention of the American Psychiatric Association. Their unusual story, heavily laced with their profound religious fundamentalism, goes something like this:

Sandra Schuster got her nursing degree from Stanford in 1961 and was ready to embark into the mainstream of American nuclear family life. "All through college, I learned Freud, Freud, Freud," she recalls. "Homosexuality was something that got left behind in the early stages of heterosexual development. I learned the perfect model of family life—heterosexuality, two children, a car, a boat, and a husband." To pay her way through her first year of college, Sandy joined the Navy, and she dutifully moved to the East Coast after graduation to fulfill her end of the naval agreement. There she met her husband-to-be.

They got married and, after the naval stint, began procreating their way into a traditional American family. Two boys, two girls, a home in the suburbs—but something wasn't right. "I knew there was an emptiness within me, but I didn't know what it was," says Sandy.

At one point, Sandy fasted and prayed for two weeks in an attempt to

"If you're a homosexual and you're ashamed of it, or you know your parents are going to have a fit and will turn from you, it must be terribly guilt-inducing. I think guilt is the most awful thing that anyone can feel. It's a great contributor to neurotic behavior."
—PAT LOUD, MOTHER OF GAY SON, LANCE

A LETTER HOME

"Fifteen years ago my parents found out that I am gay. Since then the three of us have been on a hectic roller-coaster ride of acceptance, rejection, joy, sorrow, communication, silence....

Probably the most important thing to have helped me in my own relationship with my parents happened two years ago. I had agreed to baby-sit a very young child for two friends for a long weekend. I, the unattached, totally mobile gay man, experienced diaper-changing, being awakened at four A.M., and the total insensitivity of friends to my lack of mobility. It dawned on me that when my parents were my age, I was already seven, my sister was two, and there were three more children to come.

How could these two people have given up their youth? Their freedom? How much resentment must have been generated? How did they feel now?

In my typical way, I wrote a too long, too heavy, too intense letter home telling my mother and father about this awesome thought. In their typical way, they sent back a letter three weeks later with items on local politics, news of high school friends, reports on relatives' marriages, and a P.S.: "The joys outnumber the sorrows. We wouldn't have done it any other way."

—JOHN PRESTON

AVOIDANCES

OH, FREDDIE'S HAD LOTSA ROOMIES. ALL NICE BOYS, BUT A REAL TURNOVER. HE CAN'T EVER LIVE ALONE. DOESN'T EVEN BOIL WATER.

A'COURSE HIS DAD AND ME'VE ALWAYS HOPED HE'D SETTLE DOWN ONE OF THESE DAYS WITH SOME NICE GIRL TO TAKE CARE OF HIM.

BUT AT 30, WHO KNOWS? THEY SAY IF A BOY ISN'T MARRIED BY 30 HE'S PROBABLY A CONFIRMED BACHELOR.

—DENNIS FORBES

resolve the failing relationship with her husband. She studiously worked at her friend's church, waiting for an answer. "I wasn't looking for anybody, either a man or a woman," she says. Then, in April 1970, came the second miracle. "During an evening service at the church, I saw this woman walking down the aisle with a boy at each hand. I swore that I saw a glow around her head. I thought, *Listen girl, you're really sick!*" The next Sunday, one of Sandy's sons eagerly ran to her, telling about this great Sunday school teacher whom Sandy would have to meet. They did, and the Sunday school teacher was the person with the glow around her head—Madeline Isaacson.

Madeline herself was in much the same situation as Sandy. Like Sandy, she had been married eight years in a union that was less than joyful. She, too, had been praying for God to save the marriage. Then she met Sandy. "I remember when we first shook hands. My knees got weak. I had this funny feeling all over. Then we started talking to each other, and I realized that we had a lot in common."

The relationship they began to develop was the answer to their marital problems, but they soon found that other problems had just begun. When they moved to California to live together, their two ex-husbands teamed up, followed them and kidnaped one of Sandy's children and both of Madeline's sons.

The costly court battle began. Sandy and Madeline gathered droves of witnesses, all expertly testifying that the Schuster-Isaacson home was a healthy environment for the six children. The first day in court, however, brought only a half-victory when the pair got divorces and were granted temporary custody of the children with one weighty stipulation. They could no longer live together. "We won the kids and lost each other," says Sandy. So they found two neighboring apartments where they lived "separate and apart," but were still able to maintain the family—albeit across halls.

Sandy and Madeline began tours of college campuses, raising money for their defense. Their next day in court, in September of last year, brought what they termed another miracle. Their husbands, both remarried, went to court for permanent custody of the children. Instead of granting custody to the men, however, the court reversed its previous order and said Sandy and Madeline could have the children and live together.

But the fight isn't over. The two ex-husbands have moved on to the state appeals court for a custody hearing, set in late October. Their appeals brief says that two lesbian mothers could cause the children to "have a greater acceptance of homosexuality." Sandy and Madeline don't expect the case to see final resolution until it reaches the only judicial body from which there can be no appeal—the U.S. Supreme Court. Their American Civil Liberties Union attorney expects the custody battle to consume another four years.

Madeline says the two are trying to bring up the children outside of strictly defined male/female roles. "We both discipline the kids. We both do outside jobs. We both do inside jobs, and so do all the kids. We try to impress on them that there are no masculine jobs or female jobs. There's just jobs."

The couple bristles at the suggestion that their homosexuality could in some way be detrimental to the children. "A lot of people talk about role models," says Sandy, who just picked up a master's degree in psychosexual nursing from the University of Washington. "But the kids aren't watching parents to see how they relate sexually. They're watching to see how adults get along, how they relate. Whether the parents are of the opposite sex isn't the issue. The kids just want to see some good ways to relate to other people." —RANDY SHILTS

CANNIBALIZATION OF A HERO

On August 28, 1975, the organized gay movement was presented, once again, with a genuine gay celebrity. In 1972 the movement got Dr. Howard Brown. This is the year it got Leonard Matlovich, complete with *Time* magazine cover story and a press following in almost every city's daily newspapers.

His statement "The military gave me a Bronze Star for killing two men and discharged me for loving one," is by now a classic quotation packaged and ready for future almanacs and yearbooks.

Matlovich has a way about him—a way of convincing heterosexual, middle-class, conservative, even redneck audiences that it is "okay to be gay"—that gay people are human beings, too. Matlovich is a person heterosexual America can swallow.

The organized gay movement has recognized this potential and has tried, for four months, to latch on to it. But Matlovich now feels "used," he told *The Advocate*. It all happened to him quite suddenly. He chose to come out of the closet as an open homosexual in the military in March. The decision was made quietly, after a few talks with attorneys, and without fanfare.

"My whole experience of the gay 'movement' had been the gay bars near the military bases in Pensacola, Florida, and Alexandria, Virginia. I may have heard *The Advocate* mentioned once, I don't know. I didn't even know there was such a thing as the National Gay Task Force," Matlovich recalls.

After he launched his battle with the military—a battle that was as yet unpublicized—he lost what few gay friends he did have. "They were afraid of me," he says. "Afraid of the investigation. Afraid they would be implicated. I was completely alone."

Then came the date that by now is engraved in his mind as the turning point of his life—the day *The New York Times* published its Matlovich article, the day citizen Matlovich became media fad Matlovich.

When he was catapulted, August 28, into media stardom, he was still alone—without advice, without friends, and without help.

He was alone, that is, for about a day. His telephone began to ring continually at all hours of the day and night. Demands, requests, invitations, calls for help, offers of help. These were only nibbles—a foretaste of the full-scale cannibalization that was beginning.

Among the callers and visitors, Matlovich found one person he felt he could trust, who would stand by him—Al Seviere, a disabled veteran. He clung to Seviere like a drowning kid clutching a life raft. Together they tried to cope with the flood of demands. Every gay group in the country, it seemed, wanted Matlovich for a personal appearance. And every television reporter and news

LESBIANS IN THE MILITARY

by Sasha Gregory-Lewis

We lesbians in the armed services share, by and large, most of the discrimination suffered by gay men.

Additionally, we are continually faced with sexism in the military—both on an institutional level and on a personal level.

There are lesbian purges, relying, just as they do in the male service majority, on rumor, innuendo, jealousy, and informants.

Suspicions are aroused by default. There is overwhelming pressure to have sex with males, to socialize with males.

Table talk centers around dates, boyfriends, husbands, good-looking men.

The lesbian must either play the heterosexual game or arouse the suspicions that will result in a viciously maneuvered exit from the service.

Most of my lesbian military friends cave in and play the game—they like the service, or they need their jobs badly. They save their lesbian souls for brief exploits during liberty or leave.

I ran into this kind of lesbian invisibility one weekend in the Coast Guard Reserve typing pool when another female yeoman noticed my gold ring (which looks like a wedding band).

"What does your husband do?" Sue asked.

"Oh, I'm not married," I told her.

"Well," she stuttered, "what do *you* do?"

"My lover and I have a contractual relationship," I explained, continuing with a discussion of the pitfalls of marriage and the values of contracts.

I could see that Sue thought I was weird—she was standing two feet farther away from me than when we began the conversation. After all, living together isn't exactly acceptable in the conventional military mind.

But she never caught on to the fact that my "lover" wasn't a man. That would not only have been weird. It would have been inconceivable.

We became fairly friendly during the rest of my stay in the unit—at least, I didn't have to talk about my "boyfriend," and when I shared my experience of building my own home, she became (as did everyone else) more convinced that my mysterious "lover" was a man.

Whatever bit of humor can be salvaged from a lesbian's military experience is soon lost amidst the other forms of institutionalized discrimination which gay men also face.

There are no travel or survival allowances made for lovers—only spouses. Lovers are banned from military exchanges and commissaries—only spouses and other "dependents" are allowed. Lovers don't get medical care; that also is only for spouses and dependents.

Then there is the end of service—the discharge. In one way lesbians benefit from the sexism of the civilian world in the less-than-honorable or dishonorable discharge situation. While men are nearly always required to show their discharge papers before getting a job, women aren't—most employers don't really conceive the possibility that a woman may have had military experience (military women aren't really taken seriously—in or out of the service).

But women get a bum deal in other ways which their gay male counterparts don't encounter. Despite the publicity about recent attempts by the military to provide a degree of equality to women, the armed forces are light-years away from achieving that goal.

Typing—or some form of nursing—is always available as an "opportunity" for the enlisted woman, but the more challenging and exciting jobs don't have room for more than token women.

Women are relegated to serving their country in traditional women's jobs, whatever their desires or capabilities; and despite the promises of recruiters generously depicting the "career training" available in the military, few women are given these opportunities. Women are still girls in the armed services—in every sense of the word.

writer in the country was pounding on his door for the precious exclusive interview. Every gay group in the nation was trying to organize a benefit for Matlovich—without, on many occasions, checking first to see if he needed money or for what he needed it.

Speaking agendas were arranged for him—by just about everyone, often without contract or written confirmation. Speaking engagements were canceled. Media representatives were stood up. Airplanes were missed.

Schedules were upset. Agreements were ignored or forgotten. It seemed impossible to make sense out of what had become the "Matlovich mess."

Then the complaints began. Volunteers who couldn't take the confusion began to abandon Matlovich like rats scrambling off a sinking ship.

Demands on him continued to increase; it seemed as if every gay individual in the country felt he had a right to the gay celebrity's time. Gay people acted as if they owned him. Citizen Matlovich became property Matlovich. The cannibalism was nearly complete.

No one, it seemed, noticed that he was becoming a shell of a person—worn out, tired, confused. Anyone could see it, but no one looked. He was, after all, a property, an object, a tool, a machine, a media feast for publicity-starved activists.

If the organized gay movement has gone sour on Matlovich, he has also gone sour on the organized gay movement. It's not gay people—"the man on the street, I don't want to lose touch with him"—that he's running from, but the rest; the people who think they know what he should be doing and where and when. The people who think they own him.

Matlovich accepts his share of the responsibility for the ritual slaughter of citizen Matlovich, but only his share. He has concluded, he told *The Advocate,* that the further away from the gay "movement" he stays, the happier everyone will be.

Matlovich, in fact, does not need any money for his own case. This is amply being taken care of, his attorney, David Addlestone, told *The Advocate,* by the Carnegie Foundation through the Georgetown University School of Law. Matlovich does need money to live on. He also wants to raise money for other gay causes and cases, but this hasn't been clear until now.

In an effort to straighten out his personal and public affairs, Matlovich has retained another attorney to set up a foundation to handle all of the benefit money he raises. "I have a tremendous potential to raise money for the movement," Matlovich realizes, and he is apparently beginning to get worldly-wise and serious about cashing in on his celebrity status to benefit the cause of gay rights.

He is also planning a vacation, a breather to straighten out his head, his feelings. His volunteer gay booking agents have, it seems, failed to schedule regular days of rest. He isn't left with time to get his laundry done while he's on the road.

Meanwhile, observers are taking a "wait and see" position—waiting to see if Matlovich can make the tough decisions required to clean up the carnage of four months of celebrity status.

Dr. Howard Brown went through the celebrity wringer a few years ago. He had expansive plans for what he thought he could achieve on behalf of the gay-rights movement, but as he tried to realize those plans he became torn, demoralized, and perhaps more than a little defeated.

Howard Brown died almost exactly one year ago.—SASHA GREGORY-LEWIS

THE AGE OF DISCO

"Shame, shame, shame—shame on you, if you can't dance too." From Hollywood's Studio One to Le Jardin in Gotham, everybody's doing it: the hustle, the bump, the time warp, and the continental (not to be confused with the Fred and Ginger version).

For the entertainment industry, 1975 is the Year of the Discotheque. No doubt about it, the masses have turned on to what's been getting us off for the last four years.

In this country, discos *were* almost completely gay. During the last year, hetero clubs have been opening faster than Gloria Gaynor can say "good-bye." Independent surveys indicate that at least seventy percent of the discos are *still* gay. Many straight people confess that they have *more* fun at the gay clubs.

The disco revival began in 1971, spearheaded by the gay underground. Defunct factories, markets, and restaurants were transformed into dance meccas where gay people boogied their way to happiness. The atmosphere was wild, free, and outrageous. Attire ranged from black tie to tie-dye. Discothequers lost themselves in a frantic world of nonstop music and madness. Nobody cared who did what to whom just as long as you didn't stand still.

About two years ago discos surfaced, and now there are an estimated five hundred in New York, one hundred in Southern California, and an additional seven hundred sprinkled between the coasts. The numbers seem to change daily.

The recession seems to be primarily responsible for disco's popularity. At a time when money is as tight as one's pants, discos offer cheap thrills, entertainment, and escapism.

Discos make dollars and *sense* for club owners who can no longer afford the hefty fees commanded by the better "live" groups and attractions. And while rock groups were sometimes temperamental and undependable, hit records never have a bad night. Moreover, record companies are ecstatic over the disco boom. Platter pushers previously had to rely solely on radio airplay to make a hit record. Most radio playlists are tight and restrictive; so many discs were pressed and then never heard. Discos have changed all that.

"Rock the Boat," "I've Got the Music in Me," "Never Can Say Good-bye," and "Shame, Shame, Shame" are just a few of the smashes that owe their success to disco airplay. Stars like Gloria Gaynor, Disco Tex and the Sex-O-Lettes, Carol Douglas, and Van McCoy were born in discos. Others, such as Labelle and the Supremes, were reborn there.

Now record companies have disco reps who monitor the clubs, listen to the jocks, and supply them with new products. Major labels even supply the clubs with "special mixes" of certain songs, designed for optimum reproduction when played over a disco's elaborate sound system.

Where all of this will end, no one seems to know. It looks like discos just may be here to stay.

—STAFF REPORT

> "*I think gay people like us because...we've always been different. That's kind of being nonconformists, which is the same type of thing that gays are doing. It takes a lot of courage to be different.*"
> —THE POINTER SISTERS, POP DIVAS

BOOKS: *CONSENTING ADULT*

MARTIN DUBERMAN

Historian Martin Duberman came out of the closet in his scholarship with the publication of *Black Mountain: An Exploration in Community.* "Duberman's personal approach to his storytelling, his sharing of his *feelings* and experiences with the reader, is doubtless related to his gay consciousness as much as are the discussions of homosexuality," said critic Allen Young about the author's account of Black Mountain College, a quiet community of artists and intellectuals located in the Smoky Mountains of North Carolina from 1933 to 1956. Among the gay cultural figures who taught or studied there were writer Paul Goodman, playwright Eric Bentley, composer Lou Harrison, and poet Robert Duncan.

Duberman told *The Advocate,* "One thing I feel is very important for gay people to understand and that I have learned from my own love life and experiences is that we have to learn not to judge ourselves by straight standards of what constitutes a so-called healthy pattern in someone's sexual life or history....We have to start affirming instead of apologizing."

There has never been a book quite like Laura Z. Hobson's *Consenting Adult* simply because there has never been a book that describes what parents of gay children go through. And for that reason it is rather more difficult to evaluate from a gay perspective. This is a book for our parents, not for us.

Those of us who have come out to our parents will find it a rather discomforting reminder of the emotional risks that attended the choice. Those of us who haven't will find some of our fears confirmed by Hobson's vivid and unflinching depiction of the pain and confusion caused in some families by the disclosure. If our lifestyles and perceptions about ourselves as gay people are hard for our parents to understand, *Consenting Adult* demonstrates that misunderstanding and alienation are a two-way street.

When Jeff writes his letter from a New England prep school in 1960, it signals the beginning of an ordeal that will stretch out over a decade. Psychoanalysis, guilt, reproaches, rejection, silence—all the things that should not, very credibly do occur in this happy upper-middle-class family, proud of its easy intimacy and its liberality, but totally unprepared to deal with the "abnormality" of one of its members. Now the clever, ingenuous younger child, Jeff, good in school and crazy about sports, has been taken away from them and a gay son—a sullen, uncooperative stranger at that—put in his place.

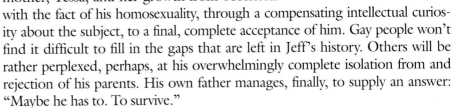

Although the events in *Consenting Adult* parallel Jeff's own coming of age and coming out in the sixties, the book's focus is on his mother, Tessa, and her growth from obsession with the fact of his homosexuality, through a compensating intellectual curiosity about the subject, to a final, complete acceptance of him. Gay people won't find it difficult to fill in the gaps that are left in Jeff's history. Others will be rather perplexed, perhaps, at his overwhelmingly complete isolation from and rejection of his parents. His own father manages, finally, to supply an answer: "Maybe he has to. To survive."

This book is bound to have its greatest impact on a gut level—for it is a testament to guts and endurance and that over-abused entity called mother love. Hobson's picture of the mother weeping over her son's letter—not "the ordinary weeping woman; it was rather, a roaring sobbing, of an animal gored"—and her solemn, near-hysterical efforts to see Jeff's homosexuality in the light of normalcy and to do right by him as well, are directly on target.

The real subject of *Consenting Adult* is not homophobia or gay liberation. It is about the struggle of a woman simultaneously locked out of her family and caught between its warring factions, living day-to-day with a consciousness of being different somewhat like our own but truly dissimilar, an outsider even to her son, the true outsider himself. There are millions of women living like that. Not all of them are as educated or advantaged as Tessa, not all of them as open-minded and earnest as Laura Hobson, but they face the same struggle Hobson writes about. For them, and for many of us, *Consenting Adult* is bound to be a moving and affirmative experience.

—GEORGE WHITMORE

Touching Your Lifestyle   Issue 197, August 25, 1976   In Two Sections, 75 cents

ADVOCATE

Reg ... takes Exotic ...
and Launches a New Career in the
California Countryside, page ...

That 'Abracadabra' man, Carleton Carpenter, is still on stage, page 27.

An affair with singer Barbara Cook, page 33.

Good News for New York

A special pull-out supplement of ADVOCATE political endorsements for the up-coming September 14 primary.

PORTFOLIO: An exhibit at Bicentennial erotica in San Francisco, page 16.

An exclusive ADVOCATE INTERVIEW: James Leo Herlihy, page 21.

ADVOCATE

Touching Your Lifestyle Issue 203   November 17, 1976 In Two Sections 75¢

Special Report BLACK & GAY

New York's Octogenarian Artist **MINNA CITRON**

Miami's Gay Cuban Connection

On Their Toes **BALLET TROCKADERO**

Exclusive Interview **SHIRLEY MACLAINE**

ADVOCATE

Touching Your Lifestyle Issue 204   December 1, 1976 In Two Sections 75¢

THANKSGIVING FEAST

In New York
LINDA HOPKINS Talks About 'Me & Bessie'
The Gossip According To **JOYCE HABER**
A Visit With **R. BUCKMINSTER FULLER**
Special Report: **GAY ORGANIZATIONS Part III**

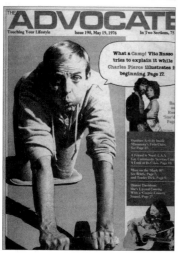

ADVOCATE

Touching Your Lifestyle   Issue 190, May 19, 1976   In Two Sections, 75

What a Camp! Vito Russo
tries to explain it while
Charles Pierce illustrates it
beginning Page 17.

DIGGING IN

1976 "Summer was an interesting time for the Archives, with a record number of visitors, including women from California, England, and Italy. Whether I was talking with lesbians from Manhattan or Europe, the concern expressed for the preservation of our herstory creates an energy that whisks the archives from the past into our daily lives....In London, women are producing street theater in the Punch and Judy tradition in support of Wages for Housework. In Italy, lesbian groups are beginning to meet in the high schools. Some of our visitors organized lesbian centers or were responsible for coordinating such notable events as the Lesbian Herstory Exploration near Los Angeles. This summer brought a feeling of universal lesbian power—women united in the celebration and adventure of pursuing our identity."

These words appeared in the fall of 1976, in the third newsletter of the Lesbian Herstory Archives, which a year earlier had taken up residence in the Upper West Side apartment I shared with my then lover, now loved friend, Deborah Edel. The idea of the Archives had been born in 1973 in a consciousness-raising group composed of lesbian members of an organization called the Gay Academic Union (GAU). Concerned with the plight of gay students and teachers in high schools and colleges, the GAU was a rallying point for gay scholarship and battles against isolation and homophobia in the city's schools. Most of us were part of the city and state university system, but soon we split into the usual early seventies factions: sexist gay men, Marxists, and lesbian-separatists. I was a member of the latter two groups.

Several of us in the group, who had come out before the Stonewall Rebellion and the advent of a formal feminist movement, felt the need to establish a grass-roots lesbian archives project. We remembered a world of lesbian culture that had nourished us but that was rapidly disappearing. We also knew, in this early heyday of lesbian publishing, that our presses and publishers were fragile undertakings, and we were concerned about preserving all their precious pro-

A fire watcher at the Michigan Womyn's Music Festival as seen through the lens of Joan E. Biren, a pioneering lesbian photographer also known as JEB. The author of two groundbreaking volumes, *Eye to Eye: Portraits of Lesbians* and *Making a Way: Lesbians Out Front,* JEB has chronicled the lives of gay people for over twenty years, gaining a reputation as one of the lesbian community's outstanding documentary artists.

ductions. But the strongest reason for creating the archives was to end the silence of patriarchal history about us—women who loved women. We wanted our story to be told by us, shared by us, and preserved by us.

By 1976, when national news was dominated by the Presidential race, the Democratic nominee paid lip service to the need for a federal gay-rights bill and a change in the military ban on gay service members. And though these issues disappeared from public debate before the year was out, the Carter-Mondale win would change the lesbian and gay community's relationship to the presidency. Carter would become the first President to appoint an open lesbian to a federal position and to whose White House gay and lesbian activists would be invited.

The pages of *The Advocate* that year are filled with examples of lesbians and gay men gaining a foothold in American culture. Dr. Tom Waddell, a decathlete, is featured in his Olympic finery. Vito Russo praises two cinematic breakthroughs: Harvey Perr's *War Widow* and *The Naked Civil Servant*. Reporter Sasha Gregory-Lewis undertakes a year-long national study of gay and lesbian organizations and concludes that religious and student groups are thriving while political organizations—with the notable exception of the National Gay Task Force under the aegis of Jean O'Leary—are struggling. We see Olga Broumas, fresh from her victory in the Yale Younger Poets competition; the Red Dyke Theater in Atlanta; Lily Tomlin announcing her Presidential candidacy; Ruth Simpson celebrating the publication of her *From the Closets to the Courts*.

The Advocate's conservative publisher, David Goodstein, ushers in the new year with an editorial warning against the gay "radical left" and "obstructionists" who could derail the movement's push into the mainstream. Immediately, in letters published in the next issue, representatives of the "fringe"—Russo, Arnie Kantrowitz, George Whitmore—decry Goodstein's narrow vision.

I was thirty-seven years old in 1976. I had entered the lesbian subculture in 1958, when I walked through the doors of the Sea Colony, a working-class, butch-fem lesbian bar in New York's Greenwich Village. I had learned, in my personal experience and in working on organizing the Lesbian Herstory Archives, how crucial memory is to a people. And in this bicentennial year, against a backdrop of a nation retelling its historical myths, a historical sense was emerging in the lesbian and gay community and in the pages of *The Advocate*.

In a February issue, a reporter pieces together a slim gay history, beginning with the sodomy laws of the thirteen colonies and ending with the witchhunting of the McCarthy period. The last issue of the year heralds the appearance of Jonathan Ned Katz's *Gay American History*, the pioneer work that will forever change our sense of ourselves in time.

Throughout the year, a steady stream of researchers and browsers walked through our kitchen to reach the small back room where the Lesbian Herstory Archives collection was lodged. Before the year was out, the collection had spilled out into two more rooms. Copies of *The Advocate*, along with *off our backs, Gay Community News*, and *Womanews*, were piled in large gray archival boxes that reached from the floor to the ceiling.

No matter how hard the national or local struggle for change was, life at the Archives always gave evidence of thriving and resistant lesbian communities. Every visitor, every phone call, and every entry in our visitors' book served as testimony to the importance of preserving our own public record. More than the Carter-Mondale win, more than our political and legal victories and losses, it was this concentration of gay men and lesbians developing our own historical sense that made 1976 a momentous year for us. —JOAN NESTLE

"*Like a large number of men, I have had homosexual experiences and I am not ashamed. Homosexuality is so much in fashion it no longer makes news.*"
—ACTOR MARLON BRANDO

"*When I was ten or eleven, I remember very vividly, I got it on with guys. But it was just experimentation....I was a gay bandido.*"
—ROCK MUSICIAN TED NUGENT

T I M E L I N E

JANUARY   San Francisco's newly elected mayor, George Moscone, appointed gay activist Harvey Milk to the Board of Permit Appeals. ❑ In a *Chicago Tribune* story, Bette Midler claimed she "did not have a gay following" and "wouldn't know a homosexual if I saw one." ❑ The California Insurance Commission issued new regulations for insurance companies, forbidding discrimination on the basis of sexual orientation. ❑ NBC Televsion's "What America Thinks" reported that 48 percent of two thousand Americans surveyed objected to their child being assigned to a class taught by a homosexual teacher.

FEBRUARY   Presidential hopeful Jimmy Carter said he opposed discrimination on the basis of sexual orientation. ❑ The San Francisco federal District Court of Appeals ruled that advocacy of gay rights and public admission of homosexuality constitute a "flaunting" of homosexuality and can be cause for dismissal from a civil service job. ❑ Malstrom Air Force Base in Great Falls, Montana, began a gay purge after a serviceman tried to commit suicide by drug overdose following the breakup of a gay love affair; forty people were investigated, but fewer than half were discharged. ❑ Sal Mineo, a gay director and actor known for his roles in *Rebel Without a Cause* and *Fortune and Men's Eyes,* was gunned down in a West Hollywood alley. ❑ A Detroit court awarded Carmen Leo $200,000 in damages after he claimed a rear-end automobile accident made him homosexual. ❑ Los Angeles Deputy Mayor Maurice Weiner was convicted of lewd conduct for groping a vice officer in a public bathroom; he later resigned.

MARCH   In *Doe v. Commonwealth Attorney of Virginia,* the U.S. Supreme Court upheld the rights of states to pass laws against private homosexual acts between consenting adults; the ruling sparked protests in at least four major cities. ❑ Rudi Cox of San Francisco became the first openly gay deputy sheriff in the nation. ❑ Harvey Milk was fired from San Francisco's Board of Permit Appeals after he announced his candidacy for City Council, a bid he later lost. ❑ Utah County police and Brigham Young University security officers raided roadside rest stops near Provo, resulting in fourteen arrests and one suicide.

APRIL   Metropolitan Life Insurance Company accorded gay couples married status for life insurance beneficiary rights if they had lived together for at least a year. ❑ National Public Radio scored a media first with its "Options in Education" series which covered the dilemma facing gay and lesbian teachers and students. ❑ The highly promoted First Annual Lavender World's Fair in Los Angeles quickly closed when a near riot occurred after the Pointer Sisters left without performing due to lack of payment. ❑ The Florida Supreme Court ruled that a playful grope in the "dark recesses" of a gay bar does not constitute "lewd and lascivious behavior." ❑ Arson destroyed the Seattle Gay Community Services Center. ❑ A new gay organization, the Association for the Protection of Individual Rights, was founded in Tel Aviv.

MAY   The Los Angeles City Council banned antigay discrimination in civic employment. ❑ Following 150 arrests, gay-bathhouse owners in Montreal, Canada, decided to close their establishments until after the Summer Olympics in August. ❑ Jeremy Thorpe, leader of Great Britain's Liberal Party, resigned over a gay sex scandal, saying he could no longer lead his party effectively, though he adamantly denied he was a homosexual.

JUNE   After Jimmy Carter withdrew his support of a gay-rights plank in the Democratic Party plaform, the platform committee of the Democratic National Committee voted to remove it. ❑ Retired Army Major General Edwin A. Walker, a longtime right-wing activist, was arrested for public lewdness in a park restroom in Dallas. ❑ After a lesbian from Philadelphia High School for Girls asked another woman to her prom, the school's vice principal informed the lesbian's mother. Dyketactics!, a radical lesbian group, picketed the school. ❑ Courts forced Rhode Island to allow gay organizations to participate in the state's bicentennial parade. ❑ The U.S. District Court of Appeals in San Francisco issued a restraining order prohibiting the Marine Corps from discharging Staff Sergeant Robert LeBlanc on the grounds of homosexuality. ❑ The Washington, D.C., City Council unanimously passed an ordinance banning discrimination on the basis of sexual orientation in child custody and visitation cases.

JULY   The Democratic National Convention in New York City did not include any discussion of gay and lesbian concerns, and a proposed ten-thousand-strong protest failed to attract more than six hundred gays and lesbians. ❑ Leonard Matlovich lost his first-round court appeal to win reinstatement in the Air Force. ❑ The Young Adult Ministry Board of the U.S. Catholic Conference voted to support gays, declaring that gay people suffer from "questionable scriptural interpretation." ❑ Three gay men faced charges of disturbing the peace after they winked at two straight men in a Des Moines restaurant; the straight men claimed the wink nauseated them. ❑ After the overthrow of a right-wing dictatorship, the first gay organization in Portugal was formed.

AUGUST   The U.S. Immigration and Naturalization Service restricted its ban on known homosexuals to those who had been convicted of a same-sex crime. ❑ The Minneapolis Civil Rights Department found the Big Brothers organization in violation of city antidiscrimination statutes for denying a gay man a position as a Big Brother. ❑ A University of California study found that 14 percent of male NCAA athletes had engaged in two or more homosexual experiences during the previous two years; 8 percent claimed to be exclusively homosexual.

SEPTEMBER   Massachusetts Democrat Gerry Studds, who would later come out as gay, won reelection to Congress despite a mud-slinging campaign by his opponent criticizing Studds for his cosponsorship of a federal gay-rights bill. ❑ The American Psychological Association adopted a policy recommending that a parent's sexual orientation not be the primary concern in child-custody cases. ❑ The Western Women's Bank—the first retail bank in Northern California organized, funded, and founded by women—opened its doors. ❑ President Gerald Ford, cornered by gay activists in Ann Arbor, confessed that he was not aware that homosexuality was used as a basis for exclusion in immigration. ❑ *Lavender Woman*, Chicago's lesbian-feminist newspaper, suspended publication after five years. ❑ The San Francisco police won the fourth annual Gays vs. Cops Softball Classic after a substantial loss to gays the year before.

OCTOBER   The San Francisco Human Rights Committee unanimously ruled that Pacific Telephone and Telegraph must publish an employment statement explicitly banning discrimination against gays; Pacific Bell was sued three years later for violating the ban and found guilty of illegal discrimination. ❑ "Blue-

In February, when law student Andy Lippincott made the above explanation to romantically inclined divorcée Joanie Caucus in Garry Trudeau's popular comic strip "Doonesbury," sixty million readers were treated to a four-day dialogue on homosexuality and society's reaction to it. Although controversy was expected, only five of the 450 newspapers carrying the nationally syndicated strip refused to run the series.

Democratic Presidential hopeful Senator Henry Jackson of Washington State confused gays and straights alike in April when he declared: "Our people want hard work. We don't want gay work. We don't want gay jobs. You have your gay jobs. You just do your own thing and stay away." Jackson further stated that he would not advocate a federal gay-rights bill.

boy Forum," a weekly television show on WKID–TV, Channel 51 in Miami, claimed to be the first weekly gay-themed show in the nation. ❑ Alfred Smith, Jr., of New Jersey, alleged that he acted in self-defense when he shot a gay man six times, explaining that the man had made a pass at him. ❑ A resident assistant at the University of Virginia who was also Gay Student Union president won the right to keep his job despite accusations of "conflict of interest." ❑ Lesbian poet Olga Broumas, a University of Oregon women's studies instructor, won the 1976 Yale Younger Poets Award.

NOVEMBER Openly gay Minnesota State Senator Allan Spear and openly lesbian Massachusetts State Representative Elaine Noble easily won reelection bids. ❑ The National Conference of Catholic Bishops called homosexuality "immoral," but also stated that gay people "have a right to respect, friendship, and justice." ❑ Controversial San Francisco gay activist the Rev. Ray Broshears, who had advocated using guns for a gay street patrol, was appointed to the Republican State Central Committee of California. ❑ In Sydney, Australia, a day-long symbolic trial called the Tribunal on Homosexuals and Discrimination prompted a deputy prime minister, two ministers, and a labor leader to urge massive reform of antigay laws.

DECEMBER The director of the U.S. Bureau of Prisons banned gay publications from all federal correctional facilities. ❑ The California state Supreme Court ruled in the case of a straight couple that unmarried couples can have binding legal property-sharing agreements. ❑ The Indianapolis Toys for Tots program, which distributes toys to needy children, declined donations from the Gay People's Union and the local Metropolitan Community Church until unfavorable media coverage forced the group to accept the offerings. ❑ Police raided the Boston Gay Men's Center after hearing reports that liquor was being served to patrons who were watching gay porno films there, but the action yielded only a print of the Judy Garland version of *A Star Is Born* and a six-pack of beer.

MURDER AS A MISDEMEANOR

In June, four teenage boys beat and killed twenty-one-year-old Richard Heakin outside a gay bar in Tucson, Arizona. Six months later, the four youths were found guilty as expected, but both gays and straights were stunned when Judge Benjamin Birdsall sentenced the youths to probation until their twenty-first birthdays. "These youths and their parents have suffered enough," said Birdsall, calling the boys "worthwhile members of the community." The judge further ruled that there was no reason for psychological treatment in what he termed "a scuttle."

The usually docile local gay community became enraged over the verdict, arousing the sympathies of the normally conservative state media, which labeled the murder Arizona's major crime story of the year.

WOMYN'S SPACE

Two thousand women descended on 120 acres of Michigan land in July for the first of what became an annual tradition: the Michigan Womyn's Music Festival. Performers included Maxine Feldman, whose two lesbian anthems, "Angry Atthis" and "Amazon," were released on a 1972 single, and Alix Dobkin, known internationally for her lesbian-produced 1973 record *Lavender Jane Loves Women.*

Also singing was Cris Williamson, whose Olivia Records album *The Changer and the Changed* sold over a quarter of a million copies, making it the best-selling lesbian record of all time. With such additional performers as Holly Near, the socially responsible musician who had joined the women's music scene with *Imagine My Surprise,* and Meg "Here Come the Leaping Lesbians" Christian, the festival was destined to become a lesbian cultural touchstone.

LILY TOMLIN

Lily Tomlin is an original and demands to be studied. Her career is unlike that of any other American entertainer in that she shows us ourselves by showing us parts of who she is through her diverse characters. For those of you who do not read, go to nightclubs or concerts, listen to radio, watch television, buy record albums, or, more recently, go to the movies, Lily Tomlin is the funniest group of people in the business.

Interviewing Tomlin, therefore, is a little like sharing a lifeboat with Sybil at the oars. *They* are there at all times, and one is almost never unaware of them. If Lily says something with which Ernestine disagrees, a snort somehow works itself into the conversation. Edith Ann comments occasionally upon the way of things and promptly disappears, leaving a smiling Tomlin.

We are at a small restaurant on Santa Monica Boulevard in Los Angeles, having dinner on our first evening together.

The fourteen people from the next table are on their way out and gather around our table. A woman says that they'd like to have her autograph because they "came all the way from Fairfield" and Tomlin is the "only movie star they've seen." A twelve-year-old girl holds out a scrap of paper, and Lily, saying "I don't sign autographs," writes: "I'm a thirty-two-year-old actress, and I'm trying to find some meaning to my life. Love, Lily." They exchange enormous smiles.

We discuss how television and movies are or are not changing with respect to stereotypes. Lily doesn't see many movies and is shocked to hear that words like "faggot" and "pansy" are still in use on the screen. "I was recently sent a script for a television movie which was supposed to have a slightly elevated consciousness," she says. "It's just so corny I can't believe it. I mean, their idea of an elevated consciousness is when the woman considers getting a part-time job. I just sent it back with a note and I said, 'Thank you for thinking of me for this, but I cannot participate in it because of my own personal views. It simply isn't radical enough from a feminist viewpoint.' Which is no big deal, but you have to do it or how will they know why you're turning it down? Gee, this piece is getting awfully dull. Isn't it?"

The following day Lily and I are driving down to Torrance to see a 1956 Corvette she's interested in buying. I'm at the wheel, and Lily is controlling the off-on switch of the tape recorder. She asks me to print whatever I find on the tape. She is interviewing me about the corduroy jumpsuit I'm wearing:

I don't know, Vito. This is going to be real duddy. That's why I stopped doing interviews. Where did you get the jumpsuit?

At Stone Free in New York.

Do you have it dry-cleaned between wearings?

Yes, every time.

Oh, well, that's quite expensive, see, because I imagine a garment like that would cost in the neighborhood of three to five dollars to clean.

Yeah, it'll cost me about four thousand dollars in the long run.

Have you actually calculated that? Because I know that the average person in their lifetime spends four hours out of 569,400 hours experiencing orgasm. And I for one spend nine hours a month conditioning my hair.

Lily, can we talk about *Nashville*?

Listen, Vito, this is for *The Advocate*. It's going to look funny if we don't discuss the gay issue.

"I'm always outraged when I hear about all this persecution and oppression of gays, and I think it's marvelous that people are now fighting for their rights. I've always felt very deeply that my first loyalty was to the homosexual situation."
—POET STEPHEN SPENDER

"What I'm trying to say with my life, with nearly everything I write and do, is 'Hey, don't change people. Don't meet somebody and see in them what might be there. See in them what is there.'"
—POET AND PERFORMER ROD McKUEN

Yeah?

Well, what did Bette Midler say about it?

She said that it's okay to be anything you want as long as you don't let your dog shit on the street.

Oh, see? Bette is wittier than I am.

Yeah, she is.

Fuck you, you commie queer....Okay, let's get down to business. Vito, do you think that there's a good reason why gay performers don't come out of the closet?

Sure. People don't come out for all kinds of reasons. Some people have families that they're considering and their state of mind.

Yeah, but that doesn't mean any of that is justified or right, even though on a professional level it's still not safe to do so. You know, I've been associated with people who consider themselves very hip, and I've sat in a room with them, and when someone overtly homosexual leaves the room, they will acknowledge among themselves that the person who has just left is homosexual and they are not. And men are the worst offenders. Very simply it can be summed up...how *can* it be summed up? It cannot be summed up, simply. And trade this Vega in as soon as possible.

We are in Torrance and the Corvette is a disaster. When Lily tries to open the door it won't open and the steering wheel comes loose in her hands. The car has no grille and someone has painted a sloppy white stripe around the body. After saying "Are you kidding?" as politely as possible, we are on our way. On her last special, Tomlin did a little sketch about a clown born to "normal" parents in Dull City, U.S.A. The clown had no friends and the doctor pronounced to the distraught parents, "In my opinion, your daughter is a clown." One day she met another clown, who took her to a place unknown to the residents of Dull City, where clowns could have fun. It was raided and she was taken to prison to be "de-clowned." Stripped of her abnormal ways, she emerged from prison an ex-clown. Her friends were waiting for her, saddened by the change. As she shook hands with one of them, though, her hand came off in his, and she smiled broadly. Once a clown, always a clown.

The next day my mother called and said, "I saw the Lily Tomlin show last night. That clown sequence was about gay people, wasn't it?" It was about people who are different, I told her.

"Well, it was really beautiful."

A few hours later, Lily calls. She doesn't even say hello:

"Listen. Don't you think our parents should all support their children's lifestyle and that it's our job to teach them the truth of a situation if they've been lied to?" I tell her yes, I believe that it is.

"That's what I thought. I can't stay on the phone. I've got work to do."

Lily's clown sequence is becoming a classic. High schools and colleges are requesting its use in minority problems classes. She is working.

Her new album, *Modern Scream,* discusses gay stereotypes from a novel and myth-exploding viewpoint. She is working.

She works at change, always with an eye toward being a little gentle with those who don't understand. She is in the business of exploration, and she's taking everyone with her. It's going to be an interesting trip. When you're as good as she is, you can get away with anything. There's no telling how far a proud clown can go.

—VITO RUSSO

DR. TOM WADDELL

"The guy who wins the decathlon is supposed to be the world's greatest athlete," muses Tom Waddell, not adding that the description would have made him the world's sixth-greatest athlete back in 1968 when he got that ranking in the Mexico City Olympics.

But that estimation of the winner of the grueling two-day track-and-field event meets with no debate from athletic observers who tout the decathlon as the sport for the "perfect athlete." Waddell's credentials in this realm of perfection are impressive. At age thirty, a time when many athletes are cashing their retirement checks, Waddell took second place in the American Athletic Union decathlon national championships. After rounding off that year with an Olympic bid, he went on to set the current world's record for decathletes in the thirty-four-year-old age group.

Despite the fact that Waddell, at thirty-eight, still has a body most men left behind in high school, you won't be hearing any stereotyped jock talk from his mustached lips. Not your all-American behemoth of hyper-masculinity, the tall, slender Waddell is more apt to talk of existentialism and social reform than God and country. He's also gay, something that he sees as neither a salient nor deplorable part of his character.

Check off the stereotype of star turns gay and hits lecture circuit. Far from parlaying his homosexuality into juicy honorariums, Waddell is peacefully practicing internal medicine in San Francisco. Though active homosexuality in sports has become a top conversation item at cocktail parties, Waddell prefers to focus on the more subtle gay aspects of big-time sports. "There's very little homosexuality in sports in terms of orgasm, but there's a lot of game-playing," he says. "There's a lot of hugs and ass-slapping—but it's all done in a very masculine context. It's like when they say, 'Hey, you caught a nice pass,' and then follow it up with a slap on the ass, okay, that's very masculine but *why* did they pick the *ass* to slap him on?"

He thinks that the recent fascination with homosexuality in sports is almost dirty-minded in its concentration on sleek, young bodies while forgetting that athletics has a bit more to offer the gay jock than hunky colleagues. Says Waddell, "When I go to a track meet, there are all kinds of attractive bodies there, but I'm not watching bodies, I'm watching a performance. I'm watching someone jumping over a hurdle, and that can be pure poetry. I'm not watching some hard-on under the trunks. People forget that you can just like sports for their own sake." —RANDY SHILTS

THE ALARMING SPREAD OF V.D.

Syphilis—a disease that can cripple, blind, lead to insanity, and kill. Gonorrhea—a disease of increasing virulence that can permanently scar the urinary tract, blind, and lead to severe arthritis.

These two venereal diseases, spreading throughout the United States at an alarming rate, have climbed to an epidemic level in the overall population. But gay V.D. workers have stopped using the term "epidemic" lately. The diseases have made inroads into the gay community that health experts now call "pandemic."

Partly due to the long-standing benign neglect that health and medical professions have showered on forms of V.D. generally unique to gay people, and partly because of the ignorance this neglect has engendered, a startling number of gay people aren't coming clean on this fundamental aspect of personal health.

The results show themselves in discomfiting figures. Data from the Centers for Disease Control (CDC) imply that half the nation's male syphilis victims are gay, a figure which would give gay men five times as many chances of having syphilis as men in the general nongay population. Norman Merino, director of the gay Los Angeles Venereal Disease Control Project, ventures to estimate that 40 percent of the nation's gonorrhea is among gay men, an estimate that would give a gay man four times as many chances of having gonorrhea as his heterosexual counterparts. This figure is rough, to be sure, but gay V.D. workers across the country, surveyed by *The Advocate,* aren't arguing.

The sheer number of gay people who will be affected by the maladies this year can give little comfort to any part of the gay community. The CDC estimates that 450,000 Americans will make personal acquaintance with syphilis in 1976. Of these, about 300,000 will be men—half of them gay.

The continued increase in gonorrhea, expected by the CDC to be between 8 and 10 percent this year, proves to be an even more formidable threat to the health of gay people. The CDC expects a whopping one million reported gonorrhea cases, but for every reported V.D. case, an estimated three to four go unreported. Says a CDC spokesperson, "Our latest estimate for gonorrhea this year is in the neighborhood of 2.6 million." And if gay people make up 40 percent of that number, it's a safe bet to estimate that once every thirty seconds, a gay person will contract gonorrhea this year.

You wouldn't expect to learn about this "love bug" from a Walt Disney movie, but you'd have about as much luck if you tried to learn about it from the public health or medical professions. The health professions do almost nothing to educate gay people on the health hazards of those deviations from the heterosexual missionary position: oral and anal copulation.

Gay V.D. workers lay much of the blame for the gay V.D. problem on the shoulders of the public health profession. Says Bob Hewes of the Gay Men's V.D. Clinic in Washington, D.C., "We have an epidemic of venereal disease in the gay community and it's primarily because of the attitudes of the straight community."

When the Los Angeles Gay Community Services Center printed its gay V.D. brochure two years ago, they found it was the first pamphlet dealing with gay V.D. problems in the United States. It took two years of prodding by gay activists before the Minnesota Department of Health would print a gay V.D. brochure. The Colorado Action Council on Venereal Disease is reported to have refused to print a gay V.D. pamphlet. Because of such attitudes, information on gay V.D remains almost nonexistent in the United States.

Gay men in the seventies had a host of sexually transmitted diseases to contend with, a fact that artist Dennis Forbes graphically illustrated.

The most telling sign of the times comes from the federal government. It sometimes bellyaches about the high V.D. rate among gay people, but it does nothing about it. The federal government last year spent $33.1 million on venereal disease control and prevention. Of that, only about $160,000—or about one-half of one percent—can be traced as being earmarked for V.D. projects specifically serving the needs of the gay community, despite the federal government's own figures that indicate a significant portion of the V.D. problem lies in the gay community.

What can be done to avoid these ills? Doctors still know very little about sexually transmitted disease. The only surefire way to avoid syphilis and gonorrhea is chastity, an alternative which most people find less than viable. A condom usually is effective against gonorrhea, but that won't do much for fellatio lovers. A good scrubbing of the genital areas with soap and water can kill off syphilis and gonorrhea germs, an alternative which doesn't help those enamored of being on the receiving end of anal intercourse.

The most prudent means of coming clean on V.D. is through a regular checkup every three months—and gay V.D. authorities are adamant about the ninety-day time limit. Yet a survey by the San Francisco Gay Health Project found that only one in three gay men has regular V.D. checkups and even fewer get regular throat and anal cultures.

The problem is compounded by the fact that many people do not know anal and throat gonorrhea exist, because of the neglect of health professionals. Few mainstream V.D. clinics in the United States regularly ask for throat or rectal cultures, assuming that the patient is heterosexual. Many gay people also feel intimidated about asking for such cultures—it can expose a homosexuality they might want to hide.

Faced with a health profession that would prefer to think gay V.D. doesn't exist and some gay people who would prefer that the health profession didn't find out, many gay organizations across the country have started their own, generally successful, V.D. clinics. The Milwaukee Gay People's Union V.D. clinic, funded through both city money and private donations, last year saw about 1,500 patients, a 50 percent increase over the previous (first) year of operation. The Gay Men's V.D. Clinic in Washington, D.C., saw only twenty-five patients a month when it began screening two years ago, but now sees nearly two hundred a month.

Since its inception less than two years ago, Chicago's Howard Brown Clinic has seen about four thousand gay people and expanded into a $12,000-a-year, privately funded operation. By far the most glittering success is the Los Angeles Gay Community Services Center Venereal Disease Control Project, which tests eight hundred gay people monthly. The project, started with CDC money and now supported by Los Angeles County, includes an epidemiology division that follows up on more syphilis cases than any other private agency in the county.

Behind much of the gay V.D. problem lies an overall reluctance of this society to deal with venereal disease at all. It continues to view the maladies in the context of Victorian morality. Venereal disease is something nice people don't talk about. Homosexuality is something that is talked about even less.

As San Francisco health worker Frank Meyers says, "V.D. is treated as a moral problem, not a health problem. There seems to be an overall feeling that V.D. is a dirty disease. Nice people don't get it. Until that changes, we aren't going to get anywhere."

—RANDY SHILTS

"Mayor Bradley turned the Fourth of July over to the [gays] in Los Angeles and gave 'em a parade down Hollywood Boulevard. I don't think the Fourth of July is a day to think of just gay people; it's a day for all of us."
—JOHN WAYNE, SUPER-BUTCH MOVIE STAR

CHARLES PIERCE
No individual has better embodied the spirit of camp than openly gay entertainer Charles Pierce. The flamboyant comedian and self-termed "male actress" has enjoyed one of the most successful and long-running drag acts in show business, performing dishy send-ups of Bette Davis, Tallulah Bankhead, Mae West, and other divas of the stage and screen to packed houses and rave reviews in theaters worldwide. But his most loyal fans over the years have been gay audiences, an allegiance he's never failed to acknowledge.

ALL ABOUT CAMP

As Susan Sontag noted in her famous essay, camp is the love of the extravagant, the exaggerated, converting the serious into the frivolous (or vice versa). It's a sensibility rather than an idea and exists in a rarefied atmosphere of esoterica. To discuss camp, therefore, is like smashing a toy to see what makes it run. The essence of camp is the unspoken amusement derived from knowing something is camp without having to explain why. Nobody asked Carmen Miranda why she wore ten-inch heels and danced around with a dozen bananas on her head. Carmen Miranda was just "too much."

To gay men, camp has been both a lifeline and an anchor. Camp humor is not necessarily gay humor. Paintings of Jesus in which the eyes follow you across the room are a camp. John Wayne is camp, but the reason for that is his exaggeration of the masculine role. No, camp is not *necessarily* gay humor, but it has been discreetly noted that gay people have been in its vanguard. Gay humor, or that famous "gay sensibility," has often been a form of camp. Since camp flourishes in urban cliques and is something of a secret code, it has become one of the mainstays of an almost ethnic humor which has been formed for defense purposes over the years. Because camp seeks to comfort and is largely a generous rather than a selfish feeling, it has also operated in a human sense, aiding people in forming images with which they feel comfortable in a hostile culture.

The relation of camp to gay humor is the same as the relation of guilt to being Jewish. It's by reputation only. And just as there are some guilty Portnoys, there are campy homosexuals. The real issue is one of vision. Because of the rarefied position of gay people, camp has seemed intrinsic to gay humor. Gay people are born into a heterosexual world and spend a lot of time being raised as heterosexual. We therefore know a hell of a lot more about being straight then straights know about being gay. We needed the training to effectively "pass." Consequently we see the culture with a dual vision, and our particular "aliveness" to the double sense in which some things can be taken overqualifies us for camp expression.

Gay humor, however, springs from *all* our experiences as gay people. While our blanket oppression has given us plenty of fuel for tough wit, we have also been shaped by other forces. Gay humor is Lily Tomlin noting that "in the fifties nobody was gay, only shy." Certainly not camp, it uses our situation in order to comment on who we are.

One of the things Bruce Rodgers says about camp in *The Queens' Vernacular* is that although camp enjoyed a general "discovery" in the late sixties, it firmly remains a form of homosexual slang. I think the reason for that is at least partially the nonpolitical nature of camp. Remember, Carmen Miranda never *said* anything. She simply was what she was.

The best camp will remain affectionate and naive. After all, Dale Evans is still alive, and if that isn't enough, we have disaster movies; Charlton Heston; plaster statues of the Venus de Milo; Los Angeles; and little telephone tables with a place for the directory. If all else fails, the next time Queen Elizabeth has a luncheon, watch it on television. She arrives from her upstairs bedroom and enters her own dining room with a smart little leather handbag hanging from her arm. That Queen is such a camp.

—VITO RUSSO

Fashion statement or camp? From lumberjack in the woods to roughrider on the range, gay men discovered they could become whatever they wanted to be, if only for a night.

BOOKS: *GAY AMERICAN HISTORY*

I first became aware of Jonathan Ned Katz in 1972, when I went to a performance of his play *Coming Out!* at the Gay Activists Alliance Firehouse in New York on the eve of the Christopher Street parade. Looking back, it seems like a magical evening—an overflow audience roaring and clapping at the jokes, the passion, the defiance. At the end, when Deanna Alida unloosed her creamy contralto on "When the gays go marching in…" we all stood—almost levitated—upward and sang along. At that moment we were all joined, brotherhood and sisterhood were here and now, justice a certainty and gay liberation a map of the future. When the lights went up, the stranger sitting next to me grabbed me and planted his lips on mine. No one minded. It seemed the only sensible response to what we'd seen and heard.

When I met Katz a few weeks later I told him about the stranger who had distributed his kisses after the show. He broke into a radiant smile. "That's exactly what I wanted to happen!" he declared. Then he told me that after another performance, a segment of the audience had surged around the corner to a bar that had been unfriendly to its new gay neighbors and "liberated" the place. They had confronted the owner, demanded a change of policy, and come to an understanding. That too, Katz explained, was the perfect ending to his play. "I wanted it to move people to action. I wanted it to be an instrument of change."

These two episodes illustrate what spurred Katz to embark on his monumental *Gay American History,* a seven-hundred-page epic just published. By bringing the past to life, he hopes to stir people to love and anger and further resistance.

With this book, Katz has become an inventor of the American gay past—those isolated moments so difficult to retrieve, so hard to string into coherent patterns, at least until now. Before he started thinking about the problem of our history (and it was a slow process, step by dangerous step), few people had sought to legitimize the subject, to bring scholarship to bear on it, or to popularize it. As Katz put it, "Something was lacking in gay life because we didn't have a sense of our collective past, our roots. Each new generation of gay people would think they were the first gay people on earth."

Katz stressed the importance of gay people knowing the history of gay resistance. "It can nourish us, fuel further resistance," he said. "Many of us don't realize that the gay movement didn't start in 1969 at Stonewall, although it became a mass movement then. I was able to discover the charter of the first homosexual emancipation society in America—the Chicago Society for Human Rights, founded in 1924 by a man named Henry Gerber. I was also able to locate and interview Henry Hay, the man who in 1948 conceived the organization that became the Mattachine Society."

Above all, Katz hopes his book will stimulate further gay research. "I hope it gains recognition for gay history as a legitimate part of American social history," he said, then wrinkled his brow. "I do worry that if the subject gets into the hands of traditional academics, they'll make it boring. I'd like to see gay history written to interest a general audience, especially ordinary gay people. At the same time, the scholarly apparatus should be there—facts verified and footnoted."

His exertions were draining, to say the least. As the months and years went

Before he authored *Gay American History,* Jonathan Ned Katz (*above*) wrote another pioneering work, the play *Coming Out!* Actor Blake Bergman (*below*) is the center of attention in a scene from this inspirational work.

Gay American Indians Claim Their Own History

Until Europeans arrived on the continent, being gay was neither a crime nor a sin in most Native American societies. Gay Indians—referred to as berdaches by French explorers—held a place of respect within tribal culture, often fulfilling roles as healers, medicine people, and craft specialists. But it would take many generations before this buried tradition could be reclaimed, a development hastened by the formation of Gay American Indians (GAI) in San Francisco in 1975. The group's co-founders, Barbara Cameron and Randy Burns, were interviewed by The Advocate *the following year, during the height of the nation's bicentennial celebration.*

"It's ridiculous. What should Indians celebrate?" asked Cameron, a Sioux. "Two hundred years of broken promises? There are plans for demonstrations at Mount Rushmore, and gay American Indians will be there."

"In the Indian community we are trying to align ourselves with the trampled traditions of our people," added Burns, a Paiute. "In the gay community, we're trying to break down the image of the Indian as a macho militant that gay white people have. Mostly, we will work among ourselves: mutual support, socializing, and help."

"Gay American Indians is first and foremost a group for each other," *said Cameron, adding that GAI represents nearly twenty different tribes. "Bringing together gay Indians is our most important task."*

by and the pile of index cards and letters and documents grew—turning his workroom into a huge, three-dimensional scrapbook—he became quieter, wearier. His voice over the telephone was faint and exhausted. At dinner parties, his old ebullience was muted. He suffered periods of discouragement. The project at times seemed physically too much for him. Now he happily credits the help he got from his extended gay family around the country.

"I couldn't have gone on without them, without their encouragement," he recalled, his voice warming as he spoke. "Doing the research put me in touch with large numbers of gay people, gave me a wonderful sense of the gay population out there that I related to."

One of the most innovative sections of the book is Part II, a chronological survey of documents on the medical treatment of homosexuals. This is a history of horrors like aversion therapy, castration, clitoridectomy, shock, hormone treatment, hysterectomy, lobotomy, and vasectomy. The earliest treatment cited used cold sitz baths to "cure" a twenty-two-year-old lesbian (1884) and the last is a terrifying story of forced electroshock of a twenty-four-year-old male (1964, interviewed by Katz ten years later).

The introduction to this section is a powerful jeremiad against the medically derived notion that homosexuality is chiefly a psychological phenomenon. In the middle of it, quite disarmingly, Katz writes of his own ten years in therapy: "I entered analysis, voluntarily I thought, with the idea that my 'problem' was my homosexuality and my goal a heterosexual 'cure'…Paradoxically, my experience in therapy turned out to be an extremely good one, helping me to know and affirm positive parts of myself, among them my homosexuality."

He terminated therapy in 1973. Looking back on that decade, Katz remarked: "I mention my own experience to suggest that the history of tortures that the medical businesspeople have inflicted on us is not the whole picture. At the same time, I continue to feel that they are among our biggest ideological enemies."

The spirit of feminism underlies his book, Katz declared, although here he is rather self-critical. "My original intention was to make the book equally about men and women—but it isn't. This is my major failure. I didn't make enough of an effort to turn up female material. It's out there—*The Ladder,* for instance, one of the main published sources on lesbians, has sixteen years of book reviews. I found bound volumes of *The Ladder* at the Mattachine library, but before I could use them, they were stolen."

He stressed again the need for continuing gay research. He was especially careful in his citations so that other historians can follow in his footsteps. Many of the documents he turned up, he pointed out, could be subjects of further analysis. "A court record of a sodomy trial, for instance, shows that homosexual activity was going on. But newspaper accounts of the trial might tell more about the gay persons involved. We might investigate the whole social setting behind the court proceedings." Above all, he believes gay history should become a cooperative enterprise, with men and women joining together.

Perhaps the best way to end this is with a quote from one of the first reviews of *Gay American History.* It appeared in the *Village Voice* and it was a rave under the headline A GOOD GAY HISTORY BURSTS OUT OF THE CLOSET: "Katz has let documents of gay history speak for themselves. And they do, at times they scream."

Yes, scream—loud and clear at last.   —RICHARD HALL

ART: PAUL CADMUS

At first, the idea of an interview didn't particularly appeal to artist Paul Cadmus. "I like reticence and discretion," he wrote in reply to our initial inquiry. "Especially about sexual matters, no matter whether hetero- or homosexual. Although I have never been stuck in the closet, I have chosen as much as possible the semi-privacy of my semi-ivory tower rather than calling from rooftops and shouting in parades."

Yet Cadmus agrees to a meeting, saying, "I am not as rigid in the flesh as in writing!" So on a glorious spring morning we drive up from Manhattan, through the wooded Connecticut countryside where gray branches are showing the first uncertain signals of coming green.

Cadmus is widely acknowledged as the dean of American social realism. His work first came into prominence in 1933, when the W.P.A. (Works Progress Administration) invited him to paint as part of a federal arts project. He completed two pictures, *The Fleet's In* and *Greenwich Village Cafeteria*. The first was selected to be shown at Washington's Corcoran Gallery. Then came the tempest.

A retired admiral was outraged by what he described as "a representation of a disgraceful, sordid, disreputable, drunken brawl with a number of enlisted men consorting with a party of streetwalkers." The painting was removed and never seen again. A storm of protest ensued from press, public, politicians, and fellow artists, guaranteeing the young artist's overnight fame.

Cadmus is perhaps best known for his drawings of the nude figure. I wonder if he has ever felt any restrictions or limitations as a result of his emphasis on the male nude. "I think the only limitation that I had is that in paintings where I might have used frontal nudity I didn't," he replies. "Like *The YMCA Locker Room*. In those days you couldn't exhibit a painting that had that sort of thing. Otherwise I've always painted more or less what I wanted."

What, I wonder aloud as the conversation drifts, does he think about today's gay scene? "Maybe I shouldn't say this," he begins hesitantly, "it's a word that's used universally now, but the word 'gay' doesn't please me. I think it sounds too frivolous. Think of calling Socrates 'gay,' or Michelangelo 'gay.' Gaiety is a wonderful thing but it does sound as though that were the whole aim in life, as though it were a career in itself. That depresses me a bit."

Looking back to the time when being "different" was *different*, does he perhaps regret the era he grew up in? "I don't feel any regret," he says. "When I go to bed at night I say 'Thank you' to whomever or whatever has caused everything to be as good as it is."

—DONNELL STONEMAN

Male Nude NM 197,
crayon on green paper.

ART: DAVID HOCKNEY

British painter David Hockney travels from place to place, experiencing what pleases him and then moving on. "My own self-image is of a student with credit cards in his pocket," he explains. "I say that as opposed to surrounding yourself with the things you like, staying in one place all the time. I could live in hotels and other people's apartments all the time, as long as I can set up my paints." No other contemporary artist has found popular and critical acclaim so quickly as the peripatetic Hockney. He arrived at the Royal College of Art in 1959, uncertain and shy, living in a shed and taking baths in a sink. He was unashamedly working-class, seemed to flaunt an exhibitionist lifestyle, and did nothing to disguise the fact that he was gay. Within a few years his name was emblazoned across the front pages of an era: "Hockney, the Sixties Swinger." "The Artist Who's Lovable and Cuddly." "David Hockney—No Dumb Blond!" He was pop artist as antihero.

Hockney's recurrent use of water imagery is related to his inherent affinity for illusion and glamour. Lawn sprinklers, showers, and swimming pools fill his canvases. Water is even the subject of one of his most famous paintings, *A Bigger Splash*. "With water you can decide where to stop looking," he tells me, amidst the clutter of his Paris studio. "You can stop at the surface or go deeper."

Man Taking Shower, acrylic on canvas.

Not surprisingly, he says he cannot resist a good beach, a predilection that led to him meeting boyfriend Peter Schlesinger. "I went to teach a course at the University of California, Los Angeles, one summer expecting a lot of classic, bronzed surfers." Hockney smiles. "Instead all I got was a lot of housewives. So when Peter walked in the door I made sure he stayed." In short order, Hockney embarked on a series of drawings and paintings with Schlesinger almost obsessively the center of focus. Through one archetypal figure, the artist had found a way to interpret a newly discovered landscape—the Southern California gay subculture.

Although a considerable period of time has passed since their romance ended, Hockney and Schlesinger remain good friends. "Would you like to meet him?" Hockney asks. He was due to meet Hockney and another friend the next day for lunch. "You come too," he insists.

We dine at La Closerie des Lilas, with Hockney and his friend doing most of the talking. Perodically Hockney stops and takes a photograph of his former lover sitting across the table. Five minutes later Schlesinger lifts his own camera and snaps back.

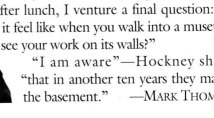

I learn that Hockney can't make plants grow ("You forget to water them," says Schlesinger); never uses yellow ("I have tubes of the stuff I bought fifteen years ago, but you never know when there might be a banana in a picture"); and quotes T. S. Eliot ("Do I dare to eat a peach?").

After lunch, I venture a final question: "What does it feel like when you walk into a museum and see your work on its walls?"

"I am aware"—Hockney shrugs—"that in another ten years they may be in the basement." —MARK THOMPSON

"WHEN THEY CAME FOR THE JEWS, I SAID NOTHING. WHEN THEY CAME FOR THE GAYS, I SAID NOTHING. AND WHEN THEY CAME FOR ME, THERE WAS NO ONE LEFT TO SAY ANYTHING..." ROMAN CATHOLIC PRIEST IN NAZI GERMANY

SAVE OUR HUMAN RIGHTS

"KILL A QUEER FOR CHRIST"

1977 The year of Anita Bryant began quietly enough, with the proposed gay-rights ordinance in Dade County, Florida, which includes Miami. In 1977 such ordinances were almost unknown. What erupted in Dade County was the model for what was to become the political battle over gay rights in America for the foreseeable future, the religious right seizing the chance to batter change with "the gay issue."

Two histories collided publicly in 1977. The history of gay and lesbian people was a history of constant self-suppression and enforced secrecy—a history of shame. Stonewall had brought the rebellious liberation spirit of the 1960s to bear on the homophile movement of the post–World War II period. The Mattachine Society and Daughters of Bilitis had been secretive organizations dedicated to making connections between people with same-sex orientation and improving the public lot of the gay person. The Stonewall Riots and the subsequent gay liberation activity had made a public issue of this hitherto secret cause. But even in 1977, the gay movement was putting its trust in the future.

Lesbians and gay men were beginning to realize that being gay was in itself no proper cause for being deprived of civil rights, and had begun to organize. Gay and lesbian Americans were beginning to come out of the closet in large numbers and to make a movement that was coming out of the shadows. One strategy of this movement was to demand equal protection of the laws in municipalities. The courts were still uncomprehending of gay rights but more and more cities, like Miami, were sympathetic to the rights of their citizens and property holders who, as they used to say, happened to be gay.

On the other side were those Americans for whom the future held not hope but terror. Christian fundamentalism had taken its modern form early in the twentieth century as a response to the changing of old-time rural Christian America into modern, industrialized, urban, pluralist America. The future for these people remained what it had always been: a future reward beyond the grave; a Life Everlasting to be paid for in suffering and moral straitjacketing now. To these fundamentalists, gay liberation was a call to battle.

Enter Anita Bryant, former Miss America, spokeswoman for the Florida orange industry, star wannabe. Bryant, propelled by God knows what private energies and fueled by a coalition of right-wing moralists and sophisticated right-wing mail-order fundraisers, formed a coalition to defeat the Dade County gay-rights ordinance as a threat to "our children."

In Anita Bryant, the gay community had met its Miss Gulch/Wicked Witch and had its first taste of the political battles that continue to rage around gay and lesbian liberation and civil rights movements.

As the months passed, the Miami ordinance was enacted, a protest coalition founded, and a referendum on the issue held. Gay people had some of the visibility they wanted and all of the hatred and opposition they had always known would accompany coming out. For all her blather about children, Anita Bryant's crusade expressed the fears and prejudices of American religious views of homosexuality combined with the American provincial fear of change and galvanized by a well-financed, purposeful, and politically conservative movement, typified by such public figures as Bryant, Phyllis Schlafly, California State Assemblyman John Briggs, and Ronald Reagan.

With the referendum's actual defeat of the gay-rights bill, the issue had been broadened into the one still with us, the way in which the right-wing and Christian alliance targets gay issues not only to force lesbians and gays back into the closet but also to mobilize bigotry and fear about homosexuality—a cultural staple in American history—into a means of undoing the gains of the civil rights, feminist, and peace movements. The troubled history to follow included the Briggs Amendment in California, a 1978 attempt to ban gay teachers from the classroom. The defeat of this proposition spurred gay organizing but established a pattern that persists.

The legacy of Anita Bryant is complex: She helped millions of gay and lesbian Americans to recognize that the closet was a prison and that the fight for safe and free lives depended on the battle being waged as something other than a jailhouse riot. Thanks to Anita Bryant the gay movement finally saw that as hard as it is to fight for civil rights in a still-homophobic America, lesbians and gays are more likely to win their rights if they come out and fight on their own side. As gay people became more forthright and more successful, their opponents would be more open and more hostile as well. Anita Bryant showed gay people what they had always feared: that to be open was to be vulnerable to hatred, abuse, violence, and discrimination. What gay and lesbian people showed Anita Bryant, America, and themselves, however, was that they were no longer willing to keep silent and that the gay liberation movement was set in its course.

Gay men and lesbians were learning, in 1977, to recognize the nature of the threat and beginning to realize the complex burdens of any fight for freedom. After being gay-bashed, San Francisco writer Joseph Torchia wrote in *The Advocate* about the connection between the out gay and lesbian person and the anti-gay movements in words that unhappily remain descriptive of American reality:

"I sobbed out loud. Not because of the pain of that violence, but because of the feeling it left inside me—the feeling that I would never laugh or smile or trust or even love in quite the same way, the feeling that I had lost the last remnant of my childhood, the childhood that Anita wants so desperately to save."

—ROBERT DAWIDOFF

DONELAN

"I DON'T KNOW! I PUT THE ORANGE JUICE ON THE TABLE, HE GLARED AT ME, SAID, 'MOTHER, HOW COULD YOU?' AND STORMED OUT."

So read the punch line of one of Gerard Donelan's first cartoons for *The Advocate*. It would be followed by hundreds more over the next fifteen years, each panel a wry, frequently hilarious commentary on the vicissitudes of gay and lesbian life. No one escaped Donelan's pen: He lampooned leathermen, lesbians, homophobic old ladies, parents, roommates, clergymen, and drag queens.

"We've got to be able to look at ourselves and not take it all so seriously," the prolific artist said. "I'm really happy that I'm gay, and hope that someday all gay people will feel the same way."

The cartoonist began his career when he moved to San Francisco from Massachusetts in 1977. "*The Advocate* used to have a wonderful cartoon called 'Miss Thing' [drawn by Joe Johnson], and I loved it," he recalled. "When it ended, I thought it was a terrible shame. So I decided to try to fill in some of the gap."

"The [gay political] rhetoric some of us believed back in 1970 and 1971 makes me want to puke when I read it. My hair stands on end when someone calls me brother. I have one brother and one sister—and that's it."
—NEW YORK JOURNALIST ARTHUR BELL

Gay and and lesbian campaign workers in Dade County celebrate despite defeat in June.

San Francisco hosted the First Annual Gay Softball World Series in November: a two-out-of-three confrontation between the hometown team and their rivals from New York. Thousands watched as the Badlands "All-Stars" defeated Manhattan.

> "*The courts have ruled over and over again that homosexuality is not a constitutional or a civil right. That's very clear. It's not a sex. Either you're a male or a female; and there are constitutional and civil rights for sex, but not for homosexuality.*"
>
> — JOHN BRIGGS,
> CALIFORNIA STATE SENATOR

T I M E L I N E

JANUARY Dade County, Florida, enacted a ban on antigay discrimination, setting the stage for singer Anita Bryant's nationwide antigay crusade. ❑ Ellen Barrett, a Berkeley, California, woman, was ordained the Episcopal Church's first openly lesbian priest. ❑ The Washington state Supreme Court ruled that a Tacoma school district was justified in dismissing an openly gay teacher on grounds of immorality.

FEBRUARY Legislators in Connecticut, Hawaii, Illinois, Maine, Maryland, Massachusetts, Minnesota, Oregon, and Washington were considering gay antibias measures. ❑ Wyoming repealed its sodomy law. ❑ The Agency for International Development and the Foreign Service lifted policies that automatically barred gays and lesbians from employment; the FBI and the CIA continued to hold out. ❑ Tucson enacted a ban on antigay discrimination. ❑ Ten students at the University of Oklahoma faced expulsion for wearing T-shirts that read "Bury a Fairy" and "Do the World a Favor—Shoot a Faggot."

MARCH Anita Bryant, whose campaign against the Dade County rights ordinance was in full force, complained of "blacklisting" after being dropped from the pilot for a television variety series because of her "controversial political activities." ❑ In the first official visit of lesbian and gay activists to the White House, fourteen gay and lesbian activists met with Presidential Liaison to Minority Communities Midge Costanza.

APRIL Rejecting a lawsuit filed by Bryant's group, Save Our Children, a Miami judge ruled that the Dade County ordinance was constitutional. Meanwhile, a Maryland firm prepared "Boycott Florida" T-shirts as a response to Bryant's crusade. ❑ More than 80 percent of Portland-area physicians who responded to a survey conducted by Oregon's Multnomah County Medical Association said they would refuse to treat gay patients. ❑ Six women sued the Boise, Idaho, Police Department, saying they were fired because their supervisors thought they were lesbians; the women were allowed to keep their jobs. ❑ The McDonald's Corporation obtained a court order forbidding an openly gay man who had once worked as a Ronald McDonald at one of its restaurants in Boston to ever dress as the clown or say that "Ronald McDonald is gay."

MAY Nine people died in a four-alarm fire at the Everard Baths, one of the most popular gay bathhouses in New York City. ❑ As activists across the country geared up against Bryant, openly gay Air Force veteran Leonard Matlovich was named cochairman of the Dade County Coalition for Human Rights, the group that organized support for the gay-rights ordinance. ❑ Iowa City, Iowa, enacted a ban on antigay bias. ❑ A Los Angeles group unveiled a proposal for an all-gay retirement home. The project was never completed.

JUNE Reaction to Dade County voters' decision to repeal the gay-rights ordinance was immediate: Jim Curasi, the openly bisexual executive assistant to Paula Hawkins, the chairwoman of the state public service commission, resigned his post under pressure from Hawkins; a daily newspaper in Florida entitled its editorial on the referendum "Shut Up, Anita"; a Florida firm began manufacturing and selling a Bryant dartboard; and a Los Angeles man said he would sue Bryant for blaming a drought on the state's tolerance of gays. ❑ Overriding

Governor James J. Exon's veto, the Nebraska legislature repealed the state's sodomy law.

JULY Gay Pride celebrations across the country took on particular intensity in the aftermath of the Dade County vote. ❑ Cities and towns nationwide reported sharp rises in antigay violence in the wake of the vote. ❑ Under congressional pressure, the federal Department of Housing and Urban Development repealed three-week-old regulations that would have allowed gay and lesbian couples to be considered for public housing. ❑ The National Gay Leadership Conference, sponsored by Dignity International, the Gay Rights National Lobby, the National Gay Task Force, and the United Federation of Metropolitan Community Churches, met in Denver; the over four hundred representatives from various lesbian and gay groups determined that the movement had to focus on education, legislation, and organization. ❑ Champaign, Illinois, enacted a gay-rights ordinance.

AUGUST The British newspaper *Gay News* was convicted of blasphemous libel in London for publishing a poem that depicted Christ as gay. It was said to

The success of Anita Bryant's "Save Our Children" campaign in Dade County, Florida, set off a wave of spontaneous demonstrations in New York and many other major cities across the nation.

be the first blasphemy conviction in Great Britain since 1922. ❑ Missouri revised its criminal code to reduce sodomy from a felony to a misdemeanor. ❑ The Association for Humanistic Psychology tweaked Bryant by voting to boycott Florida orange juice and resolving not to meet in any state that did not guarantee equal rights for gays and lesbians. ❑ *Chicago Tribune* columnist Mike Royko named Bryant one of the "ten most obnoxious Americans." ❑ Threatening to stage protests across the United States, the International Union of Gay Athletes demanded that Jody, a recurring gay character on the soon-to-debut television series "Soap," be made less effeminate; later, Jody dated a football quarterback.

SEPTEMBER The Internal Revenue Service dropped a rule that required gay educational and charitable groups to publicly state that homosexuality is "a sickness, disturbance, or diseased pathology" before they would be eligible for full tax-exempt status. ❑ The federal gay-rights bill was amended to specify that employers would not be required to hire quotas of gays and lesbians to make up for past discrimination; the bill would still not pass in this year or any subse-

"I always wanted to go into politics to be a public person, and when I realized that…I was homosexual, I was heartbroken. When it became apparent to me that sometime that might change, that someday I could be gay and in politics, I made up my mind that that would be the only obstacle that I would ever have to deal with." —NEW YORK LEGISLATOR VIRGINA APUZZO

TELL ANITA YOU'RE AGAINST DISCRIMINATION VOTE JUNE 7th

"On the third of June 1976, after serving seven years of my life in uniform, I was dishonorably discharged from the Navy for reasons of homosexuality. While taking a position, a lofty legal opposition, publicly, the Navy used covert maneuvers to pervert the concepts of due process, enabling military authorities publicly to vent their homophobia….It is clear that their tactics were little more than simple brainwashing techniques." —VERNON E. BERG, FORMER ENSIGN

quent year. ❑ Southern Bell Telephone Company refused to accept paid advertising from a Metropolitan Community Church in Miami, saying that the ad would offend its customers. ❑ Police arrested large groups of gay men at cruising areas and bars in Tulsa, Oklahoma, Kansas City, Missouri, and Provincetown, Massachusetts.

OCTOBER California activists began their campaign to fight an initiative proposed by State Senator John Briggs that would prohibit gays and lesbians from teaching in public schools. ❑ The U.S. Supreme Court declined to hear appeals from two Washington State public school teachers who were fired because of their homosexuality. ❑ A drive to recall Portland mayor Neil Goldschmidt for proclaiming a Gay Pride Day failed when not enough valid signatures were collected on recall petitions. ❑ Eight men, including a congressional aide and a pastor of the Brethren church, died in a fire at a gay porno theater in Washington, D.C. ❑ More than a thousand people demonstrated on the streets of Montreal to protest an antigay police crackdown. ❑ The International Association of Chiefs of Police voted to oppose the hiring of gay and lesbian police officers.

NOVEMBER Harvey Milk became the first openly gay man to be elected to the San Francisco Board of Supervisors. ❑ Rep. Edward Koch (D-N.Y.), a cosponsor of the federal gay-rights bill, was elected mayor of New York City. ❑ Lesbian groups across the country attended the International Women's Year

Creamed Anita: A protester made his objection to Bryant known in Des Moines, Iowa.

national conference in Houston. ❑ Eugene, Oregon, approved a gay-rights ordinance. ❑ The Florida Citrus Commission renewed Bryant's $100,000-a-year contract as a spokeswoman for the Florida orange juice industry and passed a resolution praising Bryant's "courage" for leading the fight against the Dade County antidiscrimination ordinance.

DECEMBER Dallas schools superintendent Nolan Estes retracted his statement that he would force openly gay and lesbian teachers to resign. ❑ Nine members of the New York City Gay Activists Alliance demonstrated at the offices of *The Village Voice* newspaper to protest the headline "The Coast Is Queer" on a letter about seagulls in California that have same-sex intercourse.

GORE VIDAL

    The house Gore Vidal has borrowed for three months from a famous director is high—one can go no higher—in the Hollywood Hills. The famous director clearly has a taste for grandeur: His ceilings are fifteen feet high, the furnishings are a creamy marble. Two gilded Hindu deities prance, top-lit, upon marble pillars. Palm trees droop in corners, and beyond the blue-tiled swimming pool on the terrace, L.A.'s gaudy light show glitters off infinity.

    Vidal himself—well, everyone knows Vidal. The creator of *Myra Breckenridge, Myron,* and other all-American outrages is in person very much as he appears on the box—taller-looking, perhaps, and broader in the shoulder; but the handsome Roman-coin head, the amused drawl, the weary smile are all in place as he prepares, without noticeable enthusiasm, for this latest encounter with the media.

"Let me say, a more artistic, appreciative group of people for the arts does not exist. And conceited as it may sound, I think a great deal of it has to do with their approval of my work. The seriousness of my work. They are more knowledgeable, more loving of the arts. They make the average male look stupid."

—BETTE DAVIS

"One of the main manifestations of fascism in every minority group is a kind of puritanism. I detest it. I mean, every movement develops this type of group that becomes very puritanical and, almost without knowing it, very sexist. I find many of the gay groups enormously sexist. Enormously puritanical."

—NOVELIST JOHN RECHY

What do you think of President Carter?

He seems to be showing the signs of mild homophobia—he hates the sin, but loves the sinner.

How much better to hate the sinner and revel in the sin.…For years I have been warning my countrymen that the dictator, when he comes, will not be some crazy little man like Hitler or some pompous asshole like Douglas Mac-Arthur, but somebody terribly warm and folksy and good on television who looks like Arthur Godfrey. And here, out of the South, comes Jimmy Carter, who fits the bill perfectly.

One trend among many you seem to have started is this enthusiasm for bisexuality. Suddenly, everyone is bi—or claims to be.

My line is that everybody is bisexual, although not everyone wants to go in both directions, and most end up on one side or the other. I do think there's a sizable group that goes back and forth: boys who hustle, for instance, here or in Italy. With the greatest of ease they can have very intense affairs with men and then, at the age that's expected of them, they will get married, have children, and give up sex with males. For years these boys go almost exclusively with men, and then they turn around and settle down and never revert. I could name a hundred people in that situation.

They would say they do it for the money. Whatever the official motive, the fact is that they give pleasure to men and women, and that is being actively and unambiguously bisexual. And then, of course, that most celebrated "homosexual" of the last hundred years was that devoted husband and father of two, Oscar Wilde.

In my own experience, I've met very, very few genuine bisexuals.…But you see, everybody looks at it from the faggot point of view, never from the viewpoint of the trade—as we used to call it. I reject this idea that it must always be the faggot by which homosexuality is measured. We might look at the other side; for instance, the working-class boy who seems to be hustling because he likes the money, who swears he really likes girls but gets deeper into male relationships, yet can and does switch over to the other side. Certainly, I found that in the Army you could go to bed with just about anybody, under the excuse that, well, it's the Army, it's overseas. Prisons and boys' schools are the same.…

Is there such a thing as a gay "sensibility"?

I have never seen any sign of it. I don't know what it could be. There are all kinds of attitudes among homosexuals toward homosexuality. There is this sickly Edwardian British attitude toward rough trade which you see in E. M. Forster and many others. It sends me right up the wall. Trade is the virile life force. The working class is worshiped. Butchness is all. Actually, if you want to meet real non-life-enhancing neurotics, get to know some hard-hats, or some L.A. policemen.

Do you think the gay press should sell meat the way it does? Or should it adhere to a sober political line?

You mean the sex ads? Should *The New York Times* act as a pimp for the garment trade? That's what it does, running all those lingerie ads that the squares or straights—what is their shape?—used to jerk off to. Shocking, I thought. Anyway, I am permissive if not supportive.

In European countries, attitudes about homosexuality seem to differ little from city to city: Edinburgh is no more homophobic than London, for instance. But here in America one finds the wildest swings—even in California. San Francisco is an open city, L.A. so uptight. Why is that?

It depends very much on who holds power in the local fief, and who inherits it. If New York is particularly virulent at the moment it is largely because of Cardinal Cook, who is not upholding the great homosexual tradition of Francis Cardinal Spellman, in whose seat, as it were, he is established and reigns.

The Cardinal Spellman tradition?

What was that? Oh, I thought everybody knew. A lurid queen. He used to go to the house of a friend of mine, a Catholic layman, now dead, a married man who "swung," as they say, or said. Having changed into mufti, they would leave the cardinal's Cadillac out front. Then they'd go out the back way, cross town to the house of a procurer, where this nice little bald man would be introduced to a variety of youths, make his choice, have sex, return to the house, put on his cardinal's robe and head back to the palace on Madison Avenue.

I was invited to come along on one of these thrilling adventures. I declined. My friend said that when a musical comedy called *One Touch of Venus* came to New York, the cardinal went through a good deal of the male chorus line. A friend of his—another Catholic layman—asked, "But aren't you worried? Suppose the press got hold of this?" Spellman replied, "And who would believe it?" Now that is security.

But Spellman's fault was not homosexuality; it was his very real contribution to the Vietnam War. As a power in the Roman Catholic hierarchy, which was anxious to preserve its influence in Southeast Asia, Spellman put enormous pressure to intervene on our first Catholic president, John Kennedy. He bears a large measure of blame for that disaster.

At the end of our interview, I ask Vidal to autograph two of his early books, *The Judgment of Paris* and *A Thirsty Evil*, explaining that they are favorites. I say I especially liked *A Thirsty Evil*. "Mmm," says Vidal, "it's so—short." Beneath the title he writes: "Is it ever slaked?" —W. I. SCOBIE

"What do I have to do? String myself up? For the rest of my life is the gay community going to come to me and start pulling at my skirts saying, 'Do you love me, Mommy? Do you love me?' Of course I like you. What do they want from me? I think they want me to die. I really do."

—BETTE MIDLER

TENNESSEE WILLIAMS

"Actually, we'll only have about forty-five minutes with him. He's leaving for Palm Beach at two-thirty." My heart sank. It was already past noon and we weren't even there yet. I was riding in an elevator at the Elysée Hotel with Arthur Seidelman, who is directing Tennessee Williams's new play *Vieux Carré*. He has persuaded Williams to see me in spite of imminent departure.

In Tennessee's suite there is controlled bedlam. The playwright is preoccupied with a swollen toe and the diabetes his doctor has finally told him about after "drawing blood every two hours and having me piss every hour." He can't find his brown belt that goes with his brown pants suit and is choosing a pair of dark socks as he sits firmly on the sofa next to me. I tell him that his play is very funny and he doesn't find that unusual.

"I'm a very funny man, you know. I think I'm funnier than Neil Simon. Don't you think I'm funnier than Neil Simon, Arthur?"

He turns to me and is serious about being funny. "You know, you've got to turn into a clown in your later years. People talk about my cackle laugh! Heh-heh-heh-heh. I guess I feel as though I've gone through everything there is to go through, and there's a certain relief that comes with that. I'm free of a lot of pressure." Could this have anything to do with his coming out in his recently published *Memoirs*?

"I don't think so. I'd never thought there was any question about me. *Time* magazine had been saying I was homosexual for years. But I would never have used anyone else's name unless I had permission. You know, especially for act-

*"I don't take a stand on anything....
I live on a promontory, so I truly
can shut out the world."*
—ROCK HUDSON

> **"I**n the 1940s it was
> a guessing game: Who's a
> fag? And fag-baiting was
> *the most popular game going,
> from the lowbrow* New York
> Times *to the highbrow* Partisan
> Review. *They never let up on Ten-
> nessee."*   —GORE VIDAL

ors, it's still dangerous because they can suffer." One of the actors he does not mention by name in *Memoirs* who has since discussed his bisexuality is Tab Hunter, and I tell him this. There is a pause and then the cackle. "Heh-heh-heh. Nice boy, heh-heh. But was there ever any question? Heh-heh-heh." One thing is for sure. The two gay characters in *Vieux Carré*, the Painter and the Writer, are a far cry from the horrors and self-hatred of a Sebastian Venable. There seems to be in these characters a free and honest attitude that comes naturally to them as people. Williams agrees. "Yes, there does seem to be, doesn't there? There's a kind of freedom and they seem natural and human. Well, I've never spent any time hiding my sexuality—I just never thought about it. Do you know what offended me most? A review of *Memoirs* in a magazine called *Gay Sunshine*, which said that all my long plays were lies. This infuriated me! They said that I had written love stories that were really between two men but had disguised them as being between a man and a woman. Well, that's ridiculous! Such a thing would never occur to me. Every person has in him two genders and if he's a writer he can draw upon one gender to create women and the other gender to create men. It just so happened that, being a Southerner, I found it easier to express myself in the rather poetic style of the Southern woman, in most cases.

"You know, I really don't like to talk much about sexual deviation because it makes it seem as though I were obsessed with the subject, and I am not. I am obsessed with work and the meaning of a play, not the sexual orientation of the characters. And whenever I am interviewed I am always guided toward that subject, which is really rather peripheral."

Yes, I know, but after all, *Memoirs* was rather explicit and did cause quite a stir....

"Frankly, I'm sorry I wrote *Memoirs*. I was assured I'd make a great deal of money out of it, not because of any sexual aspect of my nature about which I am quite unsure anyway, but because I was assured I would make a lot of money. Well, I didn't." He seems to be really upset by this and has a rather wild idea that the book is being suppressed.

"I never see it on the racks in airports alongside other books, even though it's in paperback now. It seems that it's being repressed for some reason. When I wrote it I had the delusion, the fear, that I would be destitute someday and the book would protect me from that, heh-heh-heh."

It begins to look as if the interview is over. Williams hands Seidelman two typewritten pages of what looks like dialogue with a lot of crossing out and rewrites. It's a scene he's been working on. "Here, see what you think of this...."

We exchange good-byes, and Williams says he'll be back from Florida in a week to sit in on rehearsals. In the elevator, Seidelman looks over the scene in his hands with amazement. "He writes all the time, Vito. It's an obsession. He's really amazing. He just can't stop writing." On my way downtown on the subway I run into an old friend who is reading *Memoirs* in paperback and I ask him where he bought it. He says that he found it on the rack at the Orlando airport in Florida.

—VITO RUSSO

OPENING SPACE

EDITORIAL COMMENT BY
DAVID B. GOODSTEIN

"Coming out" is a phrase that is used by us and other gay people almost as often as the word "gay" itself. It is a concept that troubles gay people as well as non-gay people. Many things have been written about its different meanings to different people. In order to make the concept clear for myself and others, I have developed a description that I'd like to share with you.

First and foremost, I perceive coming out as a process. It begins with the formation of our sexual identity. It ends when we die. Each gay person's experience of coming out is her/his own. Therefore, when describing it in general, non-individualized terms (a necessity for understanding and descriptive purposes), we really portray a mean of many experiences around which there is considerable variance. Most descriptions of human processes share this element of uncertainty.

A useful way of describing the process is to think of it as occurring along a tunnel. At one end is total blackness or unconsciousness; at the other, liberation into the world. The metaphor of a closet seems to be a less useful one.

For ease of measurement, I divide the process of coming out into three uneven parts,

CASTRO STREET: MECCA OR GHETTO?

with the middle being by far the longest for most people. The first part of the journey I call "personal coming out." We become conscious that we are homosexual. We acknowledge to ourselves that we feel sexual attraction to members of our own sex. For most of us, this part of the process is extremely painful. Often we feel very lonely, very guilty, and very lacking in self-esteem. We inhabit a very black recess in the tunnel of our own consciousness. But the sex urge is very powerful, so most of us move into the next part of the process, which I term "private coming out." We decide to act on our urges. We begin to meet, by means fair, foul, risky, terrible, hilarious, or whatever, other gay people. We create a group of gay friends and lovers on whom we lean for support and with whom we share our sexuality and our gay point of view. Most gay people stay in this part of the process. We activists call them closeted. They don't regard themselves so, however. And like so many other things, a description of this reality depends a lot on the place from which it is observed.

Happily, as gay people succeed in creating more space for themselves and as gay consciousness rises, more of us are expanding our coming out. We are letting more and more people in on the secret of our sexuality. A few trusted nongay friends are included and then a lot of nongay friends and even just acquaintances.

The tunnel is no longer so dark. We discover that our world continues even though some straight people know our secret. The sun rises and sets; we still have our jobs, friends, homes, etc. No one really seems to care, which is both a relief and a disappointment. Light is coming into our tunnel through a glass door out of which we see and into which a surprising number of friendly folk peer back. Sometimes a few unfriendly ones, too.

Some of us walk through the glass door into what I call "public coming out." We no longer care who knows our secret. Usually the last people we tell are our parents, our employers, our brothers and sisters, and our fellow employees—in reverse order. A few of us publish gay periodicals, work in the gay community as activists or service workers, march in parades, etc. We think life is better for us in this kind of free-from-a-secret-space. It is not free of problems. They are different and, I think, considerably more interesting.

I, for one, suffered too much during the earlier parts of the coming-out process to tell anyone that he or she is wrong to keep the secret and stay behind the glass door. We each march to our own drum. In addition, almost every day I acknowledge a new part of my consciousness that is emerging from the tunnel, so I know the process is not finished even though I experience a sense of completion from time to time. From my point of view, it is productive to be very nonjudgmental about someone else's coming out. And I perceive one of the activist's tasks to be making it safer and safer outside—and inside—the glass door.

The scene looks as if it were from a 1957 Ozzie and Harriet beach party in Tulsa, Oklahoma. Few hippies here—hair is kept closely cropped à la Korean War era. Those who dare grow more than two inches keep it tightly combed back à la Rick Nelson. The dress is decidedly butch, as if God had dropped these men naked on the street and commanded them to wear only straight-legged Levi's, or fatigue pants, shitkickers, hooded sweatshirts covered with Levi's or leather coats—and truckloads of plaid Pendleton shirts. Machismo isn't just fashionable here; it's ubiquitous.

Since no 1950s scene would be complete without a few James Deans, add a dozen bikers who rev their Kawasakis and rub their crotches as they stare down the number in the doorway. Pickup trucks with chrome mags and BALL-A-COWBOY bumper stickers lay rubber at the end of the valley as they U-turn their way back to the heavy cruising strip. Everywhere are drugstore cowboys eyeing laundromat loggers winking at barfly jocks. It's 1957 all over again—except that the air bristles with the tension of the seventies. And there are few women.

Welcome to Castro Street, San Francisco—the closest thing to a gay Harlem in the United States. For gay men from Davenports, Eugenes, Kalamazoos, Asbury Parks, and Tampas, it is nothing less than Mecca. Castro glitters like a beacon to a nation where sexual freedom is still a fantasy. Like would-be stars flocking to Hollywood, gay men migrate to the golden gates of Castro Street, where even the clothing store mannequins have washboard stomachs; a liberated zone that calls, "Give me your weak, your huddled, your oppressed—and your horny, looking for a little action."

HISTORY REPEATS ITSELF

The gay population is nothing new to San Francisco. According to San Francisco historian Terry Mangan, photo curator of the California Historical Society, local police were raiding San Francisco gay bars as far back as the Spanish-American War. Local religious leaders ominously blamed the 1906 earthquake on a city that licentiously tolerated such "deviants," and men of the cloth spearheaded an antigay campaign that put a lid on gay life until 1915.

The city has always had areas with high concentrations of gay people. The Barbary Coast of the nineteenth century, the North Beach of Bohemian times, as well as Haight and Union streets, were all at one point popular areas for the city's always large gay population. The 1970s, however, have brought a mass migration of gay people to the sexual freedom of San Francisco. One local television station recently put the gay population of San Francisco at 120,000. This may be an exaggeration; 100,000 may be a closer figure but it still represents a high proportion of an overall city population of only 700,000.

Though San Francisco may always have been home to a large gay population, Castro Street is one of the least likely locations for a gay ghetto phenomenon. Located in the geographical dead-center of the city off Market Street, the city's main drag, the Castro area was built up during the 1880s as the city burgeoned with ethnic immigrants. The area was first populated with working people—stevedores, butchers, teamsters, and carpenters. Large Catholic families stuck their roots in the rows of ornate Queen Anne houses, which were nothing more than the tract housing of the era.

John Murnin, now in his sixties, grew up there, the son of Belfast immigrants who fled the potato famine for America's West. Murnin recalls an area rich with ethnic names like O'Shea, O'Riley, Roselli, and McCarthy. He can point to the antique, record, flower, and gift shops and tell of times when the buildings housed stores selling candy, buttermilk, and kiddie-matinee tickets—all this just footsteps away from what is now called the cruisiest corner in the world. The neighborhood today is full of men who practice law, tend bar, decorate department store windows, teach historical architecture—and many who collect unemployment while spending their days cruising the other men who collect unemployment.

Enough of the old neighborhood remains, however, to resist the gay invasion—and the firsthand experience in future shock. At best, the new settlers are tolerated. At worst, the new Castro population finds itself victim to a mounting wave of beatings.

Gangs of young toughs have taken to attacking gay men in the area. The gangs don't even go through the pretense of mugging or robbing; it's violence, plain and simple. The problem has become so serious that when a new group, Gay Action, announced a meeting to try to stop the violence, over two hundred of the normally staid Castro-area residents showed up. Street patrols are now organized to thwart gangs.

THE INVASION OF THE CASTRO

The Castro ghetto began to develop during the late 1960s. Worried about the influence of the drug-oriented Haight-Ashbury neighborhood just blocks away, the working-class families of the Castro area began moving to the comfortable Bay Area suburbs. On Castro Street, as a result, rents were low, houses sold cheap, and storefronts were vacant. Single men with excess income began moving in, buying up the old houses, and using their leisure time to renovate them. By 1967, a few gay bars were doing business. By the early seventies, gay businesspeople began leasing the deserted storefronts. The trend became an explosion in 1974. Housing costs skyrocketed. Young, single men could afford it. Middle-class families, meanwhile, couldn't afford to pass up the top dollars offered for their homes. The gay population dug in.

"We're not talking about some cruisy street in Greenwich Village," says Harvey Milk, a Castro business owner whose forays into local electoral politics have earned him the unofficial title of "mayor" of Castro Street. "We're talking about a place where gay people have bought homes, where they live and work."

Historian Mangan points out, "Castro is unique because it is the quintessential takeover. I don't think you can go anywhere else in the world and see a place that has been as thoroughly taken over by gay people. There's no question that it's permanent now—and that's something new."

Roy Tackes, owner of Paul Langely Real Estate in the heart of the Castro area, recalls house prices doubling in six months and going up another 50 per-

WOMENSLINE
BY SASHA GREGORY-LEWIS

FIRST LESBIAN PRIEST ORDAINED
Ellen Marie Barrett became the first openly gay woman to be ordained by a major religious denomination, January 10, 1977. Barrett, one of forty-three women to be ordained in January to the Episcopal priesthood, is only the second openly gay person to be ordained as a priest or minister in the United States.

Barrett, who is completing requirements for a doctorate in social ethics at Berkeley, California's, prestigious Graduate Theological Union, had been ordained as a deacon in December 1975. The Episcopal Church at that time refused to ordain women as priests, a policy that was changed in 1976.

The ordination, by Bishop Paul Moore, Jr., of New York, at the Church of the Holy Apostles in Manhattan, was preceded by a joint statement issued by Bishop Moore and the Rev. Arthur W. Hargate.

"Attention has been drawn to this ordination," the statement explained, "because Ms. Barrett has not made a secret of her homosexual orientation. However, her personal life has never been under criticism. Many persons with homosexual tendencies are presently in the ordained ministry. Ellen Barrett's candor in this regard is not considered a barrier to ordination.

"She is highly qualified intellectually, morally, and spiritually to be a priest," the statement concluded.

INDIANA OKAYS WOMEN'S RIGHTS
Indiana ratified the Equal Rights Amendment January 18, becoming the thirty-fifth state to do so. Rosalynn Carter, wife of the President, was credited with influencing the final vote.

At one point, the State Senate, which had turned down the amendment two times in previous years, was deadlocked at twenty-five to twenty-five. ERA sponsor Birch Bayh (D–Ind.) called on the then President-elect to do something. Carter wasn't in, so Rosalynn went to work on the Indiana Senate.

She contacted State Senator Wayne Townsend, who was wavering, and persuaded him, Bayh aides say, to vote in favor of ratification. The ERA was finally approved, twenty-six to twenty-four. The ERA still needs ratification by three more states before March 22, 1979, to become the Twenty-seventh Amendment to the U.S. Constitution.

FBI RELEASES NOW FILES
The FBI investigated the New York chapter of the National Organization for Women for more than seven years, despite local FBI office recommendations that the investigation be canceled because there was "no evidence of the organization being influenced or infiltrated by the Communist Party or of the organization participating in or having any interest in anti-Vietnam and other New Left activities."

This revelation about the FBI comes in a package of six expurgated documents turned over to chapter president Carole De Saram in response to a year-old quest. The documents turned over to De Saram show that the FBI was already interested in the group in early 1969 and continued its probes at least until late 1976.

De Saram says that she is appealing the FBI's decision to withhold other materials from the NOW chapter.

cent six months later. Local businesspeople struggled to keep gay businesses out and would not even invite gay businesses to join their neighborhood Eureka Valley Merchants Association. So the gay businesses formed their own Castro Street Merchants Association—which rapidly surpassed the old group in membership and influence. Even the most ingrained influence soon was overcome because, if nothing else, the new population had the two most essential commodities in a capitalistic democracy: money and votes.

Milk, a onetime Wall Street financial analyst turned politico/camera shop owner, estimates that in 1976, Castro Street grossed between $25 million and $30 million—some $8 million to $10 million above what he thinks the street grossed just in 1975.

The area also carries a lot of votes, a political reality that keeps city and state politicians ready to give smiles and handshakes to all takers in Castro gay bars during election years. Milk, who has scored near-wins in races for the state legislature and the San Francisco Board of Supervisors, points to maps showing he has carried up to 60 percent of the vote in the Castro-area precincts. When Jimmy Carter was fiercely running against Governor Jerry Brown in California's Presidential primary, his son Chip Carter took time from his schedule to make a Castro-area appearance.

Is this kind of attention the end result of a decade of gay liberation? Some see it as an end, others as a beginning. But no one formula can sum up what this complex sociological phenomenon means. Ultimately, Castro Street means different things to the different people who have lived there for months, years, and sometimes even decades.

—RANDY SHILTS

> "*The people who used to live here and bitch about the gay people never did anything for the neighborhood. We're the best thing that ever happened to this place....Now that it's entrenched as a gay area, they want to stop it so there's what they call a 'better balance'— like out of Nazi Germany.*"
>
> —HARVEY MILK,
> OWNER OF CASTRO CAMERA,
> AND LOCAL POLITICIAN

THEATER: WILSON'S *WEST STREET GANG*

A new polemical satire, *The West Street Gang*, by Doric Wilson, is currently being produced by The Other Side of Silence (TOSOS) at the Spike Bar, in New York. Performing the play in a West Side leather bar is no mere whim, for it concerns the attempts of the Village gay community to defend itself against the marauding bands of juvenile punks who roam the waterfront neighborhoods attacking passersby. But the play not only calls attention to the universal threat of gay-directed street crime, it also provokes some serious thinking about the state of the gay movement today. It's also daringly theatrical and hilariously funny.

The play begins as an allusive portrait of a cross-section of gay men who drop into a butch bar on the Lower West Side to have a drink, gossip with the bartender, cruise each other, and share a few jokes. But brooding underneath the cheerful surface is a common fear of the street toughs who might attack any one of them on the way home. When a bar-hopping drag queen manages to collar the gangleader and hauls him into the bar, the tone of the play shifts into social drama as the patrons take the execution of justice into their own hands.

"I think people are terrified by the notion of the public knowing they are queer....I try to be honest; I hate telling lies, but the truth is that I don't think my life of interest—my private life, that is—to anyone but myself." —ACTOR JOHN GIELGUD

The whole thing erupts into a madcap farce with the arrival of a trio of arch-villains who conspire to exploit the young attacker for their own ends: Arthur Klang, writer for the *Greenwich Gazette* and "a close personal friend of a close personal enemy of Ann Miller," who hopes to expand the incident into a front-page story, and maybe a screenplay; Dr. Foeller McLeary, "supreme co-chairperson of the National Gay Defense Fund," who wants to settle the matter heroically, preferably with television cameras rolling; and Bonita O'Ryant, "a concerned citizen" who intends to use the occasion to plug her own civic campaign.

THE WEST STREET GANG

ROB COBUZIO

The weakest point in the play is certainly the most telling. In the middle of the second act, the bar patrons are holding captive the punk kid they all fear, but since they can't think of anything to do but let him go, the play nearly grinds to a halt. Presently the villainous trio arrive to jack the action up into the farcical climax, but in that awful moment, the play, without offering a feasible solution, poses a heavy-duty question. Suppose we get our rights in the legislature; suppose our demands for "gay power" are met. Will hatred, harassment, and exploitation cease? Isn't it time to ask ourselves, "Where do we go from here?"

—DON SHEWEY

"It seems like everybody in the world is letting it hang out. My God, people have [been gay] ever since the days of the Egyptians; it's part of life. During my MGM days, they used to sit and knit the most beautiful little booties for me to put on my feet at night and pretty little knit gloves as well." —MOVIE STAR ANN MILLER

BOOKS: *THE DAVID KOPAY STORY*

Sports fans as a whole will find *The David Kopay Story,* by David Kopay and Perry Deane Young, either delightful or appalling and, in any case, mesmerizing, since it positively reeks with juicy locker-room gossip. We see Sonny Jurgenson "so drunk at practice he couldn't pronounce the calls"; we hear Alex Karras snicker, "Maybe I'm not the only Greek around here"; we learn that as far as Vince Lombardi was concerned, "your injury was either so bad you had to be carried off in an ambulance, or you played."

At the point Kopay decides to come out publicly, he remembers how "Lombardi always told us to 'run to daylight.' That's exactly what I was doing." It was a daylight the dawn of which was years in coming, because this is also the story of a man who was once so victimized by the myth of the macho jock that he was deathly afraid of showing affection for another man, much less love or lust.

Appropriately enough, the 1975 *Washington Star* series on homosexuality in sports that triggered Dave Kopay's well-publicized coming out was in turn triggered by "a query from *The Advocate* about gay athletes." One response to that query had already achieved a modest notoriety: "Your colossal gall in attempting to extend your perversion to an area of total manhood," fumed a Minnesota Twins functionary, "is just simply unthinkable." Aside from the semiliteracy of "just simply," such mindless rhetoric perfectly illustrates what Kopay was up against in his college days and during his ten hectic years as a pro.

Toward the end of his autobiography, however, logic at last triumphs. "Homosexuality in football? I always thought football was the last bastion of masculinity," says a younger player, and Dave answers, "Masculinity? Male homosexuality is pure masculinity." Of course, and what could be more obvious? But just simply try to convince your local tight end.

Perhaps even Kopay can't do that, though his book will undoubtedly open a few eyes and maybe loosen a few ends, too. He slyly demonstrates, for example, how "the whole language of football is involved in sexual allusions. We were told to go out and 'fuck those guys,' to take the ball and 'stick it up their asses.'"

For the straight unbeliever, then, such comments may well prove a revelation. The effect on those who are gay and know it and do something about it, though, will necessarily be less dramatic.
—CARL MAVES

Artist Dennis Forbes lampooned Kopay in *The Advocate* for his refusal to participate in the Florida orange juice boycott. Said Kopay: "I switched to rum and coke for a while, but then I figured, *the hell with it.*"

ENTRANCES AND EXITS

1978 Unhinge the closet doors! Suddenly, gays and lesbians popped up as well-known athletes, next-door neighbors, authors, politicians, sons and daughters, wives and husbands, teachers, clergy, and business executives.

The glare of international media attention fueled gay liberation. There seemed little ostensible reason to stay in the closet when gays began appearing everywhere from talk shows to the front page, magazines to prime-time news. The sensation of this fresh experience was euphoric. Civil rights loomed as a promising reality for gays and lesbians on *this* side of the rainbow.

The sexually active gay male was a new media animal. Sex created its own culture, experimental and diverse, kinky and satiating. Relationships were dismissed by some gays as "hetero-imitative." Recreational sex was seen as a healthy alternative to internalized homophobia. Seeking, restless queers revealed new styles of punk, dressed in black, lived in lofts, and started shaving their hair instead of blow-drying it.

A big event of the year was NBC's broadcast of *Sergeant Matlovich vs. the U.S. Air Force*. Matlovich, discharged earlier from the service after a widely publicized trial centering on his acknowledged homosexuality, now had his story told for millions of American television viewers. In a tellingly candid *Advocate* interview, Matlovich poignantly expressed his loneliness, along with his deep yearning for love. "I've never been in a relationship...but I'm a lover-oriented and home-oriented person," the most famous gay man of the year said. "I would like it to be a relationship where we just found that we didn't really need anything outside...each other." His boyishness made him the Charles Lindbergh of the movement, a misunderstood pioneer.

Gay literature began to flourish, and gay and lesbian bookstores were transformed into burgeoning community centers. Gay novels, a New York editor opined, "won't be out of fashion until love and sex are out of fashion. There's no end to the stories that can be told." Little did he know. Gay and lesbian story-

A triumphant Harvey Milk standing in the doorway of his campaign headquarters shortly after winning a seat on San Francisco's Board of Supervisors. A year later, in November 1978, the charismatic gay leader was shot to death by political rival Dan White.

161

telling has surpassed all predictions. If we are everywhere, so are our gay books.

Gay political muscle was flexed, most notably in the emergence of a smiling Harvey Milk on the national scene following his election as a San Francisco Supervisor. His style was marked by perspicacity, energetic hard work, earthiness, and a healthy sense of humor. When gay arch-enemy California State Senator John V. Briggs of Fullerton slurred Milk's San Francisco as "the moral garbage dump of homosexuality in this country," Milk returned the serve with the agility and deftness of a Martina Navratilova. Quipped Milk: "Nobody likes garbage, 'cause it smells. Yet eight million tourists visited San Francisco last year. I wonder how many visited Fullerton?"

Still, the legal and political landscape for gays frequently mirrored the somber facade of a dark collage. Milk was assassinated near the end of the year; gay-rights ordinances were overturned or rescinded in cities around the country; the plight of gays in the military increasingly made headlines; and a local school board in Alaska decided simply to *ban* homosexuality. Politically, all this was unpredictable, precarious, heady stuff, scary and at the same time energizing.

But when the smoke cleared, following the year's political upheavals and sexual hedonism, a curious discovery was made: The closet was as dark, dank, and filled to capacity with gays as it had been at the outset. "I'm probably more representative of people who are closety than I am of people who are gay activists," said openly lesbian Massachusetts State Representative Elaine Noble. "I'm very aware of…people who can't come out, who don't want to come out, who are afraid to come out."

So, while gays were everywhere, the closet was, too. Nowhere was this more evident than in the teaching profession. Phil Sullivan, a nongay teacher with a gay daughter, had these words to say: "Many of my best teachers have been homosexuals, and as a teacher myself I have known many more. My only regret is that they could not, in their time, be comfortable with themselves, but had to be more pedantic, aloof, and distanced from their students than was good for them or us. They lost a dimension of themselves."

Nineteen seventy-eight was an incredible year for me in a personal sense. My past involvement in civil rights and the anti–Vietnam War movement made the subject of gay rights a thrilling and demanding one for me. I had been jailed numerous times during the sixties for civil protest, marched with Martin Luther King, Jr., and had been arrested twice for leading peace Masses inside the Pentagon. So, the challenge of civil rights for gays became an intensely felt struggle. I experienced the full joy of being a proud and open gay man. My gay memoir, *Take Off the Masks,* was published, I fell in love, and I appeared on national TV as a guy who was gay and happy about it. Thousands of letters poured in from gay people who responded positively to my message.

Soon, however, I would be more sober about the whole experience. Queer-haters responded to my coming out with negativism and hate. And, as a spiritual leader, I would come to grips with the savage gulf that exists between my gay brothers and lesbian sisters, on the one hand, and much of organized religion, on the other. I would also discover that while there is a gay world, there's not a cohesive, single gay community. The sheer diversity within the gay world is shatteringly robust and never-failingly creative.

From Bryant to Briggs, our enemies helped us just as much as belligerent Southern sheriffs aided the cause of African-American liberation. Despite the ambiguous and ever-changing political landscape for gay and lesbian Americans in 1978, the sheer magnitude of our mass coming out empowered us for the struggles to come.
—MALCOLM BOYD

"President Carter has difficulty with the [gay and lesbian] issue. It was on the 'Tomorrow' show, when he was a candidate, that he spoke about homosexuality and said that it puzzled him. He said that he did not approve of discrimination against any people, specifically when it was applied to homosexuals….But he still found the issue troubling and confusing."
—FORMER WHITE HOUSE AIDE MIDGE COSTANZA

"Homosexuality is a failure of emotional maturation—and it is nonsense to pretend that it is simply an 'alternative lifestyle' with the same value to society as sexual normalcy."
—U.S. SENATOR S. I. HAYAKAWA

> "*It is no longer news or a program just to be gay. It is news what gay people do.*"
> —TV HOST DAVID SUSSKIND

U.S. District Judge Ross Sterling ordered the reinstatement with two years' back pay of Gary Van Ooteghem, an assistant in the Harris County, Texas, treasurer's office. The court found that unreasonable limits stifling free speech were imposed on Van Ooteghem who had been fired for political activity on behalf of gay rights.

JANUARY *Time* magazine printed an advertisement sponsored by a Dutch-group and signed by Simone de Beauvoir, Jean-Paul Sartre, Gunter Grass, John Gielgud, Alberto Moravia, and twenty-four other famous Europeans in support of gay rights in the United States and attacking Anita Bryant and President Carter. ❑ The school board of Copper River, Alaska, banned homosexual employees. ❑ The Navy issued regulations stating that while it is not "mandatory" to discharge homosexuals, they should be "separated" from service. ❑ A Ku Klux Klan chapter for Oklahoma teenagers was formed for the purpose of attacking gay people. ❑ California Superior Court Judge John Sapunor ruled in favor of the California Department of Health, calling for the wholesaling of "Rush," one of the nitrate inhalers sold as a "room odorizer" but used as a sexual stimulant, to be halted.

FEBRUARY Senator George McGovern vaguely endorsed gay rights at a New Alliance for Gay Equality dinner in Los Angeles, stating he opposed discrimination of any kind. ❑ Josette Mondanaro, director of a statewide drug abuse program, and a lesbian, was reinstated by the state personnel board after she had been fired by California Governor Jerry Brown.

MARCH After years of being denied recognition on campus, the University of Missouri's Gay People's Union received official approval, gaining university funding. ❑ An antigay purge unleashed against enlisted men at California's Vandenberg Air Force Base resulted in twelve dismissals over a three-month period.

APRIL Nearly one thousand demonstrators marched in downtown Manhattan demanding passage of the city's gay-rights bill, introduced to the City Council and denied for seven consecutive years; the bill failed again. ❑ A dinner sponsored by the Municipal Elections Committee of Los Angeles, one of the first gay political action coalitions in the nation, raised $40,000 for Southern California candidates supporting gay rights. ❑ St. Paul voters overturned a four-year-old gay-rights ordinance. ❑ A comedian on "The Tonight Show" cracked, "I love California, but I'm a little concerned about the schools. All the teachers are heterosexual and my son is gay!" ❑ A gay film festival in Paris was attacked by twenty members of a neo-fascist group armed with iron bars; they clubbed patrons and stole the receipts while police, unaware of the attack, confiscated banned films, including three by Andy Warhol. ❑ Los Angeles's new police chief, Daryl Gates, announced in a *Los Angeles Times* interview, "Display of sexual orientation of any kind is in bad taste." ❑ Ohio's only law prohibiting gay sexual solicitation was found to be "unconstitutionally vague," and was later repealed. ❑ Openly gay student Dan Jones was elected student body president of the conservative Michigan State University.

MAY A gay-rights ordinance in Wichita, Kansas, was rescinded by a margin of five to one in a special election. ❑ Disneyland held its first Gay Night, though it closed off dance floors. ❑ Supporters of California State Senator John Briggs officially filed the 500,000 signatures needed to qualify his initiative to remove gay employees from public schools. ❑ A gay-rights ordinance in the university town of Eugene, Oregon, was overturned by a vote of 26,000 to

13,000. ❏ The Florida Supreme Court ruled that mere statement of one's homosexuality is not a failure to meet the "good moral character" standard for acceptance to the state bar.

JUNE Legislators in Alaska legalized all consensual sex acts between adults in a sweeping revision of the state's criminal code. ❏ Triangle Gay Community Center, the first of its kind in New York City, was formally dedicated. ❏ In a sold-out concert in Santa Monica, California, Joan Baez, Harry Chapin, Holly Near, and Peter Yarrow raised $25,000 to fight the antigay Proposition Six, the so-called "Briggs Initiative." ❏ A record 240,000 people turned out for Gay Pride Day in San Francisco. ❏ The U.S. Patent Office refused to trademark the title of *Gaysweek* magazine, calling the title "immoral." ❏ The American Nurses Association passed a resolution endorsing civil rights legislation banning discrimination on the basis of sexual orientation. ❏ California gay activist Frank Vel began his walk down the length of the state to raise media attention and educate rural voters about Proposition Six.

JULY Youths wielding baseball bats savagely assaulted six gay men in "the Rambles," a popular cruising area in New York City's Central Park. ❏ The Federal Communications Commission ruled that gay people must be included in the "community ascertainment" efforts of radio stations. ❏ *Homosexualities,* a widely publicized study issued by the Kinsey Institute, showed that gay men lead daily lives that are basically similar to those of heterosexual men. ❏ The Atlantic Richfield Company became the target of a gay boycott due to a two-thousand-dollar contribution the corporation made to the California gubernatorial campaign of antigay crusader John Briggs. ❏ For the first time in Mexican history, a gay group marched in Mexico City as part of a civil rights demonstration.

AUGUST The gay community lost an important political ally when Midge Costanza, the outspoken Presidential assistant who organized a meeting between gay leaders and the White House earlier in the year, resigned her position. ❏ The Pentagon gave gay veterans permission to upgrade their discharge status based on service records, which entitled them to a considerable increase in veteran's benefits. ❏ The *Los Angeles Times* described Proposition Six as "vicious," "mean-spirited," and "repugnant to basic American freedoms," joining a chorus of opposition to the measure that included Bob Hope and former California Governor Ronald Reagan. ❏ NBC broadcast the TV movie *Sergeant Matlovich vs. the U.S. Air Force.* ❏ Harvey Rosenberg began marketing Gay Bob, an anatomically correct doll packed in a closet and wearing jeans and a plaid shirt; he eventually sold over ten thousand of the dolls, priced at $14.95. ❏ Gay groups from fourteen European countries joined forces to form the International Gay Association (IGA), as an outgrowth of the conference of the Campaign for Homosexual Equality in Coventry, England. ❏ A raid on the London offices of *Cue International,* an arts and entertainment magazine for gay men, resulted in the confiscation of copies of the magazine and John Rechy's novel *The Sexual Outlaw.* ❏ More than one hundred gay and feminist Australians were arrested while counterdemonstrating at an anti-abortion rally in Sydney.

In November, hundreds of lesbians were among the thousands of participants in Take Back the Night marches protesting violence against women in major American cities.

White-haired Aileen Ryan (*below foreground*) presided over stormy hearings in November before the General Welfare Committee of the New York City Council, which defeated a gay-rights bill 6–3.

In San Francisco, two self-proclaimed faggots (*top*) and Sally Gearhart (*above*) celebrate on Election Day in November as Proposition 6, the Briggs Initiative, was defeated by a healthy 58–42 percent margin.

SEPTEMBER   Openly lesbian Virginia Apuzzo, a professor of urban sociology at Brooklyn College and co-director of the Gay Rights National Lobby, lost her bid for the state Assembly from the 57th District in Brooklyn, New York. ❑ Sergeant Bill Douglas, whose request for a discharge from the Army due to being gay had been denied, was released from military service immediately after appearing in a black lace evening gown, heels, and a wig on an army base in Fort Carson, Colorado. ❑ One of the toughest gay-rights laws in the country was approved by the City Council of Berkeley, California. ❑ Openly lesbian Massachusetts state legislator Elaine Noble lost her bid for the Democratic nomination for U.S. Senate to newcomer Paul Tsongas. ❑ A bill revising the New Jersey penal code to legalize private consensual homosexual acts was signed into law by Governor Brendan Byrne. ❑ The Gay Activists Alliance at the University of Oklahoma lost its eighteen-month battle for official recognition.

OCTOBER   Bruce Voeller, a founder of the National Gay Task Force, announced his resignation as its co-director for personal reasons. ❑ The acclaimed gay documentary *Word Is Out* was aired on most PBS stations around the nation. ❑ The Washington State Supreme Court upheld the custody award of six children to two lesbian mothers. ❑ Roman Catholic Archbishop John Quinn, California Young Republicans, and Howard Jarvis joined the opposition to Proposition Six. ❑ A concert given by Grace Jones in Washington, D.C., was attended by 4,500 and raised thousands of dollars toward building a local gay community center. ❑ An openly gay member of the Santa Clara County Human Relations Commission was unanimously voted to chair the Northern California group. ❑ Sweden, where gay male and lesbian sex acts have been legal since 1944, abolished discriminatory age-of-consent laws and set a uniform age of consent at fifteen for heterosexuals and homosexuals.

NOVEMBER   San Francisco Supervisor Harvey Milk and Mayor George Moscone were assassinated by political rival Dan White, throwing the city into mourning and Dianne Feinstein into the mayor's office. ❑ California's Proposition Six was trounced by a significant margin in what was anticipated to be a much tighter race. ❑ More than two hundred women attended the fifth annual Lesbian Writers Conference in Chicago. ❑ Seattle voters rejected Initiative 13, which would have repealed gay-rights measures. ❑ Five openly gay men were ordained as Catholic priests by the Rev. Robert M. Clement, Bishop of New York, Eucharistic Catholic, an offshoot of the Church that does not follow Rome and does not require celibacy of its priests. ❑ The Gay Activists Alliance of Washington, D.C., filed a $10 million lawsuit against the Metropolitan Area Transit Authority for refusing to rent the group advertising space on buses; two years later, the group won in federal court.

DECEMBER   Paroled killer David Likens was charged with three of five "clone murders" in San Francisco that had baffled police since October. ❑ The Gay National Education Switchboard in San Francisco pulled its plug due to lack of funding after two months of operation. ❑ A bill to exempt the legalization of homosexual acts from a recent state penal code reform went before New Jersey legislators; it later failed.

HARVEY MILK REMEMBERED

For a long time, it looked as though Harvey Milk was destined to become a gay version of perennial presidential candidate Harold Stassen. Milk first ran for the San Francisco Board of Supervisors in 1973 when, sporting a mustache and a long ponytail, he declared, "I stand for all those who feel that the government no longer understands the individual and no longer respects individual rights." He was defeated.

He ran for supervisor in 1975, calling for a program to bring San Francisco government "back to the people who actually live in the city." He was defeated again. The following year, Milk ran for the California State Assembly; to his dismay, a number of gay leaders supported his heterosexual opponent, Art Agnos. Milk had just been appointed to the city Board of Permit Appeals by Mayor George Moscone. When he decided to run for the Assembly, the mayor fired him from his new post. Milk then went on to lose the election.

So when Milk ran for the San Francisco Board of Supervisors in 1977 and won, victory was sweet indeed. Even Milk's detractors had to admire his persistence and determination. Said the exultant candidate: "I understand the responsibility of being gay. I was elected by the people of this district, but I also have a responsibility to gays—not just in the city, but elsewhere."

Milk never lost sight of that responsibility. During his year in office, he submitted a landmark gay-rights ordinance to the Board of Supervisors. The measure—which moved to end antigay discrimination in jobs, housing, and public accommodations—was passed by the board and signed into law by Mayor George Moscone. Supervisor Dan White cast the only dissenting vote.

Milk entered politics relatively late in life; he was forty-three years old when he first ran for the Board of Supervisors. He decided to become politically active out of anger over the Vietnam War and the Watergate scandal.

Born in the village of Woodmere, New York, Milk was the second son of a Jewish family. His father was in the retail clothing business. Milk graduated from Albany Teachers College in 1951. During the Korean War he became a Navy deep-sea diving officer on a submarine rescue ship in the Pacific. In 1953, the Navy discovered his homosexuality and Milk was dishonorably discharged.

The discharge prevented Milk from pursuing his teaching career, so he worked for insurance and brokerage firms. He also helped produce several Broadway musicals and plays. In 1969, he moved to San Francisco and became a securities analyst with a large company. However, his position was abolished following a merger. It was then that he came out of the closet.

As San Francisco's first openly gay supervisor, Milk came to symbolize the gay community's determination to be part of the political process. His very presence in City Hall forced all San Franciscans to acknowledge that gay people play a vibrant, important role in the life of San Francisco.

In the end, Milk—the gay Harold Stassen—was called a gay Martin Luther King, Jr.
—LENNY GITECK

Always festive: Harvey Milk in clown drag.

Thousands of San Franciscans gathered November 27 in a candlelit march honoring the slain civil rights leader.

MURDER AND MOURNING

San Francisco Mayor George Moscone, a longtime friend of gay people, and openly gay Supervisor Harvey Milk were gunned down in their City Hall offices November 27 in what was apparently an act of political vengeance.

Police charged former Supervisor Dan White with two counts of murder and with illegal firearms possession. White had resigned from his post less than three weeks earlier, saying he could not support his wife and infant son on the $9,600 annual half-time salary. Five days later, White asked for the job back. But the mayor, responding to complaints from White's constituents, decided to name someone else to the post. Meanwhile, Milk lobbied against retaining the politically conservative White.

Moscone was killed in his inner office during a private meeting with White, just thirty minutes before a press conference at which the mayor planned to name Don Horanzy, a neighborhood activist and political unknown, to succeed White. Police allege that after shooting Moscone, White crossed City Hall and shot Milk. After leaving the building, White turned himself in at a police station, where later he reportedly confessed to the killings.

Reactions to the murders came from stunned friends and colleagues of the two men. They were both remembered universally as activist politicians who listened with compassion to their constituents.

As supervisor, Milk had come to be widely regarded as a symbol of the aspirations of gay people to participate openly in mainstream politics and in society. "The fact of his homosexuality gave him an insight into the scars which all oppressed peoples wear," said Acting Mayor Dianne Feinstein.

The two liberal leaders were honored by a massive outpouring of grief unprecedented in city history. They both lay in state beneath the City Hall rotunda on November 29, as thousands of San Franciscans filed past the closed caskets to pay their respects. Various memorial services throughout the week honored the dead officials. On the evening of the shootings, more than twenty-five thousand people carrying candles marched silently from the heavily gay Castro area to City Hall to pay tribute. —SCOTT ANDERSON

ELAINE NOBLE

Senior editor Sasha Gregory-Lewis recorded the following conversation with openly lesbian Massachusetts State Representative Elaine Noble. The interview was conducted at a turning point in Noble's life, at a time when she had made the decision not to run for reelection in 1978.

Over the past three years in office I was just getting my voters and people to say, "She can deliver $2.2 million worth of street lighting, and she got through a fifty-thousand-dollar ERA commission, and she got through some good rent-control, pro-tenant legislation"—I was just beginning to have my voters and my people focus on that instead of "Elaine Noble, lesbian." But since the Anita Bryant thing happened, in many ways I've been taken back to square one. People were saying, "You have to speak on this, you have to do this, we don't have anybody with the legitimacy to speak," and everybody was asking me to comment on Anita.

So really, it's back to where I began in the beginning as being thought of as the *gay* politician. Not that that's a terrible thing to be, but the political reality is that any politician has to have a series of issues, and once you're pigeonholed with one issue it is sort of a death knell.

Basically, what I have experienced in the past three years is that because I was considered the gay politician, I had not only more work, but got more flack, more criticism, more heartache from the gay community than from the people who elected me.

I guess more than anything I'm just exhausted and very, very tired and probably disillusioned because I really tried the best I could and it wasn't good enough for the gay community. To be honest, I don't know what "good enough" is.

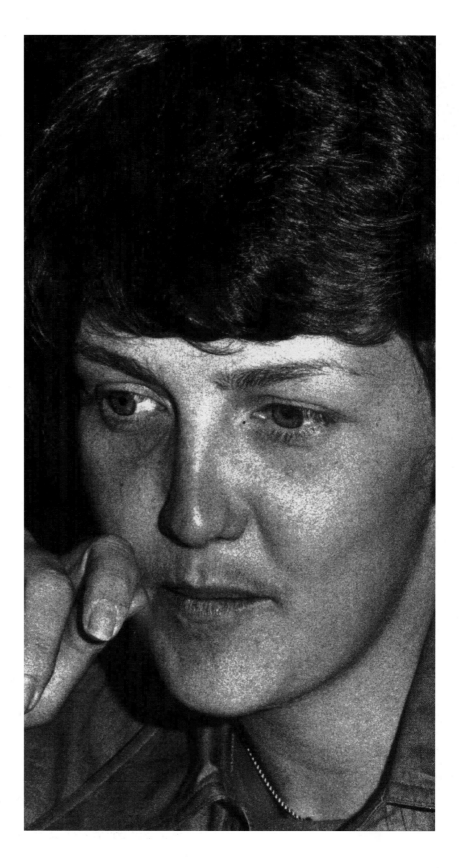

PAT BOND

To many lesbians coming of age in the seventies, Pat Bond, a San Francisco performer and activist by then in her mid-fifties, was what one *Advocate* writer called an "archetypal lesbian." She had appeared in the ground-breaking gay documentary *Word Is Out.* She performed her one-woman shows, *Conversations with Pat Bond* and *An Evening with Gertrude Stein,* around the country. And she was mouthing off at every opportunity.

She had barely begun her theater career when she joined the Army in 1945. Reminiscing, she told *The Advocate* that "the Army took in all these obvious lesbians—anybody could have seen—they were done up, most of them, in men's suits, sideburns shaved over their ears, men's underwear, and men's shoes. Once they got us in, they decided to have a witch-hunt."

The civilian world was equally unforgiving. "I worked at one point at a fruitcake factory," said Bond. "The fruitcakes came out on a belt and you stuck a cherry in the middle. We wore bandanas to cover our men's haircuts. And we got jobs driving motorcycles: I guess you went by so fast they couldn't see who you were. But forget offices, anything professional. We were stuck."

It was sort of a no-win situation with gay people. If I tried to be the best politician I could be, some gay people gave me flack because I wasn't being gay enough or responding enough to the gay community.

The gay community expected me to be on call twenty-four hours a day. It was like they felt they owned me. They think, like someone who complained that I didn't answer the phone at five in the morning, that I'm paid to be awake all the time. The irony of that is that these gay people didn't elect me. The majority of the people who are out in the gay community not only don't live in my district, they don't vote in my district. The majority of them probably don't vote.

If I were straight they probably would have thought that half of what I did was so terrific, because all the other people who get gay support don't do an iota of what I do for gay people, and in many ways they are held in higher esteem than I am.

I'm not even sure that I can even evaluate it or explain it at this point. I think I'm pretty confused about it because one part of me is saying, "What the hell did I do wrong?" I can't figure it out. Didn't I do enough? Did I do too much?

The only thing I can say is that a handful of people are far more comfortable being represented by somebody who is a straight male. It's sort of like blacks. There was a time in history when blacks, some blacks, felt they'd rather have a sympathetic liberal white speak for them. I think that's where we are.

I think the level of self-hate right now among gay people is so damn high that if, when you start trying to work in the community in a sane manner, you ask, "What are you doing constructively?" it has a self-hate backlash. They can't hit the straight world, they can't swing at the straight world, so they swing at the person who's nearest to them. Sometimes they see me as an identifiable figure, as the person nearest them.

Whenever a minority group has taken or achieved access to a political process, they assume that that process will be used negatively against them whenever they come in contact with it. It is like children who've come out of a home where they were battered. Those children will probably batter their own children, and will probably go into relationships with their hands psychologically over their face because they expect to be battered, because their only experience with close love relationships has been damage. I think that if you've been damaged by the political process you're going to want to damage back, damage others who are involved in it.

One of the things I'm very grateful for is that I will have time until 1980 to evaluate if I want to run for office again or not. I'm not sure that I want to run for public office if I have to carry the heavy burden that I've had to carry from the gay community. One of the things that's got to happen is that there's got to be more gay people who are going to take on part of that burden, or at least help.

Now that I've made the decision not to run, I've got to get a job. The political reality is that my being gay has created a real problem about going back into an even more conservative academic atmosphere. I don't have a whole lot of options, so in essence, I'm going to have to take what I can get.

I am an idealist, a dreamer. I'm also a pragmatist. But it's part of dreaming that you never quite realize those dreams; you just find ways to bring you closer to them. Gay rights is an issue that I'll never abandon, but I don't want it to be the issue that controls or destroys my life or my political future.

THE HETEROSEXUAL SOLUTION: A DILEMMA FOR GAY MORMONS

The following excerpt is taken from a major critique of the official antigay position of the Church of Jesus Christ of Latter-Day Saints, or the Mormons. It was written by an unnamed student at Brigham Young University (BYU) in response to a lecture by a psychology professor, and subsequently published in The Advocate.

The Church generally takes two approaches toward "curing" the homosexual. The first is a sort of positive-thinking approach wherein supportive counsel is given to encourage the young man to think manly thoughts, do masculine things, date, even in some cases "mess around" a little with women, and to put all notions of homosexuality out of his mind. He is urged to be prayerful, repent any past transgressions, be faithful, get married, and settle down.

This method is encouraging to the naive but quickly runs into difficulty. If the young man goes along with the persistent urging of almost everyone around him to get married, his predicament bcomes much more complicated. If he candidly reveals to the authorities that he remains homosexual in spite of all efforts to change, he is made to feel guilty and his intentions are doubted. Most quietly and simply withdraw from this kind of destructive counseling. Many are embittered permanently against the Church, while still homosexual.

The other therapy encouraged by the Church is, ironically, regarded as more professional. This is the behavioral therapist's approach. Curiously enough, BYU is coming to be preeminent in applying conditioning therapy for the treatment of homosexuality. Let me tell you briefly of a young man who recently "successfully" completed this treatment. He was popular and a good student but troubled by this problem that "wouldn't go away." He was devoted to the Church, but his talks with the Church authorities only served to confuse him. With trepidation, he finally went to the BYU counseling service. He was given a battery of tests and interviews, then was assigned to a conditioning therapy program coupled with hypnosis and supportive counseling. He came out of these sessions nauseated, shaking, and with mild burns on his arms. For nearly two years this therapy lasted, during which time he felt confident he was changing and that homosexuality was behind him.

Shortly after this, he met a friend, whom I shall call Bob. Bob was talented, intelligent, and handsome. Immediately upon his introduction to Bob, he knew that nothing really had changed. They were soon great friends, and he knew that all of what had happened in therapy, painful as it had been, had not even scratched the surface of who he always was.

This young man's experience, like many others', including my own, discredits the proposition of reconditioning the homosexual. This story is duplicated over and over. Right now, young men are going into the BYU Smith Family Living Center to be strapped with electrodes and shocked out of homosexuality.

Has it not occurred to you that in shocking the young man, you are chipping away at his ability ever to love another human being? From what set of values do you say that a man is "improved" when, following shock therapy, he can love neither a man nor a woman? Will Mormons now join the long, shameful tradition of religious fervor working its inhumanity upon mankind, epitomized in the now famous slogan "Kill a queer for Jesus"? The prospects are not encouraging. Above all, God is our judge.

Mormon fathers (*left to right*) Joseph Smith, Ezra Taft Benson, and Brigham Young cast a baleful eye on same-sex love.

Comments and Correspondence

Born and raised a Mormon, I am now not active and can identify closely with Anonymous. His shoes and mine have walked the same path. I sincerely hope the day will come when gay Mormons can openly reveal themselves to each other for mutual support.
—NAME WITHHELD, Layton, Utah

I, too, am one of the "victims" of the Mormon Church, having joined it seven years ago for the express purpose of overcoming my growing homosexual orientation. It seemed to be the thing in this world that could successfully put me on the straight and narrow path, but it failed miserably....There is no way to do justice to the feelings that dominate the body and soul of a gay Mormon, and I guess that's the real purpose of this letter. I feel the need to break the barrier that has held me away from totally admitting to myself and to my God what I am.
—NAME WITHHELD, Tucson, Arizona

Somehow I was under the impression the Mormons had their gay people under control. ...Since the article leaves me shattered, I am wondering what's left in the religious field supporting the rights of gay people.
—REV. GLENN GENERAUX, Northridge, California

THE BOYS IN THE BACK ROOM

RIGHT WATCH
BY SASHA GREGORY-LEWIS

Nearly a year ago a band of demonstrators drew national publicity at the International Women's Year (IWY) Conference in Houston with placards demanding death for all "dykes and kikes." Women's liberation activists fought off the placard bearers, preventing them from invading the IWY conclave. Across town, followers of Phyllis Schlafly were gathering for their counter-rally at the Astrodome. Again, the same extremist demonstrators were turned away, their positions too embarrassing even for stalwarts of the hardcore radical Right.

Most reporters blamed the incidents on the "Klan." The origin of at least some of these placards, however, was a self-proclaimed and government-chartered church, the New Christian Crusade Church.

The IWY incidents are just two among many that show how the racist right, or "white right," takes advantage of vague government definitions of what constitutes a church or religion to push their race-hate propaganda under cover of secrecy. Like a Swiss bank account, religious status allows a group's officers to do virtually anything with money they receive (which is tax-deductible to contributors) once it hits church coffers, without anyone being the wiser. It is only when a "religion" treads too far into politics that the Internal Revenue Service or a state tax board moves into action to withdraw a church's tax-exempt status. Even in this case "politics" is defined within the limits of electoral political efforts.

The New Christian Church claims adherents in fifty-two countries. Its chief organ is its racist and anti-Semitic monthly tabloid *Christian Vanguard*. The Church also has an "action arm"—the Christian Defense League. In practice, these three allegedly "religious" operations are part of a hybrid Klan/Nazi machine under the direction of James K. Warner, once a devotee of American Nazi Party leader George Rockwell.

Besides sponsoring the publication of racist propaganda (including such titles as *How Jews Steal Your Food Money* and *The International Jew*) and demonstrating against women's and gay rights, the group has also sponsored meetings of national and international leaders of the "white right." It has also sponsored several lawsuits, the most recent of which is aimed at the television airing of *Holocaust*. (The group, in its propaganda, denies both that the Hitler regime carried out a program of extermination of Jews and that six million people were victims of his death squads.)

Warner's New Christian Crusade Church (which will ordain ministers if they have completed the proper courses in racist theory, each course at a fee, of course) got its start in 1965 in Los Angeles as the Odinist Religion, chartered by the State of California and given its religious tax status by the IRS. Since Odinism apparently was not a satisfactory drawing card for Warner's racist ideologies, he changed the name to its Christian version in 1971. The organization has since moved to Louisiana and is said to have ties with David Duke's splinter Klan organization, the Knights of the Ku Klux Klan.

—with assistance from the Ann K. Justice Network

Staying alive. To the public eye, back rooms don't look like the land of the living. The men appear to be mere shadows, hints, suggestions. But they are men. The night seems filled with illusions, dreams, fantasies, but this is something genuine. It may be perceived through a haze of beer and grass, poppers and pills, but it remains raw reality. Sex means a lot of things to a lot of people. For some it's a sacred mystery. For others it's a pain in the ass. Some like it out of the rule books, and others like it out of their minds. Some do it in a one-family house, in the master bedroom, missionary position only, with a flag and a cross over the bed. Others do it in back rooms and baths. Some work at sex and others play.

Back rooms may lie somewhere between the borders of extravagance and excess; they may be an extreme of sexuality; but they are nonetheless a truth, necessary data for those of us who love to explore more than the socially approved aspects of our human nature. Being beyond the responsibilities and cares of the straight-ruled day, the gay promiscuity parlors—baths, backroom bars, porno theaters, and bookstores—offer the security of a crowded mother's womb in which we can touch the innermost fantasies of our community. These dark, self-contained, totally gay environments provide a temporary respite from the constraints of being "queer" in the "normal" world, whether the identity is overt or covert. Here there is the relief of shamelessness. Here we are the majority. We make the rules of social and sexual contact, and everyone is equal at the start. At the baths it's towels; at the backroom bars it may be the macho uniform demanded by some dress codes to preserve the otherworldly atmosphere. In all of them, there's the darkness to level the more drastic differences of age and appearance and manner.

There is something there in the fetid dark to which my spirit belongs—something very human and real—as real as lovers and sunlight. Promiscuity is part of the unique heritage of gay men, and because there is potential good in it, we should fight to preserve it along with the survival of our identity as a community. There is a morning after. Our lifestyle is about to come under attack, and we should defend it. It's like the song says: "Stayin' alive. Stayin' alive."

—ARNIE KANTROWITZ

PORTFOLIO

The Advocate's centerspread was frequently used to promote the work of gay and lesbian photographers, painters, and other artists. One photojournalist showcased in the Portfolio section was New York–based Bettye Lane, whose dramatic images of a movement-in-the-making appeared frequently in The Advocate during the seventies. Aside from her photographs in The Advocate, Lane's work has been familiar to readers of Newsweek, Ms., Time, People, and numerous other publications around the world. Here are a few of the veteran photographer's most memorable images.

Proud parent, New York City, 1974 (**right**).
Ready to be clubbed: *Cruising* protest, New York City, 1979 (*below*).

On the fence, New York City, 1977 (*above*).
Radicalesbians at first Gay Pride parade, New
York City, 1971 (*below*).

Malcolm Michaels Jr., a.k.a. Marsha
Johnson, at the Christopher Street
Parade, New York City, 1971 (*above*).

FILM: *WORD IS OUT*

The lifeless body of Shirley MacLaine sways gently at the end of a long heavy rope. Rod Steiger walks quietly into the green forest, carrying a loaded shotgun. Click. Sandy Dennis lies broken beneath the twisted branches of a fallen tree. A photo for the family album. Don Murray slits his throat with a razor in the oak-paneled washroom of his Senate office chamber. Our lives on film.

Part of the reason why the alleged gay experience has not been captured on the screen is because it has not been sufficiently articulated in real life. Commercial films cannot reflect what cannot be seen. With a few exceptions, the Hollywood sideshow of the past eight decades has been a strictly heterosexual view of the eternal question "Who are these people and what are they doing here?"

A hidden dream inside every gay documentarian must surely be to find a way to show "them" who we all really are, a magic trick on the order of the old "What if we were all suddenly bright blue for a day?" routine. Which is why *Stories of Some of Our Lives* is such a cunning subtitle for the new Mariposa Film Group documentary, *Word Is Out*. The expertly interwoven conversations of twenty-six gay men and women originally grew from an idea by filmmaker Peter Adair to do a film called *Who Are We?* It has evolved, after five years and over two hundred videotaped interviews, into the collective effort of three women and three men whose separate visions reshaped the scope of the film into a major documentary with implications greater than any of them had first imagined. By not trying to answer Peter Adair's original question, all six filmmakers have made *Word Is Out* an electric piece of living history.

The Mariposa Film Group worked collectively on *Word Is Out*: (*left to right*) Robert Epstein, Veronica Selver, Peter Adair, Lucy Massie Phenix, Andrew Brown, and Nancy Adair.

The gallery of twenty-six people finally chosen by the filmmakers to tell their stories on screen does so with a power and honesty that alternately tear your heart out and keep you in stitches. There is an implicit sense of community in the film and a strange sense of longing produced when gay people break their traditional silence and talk about their lives in a public way. In *Word Is Out* the subjects range in age from eighteen to seventy-seven, and their diversity is stunning. A lesbian named Whitey tells how her mother's psychiatrist treated her lesbianism by putting her on a diet of two green salads a day. We sit in the audience and think, *Jesus, imagine all the crazy things they had gay people doing all these years.*

The silence of gay people on the screen has been broken, and the voices of the twenty-six gay men and women who have broken it are so personal and so moving that they do indeed show us who we are. They point up our common experience of growing up gay in a straight world and inform us of the tremendous strength in ordinary gay people that has enabled us to survive even though we thought we were the only ones in the world.

Elsa Gidlow, a seventy-seven-year-old poet, says near the beginning of the film, "If there was ever any problem connected with my being a lesbian, it was the loneliness, the fact that I didn't know anybody like me. Where were the others, if there were any?" Well, here they are at last—some of them, anyway. Some of our lives on film.

—VITO RUSSO

BOOKS: *DANCER FROM THE DANCE*

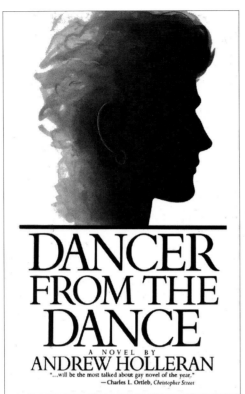

DANCER FROM THE DANCE

A NOVEL BY
ANDREW HOLLERAN

"...will be the most talked about gay novel of the year."
— Charles L. Ortleb, *Christopher Street*

> "**A**ny individual who defines himself sexually, inwardly is already less willing to become an instrument of an outward, political definition. Their connection is with the changing human condition, not with any frozen political hierarchy. That's why, perhaps, the bureaucracy fears sexual freedom....The gay movement is the avant-garde of the new self-awareness, and if it should perish, we, the heterosexual 'inneremigrés,' as I used to call myself in the U.S.S.R., won't have flanks anymore."
> —WRITER JERZY KOSINSKI

Andrew Holleran's *Dancer from the Dance* is very much about private lives led in very public places. It is also a sad story about the death of queens. Though in fact only one actually dies, another continues to reign in New York, another goes into exile and retires to the country, and the last, a macho queen of infinite tenderness, disappears entirely in the end to become for all those left alive a mystery, a living legend, a shred of gossip.

These queens—I call them that because it is the appellation they all pointedly prefer—all call each other by surnames, like Malone or Sutherland. They all come from old or rich families, are startlingly intelligent and stunningly handsome, and either have or don't have big cocks.

They shuttle between uptown and downtown discos and between New York City and the Pines in Fire Island and are generally described as "young men whose cryptic disappearance in New York City their families (unaware they were homosexual) understood less than if they had been killed in a car wreck."

The characters in this book are always sick with love: for a day, an hour, a moment. They constantly dance, pursue big cocks that they never seem to get to suck, and live in fear of three things, as one of the epistolary queens observes: "Rain at the beach, small cocks, and reality. In that order."

They finally all die, in one way or another, though some of the dead stay alive to wander, dancing still among the other living dead, clad in their obligatory uniforms of baseball hats, plaid shirts, bomber jackets, painter's pants, and vast collections of absolutely necessary shoes.

Lest it seem that I found this superficial, silly, endlessly self-involved, I did; but it is not the book that merits such description, but rather the people it so remarkably defines. *Dancer from the Dance* is one of the most brilliant gay novels I have read; its tradition is honorable. Indeed, it is probably in the mainstream of gay literature. I suspect that along with Edmund White, there may be no better contemporary writer of gay literature than Andrew Holleran.

The point of this book is that its style, its tone, its nuance, its compassion, and its broad comic range present perfectly the people it lovingly, and yet with tender loathing, describes. How can anyone who has ever been to Cherry Grove resist hearing that the Pines is a "strange seaside community where people are considered creative because they design windows at Saks"?

Holleran knows a basic truth: Gay people are romantics, only romantics; they have always been and always will be so. They are also religious, though rarely Christian, ritualistic, hierarchical, devoted to mystery and the Mysteries, whether of Priapus or Terpsichore. Though literary history has insistently divided time into cycles of romance and classicism, gay people in their literature, from Plato (who sought truth in beauty) to Wilde (who sought it there as well), have always been romantics and romancers, alive to all the possibilities of love.

In this book there are only two kinds of people, the lovers and the beloved. Plato suggested that of the two, the lover, because he gave love, was closer to the divine than the beloved. Holleran is a lover.

—BYRNE FONE

TAKING IT TO THE STREETS

1979 A decade after the Stonewall Riots, gay people took to the streets again. The defining events of the year were the first national march for gay and lesbian rights and the riot following Dan White's trial for the murder of Harvey Milk. We also took over the roads for the mushrooming local parades that celebrated the movement's tenth anniversary, a milestone in the transition from adolescence to maturity. Like any teenager confronting that marker, the second wave of activism that took shape during 1979 faced the future with both excitement and growing pains.

The spirit that sprouted in Greenwich Village had now taken root across the country and was bearing its first fruits. California Governor Edmund G. Brown, Jr., banned discrimination in state hiring; President Carter named lesbian Jill Schropp to a federal council; and the National Endowment for the Arts awarded its first grant to a gay group, The Glines theater in New York. But as the sapling grew and spread, it also ran up against hostility from threatened neighbors, and fissures began to split its once-smooth bark.

Externally, our increasing impact created another backlash like the one led by Anita Bryant. San Franciscans had mustered enough clout to elect an openly gay city supervisor, but when White made Milk our first martyr, the jury just slapped his wrist. And epochal as October's Washington, D.C., demonstration seemed to *us*, it was ignored by mainstream media and politicians—a rude reminder that we were still not taken seriously *except* by extremists. Director William Friedkin persisted despite vociferous protests in filming his sensationalistic *Cruising*. In many realms, we still did not control the "big picture."

Even so, growth was causing problems within our own community. Nineteen seventy-nine was perhaps the last year when everyone in the gay movement could still know everyone else. As each community sprouted more branches, their diversity splintered what had been an intimate, albeit fractious, small town. Two typical portents: an *Advocate* feature on racial minorities finding their own voices, and a warning from the music columnist that new styles

APRIL Governor Jerry Brown signed an executive order prohibiting antigay discrimination in California state hiring. ❑ Gays and members of other minorities demonstrated against harassment by Houston Police Department officers. ❑ Paul Guilbert, a male student at a Rhode Island high school who wanted to take another man to the junior prom, was refused tickets by the school administration; he later sued and won.

MAY In a White House ceremony, President Carter named openly lesbian Jill Schropp from Seattle to the newly reorganized National Advisory Council on Women. ❑ Chicago police carried out a week-long series of raids on the city's gay bars. ❑ After two years of deliberation on a case involving Pacific Telephone, the California Supreme Court ruled that privately owned utilities cannot discriminate against homosexuals. ❑ The Los Angeles City Council approved a comprehensive local ordinance protecting gays from discrimination, becoming the forty-fourth city in the United States to adopt gay civil rights legislation.

JUNE Carl Hill, a photographer for *London Gay News* who arrived at San Francisco International Airport wearing a "Gay Pride" button, was detained by immigration authorities; a judge later ordered that Hill be allowed to stay in the country. ❑ Thousands of gays in cities all across the nation commemorated the tenth anniversary of the Stonewall Riots. ❑ Lucia Valeska was named a coexecutive director of the National Gay Task Force.

Seventeen-year-old Randy Rohl of Sioux Falls, South Dakota, became the first high school student in the nation to take a same-sex partner to a prom.

JULY Dan White was sentenced to prison for seven years and eight months, with the possibility of parole in less than five years. ❑ The New York gay community disrupted the filming of *Cruising*, a movie starring Al Pacino as a detective who poses as gay at West Village leather bars in order to catch a homosexual murderer. ❑ California Governor Jerry Brown appointed a gay man to head the State Arts Council. ❑ The Third District Court of Appeals upheld the 1976 firing of a California Highway Patrolman who had attended a transvestite sex party that was raided by the San Jose vice squad. ❑ Gay artist Robert Opel, a vocal critic of the San Francisco Police Department's complicity in the Milk/Moscone murders, was murdered in his San Francisco gallery; the alleged killer walked out of an unlocked holding cell shortly after his arrest. ❑ *The Gay Tide*, a British Columbia gay newspaper, lost a five-year legal battle to place a classified ad in the Vancouver *Sun*, a major daily.

AUGUST The American Presbyterian Church, representing more than three million members, adopted a policy opposing ordination of gay clergy, elders, and deacons. ❑ U.S. Representative Larry McDonald (D–Ga.) introduced a measure that would put Congress on record opposing gay rights; it passed the House, but died in a Senate committee. ❑ The Metropolitan Community Church held its tenth anniversary general conference in Los Angeles. ❑ The Immigration and Naturalization Service announced that it would no longer ferret out homosexuals among visitors to the United States, and would apply the ban on homosexual travelers only when sexuality became an issue; the State Department ordered consular officials worldwide to continue to deny visas to gays.

In May, a jury found Dan White guilty on two counts of voluntary manslaughter, rather than murder, in the assassinations of George Moscone and Harvey Milk. Three thousand demonstrators rioted at San Francisco City Hall, outraged over the light verdict. Less than a day later, ten thousand gays gathered on Castro Street to sing "Happy Birthday" to Milk, who would have been forty-nine years old had he lived.

SEPTEMBER The California Supreme Court ruled that, contrary to the assumption that lay at the basis of much police harassment of gays, the state may not punish solicitation in public for a sexual act that is legal in private. ❑ Dignity, the Catholic gay organization, celebrated its tenth anniversary at an inter-

The *Cruising* Controversy

"Cruising is a film which will encourage more violence against homosexuals. In the current climate of backlash against the gay-rights movement, this movie is a genocidal act."
—GAY COMMUNITY FLYER

"This film promises to be the most oppressive, ugly, bigoted look at homosexuality ever represented on the screen, the worst possible nightmare of the most uptight straights, and a validation of Anita Bryant's hate campaign.... [Director William] Friedkin's not only playing with a keg of dynamite, he's throwing a match to it."
—COLUMNIST ARTHUR BELL

"I'm not putting anything in this film that doesn't take place every night. This is not fiction. This is the truth."
—PRODUCER JERRY WEINTRAUB

"This is a snuff film."
—PROTESTER DOUG IRELAND

"Anything that brings $7 million into our city is all right with us."
—NEW YORK CITY OFFICIAL NANCY LITTLEFIELD

"While those Cruising riots were going on, I wouldn't participate in them. As a writer I couldn't condone prior censorship of any kind of art whatsoever. People claimed that the film would incite people to violence against gay people, but I doubt it. I don't think art makes that much difference, really. Auden said that a poem never changed anything, and he might be right."
—NOVELIST FELICE PICANO

national convention in San Diego. ❑ Appointment to the Los Angeles Superior Court made Stephen Lachs America's first openly gay judge. ❑ The Episcopal Church passed a resolution opposing the ordination of gay priests. ❑ Former Florida governor Reubin Askew, nominated by President Carter to be his special trade representative, testified before the Senate Finance Committee that he would not hire a homosexual.

OCTOBER The first national March on Washington for Lesbian and Gay Rights drew more than 100,000 demonstrators. Prior to the march, hundreds attended the first National Lesbian/Gay Third World Conference. ❑ During a tour of the United States, Pope John Paul II reaffirmed the Catholic Church's position that homosexual activity is sinful. ❑ Americans for Democratic Action urged the U.S. Senate to support a bill banning job discrimination on the basis of sexual orientation. ❑ Private First Class Roger Curtsinger received an honorable discharge from the Army after acknowledging that he was gay. ❑ California Governor Jerry Brown

announced that if elected president he would sign into law an executive order prohibiting discrimination against homosexuals in federal jobs, possibly including the armed services. ❑ The American Civil Liberties Union instituted a National Gay Rights Project.

NOVEMBER New York City Mayor Ed Koch installed David Rothenberg, openly gay founder of the Fortune Society, as a member of the city's Commission on Human Rights. ❑ The European-centered International Gay Association opened an office in Washington, D.C. ❑ Seeking support for his presidential bid, Jerry Brown attended a fund-raiser in a Washington, D.C., gay disco.

DECEMBER Harry Britt won election to the San Francisco Board of Supervisors. ❑ Gay and lesbian Mormons held their first national conference in Los Angeles. ❑ Jane A. Spahr, a lesbian Presbyterian minister and director of the Council of Oakland Presbyterian Churches, resigned under pressure once her sexual orientation was revealed; in 1991, the General Assembly Permanent Judicial Commission denied her the position again. ❑ The Men's Clinic of the Los Angeles Gay Community Services Center tested a new vaccine for hepatitis B. ❑ Anita Bryant topped the *Good Housekeeping* list of the ten most admired women of 1979.

THE WHITE NIGHT RIOTS

When a San Francisco jury found former city Supervisor Dan White guilty of manslaughter rather than murder in the shooting deaths of Mayor George Moscone and Supervisor Harvey Milk, the city was stunned. And when the gay community erupted in response to the verdict, the rage shocked and scared not only the city's heterosexual population but its gay and lesbian residents as well.

In what became known as the White Night Riots, about three thousand demonstrators marched to San Francisco City Hall on the night of May 21. Scores of demonstrators and police were injured in the ensuing riot—including staunchly pro-gay Supervisor Carol Ruth Silver, injured when she attempted to speak to the crowd. Others who tried unsuccessfully to calm the crowd included organizer Cleve Jones, who tried to divert the march, and Milk's successor, Harry Britt. Damage to City Hall—where supervisors had convened for a regular Monday-night meeting—was estimated at $1 million.

Concern was compounded by a police raid on Castro Street after the riot. *The Advocate*'s Scott Anderson reported that "the police entered a bar called Elephant Walk swinging their nightsticks indiscriminately. Several patrons were injured, and the glass windows and doors of the establishment were shattered."

The following day, Mayor Dianne Feinstein, who was inside City Hall at the time of the attack, met with the Harvey Milk Gay Democratic Club and agreed to let the gay community itself monitor a celebration of Milk's forty-ninth birthday, planned for that evening. The tactic, intended to preempt violence, worked: Some ten thousand people gathered peacefully on Castro Street to sing "Happy Birthday" to Milk. The event was monitored by about four hundred lesbians and gay men in T-shirts with the message PLEASE! NO VIOLENCE!

But the celebrants hardly assumed a conciliatory posture. Speaking to the crowd, Sally Gearhart, a lesbian professor at San Francisco State University, said, "There is no way that I will apologize for what happened last night....Until we display our ungovernable rage at injustice, we won't get heard."

The Advocate ran five articles on the riots, including an eyewitness account by the magazine's typesetter and a cautionary opinion piece by editor Robert McQueen, who called the riots "a sad remembrance for a man who believed in nonviolence and a sad new chapter for a community that has patiently built a long and admirable history of peaceful, responsible behavior." He went on to wonder "how this Monday of mayhem will affect the special, though delicate, relationship the San Francisco gay community has enjoyed with the city." Readers were urged to send contributions to the San Francisco City Hall Repair Fund.

Fury over Dan White's lenient sentence for the killing of gay leader Harvey Milk erupted into the streets around San Francisco's City Hall. The angry mob set police cars ablaze and barricaded members of the Board of Supervisors within the building.

JOHN RECHY

The walls are monkey-puke green. The bedspread, orangutan-ass orange. Clearly, the Sexual Outlaw is not at home, prowling the jungle of Tropicana trappings in his San Francisco hotel room. The Sexual Outlaw is outraged. He calls the desk. The Jack Tar must, for the moment, long for the politesse of Japanese tourists.

Once we've resettled our interview in a new room consoled by cool, white walls and cooler black coffee, I discover that John Rechy is outraged and angered by many things.

He's outraged by gay politicians who prefer propaganda to art—and truth. He's outraged by the Pope and organized religion, especially homosexual churches. He's outraged by psychiatrists, the Kinsey people, Masters and Johnson, and other apologists who judge homosexuals as "not sick" in direct relation to how much we conform to their standards.

Most of all he's outraged by us homosexuals. Based on an earlier play, his new novel, *Rushes,* is set in a New York dockside heavy-leather macho bar called The Rushes and ends up in an orgy room called The Rack. *Rushes* reveals the depth of that anger as Rechy traces a number typical bar-goers through a gripping and groin-groping dark night of the soul. Rechy deplores the growing alcoholism among younger gay men, the popularity and institutionalization of sadomasochism, our reliance upon amyl rushes, and our rush for sexual experience that he considers limiting rather than liberating.

Your comments in *The Village Voice* opposing demonstrations intended to stop the filming of the movie *Cruising* are very controversial. Do you still think it's a First Amendment issue? An issue of prior censorship?

My concern for the First Amendment was actually surpassed by my concern with what would happen to homosexual causes, to homosexual rights if this immediate issue went the other way. We were setting ourselves up for enormous danger that would just lash right back at us. This was at least my equal concern.

Many gay writers are at odds with the movement's spokespeople because of the latter's fairly narrow point of view regarding what is acceptable presentation of what gay life is all about. Do you see this conflict?

One of the crucial issues to be aired is the relationship between politics and art and the responsibility of one to the other. Increasingly, you hear that artists or whoever are supposed to present *positive role models*. Positive images. It has become a cliché now. In the first place what is being called for as a positive image is really an imitation of heterosexuals. To me, that is not a positive image for the homosexual—the great surrender to being just like heterosexual society that is happening in the name of positive role models.

If we insist that *that* is the image we must give and that our artists must provide it, two things are going to happen: We're going to deny who we really are, our endemic beauty, our sensibility, what indeed makes us special; and we're not going to deal with our problems because we're going to be obsessed with presenting a so-called positive image which does not exist.

Your novel suggests that gay men hopelessly choose to participate in their victimization. For instance, the ghettoization that has been forced upon them. In the novel they seem most comfortable in the sites of their oppression.

You can't begin from that point. The book opens outside the bar in a very hostile world. Invaders raid the area, shouting, "Queers, faggots, cocksuckers!" That is what is out there. When the bar closes, one character observes that no matter how cruel the bar was, it protected the men from a greater cruelty outside. The point is not that we are participating in our victimization. The point is that we have been so victimized and so oppressed that we cannot now differentiate where victimization ends and liberation takes over.

People are going to think that I am contradicting myself because I've long upheld the abundance of sexuality. But to me what's happening on the homosexual front is a great confusion between liberation and destruction. I think we're destroying ourselves and calling it liberation.

One of the reasons I use the ritual of the mass as a metaphor in the novel is the mass makes a ritual of the original crucifixion. In our bars, and especially in our orgy rooms and our sadomasochism, we are now doing a mass to heterosexual oppression. How else to account for the fact that the uglier and dirtier the orgy room, the more popular it is?

Why are so many of the metaphors in your book related to the hunt for sex?

One of the things that we must never let go of is our abundant sexuality, which so many people call promiscuity. We are now apologizing for our sexuality. There is no reason to do that. Sexuality is one of the enriching factors in one's life; it keeps one from suicide, for one thing.

But there is a point where this book and where the "sexual outlaw" in me begins to wonder and question the direction in which our sexuality is now going. Younger homosexuals are abdicating a certain portion of their lives; they are surrendering to death at the age of thirty-five. They are creating a world which will lacerate them, which will turn back on them.

I feel responsible about the younger homosexual. We older homosexuals— and again I don't refer simply to age—have a very important duty which is being ignored. Younger homosexuals are the only children we will ever have. I have a duty to leave a world that is better for those homosexuals than the one I experienced with such pain and barbarity. Yet it almost seems as if we're trying to give the younger generation the legacy of pain.

I know that I have had as full a range of experiences as other people. Yet now as I look in alleys or orgy rooms, I see increasingly haunted faces. I think there's got to be more. What are we doing? Is it then, indeed, just a ritual of pain that we have to perform? If so, there's got to be a way to stop it.

—BRENT HARRIS

"S&M is a deliberate, premeditated, erotic blasphemy....I identify more strongly as a sadomasochist than as a lesbian. If I had a choice between being shipwrecked on a desert island with a vanilla lesbian and a hot male masochist, I'd pick the boy."
—PAT CALIFIA

"Since most gays working in the arts are in the closet, there very definitely is the end result of the gay closet sensibility, most of which is rather destructive and not very attractive— its worst excesses can be seen at the Metropolitan Opera House, New York's principal gay theater. But as far as healthy gay sensibility in the arts, that's something new."
—PLAYWRIGHT DORIC WILSON

ANDREW HOLLERAN

Apprehensively, I wait for Andrew Holleran beside the house phone in the plutocratic plush lobby of San Francisco's Hotel St. Francis. I expect the author of the best-selling gay novel *Dancer from the Dance* to be a jaded gay version of John O'Hara—worldly, sophisticated, all rep tie and tweeds.

But a tall, jaunty, trimly thin man in his early thirties, casually dressed in jeans and windbreaker, dispels my fears of a formal Fitzgerald-esque encounter. Andrew Holleran is darkly handsome and immediately likable.

I am impressed by his excitability and capacity for wonder. There is something of the innocent–abroad–in–San Francisco about him. (I learn later that he delays the "author's tour," reveling in Babylon-by-the-Bay's seductions.) Surprisingly naive in some ways, Holleran is a curious mixture of vitality verging on awkwardness, insouciance, and a touching, wistful melancholy. He's into remembrance of things past. If he is jaded, he is also a Jeremiah about the failure of the gay sensibility.

How do you answer the charges that *Dancer from the Dance* is politically retrogressive, especially in what detractors perceive to be its depiction of so many self-hating queens?

One of my characters says that the world demands that a gay novel be ultimately tragic like the life of the very rich. But I didn't want to write a novel in which people confirmed stereotypes, committed suicide, overdosed, and everything. On the other hand, I had had a certain experience of myself as a gay man, and the novel reflects that experience, no matter what detractors say. I know that it was true because in a simple, primitive sense, it happened to me. If I confirmed clichés, I couldn't help it; the only test is, "Was it true?" If it's retrograde, I don't care.

I agree that we have to get across to the American public that gay men are perfectly fine, decent citizens like anybody else, but we can also move beyond that and write about the realities of gay life.

What is distinct about those realities?

My book was written out of a certain amount of anger. I'm angry that we treat each other as shabbily as we do. We seem to be imprisoned in behavioral patterns that are just short-changing. I looked around and I thought, "Why do gays have such a lousy deal in terms of human relationships? Why are we always operating on this lousy level? Why do I sleep with someone, walk away, and have it mean nothing?" It's not right.

Whoever is writing the opening letter of the novel says, "Who after all wants to read about sissies? Gay life fascinates you only because it was the life you were condemned to live." Why the verb "condemned"? Is that your voice, your own view?

I wrote "condemned" with a little sadness and a little anger. To me, realizing I was gay was almost like being told I had cancer at the time. I thought, "My God, here I am slipping away from my family, my society; I'm going to be invisible." I felt a physical sensation of being on a ship, and the ship was leaving from the dock and everyone was standing on the dock and the ship was moving, and I could do nothing to get off that ship, and the stretch of water was getting wider and wider between us. So it's a "condemnation," yes.

Are gay men especially into sex as fast food?

> "The worst thing in the world is to be an invisible man; to have the feeling that it's not your world, it's the other people's world, and you're either not seen or you're tolerated only as a guest. I want my world, where I belong in public—and I think gay literature can help bring that about."—EDITOR MICHAEL DENNENY

When I used to go to the baths when I first came out, the baths were a cathedral to me. They were precious environments. I used to have dreams about living in the baths. I thought I'd love to stay there for a week, a month, to never come out of the place. Now, my God, I travel with a credit card for the baths. I have a little plastic magic for them. I can go to the baths any time I want now, practically anywhere, and I still love them.

But it's not a pilgrimage, is it? It's not the cathedral quest?

No, it's not. It's fast food. I know the quest is passé. I do.

One of the characters in your novel says, "Remember that the vast majority of homosexuals are looking for a superman to love, and find it very difficult to love anyone really human." Who is selling gay men the superman?

Gay men all work so hard for each other. The irony is that the closer you approach this perfection you're looking for, the better your body gets, the more attractive your clothing, the smoother you are, the more it all becomes a kind of backfiring narcissism that alienates you more rather than bringing you close. Ostensibly, we're doing all those things for vanity, but it's also ultimately to attract someone to love. You walk into rooms now and everyone has got the right body and everyone has a good haircut and everyone has got the right outfit and they're all attractive and bright. But they're all so far from each other.

So we're looking for the superman, we're looking for this person better than ourselves and at the same time working to be the superman. We seem to be going farther and farther away from the old human context of love, which is loving a man for his humor, for his character, for the way he deals with the world.

That kind of love is rare and no politics can give it to us. They could give us all the baths, all the bars, all the neighborhoods, all the acceptance in the world, and it would make no difference to the individual as to whether he's going to be happy or not. That's your own fate, your own little journey, and it's an independent thing that's subject to chance.

Is there any part of gay life that you would disown?

What I don't like is "ghettoization." Gays are defeating themselves in that. We're all coming together and we're all living the same gay life, yet paradoxically we're living less of a life because of it somehow. I was talking to a friend about buying a winter jacket in New York, and I said, "I'm not going to wear that fucking uniform. I'm not going to wear a bomber jacket with a plaid shirt when I walk down the street. If one of those guys passes me, I don't care how good-looking he is. It's as if he's invisible; it's as if I'm looking at a Barbie doll, dressing in this stupid goddamn uniform."

But then I began to think of the other coats I might wear. I worried that if I started wearing some of those coats I wouldn't get cruised. I reminded myself that the original reason we dressed in that way was to identify ourselves to other gay people in a populace that wasn't gay. So there's some happy medium between the two extremes.

Ghettoization fulfills a function; it gets us together where we can be gay, and of course I'm going to go on living in New York. I made a choice to go to a ghetto and live in the Village to be with gay people. Now that I've had my fill of it, I can remove myself a little bit from it. It seems to me stultifying at this point.

—Brent Harris

"We pulled the ugly green frogskin of heterosexual conformity over us, and that's how we got through school with a full set of teeth. We know how to live through their eyes. We can always play their games, but are we denying ourselves by doing this? If you're going to carry the skin of conformity over you, you are going to suppress the beautiful prince or princess within you."

—Pioneer activist Harry Hay

"When I do a concert now and a five-year-old girl comes up to me to ask, 'Are you going to sing "Leaping Lesbians"?' it just warms the cockles of my heart."

—Meg Christian

A Monumental March on Washington

Thousands of lesbians and gay men from every state in the Union marched in Washington, D.C., October 14, to dramatize the need for legislation guaranteeing the civil rights of homosexuals.

Although estimates of crowd size varied—the organizers' official estimate was 100,000—the first national gay-rights march was lauded by organizers and participants alike. "It symbolizes the birth of a national gay movement," said Lucia Valeska, codirector of the National Gay Task Force.

The march began near the U.S. Capitol, passed the White House, and ended at the Washington Monument, where more than thirty speakers and entertainers appeared before the throng. The lively procession was headed by Third World lesbians, followed by other lesbians from around the country. Many of the women sang "When the Dykes Come Marching In" and chanted "Two, Four, Six, Eight, Is Your Mother Really Straight?"

Gay people from the entire United States and ten foreign countries marched according to their regions. Many of the delegations carried colorful, elaborate banners and posters. The kaleidoscope of gay organizations participating included religious, social service, and political groups; parents and friends of gays; a youth contingent; college groups; neighborhood associations; and business groups.

The mass swarmed down Pennsylvania Avenue past the White House and spread onto the vast, grassy field known as the Mall, which surrounds the Washington Monument. There, activists, entertainers, congresspeople, and private individuals with views to celebrate spoke well into the afternoon. Comic Robin Tyler roused the crowd to hilarity and then to serious cheers when she shouted out, "If freedom shall ring in this country it must ring for all Americans or in time it will not ring at all for anyone."
—Scott Anderson

"A Gentle, Angry People" Come From Everywhere

"We are a gentle, angry people," Holly Near was to chant later that day to 100,000-plus deeply moved gay men and lesbians. But the six hundred of us monopolizing the coffee concession in New York's Penn Station at six A.M. were as yet less teary-eyed than bleary-eyed. Not counting those who arrived by taxi from the tail end of a prolonged evening, the chartered "Disco Express" to Washington was obviously forcing many present to greet Sunday dawn for the first time since a high-school Easter service.

Never ones to lose an opportunity, however, the assembled crowd soon

James M. Saslow, *The Advocate*'s **New York editor from 1978 to 1985.**

broke out bags and baskets of bagels and lox, homemade muffins, and Bloody Marys, and settled in for a four-hour brunch/musicale/ occasional backroom. It was the start of a day that reminded us why we chose to call ourselves "gay."

The generally festive mood of this first-ever gay March on Washington was only one of several contrasts with the first anti-Vietnam march, held on the same Capitol Mall ten years ago almost to the day (October 15, 1969). Then the order of the day was Quaker solemnity, panicky outrage, and some rather naive notions about the ingredients of social change. The men made speeches, and the women made coffee. I am a decade older now, and so is Stonewall; today the women lead off the march, and there is a mood of celebration, a sense that

this time we're all marching not merely against something, but *for* something.

Besides the distances traveled by everyone assembled here, today's march draws its magic from the place traveled to. It's impossible not to feel somehow sanctified marching along the same route used by Presidents en route to inaugurations. When the endless line finally spills out over the Mall at the exact intersection of the capital's grand axis, we know we have reached the symbolic center of America's consciousness. East to the Capitol, north to the White House, west toward Lincoln, and south toward Jefferson—who once prayed appositely for "equal and exact justice for all men [*sic*] of whatever state or persuasion." Live up to your credo, America, or we'll know the reason why.

And yet, I feel little need to listen attentively, as I did in 1969, to every speaker, every idea. The once novel preachings of feminists and gay activists seem familiar now—a word, lest we forget, that comes from *family*. I have a sense of family here—the assured relaxation of being with people with whom I have shared, and grown, and put in a lot of emotional/philosophical work. We have already heard today's gospel and absorbed its healing message as part and parcel of our individual and collective identities.

Yes, we *are* a gentle, angry people. And after today—thanks to today—a bit less angry, and a bit more gentle.
—James M. Saslow

QUENTIN CRISP

"In an expanding universe," wrote Quentin Crisp in his autobiography, *The Naked Civil Servant*, "time is on the side of the outcast. Those who once inhabited the suburbs of human contempt find that without changing their address they eventually live in the metropolis." In other words, Crisp advised us, "if you stay in the same place for long enough, the world will come to you."

Crisp learned this the hard way. Born into a middle-class family in suburban London on Christmas Day 1908, he grew up hated and ridiculed by most of the world, frequently beaten up in London streets for daring to flaunt his eccentric looks (hennaed hair, painted lips and nails), and homosexuality. He was sixty before his autobiography was published in England, seventy before his book, an acclaimed television film based on it, and the man himself debuted in the United States.

Crisp is an outcast unlike any the world has yet known, a provocative, witty, violet-haired, elderly "self-evident effeminate homosexual" to whom John Hurt, who brilliantly portrayed him in the BBC television movie of *The Naked Civil Servant*, brought fame. In the wake of the film's success, Crisp has now unveiled himself in a one-man show titled *An Evening with Quentin Crisp*. It consists of Crisp, alone on stage, chatting about his life for the first half, and answering bewildered questions from the audience in the second. After a tour which took him from England to Australia, Crisp opened in various cities across the United States, including New York in 1978 and Los Angeles this year. After decades of invisibility, he is—to his astonishment—a big hit.

Despite his newfound fame, and a reputation for witty one-liners which makes him seem like a latter-day Oscar Wilde, Crisp is by no means embraced by everybody. *The Naked Civil Servant* and some provocative opinions he's expressed about homosexuality in interviews have not won over gay activists. "I think it's a great mistake for minorities to assume they can demand anything," he says. "They tend to say, 'We have our rights.'...I don't think anyone has any rights. I think you fall out of your mother's womb; you crawl across open country under fire; you grab at what you want, and if you don't get it you go without; and you flop into your grave. So you have to make up your mind whether to grab what you want, fight for it, or ask for it. Now if you're in a minority, the only thing you *can* do is ask for it, because otherwise you will lose."

Homosexuality doesn't interest Crisp as much as individuality: "I do not regard myself as a symbol of anything except myself. If I represent anything beyond that, I represent the idea of living your own life without doing any particular harm to the world." He eloquently admonishes us to be ourselves, as fully as possible, in public—even if we are "ordinary."

As he says at the end of his one-man show: "I'm trying to speak to anybody who may feel that the band always seems to be playing in another street. And when I say, 'The door is not locked, go to where the band is playing,' I don't want anyone to say, 'But I haven't a thing to wear!' All you have to wear are your wonderful selves."

—GUY KETTELHACK

VILLAGE IDIOCY

"I am the number-one public relations man for the gay world. I've never made any excuses for my gay lifestyle, or denied being gay… [but] there is always a danger of being too political. If you become too political you become provocative, and you risk provoking a backlash, a reversal. Don't forget, no matter how understanding, most parents don't want their children growing up gay."
—VILLAGE PEOPLE PRODUCER JACQUES MORALI

"You don't spend $13 million to make a minority movie."
—HOLLYWOOD MOGUL ALAN CARR, on why the Village People movie, *Can't Stop the Music*, would not be gay-identified

"One of the fabulous things about what happened to us is meeting the people we have. I mean, I used to sit on my parents' living room floor and watch 'Sonny and Cher.' Now we hang out a lot at Cher's. It's great to find out stars like that are so real."
—VILLAGE PERSON RANDY JONES

THEATER: *BENT*

What does it mean to survive in a society where even fantasizing about gay contact is punishable by internment in a concentration camp? Even more, how does a gay man survive in Hitler's Germany after he has already, through a baroque chain of circumstances, found himself locked behind the electrified barbed-wire fences of Dachau?

If that man is Max—crudely handsome petty con artist and prime mover of Martin Sherman's hit London drama *Bent*—survival at first means what it has always meant: lie, bargain, hustle. When he and his young lover, Rudy, are imprisoned (for picking up a trick whom the Nazis assassinate during a purge of homosexuals), Max quickly sizes up the situation. Observing that gays rank lowest on the Nazi totem pole, he falsely declares himself Jewish: While pink triangles on the chow line get bare broth, Max's yellow star means that "I got meat in my soup." Yet Max's seemingly amoral opportunism is sustained at great psychic cost. When Rudy is savagely killed, Max begins compulsively repeating numbers, then blocks out even Rudy's name in a desperate attempt to defuse the inescapable horror that surrounds him.

Not a pretty subject, this—and not a pretty play. *Bent* is gay theater with a vengeance, for the Nazi horror is easily read as a grotesquely extended allegory of the (usually more subtle) oppression experienced under all regimes.

The greatest danger in the camps is dehumanization: Total isolation reduces many prisoners to "Muslims," camp slang for brutalized zombies. Resourceful Max (played by Ian McKellen) pulls more strings—and a cock or two—to procure the transfer of a pink-triangled inmate, Horst (Tom Bell), to duty on the same rockpile. Although Max's initial motive is simply companionship, the two men gradually develop a grudging fondness for one another that becomes their only bulwark against despair. This "endgame" situation is replete with sardonic humor: When Horst admires Max's muscular build, Max replies, "I exercise."

Always wary of discovery, they have only one opportunity for sustained conversation: during rest breaks, when they must stand ten feet apart at attention. They fantasize making love to one another, describing every action with mounting excitement until, miraculously, they both reach orgasm. "They're not going to kill us," whispers the astonished Horst after a moment of stunned silence. "We made love." Ever wary of the dangers of openness, Max says brusquely, "I love you, but I won't help you." In time, however, his latent instinct for devoted concern leads him to pull one more deal—to get medicine for Horst's worsening cough. The ploy is discovered and Horst is killed. Numbed, furious but helpless, Max changes uniforms with the crumpled Horst, emerging from the grave wearing for the first time the fatal pink badge of his own denied identity. Mindful of his own earlier statement that, inside the camp, suicide becomes an act of defiance, he strides purposefully to the electrified fence and resolves everything in a flash of sparks.

In Max's final moment, his two hands grasp only the crackling voltage of a prison fence. In the context of a culture that makes of all gays prisoners in one sense or another, the ending becomes a triumphant gestures of hope.

—JAMES M. SASLOW

Form and Color of Markings

	POLITICAL	HABITUAL CRIMINALS	EMIGRANTS	JEHOVAH'S WITNESSES	HOMO-SEXUALS	VAGRANTS
Basic Colors	▼	▼	▼	▼	▼	▼
Markings for Repeaters	▬▼	▬▼	▬▼	▬▼	▬▼	▬▼
Inmates of Penal Battalions	▼⊙	▼⊙	▼⊙	▼⊙	▼⊙	▼⊙
Markings for Jews	✶	✶	✶	✶	✶	✶

Markings of inmates in the concentration camps. Gay prisoners wore the pink triangle.

PHOTOGRAPHY: ROBERT MAPPLETHORPE

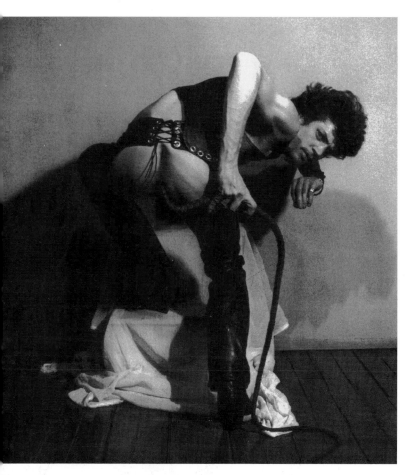

The art world collectively gasped when Robert Mapplethorpe appeared on the scene with his sensational photographs of leathermen in hard-core poses. Almost ignored were his meticulously composed and lit images of flowers, cut and arranged in vases and bowls, and striking portraits of the rich and the beautiful. "Most evident in these images is the force of total control that the artist has drawn over his work," said *Advocate* critic Scottie Ferguson in reviewing a limited-edition portfolio of Mapplethorpe's work released in 1979 by a small Dutch publisher. "The subjects are already frozen in their poses long before the camera clicks. Nature is completely eschewed— available light banished. The personalities of the portraits all partake of defiant arrogance; with few exceptions they look into the lense with no apologies."

Mapplethorpe's cool and objective worldview seemed all the more unsettling when focused on S&M sexuality. "That Mapplethorpe is an artist, albeit of the agent-provocateur school, there can be no doubt; he is there not just to please—but to upset and disturb the beholder," continued Ferguson. "Yet ultimately the scale of his work dips to shallow depths. A body of creation that goes no higher than carefully executed tongue-sticking has its limitations."

A year later, while in San Francisco attending an exhibition of his notorious images, Mapplethorpe told *The Advocate,* "I would prefer a sexual experience to photographing one. The camera gets in the way, although I have always made an effort to use it. I think I have been one of the first to really approach sexuality with an eye for lighting and composition and all the other considerations relative to a work of art. I recorded it from the inside. I

Mapplethorpe on Mapplethorpe (*above*) and on flowers (*right*).

guess all photographers are in a sense voyeurs. But I don't like voyeurs, people who don't like to experience the experience, who view life from the outside. I resent that.

"I don't understand the way my pictures are," the unassuming artist concluded in response to his critics. "It's all about the relationship I have with the subject that's unique to me. Taking a picture and sexuality are parallels. They're both unknowns. And that's what excites me most in life—the unknown."

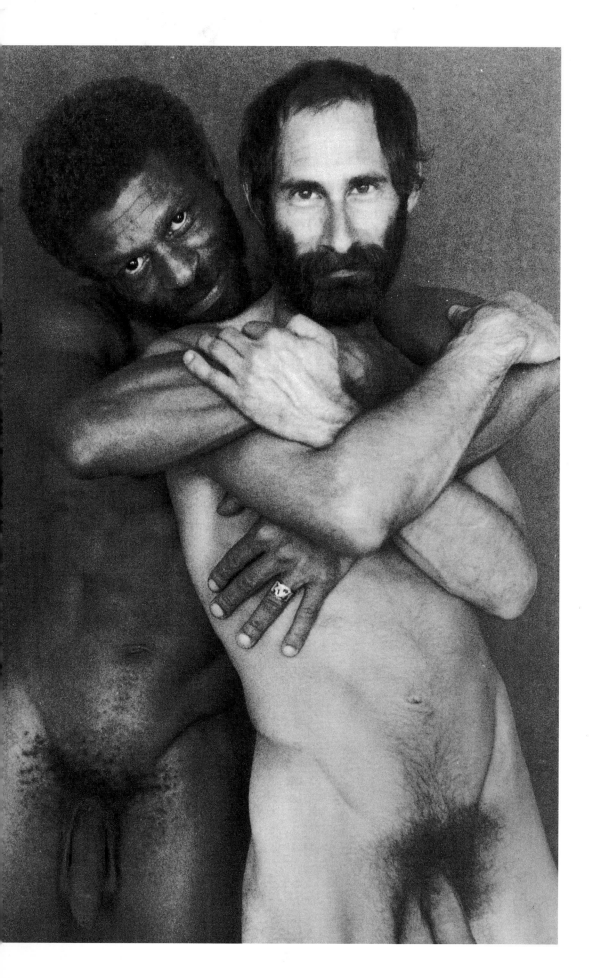

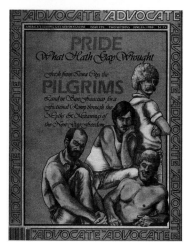

CALM BEFORE THE STORM

Crawford Barton's portrait of two men in a loving embrace is filled with the steady self-assurance many gays and lesbians felt at the turn of the decade.

1980 The year started off with high hopes. David Goodstein's first editorial of the year predicted: "I foresee the next ten years to be the best in the history of humankind." And, indeed, there seemed reason enough to think so. We were making our mark: Gay and lesbian culture was burgeoning. Individual empowerment and entrepreneurial ingenuity flowered. Growing community discourse, generated by our blossoming self-awareness, excitedly encompassed a range of topics—coming out, our creative families of choice, religion, and sexuality.

The National Gay and Lesbian Archives was inaugurated in Los Angeles. The letters of Lorena Hickock, Eleanor Roosevelt's longtime lesbian lover, were published. "If it was good enough for Eleanor Roosevelt, it's good enough for me!" declared a popular T-shirt at gay resorts that fall. Avant-garde art like Robert Mapplethorpe's, and plays like *Bent* and *Last Summer at Bluefish Cove* were the rage, and gay and lesbian scholarship began to come into its own with the publication of John Boswell's monumental *Christianity, Social Tolerance, and Homosexuality*. We were taking up the core question of how to balance identifying and expressing our unique voices with confronting and interacting with mainstream America.

Yet despite this cultural health, 1980 still saw the deep divide between the gay men's community and the lesbian community. Those of us in the largely separate lesbian world barely paid attention to the misinformed and often misogynist sentiments reflected in *The Advocate* and elsewhere. We were busy. We were building a vibrant independent lesbian culture for the first time ever. We were saddened that year by the closing of Jeanne Cordova's *Lesbian Tide* magazine, a pioneering journal that bridged the "old gay" pre-feminist lesbian world and our lesbian-feminist era. On the other hand, that unique lesbian subcultural phenomenon, "women's music," was hitting its peak. Over a million records had by now been sold, and tens of thousands of lesbians' lives were touched by the concerts and festivals flourishing around the country.

These annual festivals were uniquely lesbian-feminist events. First and foremost, no men were allowed. (Bitter battles were fought over the years about even allowing boy children to attend.) I remember a gay male friend of mine begging to come, promising exquisite drag as cover. "But you don't understand," I told him. "All the dykes wear is a leather strap around their naked waists with their Swiss army knife attached—lipstick and heels would give you away in a second!"

Imagine up to ten thousand women on hundreds of self-contained acres of forest and field land in "women's space," reveling in rare freedom, with three stages running all day showcasing theater, poetry, all kinds of dance and music, political lectures and workshops. It is a true cultural revolution. It is all women. It is safe and anarchistic, spontaneous and skillfully assembled. We call the festival space "The Land." Festival time and energy are separate from "real life." Women fall in love with themselves, with a newfound sense of identity and independence. Women fall in love with each other. Sex abounds.

Meanwhile, in real life in 1980 we suffered humiliating defeats at the ballot box, like the three-to-one repeal of a gay-rights ordinance in Santa Clara County, California. In this Presidential election year, Senator Ted Kennedy was the gay and lesbian community's favorite candidate, but the party's nomination went to the hopeless Carter-Mondale ticket instead. We had had great hopes. The National Gay Task Force's annual budget reached $260,000; the Human Rights Campaign Fund was founded; MECLA, Los Angeles's gay PAC, raised what was then a phenomenal amount of money, $50,000, at one fund-raiser alone.

At the Democratic National Convention in July there were an astounding seventy-seven lesbian and gay delegates. In a stunning and historic speech, Mel Boozer, a brilliant black gay delegate from Washington, D.C., sang out these profound words: "Would you ask me how I dare to compare the civil rights struggle with the struggle for lesbian and gay rights? I know what it means to be called a nigger and I know what it means to be called a faggot, and I understand the difference, in the marrow of my bones. And I can sum up that difference in one word: nothing. Bigotry is bigotry."

But with the election of Ronald Reagan in November, the rising New Right and its politics of division gained momentum and visibility. Jerry Falwell was a name unfamiliar to us, but not for long. The U.S. Navy's *Norton Sound* antilesbian witch-hunts captured the headlines. And antigay violence was rapidly rising, signaling to many of us the absolute ending of those wide-open horizons of the seventies.

CBS battered us with the insidious documentary "Gay Power, Gay Politics," which foreshadowed the Right Wing's later disinformation campaign. The program portrayed gays as white, rich, male, and having endless sex in public places in front of children. We were outraged; five hundred of us protested in Los Angeles. I can still remember our rage over that betrayal—many of our leaders had cooperated with the filmmakers, believing they would portray us fairly. We still had a naive and optimistic, almost childlike hope that the nongay establishment would realize just how wonderful we are if they only knew us.

Like a sudden eclipse, the advent of the Reagan Administration darkened our hopes for continuing cultural and political progress. As robust as our communities seemed in 1980, giddy from the rising high of the seventies, we were far from ready for the bitter realities of the eighties. —TORIE OSBORN

"We all know Reagan is an enemy of gays. He's an enemy of women, of the ERA, of the twentieth century. I think his chances of election are depressingly good. He started out in Des Moines, Iowa, as a sports announcer. ...He would surely be the dumbest President we ever had. And we can't afford him. Think of Reagan running American foreign policy. Think of the kind of men he might appoint to the Supreme Court."
—PRESIDENTIAL BIOGRAPHER MERLE MILLER

"You smile, but if more gay politicians went boogeying they'd understand their constituents a bit better."
—NOVELIST GEORGE WHITMORE

T I M E L I N E

At Washington University, openly lesbian filmmaker Barbara Hammer headlined the St. Louis Women's Film Festival. Audiences jammed the theater to watch *Dyketactics, Women's Rites, Superdyke,* and other works by the pioneering artist.

In November, Briton Carl Hill filed his second challenge to U.S. immigration law. Arriving at San Francisco International Airport after a direct flight from London, he went directly up to a customs official and said, "I must inform you that I am a homosexual." Hill was taken into custody under a law that prohibited self-declared homosexuals from entering the United States. Two days later, an immigration judge ordered Hill's release, calling the current law unenforceable.

JANUARY Fifty Christian businessmen pledged to raise $10,000 each for the Presidential campaign of fomer California Governor Ronald Reagan, saying they liked his conservative stand on abortion, drugs, and gay rights. ❑ Gay and Young, a youth advocacy program in New York City, was granted $35,000 in state funds. ❑ Lesbians and gays picketed the opening of *Windows*; the film portrayed "a psychotic lesbian killer who hires a man to rape her best friend with whom she is secretly in love." ❑ Lesbian activist Del Martin was named to the California Commission on Crime Control and Violence Prevention by Governor Jerry Brown. ❑ Mexican dress designer Jaime Chavez, refused entry into the United States because of his alleged homosexualty, sued the U.S. government for $1 million.

FEBRUARY Dr. King Holmes, a Seattle public health official, announced that twenty types of venereal disease had reached epidemic proportions in the nation. ❑ The Lyon-Martin Medical Clinic, serving the Bay Area lesbian community, opened in San Francisco. ❑ Gerd Bloemer, a gay German socialist, was jailed on a slander conviction for demanding the destruction of a "secret gay list" compiled by police in Cologne. ❑ SOMOS, a gay group, was founded in São Paulo, Brazil; it was one of the first gay organizations in the country.

MARCH The National Lesbian and Gay Archives, containing more than ten thousand volumes and twenty thousand periodicals, officially opened in Los Angeles. ❑ After more than a hundred men were arrested at a gay bar in January, Chicago mayor Jane Byrne publicly chastised police officers for campaigning against homosexual prostitution rather than "true crime." ❑ A church near Seattle sued a gay disco when parishioners became confused over the name The Sanctuary, which they shared. ❑ Ronald Reagan said that he would not condone homosexuality; at the same time, the Christian Voice, a group opposed to gay rights, women's rights, and abortion, announced that it would undertake a major fund-raising effort for his Presidential campaign. ❑ President Carter issued a formal statement dashing hopes that his administration would issue an executive order banning antigay discrimination in the federal government or supporting a gay-rights plank at the Democratic convention.

APRIL "Washington for Jesus," a fundamentalist Christian campaign to support right-wing legislation, drew 200,000 marchers to the nation's capital. ❑ Five hundred people participated in the first Gay Pride celebration in St. Louis, where a lesbian bar was fire-bombed the previous year. ❑ In a reversal of policy, Federal Bureau of Prisons Director Norman Carlsen allowed inmates to receive some gay publications. ❑ *Time* magazine revealed that its best-selling issue for 1979 featured the cover story "How Gay Is Gay?" ❑ Dutch officials announced plans to challenge American antigay immigration laws in the Council of Europe.

MAY The American Jewish Congress adopted a resolution that recommended abolishing antigay discrimination in employment, housing, and military service. ❑ San Francisco's Buena Vista Park, which was condemned as a public sex scandal in the CBS special "Gay Power, Gay Politics," was called the safest park in the city by elderly resident Grace Wade, who said, "If you scream, you know fifteen guys will pop out of the bushes to help you, and a lot of them carry whistles." ❏ An information hotline for young homosexuals opened in Marseilles, France.

JUNE The Democratic Party adopted a plank insisting on protecting "all groups from discrimination," and opposing the ban on homosexual visitors and immigrants. ❏ The U.S. District Court in Chicago ordered that the Army reinstate Sergeant Miriam Ben-Shalom after her dismissal because of her homosexuality; the Army later appealed and won. ❏ Two new lobbies targeted the gay-rights movement, the American Family Institute and Americans Against H.R. 2074 (the federal civil rights bill). ❏ Archbishop John Quinn of San Francisco called homosexual acts "pathological" in an open letter to his Roman Catholic archdiocese.

JULY The U.S. House of Representatives voted overwhelmingly to deny federal funding to legal groups that work for equal rights for homosexuals. ❏ While eight of sixteen women accused of homosexual activity aboard the U.S.S. *Norton Sound* were cleared by the Naval Investigative Service, four others were found guilty and discharged; proceedings against the remaining women were dropped because the negative publicity was disruptive for both the Carter Administration and the Navy. ❏ In a diplomatic first for the United States, lesbian concerns about health and sex education were included by the U.S. delegation to the United Nations World Conference for the Decade for Women. ❏ More than two hundred members of the Committee of Black Gay Men from around

After more than five thousand Cuban refugees were released as "undesirables" by Fidel Castro's government, twelve hundred gay immigrants found sponsorship from lesbian and gay Americans through the Metropolitan Community Church in July.

the country attended a major planning conference in Chicago. ❏ A statewide Gay Pride picnic in Bozeman, Montana, drew a mix of more than two hundred activists, cowboys, and cowgirls.

AUGUST Oklahoma television station KOTV decided not to air a Jerry Falwell special titled "America, You're Too Young to Die," which condemned homosexuality and abortion. ❏ More than five hundred Christian fundamentalists demonstrated against the Fifth Annual Southeastern Conference of Les-

the Moral Majority is Neither

"Gay Vote 1980," a nationwide drive to secure a gay-rights plank in national party platforms, resulted in about a dozen gay delegates in the Iowa Caucuses.

CBS Stirs Protest

"Very soon attacks on gays will take place all over Los Angeles–Hollywood. The young, good-looking ones will be the chief targets. Gay businesses will be sabotaged. Gay political ambitions will fail. Gays will be beaten and stabbed, shot and mugged. They deserve it. Der Fuhrer."

—A LETTER RECEIVED AT *THE ADVOCATE* AFTER THE AIRING OF *"GAY POWER, GAY POLITICS"*

It is impossible to know if "Der Fuhrer" actually watched "Gay Power, Gay Politics," the CBS news special that was broadcast the evening of April 26—the reference to gay political ambitions would seem to indicate he did see the program—but in any event, starting a dialogue, hammering out differences, reaching a compromise, and living in harmony seems highly unlikely in this instance. Response to the sensationalistic San Francisco–based documentary, from gay leaders and city officials alike, was outrage.

The broad impact of the program is more difficult to gauge. (According to CBS, it garnered a 25 percent share of the audience.) Notes Charles F. Brydon, codirector of the National Gay Task Force, "The show just reinforced all the old stereotypes; it told people that when they speak about homosexuals, they're only talking about sex."

Yet even in this gloomy Nielsen cloud Brydon finds a silver lining. "The program," he contends, "was so extreme and inconsistent that it was inherently self-discrediting. I think it will have a positive effect over the long term. It has started gay groups talking to their local TV affiliates. It will be a powerful organizing tool." —LENNY GITECK

bians and Gay Men, held in Memphis, Tennessee. ❑ The Screen Actors Guild added sexual orientation to its nondiscrimination clause for employment.

SEPTEMBER Calling the move a "softening" of antigay practices, gay leaders hailed a Justice Department ruling that immigration officials may enforce antihomosexual provisions only if arriving foreigners voluntarily admit they are gay. ❑ At their semiannual convention, American Bar Association members overwhelmingly defeated measures in support of gay civil rights. ❑ A postcard campaign by the American Christian Cause attacked "Adam and Yves," a proposed ABC network series about a gay male couple; the show never aired. ❑ Nineteen-year-old Andrew Exler filed suit against Disneyland after having been ejected for dancing there with his male date a month earlier; eight years later, he won the case. ❑ An investigation of alleged homosexual activities by a Hong Kong police inspector was closed following the man's suicide.

OCTOBER Conservative Congressman Robert Bauman (R–Md.) confessed to the afflictions of "alcoholism and homosexuality" after he was accused of soliciting a sixteen-year-old boy for sex; he lost his reelection bid in November. ❑ John Farrell, an openly gay man, was appointed to the Police Review Commission of Berkeley, California. ❑ The county medical examiner ruled accidental the death of Houston gay activist Fred Paez, who was shot in the back of the head by an off-duty police officer. ❑ An eighteen-year-old Ontario man was sentenced to life without parole for pushing two gay men off a cliff; one died and the other testified. ❑ The Human Rights Campaign Fund, a new political action committee to support pro-gay candidates at the federal level, was established in Washington, D.C.

NOVEMBER Atlas Savings and Loan, founded by and for gays, opened in San Francisco. ❑ Following the election of Ronald Reagan to the White House, gay activists debated whether moderates might be afraid to support gay-rights legislation. ❑ Thirty-eight-year-old Donald Crumpley murdered two gay men and wounded six others when he sprayed two Manhattan gay cruising places with machine-gun fire; Crumpley later told police, "I'll kill them all, the gays. They ruin everything." ❑ Sixteen random homicides of gay men in the Hollywood and West Hollywood areas during the year prompted a community meeting between law enforcement representatives and gay citizens who complained of police inaction or bias. ❑ The *Houston Chronicle* reported that Boy Scouts at a Ku Klux Klan "survival camp" were being taught how to use guns and strangle people, specifically Communists and homosexuals. ❑ A group of one hundred people, including Protestants and Catholics, assembled in Dachau, West Germany, to honor the memory of homosexuals who were imprisoned, tortured, and killed under the Nazi regime.

DECEMBER Gay Expo, featuring products from lubricants to designer fashions, attracted nearly 35,000 visitors to the Los Angeles Convention Center. ❑ At its annual meeting in Cincinnati, the National Council of Teachers of English approved resolutions prohibiting sexual orientation discrimination in hiring and firing practices. ❑ A law making it criminal to be a "lewd, wanton, and lascivious person...in speech and behavior" was struck down by the Massachusetts Supreme Court. ❑ The Human Relations Commission of Austin, Texas, awarded the Lesbian/Gay Political Caucus a cash settlement from Jim and Ginger's Northside Kwik Kopy, which had earlier refused to print the group's material.

MILTON BERLE

Milton Berle glides into the library of his home, grabs a cigar, and stalks the room in search of a match. He's beat. Yesterday, he did his first set of matinee and evening performances in a revival of *Guys and Dolls*, in which he plays "de lovable, de no good Nathan Detroit." He'd opened to very good reviews, though all the critics seemed surprised that Uncle Miltie had played it straight and hadn't stepped out of his character to do Berle ad-libs.

Berle has been kicking at this thing called show business for seventy-two years. At five he was Marie Dressler's baby in *Tillie's Punctured Romance*, graduating in his teens to vaudeville and, later, to clubs, Earl Carroll's *Vanities*, the Ziegfeld Follies, more films, radio, and, of course, on to become the kingpin of early television, where he was the pioneer of comedic cross-dressing.

"On television, I was the first man to ever put a gown on," he says with a chipmunk grin. "I was even Number Eight on Mr. Blackwell's list of the ten worst-dressed women. Before television, when Gypsy Rose Lee became popular, I was doing my nightclub act, so I'd start with my street clothes and take off everything down to a bra with tassels and a gold thing on my crotch with a heart right in the middle.

"You're going to flip," says Berle, sucking on his cigar, "but the first person that I ever saw in drag was Wallace Beery. Of course they didn't call it drag then, they were female impersonators. I appeared on the bill with Julian Eltinge, who was, I think, the only female impersonator to have a theater named for him. Another one was Karyl Norman, a fantastic impersonator, who was known as 'The Creole Fashion Plate.' I saw Francis Renault. I saw Bert Savoy. In the thirties, I used to go down to the Village, and one of the greatest ones I ever saw was Jacki Maye. He had long hair, he never wore wigs, and in those days there was never any talk of homosexuality. It was a profession, that was their job." Berle is pulling laughs out of his memories.

"When Christine Jorgensen came back from Denmark after her operation, we were appearing on the same benefit together. Walter Winchell brought her over to meet me and introduced us. I'd just had a nose job, so when we were introduced I said, 'I'll show you my old nose if you show me your old cock.' Christine looked at me and said, 'Very funny, *Miss* Berle.' Phew! She's sharp as a bastard. We became good friends after that.

"Here's one," he says, striking another match to his cigar. "Jan Murray, myself, and our first wives went off to Lake New Jersey. While the girls were off swimming, Jan and I went downtown to shoot a little pool. So while we're playing, Jan keeps stroking his cue stick and scratching his crotch. I said, 'What's the matter with you, you got the crabs?' He said, 'No, I've never had anything like that.' A few minutes later he's scratching again. I said, 'Come on, I think you got the crabs, let's go back to the hotel and check you out.'

"Instead of going to one of our rooms we went to the men's toilet and into one of the enclosed booths. I told Jan to take his pants down and to sit on the toilet. Then I got down on my knees and was going through his pubic hair. There wasn't enough room to get the booth door shut. About this time a big tall guy comes walking in. Now, I'm in a very compromising position. Well, the

OPENING SPACE
Editorial Comment by
David B. Goodstein

Recently, the former wife of one of my colleagues—a wonderfully supportive, loving woman who likes sex and has a great sense of aliveness—took a walking tour of San Francisco's Castro district. She found the experience highly depressing. "Everyone seemed so serious, so intent, so heavily into sex," she reflected. "Nobody was laughing, and they all looked alike. It was like visiting a communist country."

For several years, many observers have criticized the overwhelming role sexuality plays in the lives of gay men. That hue and cry has now been taken up by a number of influential lesbians. We gay men have usually reacted defensively to such comments, and have been blind to the basic support that often underlies them. Like all oppressed minorities, we can be victimized by our own paranoia.

Sexuality is neither right nor wrong—it just *is*. It is simply a part of the behavior of human beings and other living creatures. But when orgasmic gratification becomes the sole source of satisfaction or the standard against which all satisfaction is measured, we deprive ourselves of a great many other forms of pleasure. We become driven by our genitals instead of being in charge of our lives.

A great deal of the satisfaction in all sex, gay or straight, lies in the excitement of the hunt—including the risk of exposure, disease, robbery, or injury. In comparison with some of our current sleaze palaces, the bars of ten years ago maintained a high level of light, cleanliness, and fire protection. Today we are accustomed to having sex on floors, through holes, and even in simulated bathtubs. The prevalence of more exotic forms of sexual practices and the routine inclusion of pills, poppers, and piss

are taken for granted. Only discomfort and disapproval are now considered out of place.

It's easy to see how we can feel confused about all this. Judaeo-Christian morality has been hostile to most forms of human sexuality. Our cultural heritage has made sex wrong, and often our parents have, too. As we come to understand the absurdity of that position, we tend to take the opposite stance, making *sex* right and our *past conditioning* wrong. Our new position may not always be conscious, humane, or romantic, but like the orgasm it tends to be exciting.

And that's fine; excitement is certainly enjoyable. However, when the general agreement is that sex is what matters most, our satisfaction in the rest of human experience is lost. It seems as though serenity has to be sacrificed for ecstasy, or vice versa. To be sure, cosmic orgasms are wonderful, but part of what makes them so wonderful is their rarity. Getting lost in the search for the cosmic orgasm is no better than being denied that orgasm altogether. The endless, frantic search can only keep us dissatisfied and separate from others.

Sex is wonderful, but it is not all there is in being alive. Whenever we make the next orgasm what our life is about, we deprive ourselves of the richness of most of our moments—including moments of romance, beauty, intimacy, and accomplishment. It is a very heavy price to pay to make our parents and our culture wrong.

The time has come when gay men must validate more than the piece of meat between our legs. We have much more to offer than sleaze. It's time we contribute more than our sexuality to each other and to the rest of society.

To do that, we simply have to make something other than tonight's sex more important than…tonight's sex.

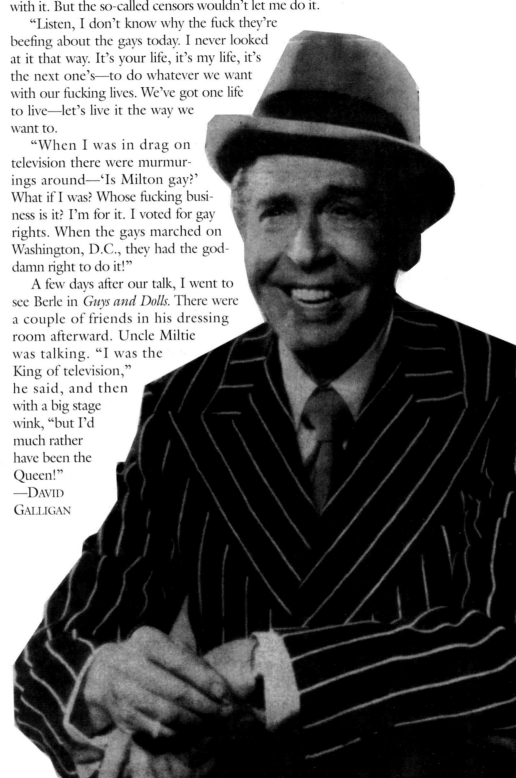

guy looks at us and is shocked. Jan looks at him and points at me and says, 'This is Milton Berle—he loves me!'

"I camp a lot on the stage," Berle continues. "When I first did it on television, I'd say, 'I swear I'll kill you…I'll kill you a million times!' I wanted to do it as a gay throwaway with a little lisp. Not as a put-down, but just having fun with it. But the so-called censors wouldn't let me do it.

"Listen, I don't know why the fuck they're beefing about the gays today. I never looked at it that way. It's your life, it's my life, it's the next one's—to do whatever we want with our fucking lives. We've got one life to live—let's live it the way we want to.

"When I was in drag on television there were murmurings around—'Is Milton gay?' What if I was? Whose fucking business is it? I'm for it. I voted for gay rights. When the gays marched on Washington, D.C., they had the goddamn right to do it!"

A few days after our talk, I went to see Berle in *Guys and Dolls.* There were a couple of friends in his dressing room afterward. Uncle Miltie was talking. "I was the King of television," he said, and then with a big stage wink, "but I'd much rather have been the Queen!"
—DAVID GALLIGAN

WILLIAM S. BURROUGHS

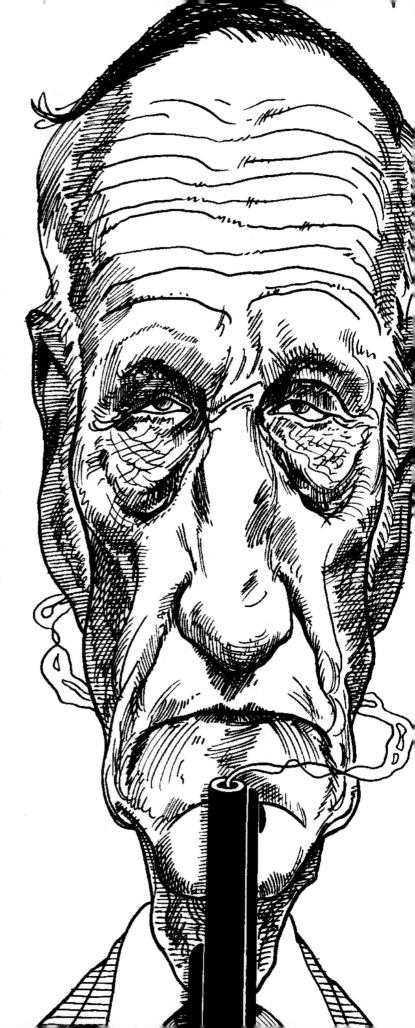

The lunch is indeed naked. William S. Burroughs hovers aquiline over a table of early afternoon snacks, occasionally pecking at the predictable cold-plate party goodies in the kitchen of his San Francisco hosts. We begin the interview, drawing his attention away from newspaper and magazine clippings about mass murderer John Gacy and the Rev. Jim Jones pinned to a bulletin board on a nearby wall.

Is sex really a political issue? If so, why?

One of the most potent weapons in the hands of the people in control is sexual suppression. It is very definitely a political issue.

What is your view of the power that churches have—especially aggressive Christian fundamentalist denominations—in regulating sexual morality at this time in history?

It's absolutely terrible. I am almost violently anti-Christian. It is one of the real disasters that have ever occurred on this disaster-prone planet. It has caused untold misery. They are just congenitally unable to mind their own business—fundamentalist Christians; they're dangerous lunatics.

Is the codification of gay rights something to be objectively pursued or is it a lost cause?

The gay liberation movement serves a very useful purpose. What it is really doing is stating something that was already there. As we know, long before anyone could publicly admit it, there were gay things going on, and that was well known to the general community. They just didn't want it brought to their notice. What is new is confrontation, which is very valuable since "gay" has now become a household word and people realize that it is not all as sulfurous and evil and distressing as it was once thought to be.

Has the gay movement become too serious? In your view, does it lack humor and irony?

There is a basic lack of humor implicit in any political action. Humor isn't the way politics operates. Revolutionaries are usually very, very serious. There seems to be absolute incompatibility between humor and revolutionary politics.

What do you make of feminist objections to gay male pornography?

"The American gay movement suffers from an excess of seriousness and an absolute lack of irony....One can't talk about homosexuals as if a gay man or woman in Los Angeles is the same as a homosexual in Bangkok or Tehran—it means such different things." —WRITER DENNIS ALTMAN

"I decided some years ago that if I was to be labeled a queen, I would be the biggest, best queen there was. Our humor is our key. If we lose that we're dead. I think that the gay community is beginning to take itself a little too seriously."
—DRAG PERFORMER/POLITICAL CANDIDATE JOSE SARRIA

I cannot see how gay male pornography could possibly incite anyone to rape. It seems to me an absolute lot of nonsense.

What is your opinion of the S&M phenomenon? What do you make of men who want to dress up as SS officers?

(*Laughs.*) Gore Vidal once said, "I believe in corporal punishment between consenting adults." Well, I feel about the same way. If they want to get themselves up as SS officers or medieval executioners, it's just costume.

You seem to have very expansive views about human sexuality.

We assume that we know what sex is. But we don't at all. For example, we don't know about orgasm and what it means. The moment of orgasm is very mysterious—it may be prophetic. I used to play the horses. I'd get a horse's name in a sort of silver flash at the moment of orgasm. I'd get up, put on my pants and rush down...too late...the horse had already won. There's something about prophecy as regards gambling that always fucks you up. You can't use it. You get there too late.

The mystery is related to the whole dream phenomenon—the fact that males always have erections during dreams even while the content of the dream may not be sexual at all....We don't know *why* people have to dream. We just know that they do and that it's a biological necessity. If you deprive people of dream sleep, they'll eventually die—no matter how much dreamless sleep they've had. This is an established fact. We don't know why it should be that this is a necessity of all warm-blooded animals, including birds. Apparently, cold-blooded creatures don't dream. It may be because their neural tissue is renewable and ours is not. We don't know the exact function of dreams.

Your detractors often condemn you, like Timothy Leary, as an apostle of drugs. Do you regard yourself as a proponent of their use?

I never had any sort of messianic attitude. I hate LSD myself. I've taken it twice and it's terrible stuff. But if you get something out of it, that's fine. More than any other drug, I've got a lot out of *cannabis*. It is useful. If you don't see where a story is going, a couple of drags may lead you to see a number of alternatives. Actually, it stimulates the whole associative process in some way—the whole process of visualization and recall. That has a certain use.

What, in your view, is the function of art?

The funtion of art is to make people aware of what they know and *don't know* that they know. I'm talking not only about art, but about any sort of creative thought. (*Burroughs then cites the theories of Galileo, the aesthetics of Cezanne, and James Joyce's use of stream of consciousness as examples of creative thought processes that have altered people's perceptions of reality.*)

In what literary tradition would you place yourself?

I consider myself in the *picaresque* tradition—like Petronius's *Satyricon* and Thomas Nashe's *The Unfortunate Traveler.*

Do you read a lot of the new gay writers?

No. A lot of my reading is just entertainment reading, particularly on airplanes. I prefer horror stories—un-speak-a-ble evils. Yup.

As we leave the study, I notice an "unspeakable evil" sitting on a coffee table in Burroughs's host's sitting room. It is the severed head of a crocodile, bleached white, still drying, jaws frozen in a formal smile that knows the ironies of nature's ways. It liked to terrorize with truth, I think.

Burroughs, too, is smiling. Yup.

—BRENT HARRIS

THE MYSTIQUE OF THE TATTOO

Tattooing has had a strange history, with many alternating periods of strong favor and intense loathing. Wars and depressions mark periods of its highest vogue. At one time in America it was associated with the criminal classes, as the only tattoos were applied by hand-pricking in prison. In the early years of this century, even some of the "400" in the best circles of New York society wore them.

With apology, it is necessary here to establish certain *bona fides* of my own, and to say that after twenty years of university teaching I resigned to become a tattoo artist in Chicago, working under the needle-name of Phil Sparrow. At Dr. Alfred Kinsey's request I kept a journal relating to the sexual implications of tattooing, in which Kinsey was interested before his early death in 1956. Later I moved to Oakland, California, where I worked for five years, making a total of eighteen in the racket.

In the early part of my experience with tattooing, before the leather movement began in the middle fifties, there were very few homosexuals getting tattooed. I kept a running count of the overt or obvious ones who got a tattoo in those first years, with some interesting results: Out of the first fifty thousand tattoos, only forty-three were put on recognizable homosexuals. This led to a great deal of head-shaking between Kinsey and myself, and to a conclusion that narcissism played a large part in one's decision about a tattoo. Since narcissism is one of the important elements of homosexuality, it might follow that many homosexuals did not want to spoil their pretty pink bodies with a tattoo, being satisfied with themselves as they were.

Lines of questioning revealed other reasons for disinclination: One said, "I can't imagine myself being permanently satisfied with one design—I'd be wanting to change it." Another was sure he couldn't stand the pain, and a young Chicago elegant said, "Really, m'dear, it's too low-class for words."

In the journal I kept for Kinsey—which totaled close to a million words in eight years—I found thirty-two motivations for getting tattooed, of which twenty-five were sexual in whole or in part.

Of the twenty-five with sexual motivations, by far the most heavily weighted reason for getting one was an assertion of masculine status, so much so that early on I made a sign for my shop which said: "Depressed? Downhearted? A good tattoo may make you feel like a man again."

How male an ineffectual little pipsqueak could feel as he looked into the mirror at the new tattoo that first night and masturbated, certain that he was at last a Man! Recorder that I was, I kept a tally of persons who returned for a second tattoo, casually probing their reactions to the first one. I asked some questions in phrasing like: "Well, how did you enjoy your first tattoo? Lotsa guys tell me they went out and got fucked, or got in a fight, or got drunk, or jacked off in front of a mirror. What did you do?"

Many, of course, simply laughed and made no reply at all, but certain totals appeared after about five years: those who got laid, 1,724; in a fight, 635; who got drunk (over 800 of those who got laid also said they got drunk), 231; those who masturbated in front of a mirror, 879. Even after making allowances for braggadoccio, the proportions between the answers were interesting.

The close corollary of narcissism is exhibitionism. People always seemed to want to show off their tattoos. If one happened to ask a prospective customer if

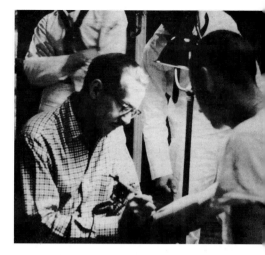

Samuel Steward at work in his Chicago tattoo parlor.

he were already tattooed, there would rarely be a simple "yes" for an answer. The sleeves would be rolled up, the jacket removed, or the pants dropped to show what he had—in the way of tattoos, that is. Curiously, it took two or three years for me to find out why so many young men had their first tattoo on the left bicep rather than the right. If it were on the left arm, that arm could be hung out the window while driving a car, to impress the girls. Or boys.

The scarcity of homosexual customers has been noted, but after about 1956 that all changed. When the "leather movement" began, the numbers of homosexuals rapidly increased. Most of the tattoos on the S&M crowd were masculine symbols—tigers, panthers, daggers with snakes entwined around them. Oddly, they were placed mostly on those who were predominantly masochistic, and these persons stood the pain very well, whereas the "real" sadists often fainted.

Of the many homosexuals who fooled me for a while there was Ed, a sailor from the Great Lakes. Because of some defect in his skin, the first coloring of his rose did not take well. He came back to have it recolored. Then he disappeared for four years during his Navy hitch. When he returned just before his discharge he had a great many tattoos. He came in the last time with a buddy of his, and in a double scroll under a flower got the names Ed and Chuck, they having successfully been lovers in the Navy for four years without having been discovered and thrown out.

A young Polish homosexual of about nineteen once brought in a curious design for his arm. It was an outline drawing of two men kissing, but their profiles had melted into each other so that the nose of each was in the center of the other's head. At first I objected, saying that he was advertising his preference and might some day regret it. "What would your mother say?" I asked. "She'd know at once you were gay."

"Oh, she already knows," he said. "She don't care. Matter of fact, she said that my goin' out with boys saved her a lotta money, and was cheaper'n given' me the bread to take girls out."

There were other examples of advertising, some subtle, some direct. On the buns of one young man I once printed "Screw" on the left side and "Me" on the right, with appropriate arrows. On another I put a rose tree, the idea having come to this particular hustler from a fake photograph he had seen: The rose tree began in the cleft of the ass near the anus, branched out into the gluteus, and gracefully wandered up the spine with flowers here and there, branching finally into two divisions at the shoulders, each ending high on the peak of his deltoid. It was a charming *divertissement* for those who screwed him. Tattoos *do* have their place in the business world.

Tattooing has always had the basic puritanism of America against it. It has been considered faintly evil, criminal, and nasty. Right-wingers and little old ladies have always denounced it, seeing it as the *cause* of criminal behavior, or believing it to be prohibited by religion. Tattoos do not turn people into criminals any more than they turn them into saints. But for the puritans the world of tattooing is strange, dark, and should therefore be outlawed.

It is, of course, no such thing. But the aura of mystery remains. Tattooing is merely the last of the unchanged folk arts, a highly lucrative calling for the ones who practice it skillfully, and the most superb substitute for cruising that ever has been invented. If you become a tattoo artist, you will never have to go searching into the bars or the baths again... for all the beauties will then come looking for you.

—SAMUEL M. STEWARD

TALK OF THE TOWNS: GENTRIFICATION

The Advocate declared that it was "happening everywhere": Gay men were buying up buildings in poor inner-city neighborhoods and remaking them—and the neighborhoods—after a new upscale image. From Boston to San Francisco, gays seemed to be leading a process that drove real-estate prices up and poor longtime residents out of changing urban areas.

Hippie communes of the seventies were replaced with the comfortable neighborhoods of the eighties. In Boston, where a gay commune called Fort Hill Faggots for Freedom had flourished through the seventies in the city's Fort Hill neighborhood, gay men moved a dozen blocks closer to downtown, into the South End, whose magnificent Victorian townhouses stood boarded up in the wake of the busing riots. In Philadelphia, gay men moved in on South Street, also decimated by race riots. Gay businesses and a gay community center soon followed.

"Soon the rush is on," wrote *The Advocate*'s Thom Willenbecher, describing the pattern. "Middle-class whites 'discover' the area, and the real-estate speculators buy, refurbish, and resell buildings at huge profits. Rents soar, and some minority group members—usually blacks—who have been longtime residents of the neighborhood are forced out. Blacks resent the newcomers' muscling them off their home turf, and black leaders attack the whole process, blaming gays."

By 1980, big-city newspapers were beginning to take notice of the new urban tension between the white gay male and African-American communities. The *San Francisco Chronicle*'s columnist Charles McCabe railed against the "homosexual invasion." By then San Francisco had several neighborhoods that were seen as "gay" and several more with a high concentration of lesbians. The best-known of these—the Castro—had elected Harvey Milk in one of the earliest demonstrations of gay neighborhoods' voting power. But much of the massive migration of gays to San Francisco and the building of gay neighborhoods had happened at the expense of the areas' black residents. Writes historian John D'Emilio in an essay on the city's gay community: "Gay male real-estate speculators displayed little concern for 'brothers' who could not pay the skyrocketing rents."

Taking a kinder lens to the phenomenon, *The Advocate* asserted that most of the real-estate speculators were heterosexual. "Basically, the speculators are the realtors, big landlords, and banks who have *always* decided which neighborhoods will go back and which will be restored," wrote Willenbecher. He added that many blacks were staying in the refurbished neighborhoods, living peacefully side-by-gentrified-side with the gays.

Still, the magazine had to acknowledge the rising tensions—though it framed the picture in terms of white gays and straight blacks only. "Resolving the problems that gentrification brings will require much self-examination, hard work, and good will from gays and blacks alike," concluded Willenbecher. "It's no simple task to cure black male homophobia, just as it's not easy to root out racism among gays."

KNOCKING ON RELIGION'S DOOR

The Perils of Churchianity

"As gays, we must not beg anymore. We claim freedom that is our authentic right. No one can 'give' it to us. The establishment churches, as part of the power structure, respect power. We must show them ours....

"Never forget: The religious question is central to gay politics. The antigay position is predicated on the fundamentalist religious proposition that, in effect, 'The majority of American Christians, which is the majority of Americans, are not and never will be prepared to approve or accept the open practice of homosexuality.' What the Bible is construed to say about homosexuality is the bottom line of the gay political struggles.

"It is necessary for gays to deal with the religious question creatively and take the initiative rather than be put on the defensive about it. If gays let the religious question go by default, a major communications disaster will occur. Gays need to approach the religious question in a very positive way. Untapped political strength will be the result. God is not antigay, nor is the Bible. Only churchianity is....

"Jesus speaks of love. He acts out of love. If many of his so-called followers openly deny love and show hate, they're not the 'good people' at all."

—AUTHOR/PRIEST MALCOLM BOYD

Not long ago churches burned homosexuals at the stake, and to this day most denominations still decry homosexuality and refuse to ordain openly gay clerics. Yet religious gays today are struggling to have a stake in how their churches are run, and in so doing are urging an affirmative answer to the question: Can religion and homosexuality mix?

Gay caucuses have sprung up in every denomination, from the Mormons to the Jews. These unofficial groups are beginning to gain the attention of church leaders and to lobby for a new view of homosexuality. While many mainstream churches at least grudgingly accept the presence of homosexuals in their congregations, few are willing to ordain up-front gays.

The ordination issue has done for religion what battles over gay rights have done in politics: publicized the existence of homosexuals and made it clear they're not going away—even from the pulpit. "Civil rights are one thing, but ordination is another—it's a very emotional issue," says John C. Lawrence, president of Integrity, Inc., an Episcopalian group with chapters in thirty-eight cities. "There are a lot of closeted gay laity and clergy who act out of fear," reports Lawrence, "although there is an implicit recognition that there *are* gay people in the church and that we have legitimate grievances." One church insider, in fact, claims that a "conservative estimate" would put the number of homosexual priests in the Episcopal Church at 30 percent. Such a high number of gay clerics—albeit closeted—can have an eventual effect on official church views of homosexuality.

The ordination issue first came out of the closet in a big way in 1978, when the Presbyterian Church's general assembly voted against ordination of openly gay candidates. Despite this, the church hierarchy remains open to homosexuals, says Chris Glaser of Presbyterians for Gay Concerns.

Gay Catholics, too, are tackling their church's age-old opposition to homosexuality. Frank Scheuren, president of Dignity, Inc., with eighty chapters and six thousand members throughout the United States and Canada, says his group has been making "very positive inroads" with church officials.

Gay Jews are also trying to moderate traditional opposition to homosexuality. A dozen gay synagogues have been established across the country, and two of them have been admitted to the prestigious Union of American Hebrew Congregations. "The Reform Movement has been really super about receiving us," says Louis Hirsch of Los Angeles's Beth Chayim Chadishim. "The onetime oppressor has become our defender."

Everywhere, a dialogue is under way. That dialogue has already borne fruit in several denominations. The United Church of Christ has ordained open homosexuals. The Quakers are enthusiastic supporters of gay people's right to be themselves. And the Unitarian Universalist Church even has an official Office for Gay Concerns.

To speed the arrival of such healthy developments, the various gay religious groups are cooperating more and more closely. There is even talk of a national ecumenical conference. It may be a long time before your minister, priest, or rabbi casually mentions that he (or she) is gay. But when that day comes, it will be the result of the groundwork being laid by gay religious groups today.

—SCOTT ANDERSON

BOOKS: *CHRISTIANITY, SOCIAL TOLERANCE, AND HOMOSEXUALITY*

Historian John Boswell

Christianity, Social Tolerance, and Homosexuality: Gay People in Western Europe from the Beginning of the Christian Era to the Fourteenth Century will likely be the most important book on homosexuality published this year. John Boswell's long-awaited survey of attitudes toward homosexuality during the first thirteen centuries of Christianity furnishes the evidence to support his claim, made to gay groups across the country for several years, that the severe moral condemnation we experience today dates only from about the thirteenth century. But Boswell does more than merely point out that attitudes have changed; he convincingly demonstrates that many arguments Christians have used to support their homophobic views are based on mistranslations and misinterpretations of their own scriptures. All future writers on the subject must take into consideration this pioneering historical work on social attitudes toward gay sexuality.

The book is in four sections. The first, "Points of Departure," not only sets the stage historically, with a discussion of the widespread acceptance of gay sexuality in Greece and Rome, but also sets out the problems of studying social history. In particular, Boswell's decision to use the modern term "gay" in a discussion of an earlier period will probably set the pattern for future writers.

"The Christian Tradition" discusses scriptural passages dealing with homosexuality and the role of Christians in the Roman Empire. Boswell concludes: "Not only does there appear to have been no general prejudice against gay people among early Christians; there does not seem to have been any reason for Christianity to adopt a hostile attitude toward homosexual behavior." But if prejudice was not general, there were individual church fathers who severely condemned homosexuality, and it was their opinion that eventually became the official justification for the oppression of gay people.

"Shifting Fortunes" includes the early Middle Ages and the urban revival, which led to a flowering of gay literature in the period 1050–1150, a century that saw tolerance of gay people in the highest places of church and state. The following two centuries, discussed in "The Rise of Intolerance," saw a continual increase of hostility toward homosexuality, culminating in the argument against its "naturalness" by the philosopher-theologian Thomas Aquinas, whose writings became the touchstone of orthodoxy for the centuries to follow.

In exploring the "social topography of medieval Europe" Boswell modestly contents himself with "the belief that he has at least posted landmarks where there were none before and opened trails on which others will reach destinations far beyond his own furthest advance." He has surely done both of these; seldom has previously unexplored territory been so thoroughly posted all at once, and Boswell demonstrates that he has the historical skill and, above all, the linguistic ability to do it. Such a rational discussion can only lead to a greater understanding and therefore acceptance of gay people, and for that reason the book is doubly welcome. —HUBERT KENNEDY

Christianity, Social Tolerance, and Homosexuality

Gay People in Western Europe from the Beginning of the Christian Era to the Fourteenth Century

John Boswell

Theater: Chambers's
Bluefish Cove

Jane Chambers's new play is more than a lesbian love story. The March premiere of *Last Summer at Bluefish Cove,* the pilot production of the Women's Project at The Glines in New York City, is also the story of a death in the "family" of women who spend each summer together in cabins on the cove. The parallel themes of the imminent death of Lil and her brief love affair with Eva are intriguingly intertwined.

The unfolding story of Lil and Eva is watched over and discussed by six other characters. They are onstage observers of the main drama; their reactions to events at the cove make the play startlingly affecting.

Insights come frequently, about themselves—as when Rita describes her life as the woman behind the successful woman—and about each other—as when Kitty, high priestess of feminism and human relations, comically but truthfully analyzes the decrepit relationship between the wealthy Sue and her sycophantic lover. There is no shame in these frank observations. They are spoken among family—not the inherited one, but the family chosen by those who, moving out of the closet, moved away from the stifling responses of the former to the sympathies of the latter.

Into this conclave of self-aware women stumbles Eva, who has just left her husband of twelve years and who has come to Bluefish Cove for a summer of soul-searching, unaware that it is a lesbian colony. After a comically awkward introduction to the place, she strikes up an affair with Lil.

The only character approaching a stereotype is Eva, the quintessential straight woman from Westchester who has all her life done what everyone else wanted her to do. Through her experiences at Bluefish Cove, she is transformed and eventually declares her independence.

"I spent years making excuses," said Jane Chambers, who began her professional theatrical career in the late 1950s as an actress and playwright, off-Broadway and in coffeehouses. "I'd get so depressed over being a woman that no one was going to hire, writing about lesbians in a play which nobody was going to produce, that I became immobilized....You can't keep that in your head. You keep on going."

Chambers's play is bittersweet. It is full of humorous moments; there is little of the sentimentality and anguish that surround the dying patients in Michael Cristofer's *The Shadow Box.* Chambers's characters are not merely determined to have a good time during this summer that happens to be Lil's last; they genuinely enjoy themselves. There is sadness, but always an awareness that life goes on for them, right through the end. They are not unfeeling, they are accepting. Out of this attitude emerge clearly defined, attractive characters. —Jessica Abbe

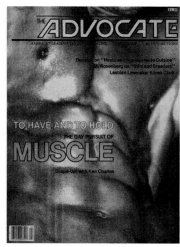

EARLY WARNINGS

Photographer Mick Hicks caught this moment of quiet reflection on California's Russian River.

1981 I remember my "first time." It was the winter of 1981. Brent Harris was my first editor at *The Advocate,* the first of my colleagues to be diagnosed with what some were calling "gay cancer," and the first of my friends to die in what has become one of the greatest pandemics in recorded history. Brent's condition, he was told, was an atypical and very rare form of malignancy called Kaposi's sarcoma. It was so rare, in fact, that even though I was a physician, I had barely heard of it.

At the time of Brent's disclosure, neither Brent, his doctors, nor I had any inkling that we were dealing with an epidemic. Even several months later, as I wrote the first press report and the first feature article (both for the gay newspaper the *New York Native*) on the clusters of cases that had appeared in Los Angeles, San Francisco, and New York—we could not say with certainty that the epidemic of a new disease we were now unquestionably dealing with was sexually transmissible.

Not unpredictably, there was pervasive denial of the seriousness of the epidemic in our community. During a period when no other such information was being featured, *The Advocate* declined to publish my "Basic Questions and Answers About AID [acquired immune-deficiency]" and *The Village Voice* killed the big report they had reluctantly commissioned me to do, which I had titled "The Most Important New Public Health Problem in the United States." Meanwhile, Canada's gay publication, *The Body Politic,* launched an attack on writers Larry Kramer and Nathan Fain, Dr. Dan William, and myself, alleging that we were fomenting hysteria and trying to return to the old concepts of homosexuality as sin and sickness.

As hugely important as AIDS has been from the earliest cases, it has, in fact, never overturned the greater tide of history that sexologist John Money called "the birth control age" and what we called "the sexual revolution." Surrounding the AIDS epidemic, which mirrored parallel STD epidemics of chlamydia, gonorrhea, and herpes among sexually active heterosexuals, 1981 saw battles on other fronts of the struggle for sexual liberation.

With the publication of *Sexual Preference*, the second of the Kinsey Institute studies on homosexuality, the long-standing debate about whether "sexual orientation" was inborn or learned took one of its biggest steps. The conclusion of authors Alan Bell, Martin Weinberg, and Sue Hammersmith was that lifelong gender nonconformity and homosexual preference are probably biological. Rather than settling the nature-versus-nurture debate, however, their book demarcated an expansion of this discourse.

Sexual Preference highlighted two other important changes in thinking about homosexuality that had been taking place since the early seventies. The first of these was the shift in credibility of "expert opinion" about sexual preference from psychiatry to sex research. From the worlds of medicine and science, nearly all of the new thinking about homosexuality and sexuality was coming from sex researchers such as Masters and Johnson, Money, Bell, Weinberg, Hammersmith, and Shere Hite. In her *Hite Report on Male Sexuality*, Hite asked one of 1981's most penetrating questions: Why should the anus be any less erogenous in a heterosexual male than in anyone else?

At the start of the new decade, a bigger and far more important shift in thinking was discernible: from a reliance on outsiders to a new recognition of and respect for the testimony, research, and opinions of lesbian and gay people ourselves. Just as whites were no longer preferentially sought for opinions about blacks, or men for understanding women, or Christians to explain Jews, the time for relying on heterosexual expertise for matters homosexual was finally beginning to pass. With the publication of John Boswell's monumental *Christianity, Social Tolerance, and Homosexuality*, a new era of lesbian and gay scholarship had arrived.

While Boswell's book received mainstream acclaim unprecedented for a study of homosexuality by an openly gay scholar, Vito Russo's *The Celluloid Closet* had a much tougher time. Turned down by twenty-two publishers before being accepted by Harper & Row, the book was not deemed worthy of being reviewed by the then pervasively homophobic *New York Times*, which featured a front-page story on an outbreak of viral illness in Lippizaner stallions when it had yet to publish a front-page or in-depth feature article on the epidemic making deadly inroads into our community.

The year saw the release of several other important, self-defining works by gay and lesbian authors: *Homosexuality and the Law*, edited by Don Knutson; *Sapphistry: The Book of Lesbian Sexuality*, by Pat Califia; *Man to Man: Gay Couples in America*, by Charles Silverstein; and *Meat*, the first of Boyd McDonald's many collections about gay male eroticism. It was the year of the shocking Toronto bathhouse raids. And it was the year that AIDS education and fundraising in New York City coalesced to the extent that Kramer, Fain, Edmund White, Paul Popham, Paul Rapoport, and I were able to establish what became and has remained the world's largest AIDS information and service organization, Gay Men's Health Crisis.

If the queers at the Stonewall didn't know their battle would turn out to be a historical watershed, neither did those of us who tried to defend affirmations of "sexual freedom" and "recreational sex" against denunciations of "promiscuity" and "sexual compulsion" in the wake of the epidemic's first cases. Nineteen eighty-one: a sentinel year for the cataclysm to come. The floodgate for a tidal wave in the history of the gay community and the sexual revolution. —LAWRENCE D. MASS

"The majority of gay white men are real self-serving and don't get any further than their needs....There doesn't seem to be a commitment to anything other than getting the right to screw whomever you want. After that, it's fuck everybody else."
—FOLK SINGER BLACKBERRI

"All these dancers from the dance are running around like a bunch of Rotarians in Omaha."
—ANONYMOUS AIDS VOLUNTEER, commenting on the sudden rise of fund-raising within the gay community

T I M E L I N E

JANUARY The Gay Press Association, comprising more than eighty publications from around the country, was founded at a New York conference. ❑ Delaware's only gay dance bar had its windows broken and received repeated bomb threats. ❑ Cary Grant slapped a $10 million lawsuit on comedian Chevy Chase, who had called Grant a "homo" on the "Tomorrow" show and added, "What a gal"; the suit was later dropped.

FEBRUARY John Hinson, a Republican Congressman from Mississippi, was arrested in a Capitol Hill bathroom and charged with "oral sodomy"; he pleaded no contest and was given a thirty-day suspended sentence. ❑ "The Moral War," a series of reports aired by San Francisco television station KRON, revealed that a right-wing religious group, In God We Trust, had raised $100,000 for a media campaign designed to purge homosexuals from the city. ❑ Calling the event "our Stonewall," three thousand Canadian gays rioted in Toronto following police arrests of 273 men in local bathhouses.

MARCH The San Francisco Freedom Day Committee sued the *National Enquirer* for publishing articles in which gay parade-goers were labeled "mentally diseased"; a U.S. District Court dismissed the case later in the year. ❑ After broadcasting a humorous segment about lubricants and sex toys on his Cincinnati radio show, "Gaydreams," reporter John Zeh was arraigned on felony charges of obscenity, lost his job, and was evicted from his apartment; in September, the case was thrown out and the charges were dropped. ❑ A police crackdown on gay cruising at Allsopp Park in Little Rock, Arkansas, drew complaints from local activists. ❑ San Francisco coroner Boyd Stephens caused an uproar among city officials when he offered a series of S&M safety workshops. ❑ In New London, Connecticut, Jim Revering, a twenty-two-year-old sailor, shot himself in the head aboard his submarine after being taunted by his shipmates as a "sissy." ❑ A Chicago jury convicted James Lavas of beating and robbing two gay men in one of the first gay-bashing cases ever to go to trial in that city; Lavas was sentenced to four years in prison.

APRIL More than fifty gay and lesbian students at Michigan State University danced at a fraternity-sponsored marathon to raise money to fight multiple sclerosis, defying official rules that required dancing couples to consist of one male and one female. ❑ Even though the Carter White House had been an uncomplaining subscriber, Ronald Reagan's administration asked that it be removed from *The Advocate*'s mailing list. ❑ Shouting, "We're gonna beat some faggots," four men and two women roamed a gay sunbathing area near Durham, North Carolina, assaulting four men, one of whom died. ❑ Ten thousand people marched in Paris to protest the World Health Organization's classification of homosexuality as a mental disorder, and to demand lowering the French age of consent for homosexuals to fifteen, the same as for heterosexuals; a year later, the French law was changed, but the W.H.O. would take another ten years to remove homosexuality from its list of diseases.

PRO-CHOICE PROTESTS

During April U.S. Senate hearings on the Human Life Amendment, an antiabortion proposal sponsored by Senator John East of North Carolina, no pro-choice speakers were permitted to testify. But after one anti-abortion activist claimed that "a fetus is an astronaut in a uterine spaceship," three lesbian members of the Women's Liberation Zap Activist Brigade stood up, chanting, "A woman's life is a human life." Mildred Jefferson, leader of the Right to Life movement, winces as the demonstrators are being arrested (*above*). Their action drew national attention as all three major networks covered the story.

At the women's trial for "disruption of Congress," arresting officer Billy Joe Pickett testified that they had been chanting "A lady has the right to choose." Washington, D.C., trial court judge Harriet Taylor found them guilty, but merely fined them $100, the lightest possible sentence.

MAY Rolling Hills Memorial Park in Morganville, New Jersey, set aside ten thousand burial plots for gays as a marketing ploy to attract same-sex couples who were often unable to be buried together in other cemeteries. ❑ Timothy Curran, a nineteen-year-old Eagle Scout from the San Francisco Bay Area, sued the Boy Scouts of America for ousting him over his homosexuality; he later won. ❑ Fund-raising began in Amsterdam to contruct a monument commemorating the Dutch gays who died in Nazi concentration camps. ❑ Turkish security forces shut down several Istanbul nightclubs that employed homosexuals, and arrested, detained, and eventually expelled from that city twenty-two gay men.

JUNE The Centers for Disease Control announced that five previously healthy gay men in Los Angeles had been diagnosed with Pneumocystis carinii pneumonia (PCP). ❑ In *Baker v. Wade,* Dallas County District Attorney Henry Wade filed legal documents stating that laws against sodomy were as important to the public well-being as laws against rape and theft. ❑ A lesbian who went to court to be accepted for training as a sheriff's deputy graduated first in her class of thirty-nine in Contra Costa, California. ❑ Under pressure from gay scientific groups, *Science* magazine banned antigay bias in its staff hiring and advertisements. ❑ A Missouri man who admitted murdering popular Midwestern drag performer Stephen L. Jones (a.k.a. Wanda Lust) received the lightest possible sentence for his crime, with elegibility for parole after one year. ❑ In a first for her city, Chicago Mayor Jane Byrne officially proclaimed June 28 "Gay Pride Parade Day."

JULY The largest San Francisco fire since the 1906 earthquake reportedly started in the Barracks, a gay bathhouse, with local news coverage blaming the blaze on the use of nitrite inhalers. ❑ Eight Texas transsexuals successfully challenged a Houston ordinance that forbade cross-dressing, forcing the city to drop the law. ❑ The Equus, a gay bar in Washington, D.C., reported a series of vandalizations by Marines from a nearby barracks. ❑ More than 250 people from six countries attended the Sixth Annual Conference of Gay and Lesbian Jews in Philadelphia. ❑ Dr. Jeanette Howard Foster, pioneering lesbian scholar and author of *Sex Variant Women in Literature,* died in Arkansas. ❑ Lavender University of the Rockies, in Denver, began offering classes ranging from "Lesbo Lit" to "Country Disco."

AUGUST Tennis star Martina Navratilova, after a well-publicized relationship with lesbian author Rita Mae Brown, expressed concern that her application for U.S. citizenship might be threatened by public comments about her sexual identity; she received citizenship, however. ❑ Stripped of his Army security clearance on grounds of being a homosexual, Sergeant Perry Watkins sued to halt attempts to discharge him; after a series of court decisions, he was discharged but given all back pay and retirement benefits. ❑ Leaders from seventeen local gay and lesbian groups formed a town council in Lincoln, Nebraska, to work for gay legal concerns in their state. ❑ In response to police repression of gays in the south of Spain, three gay groups united to form the Homosexual Liberation Front of Andalusia.

SEPTEMBER From his Manhattan apartment, author Larry Kramer spearheaded mobilization of gay New Yorkers stricken by Kaposi's sarcoma, of which more than a hundred cases had been reported. ❑ Mary Morgan became the first openly lesbian judge in the country when California Governor Jerry

Women's tennis champion Billie Jean King admitted in May that she had been lovers with Marilyn Barnett, who sued her for palimony, but the athlete then called the lesbian relationship "a mistake" and asked for "compassion and understanding" from her fans. A year later, Barrett's suit was thrown out of court.

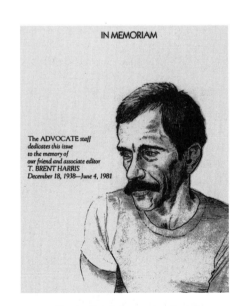

IN MEMORIAM

The ADVOCATE *staff dedicates this issue to the memory of our friend and associate editor T. BRENT HARRIS December 18, 1938—June 4, 1981*

This notice in *The Advocate* marked the passing of associate editor Brent Harris on June 4. He was the first staff person to die of complications due to AIDS. Harris was forty-two.

First AIDS Reports from the News Pages

JULY 23: "Recent media reports have trumpeted a new form of pneumonia that supposedly attacks gay men, but Dr. Alexander Carden of the National Centers for Disease Control says it's not so....The disease in question, Pneumocystis carinii, is caused by a protozoan. Its victims are almost always people with weakened immunities, Carden says: cancer patients, people recuperating from transplants, or others taking medication that suppresses their immunological systems."

"The quality of my life has been reduced to such a miserable level that I don't think it's worth going on,' said Advocate *associate editor Brent Harris the day before he died from a rare form of cancer."*

AUGUST 20: "Medical authorities across the country are hopeful that a recent outbreak of a rare cancer among male homosexuals might eventually shed light on the causes of all cancers. Reports of the disease sent shock waves through the gay community just weeks after it has been learned that one type of pneumonia among gay men might be sexually transmitted. 'We are seeing the beginning of a major epidemic of cancer,' said Dr. Alvin Friedman-Kien of the N.Y.U. Medical Center. 'We are very concerned to head off a panic.'"

SEPTEMBER 17: "A group of physicians at the U.C. Medical Center in San Francisco has undertaken a study to learn if an epidemic of Kaposi's sarcoma, an extremely rare form of cancer, has broken out among gay men."

Brown appointed her to a Municipal Court judgeship in San Francisco. The country would get its first elected openly lesbian judge nine years later, with the election of Donna Hitchens in California. ❑ Two hundred Christian fundamentalists marching to "bring San Francisco back to Jesus" were met by two thousand gay demonstrators, including dozens of bearded men in nuns' habits. ❑ A San Francisco tourist was stabbed to death and his companion wounded by a youth who shouted, "Are you dudes gay?" ❑ The California Office of Post-Secondary Education granted Los Angeles's ONE Institute recognition as a Graduate School of Homophile Studies able to grant master's and doctoral degrees. ❑ Despite protests from the Moral Majority, the Ku Klux Klan, and other opposition groups, the Tenth Annual Miss Gay America Pageant took place at the Dallas Convention Center Theater. ❑ Protests against the United States' antigay immigration policy were held simultaneously in Amsterdam, Dublin, London, Oslo, Ottowa, Stockholm, and Toronto.

OCTOBER   After the Moral Majority warned that Washington, D.C., was on the verge of becoming "the gay capital of the world," the U.S. House of Representatives overwhelmingly vetoed a sex-law reform bill proposed by the District of Columbia's City Council. ❑ A gay-rights bill was reintroduced in the U.S. Senate by Paul Tsongas; cosponsors included Edward Kennedy, Alan Cranston, Daniel Inouye, Lowell Weicker, and Robert Packwood. ❑ The Coalition of Lesbians Against the Harassment of Lesbians announced the boycott of a Minneapolis gay paper because of its supportive positions on female impersonation and pornography. ❑ Gays won a victory when the European Court ruled that Britain had denied the rights of homosexual men in Northern Ireland. ❑ Tony Sullivan, a gay Australian, fought efforts to deport him from the United States, arguing that he had married an American man, Richard Adams.

NOVEMBER   A New York City gay activist who sued police for beating him during a demonstration against the film *Cruising* was awarded $125,000 in damages by a federal jury. ❑ The University of Oregon Law School canceled recruitment interviews by the FBI because of the agency's refusal to hire homosexuals. ❑ Marjorie Rowland, a counselor from the Mad River School District in Greene County, Ohio, who was fired when she revealed her bisexuality to another employee, was awarded $40,437 in back pay and damages by a U.S. District Court.

DECEMBER   A gay black student activist at the University of Massachusetts was placed under police protection after receiving four letters threatening his life. ❑ The student government of Western Connecticut State College voted to allow Spartacus/Sappho, a gay students' group, to meet on campus. ❑ California State Senator John Schmitz was stripped of his committee positions for bigoted remarks made in a press release entitled "Attack of the Bulldykes," which criticized "lesbians and the murderous marauders of the pro-abortion encampment." ❑ The Indecency Displays Control Act took effect in England, while antiporn crusader Mary Whitehouse proclaimed that Britain had not yet vanquished "the tide of titillation engulfing civilization as we know it." ❑ Prostitutes in Athens's six hundred brothels went on strike, demanding that the new socialist government of Greece repeal laws barring homosexuals and transvestites from brothel employment.

BOYD MCDONALD

"My magazine is more respectable than *The Wall Street Journal*," Boyd McDonald says, lighting a cigarette and squinting as he takes a drag. "It's so honest and innocent—and Wall Street is anything but. The best point you can make about *Straight to Hell* is that it's a kind of history that no one else is recording so extensively."

Extensive is right. *STH,* which also styles itself the *Manhattan Review of Unnatural Acts* and the *Archives of the American Academy of Homosexual Research,* aims to take up where Kinsey left off. First of all, it's hot. "The truth is the biggest turn-on," writes McDonald. And, indeed, most of the reader-contributed stories that make up the thirty or so pages of each irregularly published edition are arousing. An astonishing variety of men is represented—straight and gay (though within *STH*'s pages these categories quickly break down), married and single, urban and rural, young and old, important and obscure. You can depend on finding something to your liking.

Such stories as "Reader Jacks Off with Fat-Cocked Puerto Rican Youths," "Trainer Wants to Sniff Boxer's Groin," and "School Cook Licks Guard's Boots"—all from the current issue—are interspersed with book reviews and McDonald's entertaining and politically astute commentary.

It doesn't seem so farfetched to envision *STH* as a huge switchboard of sexual styles and erotic language, with McDonald himself at its center. "I get letters from guys who tell me, 'I never knew anyone else did this,'" McDonald relates. "And then there are the guys who have been doing certain things all their lives but have never seen them in print before—which kind of makes a difference. It has a liberating effect on them."

McDonald's background is unremarkable. He was born in South Dakota to a middle-class family. After a stint with the Army and a Harvard education, he worked for twenty years as a staff writer for such publications as *Time* and *Forbes*—years he also spent as an alcoholic. In 1968 he got off the bottle and on to welfare. "I took my suits to the pawnshop," he recalls. "It was like burning the mortgage: I remember the feeling of exhilaration when I realized I couldn't have gone back into an office as a writer even if I'd wanted to. When you write what I write, you're bound to be unhappy writing for *Time.*"

Does McDonald have any advice for those interested in following in his footsteps? "All you need is to be a real sex hound like me," he says. "Recently I jacked off almost constantly for five days—except for when I went out for food. I was in ecstasy. And you have to be intelligent enough to know that it's okay, that you don't have to do what the Church and the government, for dirty reasons, say you should do." —STEPHEN GRECO

Fran Lebowitz

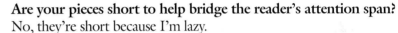

Fran Lebowitz is miserable. At age thirty, the woman who is undoubtedly one of the funniest writers in America is afraid she may be coming down with the mumps, the one childhood disease, she informs me, she managed to miss during an otherwise uneventful preadolescence in suburban New Jersey. Lebowitz is in San Francisco to deliver one of her acclaimed comic lectures, but the glands in her throat are swollen, and every newspaper and TV station in town is clamoring for an interview. In a manner befitting a professional curmudgeon, Lebowitz is clearly enjoying every minute of her discomfort.

Certain that the condition of her glands will prevent her from being the onstage hit she knows she deserves to be, Lebowitz grumpily admits me into her hotel room and lights up the first of what will be an unbroken series of low-tar cigarettes. With a surly nod in my direction, she settles into an armchair.

Are your pieces short to help bridge the reader's attention span?

No, they're short because I'm lazy.

Do you watch TV?

Yes I do. Mostly during the daytime. "Family Feud" is the only show I watch with any regularity. It makes me feel more American.

Who do you think is winning the battle of the sexes?

I don't know. That war is not one I'm participating in.

Is romance fading?

Do you mean here, or in general?

In general.

I think that what people think of nostalgically as romance was just people trying to get laid. It kind of makes you feverish. I think that was really the genesis of romance. Now that sex is more acceptable, people probably aren't as romantic. I don't think it's a great loss, however.

What about homosexuality?

Is it fading? No.

It would appear to be prospering.

I don't think there are any more homosexuals now than there used to be. Why would there be? I just think that more people get to be queer if they want to be; it's a big difference. I don't know—maybe there are more. There's certainly less reason to be heterosexual. Heterosexuality is kind of old-fashioned. Marriage really seems to be enormously outmoded, in every possible way. If half the marriages fail, and if you can be sued for living with someone anyway, there would seem to be zero reason for getting married. Marriage was just a contract made because women were dependent on men financially; it was like ownership, like holding a slave. So there's no reason for marriage anymore. If you think of heterosexuality as being more natural in the sense of being more primitive, then I think that probably homosexuality will become more prevalent, because it's more modern.

What do you think of San Francisco?

I think it's very cute. I've never been here without getting sick. I never leave San Francisco without a sore on my mouth; I don't know why that is.

—Steve Beery

FIRE ISLAND: GOOD-BYE TO ALL THAT!

I didn't go to the Island last summer. Instead, I stayed home and wrote a book about it. In the first place, I couldn't afford it any longer. The price of a share (or even a quarter share) has skyrocketed. The Island is now probably the only place on the East Coast—save for certain Georgetown dining rooms— where they discuss real estate as much as they do in Los Angeles. My friend Chuck used to say that you could tell the Californians in the Pines from the New Yorkers quite easily: The Manhattan queens had analysts, while the faggots from West Hollywood had real-estate agents. This is no longer so.

Real estate. The number of friends I had with houses on the Island had suddenly diminished to two. We heard that a lot of houses were going empty because no one could afford them and that there was a mad scramble at the eleventh hour to rent them to straights. My closest friend out there, who'd lived in blissful solitude in a little house in the Pines for five years, was informed that winter by the owner that the house wasn't available. It was being renovated. So, over the summer, a second story was added on; another huge monstrosity was erected on the vacant land next to it; and my friend lost a large, important chunk of his life.

Real estate, but also overpopulation. The rural had become crashingly urban. No longer could you expect to sit out on your back deck of an evening and hear deer rustling through the foliage. Now it was disco from *The Love Boat* next door.

No, the early reports last year weren't good. My friend Ed has been going to the Island for twelve years now. He lives with the same cast of characters year in and year out. They have it down to a science. Or thought they did.

"The only problem is," Ed told me over dinner one night, "we can't go out

alone after dark. The beatings. Straight kids come over from Sayville and jump people on the walks. I never go to the Ice Palace on weekends anymore. And remember those nice breaks you'd take after reading all evening? I'm afraid to go down to the Meat Rack."

I'd heard stories of straight couples, and even single women, invading the Meat Rack for action, voyeuristic or otherwise, but this wasn't funny.

"Why don't the cops confiscate the six-packs off these kids when they get off the ferry?" my friend asked rhetorically. "I hate it. I have a feeling that in two or three years it'll be completely straight. The Island doesn't *belong* to us anymore and I don't know what we're going to do about it. You can't mobilize these queens, you know."

It's true that, while the Island is probably (even now?) the most completely gay environment on the face of the earth, gay lib didn't bring it about. Initially, gay ingenuity built it. That was before there was electricity out there. Then, gay

style and a sense of play developed the ambiance. The Island used to be *fun*. Now the improvisational spirit of the place has been overwhelmed by issues of property and turf. Unfortunately, however community-minded they might still be, the people who live out there are not noted for their political sense. The problem with the Island is one of the cardinal problems of gay life writ large: They can manage to get the wooden walks painted out there, but they can't protect themselves—either from the "isolated" beatings or from the publicity.

On the other hand. Though again and again, usually from people like Ed who I knew loved the Island for the same reasons I did—for its quiet domesticity and its natural beauty as much as for the nightlife—I heard stories about how the Island was changing for the worse, just as often I heard how great it still was—this mainly from people who'd vacationed there for the first or second time. According to them, the heady mix of sun and drugs and more beautiful men than you've ever seen in one place in your life was still dazzling. The Island still delivered its now legendary punch, with the concomitant and equally legendary hangover, perhaps. Life out there was still a cabaret.

It was interesting to get this pro-Island propaganda from "outsiders" for a change, from people who (because they've been relegated to the "out" side by the "in" residents) traditionally have had a lot invested in criticizing the Island for its insularity and snobbery. The criticism came mostly from "insiders" who felt they'd created a monster of some sort.

I was willing to accept the paradoxes and all the conflicting judgments that would sometimes circulate like angry wasps over the brunch table on a sweltering Sunday afternoon in the city. People do seem to *care* a great deal about the Island, one way or the other. And whatever it might be in reality, the Island has always been less a real place than it is a state of mind—of fantasy. There are, I suspect, as many Fire Islands as there are people out there.

"What you see out there," says a philosophical friend of mine from Toronto, "is what you get. But it depends on the extent of your myopia. What you get is usually what you deserve." Suffice it to say for now, the Island is no longer a very safe place for the uninitiated, the unattractive, the uncloned, or the uncool.

Age. There's no doubt that the image of the Island, if not its vitality, as compared to way back there in the late sixties, is on the wane. Its inhabitants—those responsible for the special context so seductive to visitors and weekenders alike—have aged. Contrary to popular opinion, you can't boogie all your life. The Island couldn't remain unchanged, if only because the people who supplied the energy for it had to change. "I decided it was time to get a real job," one old Island hand announced to me one day last fall. "I don't mean 'grow up' or anything like that. It's just that I realized working at the card shop all day was a pretty high price to pay for a share on the Island—or for dancing all night with oil barons at Bonds."

But lest this become a eulogy. I have a sneaking suspicion that on Memorial Day some young man (perhaps you, dear reader) who's hocked himself to the tits (as I once did) for that weekend at the Cherry Grove Inn (fine, accommodating people) is going to step off the ferry from the mainland and have the time of his life. Stranger things have happened. It's a nice place to visit, still—but you know the rest.

—GEORGE WHITMORE

"Rollerena is New York City's fairy godmother. She has captured the entire city in the palm of her hand. When she skates down the street, it's magic.... She likes to wear her nails long because they are an extension of her personality—sharp and growing. She has a dingleberry ring, the most sought-after dingleberry ring in the city. More tongues have kissed it than the Pope's." —ROLLERENA

Perpetually Indulgent Sisters

For all their good deeds—risking leprosy in the Congo or baleful glares in the classroom—nuns have seldom been known to have a sense of humor. Despite occasional outbursts of flying or singing, most sisters' stock-in-trade seems to be suffering, silence, and sobriety. But in San Francisco there is an order with vows for just about everything except these dour duties. The laying-on of hands and the missionary position are among the well-practiced techniques of this order, and converts are easily made.

They've been raising wimples, eyebrows, and more than a little hell since publicly manifesting on city streets last year. Newspaper editors have frothed, pious Catholics have fumed—yet no one forgets the sight of them. Immodest, perhaps, and certainly not immaculately conceived, the Sisters of Perpetual Indulgence is an order of gay male nuns dedicated to promulgating joy and expiating guilt.

"We are doing important work," says Sister Hystorectoria, one of the group's sixteen members. "Our mission is much bigger than we could ever have imagined. Our ministry is one of public manifestation and habitual penetration. Our motto is 'Give up the guilt.' And we're going to do that through any form at our means. The truest religion in the world is theater, or ritual. On a broad philosophical range, we are being religious in the truest sense, but merely by a different definition."

"THIS IS SISTER MARY RALPH FROM OUR ALTERNATIVE-LIFESTYLE CONVENT."

The order began three years ago in the Midwest, explains Sister Missionary Position. "We went to an actual convent in Iowa to get our first habits. They were the habits of nuns who died. We asked if we could borrow a few from storage so we could do *The Sound of Music*. What we were actually doing was drag shows in gay bars. They were later brought to San Francisco."

"People come up and say that they love us," says the group's Reverend Mother. "We have discovered a specific need in the community—that people live vicariously through us. We live out different aspects of personality for them. People come up and say that they've sinned, usually only half-jokingly. We always tell them that they're forgiven, that there is no more sin, so they can enjoy what they're doing."

But not everyone agrees with their mission. "One man just couldn't relate," says Sister Sensible Shoes, "so he threw a firecracker right at me. It blew a stigma right into my habit. It's a good thing I had on Sister's crinolines." And a recent letter to the editor of a local newspaper bannered the impious admonition to "Nix the Nuns."

One reason why some people get upset with them, the Sisters explain, is that they challenge conformist notions. "Gay ghettos are places for people to find and create fantasies," says Sister Searching for Men. "But people have gotten into a kind of rut, so we're enriching that fantasy. It's too easy to say, 'Don't do this or that.' We're saying, 'Push those boundaries back, transcend the limitations you've set on yourself.' You can be a lot of things, so take a chance and find out." —Mark Thompson

A Remedy for Queer-Bashing

I've been publicly identifiable as a lesbian for ten years now, and I've been insulted, threatened, followed, and assaulted so many times that I'm sure I've forgotten half the incidents. *But it's getting worse.* Ever since Dade County, gay people are being beaten and murdered in increasing numbers—all over the United States. This violent backlash has caused gays in Chicago, Seattle, New York, San Francisco, and other cities to start learning self-defense, carry weapons (both legally and illegally), organize street patrols of gay neighborhoods, and open crisis lines to keep statistics on antigay assaults and offer help to the victims. We are under siege, and people are reacting to it with anger and grim determination to retaliate.

Why is this happening, and what can we do about it? The media are being used to turn gays into a target for the frustrations of Middle America. Instead of blaming our economic woes on multinational corporations and an inflated defense budget, the American people are being encouraged to blame them on Communists, uppity Third World nations, and morally degenerate queers who somehow evade pulling their fair share of the load. We are repeatedly portrayed as economically privileged and sexually depraved. Our political clout is exaggerated and attributed to the cowardice of public officials. That image encourages people who have been deceived and cheated, people who work hard and get too little in return, people who don't get enough pleasure—especially not sexual pleasure—out of their lives, to turn on us.

If we are going to get anywhere, gay politics must become coalition politics, all the way from the federal government down to your block of the neighborhood. Straight feminists and ethnic communities are as threatened by increasing violence as lesbians and gay men. We can't form coalitions, however, if our own community is divided. Lesbians and gay men need to learn how to work together, no matter how painful this is for both parties.

A lot of lesbians and gay men move to the city to achieve a degree of anonymity. We want the privacy an urban environment can provide. But thanks to our own political efforts, we can no longer count on being anonymous in the city. Your average heterosexual citizen knows what a lesbian or a gay man looks like now. So do the queer-bashers. It's hard, time-consuming, and risky for us to ask help from our neighbors, organize meetings with them, find out what our common problems are, and start pressuring our elected officials to earn their keep. It can be boring, it can be discouraging, and there's no money in it.

Working for a constitutional gay-rights amendment, building coalitions with other oppressed groups, organizing our neighborhoods, and insisting on complete sex education for young people are all long-range goals that will require a lot of persistence and hard work. But would you rather be straight? I'm not being flippant. That really is the choice America is offering us. So roll up your sleeves, crank up that mimeo, dust off your clipboard, limber up your doorbell-ringing finger, and remember what they say in the cavalry—when the going gets tough, the tough get going!

—Pat Califia

THE MADDING CROWD

"The parts of the body that seem to be weaker are indispensable and those parts of the body we think less honorable we invest with the greatest honor.

"St. Paul's remarks about the less honorable or less presentable parts of the body reflect the sense of shame felt by mankind since the loss of original innocence and the subjection to concupiscence, particularly to the lust of the flesh.

"The parts in question are not objectively less honorable or respectable in themselves. They are such only on account of that sense of shame that urges us to surround our body with honor—to control in holiness and honor.

"It is precisely by controlling the body in holiness and honor that we overcome the present discord within us. We restore harmony by purity of heart."*

—Pope John Paul II, on St. Paul's
Letter to the Corinthians

*Papal double-talk translation: Be ashamed of your genitals and enjoy holiness as the consequence.

MUSIC: HOLLY NEAR

Holly Near is aware that, as a pop vocalist, she represents an unusual combination: "Politically, I identify with the radical folk tradition associated with Paul Robeson, Woody Guthrie, Pete Seeger, and the Weavers. But artistically, I was most influenced by Broadway, by Judy Garland, Edith Piaf, Barbra Streisand, and Aretha Franklin. There's always been a split in this country—protest music was sung in union halls or at rallies, and pop music just entertained. I do pop music that entertains while being political."

Near has solid roots in show business. Singing at community events in her rural Northern California hometown of Ukiah from the age of seven, she later did summer stock and musical comedy as a teenager, appeared in the Broadway version of *Hair,* and ended up in Hollywood at age nineteen with parts in a dozen TV shows and five movies. "I enjoyed it," she says of her acting roles, "but I felt so empty after all the performances. The material was so shallow."

Fonda and Donald Sutherland helped Near unify her art and politics by signing her up for their anti–Vietnam War "Free the Army" worldwide tour in 1971. As the war wound down in the mid-seventies and the women's movement wound up, Near's songwriting and performing increasingly focused on feminist consciousness, reflected in her next two albums. Her lesbian following grew accordingly, and she began to link up with the developing "women's music" circuit. In 1973, Near started her own Redwood Records label after walking out of a meeting with a record company executive who told her that her voice was "terrific, but not submissive enough."

Following the historic 1975 "Women on Wheels" tour by Near and lesbian performers Meg Christian, Margie Adam, and Cris Williamson, Near came out as a lesbian. Because of support from a growing lesbian-identified alternative feminist culture, coming out as a lesbian was far from detrimental to Near's career. In fact, her audiences grew even larger. "My work as a lesbian is to help others be as proud of who they are as I am. It's real painful how many people, like lesbians and gays in the entertainment industry, spend so much energy keeping their gay identities quiet. Perhaps by my being out, eventually they will." Near's "Singing for Our Lives," a song written as a tribute to Harvey Milk, has become an anthem of the gay movement.

The singer says she is "concerned about military madness and nuclear power, but also about the whitewashing of so many cultures that's been happening for so long—nonwhite cultures, lesbian culture, and gay culture are all threatened with assimilation. It shouldn't be 'Let's all be the same' as the straight white men are. We aren't the same. I don't want a melting pot. Let's have no more invisibility of our differences; let's celebrate and build our differences—they are our strengths."

—TORIE OSBORN

Two women build a wheelchair ramp in preparation for a women's music festival.

BOOKS: *THE CELLULOID CLOSET*

"I've been working on this book for so long people are convinced they've already read it," Vito Russo says with a laugh. His *The Celluloid Closet: Homosexuality in the Movies* has finally seen print. "For years, people have been coming up to me and saying, 'Hey, you wrote that book on gay cinema.' Now I won't have to tell them it's not finished yet."

It has indeed been years since Russo began touring the country with his remarkable show of clips from films with gay characters. He got the idea for his show, and for the book that eventually grew out of it, while working in the film department at the Museum of Modern Art in New York in the early 1970s. From the clips he collected, he put together a formal presentation about homosexual stereotypes in film.

Supporting himself by working in restaurants and bathhouses, Russo kept plugging away at his labor of love. Research for the book took four years, and the actual writing another two. Because Russo thought photos were essential, and since most gay characters are minor ones and rarely appear in studio stills, he took his own photos. Using a light box, Russo blew up the frames from 16mm prints to make the 130 photos that appear in the book. That process alone took an entire year.

Finding a publisher for his ground-breaking book proved to be an even more difficult process, however. The reluctance of many mainstream houses to take on the project seems only to confirm Russo's trenchant views about homophobia elsewhere in the world of mass communication—specifically, the dream factory known as Hollywood.

Film historian Vito Russo

Actor Ryan O'Neal played gay in *Partners*, although the film's producer, Aaron Russo, denied any overt gay message. *"Partners* is not a homosexual movie," he said. "One of the characters is homosexual. But it's not making a statement about anything."

What were the problems in finding a publisher?

My agent took my proposal around to every publishing house in the world and everyone turned it down. They said Parker Tyler had already written a book called *Screening the Sexes: Homosexuality in the Movies* and that therefore the subject was exhausted. Tyler's book is good, but it's also very esoteric. I wanted something that would have appeal on a wider basis. I mean, my mother doesn't know from Kenneth Anger and *Scorpio Rising*.

I set out to write not a book about homosexuality in cinema, but a very subjective, political view of gay film-history as put forth by Hollywood. I wanted to explore American attitudes toward male and female roles as expressed in film. Because I talk so much about changing concepts of masculinity, I consider it a feminist book. It's not a coffee-table book. It's a history. I think the audience for the book will go beyond gay people. I would like, for example, to reach straight men and have them think about a possible redefinition of traditional sex roles and American ideals of masculinity.

Is there a direct connection between the way gays are treated in real life and how they are portrayed in the movies?

To some extent, yes. Movies can only reflect what we see in society. The people who complain that movies don't reflect their lifestyle are the same people who are in the closet, and their lives are not widely visible in society. On the other hand, even if they

"Taxi Zum Klo shows that gays are as normal as heteros, and many gays will not stand for this. They feel somehow special—crème de la crème. Queens. That's ridiculous. Maybe we are a little bit more colorful and we like to gamble and differ in sexual play, but concerning love we are as helpless as anybody—hysterical and weak. None of us has learned to love."
—DIRECTOR FRANK RIPPLOH

"Suburbia is the only place where I'm scared. I can walk through Harlem and not feel uptight, but when I go into the suburbs, I feel I'm in outer space. Polyester is a movie about enemy territory."
—FILMMAKER JOHN WATERS

were widely visible—as Chicanos, blacks, and Third World people are—I still don't think Hollywood would reflect the reality of their existence, because Hollywood is in the business of creating an illusion.

So you think Hollywood might never make a positive gay movie?

To expect Hollywood suddenly to come of age is really naive. Hollywood is simply not going to start making positive films with gay themes. The only place gay reality will be reflected is in independent films, and I think that's the direction gays should be going. We need to support gay filmmakers and straight filmmakers who are positive about gay themes. The thrust of my book is that the dream of gay people should *not* be to become part of that Hollywood illusion, because it's empty. They should be looking for something more lasting. You think having a gay version of "Charlie's Angels" will make our lives better? Bullshit.

But isn't this just a transient period, as gays find legitimization in the larger society?

The basic issue is the conflict between the majority of gays, who want to be assimilated, and the minority who do not. The minority want to stay different, to teach society the beauty of that difference, and to respect those differences. Gay people get on TV and say, "You should like us because we're just like you." Of course that's true—we're all people. But what they should be saying is, "You should like us in spite of the fact that we're different from you," or even "You should like us *because* we are different."

One of the problems in all media seems to be that gay people are just left out, even though we're there. Can you give an example of how gay characters and situations simply disappear by the time a screenplay is turned into a movie?

According to Arthur Laurents, there was supposed to be a long-standing gay relationship in *The Turning Point*, to be contrasted to the heterosexual marriages in the film. The point was to show the similarities and differences in relationships. All that was lost because, according to Laurents, Herb Ross was nervous about using the gay relationship, so most of the scenes were never shot or else they were cut. And Laurents was remarkably courageous about sticking to his guns. When the film came out, he gave an interview with the *Los Angeles Times* in which he blasted Ross for cutting the gay characters. Ross squealed like a stuck pig, but Laurents told me he stands by every word of the interview.

Is there any difference between the way European and American films handle homosexuality?

The difference seems to be that in European films homosexuality is seen as part of the whole person. American films reflect the assumption that homosexuality is something one does and not something one *is*. Even if gay characters are portrayed negatively in European movies, they are viewed as people whose homosexuality is part of their totality.

Just how supportive do you think gay people are of filmmakers who make realistic films about gays?

Gay people spend millions of dollars in the United States and in Europe seeing stuff like *Can't Stop the Music*. If they would give only part of that money to support gay artists, even if they don't like the product, they'll be helping to create a diverse spectrum of gay images on the screen. A low-budget, independent film like *La Cage aux Folles* proves that we can have a hit. Now we just need to go on and create different images of gay people.

—SCOTT P. ANDERSON

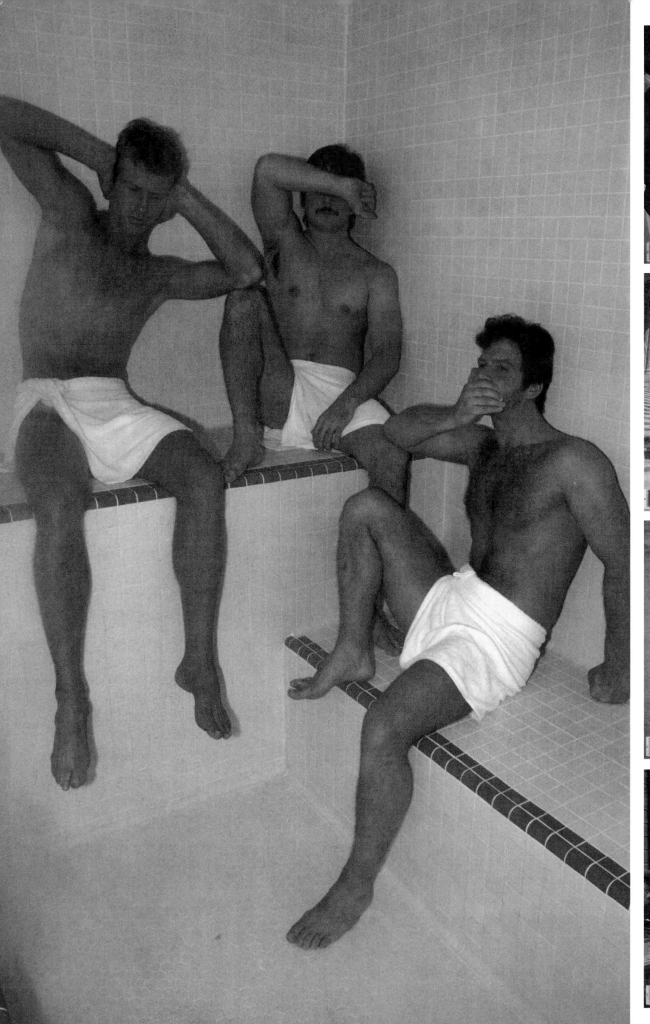

THE BIG SECRET

1982 For one week at summer's end throughout San Francisco, hundreds of perfectly muscled, beautifully toned bodies arched and soared, raced and lunged at the First Gay Games. The Games quickly became the focus, the epicenter of American lesbians and gays as we celebrated our prowess, our ability, our power—and our health.

Healthy was how lesbian and especially gay male life looked and acted in 1982. Fourteen years after Stonewall, it seemed that the revolution was complete. Our photos, paintings, all our images of ourselves show it: We're stalwart masculine men and handsome women. We face forward, look you in the eye, unafraid, individual, even in a couple. If you'd attended the National Gay Rodeo in Reno, Nevada, earlier that summer, you saw us take the American cowboy/cowgirl icon and remake it in our image.

Not that all was perfect. Politically, it was the usual mixed bag. With Ronald Reagan in office a year, it was clear he would remain uninvolved in lesbian and gay issues. Nor would he stop the Moral Majority, which had targeted us in the most concentrated way since Anita Bryant, raising $83,000 from one antigay mailing alone.

Balancing that were gay inroads. When Texas became the twenty-sixth state to repeal its sodomy laws, it showed the power emerging from Dallas and Houston with their large homosexual populations. Mayoral candidates Tom Bradley of Los Angeles, Kathy Whitmire of Houston, and Andrew Young of Atlanta were only the most overt in their wooing of gay voters—and when elected, in their work with lesbian and gay groups. By 1982, Seattle; Portland, Oregon; Philadelphia; and Boston also had thriving gay centers.

But for every progay law passed there seemed one step backward. Olympian Tom Waddell, who'd begun the Gay Games, lost the right to use of the name "Olympics" in court. At Blue's, a mid-Manhattan African-American bar, twenty-five people were injured in a police raid. In Boston, the building containing *Gay Community News, Fag Rag* magazine, and Glad Day Bookstore was destroyed in a fire after phoned threats. They all relocated, the store eventually to the Back Bay's most prestigious shopping boulevard.

Culturally, lesbians and gay men never looked healthier. Theater and dance, music and poetry blossomed. New York's The Glines and San Francisco's Theatre Rhinoceros were only the most successful of the many gay theater companies across the nation. The Glines's production of Harvey Fierstein's *Torch Song Trilogy* moved to Broadway, becoming the hit show of 1982. When the Tony Awards were given on TV, Fierstein thanked his lover and the producers smooched.

The actor-playwright also thanked Gay Presses of New York, which had published the trilogy before it was staged. Larry Mitchell, Terry Helbing, and I formed the press, and we each operated a small imprint—Calamus, JH, and Sea-Horse—devoted to lesbian and gay literature. Gay Sunshine Press, Daughters Press, Spinsters Ink, Alyson Publications, and Naiad were among the other independent publishers establishing a solid source for uncensored gay and lesbian writing.

Then, too, in 1982 Hollywood seemed to discover homosexuality. While the movie adaptation of *The Front Runner* languished, *Making Love,* starring hunks Harry Hamlin and Michael Ontkean, opened with much fanfare on screens across America. But it was surpassed by Mariel Hemingway and Patrice Donnelly's heat as athlete-lovers in *Personal Best,* and by a transvestite Julie Andrews and a gay Robert Preston in the hysterically funny gender-bending *Victor/Victoria.* From Germany came Frank Ripploh's *Taxi Zum Klo,* shot in a Berlin so open that strangers engaged in water sports and had glory-hole sex on the way home from work. But nothing topped public television's immensely successful *Brideshead Revisited.* Not only did the Evelyn Waugh adaptation make Jeremy Irons a star overnight, it made gay romance glamorous.

With twenty-two gay and lesbian radio shows across the country and scores of burgeoning film and video companies, with homosexuals plugged in to the future world of computer electronics, and Gay Pride parades erupting in two dozen cities, no wonder we were congratulating ourselves.

Too soon. If 1982 appeared to be the year homosexuals finally came into empowerment, it was also the year a thousand cases of an unnamed disease were certified by the Centers for Disease Control, a disease that had already afflicted an unknown number of gay men with Kaposi's sarcoma, toxoplasmosis, and Pneumocystis carinii. It was the big bad secret even the most outspoken gays kept hidden. But some of us, fueled by Larry Kramer's outrage in *New York Native* articles, even as we nursed our loved ones and feared for ourselves, tried to awaken our community to the last thing it wanted to hear: that sex was killing us. Many activists had fought so long for gay rights that giving up anything won—sexual freedom, drugs, the right to go to bathhouses—was seemed as deadly as AIDS itself.

In retrospect, 1982 is perhaps the saddest year since Stonewall. On the surface, a model year of achievement, of what might have, indeed what I believe *should* have become of gay life. Instead, it was the year of the big secret that could not be kept quiet. Soon AIDS would explode, decimating our community, changing our lives forever.

—FELICE PICANO

"What do you mean by 'natural'? If you say 'natural' in terms of how people love each other, then who cares if the relationship is gay or straight, as long as the love can be expressed and received? That is what's natural—not to be able to love is what's unnatural."
—REV. WILLIAM SLOAN COFFIN, JR.

The lesbian community had coalesced as never before by the early eighties. This gathering of San Francisco lesbian leaders included *(top, second from left)* Phyllis Lyon, *(top, third from right)* Del Martin, and *(bottom, left to right)* Roberta Achtenburg, Gwenn Craig, Carole Migden, and Dianne Barton-Paine.

"I don't think there is a 'gay lifestyle.' That's superficial crap, all that talk about gay culture. A couple of restaurants on Castro Street and a couple of magazines do not constitute culture. Michelangelo is culture. Virginia Woolf is culture. So let's don't confuse terms."
—AUTHOR RITA MAE BROWN

When Los Angeles radio station KROQ–FM played "Johnny, Are You Queer?," Josie Cotton's New Wave hit, born-again Christians and antipornography zealots picketed the station, claiming the song would encourage teenagers to "try" homosexuality.

Among the offending lyrics: "I saw you today, boy, walking with them gay boys.... I'm so afraid I'll lose you, if I can't seduce you. Is there something wrong, Johnny come on strong."

Gays defended the song as humorous and non-derogatory, and the single was in heavy rotation at local gay hot spots.

**HOMO-HATING GREEKS
GO BOTTOMS UP FOR BIGOTRY**
In March, members of Sigma Epsilon Phi celebrated the ousting of the University of Florida Lesbian and Gay Society (UFLAGS) from its campus office in Reitz Union. The mooning incident resulted in the expulsion of the fraternity brothers involved and the fraternity alumni council put the frat on a year's probation for "conduct unbecoming a fraternity." The publicity brought campus adminstrators to reverse UFLAGS's eviction.

JANUARY Voters in Austin, Texas, overwhelmingly rejected a measure that would have specifically allowed antigay housing discrimination. ❑ The Georgia Supreme Court overturned a lower court ruling that voided the registration of nearly 77,000 voters, many of them black or gay. ❑ Friends of Families, a progressive answer to conservative advocates of "family values," held its first conference in San Francisco. ❑ A Baltimore television station was forced to stop airing public service announcements encouraging children to report abuse to a teacher or friend; the right-wing Family Protection Lobby claimed the ads undermined parental authority. ❑ Methodist Church officials cleared a Denver bishop and the openly gay minister he had appointed; local parish members had asked that both be put on trial for disseminating false doctrine. ❑ A married professor in Clarksville, Tennessee, committed suicide after being arrested with twelve other men in a public park. ❑ An Australian postoperative transsexual was convicted of making false statements on her marriage certificate by claiming "spinster" status. ❑ A lesbian teacher in Belgium began a hunger strike to protest her dismissal as assistant headmistress at a girls' school.

FEBRUARY Wisconsin became the first state to pass a gay-rights law. ❑ Under pressure from a coalition of ethnic, gay, and women's groups, President Reagan withdrew his nomination of the Rev. Samuel B. Hart, a vociferous reactionary, for a seat on the U.S. Civil Rights Commission. ❑ All seven justices of the Florida Supreme Court agreed that the Trask-Bush Amendment, aimed at forcing gay college groups off campus, was unconstitutional. ❑ The FBI seized two mail-order gay erotic films in Dade County, Florida, claiming that one was

"sadomasochistic" because an actor slapped his fellator's face with his erect penis. ❑ Minneapolis Police Chief Anthony Bouza announced that officers using ethnic or antigay slurs, including "queer," "faggot," and "nigger," would be disciplined. ❑ Two women were arrested for kissing in a Sicilian public park.

MARCH New Right strategist and closeted homosexual Terry Dolan told *The Advocate* that he endorsed gay rights, a statement he later denied making;

four years later, he died from an AIDS-related illness. ❑ A Cincinnati woman who said she was kidnaped by people hired by her parents to "deprogram" her from becoming a lesbian filed a $2.75 million suit against her parents and her alleged assailants. ❑ A Dallas woman who had been selling sex toys at Tupperware-type home parties was arrested on a felony charge under a Texas law that forbids the sale of devices designed or marketed to stimulate human genitals. ❑ The National Gay Task Force launched the Violence Project in an attempt to combat the rise of homophobic violence in the United States. ❑ Two men were attacked and one was castrated in a gay-bashing incident at the West Street piers in New York City. ❑ The San Francisco Board of Supervisors unanimously ordered the city's police department to recruit gays and lesbians.

APRIL The House Subcommittee on Health and the Environment, chaired by California Representative Henry Waxman, held the first federal hearing on Kaposi's sarcoma and related opportunistic infections. ❑ A Florida deputy who arrested two men for kissing each other good-bye at an airport was dismissed from his job.

MAY More than five hundred gay men packed a New York University auditorium for a briefing on Gay-Related Immunodeficiency (GRID). ❑ The song "Homosapien," by British rocker Pete Shelley, was banned from daytime airplay by the BBC. ❑ More than a thousand Texans rallied in Dallas to protest poor treatment of gays by the police department. ❑ Voters in Lincoln, Nebraska, rejected a charter amendment that would have extended civil rights protection to the city's gays. ❑ All nine members of the publishing collective of the Canadian gay newspaper *The Body Politic* were charged with printing obscene material; later in the year, the state dropped its case. ❑ After thirteen years of lobbying, the Pink Triangle, a gay advocacy group, convinced the West German goverment to pay reparations to surviving gay victims of Nazi prison camps.

JUNE Over four hundred New Yorkers protested the brutal police raid on Blues, a Manhattan gay bar; in the raid, twelve patrons had been seriously injured. ❑ The American Nazi Party held an "antihomosexual" rally during Gay Pride Day in Chicago, with two thousand people showing up to salute the effigy of Harvey Milk's assassin, Dan White. ❑ More than sixty-five lesbian and gay activists attended the Democratic Party's midterm convention in Philadelphia, pressuring for gay civil rights. ❑ Chicago Mayor Jane Byrne issued an executive order banning antigay bias in city jobs and services. ❑ A federal court in Oklahoma upheld a law aimed at firing gay teachers. ❑ Boston gays carried signs saying "Big Mother Is Watching" after the Christian Science "Mother Church" fired two gay employees. ❑ Following an *Advocate* report on surveillance, three U.S. Congressmen asked the FBI for a full disclosure of agency probes of gay individuals and organizations.

JULY By a wide margin, the 194th General Assembly of the United Presbyterian Church in the United States voted to exclude lesbians and gays from ordination as ministers or lay elders. ❑ Gay and feminist demonstrators disrupted nearly every public appearance of conservative fundamentalist minister and Moral Majority founder Jerry Falwell during a four-day tour of Australia. ❑ British Commander Michael Trestrail, Queen Elizabeth's personal bodyguard of sixteen years, resigned following the exposure of his sexuality by one of his male sex partners.

In her hometown of Houston, feminist author and publisher June Arnold died of brain cancer in March. She was fifty-five. As founder of Daughters, Inc., Arnold quickly established herself as the mother of the women-in-print movement, publishing Rita Mae Brown's *Rubyfruit Jungle.* She also authored several books, including *Sister Jen.*

"*D*oing Making Love has had a profound and recognizable effect on my personal life. Once you acknowledge to the world, once there are no more secrets, you're no longer concerned about going to a party with another guy. I don't give a shit anymore. This is who I am."
—SCREENWRITER BARRY SANDLER

The First Gay Games, organized by former Olympic champion Dr. Tom Waddell, were held in San Francisco. The week-long August event featured thirteen hundred athletes from twenty-eight states and ten nations.

In December, San Francisco's gay community launched a "Dump Dianne" campaign after Mayor Dianne Feinstein vetoed a domestic partnership bill that would have permitted homosexual city employees and their partners to receive health benefits, sick leave, bereavement leave, and jail and hospital visitation rights.

AUGUST The Centers for Disease Control in Atlanta reported ten to twenty cases of AIDS being discovered every week across the nation, with a total of 202 deaths attributed to the syndrome so far. ❑ A U.S. District Court judge in Dallas struck down as unconstitutional a Texas law that made private homosexual sex a criminal offense. ❑ The U.S. Olympic Committee secured a court order preventing the word "Olympic" from being used by organizers of the Gay Games, even though other groups had been allowed to used the term; the Supreme Court later upheld the ruling. ❑ The International Gay Association held its fourth annual conference in Washington, D.C.

SEPTEMBER Former Major League baseball player Glenn Burke of the Los Angeles Dodgers came out. ❑ A ground-breaking report issued by a task force of the San Francisco Archdiocese of the Roman Catholic Church made fifty-four pro-gay recommendations, calling for an end to antigay violence, for equality for women, and for the recognition of the spiritual value of gay sexuality.

OCTOBER Gay rights were endorsed by the Industrial Union Department, making it the second major labor group in the country to adopt a pro-gay stance. ❑ Virginia Apuzzo agreed to replace Lucia Valeska as head of the National Gay Task Force. ❑ Roman Catholic Archbishop William Borders of Baltimore celebrated Mass for more than three hundred members of Dignity, a gay Catholic organization. ❑ In an unprecedented move, the Army heeded a judge's order to allow Perry Watkins, an openly gay soldier, to reenlist. He would later be discharged again. ❑ A YMCA in Phoenix was converted into a gay community services center. ❑ The Salvation Army in Chicago refused a donation of $1,400 raised by a gay motorcycle club, then reversed itself, but the funds had already been given to other charities. ❑ Despite a "Save Ulster from Sodomy" campaign, gay sex was legalized in Northern Ireland.

NOVEMBER The Centers for Disease Control reported 775 cases of AIDS nationally, with 294 deaths. ❑ Merle Woo, an Asian-American lesbian teacher of ethnic studies at the University of California, Berkeley, claimed sexual and racial discrimination in her suit for reinstatement after being fired.

DECEMBER The immune impairment of a twenty-month-old baby was traced to the blood donation of an AIDS patient, suggesting that the disease could be transmitted by transfusion and that it might have a long incubation period. ❑ Police in Dade County, Florida, conducted simultaneous raids on forty-three Miami-area adult bookstores; eighty-six officers arrested fifty-one people in the operation. ❑ In an attempt to obtain names of its political opponents, the Adolph Coors Company sued for the membership lists of Solidarity, a San Francisco gay organization that organized a boycott of Coors products; a U.S. District Court rejected the beer corporation's request six months later.

A Spy Infiltrates a Falwell Dinner

When Philadelphia gay activist Scott Tucker heard that televangelist Jerry Falwell was coming to town, he decided to meet the man. Tucker and friends put on conservative attire and infiltrated a Falwell rally. Here's what happened to them.

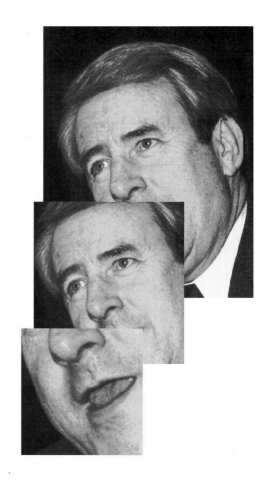

On the evening of November 3, we drive to the Marriott Hotel. Plainclothes and uniformed security is evident everywhere in the hotel and parking lot. Our group, all dressed properly for the event, gathers while the other demonstrators (numbering in the hundreds) begin chanting: "One-two-three-four: We Don't Want Your Holy War! Two-four-six-eight: Falwell Preaches Christian Hate! They Say No Choice—We Say Pro-Choice!" The dozen of us who are undercover feel as though we are walking into the lion's den.

There in the hotel lobby stand hundreds of Moral Majoritarians, and most of them look like just plain folks in their Sunday best. Not many black people, lots of people holding Bibles, lots of polyester and "Jesus First" lapel pins. We proceed to a large anteroom full of hundreds more people.

We mill about in the crowd for nearly a half-hour. One couple with cheerleader charm strikes up a conversation, asking us if we've seen "the gays and the feminists outside." I say, "No, we haven't, but Falwell must be used to *them* by now." One lesbian in our group, being quite fluent in fundamentalism (her parents having long been Falwell supporters), converses calmly and at some length.

Finally we are allowed to file into the banquet hall, with security making spot checks of our reservations. The occasion is "The Friends of Liberty Dinner," a public boosting for one of Falwell's ventures, the Liberty Baptist College, "where new generations are trained to carry on the work of Christ." Almost as soon as our group has seated itself at a big round table, a security guard comes over to ask us what our religious affiliations are. (Are we giving off a telltale scent?) The lesbian fluent in fundamentalism gives likely answers, and the guard withdraws, though men with walkie-talkies keep a steady eye on us.

The meal is edible, but how to describe the water-torture of the next two hours? Falwell inveighing against "the feminists, the abortionists, the homosexuals who threaten the Traditional Family." (And of course he's right, we do.) At one point Falwell asks all the ministers and pastors in the audience to rise, and a formerly Jewish, transsexual member of the Metropolitan Community Church stands up from our table to be counted among them.

At the end the lights come up again, and I feel like a deep-sea diver with the bends. Falwell begins delivering another homily. Like Reagan, he comes across really homey and folksy, a wolf in sheep's clothing. We rise from the table, and unravel squares of cloth with slogans like THE MORAL MAJORITY IS NEITHER.

First there are stunned stares, then currents of muttering pass through the hall. Guards rush from all corners to grab us and hustle us out the door. Falwell expresses his regret that "there are people among us who do not have Jesus."

We regroup outside the hotel and talk to the press. What, finally, was the point of it all? Symbolic action and acts of silent witness have a modest, yet significant, purpose. There is a time and place for aggressive and passionate resistance, but we wanted to walk out of the lion's den unpawed. Speaking for myself, I wanted to know and deal with my enemy face to face, instead of frowning at newspapers and the TV screen. I can only say I feel stronger now.

CRAIG CLAIBORNE

"In science fiction, you can write about sex the way it really happens, whereas in mundane fiction you are more or less restricted—oh, not to the standard missionary position, but at least to the standard missionaries doing it." —AUTHOR SAMUEL DELANEY

For every American even remotely interested in fine food, the name Craig Claiborne is legendary. *The New York Times* food editor and prolific author of cookbooks is one of a handful of men and women who have helped transform the American dining scene and, in fact, the entire national consciousness about good eating.

Most recently, Claiborne has gained notoriety for his book *A Feast Made for Laughter,* subtitled *A Memoir with Recipes* (his one hundred favorite). In the book he writes candidly about his sexual feelings for his father and is forthcoming on the subject of his own homosexuality.

We met the grand old man of American eats during his recent book tour, at breakfast in the bright pink and green Polo Lounge in the Beverly Hills Hotel.

Through the years, Claiborne says, his sexual orientation has never been a handicap to him. "I've never felt put upon by society because I was gay. I've never made a big number about it, I'm no crusader. I presume that if people think about it they know that I'm gay. I've had lovers and have never hidden that from people. I've been at *The New York Times* for twenty-five years, and I don't think there's a single person at the executive level who doesn't know I'm a homosexual."

Claiborne spent years in psychotherapy dealing with issues related to his sexuality, including the relationship with his father. For two years, because of family finances, young Craig and his father shared the same bed. The contact spurred Claiborne's sexual awakening. In his book he describes his nightly explorations of his father's body: "It was as though all my being were inundated with warm waves of ecstasy, the sensation of drowning and awakening shaken but on a safe and hitherto unexplored island." Though their sexual relationship was never consummated, Claiborne is sure that his feelings for his father affected his own sexual development.

"People seem to think I am accusing my father of being responsible for my homosexuality, which is not what I intended. I was totally aware of my homosexuality when I was in my crib. In my early childhood, we had a black man, Albert, on whom I had a terrible crush. Sometimes he'd keep [an eye on] me and put me in his own bed for a nap. So I was terribly involved with wanting Albert—and that was long before puberty."

Like millions of other gay servicemen after the war, Claiborne headed for a big city—in his case, Chicago—so he could come out. He didn't become involved with anyone right away, however. "I was having too much fun." He chuckles. His first serious affair was with a man, since dead, who worked for a major corporation. "We lived together for two years, and it was total, absolute bliss," he recalls softly. "It was a perfect sexual liaison for two solid years. Then my mother came to visit, and things were never the same between him and me. I don't know what she did, but suddenly he and I were no longer." Today Claiborne's love life is happier. He is involved with a man his own age, and they both believe things will work out for them in the long run. "We've already planned that New Year's Eve at the advent of 2000 we'll be at Windows on the World celebrating with champagne," says Claiborne. "And we'll be spending the rest of the evening *very close.*"

—SCOTT ANDERSON

Is Our "Lifestyle" Hazardous to Our Health?

By early 1982, it could no longer be ignored but it didn't yet have its name. It was referred to sometimes as "the gay cancer," sometimes as GRID (gay-related immunodeficiency), and most often as Kaposi's sarcoma, the illness that was, at the time, most strongly associated with the new epidemic. And though by the end of the year it would be clear that the epidemic was affecting injection drug-users and hemophiliacs in addition to gay men, the year started with the frightening question: Were the hallmarks of the urban gay lifestyle—sex and drugs—making gay men sick?

The question sparked an angry debate on the pages of the gay press, including *The Advocate,* and in gay communities in New York, San Francisco, and Los Angeles. On one side of the controversy was the medical establishment, historically no friend of the gay community and ill-equipped to deal with the questions raised by the new epidemic. On the other side stood the urban gay male communities, determined to hold on to their hard-won culture of fast sex and easy drugs. Some gay men weighed in on the side of the "lifestyle" theory of the origin of the epidemic—only to be immediately rebuffed as "gay homophobes."

And professional homophobes were starting to recognize the propaganda opportunity presented by the outbreak. Early in 1982, gay men leaving a West Hollywood bar found leaflets under their windshield wipers. The fliers featured a December 1981 *Newsweek* story entitled "Diseases That Plague Gays" and an invitation to come to a fundamentalist Christian church for salvation—and, perhaps, a cure.

In July 1981, *The New York Times* reported the appearance of Kaposi's sarcoma in forty-one gay men in New York and Los Angeles. In August, New York writer Larry Kramer published a tiny story in the biweekly gay paper *The New York Native* entitled "A Personal Appeal." "The men who have been stricken don't appear to have done anything that many New York gay men have not done at one time or another," wrote Kramer, asking gay men to contribute to a study of Kaposi's undertaken by Dr. Alvin Friedman-Kien at the New York University Medical Center. "It's easy to become frightened that one of the many things we've done or taken over the past years may be all that it takes for a cancer to grow from a tiny something-or-other that got in there who knows when from doing who knows what."

The last statement set off a barrage of angry letters to the *Native* from men who saw the writer seizing an opportunity to reiterate what many saw as the central message of his 1978 novel, *Faggots:* Gay sex (and drugs) equals death. Six months later, *The Advocate* printed a two-part article by New York writer Nathan Fain giving both sides of the controversy, which continued to rage. Fain quoted another New York writer, the novelist Edmund White—an expert on gay life by virtue of being the author of the gay travelogue *States of Desire* and coauthor of *The Joy of Gay Sex*—warning, "Some moralists are using the appearance of Kaposi's sarcoma as a pretext for preaching against gay promiscuity under the guise of giving sound medical advice. In fact, no one knows the causes of *any* kind of cancer, much less a kind to have emerged so recently among young and middle-aged, gay male Americans. True, most of the new

One of *The Advocate*'s most popular and long-standing features is Pat Califia's no-holds-barred column advising readers on matters of sex, relationships, erotic fantasies, and fetishes. Here is a sampler from a typical column.

I am really into having sex with jockey shorts on, or wearing some types of cotton, silk, satin, rayon, or synthetic-fabric underwear. Are there other gays into such a fetish?

A fascination with underwear is probably one of the most common fetishes, since you are heightening the significance of the genitals and prolonging or postponing the moment when you finally get to touch naked flesh. It's a tease and a tribute.

Are there bathhouses for women? It's so easy for gay men to get a lot of casual sex with no strings attached. I want some too!

Unfortunately, the few women's bathhouses that exist are there to provide a hot tub—not hot sex. A lesbian who would like to have sex without the complications of a romantic relationship has a fairly difficult time meeting women with the same goal. However, with patience and courage, you can build a network of women who also enjoy casual sex.

I have discovered "water sports." In group sessions, we all drink plenty of liquids, not only during get-togethers, but hours before as well. The result is piss that is as clear and unpolluted as a mountain stream. I have been on the giving and receiving side, including drinking, and feel very comfortable about it. But what are the health risks?

It sounds like you've fallen in with a group of responsible and intelligent perverts. That's wonderful! Piss has a terrible reputation among those with secretion phobias. I often wonder how some people manage to

live inside their own bodies. Can they savor (even in the privacy of the bathroom) the pleasure of a good piss or a healthy shit?

Piss is sterile, and it is safe to drink the piss of a healthy person. There is a phenomenon known as viral shedding, which means that if someone is carrying a virus, viral particles are shed in their sweat, semen, spit, urine, shit, tears, and blood. However, you are no more likely to contact viruses from drinking piss than you are from licking a sweaty armpit, or giving a deep-throat kiss.

I've heard that in lesbian hanky codes, white lace indicates women interested in "Victorian scenes." What in heaven's name is a Victorian scene?

A Victorian scene has different costumes, roles, and plots than a typical leather scene. Participants wear long dresses, high heels, and feminine underthings. Canes, birches, riding crops, and hairbrushes are used for chastisement. For example: The "maid" is spanked for pulling her "mistress's" hair while brushing it out.

My boyfriend told me he caught gonorrhea from me and suggested I get a rectal examination. I had cultures taken and tested negative, so I told my boyfriend I was clean. But after he was treated and cured he got it again! Why should this happen?

First, it's possible that your boyfriend didn't get gonorrhea from you. Unless he was absolutely one hundred percent monogamous, it's impossible to tell just who gave him what. It's also possible that he never really got rid of his first infection. The third possibility is that your tests were inaccurate.

People's attitudes toward sexually transmitted diseases rarely take into account the nature of the diseases or the methods of treatment and diagnosis. Your boyfriend apparently still has a horror of STDs and a need to blame somebody else for giving it to him, instead of viewing it as a risk that one takes.

KS victims are sexually active, but they also share many other attributes. Given how conformist gay life has become, one could just as easily single out any other feature of a clone's existence as being carcinogenic—wearing button-fly jeans, perhaps, or weightlifting, or excessive disco dancing."

Desperate as this debate could sound, some prominent gay minds refused either to take sides or to take it seriously. Contacted by Fain, San Francisco writer Armistead Maupin asked, "Can't I just be a Concerned Whore?"

"Nothing anyone has said so far so neatly puts the dilemma," wrote Fain. "The outbreak of disease appears in a way like the face of Death itself—fascinating, horrifying, a figure guarding a threshold. As it poses a supreme challenge to medical science, it poses an equal challenge to the very idea of free sexual expression and a sense of social integrity. There remains, on every side, much work to be done."

In his two-part report on the epidemic, Fain plunged into the nature of this work sounding at times more like a private investigator than an investigative reporter. He identified the major suspects: cytomegalovirus and the related Epstein-Barr virus; the use of the drug Flagyl to treat amoebiasis; and "poppers," the nitrite inhalants then ubiquitous in urban gay male communities. The case for the prosecution was made by Dr. James Curran, whose team of investigators from the federal Centers for Disease Control had been surveying 150 gay men—fifty of them ill and one hundred healthy—about their lifestyle. Speaking for the defense were gay writers and activists and the president of Pharmex, a San Francisco company that made nitrite inhalants under the brand names Rush and Bolt.

Some attempted to find a middle ground. Speaking in *The Advocate,* Lawrence Downs, a New York physician with a large gay clientele, counseled moderation. "We've been rotting ourselves out with ethyl chloride and butyl nitrite in our lungs, and amoebas in our intestines," said Downs. "I tell my patients, there are no *bad* drugs as such. There is *abuse* of drugs."

As the year went on, most of the voices in *The Advocate* tried to hold this cautionary middle ground. In the summer the magazine reprinted a pamphlet distributed by the Sisters of Perpetual Indulgence during San Francisco's gay pride festivities. Entitled "Play Fair: A Sisterly Sermon," it listed among its authors Sister Florence Nightmare—Bobbi Campbell, a registered nurse who would go on to become an AIDS poster boy. The sisters gave basic information about sexually transmitted diseases, outlined the symptoms of KS and *Pneumocystis carinii* pneumonia, and, for the first time in *The Advocate,* suggested that condoms may "actually prevent the spread of certain diseases."

Illustrations from a safe-sex instruction pamphlet produced and distributed by the Sisters of Perpetual Indulgence and later reprinted in *The Advocate.*

By November, when *The Advocate* printed a report on an AIDS symposium at the University of California medical school in San Francisco alongside a profile of the city's five-month-old Kaposi Foundation, 735 people had been diagnosed with the newly named syndrome. Though the specifics of either risk factors or prevention techniques were still hazy, a consensus about the dangers of gay male sex was emerging.

"Physicians no longer should be afraid to appear moralistic when they tell their patients about the dangers of promiscuity," the magazine quoted Dr. Robert Bloan, medical director of the Gay Clinic at Presbyterian Medical Center in San Francisco and a member of the gay group Bay Area Physicians for Human Rights. "In this environment, it's probably best to do away with things that are not necessary."

Manhattan Hunting Grounds

For those of you who don't read, never go to movies, and otherwise know nothing of the world in which you live, tearooms are public men's rooms—so-called, it is said, because the English refer to urine as "tea." Tearooms are found in parks, along highways, at airports, within landmark skyscrapers on Fifth Avenue, and everywhere else there are men and a thought of "public comfort." And everywhere they exist—I'm speaking empirically now—they are used for sex. Don't balk. Some of these shrines are quite popular, even legendary, and are known to those who care to know such things. More men than you might think, both straight and gay, make a pilgrimage as part of their daily routines—though categories like "straight," "gay" and "indifferent" don't hold up for long in tearooms.

Compelling reasons for not patronizing tearooms have been well rehearsed—you'll get mugged, you'll get arrested, you'll get sick, you'll deny yourself the opportunity to forge the well-integrated sexual identity that an openly gay lifestyle affords. And all of this is true. I especially don't want to minimize the emotional toll exacted by a gay life based *solely* on tearooms. But in the years since Stonewall it's gotten harder to spend your life in a toilet, what with gay choruses, gay clinics, gay softball teams and all. Nowadays, twelve years after Laud Humphreys revealed the workings of a shadowy underworld in his landmark *Tearoom Trade,* burgeoning gay culture provides a somewhat brighter background against which to look at these more ill-appreciated of homosexual institutions.

What do most people know about tearooms, anyway, except for gossip? Veterans who have endured even one well-intentioned lecture on "the shame of the tearooms" find it tempting to conclude that those who talk most about such things often know them least. And vice versa.

My local tearoom is on the RR train of the BMT line, one of three inter-connected lines that make up the sprawling New York subway system. The line is immaterial, really, since superior cruising is available anywhere at the right time. Success depends on many variables: skill, luck, patience, instinct, phases of the moon. Good architecture is paramount: The best tearooms offer the security of long entry hallways and noisy doors, making it impossible for someone to enter unobtrusively. Naturally, cruising strategies vary: Some invest time in loitering, others flit. Many cruise locally, on one line, within a few stops of their place of work or residence. Others—the real virtuosos who know the subways better than migrating birds know the constellations—think nothing of covering four boroughs using all three lines. Sadly, subway service is deteriorating. Now that waits between trains are longer than they used to be, one passes up the two-star tearooms in favor of the three-star; and since reading helps pass the time, one sees more paperback editions of *Middlemarch* hanging out of the pockets of bomber jackets.

I didn't realize how fond of tearoom society I'd become until the New York City transit strike two years ago. Thousands of us who normally take the subway to work were left to our own devices. In a quandary, I resorted to hitchhiking for the first time since college. It was a chore, but it worked. The worst of the strike for me, however, was not standing at the entry ramp of the Brooklyn Bridge in the pouring rain at seven-thirty in the morning. Nor was it, when finally picked up, having to put up with some other guy's idea of early morning radio. If the truth be told, the worst of it was not being able to stop in at my friendly neighborhood tearoom.

"What's a guy supposed to do with his cock?" my friend Albert lamented at the time. Albert is an account executive at a major downtown bank, a serious collector of Chinese porcelain (Sung) and an inveterate tearoom cruiser. We met years ago in pursuit of a since-forgotten number in black leather and have been chums ever since. Albert was heartened somewhat when I reminded him of all the other ways to have sex in this city I also told him I was confident that city and union officials were working day and night to solve the problem.

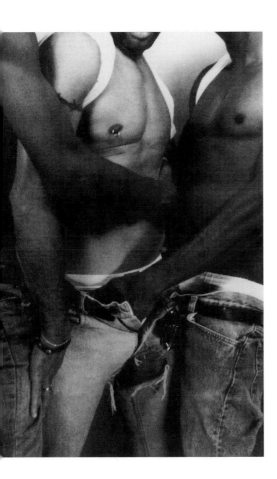

What became clear to me after a few days of strike was that my cock was not quite the epicenter of my concern. To be sure, fast, easy sex can become a habit—and why not?—but the "compulsion" of many tearoom regulars is actually as much of the spirit as of the body. In fact, I wouldn't be surprised if some future study showed that men have sex in subway tearooms in inverse proportion to the regularity of their visits. Why? Surprisingly, there is in tearooms some of the same atmosphere of fellow feeling and camaraderie more often associated with clubs and corner taverns. I don't know about Albert—I think he said he managed to sneak into a locked station somewhere—but I missed "the guys." I'd come to enjoy the fraternal contact, nodding hello to men I've seen before, respecting with them the unwritten rules of tearoom etiquette, sharing an occasional raised eyebrow at the extravagant behavior of a newcomer. Such small sociabilities among men are as important as sex, even in tearooms. Here, as elsewhere, they function as a sort of common language.

Taken together, tearoom conventions and their universality say more to me about the much-vaunted democratic element of gay life than anything else I've seen. And shared metaphors are the least of it. Sex, of course, is the preferred language of tearooms. Take a typical day in my local tearoom. The place is filled with assorted types who would probably pass unnoticed and unconnecting in the intersection aboveground, let alone in a gay bar. There's an extremely fit, sixty-year-old married guy who superintends a nearby apartment building; a young black messenger whose street-worn clothing belies his gentlemanliness and desire to please; a wormy but likable fellow in a pilled polyester sport coat and Dr. Zorba hairdo who knows more about this particular tearoom than anyone else I've talked to—what it's like very late at night, when the cops last wandered in, what the porters use to clean it; a surprisingly affectionate Puerto Rican high school student with sublimely satiny skin; a tall, handsome upwardly mobile gay businessman dressed impeccably in Armani, reeking of Halston Z-14.

What had I known before of such men? Except for my grandfather, I'd never even *touched* a sexagenarian, much less dallied with him. In an all too inhibiting world, the tearooms are places for sexual experiment, for trying new things with new people. They are places where the very absence of tedious preliminaries and meaningful relationships—both available elsewhere in greater quantity than ever before—make it easier to break through the web of sexual prohibitions that constrains gays as well as straights. Moreover, tearooms engage a facet of the gay imagination seldom touched by bars and baths: the belief that the terrain of *everyday life* is rich with erotic possibilities. Many men, I have found, share this belief. It is the very promise of cruising. This is why the men in my tearoom can enter expecting an intimate moment with a stranger at eight-fifteen in the morning and, extraordinarily, can find it. Thus a simple ride to work can metamorphose into a journey of discovery of desire.

—STEPHEN GRECO

THE BUTCH QUIZ

Does anyone get laid enough?

Did you feel like you were finally getting somewhere in the self-esteem department? You stopped trying to deepen your voice when you met new people. You stopped worrying if you crossed your legs the wrong way. You finally liberated youself as a free spirit—only to find that free spirits had gone out of season!

The most inconsequential decision is now grounds for a major identity crisis. Which color is more fun: party pink or olive drab? Which article of clothing is more festive: a feather boa or a construction hat? Who would it be more fun to imitate on a New York subway grating: Marilyn Monroe or R2D2?

So why is everyone walking around acting like R2D2? Because R2D2 is Butch, and Butch is getting laid. Throw out the heels and get out the construction boots. There's a whole new drag, and it's called Butch.

Relax. No one was born Butch. People were born babies and promptly burst into tears, which was most un-Butch. Yet when some people grew up, they became inescapably Butch, while others are still sitting on the sidelines waiting for a Miracle. Is it in the genes? Natural selection? Divine intervention?

No. These people have done their homework. And so can you. Here it is, to better see if you, too, have potential.

—CLARK HENLEY

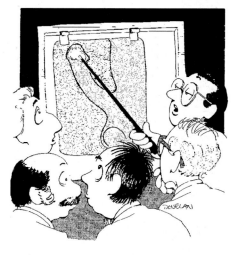

"AS YOU CAN SEE, WE HAVE DISCOVERED THAT IT DOES, IN FACT, HAVE A MIND OF ITS OWN."

1. In the first grade you received a box of crayons; the first crayon you grabbed was:

A. gray   D. silver
B. navy blue   E. magenta
C. red

2. In the second grade your favorite thing to do at recess was:

A. hide in the school's dumpster
B. play "crack the whip"
C. play tether ball
D. sneak into the cloakroom and try on everyone's coats
E. hitchhike to the nearest movie theater and see the latest Bergman film

3. The sound most reminiscent of your childhood was:

A. the school lawn mower finding a Coke bottle on the athletic field
B. the recess bell
C. your name being chosen to be on a team for Phys. Ed.
D. your mother talking on the telephone
E. the nurse reading your name on the "Excused from Phys. Ed." list

4. In the fifth grade each person chose a state to do a report on. You chose:

A. Arkansas   D. The Côte d'Azur
B. Colorado   E. Depression
C. Washington, D.C.

5. In the sixth grade, at graduation, the teacher asked everyone what they wanted to be when they grew up. You said:

A. a fireman   D. a makeup artist
B. a realtor   E. young
C. a husband

6. In seventh grade you suddenly found yourself extremely unpopular. You attributed this to:

A. the scar you got when you fell out the window of the school bus
B. your inability to use the guide words in the dictionary
C. your braces, your zits, your height, your weight, and seven cowlicks all in front
D. throwing like a girl
E. the fact that your class was mildly retarded, aesthetically if not academically

7. Disney was your religion as a child. Your most memorable movie moment was when:

A. the alligator ate Captain Hook
B. Snow White's stepmother was crushed by rocks
C. Pinocchio turned into a donkey
D. the mice made Cinderella's dress
E. Bambi's mother died

8. In eighth grade, Prom Night finally arrived. You:

A. took the fattest girl in school and cut up the dance floor
B. took the most beautiful girl in school and lost your virginity on the ninth hole of the nearest golf course
C. went with the guys and spent the evening getting drunk in the locker room
D. went by yourself and asked a girl to dance; when she said no, you went outside and threw up
E. decorated the gym within an inch of its life, then stayed home and watched reruns of "Leave It to Beaver"

Answers:

If you chose lots of As, you are already extremely Butch. You are also a Dyke, no offense intended. If you chose lots of Bs, you are almost as Butch. You are also a heterosexual male, no offense intended. If you chose lots of Cs, this book is what you've been looking for your whole life. Proceed with renewed vigor and memorize every detail. If you chose lots of Ds, you are an accomplished Queen. You could skim this book and have the whole routine down perfectly in fifteen minutes, but you'd give it up immediately because olive-drab bugle beads do not look attractive in a spotlight with a bastard amber gel. If you chose lots of Es, you are an accomplished eccentric. This quiz will not make any sense to you.

BOOKS: *SURPASSING THE LOVE OF MEN*

Historian Lillian Faderman

"Because I lived with a woman for forty years, people assume I'm a lesbian."
—NOVELIST MARGUERITE YOURCENAR

Lillian Faderman's *Surpassing the Love of Men: Romantic Friendship and Love Between Women from the Renaissance to the Present* is a great achievement. It gives lesbians the significance in literary and intellectual history that has sometimes been claimed for us but has never before been so convincingly demonstrated.

Based on material from France and Germany as well as England and America, the book covers five centuries, although two-thirds of it is devoted to the nineteenth and twentieth centuries. The writing is concise and its narrative flow impressive, given the great number and variety of sources.

The story Faderman tells is as interesting as a novel. For a long time, passionate relationships between women were accepted (unless women dared to dress as men and thereby claim some male power). Then, in the nineteenth century, a reaction began, and lesbians were seen as evil, unnatural, and sick (often by themselves as well as by male authorities). Finally, with the rise of lesbian-feminism in our time, the myths and stereotypes have been exposed, and we ourselves have become the authorities on lesbianism.

One of the main themes of Faderman's book is that literary treatments of lesbianism, based on male fantasy, were mistaken for reality; these distortions influenced other writers and in time were internalized by lesbians themselves "and became self-fulfilling."

Another theme is that women's romantic friendships were not sexual. Faderman values them highly and assumes they were whole, healthy relationships, an unorthodox view in our sex-charged times. Her evidence is persuasive, and probably only the discovery of sexually explicit letters or diaries would refute it. The advantages of Faderman's conclusion are that it carefully avoids interpreting past experience through present values and assumptions, and that it works against the simple-minded reduction of lesbianism to sex.

Surpassing the Love of Men uncovers an astonishing amount of ignorance on the part of doctors, historians, writers, and sexologists. Often when scholars challenge received opinion with weighty evidence, they become righteous and rancorous, but Faderman corrects error in a calm, even-tempered way.

The book is full of fascinating details: lesbian vampires; lesbians in Utah; a theory linking lesbianism to birth order (oldest daughter); the name of Edna St. Vincent Millay's early lover; the lesbianism of Minnie Benson, wife of the Archbishop of Canterbury; the Boston marriage of Sarah Orne Jewett and Annie Fields; and the circle around Harriet Hosmer, the nineteenth-century American sculptor who lived in Rome—these are only a few, not to mention countless diverting plot summaries and quotations revealing the wacky ideas about lesbians that danced in the heads of psychiatrists.

A great deal more could be said about Faderman's book, which in its originality, scope, and sheer mental energy challenges a reviewer to respond to it adequately. Valuable in itself, the book is also valuable for the creative scholarship it may inspire and the fruitful paths of investigation it may suggest to others. *Surpassing the Love of Men* is a pioneering work of recovery and reinterpretation that becomes a celebration of women. —MARGARET CRUIKSHANK

CONFESSIONS OF A GAY ROCKER

Adam Block began his decade-long tenure as the first openly gay rock colum-nist in a national magazine with the self-revealing essay excerpted here.

In 1971 I was a teenager struggling with coming out. The hard part wasn't my family, and shucks, I knew I liked boys. The scary part was my music. I fig-ured you could always spot a homo by his record collection, and mine was a disgrace. How was a kid raised on the Rolling Stones, the Animals, and the Who supposed to relate to a world where the reigning deities seemed to be Judy Garland and Barbra Streisand, where polite conversation required a fasci-nation with the minutiae of show tunes and opera? "You can't be a homo," I kept thinking. "Homos don't like rock 'n' roll."

Rock was more than the soundtrack of my youth. It was a shared secret lan-guage that linked me to every other fan. It was unnerving and invigorating: the sound of lust and revolt, passion and humor. The problem was that rock, for all its daring celebrations, stopped short at the ultimate taboo: Boys don't kiss boys. That had me spooked. There *seemed* to be plenty of gay rockers out there, but you could look in vain for an openly gay rock star. Rock was still a part of main-stream culture; a place, as Vito Russo said of the movies, "where one learned to pass for straight, where one learned the boundaries of what America would accept as normal."

Bruce Springsteen and Clarence Clemens (*above*); **Mick Jagger and his guitar** (*below*).

The next year, I was in London and thinking about the ways that rock and gay lib touched each other, when those boundaries began to stretch to the breaking point. In the summer of '72 the British press was full of David Bowie, an admitted bisexual who was releasing his *Ziggy Stardust* LP and inspiring young boys to pile on the makeup and glitter. I also read an account of a sixteen-year-old who said he felt strange getting a hard-on while he watched Mick Jagger perform. That made me grin. "I think that teenager's hard-on says more about rock as gay lib than Bowie's notoriety," I told a fellow writer. "Bowie may be claiming the form, but a hard-on, that's *function*."

In fact, both said a lot. If the gay revolution never took hold in rock, that said as much about gay lib as it did about music. Rock's strongest appeals have always been more implied than overt: sly promises, ambiguous in the same way that sexual ambivalence can be. Forthright celebrations and denunci-ations were folkie tools that often preached to the converted. Rock was more shadowy and subversive; the walk often was the talk.

The fact is that to this day I can't think of one rock artist who has been gay and proud, erotic and liberating—seizing the airwaves and giving the boys bon-ers. Many who claim to be bi or straight have touched on the subject in excit-ing ways, but the fear and resentment of gays and gay impulses runs deep, and hip rock is no exception. I began to look for music that expressed those fears and even dismantled them. Rock was built by voices that wreaked havoc with a nation's notion of deviance and decency. I watched for the impulses of rock to cross paths with the fact of being gay.

That same summer of '72, Little Richard appeared at a rock revival show at Wembley Stadium. Mascaraed to the tits, under a lacquered bouffant, the self-proclaimed Georgia Peach was grotesque and a little magnificent. Though he was acting like an outrageous queen in the seventies, Little Richard had been

GEORGE CUKOR

After considerable coaxing, Hollywood legend George Cukor consented to sit down and speak with The Advocate *in April 1982. Cukor was the director of such enduring film classics as* Dinner at Eight, Camille, The Women, The Philadelphia Story, Adam's Rib, A Star Is Born, My Fair Lady, *and two dozen other movies that set new standards of cinematic sophistication and polish.*

Although Cukor kept a discreet silence about being gay throughout his long and distinguished career, never was he totally in the closet. He led a quietly sheltered life in a richly appointed home in the Hollywood Hills, dividing his time between a circle of movie-colony luminaries and a coterie of other gay men working in the film industry.

From the onset of his Hollywood career in the early thirties, Cukor had a reputation as a "women's director." He was known for his talent to bring out the best in the screen's most fabled leading ladies—Hepburn, Greta Garbo, Norma Shearer, Jean Harlow, Joan Crawford, Judy Garland, Marilyn Monroe, and Judy Holliday, among others. But the appellation was also no doubt a thinly veiled reference to his homosexuality. Reportedly, it was Clark Gable's homophobic response to Cukor shortly into the filming of Gone With the Wind *that led to the director's dismissal from that production.*

Still, whatever slights he might have suffered for being gay, Cukor kept a tight rein on his feelings, letting candor seep out only near the end of his life. "I didn't put on any big act," he told Advocate's *publisher, David B. Goodstein, and Los Angeles editor, Douglas W. Edwards. "You know, a lot of people are so funny. They go out with the girls and all that, and that's absolutely ridiculous. I didn't pretend."*

When asked if he thought Hollywood was ready to portray gay characters in non-stereotypical ways, Cukor replied, "No, quite candidly. It scares the studios to death. They always make them camps....The audience is accepting things by leaps and bounds, but I don't think they're ready to accept a frankly gay—I hate that word—relationship yet."

an apparition in a zoot suit in '55. The man was beyond camp, beyond macho—he *was* rock 'n' roll. Arrogance, humor, and delight have always been our most effective weapons against despair and censure.

A decade after Little Richard burst upon the scene, a major rock band, the Rolling Stones, appeared in drag on a record sleeve. Camp and drag were comic traditions in England, but the rockers were willing to make them threatening. The Stones aren't a gay group, but they have played with the fear and allure of faggotry more cleverly than anyone else in rock. Jagger's marriage of camp to macho expressed an ambivalence that wasn't willing to choose one over the other. But even though he recorded the song "Cocksucker Blues," Jagger never exposed any male liaisons. He got married and had a kid. And though Bowie *admitted* to sleeping with boys, and seemed poised to bring rock and gay lib together, he, too, married, and grew richer and more conservative.

As gay glitter was consumed in its own glare, I was thrown by a rear-flank attack. Gays, blacks, and Latins, shut out of music's mainstream, were building a scene on the fringes: places to meet and dance. Disco sidestepped the world of rock prophets and celebrities. The artists were faceless, the stars were on the dance floor. Why worry about when the first rock star would come out on the radio? Boys were kissing boys in these clubs.

By 1975 I was feeling a bit schizophrenic. By day I was writing about rock, but at night I bumped to the thump of that divinely enforced rhythm track that even a spastic on Quaaludes could follow. Disco seemed like some secret gas—turn the stuff on and suddenly you were aflame in a queer bar. I never brought it home. If my heart was in rock, well, at least my crotch was in the discos. After all the agony and hurt, all disco insisted on was seamless celebration.

Still, there seemed to be nothing *but* disco in gay bars, and I found that more than a little irritating. The ugly thing about disco was that it seemed to announce and enforce an overwhelming conformity. I'd always thought that the liberating secret of coming out was, "Hey, it's okay to be different."

Yet, even while disco was busily announcing a society of "insiders" appropriating the emblems of success, the punk scene emerged as a society of "outsiders" attacking those emblems. Disco perverted legitimacy. Punk made perversity legitimate. Homos who had grown up in the sixties flocked to both scenes. But if disco was upwardly mobile and coolly hedonistic, punk was downwardly mobile and aggressively nihilistic. Though both developed in alternative "fringe" music scenes, they came to view each other as the enemy. The diverse motley of homos that I had met in the bars in the early seventies were facing off against one another five years later. And a lot of the punks were as insufferably insular as their disco counterparts.

When I had to pick a side, it was with the underdog punks who insisted that music could still be a scary brand of fun. Gay punks were rejecting both the mainstream rock and mainstream gay scenes. They were creating an arena that welcomed ambiguity and revolt. They were also a declaration against mainstream gay sterotypes.

While I'd still like to see a homo Springsteen, maybe it's time to give up on the idea. Besides, the whole notion seems hopelessly at odds with both gay and rock traditions. Both cultures favor innuendo—the suggestive attitude or lyric that makes the listener a conspirator in determining meaning. For gays, the choice has been camp over candor; for rockers, sly sexy promises over overt declaration. Ambiguity, in any form, forces the listener to think twice, to consider the alternatives.

COPING WITH A CRISIS

1983 Summer grasses, bleached white, danced against a hot blue sky. I lay in a field northeast of San Diego, my arm comfortably around a comrade at a Radical Faerie gathering. The setting—dry, stony hills and low scrub—seemed lyrical compared to my Los Angeles home. So much so that, for the first time, I let something into my heart that I had been determined to avoid: AIDS.

The faerie movement was at its peak. For the fourth year, its rural retreats, miles from anything resembling "gay lifestyle," drew increasing hundreds to dispute the conventional wisdom that sex provided the sole path to gay liberation. Some of the new gay therapists had recently counseled gay men that failure to go to the baths meant internalized homophobia. Titles of the year's best-sellers reflected the preoccupation: *The Butch Manual, Foreskin, Working Out*. Babybuns lubricant ("baby your baby") bought big ads in *The Advocate*.

Becoming a sexually liberated consumer, while a deliriously attractive goal, was not, however, always an easy one. Navigating a culture of bars and baths meant overcoming both homophobia and attitude. And with the introduction of this fatal uncertainty, that once-clear path became overgrown with thorny dilemmas, a problem my faerie friend succinctly stated.

"It's like you finally learned to play the game," he said, "then all the rules change." He was a medic with the Navy, and had already seen this still-rare terror up close, in VA hospital beds. "Believe me," he said, "you do have to change."

"Yeah," I whispered. "All the things I learned: I have to forget a lot of them." Gay life had done this before, only in a much more pleasant way.

The "everything you know is wrong" aspect to coming out had been an invitation to completely reassess life, but in one's favor—trading individuality and sex for guilt. The Bible was wrong. The government was wrong. Your parents were wrong. The reversal of values felt delightful.

Now AIDS demanded a counter-adjustment, one that caused a psychic whiplash. The fever of unknown origin, which turned up in every corner of the

New York photographer Lee Snider was among this crowd of more than one thousand in a June 13 Central Park memorial service for those recently lost to AIDS, the first such event held in the city. "For me, the most dramatic and poignant moment of the service came at dusk as those assembled held up placards bearing numbers showing the death toll," Snider recalls. "In 1983, the highest numbers were under six hundred. How were we to know how this number would soar to so devastate the gay community?"

world, had so far left one thousand dead and nearly three times that many infected. It insisted we address it.

The awful truth of 1983, however, was that no one *knew* anything. The agent of the disease awaited discovery. Whether at a rural conclave or in an urban bar, gay men foundered in the realm of theory—and wishful thinking: "It's just New Yorkers who get it." "It's just leather guys." "Fisting. That's what causes it." "Poppers! Death in a bottle," said one friend, jumping on 1983's biggest bandwagon. Indeed, *The Advocate* ran a piece on the $25 million industry, asking "Is It Safe to Sniff?"—with no firm conclusions.

In personal ads, the term "safe sex" had not yet usurped the honestly vague term "health conscious." The new phrase "get into rubber" brought wetsuits to mind more easily than condoms, the effectiveness of which we still doubted. Officials cautioned "Limit your partners," but to what number or activities remained unclear. Many men just had the same-style sex twice a month instead of twice a week. Such was the hard work of forgetting what we'd learned before the new rules were tidily in place.

This uncertainty gave rise to bitter debates within the community. Some insisted damage by the "media plague" exceeded anything biological. A writer in the *New York Native* spoke for many when he claimed that no health crisis existed at all. He went on to chasten a doctor who had advocated sexual restraint by saying he was "pushing morality under the guise of medical expertise." Such impassioned contradictions, regrettable as they might seem later, were a necessary part of coping with the crisis as we then knew it.

Henceforth, every year would be the biggest year for AIDS. But 1983 saw the settling in of planned response to the problem. Candlelight vigils illuminated major cities. AIDS Project Los Angeles marked its first birthday. And the first major Congressional hearings on AIDS featured testimony from gay men with AIDS, resulting in dramatic increases in federal funding.

In May, Nathan Fain launched a regular health column in *The Advocate* ("health" being a code word for "AIDS"). A tenacious and insightful chronicler of the plague, Fain perfectly reflected the anguish of conflicting political and medical strategies when he wrote in an early column that "heroism is everywhere, as are mistakes."

The world, meanwhile, got steadily gayer. Two Presidential hopefuls openly courted the gay vote, and two members of Congress came out.

Art and pop culture continued, with androgynous if uncommitted influences. Michael Jackson's "Billie Jean" and "Thriller" were inescapable. Prince and Boy George eclipsed the return of David Bowie. Hollywood offered *Flashdance*, which prompted gay boys nationwide to shred their own sweatshirts and tug them past their deltoids. Song-and-dance man Peter Allen, former husband of Liza Minnelli, toured the nation's stages coyly billing himself as "Mr. Bi-Coastal."

Disco having gone the way of dinosaurs, underground scenes began to burgeon. Proto-queers slam-danced to punk and techno-pop, and gawked at an often empty spectacle called performance art. The most substantial of the performance set, such as John Sex at the Pyramid Club in New York and John Fleck at Los Angeles's Anti-Club, made a wild mockery of gay sex roles. The brave new world of bravely redefining gay identity began to take hold.

But only among the converted. The still-evolving lessons of AIDS remained unspeakable to the public at large. The straights' breakthrough—seeing the enormity of what was happening to gays, and realizing that it could happen to them—would take years to come. —STUART TIMMONS

"It's curious that the great thing that's developed out of gay liberation, one of its most visible artifacts, is all those bars where guys go and piss on each other, with all due respect to their tastes. This has become so much a part of the culture—or is it really?"
—AUTHOR KATE MILLETT

"Houses of death, says one side. Nazi, genocidal homophobia, says the other....Nearly everybody sees symbols in the bathhouse and its closure. To some, closure would be not only a sign to the gay community but an assurance to the nongay community that gays are not ambitiously and self-indulgently spreading the disease while demanding money and sympathy. But, like it or not, the baths do symbolize gay liberation—or a part of it—to many."

—JOURNALIST RAY O'LOUGHLIN, reporting on the bathhouse controversy

Torch Song Trilogy, **a play about a tough drag queen's struggle with his even tougher mother, won Best Play at the Tony Awards: its author, Harvey Fierstein, who played the lead, was named Best Actor.**

"The poor homosexuals. They have declared war on nature and now nature is exacting an awful retribution."

—CONSERVATIVE COMMENTATOR
PAT BUCHANAN

JANUARY   America's largest blood banks, the Red Cross, the American Association of Blood Banks, and the Council of Community Blood Centers, issued a joint rejection of proposals to ban blood donations from gay males. ❑ A citizens' petition to close down a strip of five gay bars in Oklahoma City won qualified support from the City Council, but the bars did not close.

FEBRUARY   In a startling turnaround from years of hostility to the gay community, the Los Angeles Police Commission adopted recruitment policy reforms recommended by gay activists. ❑ An Illinois appellate court struck down gay-rights ordinances in the cities of Urbana and Champaign. ❑ The Lesbian Rights Project of San Francisco took on its first male client, Boyce Hinman, who sued his employer, the State of California, to receive dental benefits for his male lover; he later lost. ❑ A gay organization in Lakewood, Ohio, raised a $10,000 donation to the Centers for Disease Control for research and treatment of AIDS.

MARCH   Describing them as "prudent and temporary measures," the Department of Health and Human Services suggested that the government recommend voluntary screening of sexually active gay and bisexual men from blood donation programs. ❑ An "anticruising" law, which prohibited loitering with intent to arrange gay sex, was struck down by New York State's highest court. ❑ A Washington state gay group denounced Seattle's major media for front-page characterizations of AIDS as "the gay plague," "the gay cancer," and "the gay disease." ❑ In a first for that state, Ohio Governor Richard Celeste created a blue-ribbon commission on discrimination and sexual minorities. ❑ A London warehouse was selected to be the site of England's first government-funded gay center.

APRIL   Democratic Presidential front-runner Gary Hart addressed MECLA, the major gay political fund-raising group in Los Angeles. ❑ The Associated Press turned down a union request to include job protection for gay employees; the provisions were modeled after those approved by United Press International in January. ❑ The gay-rights movement lost one of its Congressional champions with the death of California's Representative Philip Burton. ❑ Pioneer checkbook activist Gayle Wilson, whose successful Los Angeles real-estate business helped her pump vast sums of her own and others' money into gay causes, died of cancer at age forty-nine. ❑ Demonstrators in Santa Rosa, California, protested acquittal of a gay man's confessed killer. ❑ In a fund-raising letter to Mississippians, the Moral Majority blasted the Metropolitan Community Church and its proposed new building for the Jackson area, warning that homosexuals were "invading" the state capital. ❑ Police raided and took names and addresses of patrons of two gay bars in Hong Kong, where gay sex is a crime carrying a possible life sentence.

MAY   Close to nine thousand demonstrators in Manhattan and ten thousand in Los Angeles, marched to demand federal action on AIDS; similar marches took place in San Francisco, Chicago, and Houston. ❑ The Reagan Administration proposed to reduce federal funding for AIDS programs at the Centers for Disease Control. ❑ San Francisco Mayor Dianne Feinstein declared the first week of the month "AIDS Awareness Week." ❑ Wisconsin became the twenty-seventh state to legalize gay sex. ❑ Mario Cuomo made the first appearance ever by a New York governor before a gay group when he spoke at a dinner for the Fund for Human Dignity. ❏ At its thirty-eighth conference, the International Ladies' Garment Workers Union unanimously adopted a gay and lesbian rights resolution. ❏ Angry over the New York City Council's repeated defeat of a gay-rights bill, organizers rerouted the fourteenth annual Gay Pride March in order to snarl traffic on Manhattan's West Side.

JUNE After reaching an agreement with the state health department, New York funeral directors ended their refusal to embalm people who had died of AIDS-related illnesses. ❏ In a sermon to his Lynchburg, Virginia, congregation, the Rev. Jerry Falwell called AIDS "the judgment of God" and characterized the epidemic as "hopeless." ❏ After seventy employees of the *Washington Times* protested the publication of a cartoon antagonistic to people with AIDS, the conservative newspaper ran an editorial sympathetic to AIDS patients and supportive of federal research funding. ❏ Gay and lesbian activists organized a boycott against *The New York Times,* protesting the newspaper's meager coverage of the AIDS epidemic and of the gay movement.

John Sayles's low-budget independent film *Lianna* played in several major cities around the United States. The movie, about a woman who leaves her husband for a lesbian, only to find that she has a girlfriend elsewhere, enjoyed critical success.

JULY In a dramatic statement from the floor of the House of Representatives, Gerry Studds (D-Mass.), facing censure for his relationship with a seventeen-year-old Congressional page, became the first member of Congress to come out as gay. ❏ A nation-wide toll-free AIDS hotline began operation as a project of the U.S. Department of Health and Human Services. ❏ Gays called *California* magazine biased and bigoted for publishing an article charging San Francisco gay activists with "whitewashing" AIDS dangers to protect the gay movement and business interests. ❏ Anita Bryant emerged from a self-imposed silence to promote a line of sunglasses decorated with religious symbols. ❏ Gay organizations participating in an outdoor fair and exhibition made their first public appearance in East Germany since before the Nazi era.

AUGUST After lesbians and gays staged a sit-in to protest her exclusion from the program, African-American lesbian author Audre Lorde spoke at the twentieth anniversary of Martin Luther King, Jr.'s March on Washington. ❏ Activist Michael Callen was among those who testified at the first Congressional hearing on AIDS. ❏ Lawyers for a Seattle man who was sued for injurious assault on another man in a gay bathhouse claimed that the victim was a "known sado-masochist" who had provoked the attack; a jury awarded the injured party, who claimed the attack was not sexual, $40,000.

In August, the National Reno Gay Rodeo was held without incident despite warnings by a local fundamentalist leader that "un-American" sexual activities at the event would spread AIDS.

SEPTEMBER At a fund-raising banquet for the Human Rights Campaign Fund in New York, the Rev. Jesse Jackson publicly invited gays to engage in "meaningful dialogue" with the civil rights movement. ❏ A Denver police officer fled the apartment of a burglary victim after learning the man had AIDS. ❏ The Miss Gay America Pageant, a drag competition, was held in Oklahoma City after the sponsors won a court injunction ordering the city to reissue a permit it had granted and then rescinded. ❏ Seattle's gay leaders, along with the American Civil Liberties Union, called on the city's police chief to investigate an AIDS patient list, called "AIDS Alert," that was circulated among local police officers; the chief apologized and had the list destroyed.

OCTOBER In the first case of AIDS patient "dumping" to receive public attention, Florida officials sent an indigent hospitalized man to San Francisco, where he died. ❏ The prestigious *Columbia Journalism Review* castigated the

In October, a national AIDS vigil was held in Washington, D.C. (*above*), following a series of similar events in cities across America. In Los Angeles (*below*), over ten thousand massed for the solemn gathering.

Kentucky Journal of Commerce and Industry and the Sarnia, Ontario, *Observer*, two regional publications, for distorted coverage of gay rights. ❑ The Los Angeles City Council unanimously endorsed a resolution urging the U.S. Department of Justice to prosecute convicted assassin Dan White, who was scheduled to be released from prison in January 1984; the Justice Department did not prosecute. ❑ An epidemiologist with the Centers for Disease Control announced that AIDS was rapidly becoming the leading cause of death in the nation's prisons. ❑ The American Academy of Pediatrics approved a proposal that homosexuality be considered an "alternate choice of sexual expression."

NOVEMBER   Openly gay mayors were elected on opposite coasts: Richard Heyman in Key West, Florida, and John Laird in Santa Cruz, California. ❑ A Virginia man was fired from his job as an editor of *The Military Engineer* five days after he told another publication that he rarely faced discrimination for being gay. ❑ Gay leaders cried betrayal when New York Governor Mario Cuomo watered down his long-awaited and long-postponed executive order banning antigay discrimination. ❑ The National Council of Churches of Christ voted to "postpone indefinitely" action on the membership application of the gay-oriented Metropolitan Community Church. ❑ David Scondras narrowly defeated Mark Roosevelt, great-grandson of Theodore Roosevelt, to become Boston's first openly gay city councilor. ❑ An Auckland judge ruled that *The Advocate* is "not indecent" and that New Zealanders may continue to subscribe.

DECEMBER   Protesters followed Senator John Glenn after the Presidential hopeful questioned the fitness of gays to serve as schoolteachers or soldiers. ❑ Denver's new mayor, Frederico Peña, issued a gay-inclusive policy of nondiscrimination in hiring, employment, housing, and provision of services. ❑ The head of the Phoenix County Board of Supervisors proposed that medical experiments be performed on homosexuals instead of animals; he later said it had been a joke, but was forced to resign under public pressure a month later. ❑ Mary Renault, whose portrayals of historic gay characters filled sixteen popular novels, died at her home in Cape Town, South Africa. ❑ *Screw* magazine publisher Al Goldstein called AIDS a "wonderful disease" that transforms those infected "from fruits to vegetables." ❑ An electronics engineer filed suit against the Central Intelligence Agency, seeking to overturn its antigay security policy.

FRANCO ZEFFIRELLI

"Disastrous!" the director exclaims, his eyes flashing with anger, his sudden animation disguising the exhaustion of a full day's battery of interviews. Franco Zeffirelli, whose deportment with reporters is analogous to the lush histrionics of his film and stage work, is in San Francisco to launch his new $8 million production of Verdi's *La Traviata*.

For the moment, though, the tempestuous Florentine is recalling Joseph Losey's 1979 version of Mozart's *Don Giovanni*. "I was furious, so *fucking* furious that he could destroy this incredible work! The man doesn't know the first thing about directing opera." Now, as for *La Traviata*: "I've finally managed," Zeffirelli is fond of saying, "to make my two mistresses cohabit." His picture, featuring Teresa Stratas as the doomed, consumptive Violetta, is the first true fusion of opera and film in the director's forty-year career. It has already won two Oscar nominations and received bouquets of praise from Zeffirelli's bête noire, the American press.

When Zeffirelli first envisioned his film, it was with Maria Callas in the demanding role of Violetta. Callas died in 1977, and the director now realizes that she might have overwhelmed the film with her tremendous force of personality. "Callas was more than a singer," he says. "She was a phenomenon… the top. *The best*. Ever."

Zeffirelli is no stranger to hyperbole: indifference and complacency are anathema to him. His personal extravagance, the theatricality of his gesture, the immoderateness of his speech are not only essential components in his personality but recognizable traits in his work. When he is chastised for garishness, for window-dressing, for emotional excess, he sees no fault, because to Zeffirelli these are natural states of being and require no apology.

Zeffirelli is, first and foremost, an entertainer. "The reason I am box office everywhere," he has said, "is that I am an enlightened conservative continuing the discourse of our grandfathers and fathers, renovating the texts but never betraying them." Bravura statements such as this have triggered my curiosity, relaxed my journalist's politesse, and driven me to delve more provocatively into the nature of Zeffirelli's work. The replies I get, to my astonishment, are more personal and revelatory, perhaps, than any he has given in print before.

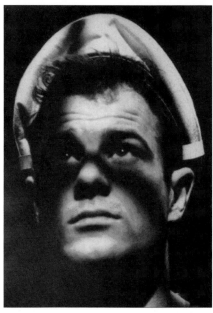

How important is the gay audience to your films?
I hate to call certain human beings "gay." The moment you say "gay," I see already a movement or a category or a ghetto. I don't like that at all. It so *happens* that gay people—or the gay community—is composed of sensitive, cultivated, attractive people who give a lot of space in their lives to education and to enjoying the important, valuable things in life. In that sense I have to say the gay community is a higher "rung" of community than the normal community.

That doesn't mean it has to be a "community." I don't understand that; I like to see a gay person as a person. I'm gay too, so…what makes us different from the others? Just because of our private sexual preferences? It's very stupid.

"Querelle is the blueprint of a man who is possessed, who's not like other men, who is alone and has a voice of the dark angel over his shoulder that says he's protected as long as he lives in total danger. This was not hard for me to understand. I've been through a lot of things in my life, and I'll continue to in the process of searching for who I am, and a lot of it has been very destructive."

—ACTOR BRAD DAVIS

"In my case, I'm not a victim of sexual discrimination. I'm just a victim of myself. When you build a reputation as being a wild and zany character, you don't get many calls to play Lady Macbeth."
—ACTRESS HOLLY WOODLAWN

Has your sexuality ever been a detriment to you in your career?

No, I never talked about it! Nobody seemed interested in what I was doing in bed. I've always been considered for what I had to offer, as a human being or as an artist. First of all, I never talked about it. This is the first time I have talked about it openly. I don't like to talk about my sexual inclinations. People are not special because they like one thing better than another in bed.

But mind and spirit are something else. It happens that people who have to go through this particular sexual syndrome are forced to refine certain receptive instruments in the mind and soul: They become much more sensitive, more ready to talk and to deal with the things of the spirit. They suffer more than the normal person. I think it is not easy to be a gay. I know this. You have to go through a very, very anguishing time.

The profile "60 Minutes" did on you two years ago came very close to saying you live with a male lover.

Yes, that's right: "He lives with a male companion who doesn't want to be photographed."

Well, what's his name?

Was his name.

Well, who are you living with now?

Well, listen…

[The reporter laughs nervously. The publicist, who has reentered the room, glares. The director squirms.]

Reporter: This is getting to be like Barbara Walters.

Zeffirelli [half-mocking, to reporter]: Why don't you mind your fucking business?

Publicist: Why don't you think about wrapping up?

Reporter: Is that a quote: "Why don't you mind your fucking business?"

Zeffirelli: No, really, I am very serious about this. It happens that the so-called gay community is immensely more sensitive and attractive. In fact, my audience—half of my audience throughout the world—again in quotes, is "gay" people. But…who cares?

Zeffirelli's coming out, completely unexpected and unsolicited, gives rise to dozens more questions, but—as frequently happens in such situations—my allotted time is winding down and the gorgeous, non-English-speaking young man who is Zeffirelli's traveling companion is pacing just outside the suite where we speak. Still, the director talks, in fact, persists, in the line of conversation that I had imagined might be a touchy one for him.

"I don't really see the point," Zeffirelli says, "to be ashamed in homosexual love affairs, or to make a point—plus or less."

"That's the objective, isn't it?" I hastily add. "To get to where people don't even care, where there is no shame attached, and it's never an issue. But for now, don't you think the gay-rights movement, the political thrust, is still necessary?"

"No, it *was* necessary," the director emphatically concludes. "I must correctly say it was absolutely necessary to break up this kind of guilt and shame structure around certain natural problems. Now that it has been achieved fully, I don't think we need to dwell more about it." —EDWARD GUTHMANN

GERRY STUDDS

There is perhaps some irony in the fact that the nation's first openly gay member of Congress represents the district that includes Plymouth Rock, the land of our Pilgrim forebears. The Puritan values of that early-seventeenth-century settlement have been passed down through three centuries of American history. But then, the voters in Massachusetts's 12th Congressional District had no idea that they were casting ballots for a man who would break the traditional reticence of all previous—and current—gay members of Congress. It was enough that they were electing a Democrat in 1972, after years of Republican rule.

Gerry Studds, who became that congressman, stands out not because of an indiscreet and inappropriate sexual relationship with a male page that resulted in a house censure of Studds in July, but rather because of the way he handled it. He was, in fact, the fifth member of Congress in five years to have his homosexual conduct made a public issue; but he was the first who responded not by publicly scourging himself for "homosexual tendencies" but by affirming his gay identity and discussing the difficulties of balancing a private life and public responsibilities.

His response appears to have been favorably received by the district's voters, who have reelected Studds to Congress five times. In August, when he walked in a New Bedford parade to celebrate the annual Catholic blessing of the district's numerous Portuguese fishermen, he was enthusiastically applauded.

How do you feel now that you have publicly declared you are gay?

Better than I've ever felt in my life....Any person who has ever gone through the experience of coming out will understand that. I feel as if the remaining seven cylinders had just kicked in for the first time in forty-six years. And that's a very powerful feeling.

What would you now advise other closeted political figures to do?

I would not in a million years urge a prominent Washington person who was a friend of mine to make that decision one way or another. I would be perfectly happy, if asked, to share my experiences. But it seems to me that it is essentially a personal decision.

You've spoken out on the House floor on behalf of gay-rights concerns in the past, and of course you are a cosponsor of the federal gay civil rights bill. Do you think coming out will affect your effectiveness on those issues?

Part of what I feel so magnificent about now is the nature of my relations with my colleagues. They are fundamentally changed, at least in my perception, and I suspect in theirs....I have not had the slightest difficulty, to put it very mildly, looking anyone in the eye, and to my knowledge, no one has had any problem returning that look. The ability, not only to be candid and no longer timid, but to be able to use outright humor, is wonderful. Just wonderful. Colleagues are on their toes now. I caught somebody using one of the old code words the other day, and he nearly collapsed when I called him on it.

I think that people of good will, and I think that's most members of Congress, are now going to listen a little more carefully on this subject.

—LARRY BUSH

AIDS: Mysteries and Hidden Dangers

The only fact about AIDS is that it exists. It is probably fatal, but not enough time has elapsed to determine that, extending needed hope to patients. Beyond that fact, assertions range from reasonable conjecture to cruel fabrication. Suspected, even invented horrors pour out as facts from a hostile press in gloating obituaries on our sexuality; some of our own publications borrow these assumptions; too many homosexuals accept them. Caught in this rampage of conjecture, we are endangered by another illness, the exhumation of guilts and self-hatreds we insisted were buried forever. This may go on killing us even after a cure for the diagnosed illness is found.

A homosexual in a Hollywood store cackles, "Know what gay *stands for?—'Got AIDS Yet?'" In a New York bar one man screeches at another, "Bitch! I bet you've got AIDS!" Accusing him of being "responsible" for present dangers, a heavyset man savagely pummels and kicks a slender, shirtless homosexual cruising the Silver Lake turf of Los Angeles. But this time the attacker is not a heterosexual thug—he too is homosexual.*

AIDS commands our lives. Every homosexual has contracted a form of it, in fear, suspicion...and accusation.

Cruelly, viciously, a homosexual writer asserts in *The Village Voice* that AIDS patients lurk in darkened doorways. However genuinely motivated, a homosexual reporter in San Francisco provides two journalists of doubtful credentials the flimsy basis for *California* magazine's violent accusation that homosexuals are hiding the danger of AIDS. Instead of questioning the spurious allegations, several homosexual newspapers carry those spewings as facts. In the boredom-of-it-all tone that afflicts that magazine, a *Christopher Street* columnist writes: "And so the recent comparison of the behavior of pigs infected with African Swine Fever Virus—pigs observed to lick sperm up from the floor, to fornicate with each other—and male homosexuals is not merely darkly amusing, it is quite accurate."

Time magazine crows: "The flag of gay liberation has been lowered...and many do not regret it." Even "good heterosexuals" find bonds with Jerry Falwell. In one of the meanest articles—its prejudices are masked as "intellectual concern"— Jonathan Lieberson in *The New York Review of Books* applauds homosexuals who have "become 'twice born,' despising their former promiscuous selves." The self-avowed "liberal" *New Republic* finds in AIDS a "metaphor" symbolizing "the identity between contagion and a kind of desire."

Chilling in their lack of compassion, these journalistic assaults have in common the rancid stench of repression, a note of harrowing triumph in the authentication of bigotry.

They attempt to make AIDS patients accountable for their illness—much as blacks have been blamed for their poverty, women for rape, Jews for the Holocaust. AIDS affirms Susan Sontag's powerful observation: "Nothing is more punitive than to give disease...a moralistic meaning."

On a hot afternoon in Beverly Hills a slightly effeminate man waits for a bus in the shade of a park. A man identifying himself as a cop orders him out: "We don't want queer disease." A few miles away, in Santa Monica, a homosexual gets knifed by a man screaming: "Diseased pervert!"

Hidden dangers: namely, the emergence of a pressurized generation of once-healthy homosexuals branded by assumptions of mutual contagion—murderous lovers. Impotence, alcoholism, addiction, suicide. If old guilts are entrenched as new ones, there will be a return to institutions of our oppression: religion, psychiatry, the tenets of repressive politics. Darker closets more difficult to break out of because we are helping to shut the doors.

What outlet for a young man just coming out, what of him, with eager yearnings, when his first contact may be fatal? As the projected period of incubation is extended without evidence—from months to years—how will living under a lingering sentence of death affect every single area of endeavor among homosexuals?

A psychological time bomb, its forms of implosion and explosion another unpredictable aspect of AIDS.

"Sure, we had raids, arrests, jailings, but we kept on living, and fully—and having sex; if nothing else, that got us through," says a middle-aged man. "What now?"

Because our sex was forbidden harshly and early by admonitions of damnation, criminality, and sickness, sexual profligacy became—not for all of us but for many more than we claim—an essential, even central, part of our lives, our richest form of contact, at times the only one. Because our profligacy questioned their often-gray values, the enemies of desire supported our persecution. With AIDS their sexual envy was avenged: The illness was "created" by promiscuity! they exulted.

But was it? Promiscuity occurred virtually as often before the late sixties as after; the literature of those times confirms that unequivocally. It merely shifted to safer locations, and there was wider knowledge of it. Then why now?

Two men go home together. They strip. Cocks rise in ready desire. (Will he be the one who kills me, the one I kill?) They press sealed lips, trying to awaken softening cocks.

We prevailed over torturing inquisitions, concentration camps, jailings, registration as "deviants," aversion therapy. Then in 1969 a few courageous transvestites, male and female, resisted arrest at the Stonewall Inn, other homosexuals rioted, and gay liberation was officially born. Then it all changed! Instantly! We paraded, chanted prideful slogans, linked hands! *And left the unjustified, heterosexually imposed, but now powerfully absorbed guilts in the darkest closets of ourselves.* Mean bars proliferated. We ritualized fantasies of punishment without exploring origins. Discarded: "fats, femmes, trolls!" Banished: defiant "stereotypes!" The young exiled the now-old fighters—and cut themselves off from a heritage of endurance. Older homosexuals who qualified as "hunks" were granted extensions on their sexual passports—too often to act as punishing "daddies," instead of as needed, experienced guides through still-mined territory.

Yes, there was courage, abundant courage. We vanquished Anita Bryant, crushed the Briggs Initiative. In prideful triumph, we thrust our vast energy outward as anger, and we overcame again.

Why—now—the threatening chaos, the blind meanness turned against our own? Because the rallying crises of our immediate past had demanded no introspection. The enemy was outside, identifiable. AIDS, with its mysteries, tapped our unjustly inherited guilts where we had left them unexplored:

Inside.

—JOHN RECHY

Tough Questions

Who Gets AIDS, and How?

There are two kinds of answers to all questions about AIDS. One kind is the cold, hard truth, and that is what remains elusive. It will continue to remain that way until someone proves beyond a shadow of a doubt exactly how the disease is induced. Theories abound.

Still to be solved, however, is the grittier question confronting gay men, who would like to express their sexual longing without going, as Richard Goldstein wrote recently in The Village Voice, "heartsick" over the "devastating task" of choosing between love and possible death. The dilemma is, indeed, Wagnerian.

What About Poppers?

The inhaled nitrites—amyl and butyl—may no longer be in the top ten among what-causes-AIDS theories, but as major culprits these chemicals still have a devoted following of detractors. One gay newspaper recently took this gay newspaper to task for publishing an advertisement for butyl nitrite that quotes CDC authorities on nitrites' role (or lack thereof) in bringing on the epidemic....

In any event, whether to use poppers or not remains a personal decision, much like smoking. The statistics may not look sunny, but life is more than statistics. In the current tense climate of self-consciousness, many gay men see any form of sexual expression as deadly and thus subversive to a stronger sense of community. It is unfortunate that, in rare cases, sniping has replaced a cautious review of the available facts.

—FROM THE HEALTH COLUMN

STRONG BODIES GAY WAYS

When I started bodybuilding, I knew that strength and definition wouldn't save me from Kaposi's sarcoma or from petty squabbles at the office. Still, I imagined I was becoming encased in a kind of protective shell. That illusion of invulnerability was nice, but illusions—as was brought home to me recently—have their limits.

A new piece of equipment arrived at my gym the other day—a Nautilus abdominal machine. After a brief demonstration by an instructor, each of the half-dozen or so weekday-morning regulars I work out with tried the new machine as the others watched. I've been doing sit-ups and leg lifts for months now, so when it was my turn, I decided to set the weight at twice what the guy before me—a bulky, macho type—had used. Well, he had trouble completing six repetitions; I punched out a neat twelve and, hopping out of the machine's seat, made a mental note for the next time to raise the weight a notch.

As I headed for the paper-towel dispenser, I caught the guy staring at me. "How did he do that?" I overheard him ask the blond woman who always wears matching purple leotards and tights. At first I was amused that this bruiser should find it incredible that a modestly built fellow like me could move more metal than he. Then the woman, with whom I have only a nodding acquaintance, replied, "He's skinny, but he's strong."

Bells went off. Positioned on the next machine, I found myself grinning. "Yeah, I'm strong," I repeated silently. It had never occurred to me that I could really achieve physical strength, much less that a glorious sense of spiritual well-being might result from it. "He's skinny, but he's strong." The remark stuck with me. I found myself remembering it later that day at my office, during an unpleasant confrontation I wasn't even part of—as if muscles could be of any use in such matters. And I remembered it again that evening when a sudden rush of panic overwhelmed me during a public briefing on the AIDS crisis.

Like so many other red-blooded American homosexual boys, I hated gym in school. The indelicacy of public disrobing; the absurdity of having to jump higher and shout louder than other little boys; Coach Halbig, who was a Nazi—these things tipped off a sensitive young bookworm that gym was not for him. Institutionalized physical education did little for me except make me wish I didn't even have a body. In high school I was not able to negotiate the kind of open-ended medical excuse that my friend Andy says he managed to wangle from a suspiciously sympathetic family doctor. By then, however, I discovered that my brains and flair for dressing could help compensate for what I accepted as my constitutional weakness. These helped; but in a boys' world, where the parody of power is taken as the real thing, they were only substitutes.

Bulk and definition carry a symbolic charge in our culture, representing presence and identity. They can even promise to function as the kind of protective shell I felt my strength gave me (for a while). Gay amateur bodybuilders can compensate for the powerlessness and invisibility some say are ours as "marginal" members of society. Which seems fine, to a point—recolonizing the gym, and all that. But you know, this rosy, self-actualized inner strength is no more useful than blobs of muscle against life's little uncertainties. How disillusioning! "He's skinny, but he's strong." Sure, I loved hearing it, but since the AIDS briefing I mentioned, the phrase doesn't enchant me the way it used to.

You see, what got to me this time was not just the number of hands that went up—nearly all—when a speaker asked who personally knew an AIDS vic-

tim. It wasn't the man weeping softly in the row ahead of me, or the anger with which questions from the audience were raised at the end. What got to me was a photograph. There have been so many recent cases of Kaposi's in New York that the doctors who throw these grim parties no longer need use as illustrations those outdated slides showing the so-called classic cases of the disease as manifested in older Jewish and Italian men. Now we have *our* own cases, and what appear before us in darkened auditoriums, ten times life-size, are pictures of our own bodies. It makes you think.

In this instance, it was a picture of a young man's chest from his neck to his navel, incorporating the most carefully inflated pectorals imaginable. The audience gasped: Those luscious pectorals were covered with Kaposi's hideous purple lesions. There were also pectorals that, considering the size, shape, and color of the nipples, I suspected with a flash sweat I had once kissed. I shuddered and automatically slid my hand under my jacket to feel my own chest to see, I guess, if my own flesh was still as firm as it had been during my morning workout.

Afterward, it was a slow walk to the subway. So much for spiritual well-being, I thought: *He was strong, too.* Strong but still vulnerable. I kept wondering if the man whose picture I'd seen was still alive. Hadn't he said his name was Ed? Hadn't I gone no further than to explore his chest? I've been to a lot of meetings on the AIDS crisis, but previously my reaction had been a bit too of-the-mind when I acknowledged—as we all must—the proximity of death to our community. Now I find I cannot write the reasoned paragraph on mortality an essay like this might logically require. Death observes no logic, anyway. I haven't stopped going to the gym, of course. I still work out; I still believe bodybuilding is important. But somehow the honeymoon is over. My body and I are on too-familiar terms now, if you know what I mean. —STEPHEN GRECO

TILL DEATH DO US PART

"The quest for the Holy Male was a nice joke, but at the same time it's also true. Men have to come to look for the divine in one another, that is, to meet on a soul level. The ecstatic as a dimension of cruising is not simply to get it on and get it over with, and chalk up one more conquest. That isn't the point."

—POET JAMES BROUGHTON

"When I read the articles on AIDS and look back on those seventies experiences where I was in the thick of an orgy bar, I say, 'Good grief, what the hell was going on?'"

—NOVELIST PETE FISHER

Over the years since Stonewall, we gay people have attracted more than our share of enemies, but few of them have been as vehement in criticizing the ways we live as we ourselves have been. Whether the goal is physical health or political progress or just plain happiness, we are a tribe of idealists, and no one is as ferocious as an idealist when it comes to finding fault. Of all the things that separate gay people from one another—class, race, religion, philosophy, you name it—the one thing that divides us most is the same thing that brought us together in the first place: the quest for sexual freedom. Our differences over the ways in which we make love and the lifestyles that grow out of them are threatening to tear us apart.

Is *promiscuity* a dirty word? I never used to think so. I practiced it gladly, making love to as much of mankind as I could get my mouth on, and enhancing my pleasure with an artful palette of drugs. Too bad I can't seem to remember all the details. With a head full of chemistry all things are possible. On only a joint, a backroom bar or a bathhouse can become paradise. On a Quaalude, you can kiss total strangers and not care who they are. On acid you can find yourself confronting a new acquaintance's ass and realize that you've already forgotten his face. On poppers you can rim Frankenstein and love it. Such pleasures aren't easy to give up. But what if they prove dangerous?

The argument that is shaping up in the gay press over promiscuity and health has the same tone as the earlier divisions in the gay community. One group says that promiscuity is ruining our public image. Some of them are turning it into a moral issue and demanding that respectable gays denounce practitioners of promiscuity as "bad." Others say that sexual freedom is the reward we have earned for coming out of the closet, that it is gay liberation in action.

My lover, a doctor, now finds himself in the middle of this age-old dispute about monogamy versus promiscuity. He is called homophobic for suggesting that the exposure risk to sexually transmitted diseases is higher with a greater number of sexual partners. On the other side, angry AIDS patients denounce him for not asserting that promiscuity itself is the *cause* of the epidemic. As he philosophically puts it, "They're angry at the messenger who brought them the bad news." And what is the bad news? Is sex dead? No. Is God wreaking cosmic vengeance on us? No. The bad news is simply that we have to take responsibility for our actions, and that goes for our self-criticism as well as our sex lives.

We may deny our relationship to those gay people whose practices or beliefs differ from ours, but we are related nonetheless. The issue for us is not monogamy versus promiscuity. The issue is solidarity versus collapse, at least insofar as our dream of living outside the closet is concerned. In Ben Franklin's words, "We must all hang together, or assuredly we shall all hang separately." Before we pick our pleasures or mold our morals or fall in love or see our politics prevail, we must first learn how to survive. The only way members of any gay minority can succeed is together. We are one another's family more than we belong to those who gave birth to us. That doesn't mean we must tolerate evil in our midst, but it does mean we should tolerate one another's differences.

In the long run, it is not one man I am married to. It is all of you, as diverse as our lives are and as cantankerous as we may be about the differences. Whatever kind of gay love we seek, each of us is part of the gay community, "for better for worse, for richer for poorer, in sickness and in health ... till death us do part."

—ARNIE KANTROWITZ

BOOKS: AUDRE LORDE'S *ZAMI*

Audre Lorde grew up in Harlem, black and gay. In high school she belonged to a gang called The Branded. By the time she was seventeen, she had saved enough money, working in a factory, to go to Mexico. Inarticulate as a child, and an outsider everywhere, including the gay bars of Greenwich Village in the fifties, she wrote poems because poetry was the language she understood best.

Lorde's third book of poems was nominated for the National Book Award in 1973, and she is now one of the most inspiring contemporary writers of both poetry and prose. Not only is Lorde's writing beautiful, it is consistently political. An early pamphlet, "The Erotic as Power," makes a radical statement about sexuality in American society, and her poetry draws directly from her black lesbian experience, never failing to incorporate her radical view of the world.

A collection of Lorde's work, *Chosen Poems: Old and New*, was released last year; an autobiography relating the early years of her life, *Zami: A New Spelling of My Name*, has just been published.

How do you want people who are neither black nor lesbian to relate to *Zami*? Have you had responses from them?

Our lowest common denominator of similarities is the fact that we're all human beings, and [people who have read the book] see that. There are things that we all feel, that get lived out in the particular details of our lives....But there is also a particularity of experience that I claim and own. We can use what is different between us to illuminate what is similar. I'm very involved with this question of difference, and how we need to make it not a barrier—not to ignore it, nor to pretend it doesn't exist; not to use it as a reason to kill each other, but to use it as an active way of reinterpreting our experience.

It seems that the ability to accept and appreciate those things that are different about other people is an integral part of gay and lesbian strength.

It is an integral part of our strength, and it's very difficult. But without it, we cannot love those things that are different about ourselves—you know, the things that are neither perfect nor acceptable nor "politically correct." We tend to ignore those things, which takes an enormous amount of energy—I'm talking about just within one person, before we even start to deal with what goes on between two of us....I wrote a poem once, a while back, about figuring in the dreams of people who do not even know me. Yes, it happens. Growing up black in this society, you recognize very early what it means to be objectified—to have the kind of hate that comes down on black people in general, walking through the street, living a life, you know, where it has nothing to do with who you are. It is a viable, tangible force. This teaches you.

We have so many different kinds of invisibility. There are even ways we are invisible to ourselves.

—JUDITH BARRINGTON

"I am not playing a homosexual [as the lover of a drag queen] in La Cage aux Folles. *I am playing a person who cares deeply about another person. The role is loving another person onstage; it doesn't matter whether it's a man, a woman, or a giraffe; it has nothing to do with sexuality."*

—ACTOR GENE BARRY

"You know and I know that black is not beautiful. Neither is it ugly. Gay is good? Well, gay is not good—but neither is it bad....I was once asked to be on a program of all gay composers and I refused. I don't want to be asked because of my sexuality. Anybody can be gay. Only I can be me."

—COMPOSER/DIARIST NED ROREM

ART: TOM OF FINLAND

For nearly thirty years, Tom of Finland has celebrated his vision of the unmitigated masculine and in the process has helped gay men around the world to redefine their own sense of sexual self.

The Helsinki-based artist's drawings, which have appeared in publications throughout the United States and Western Europe, seethe with an overt male energy. Tom's subjects are robust, playful, and self-sufficient, his heroes street-wise and working-class. But above all, the muscled and generously endowed men in a Tom of Finland picture exude self-congratulatory eroticism without a trace of sentimentality or doubt.

Curiously, the artist whose work has inspired men all over the world remains underappreciated in his native Finland. Most of his art is considered pornographic by Finnish standards and consequently has never been widely circulated there. "People think Finland is as liberated as Sweden or Denmark, but that just isn't the case," says Tom. "Most of my work *is* pornographic—it *is* meant to excite." Although gay life in the Scandinavian country has become more open in recent years, the artist admits that he preferred when "things were less free. I always found something really stimulating about the sexual encounter steeped in an atmosphere of danger."

Tom of Finland's drawings usually depict a sunlit world of healthy sexual seduction where the men are uninhibited and virtually guilt-free. But there is another side to the Finnish artist's work: slightly more somber, chiaroscuro settings where S&M and military-style discipline are the subject.

Some of these more overt drawings have proved controversial, with critics accusing the artist of possessing a fascist mentality. Although the complaint is a familiar one, it still disturbs Tom a great deal. "In the sixties, a French publication printed a story which said I was a Nazi," he explains, "and they advised their readers not to buy my work. It's a nasty rumor, and, much to my dismay, it continues to surface from time to time.

"All I want to communicate through my art is that it's okay to be gay and masculine. Certainly just as masculine as the hetero version. When I first came out, the only gays I met were extremely affected and effeminate. I even tried to emulate those kind of people. Then I started meeting more masculine gay men, and I realized that there were choices. Just because you were gay didn't mean that you had to swish around. I instantly knew that for me a sense of strength was appealing.

"Gay men who feel uncomfortable with the limp-wristed set usually respond quite positively to my drawings," he continues. "That's one of the reasons I enjoy visiting the United States; so many gays there are unafraid to show the strong masculine side of themselves."

In fact, the sixty-two-year-old artist is planning to spend more time here in the coming months. He is currently establishing a foundation in Los Angeles, where much of his work will be housed, marketed, and periodically exhibited.

"I'm hoping that collectors of my work will make arrangements to eventually donate it to the foundation," the artist says. "Certainly it would be comforting to know my work—even if it isn't great art—would live on after I'm gone. If for no other reason, sociologists could examine the drawings and come to some conclusions about how gay men chose to live during this period. Hopefully, they'll realize at least some of us were having a rather good go of things."

—WILLIAM FRANKLIN

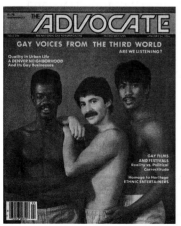

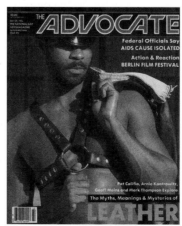

CULTURE CLASH

1984 AIDS, *Tootsie*, Robert Mapplethorpe, *La Cage aux Folles*, Ethyl Eichelberger; these were some of the "culture clashes" of 1984. I remember that my own life—as a gay man as well as a social critic—during this time was rich, full, and, well, confusing. While I, at first, viewed the new burgeoning of "gay culture" and gay male life as a manifestation of the new freedoms brought on by gay liberation, it was becoming clearer that the situation was more complicated: Every new sexual freedom brought a backlash of attempted repression, every new cultural gain brought with it the promise, and the threat, of assimilation.

The history and ongoing struggle for gay rights is an endless negotiation between private and public space. It is not simply the individual act of leaving the world of the closet that moves us forward, but the communal staking-out and claiming of physical, emotional, and psychological space in the material world. Once that queer space is established we are under constant pressure to maintain and defend it. The threat of gay sexuality is measured for the most part by the imperative of its visibility.

Nineteen eighty-four was a pivotal year in this struggle between public and private on two very separate, though not unconnected, fronts. The first was the undeniable recognition that AIDS was the most crucial problem our community had ever faced; the second was the emergence of a gay sensibility in mainstream popular culture. These two facts, at first glance unconnected, were emblematic of the struggles for the next decade.

Throughout the seventies gay male sexuality had become more and more visible. It was reflected not only in the backroom bars and bathhouses that flourished in most urban centers, but in the industries that were created to cater to it: a plethora of slick pornographic magazines, companies that produced as many as thirteen brands of butyl nitrite, mail-order firms that specialized in sex toys, a now-above-ground film and video porn culture—all of which answered with alarming accuracy the age-old question, "What *do* they do in bed?" This newly liberated gay male sex culture was reflected in advertising (Calvin Klein ads), in styles (the invention of "the clone"), and in attitude (a new permission in sexual frankness for heterosexual women and men). A decade of new sexual freedom thrived, and AIDS threatened to put a stop to all of that.

Although the gay community was taking the appropriate steps to safeguard its health, it was clear that gay male sexuality was under fire: Bathhouses were under threat of closure; some critics, both straight and gay, claimed that the sexual revolution was a failure and called for a return to monogamy; and experimentation with S&M and leather was being called into question. The very *idea* of sexual liberation was becoming suspect. The advances that gay men had made in building a new visible public culture of sexuality were clashing with a backlash of fear engendered by the emerging epidemic.

This culture of open gay male sexuality did not exist independently, but was supported and energized by a whole range of cultural and artistic endeavors. Gay writing flourished as the poems of James Broughton, Robert Peters, Dennis Cooper, and Walta Borawski were published by small and independent gay presses. Robert Chesley's shocking AIDS phantasmagoria *Night Sweat* played in gay-run theaters, and drag diva Eichelberger enacted his blatantly feminist, historical travesties *en travesti* in performance spaces on both coasts. Small, independent film companies were producing the likes of *The Times of Harvey Milk,* and annual lesbian and gay film festivals were drawing big crowds all over the country. The grassroots lesbian and gay culture that had been fermenting for a decade and a half was finally coming into its own.

Still, as often as not, this work remained within the community. With few exceptions—the photography of Robert Mapplethorpe being the most famous—this gay art and sensibility remained an influence and cultural instigator rather than being widely accepted and acknowledged.

What did occur, however, was that mainstream culture did *allow* some gay influence to become more prominent: British rock gave us The Smiths, Bronski Beat, Marilyn, and Boy George; Jerry Herman and Allan Carr gave us *La Cage aux Folles* on Broadway. Barbra Streisand gave us a gender-bending *Yentl,* and Cher gave us a lesbian in *Silkwood.* All of this was well-noted. Mainstream critics talked about how popular culture was becoming homosexualized, homosexual critics talked about the gayification of the arts. Neither was quite right.

Contemporary culture has always been fueled by a gay sensibility. The now noted "homosexualization" of popular culture was simply a long-overdue recognition of this situation. On the other hand, the gay critics who rejoiced in the emergence of a gay sensibility within the mainstream overlooked the fact that such "mainstreaming" was quite distinct from the cultivation of gay culture either *within* the community or the acceptance of this authentic culture outside of it.

Because so much of gay influence was still fairly covert and mostly in the service of heterosexual contexts, in a very real way queerness remained private and did not emerge full force into the public arena. Few gay artists were allowed into the mainstream with their *openly* queer sensibilities intact, and truly gay writing, painting, composing, performing, and sexuality remained on society's edge. This continued marginalization dovetailed with the backlash against gay sexuality that coincided with AIDS: public space and private space in conflict again.

In 1984, gay male sexuality and culture came as close as they ever have to establishing themselves as open, public, and flagrant possibilities. The clash began, but the explosion is still waiting to happen. —MICHAEL BRONSKI

"In San Francisco, we actually saw homosexuals sharing a public platform in Union Square with transvestites, communists, Central American terrorists, punk rock anarchists, unionized prostitutes, people who would legalize marijuana, and other radicals."
—FUNDAMENTALIST JERRY FALWELL

"Eddie Murphy's tirade is no different from any uneducated bigot's. It's not just the casual use of the word 'faggot' that is objectionable. His remarks on AIDS are not only inaccurate, they are dangerous."
—D. FRANK CULBERTSON, reporting on the comedian's antigay remarks

T I M E L I N E

Flamboyant pianist Liberace, sued for palimony by animal trainer and chauffeur Scott Thorson, won a victory when a major part of Thorson's suit was thrown out of court in March.

GAY LIBERATION VANDALIZED
Statues of male and female couples by acclaimed sculptor George Segal were attacked in March by a man with a hammer at their new location at Stanford University in Palo Alto, California. The sculptures, originally exhibited in New York City's Sheridan Square, had been moved west after protests by both gay and straight city residents. The gay men and lesbians complained that Segal was heterosexual and that the sculptures were too bland, while some straights were offended by the positive portrayal of homosexuality.

JANUARY Dan White, called "the luckiest assassin in history" by gay activists, was released on parole after serving only five years in prison for killing San Francisco Mayor George Moscone and Supervisor Harvey Milk; one year later, he committed suicide. ❏ Boston Mayor Raymond Flynn signed an executive order protecting gays in city employment and appointed openly gay people to posts in his administration. ❏ The Ice Palace, a defunct gay disco in Manhattan, was found guilty of racial discrimination and fined $6,000 by a New York State human rights commission. ❏ The U.S. Conference of Mayors passed a resolution calling for an end to antigay bias. ❏ Two hundred mostly gay participants converged on Amsterdam for the first European AIDS Conference.

FEBRUARY After years of debate, a comprehensive bill protecting gays from job discrimination was passed by the California legislature, only to be vetoed by Governor George Deukmejian, who claimed it was "divisive"; gay activists protested at his public appearances for moths to follow. ❏ An Atlanta meeting of the Federation of AIDS-Related Organizations proposed an expanded definition of the disease. ❏ Green Party representative Herbert Rusche, the only openly gay voting member of West Germany's parliament, began to campaign for gay rights and AIDS reforms.

MARCH In *Board of Education of Oklahoma City v. National Gay Task Force*, a law prohibiting teachers from discussing homosexuality in the classroom was struck down by a federal appeals court; a year later, the U.S. Supreme Court, taking its first gay-related case in seventeen years, affirmed the lower court's ruling on First Amendment grounds. ❏ Mayor Federico Peña and Representative Pat Schroeder were among leaders who boycotted Denver's annual St. Patrick's Day Parade after the parade's organizers decided to exclude gay marchers. ❏ Presidential candidate Jesse Jackson attended a meeting at New York's Lesbian and Gay Community Services Center. ❏ Gay blood donors could be subject to jail under a law proposed in Florida; the bill failed to pass.

APRIL Health officials in the United States and France announced the discovery of a virus thought to be the cause of AIDS, which so far had claimed 1,807 lives in the United States alone. ❏ Only two years after gay sex was legalized in Texas, conservatives urged a ban on homosexual acts to prevent the spread of AIDS. ❏ British customs officials raided Gay's the Word, London's largest gay bookstore, seizing more than eight hundred imported books they claimed were obscene.

MAY The United Methodist Church voted to ban the ordination of gay ministers. ❏ A gay group was denied official recognition and gay speakers were heckled at Gallaudet College in Washington, D.C., the nation's only college for the deaf. ❏ "The threat of homosexuality" was the theme slated for a pro-family rally planned by Reagan Administration officials and Christian Right leaders to precede the Democratic National Convention in San Francisco. ❏ Richard Longstaff, a gay Texas businessman originally from Great Britain, lost a court appeal to become a United States citizen; a year later, he was granted citizenship by Congressional order. ❏ A lesbian couple in Los Angeles won a discrimination suit against Papa Choux restaurant, which had refused to seat them in a couples-only section.

JUNE   Seattle Mayor Charles Royer signed an ordinance making the physical assault or verbal harassment of lesbians and gays a criminal offense. ❏ Two gay men won a discrimination suit against—and the right to dance together in—Disneyland. ❏ Arthur Bell, the colorful and outspoken gay columnist for *The Village Voice*, died of complications from diabetes. ❏ Gay activists in the nation's capital called for the removal of a judge who gave probation to two teenagers who took a gay man to the woods, attacked him with a knife, and left him naked and bleeding.

JULY   As 100,000 lesbians and gays marched for gay rights in the streets outside the Democratic National Convention in San Francisco, Presidential nominee Walter Mondale made history by choosing Geraldine Ferraro for his running mate. ❏ Boston passed a gay-rights ordinance while Columbus, Ohio, rejected one. ❏ The City Council of Berkeley, California, passed a domestic partnership bill granting equal benefits to members of long-term gay and unmarried heterosexual couples. ❏ San Francisco police charged five men with going on an antigay rampage in the city's Polk Street neighborhood that left one person dead and three others injured; gay activists protested that the chief investigator in the case belonged to an overtly homophobic group called Cops for Christ.

AUGUST   For the first time, an organized gay presence was visible during the Republican National Convention. ❏ Dr. Mervyn Silverman criticized health authorities in San Luis Obispo, California, for hastening the death of an AIDS patient by sending him without supervision two hundred miles to San Francisco to seek treatment; the patient was given a note saying that his care "would not be suitable in our city." ❏ In a major blow to gay rights and privacy rights, Judge Robert Bork, writing for the District of Columbia Court of Appeals, found it "impossible to conclude that a right to homosexual conduct is 'fundamental' or 'implicit in the concept of ordered liberty' unless any and all private sexual behaviors falls within those categories, a conclusion we are unwilling to draw." ❏ Truman Capote, acclaimed chronicler of high society and low deeds, died in Los Angeles. ❏ Bobbi Campbell, a tireless activist and the first person with AIDS to appear on the cover of *Newsweek* magazine, died in San Francisco. ❏ An all-male version of *Who's Afraid of Virginia Woolf?*, Edward Albee's award-winning play about battling heterosexual couples, was closed after Albee threatened to sue.

SEPTEMBER   A federal government proposal for a list of Americans exposed to the AIDS virus drew fire from gay and civil rights leaders; the proposal was dropped. ❏ Michael Jackson's representative announced at a press conference that the pop star is *not* gay. ❏ Scientists created a clone of the AIDS virus; they considered this an important step toward developing a vaccine against the disease. ❏ In what was considered a victory for the Catholic Archdiocese of New York City, a state

In November, top West Hollywood vote-getter Valerie Terrigno became the focus of international media attention as the nation's first openly lesbian mayor. Shortly thereafter, Terrigno was forced to resign after she was caught embezzling funds.

San Francisco's gay bathhouse patrons protested the closure of the city's bathhouses as an irrational and overly simplistic response to the AIDS epidemic.

AIDS WATCH

trial court struck down an executive order by Mayor Ed Koch barring antigay discrimination by firms doing business with the city.

OCTOBER After months of rancorous debate, San Francisco closed the city's gay bathhouses. ❑ The Federation of AIDS-Related Organizations hired a lobbyist in Washington, D.C. ❑ California Governor George Deukmejian signed a bill making antigay violence and harassment a crime. ❑ The General Accounting Office revealed that the military's antigay exclusionary policy cost taxpayers millions of dollars annually—$23 million in 1983 alone. ❑ An AIDS study conducted at the University of California, Berkeley, was nearly canceled when confidentiality issues scared off participants.

NOVEMBER West Hollywood residents voted for incorporation and elected a majority of openly gay City Council members, making the popular Los Angeles district America's first gay-controlled city. ❑ Massachusetts Democrat Gerry Studds, the first openly gay member of Congress, easily won reelection after being forced out of the closet by a congressional investigation. ❑ Ronald Reagan's landslide election to a second term sent a threatening message to gay activists about the Christian fundamentalist influence on federal policy. ❑ The FBI released more than 7,500 pages of material gathered on gay groups over a period of more than thirty years. ❑ Los Angeles gay activist Duncan Donovan received a death benefit check on a policy for his late lover after an eight-year legal battle to pursue the claim.

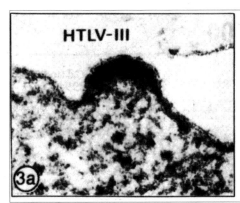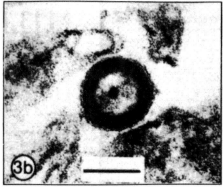

A microscopic photograph of the virus (later renamed HIV) believed to cause immuno-deficiency.

DECEMBER Two flight attendants, placed on medical leave by United Airlines because they had AIDS, filed a $10 million reinstatement lawsuit; three months later, they settled out of court for back pay and full benefits. ❑ A gay minister sued Jerry Falwell for calling the gay-oriented Metropolitan Community Church a "vile and Satanic system that will one day be annihilated...[causing a] celebration in heaven." ❑ The Public Broadcasting System announced the forthcoming broadcast of a show in its NOVA series titled "AIDS: Chapter One." ❑ A New York group took up the campaign for historic landmark status for the Greenwich Village building that formerly housed the Stonewall Inn, site of the 1969 riots that marked the beginning of modern gay liberation. ❑ Carol Lease, an open lesbian, was elected chairwoman of the Colorado chapter of the American Civil Liberties Union.

ALLAN CARR

"Come up! Let me tell you what my life is like today." Allan Carr stands on a small hill near his swimming pool outside his stunning house, which, as everyone knows, was built by MGM for Ingrid Bergman in the late thirties, when she came from Sweden to do *Intermezzo*. In the driveway are parked maybe seven cars, from a Porsche to a pickup. In the elfin guest house at the foot of the hill toils a small army of aides and secretaries, who answer the constantly ringing telephones with a cheery "Allan Carr Productions!" A young man gestures toward the house and says, "Go on up, he's waiting for you." Just for a second I think of Anne Francis pointing out Ziegfeld to Streisand in *Funny Girl*. "He's up above, honey. Like God."

But Carr doesn't act like God. He acts like Ziegfeld with a sense of humor. The man who manages Ann-Margret's career and gave us The Village People in *Can't Stop the Music* has the artless enthusiasm of a child whose favorite toy is show business.

It's one of Carr's dreams come true to have a movie and a hit Broadway musical playing a few blocks apart at the same time—which he does with *Where the Boys Are* and *La Cage aux Folles*. "*Where the Boys Are* was my college fantasy," he says with a grin. "Now I'm ready for postgraduate work, and I'm very happy."

Hollywood mogul Allan Carr (*right*) with gay recording artist Sylvester, who was rumored to have been considered for a starring role in an all-black version of *La Cage aux Folles*.

He's been wanting to do *La Cage aux Folles* since 1976, and kept the project in development with his own money for years. Based on the long-running French play and subsequent film about the family intrigues of a gay nightclub owner and his aging cross-dressing lover, Carr's version trades glitzy excess for the original story's more homoerotic content. "As it's presented on Broadway, people can relate to it in the most simple 'Father Knows Best' way," he claims. "They have to be either rock hard or have no emotions at all not to come out of that show wanting to call someone to say 'I'm sorry.'"

Recently Carr has made what some would call an uncharacteristic gesture toward the gay community, pledging to hold a benefit of *La Cage aux Folles* in San Francisco for that city's AIDS Foundation. "I feel *La Cage* is a statement, and also that the AIDS crisis is very, very serious. It's such a myth out there that it's only affecting gays. The misinformation is shocking," he says.

As for Hollywood's traditional attitudes toward gays, Carr sees a change as inevitable. "We cannot go backwards," he says. "There have been a few breakthroughs in what I call popular entertainment. People think *Guess Who's Coming to Dinner* was tame, I know. But I'm sorry, you just didn't *do* that subject before that picture. For gays, the contribution of *A Chorus Line* was enormous. Now, fourteen-year-olds are going to see *La Cage* because they saw the 'I Am What I Am' number on the Grammy Awards. Today people are a little more tolerant if a son or a daughter comes home and says, 'Guess what…?' Everyone's growing up, I think. It's just a question of time and of people being more tolerant and not questioning so much what people do in bed but what they're doing to prevent [a nuclear holocaust] from coming."

Concerning his own public image, Carr is adamantly uninterested. "People can think whatever they like about me," he says. "It doesn't make any difference. I am what I am. That's how the song goes, and that's how people live their lives."　　　　　　　　　　　　　　　　　　　　—VITO RUSSO

MICHEL FOUCAULT

Michel Foucault was a historian, philosopher, critic, and social theorist. He taught the history of systems of thought in Paris and Berkeley, and was author of the revolutionary *History of Sexuality,* a three-volume work in which he challenged Freudian theory and denied the essentialism of "human nature."

Foucault's notion of sexuality, some people say, denies gay and lesbian people a history that allows us to name Plato, Michelangelo, and Sappho as our ancestors. Furthermore, his ideas undermine our ability to defend our lives by claiming to be a minority in need of protection, for our minority status is based on our assertion that we have a sexual *orientation*. But if gay sexuality is not based on some kind of orientation, then that whole politics becomes questionable.

This is a welcome controversy. For some time now, there has been a pressing need to reexamine the theoretical underpinnings of a sexual politics. The following observations are excerpted from one of the last interviews conducted with Foucault before his death on June 25 from complications due to AIDS.

You suggest in your work that sexual liberation is not so much the uncovering of secret truths about one's self or one's desire as it is a part of the process of defining and constructing desire. What do you mean?

What I meant was that I think that what the gay movement needs now is much more the art of life than a science or scientific knowledge (or pseudo-scientific knowledge) of what sexuality is. Sexuality is a part of our behavior. It's a part of our world freedom. Sexuality is something that we ourselves create—it is our own creation, and much more than the discovery of a secret side of our desire. We have to understand that with our desires, through our desires, go new forms of relationships, new forms of love, new forms of creation. Sex is not a fatality; it's a possibility for creative life.

That's basically what you're getting at when you suggest that we should try to become gay—not just to reassert ourselves as gay.

Yes, that's it. We don't have to discover that we are homosexuals.

Or what the meaning of that is?

Exactly. Rather, we have to create a gay life. To *become*.

And this is something without limits?

Yes, sure. I think when you look at the different ways people have experienced their own sexual freedoms—the way they have created their works of art—you would have to say that sexuality, as we now know it, has become one of the most creative sources of our society and our being. My view is that we should understand it in the reverse way: The world [regards] sexuality as the secret of the creative cultural life; it is rather a process of our having to create a new cultural life underneath the ground of our sexual choices. Not only do we have to defend ourselves, we have to affirm ourselves, not only as an identity but as a creative force.

A lot of that sounds like what, for instance, the women's movement has done, trying to establish their own language and their own culture.

Well, I'm not sure that we have to create our *own* culture. We have to *create* culture. But it must not be a translation of gayness in the field of music or painting or what have you, for I do not think this can happen.

—BOB GALLAGHER AND ALEXANDER WILSON

THE RADICAL FAERIES OF SHORT MOUNTAIN

When I was a little boy on the farm, I fancied myself Puck, the fairy child who flits naughtily through the enchanted forests of *A Midsummer Night's Dream.* As I grew toward adolescence, my alter ego was gradually drawn to the more ethereal elegance of Titania, the original Fairy Queen. Upon learning in the usual rude ways that such fantasies were not to be acted out in public, I moved to New York City, grew a beard, and settled somewhat reluctantly into the more suitable role of Oberon, Puck's sprightly but masculine Fairy King.

So it seemed an omen of sorts when, stopping off at Virginia's Luray Caverns en route to a rural gay commune in Tennessee, I came upon one of the ancient cave's stalactites, a delicate white cascade of stone icicles named Titania's Wedding Veil. Was it merely the echo of fellow tourists, or did this graceful embroidery of Mother Nature really seem to call up the ghosts of ancient desires and knowledge, murmuring urgently to be released from the limbo of dreams deferred?

Short Mountain Sanctuary is a two-hundred-acre farm tucked into a leafy hollow in the hill country of central Tennessee. It was founded in 1972 by a small group of counterculture folks—including several lesbians and gay men— who were seeking the benefits of healthful country living, communal society, and escape from the technological and cultural pressures of urban life. The current residents—about a dozen in the prime spring season—are the hub of a network of gay and lesbian neighbors, visitors, and sympathizers that stretches from nearby farms to Boston, Atlanta, rural parts of North Carolina and Mississippi, and even to California, Canada, Europe, and Australia.

Short Mountain is operated as a nonprofit land trust dedicated to ecologically sound, low-technology agriculture. The antebellum log cabin that houses cooking and dining facilities has no electricity, toilet, or telephone; water

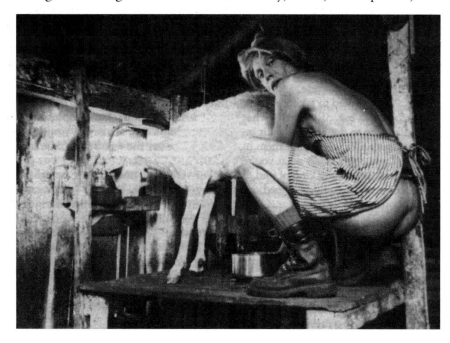

Floating Eagle Feather, a Native American of Mayan descent, spent the year touring the continent as an openly gay professional storyteller. Charged with the belief that his stories could help create international peace, he entertained audiences from Alaska to Nicaragua. "I'm a weaver of social fabric," he told *The Advocate*. "As I travel and relate the stories of different cultures that people have told me, I help to create a more direct link between cultures and among individuals. If we all realize how much we have in common, then the craziness of our world leaders will start to evaporate."

As a young boy growing up in New Orleans, Eagle Feather said he knew better than to talk about being gay. "I had to speak through the heterosexual mouth," he explained. "I learned how to use pronouns and how not to use pronouns—'My friend and I went for a walk.' Things like these were chipping slowly away at my consciousness and making me become a revolutionary."

> "*I think the flaming, flagrant antigay population is even smaller than the gay community. But what could be flamed up in that population—the feelings hidden there—is an altogether different subject.*"
> —PLAYWRIGHT LANFORD WILSON

comes from the spring, heat from an ancient woodstove. Some residents live in smaller cabins or barns nearby; one built himself a round house similar to a Mongolian yurt. Although far from self-sufficient, the "mountaineers" are quite serious about their plentiful vegetables, fruits, and herbs, and about the ever-present chickens and goats that provide dairy products and an occasional roaster.

But one glance at their visitor's brochure listing "Whatcha need to bring" reveals that this is no austere, grown-up version of Boy Scout camp: "Sleeping bag, eating utensils, flashlight, costumes, and makeup." Living in the country is motivated by more than sociology and economics; it is also a spiritual opportunity to reacquaint oneself with the eternal cycles of nature and with the neglected potentials of human nature. Words like "ritual" and "androgyny" are too abstract to convey the impression that living among these "radical faeries" is also a lot of fun. Sharing the barn with eighteen goats is an entire storeroom for the colorful costumes and props used during their gatherings, week-long parliamentary-sessions-cum-druid-Woodstocks celebrating the equinoxes and, once a year, culminating in the coronation of the group's administrative Empress:

I'll give thee fairies to attend on thee,
And they shall fetch thee jewels from the deep,
And sing while thou on pressèd flowers dost sleep;
And I will purge thy mortal grossness so,
That thou shalt like an airy spirit go.

So sings Titania in Shakespeare's forest, and she should know. To really appreciate the lure of country life, you have to wake up with the smell of honeysuckle floating in from the bushes and no sound but the rooster crowing, and pad downstairs to join in planning the day's schedule over coffee and cereal laced with frothy-fresh goat's milk. Although some detailed ground rules are necessary here, day-to-day operations are decided by consensus. Division of labor depends on the shifting talents and interests of available residents, most of whom also spend portions of the year elsewhere or work part-time in nearby towns to earn the farm's "foreign exchange." Today, Edwin, a knowledgeable herbalist, will be gathering plants to dry for tea and medicine; the goats will be looked after by Perlie Sudds, an ex-naval trainee dressed for milking in combat boots and a striped pink apron; Mike, the mechanical wizard, will be running errands in the village. Kitchen patrol rotates weekly, with the culinary supervisor receiving the temporary title "Mom." Like "Empress," the name does not vary with the sex of the functionary—its whimsical androgyny suits a world where in an average day the same person may be called upon to cook a soufflé and change an axle.

Some days, of course, are marked by more than average activity. The afternoon of my arrival is set aside for the ancient Indian ritual of the "sweat"—urbanites might call it a sauna, but it's as far removed in spirit from that commercialized pastime as it is in distance from the typical sanitized downtown bathhouse. To start with, we heat the rocks in an open bonfire, then carry them to a pit in the center of the low, tarp-covered "sweat lodge." Eight or nine of us strip off our clothes, huddle around the steamy heat, and throw into the pit sprigs of fragrant herbs that cleanse the nose and mist the brain like pungent incense. Someone chants, filling the tiny chamber with a heady drone; two others whistle softly.

When sound, smell, and sweat reach a level of woozy exaltation, we wobble back out into the glade and douse ourselves in the frigid mountain stream. Earlier that day an eclipse of the sun cast an eerie green half-light across the noonday air, stilling the animals and awing the humans into silent recognition of the vast rotating universe in which we are a mere speck. Later, I splash naked in the clear waterfall, shrieking from cold and delight.

Wednesday dinner is another special occasion, a weekly potluck open house for friends and neighbors who don't live at Short Mountain. Before the meal, the dozen and a half guests link arms in a circle of welcome. We eat on the wide porch, quietly watching the sunset, which is almost as long and colorful as a movie. As darkness falls, we adjourn to the living room, sprawling before the fire to trade gossip, farm advice, and soothing massage.

My wistful reverie is soothed by an invitation from Stevie to cuddle in his home this evening. New faces, being much rarer than in the urban ghetto, attract immediate attention; as Perlie later confessed, "I mean, *everyone* got dressed up for your arrival, dear." Relationships can be a problem here: If you've got one, it suffers the strains of both isolation and communal living; if you haven't, you may make do with intermittent long-distance affairs and the occasional visitor or local pickup.

Yet, the Short Mountaineers generally feel that the advantages of their life outweigh this dilemma. Their need for intimacy is more than satisfied by frequent hugs and companionship that bespeak a genuine caring and sharing. More broadly, as Perlie puts it, "Everyone here is in love with the farm, and with each other, and with being in the country."

Like centuries of monastics who also lived in isolated all-male or all-female enclaves, the mountaineers distinguish between *eros* and *agape*, the Christian/Greek division of love into body and spirit—and come down, though less exclusively, on the side of agape. If the cost of intense, undiluted communion with Mother Nature and Brother Man is cutting down on some of the more literal forms of intercourse—well, it's a tempting bargain, especially in these times of plague. There's a lot to be said for cuddling; as I dozed off later that night in Stevie's cozy attic, his heartbeat next to my ear seemed to thump the iambics of Titania's blessing on Bottom:

> Sleep thou, and I will wind thee in my arms...
> So doth the woodbine the sweet honeysuckle
> Gently entwist; the female ivy so
> Enrings the barky fingers of the elm.
> Oh, how I love thee! How I dote on thee!

— James M. Saslow

"*Falling in love has never not had a challenge....In the days of the plague, even saying hello to somebody was a dangerous proposition. In AIDS, liberation doesn't meet its defeat at all, it meets a test, which is a very different thing.*"
—Poet Robert Duncan

"A relationship too inflexible to cope with the variety within the human race is probably doomed to be one of those short ones which disillusion so many gays who ask so much of others and so little of themselves."
—Essayist Donald Vining

SAFE-SEX PARTIES

POLICE ABUSE AGAINST GAYS

For the first time, a Congressional panel heard testimony on police harassment of gays during a New York City hearing last November. James Creedle of Black and White Men Together and Kevin Berrill, director of the National Gay Task Force's Violence Project, told the House Subcommittee on Criminal Justice that gays and lesbians face abuse from police because of their sexual orientation, and called on Congress to take steps to correct the problem.

"If we are serious about the eradication of [police] brutality from [the black] community," testified Creedle, "then we must acknowledge the widespread abuses which occur daily against lesbians and gay males. The point is that as a black gay man, I often ask, 'From whom do I need protection?' And more often than not, the answer is, 'I need to be protected from the police!'"

Creedle recounted his visit to Blues (a Manhattan bar frequented by black gays) the day after a police raid that received substantial press attention and is now being investigated by the office of New York Mayor Edward Koch.

Creedle likened the destruction to what he had seen during his tour of duty in Vietnam. "Broken bottles, glasses, and mirrors were strewn about the floor. Blood was everywhere splattered on the floor, on the walls, on equipment—a total wasteland."

"To be a victim of a crime, especially a violent crime, is a terrible ordeal," Berrill said. "But when that crime against you is committed by those who are responsible for protecting you, the pain and rage are even greater."

HOUSE REPORT LAMBASTES FEDERAL HANDLING OF AIDS

A House committee report on the federal response to AIDS was released last December, documenting findings that the Public Health Service (PHS) has had insufficient funds to fight the AIDS epidemic; that the PHS lacks the mechanism to quickly fund health-emergency activities without diverting funds from other health programs; that inadequate funding has undermined the PHS's surveillance, epidemiology, and laboratory research activities; that AIDS grants to researchers have been unnecessarily delayed; and that the Department of Health and Human Services (HHS) has not adequately planned and coordinated the federal response to the epidemic.

The report provides a sometimes startling contrast between what federal health researchers were saying privately and what officials were willing to say publicly about the funding required to respond effectively to the emerging AIDS crisis. In each of the hearings at which AIDS funding needs have been discussed, Reagan Administration officials have sought to hold the line on funding requests, only to increase the budget proposal later—often within weeks.

One subcommittee document in particular—a letter dated April 12, 1983, from Dr. Donald P. Francis, assistant director for medical science at the Centers for Disease Control, to Dr. Walter Dowdle, director of the Center for Infectious Diseases—makes an urgent plea for increased federal funding.

"The number of people already killed is large, and all indications are that this disease will not stop until thousands of Americans have died," Francis writes. "Our government's response to this disaster has been far too little. The inadequate funding to date has seriously restricted our work and has presumably deepened the invasion of this disease into the American population.

"For the good of the people of this country and the world, we should no longer accept the claims of inadequate funding and we should no longer be content with the trivial resources offered," Francis writes in his concluding paragraph. "Our past and present efforts have been and are far too small and we can't be proud. It is time to do more. It is time to do what is right."

—LARRY BUSH

"There was so much liquid protein splattered on the floor, Adele Davis could have sniffed herself into ecstasy." Am I describing a Kansas health-food store hit by a tornado? No, Dorothy, just a jerk-off party held at a New York club, a simple gathering of two hundred homosexuals who'd checked their street clothes and were wandering about stroking themselves and others into the throes of passion.

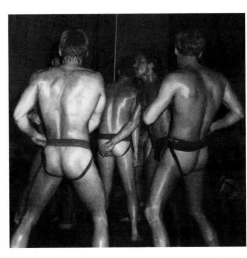

"So what?" you ask.

So what!

For the uninformed, this was no ordinary Crisco orgy. Within the confines of the two-story cruise bar, a safe-sex J/O gathering was gathering momentum. Yes, safe sex. No amoebas, parasites, or AIDS germs were being allowed to switch partners at this, the newest phenomenon to hit the nation since the arrival of Boy George's dreadlocks and Soloflex videotapes.

How did I latch on to this trend? It was all very unexpected. I opened my morning mail and there was an invitation that read: "Solo and mutual masturbation and touch only so as not to exchange body fluids, i.e., no French, Greek, WS, etc.—relax and enjoy, we are all friendly and horny!"

"At last," I exclaimed, "Gloria Vanderbilt has invited me to one of her functions." But my jet-set euphoria was short-lived. This invite was from White Productions—the numero uno sponsor of stud ejaculations. Faced with reality, I immediately started trying on my jockstraps, applying pancake powder to my buttocks, and doing tit exercises. I had four days to turn myself into a specimen certain to inspire erections on the jaded masses. Of course, the morning of the gala I had gas and looked like I was giving birth to Rosemary's baby. But with the aid of a few Gas-X tablets, I soon returned to my natural virile physique.

After arriving at Alex's, I checked everything but my jock and ten dollars, which I wedged into my sneakers. I then ran into the bathroom and jerked off a little, so my basket would look full. Pleased with the result, I strutted into the upstairs sex room only to be greeted by my ex-lover's laughter. He explained, that the prodigious sight of his sexy old flame had caught him off guard.

Knowing an honest compliment when I hear one, I didn't pull his nipple chain violently. Instead, I drank two Lite beers to loosen up. On reaching the desired state of mind, I grabbed a handful of grease and started massaging my flaccid member. Again aroused, I slowly trod around the bar, approaching and departing from couples and groups, partaking of lusty gropes. At last, after hooking up with a well-equipped chap, I spurted with the best of them.

Using just twenty-four jars of Albolene cream and fifteen rolls of paper toweling, White Productions is giving sex back to the gay populace who had grown schizo about sex. Not surprisingly, one of the few problems the group faces when renting spaces is that owners are nervous about sperm stains on their floors. "Don't worry," they're reassured, "most people enjoy coming on each other!"

—BRANDON JUDELL

THEATER: ROBERT CHESLEY'S *NIGHT SWEAT*

He was a devoted, if unorthodox, teacher for nearly a decade, the partner in an intensely devoted, if sexless, marriage for almost as many years, and, at age thirty-two, a born-again gay adolescent. Now, at forty-one, Robert Chesley is emerging as one of the gay community's best playwrights, tapping collective dreams, fantasies, and sometimes nightmares, and transforming this potent material into the stuff of dark romantic comedy. Chesley's last play, *Stray Dog Story*, a fairy tale about a dog magically transformed into a gay man, received back-to-back productions in New York and San Francisco; his latest, *Night Sweat* ("a New York problem play with a San Francisco solution," the playwright notes), opened in New York this spring.

Chesley refuses to label *Night Sweat*, a play that is concerned with AIDS. "The current health crisis is the context for the play; it's not the subject for the play," Chesley says. *Night Sweat* is a gay dream-fantasy version of Robert Louis Stevenson's "Suicide Club." "That's where the germinal idea came from, actually," explains Chesley. "The only fact you know about my play is that the hero, Richard, is having a nightmare because of his worries about his health. Richard's nightmare is about a super-glitzy, urban gay male, high-tech, state-of-the-art, 'we can do it more beautifully than anyone' suicide club. This play will push a lot of buttons because it brings to the surface feelings and violent fantasies that are usually kept on a very tight leash or completely buried in the unconscious."

Chesley insists that all of his major plays contain universal themes but does admit that the target audience for *Night Sweat* "is the visible, urban gay male population," he says. "It also reworks 'the tragic queen syndrome' that was rejected and attacked by the gay movement after Stonewall. The correct line was how terrible it was that gay literature always ended in murder or suicide. Unhappy, tragic endings were part of the old gay sensibility. But Tennessee Williams showed how artfully the tragic-queen sensibility could be brought to bear in the theater. It's related to the appreciation of beauty and to masochism." Chesley admits that some of the scenes in *Night Sweat* depict his own personal death fantasies, while some have been borrowed from friends. "It's not just fantasy material," he says. "I'm also making political points because I'm a little preacher. I couldn't resist the scene where the gay businessman is tortured to death, when his executioners put him on the rack and make him confess that he has served little dishes of cassis sorbet between dinner courses because he knew it would impress his guests." Chesley is concerned with the extent to which his audience will be focusing on the AIDS crisis as they view *Night Sweat*. "This is a real problem, because the play comes from my own real fears and real grief," the writer notes. "At this point, I've lost five people I know to AIDS. The play was influenced, too, by my own unduly morbid look at life.

"It's peculiar to the gay and women's communities that they've chosen to make leaders of their writers....Writers are by nature solitary, willful, and perverse and have no business leading anybody anywhere."
—AUTHOR JANE RULE

"Some of my friends are horribly disturbed that I can think this way or would own up to these morbid fantasies," Chesley admits. "My best buddy in New York is sorry I wrote *Night Sweat*. I told him that there are people who really like the play. He said, 'I never want to meet those people.' "

— DAVID LAMBLE

FILM: *THE TIMES OF HARVEY MILK*

"When I wrote an obituary for the Flamingo [a New York City disco], some men were angry. This was politically incorrect: You couldn't talk about the value of a disco as forming a gay community. Disco was for frivolous people, while good, serious people were out there marching. What made anybody think that one of those things excluded the other? Communities are formed in bed, on the dance floor, marching, working...they are also formed out of the threat of death."

—EDITOR GEORGE STAMBOLIAN

There was a moment of panic, not long ago, when Rob Epstein and Richard Schmiechen, the director and producer of *The Times of Harvey Milk,* thought they'd hatched a dud.

It happened Labor Day weekend at Colorado's Telluride Film Festival—a prestigious, four-day hothouse that's considered a crucial springboard for independent films. *Harvey Milk*—the story of San Francisco's first openly gay politician, and his assassination by fellow supervisor Dan White—was finally making its debut, nearly six years after its conception.

"By the time our film started," the soft-spoken Epstein recalled recently in San Francisco, "people were walking out and continued to do so in order to go see other films. We were completely devastated." But something happened the next morning, when *Harvey Milk* was given a repeat screening. That time, Epstein said, "nobody walked out. Everybody stayed; the response was tremendous."

Since then, *The Times of Harvey Milk* has played to similarly enthusiastic audiences, and won rave notices, at the New York and Toronto film festivals. "One hopes for this kind of reaction," Epstein said, "though it's hard to expect." What's clear from the response is that *The Times of Harvey Milk* transcends sexual and attitudinal barriers. It's a potent, emotionally overwhelming film—for men or women, gay or straight—and it made this writer, for one, cry like a baby.

An emotional roller coaster, *Harvey Milk* opens with the assassination of Milk and San Francisco Mayor George Moscone, accompanied by the eerie recording that Milk made shortly after his November 1977 election, in which he said: "To be played only in the event of my death by assassination." The sobriety of those early moments is then replaced by humorous accounts of Milk's early life, his careers as a stockbroker, a theatrical producer, and a camera shop owner, and his lively eleven-month term as a member of San Francisco's Board of Supervisors. Abruptly, the mood turns deeply sad again when the filmmakers recap the City Hall murders and the quiet eloquence of the candlelight march that proceeded down Market Street that·evening.

From the beginning, Epstein said, he envisioned a film that worked emotionally rather than intellectually—one that would capture the soul and the flair of Milk without pedantry or soapboxing. "I wanted the film to be experiential," Epstein said, "in that people would feel the emotions that were felt during each of the events. And that's what we tried to draw from the interviews and the construction of news material. We wanted to tell the story responsibly, unsensationally."

The filmmakers interviewed a cross section of people whose lives Milk touched, from Sally Gearhart, a lesbian educator who joined Milk to defeat the Briggs Initiative, to Jim Elliot, a straight car mechanic and labor advocate. Their testimony, occasionally punctuated by tears as they recall the tragedy of Milk's death, is forthright and heartrending. The Harvey Milk who emerges is neither saint nor fool—but a complicated, clowning, exasperating, ultimately generous and idealistic man with a gift for drawing people together and vitalizing social issues.

Ironically, Epstein said, "I think I really got to love Harvey making this film. Looking at all the news footage and talking to his friends, what emerged was this guy who was pretty special. The fact that his loss was felt so deeply, I think, says something about who he was and whom he had affected and reached."

—EDWARD GUTHMANN

BOOKS: JUDY GRAHN'S *MOTHER TONGUE*

Poet Judy Grahn fought for gay rights long before Stonewall. Born into a working-class family in New Mexico, she was drummed out of the Air Force in 1960 for being lesbian. In 1963 she joined the Mattachine Society and picketed the White House for gay rights.

In 1969, Grahn moved to San Francisco, where she helped found an all-women's press that published books of lesbian poetry, prose, and graphics. Her own major collections of poetry to date are *The Work of a Common Woman*

and *Queen of Wands*. Grahn's latest book, *Another Mother Tongue*, is provocative and controversial—part autobiography, part gay etymology and history. The writer recently spoke to *The Advocate* about the implications of her new work.

I'm impressed with how you weave anthropology in with your own autobiography. How did you choose this form?

I began with a list of slang words I learned when I first came out in the early sixties: *camp, buggery, faggot,* and *gay,* among others. These words, it seemed to me, held clues. This led me to the tradition of being called queer if you wore green on Thursday. I traced that to the witches and fairy people. Eventually I had a rough dictionary that told me there was a tradition, but I didn't have contemporary examples, and this history is totally alive: It's walking down Polk Street, it's holding hands on subways, it's everyplace. Then I remembered that I could use myself as an example.

When there's a gay march, some say, "Now don't get outrageous." They forget drag queens are the ones who fought at Stonewall, who enlarged freedom for all of us.

Right! If gay is more than just behavior in bed, if it's a culture, then it's the dykes and drag queens who have the culture in their hands. Giving that up in order to march is giving up gayness in a sense. It's saying, "Look how straight we are," rather than saying, "Gay people are okay." Maybe it's necessary for certain civil rights issues, but if we do that too much we lose our essence, the meaning that's in us as a group.

What are some of the key distinguishing aspects of our culture?

We're a people who keep things in motion. We represent what the Trickster does in tribal society, the chaotic wilderness part of social interaction. We're overtly sexual, for one thing. There's an electric spark in that. We're willing to take risks, to take an idea like gender, which seems so biologically fixed, and reverse it....I believe there's a men's culture, a women's culture, and a children's culture. One of our tasks as gays—and we haven't even begun to define them all—is to take information developed in one group and pass it to another. We pass it in particularly gay ways, totally identifying with members of the opposite gender, for instance, then changing in mid-life and becoming the other kind of person. Or acting it out more theatrically. After just a decade, we've changed centuries of rigid attitudes [about men's and women's roles]. Who would have thought this possible in 1965? —STEVE ABBOTT

"I relate to greed....It's rampant in this country right now. I see it everywhere I go in New York. I've never seen so many limousines, and I've never seen so many people sleeping on the streets. That's greed."

—DRAG PERFORMER
ETHYL EICHELBERGER

MUSIC: ENGLAND'S GENDER WARS

The British pop press loves a bitch fight. They've dubbed the latest round the gender-bender wars. What's unusual is that these brickbats have been flying between a roster of increasingly out pop stars.

First there was Boy George, disarming the planet with his cheeky, cuddly androgyny. Since then, five acts (all marketing homosexuality as part of their work) have scaled the British charts, though they haven't been quick to embrace one another.

Marilyn was next off the mark. Where Boy George affects a nearly asexual camp, Marilyn countered with a haughty Dietrich vamp, but his limited vocal skills left him a media novelty with little musical appeal. Frankie Goes to Hollywood hit the charts last fall, draped in leather, the band's two leaders openly announcing that they were S&M lovers. The ludicrously sleazy video that accompanied their first smash single, "Relax," showed a fat old man, naked in a G-string, playing emperor to a team of leather lads who offer a golden shower baptism to a lost youth who stumbles into their lair.

When Boy George criticized the video as "cheap, disgusting, and very childish," Frankie's Paul Rutherford told a reporter, "Boy George—the guy's an idiot if overt things freak him out. How can he say that when he's got eye makeup on?"

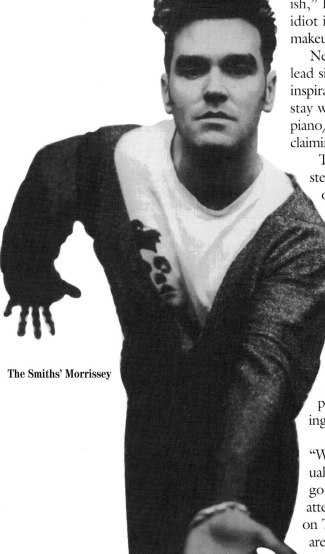

The Smiths' Morrissey

Next, out of left field, came the Smiths—no leather or makeup, but their lead singer, Morrissey (who credits Oscar Wilde and James Dean as his twin inspirations), offered telling lyrics: "I lost my faith in womanhood," "Please stay with your own kind/And I'll stay with mine," and "Shove me on the piano/I'll take it slowly." The Smiths have generally disdained the bitchy fray, claiming their aim is not to bend gender but to transcend it.

The fourth act in the sweeps, Dead or Alive, is fronted by macho-glamster Pete Burns. With a recent U.K. hit, the outrageous dresser performed on British TV in a jockstrap, gauntlets, and a ripped rubber T-shirt. Burns, who is married, has delighted in telling the press that his favorite fantasies would be "sucking on Muhammad Ali's knob" and in savaging Boy George. "I got a message from Boy George saying let's be friends," he reported. "I said, 'Fuck off, I don't speak to men in dresses.'"

The latest act out of the gate is Bronski Beat, a trio of nerdy-looking lads, two of them from Scotland. They aren't arty inverts like the Smiths. They don't dress up like Boy, Marilyn, Frankie, or Pete, but offer forthright falsetto assaults on homophobia. The voice is diminutive Jimmy Somerville's, who complains that Marilyn and Frankie's outrages simply exploit gay sleaze for its shock value: "It's so boring, so played out. There's no creativity." Boy George responds, "Talk about boring—he looks like a potato."

Amidst all the flying fur, though, Boy George recently proposed a truce: "We all try so hard to be individual yet we resent any other form of individualism....If you think that Boy George is the acceptable face of eccentricity, go tell it to the skinhead who wants to break my nose. Fame brings mass attention, but how many he-men who sit down to watch 'Top of the Pops' on Thursday would love to stomp on our heads? I can assure you that there are plenty, and that's what we should be fighting, not each other."

Boy George can talk. He has taken *his* show on the road.—ADAM BLOCK

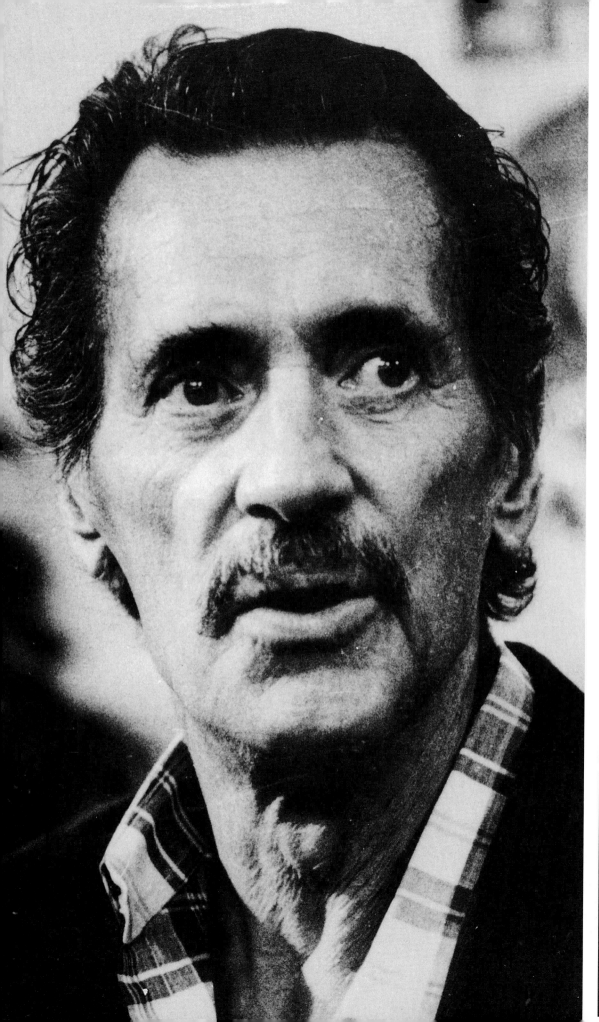

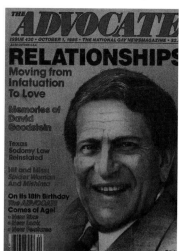

THE ADVOCATE
ISSUE 430 • OCTOBER 1, 1985 • THE NATIONAL GAY NEWSMAGAZINE • $2.

RELATIONSHIPS
Moving from Infatuation To Love

Memories of David Goodstein

Texas Sodomy Law Reinstated

Hit and Miss: Spider Woman And Mishima

On Its 18th Birthday The ADVOCATE Comes of Age!
• New Size
• New Look
• New Features

THE ADVOCATE
$2.50 • OCTOBER 15, 1985 • THE NATIONAL GAY NEWSMAGAZINE • ISSUE 431

AMAZING GRACE
Grace Jones On Gays, AIDS, Hollywood and Black & White

FDA Guidelines Restrict Gay Blood Donations

Relationships: How Important Is Hot Sex?

N.Y.'s 10 Most Eligible Gay Bachelors

PLUS: AIDS Crisis Update • Fast Forward • The Classifieds

THE ADVOCATE
$2.50 • OCTOBER 29, 1985 • THE NATIONAL GAY NEWSMAGAZINE • ISSUE 432

HOORAY FOR HOLLYWOOD!
The Stars Come Out To Fight AIDS

Paul Cameron: Most Dangerous Antigay Voice in America?

African Swine Fever Theory Discredited

Gay Native American Awakening

PLUS:

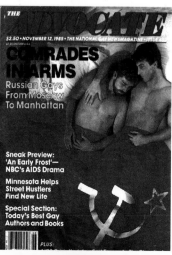

THE ADVOCATE
$2.50 • NOVEMBER 12, 1985 • THE NATIONAL GAY NEWSMAGAZINE • ISSUE

COMRADES IN ARMS
Russian Gays From Moscow To Manhattan

Sneak Preview: 'An Early Frost'— NBC's AIDS Drama

Minnesota Helps Street Hustlers Find New Life

Special Section: Today's Best Gay Authors and Books

PLUS:

TURNING POINT

1985 In late October, the New York State Public Health Council, acting on Governor Mario Cuomo's initiative, passed a sixty-day emergency measure giving local officials the power to shut down any public establishment that made facilities available for anal or oral sex. Despite a letter from New York City Health Commissioner Dr. David Sencer to Mayor Edward Koch, which said, in part, that "closure of the bathhouses will contribute little if anything to the control of AIDS," by early November the *New York Daily News* announced, "City Wants to Shutter Whips-&-Sex Gay Club."

This club was the Mineshaft, which the *New York Post* referred to as "a homosexual leather bar on the fringes of Greenwich Village." It was padlocked on November 7 as a "public nuisance." For several days afterward, the tabloid press was full of lurid accounts of the "high-risk sexual activity" reportedly witnessed by three inspectors from the city's Department of Consumer Affairs. "While I was near the back room, I heard sounds of whipping. I could hear men moaning," one inspector explained. "I chose not to attempt to enter this area for reasons of personal safety," said another. Almost as an afterthought, the inspectors noted that patrons did not seem to be using the bar's free condoms.

The next day, Koch warned ten more New York gay bars, bathhouses, and clubs that they could be closed down as well. On November 12, the *Post* announced in headlines nearly two inches high: "AIDS Den Closed for Good." Manhattan Supreme Court Justice Francis Pecora had signed a preliminary injunction to make sure "no similar use" would ever be made of the space at 835 Washington Street. The Mineshaft had ceased to exist.

The owner of the St. Mark's Baths, Bruce Mailman, called the state regulations "the worst kind of sloppy, craven legislation...I think it's a nightmare." Patrons at St. Mark's received prophylactics and a safe-sex brochure, and had to sign an agreement that they would comply with safe-sex guidelines while on the premises. Nevertheless, on December 6, the St. Mark's Baths was closed.

World attention was focused on Rock Hudson when French doctors released a statement that the American screen legend was suffering from AIDS and seeking experimental treatment at a hospital in Paris.

The city's Department of Consumer Affairs had made thirty-five visits to the baths and cited a total of forty-nine separate acts of "high-risk" activity. A news story about the closure in the December 23–29 edition of the *New York Native* was accompanied by a photo of the closing order on the bathhouse door. Graffiti on the closing order said "Finally" and "Fuck fags."

The crackdown on New York sex clubs was only one battle in an escalating national war against public sex. Under orders from Mayor Dianne Feinstein, San Francisco's public health director, Dr. Mervyn Silverman, had closed the bathhouses in San Francisco in 1984. Los Angeles; Atlanta; Orlando, Florida; East Hartford, Connecticut; Newark, New Jersey; Indianapolis, Indiana; and other cities had also cracked down on public sex arenas in 1985. In October, the U.S. House of Representatives even passed an appropriations bill with an amendment providing that certain AIDS research funds "may be used by the Surgeon General for closing or quarantining any bathhouse or massage parlor which…can be determined to facilitate the transmission or spread of…AIDS."

The lesbian and gay community's response to this moral panic was fraught with ambivalence. Many segments of the gay community had never approved of the sexual license the bathhouses represented. The fact that the Mineshaft was an S&M club made many gay men and lesbians reluctant to defend it. A notable exception was Sarah Schulman, who published an article entitled "Wake Up—AIDS Hysteria Will Change Your Life" in the December 1985/ January 1986 issue of *Womanews*. Schulman wrote: "When the organized meeting places are closed, gay sex will go underground where it was before, far from any health information."

City officials and gay activists seemed to be confused about their strategy for attacking AIDS; they stigmatized identities ("bathhouse sluts") and places ("AIDS dens") instead of focusing on risky behaviors. When he announced that the state would be targeting gay sex spots, New York State Health Commissioner Dr. David Axelrod told reporters, "We're trying to deal with dangerous sex….What individuals do…in their homes is in no way prohibited by the actions taken today." This would seem to indicate that Axelrod felt that public sex itself was the problem, not the presence of a virus or the absence of condoms.

Michael Callen, a member of the Coalition for Sexual Responsibility and the New York State AIDS Advisory Council, said in the November 11–17 issue of the *Native* that his group had told the bathhouses, "We wanted the lights turned up….We asked them to keep the place clean, to remove glory holes, bathtubs, and slings." This would seem to imply that someone was more likely to contract AIDS in a bathtub or a sling than in a private bedroom.

However, it would be a mistake to conclude that the closure of the Mineshaft and other sex clubs did not create any opposition. Reeling from tabloid coverge of the bathhouse controversy, on November 17 more than seven hundred people attended a town meeting called by a group that would go on to form the Gay and Lesbian Alliance Against Defamation. Activist Andy Humm pointed out that it was outrageous for the city to attack gay public space when the gay-rights bill could not be scheduled for a vote by the City Council.

By 1985, the gay community was exhausted by the epidemic, deep in mourning, sickened by the specter of death, and simply not up to the challenge of defending deviant pleasure on the evening news. So the sexual territories of the baths were lost to us for the remainder of the decade. The year's lesson was sobering: At any time, the state could step in and shut down gay space.

—PAT CALIFIA

"From the beginning, we were adamant that throwing pennies at the AIDS problem was not going to make it go away. It became clear to us very early that $100 million was the level of research money needed immediately….Gays were not going to be nickeled-and-dimed on a life-or-death issue."
—VIRGINIA APUZZO, OUTGOING HEAD OF THE NATIONAL GAY TASK FORCE

"It's all about how people insert the penis into the anus and how they insert the fist into the anus, etc. That was all very interesting, but it seemed to me that the most interesting question was how the people of Orange County came to insert an anus into the House of Representatives."
—U.S. REPRESENTATIVE BARNEY FRANK, on conservative Congressman William Dannemeyer's description of how AIDS is transmitted

T I M E L I N E

In November, participants in San Francisco's annual memorial march for Harvey Milk plastered the side of the Federal Building with the names of those who had died of AIDS. The dramatic display inspired the march's coordinator, Cleve Jones, to conceive the Names Project AIDS Memorial Quilt.

Openly gay producer Richard Schmiechen (*right*) and director Robert Epstein won Best Documentary Oscars for *The Times of Harvey Milk* in March.

JANUARY The day after federal officials announced the availability of a blood test for HTLV-3, the virus suspected to lead to AIDS, sixteen gay organizations joined the National Gay Task Force in urging gay men not to take the test on grounds of potential discrimination, unreliability of tests, and questionable confidentiality. ❑ In what was called the ugliest gay-rights referendum since Anita Bryant, Houston voters repealed an ordinance prohibiting antigay discrimination by a four-to-one margin. ❑ Virginia Apuzzo, acclaimed for rejuvenating the National Gay Task Force, resigned as executive director and was replaced by Jeff Levi.

FEBRUARY The Reagan Administration's proposed budget for 1986 revealed a $12 million cut in AIDS-related funding. ❑ California state senators Milton Marks and David Roberti introduced legislation to ensure confidentiality in AIDS research. ❑ The London publishers of *Burke's Peerage* began excluding the names of people with AIDS from their list of eligible marriage partners for British nobility.

MARCH The Food and Drug Administration licensed the ELISA (enzyme-linked immunosorbent assay) test, the first procedure to detect the presence of HTLV-3. ❑ For the first time, police recruits in Milwaukee were given sensitivity training on dealing with gays and lesbians. ❑ At WNBC in New York, a television crew refused to interview two AIDS patients until the PWAs agreed to pin on their own microphones and then dispose of them. ❑ Air Force Sergeant Leonard Matlovich, on the tenth anniversary of his challenge of the government's policy against gays in the military, launched a petition drive for a ban on sex in Washington, D.C., bathhouses.

APRIL Two thousand scientists and thirty nations were represented when the first International Conference on AIDS was held in Atlanta. ❑ John Quinn, San Francisco's Roman Catholic archbishop, was ordered to pay $2,250 to the Dick Kramer Gay Men's Chorale for breach of contract; Quinn had canceled a concert in a church facility because of the word "gay" in the group's name. ❑ Reflecting a nationwide trend, the Kirk and Nice Funeral Home of Philadelphia refused to handle the corpse of a person who died of AIDS. ❑ The owner and two employees of Chase's, a popular gay bar in Charlotte, North Carolina, were charged with the Christmas Eve burning of the Scorpio Lounge, a competing bar; four months later, a grand jury convicted them of arson.

MAY Mayor Ed Koch's ban on antigay discrimination in New York City hiring, overturned by one court, was reinstated on appeal. ❑ Under threat of a discrimination lawsuit by a gay advocacy group, the Big Brothers/Big Sisters organization of Sacramento reversed its practice of excluding gay men and lesbians as volunteers.

JUNE Longtime *Advocate* owner David B. Goodstein died of colon cancer in Los Angeles; the fifty-three-year-old publisher was succeeded by Orange County businessman Niles Merton. ❑ Massachusetts Governor Michael Dukakis earned the wrath of lesbian and gay activists when he ordered the removal of two children from the care of gay foster parents. ❑ Harvey Milk High School, an education alternative for lesbian and gay youth, opened in

New York City's Greenwich Village. ❑ The United Way of the Texas Gulf Coast refused a funding request made by the Houston KS/AIDS Foundation, stating that the Texas chapter of the nation's largest charitable group "would not fund AIDS-related projects." ❑ A meeting of fifty-three bathhouse owners from around the country unanimously agreed to promote "sexual responsibility" by distributing AIDS literature and condoms in their establishments. ❑ Gay's the Word, London's only gay bookstore, went to trial under an 1876 indecency law. ❑ Indonesian street transvestites were given government-sponsored training as hairdressers and dressmakers in an effort to keep them from becoming "tramps in their old age," according to Dr. Gatlot Hadisantoso, head of the Municipal Social Action Department.

JULY A Minnesota judge denied custody of Sharon Kowalski, a paralyzed lesbian, to her lover; Kowalski's father was named conservator instead. ❑ Entertainer Ann-Margret and Los Angeles Mayor Tom Bradley led the city's first "AIDS Walk" to raise funds for AIDS Project Los Angeles. ❑ Johnson and Johnson, makers of Band-Aid brand bandages, told the San Diego AIDS Project to "cease and desist" its campaign called BAN-AIDS. ❑ As many as three hundred New York City children were suffering with AIDS or AIDS-related symptoms, according to the city Department of Public Health. ❑ At a briefing on AIDS issues two U.S. Senators arranged for their Republican colleagues, only staffers—no Senators—showed up. ❑ An emergency quarantine was instituted in China after an Argentine tourist became the first known AIDS fatality in that country.

A pink granite monument was erected in May at Neuengamme, a former concentration camp in West Germany, as a memorial to gays killed by the Nazi regime.

AUGUST Dapsone, a drug used to treat leprosy, was reported successful in treating AIDS-related pnuemonia. ❑ The French National Assembly passed a bill protecting lesbians and gay men from discrimination in employment and access to services.

SEPTEMBER Elizabeth Taylor announced that she was the chairwoman of the newly formed American Foundation for AIDS Research. ❑ The Defense Department announced that it would test all military recruits for exposure to HTLV-3 and bar those who tested positive. ❑ After an announcement by the New York City Board of Education that it would allow children with AIDS to

Jack McCarty and Victor Amburgy, a gay couple from San Francisco's Castro district, were among hostages held for seventeen days by Lebanese Shiite terrorists.

AIDS Watch

Several important California scientists published a letter in the March 2 issue of The Lancet, *covering all the same major points of objection to the federally patented AIDS antibody test as those voiced by gay and lesbian groups. Though these groups remain, on the whole, outspoken and unfriendly to federal approval of such a test, the objections from critics in other quarters are more likely to reach federal ears.*

One of the most important points in question is exactly how a positive test result is to be confirmed. The U.S. Public Health Service had elected to have the test-positive blood run again through the original (ELISA) test for certainty. Many scientists would prefer that confirmation come from other, better tests—the Western blot and the immunofluorescent assay; federal policy calls for neither.

The California authors made their urgent point clear: Because in some cases up to six months pass between the time of infection and the moment of seroconversion—when antibodies against the AIDS virus appear—no test looking for those antibodies will find them in that six-month period. For this and other reasons, gay health groups are eager to remind all gay men that they should not donate blood, plasma, semen, or body organs until the situation is generally straightened out. Nor should they drop their guard when having sex.... This forbidding stance owes much to the general panic among physicians who treat AIDS. They do not wish to "mix the message," as they say. And that message is clear: Use extreme care in sexual encounters.

—From the Health column

attend school, nearly ten thousand parents in the city borough of Queens kept their children home in protest. ❑ West German prosecutor Manfred Bruns, one of the highest-ranking politicians in the country, shocked his colleagues when he came out in a newspaper interview. ❑ David Norris, a prominent Irish scholar, won an agreement from the European Court of Human Rights to hear his suit against Ireland's laws prohibiting gay sex; three years later, the court ordered Ireland to decriminalize homosexuality. ❑ The authors of *Lesbian Nuns: Breaking Silence* were evicted from a Dublin hotel during their European book tour; British tabloids headlined "Get Thee from the Nunnery."

OCTOBER Hollywood leading man Rock Hudson died in his Beverly Hills home, a year and a half after being diagnosed with AIDS. ❑ The AFL-CIO went on record opposing HTLV-3 testing of workers by employers. ❑ A survey of five hundred gay men and lesbians in Philadelphia found that 63 percent of the men and 39 percent of the women had suffered from antigay violence or threats of violence. ❑ Four female impersonators in Meridian, Mississippi, were arrested during an AIDS benefit and charged under an obscure city ordinance banning cross-dressing. ❑ In the first incident of its kind reported by *The Advocate*, a Florida judge ordered a man charged with a sex offense to take the HTLV-3 test. ❑ More than half the female prostitutes in Nairobi tested positive for AIDS antibodies.

NOVEMBER Attorney Marvin Mitchelson filed a $10 million claim against the estate of Rock Hudson on behalf of Hudson's ex-lover, Marc Christian, who tested negative for HTLV-3 but cited "extreme and constant fear"; five years later, a jury awarded Christian $21.75 million. ❑ Warning that the AIDS epidemic was "more dangerous than nuclear war," right-wing extremist Lyndon LaRouche launched a campaign against gay civil rights, using the slogan "Spread Panic, Not AIDS." ❑ The Mineshaft, a legendary backroom bar in lower Manhattan, was closed by order of New York City health authorities. ❑ A Denver company began selling an "AIDS-Free" identification card for $20. ❑ Four British Royal Air Force officers, charged by their government with operating a "homosexual spy ring," were found innocent of all counts by a London jury.

DECEMBER A University of California, San Francisco, study found that condoms definitely block transmission of HTLV-3. ❑ Gay activists demonstrated against the *New York Post* for homophobic news stories, editorials, and headlines that referred to gay bars as "AIDS dens." ❑ The Centers for Disease Control put funds for fourteen safe-sex education guides "on hold" because they were embarrassed about the sexually explicit content of the pamphlets. ❑ A group of excommunicated Mormons formed a new church to include a large pool of lesbian and gay ex-Mormons. ❑ The $750,000 estate of a New Orleans gay man whose handwritten will said "I leave all to Danny" was contested by three ex-lovers, each of whom was named Danny. ❑ An Atlanta man, infuriated by antigay and AIDS-related remarks made by fundamentalist preacher Jerry Falwell, programmed his computer to call Falwell's toll-free fund-raising line every thirty seconds for eight months to keep the line busy so no one could make donations. ❑ The International Gay Association held its annual European conference in Cabrera de Mar, Spain.

ROCK HUDSON

It had become a cliché among AIDS activists: The press and the politicians would pay attention to the AIDS epidemic only if it struck someone white, wealthy, and heterosexual. In 1985, the press and the politicians were compelled to take notice of AIDS because it had struck Rock Hudson—a Hollywood star who was white, wealthy, a symbol of robust heterosexuality, and a Republican to boot.

The rumor that he was gay had circulated for decades. The rumor that he had AIDS had been around for months by July, when his publicists and doctors addressed the issue of Hudson's health in a confusing week-long chain of announcements that had him suffering from liver cancer, being cured of AIDS, and, finally, being gravely ill with AIDS-related diseases. Suspicion had taken shape the previous fall, when Hudson appeared on the television series "Dynasty," looking jarringly aged and gaunt. Word had it that he had been in Paris to receive treatment for AIDS at the Pasteur Institute. But his representatives continued to deny all rumors of AIDS even after he was hospitalized in July and UPI reported that he had fatal liver cancer.

While television and print pushed for details of Hudson's illness and pursued every conceivable angle—exploring, for example, the question of whether Hudson's "Dynasty" costar might be infected—they walked gingerly around the issue of Hudson's sexuality, wondering in print and on the air how the star could have become infected with HIV. Finally, the *San Francisco Chronicle* put an end to this contrived speculation by publishing a story in which longtime friends of Hudson's talked about his gay life. Relieved of the burden of having to be the first to tackle the titillatingly taboo issue of celebrity homosexuality, other media outlets immediately picked up the story.

The press that had for four years ignored or downplayed the AIDS story suddenly couldn't get enough of it. Painful as the irony of this newfound interest was for gay and AIDS activists, they tried to capitalize on it, holding press conferences and giving interviews to publicize the number of AIDS diagnoses in the United States—which had just passed twelve thousand—the lack of resources in fighting the epidemic, and President Reagan's continuing silence on the subject of AIDS.

It would take Hudson's longtime friend Ronald Reagan another two years to address the issue of AIDS publicly. Still, the impact of the publicity surrounding Hudson's illness and death could not be overestimated. As Randy Shilts wrote in the opening statement of his history of the first five years of the AIDS epidemic, *And the Band Played On*, "By October 2, 1985, the morning Rock Hudson died, the word [AIDS] was familiar to almost every household in the Western world."

Four years later, *The Advocate*'s media critic, Stuart Byron, would comment: "Rock Hudson's illness and death marked the turning point in opening up funding for and public sympathy to the AIDS epidemic. How many lives might have been saved had there been...uncloseted stars and athletes testifying before Congressional committees and leading AIDS marches?"

The Rock Crisis

"Now the militant homosexuals have a celebrity disease of their own," wrote Wesley Pruden in the Washington Times.

Time *magazine reported, "Last week as Hudson lay gravely ill with AIDS in a Paris hospital, it became clear that throughout those years the all-American boy had another life, kept secret from his public: he was almost certainly homosexual." People magazine, in a cover story on Hudson, drew more pointed conclusions from Hudson's Aunt Lela: "Never would we think that he would be [gay]. He was just always such a good person."*

"Is it possible that Rock Hudson transmitted AIDS to actress Linda Evans during love scenes on 'Dynasty'?" asked TV anchorman Harold Greene. "I am not sick and I'm not frightened of anything," responded Evans, "Where do these stories get started?"

"It began like a cheap melodrama," wrote Los Angeles Times *commentator Howard Rosenberg. "Rock Hudson was near death; Rock Husdon wasn't near death. He had AIDS; he didn't have AIDS. Film at eleven. In a matter of weeks, TV had hopscotched from hostage crisis to Rock crisis." A spokeswoman in Paris claimed that Hudson had been cured of AIDS; one TV reporter speculated that since Hudson had gotten AIDS, now more than just gays and IV-drug users were at risk.*

"It was tacky," concluded Rosenberg. "The coverage has bordered on sensationalism....Everyone, movie star or not, is entitled to a certain amount of respect and consideration at a time of personal tragedy. But TV, in its vulturous scramble for competitive advantage, sees it differently."
—MATTHEW DANIELS

MALCOLM BOYD AND TROY PERRY

The voice of Christian fundamentalism in the past several years—especially on the issue of homosexuality—has led many to believe that gayness and religious experience are antithetical to each other. Nothing could be further from the truth, according to Troy Perry and Malcolm Boyd, probably the most articulate and outspoken openly gay religious leaders in the country. *The Advocate* spoke with the two men about a wide range of topics: sexuality, gay spirituality, and the closeted clergy.

Boyd is a writer-priest in residence at St. Augustine-by-the-Sea Episcopal Church in Santa Monica, California. He is the author of twenty books, including *Are You Running with Me, Jesus?, Take Off the Masks,* and *Look Back in Joy: Celebration of Gay Lovers.*

An ordained Protestant minister, Perry is the founder and spiritual leader of the Universal Fellowship of Metropolitan Community Churches, a group of more than two hundred predominantly gay congregations in nine countries. Here is what Perry and Boyd had to say:

Many gay people view organized religion as their main enemy, and they consider participation in religion as trading with the enemy.

PERRY: I don't look at organized religion as our enemy. In some ways, I think our long-term deliverance will come through organized religion. But we don't have to wait for religion to do anything for us. In 1968, when I founded Metropolitan Community Church, I decided that my days of waiting were over. There was no way I'd ever go back to the Church of God, the denomination that had excommunicated me because I was gay. The most important thing is that gay people not allow organized religion to steal their spirituality from them....I say up front, homosexuality is a gift from God. And I believe that with all my heart.

BOYD: In the past, I've felt very alienated from the church, and have been very critical of it. Yet I continue to function in the church, because I think you cannot change it from the outside. The enormous institution of the church exists; we must engage it in dialogue, work to change it.

Why don't gays who hold powerful positions in the various denominations come out?

BOYD: Many gays don't come out of the closet because they *themselves* still don't consider being gay as something good. They hate *themselves,* and as a result, they also hate other gay people. For many of these individuals, the hierarchy of the church is, in effect, Daddy. They're in a love-hate relationship with Daddy, yet they still want his acceptance.

What would happen to organized religion if the leaders somehow could identify every gay person in their denominations and felt compelled to boot them out?

PERRY: Of course, some of them get into religious work for the wrong reasons. Some want to punish themselves for their sexuality. I've talked to former monks who were in orders where they had to do penance because of their "evil sexual thoughts," and they loved it!

Sexuality and spirituality have often been pitted against each other by traditional religions. Are there links between the two, and do gays have a special contribution to make in understanding this?

PERRY: If I believe in the Incarnation, if I believe that Jesus was God in the flesh, then I have to believe that sex is part of creation—God invented it. It wasn't something that was an afterthought; it was totally integrated into the human personality—spirituality in sex works. God didn't give us our sex drive to say that we could never use it because we were different.... Jesus never married, we know that, but we don't know what his relationship was with other people. We do know that he had some very unusual, healthy, happy relationships with men *and* women.

BOYD: I find spirituality and sexuality inseparable. A holistic view claims that body, mind, and spirit are inextricably linked; disease is the denial of this. Holy Communion for me is found in very different ways—sometimes at a ritual at the altar in a church, a walk on the beach, sometimes a tender and intense sexual act that also combines love. An attempt to have spirituality without integrated sexuality tends to be arid, unreal, denies raw nakedness, therefore life, and is phony. A struggle in my life, of course, has been to integrate the two.

What meaning or purpose does God have for gay people? And how do you view your own role as a spiritual leader?

PERRY: I believe that God called me to prophecy, to say to the established church that God created everyone, and there's a place in the kingdom, not a second-class citizen's place, but a place for everyone. My message is the same as Isaiah's and some of the other prophets': "God always makes room for the exception." My sense of my calling is to give direction to gay people and say unto them: "Don't let people steal your spirituality, it's real, it's yours."

BOYD: I think we are a special people, that there is a holy purpose for us as gay people. Our vulnerability, tenderness, our yearning and longing, are very close to the heart of God. So, quite the opposite of being damned or excluded, I think we are very much like the beloved disciple John, with our head on the bosom of Christ.

What does God ask of anyone in the world? It is to risk, to grow constantly, to have the capacity for change. We all know how little justice has been done and how little mercy has been shown by so much of organized Christianity. I believe God wants us to express the divine will in this way. We are all called to be prophets.

What would you say to those thousands of gay people who feel wounded and rejected by organized religion?

BOYD: I've got open wounds; so does Troy. We're among the walking wounded.

PERRY: I consider myself a wounded healer, too—precisely. I hope I bring about healing by being myself, by talking to people. I would say to those millions of people who have difficulties with the church: Don't lose your birthright because someone has told you a lie. Don't let them do that.

BOYD: Neither Troy nor I am saying there is a specific answer of where in religion you should go. The point is: Quit being the walking wounded. Get healed. You've got to deal with your spirituality in order to deal with your sexuality, and for gay people this is a very important truth.

OPENING SPACE

EDITORIAL COMMENT BY DAVID B. GOODSTEIN

Among the most powerful of human longings is wanting to make a difference. Nevertheless, American society, in general, and gay society, in particular, do not acknowledge this need. Instead, we are urged to be consumers and to be victims waiting for some powerful bureaucracy to provide for us and/or rescue us.

Some, however, do acknowledge the need. I know many gays who have spent time—from a week to a year—working in community efforts; they quit because such work, gay or nongay, is frustratingly difficult. Community problems are not solved in one meeting or in one year.

Professor Ben Barber, in his book *Strong Democracy*, calls these problems of community the issues of the "public space." That Americans have allowed bureaucrats, experts, and elitists to take over the public space would amaze our Founding Fathers. As early as 1816, Thomas Jefferson worried about this in a letter to Joseph Cabell; he suggested that counties be broken into wards of about one hundred families. These groups would then be like little republics, and *every* citizen would have to be involved in and responsible for the public space. Jefferson was clear that unless individual citizens retained responsibility for the public space, an aristocratic elite would take over; his contemporaries believed that Americans would never let that happen.

As a citizen, each of us has a variety of public spaces. There are the obvious ones—our neighborhood, town, state, and nation. There is the one where we work. There may be one based on our religion or ethnic background. And for most of the readers of this magazine, there is a gay public space.

In the gay public space, issues of magnitude are decided: life and death as it pertains to AIDS, other sexually transmitted diseases, and alcohol and drug abuse; the right to privacy in our bedrooms, including the assurance that what we do there does not cause us to lose jobs, housing, credit, etc.; respect and acknowledgment of our significant relationships; care for our aged and support for our young; culture; and more.

Democracy is not about voting; it is about self-government. Self-government requires citizens to come together for civil conversation to solve the problems of the public spaces. The conversations can and do get heated and emotional; but it is up to the citizens to make sure they remain civil. My experience of hundreds of such conversations, gay and nongay, is that when democracy is operating, the issue is not majority rule. Rather it is likely that almost 100 percent of the participants will agree on a solution to a problem. Furthermore, if the first solution doesn't work, those involved can correct their mistake and try another solution. Any solution they attempt will be better than one imposed on them.

Traditionally only citizens have had the right to speak in the public forum. Television cannot replace the public forum, though it has gone further to do so than all the tyrants in history. In the forum *many* voices talk to and hear *many* other voices. Television is *one* voice talking to *many*. You must stop giving your power away to television and to elites of any persuasion, and get your gay voice and ears to the public forums that matter to you. There are hundreds of public spaces for every American; there are dozens of gay ones. If they are weak and dominated by bar culture or silliness, then take them over.

What is needed and wanted for the gay community is for its citizens to get involved, and stay involved, in its public spaces.

ARMISTEAD MAUPIN'S DESIGN FOR LIVING

One of the most widely quoted articles The Advocate *ever published was this essay by Armistead Maupin, outspoken champion of gay rights and best-selling author of the* Tales of the City *series.*

Several months ago my friend Timothy Leary gave me some advice about my upcoming national book tour.

"Before you go," he suggested, "figure out exactly what you want to say, and don't be embarrassed to say it over and over again. It may be the hundredth time you've said it, but it's the first time they've heard it, so make sure you sound like you mean it. The hundredth time is just as important as the first." He was so right.

Three weeks and fifteen cities later, I had summoned up the same answers so often that I felt like a cross between Dr. Ruth Westheimer and the audio-animatronics Abe Lincoln at Disneyland. Most of the questions were about my books ("When will Mouse find a lover?" and "Didn't you kill Connie twice?" were two of the biggies), but a surprising number of them cast me in the role of Coming-Out Consultant, a keeper of the mysteries of happy Homohood.

Remembering Tim's suggestion, I surveyed my most frequent responses and discovered the following blueprint for a more fulfilling life. Read it once, and I promise I won't bring it up again:

1. Stop begging for acceptance. Homosexuality is still anathema to most people in this country—even to many homosexuals. If you camp out on the doorstep of society waiting for "the climate" to change, you'll be there until Joan Rivers registers Democratic.

Your job is to accept yourself—joyfully and with no apologies—and get on with the adventure of your life.

2. Don't run away from straight people. They need variety in their lives just as much as you do, and you'll forfeit the heady experience of feeling exotic if you limit yourself to the company of your own kind.

Furthermore, you have plenty to teach your straight friends about tolerance and humor and the comfortable enjoyment of their own sexuality. (Judging from "Donahue," many of them have only now begun to learn about foreplay; we, on the other hand, have entire resorts built around the practice.)

Besides, it's time you stopped thinking of heterosexuals as the enemy. It's both convenient and comforting to bemoan the cardboard villainy of Jerry Falwell and friends, but the real culprits in this melodrama are just as queer as you are. They sleep with you by night and conspire to keep you invisible by day. They are studio chiefs and bank presidents and talk-show hosts, and they don't give a damn about your oppression because they've got their piece of the pie, and they got it by living a lie.

3. Refuse to cooperate in the lie. It is not your responsibility to "be discreet" for the sake of people who are still ashamed of their own natures. And don't tell me about "job security." Nobody's job will ever be safe until the general public is permitted to recognize the full scope of our homosexual population.

Does that include the teachers? You bet it does. Have you forgotten already how much it hurt to be fourteen and gay and scared to death of it? Doesn't it gall you just a little that your "discreet" lesbian social-studies teacher went home every day to her lover and her cats and her Ann Bannon novels without once giving you even a clue that there was hope for your own future?

What earthly good is your discretion, when teenagers are still being murdered for the crime of effeminacy? I know, I know—you have a right to keep your private life private. Well, you do that, my friend—but don't expect the world not to notice what you're really saying about yourself. And about the rest of us.

Lighten up, Lucille. There's help on the way.

4. Stir up some shit now and then. Last spring I wrote a commentary for the *Los Angeles Times* on the subject of television's shoddy treatment of homosexuality. The piece originally contained a sentence to the effect that "it's high time the public found out there are just as many homosexuals who resemble Richard Chamberlain as there are who resemble Richard Simmons."

The editor cut it. When I asked him why, he said: "Because it's libelous, that's why." To which I replied: "In the first place, I'm not saying that Richard Chamberlain is gay; I'm simply saying there are plenty of gay men who resemble him. In the second place, even if I were saying that Richard Chamberlain is gay, it wouldn't be a libelous remark, because I'm gay myself and I don't say those things with malice. I don't accuse anyone of being gay; I state it as a matter of fact or opinion." When the new city of West Hollywood assembled its council last month, the Associated Press identified the three openly gay members as "admitted homosexuals." Admitted, get it? Fifteen years after the Stonewall Rebellion, the wire service wants to make it perfectly clear that homosexuality is still a dirty little secret that requires full confession before it can be mentioned at all.

If you don't raise some hell, that isn't going to change.

5. Don't sell your soul to the gay commercial culture. Well, go ahead, if you insist, but you'd better be prepared to accept the butt plug as the cornerstone of Western civilization.

I am dumbfounded by the number of bright and beautiful men out there who submerge themselves completely in the quagmire of gay ghetto life, then wonder why their lives seem loveless and predictable.

What the hell did they expect?

If you have no more imagination than to swap one schlock-heavy "lifestyle" for another, you haven't learned a goddamn thing from the gay experience. I'm not talking about sex here; I'm talking about old-fashioned bad taste.

No, Virginia, we *don't* all have good taste. We are just as susceptible to the pitfalls of tackiness as everyone else in the world. Your pissing and moaning about the shallowness of other faggots falls on unsympathetic ears when you're wearing a T-shirt that says THIS FACE SEATS FIVE.

Not long ago I sat transfixed before my TV screen while an earnest young man told a gay cable announcer about his dream of becoming Mr. Leather something-or-other. He was seeking the title, he said, "in order to serve the community and help humanity." He wore tit rings and a codpiece and a rather fetching little cross-your-heart harness, but he sounded for all the world like a Junior Miss contestant from Modesto.

If our fledgling culture fails us, it will be because we forgot how to question it, forgot how to laugh at it in the very same way we laugh at Tupperware and Velveeta and the Veterans of Foreign Wars.

6. Stop insulting the people who love you by assuming they don't know you're gay. When I began my book tour, a publicist in New York implored me to leave his name out of it, because "my family doesn't know about my…uh, lifestyle."

Maybe not, but they must be the dumbest bunch this side of Westchester County; I could tell he was gay *over the telephone.* When my own father learned of my homosexuality (he read about it in *Newsweek*), he told me he'd suspected as much since I'd been a teenager. I could've made life a lot easier for both of us if I'd had the guts to say what was on my mind.

7. Learn to feel mortal. If AIDS hasn't reminded you that your days are numbered—and always have been—then stop for a moment and remind yourself. Your days are numbered, babycakes. Are you living them for yourself and the people you love, or are you living them for the people you fear?

I can't help thinking of a neighbor of mine, a dutiful government employee who kept up appearances for years and years, kept them up until the day he died, in fact—of a heart attack, in the back row of an all-male fuck-film house.

Appearances don't count for squat when they stick you in the ground (all right, or scatter you to the winds), so why should you waste a single moment of your life seeming to be something you don't want to be?

Lord, that's so simple. If you hate your job, quit it. If your friends are tedious, go out and find new ones. You are queer, you lucky fool, and that makes you one of life's buccaneers, free from the clutter of two thousand years of Judaeo-Christian sermonizing. Stop feeling sorry for yourself and start hoisting your sails. You haven't a moment to lose.

THEATER: SPOTLIGHT ON AIDS

More than television or film, the stage has provided a forum for expressing gay concerns. Unfortunately, the bulk of gay theater has remained underground, never reaching a mainstream audience. But with the mounting crisis of AIDS, the need of gay people to be heard—and the willingness of nongay people to listen—have both increased. Playwrights and producers, from Honolulu to New York City, are now responding with important new works dealing with the epidemic. The tragedy of AIDS, dramatically speaking, is prompting gay theater to a new level of maturity.

"I want to get the message of what's happening to us out to the world," says Larry Kramer, whose new play, *The Normal Heart*, debuted at New York's Public Theater in March. "The play is both an attempt to get the message across and an attempt to dramatize how almost everything seemed calculated in advance to prevent anything from happening: It happened to gay people; the community is not organized politically; we're in a city where the mayor doesn't want to help us because he's afraid he'll be perceived as being gay; the medical community itself doesn't want to help."

The writer initially intended *The Normal Heart* to be a novel. But after seeing a number of plays in London, he decided to express his message theatrically. "I realized you could deal with political issues in a theatrical way," he says. "Political theater has succeeded in other countries for centuries. Americans don't like to be criticized, and they don't like to think things can be made better—otherwise they would never have elected Ronald Reagan."

Although William M. Hoffman admits there are "implicit political statements involved" in *As Is,* his new drama about AIDS, which opened in February at New York's Circle Repertory Company, he's deliberately avoided "the politics of it." Says the playwright, "I'm much more concerned with what it's like to have AIDS: the reactions of the people around the person and how people behave.

"I didn't write a play about a disease; I wrote a play about people," Hoffman explains. "*As Is* is a play about *acceptance*—acceptance of having a a dangerous disease, acceptance of death, acceptance of living. The impulse when I write a play is internal—I'm working things out for myself. If it were going to be educational, I'd have written a pamphlet."

"There are a lot of ways to make people aware," says Dr. Marshall Kreuter, "and art is one of them." Kreuter, director of the Division of Health Education at Atlanta's Centers for Disease Control, is referring to Rebecca Ranson's play *Warren,* which is being produced in Honolulu after two successful runs in Atlanta. "*Warren* should be helpful in getting people aware of, and sensitive to, a variety of psychosocial issues related to the AIDS dilemma," states Kreuter. "We're very intrigued by the potential educational benefits of using her play."

> "The Normal Heart contains passage after passage of impassioned writing, elegantly literate and emotionally raw; strung one after the other, however, they bombard rather than persuade. Too many scenes center on an explosive confrontation; they leave us exhausted....Larry Kramer vehemently retells his trials—protagonist [and alter ego] Ned Weeks tirelessly fights inertia, denial, and closeting. But though there are occasions when screaming insistence is what is needed, perhaps a play isn't one of them. It can discourage an audience, rather than invite their involvement."
>
> —MARCIA PALLY, *REVIEWING* THE NORMAL HEART

> "*I*f it hadn't been for Rock Hudson, An Early Frost [an NBC movie about a young man with AIDS coming out to his family] would never have been done. But he created such a worldwide impact because he was so loved and adored…that I believe most people are taking a different view of the homosexual impact and of the disease."
>
> —ACTRESS SYLVIA SYDNEY

Sound and fury: scenes from William M. Hoffman's *As Is* (*above*) and Larry Kramer's *The Normal Heart* (*below*).

Ranson wrote *Warren,* she says, "partially as education, yes, but more as a natural response to a friend's death. In places other than Los Angeles or San Francisco or New York, lots of the men I run into say, 'That's one of *those* cities' diseases; it doesn't happen here.' The play entertains the notion that AIDS happens everywhere, and of course it does." Robert Chesley's controversial *Night Sweat* has been labeled "an AIDS play," even though Terry Helbing, artistic director of New York's Meridian Theater, where *Night Sweat* was recently produced, says Chesley "would object to it being called an AIDS play. He thinks it's about a lot of other stuff too—like gay capitalism and its effect on the health of the community. People either really loved it or hated it." According to Chesley, "Gay theater has not, by and large, developed a theatrically adventurous audience, an audience that enjoys being confronted by unpleasant issues. For the most part, the plays have been—properly—supportive. I'm not saying that gay theater is 'bad,' but it has resulted in an audience that enjoys being coddled. *Night Sweat* demands that the audience think about the many issues it raises."

Portland, Oregon, is one of the many cities to host Jeff Hagedorn's *One,* a thirty-minute monologue depicting a man dying of AIDS. Originally produced in Chicago in 1983, *One,* written as a response to the irrational fear surrounding AIDS, has since been staged in San Antonio, Los Angeles, Schenectady, Milwaukee, New Orleans, and Kansas City. Hagedorn says, "The point of *One* is to present an average, normal human being who happens to have this disease, and make you like him." "Using the term AIDS is very off-putting to some people," says Bill Oxendine-Santana, whose comedy about contemporary gay life, *Pumps,* is finding a supportive audience in Los Angeles. "So we took out specific references to the word, replacing it with 'this new disease' or 'the gay disease.' Some people feel it's wrong to call it 'the gay disease,' but in terms of the general public, the AIDS question is still pointing a finger at gays. The objections have been from gay people who say I shouldn't be writing negative stuff about gay people. But I think there's danger in having everything come out like *Making Love*—all so prettied up."

Chuck Solomon, director of San Francisco's Theater Rhinoceros, won't consider "a contemporary gay play which propagates old values and dangerous practices unless there's some qualification. It's something I look for in every new gay play I read: How does it deal with the horror of everyday life?" Solomon says that 90 percent of the scripts received by the theater "have references to AIDS—it doesn't matter where in the country they're from.

"When I read a contemporary gay play that doesn't refer to the AIDS crisis, I have a tendency to trivialize it, which I shouldn't," he says. "Even though, for me, AIDS is the *only* issue there is, our audience doesn't want to see six new AIDS plays." Solomon's audience, however, apparently does want to see *The AIDS Show* (Artists Involved with Death and Survival). Currently in an extended run, the play consists of twenty-four segments that "[try] to cover the health crisis from as many different perspectives as possible," the director explains.

"The medium of theater is very good at personalizing a general problem," concludes Helbing. "You can't have somebody get on stage and recite dry facts about AIDS—that's not very dramatic. But if you make it personal, people might learn the personal one-to-one effect of AIDS, rather than just a statistic."

—MICHAEL KEARNS

THE **ADVOCATE**
$2.50 • MARCH 18, 1986 • THE NATIONAL GAY NEWSMAGAZINE • ISSUE 444

Lily!

Tomlin Proves There *Is* Intelligent Life in the Universe

Success Story: Michigan Gay Rights Organization

THE **ADVOCATE**
$2.50 • JUNE 24, 1986 • THE NATIONAL GAY NEWSMAGAZINE • ISSUE 449

GAY DRUG ABUSE

- Why We're More Susceptible
- Overcoming Bad Habits
- The AIDS Connection

Special Travel Guide: **AMAZING AMSTERDAM!**

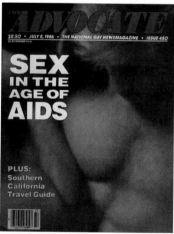

THE **ADVOCATE**
$2.50 • JULY 8, 1986 • THE NATIONAL GAY NEWSMAGAZINE • ISSUE 450

SEX IN THE AGE OF AIDS

PLUS: Southern California Travel Guide

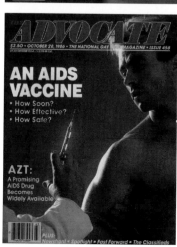

THE **ADVOCATE**
$2.50 • OCTOBER 28, 1986 • THE NATIONAL GAY NEWSMAGAZINE • ISSUE 458

AN AIDS VACCINE

- How Soon?
- How Effective?
- How Safe?

AZT: A Promising AIDS Drug Becomes Widely Available

PLUS: Newsbrush • Spotlight • Fast Forward • The Classifieds

SPIRIT AND THE FLESH

1986 *in basements/attics/alleyways/and tents/fugitive slaves/pets and griots/seminoles from Singhay/vodun queens/all in drag,/stumbling over discarded fetuses/hitching/dodging state troopers behind shades/searching for safe houses/uptight but cool:/the tam/the aviator frame/the propped cigarette/and singing:/'I was born in Georgia./My ways are underground./If you mistreat me,/I'll hunt you like a hound.'/Lack of money produces such atavism.*

These lines are from a poem called "living as a lesbian underground: a futuristic fantasy" and express for me the anxiety of this year. They are from my second collection, *Living as a Lesbian*, released in 1986. Midway into Ronald Reagan's second term, New York City passes a gay-rights bill while Chicago defeats one. Unprotected anal sex is still the number-one cause of HIV transmission in the United States. Jerry Falwell forms the Liberty Foundation to garner support for conservatives and to take on any "family form" that isn't "moral or traditional." The Supreme Court upholds Georgia's sodomy law in *Bowers v. Hardwick*. "It is the very act of homosexual sodomy that epitomizes moral delinquincy," writes Georgia's attorney general, Michael Bowers, in his brief to the court. Citing the Bible, the court agrees, pushing us further underground.

Travel light/and don't wait til morning./Quadafi is only a fleeting distraction/radiating the 3rd world with his/macho, mercurial, maligned smile./A scapegoat./Uptight but cool./The terror is here somewhere/in Detroit.

In Kalamazoo, Michigan, a gay man named Harry Wayne Watson is bludgeoned to death, his face so misshapen that he is unrecognizable at first. His seventeen-year-old murderer, Terry Kerry, is acquitted. Another judge, in Chicago, orders a divorced gay man to take the HTLV-3 antibody test before his child can visit. "Instead of calling us queer…now they have something that's more legitimate-appearing to hide behind," says Roberta Achtenberg, directing attorney for the San Francisco–based Lesbian Rights Project, in *The Advocate*. "AIDS provides a veil for basic homophobia."

In an acerbic opinion piece, critic Michael Bronski responds to the mounting conservative trends of the AIDS era: "Monogamy, dating, and romance are not solutions....They are culturally dictated and enforced illusions of safety that have resurfaced in response not only to AIDS but to the freedom brought by fifteen years of gay liberation.... Gay men have always been on the cutting edge of sexual and personal freedoms." A few months later, New York writer and cofounder of the Gay and Lesbian Alliance Against Defamation Marcia Pally similarly encourages a liberated approach to sexuality: "It's in the women's interest, you might say, to unhitch the pleasures of objectification from danger and discrimination...to keep objectification in the realm of play. But to keep it." Still the conservative pressure keeps growing.

And...don't sleep before midnight./And don't fret over the Poles./We in the same fix/with the Pope's position on lust/and family protection/a storefront on every corner/in Manhattan.

After eighteen months of hearings, deliberations, and controversy, the Meese Commission releases the 1,960-page *Final Report of the Attorney General's Commission on Pornography.* "Reading it is about as much fun as listening to the Mormon Tabernacle Choir," writes *Advocate* columnist Pat Califia. She pronounces the report "the harbinger of the new sexual McCarthyism."

Don't be fool, now, cool./Imperialism by any other name/is imperialism./Even Vietnam was finally over./It's all the same—/a-rabs, gooks, wogs, queers—/a nigger by any other name...

For the first time since Stonewall, lesbians and gay men of color are asserting their contributions to the overall movement, issuing a clarion call that is in all of our best interests to solve the problems posed by monocultural leadership. In a rare interview with *The Advocate,* legendary author James Baldwin seems evasive when answering the question of what is the most important issue facing gay people in 1986. "It's not important to be gay," says Baldwin, "or important to be white...or important to be black. What's important is to be *you.*" Still, Baldwin's public persona as a black and marvelous homosexual is, I am certain, one of the most important factors in the choices of many gay and lesbian writers—black and white—to live as queers.

So...don't be taken in your sleep now./Call your assailant's name now./Leave the building empty/the doors unlocked/and raise the windows high/when they pass by./Leave signs of struggle./Leave signs of triumph./And leave signs.

Issues of race, class, and ethnicity are placed at the top of the agendas of all the women's organizations I find myself a part of in 1986. Anti-Semitism in the lesbian community is challenged in writings by Elly Bulkin, Irena Klepfisz, Melanie Kaye/Kantrowitz, Adrienne Rich, and Evelyn Torton Beck. All of us—no matter what our backgrounds—are expected to examine our heritage of prejudice, our class positions, and the ways in which we act out our privilege. Being "out" is not enough. One's antiheterosexist practice needs to be defined in relationship to one's diverse anti-oppression stances. Lesbian leadership at all levels is becoming visible in the pursuit of multicultural leadership and community.

My second book is published during a watershed year for lesbian poets. Audre Lorde publishes her seventh book of poems, *Our Dead Behind Us.* Marilyn Hacker's multipart sonnet sequence of a failed lesbian love relationship, *Love, Death, and the Changing of the Seasons,* stuns queer and straight readers alike. And Joan Larkin's long silence about alcohol and her hard-won recovery shatters like the family crystal in *A Long Sound.* We leave signs of struggle. We leave signs of triumph.
                                                    —CHERYL CLARKE

"If I can help make a dent by showing that a sex therapist who's old-fashioned and square like me can talk about homosexuality, accepting that people live in homosexual relationships, without my thinking, 'Oh my gosh, what is happening?' then I'm doing some good."
—SEXOLOGIST DR. RUTH WESTHEIMER

"The cop stood there for like...thirty-five seconds while I was engaged in mutual oral sex. When I looked up and realized he was standing there, he then *identified* himself. He said I was under arrest for sodomy. I said, 'What are you doing in my bedroom?'"
—MICHAEL HARDWICK,
SUPREME COURT PETITIONER

T I M E L I N E

Lesbian drill sergeant **Miriam Ben-Shalom** won a ten-year battle with the U.S. Army Reserves when a court ordered her reinstatement in February.

In an action that sent shock waves through gay America, the Supreme Court upheld the Georgia sodomy law, ruling in *Bowers v. Hardwick* that gay people have no constitutional right to engage in consensual sex in private.

JANUARY   The Texas Board of Health gave tentative approval to add AIDS to the list of the state's diseases requiring quarantine; the idea was eventually dropped. ❑ Michigan lesbians held the fourth in a series of blood drives organized to show support for gay men. ❑ Five persons in Singapore who tested positive for HIV antibodies were put under "close surveillance."

FEBRUARY   The Reagan Administration proposed to screen out immigrants who test positive for HIV antibodies. ❑ Following a bitter debate in which one legislator referred to two others as "queer-lovers," the Idaho House of Representatives acted to prohibit school employees from teaching that "homosexuality is a normal or acceptable form of behavior"; the bill died in the State Senate a few months later. ❑ James Miller, Ronald Reagan's budget director, told a U.S. Senate panel that care for AIDS patients should be a "state and local concern," not a federal one. ❑ Murteza Elgin, a popular male movie star in Turkey, was trumpeted in that country's tabloids as "Turkey's first AIDS case."

MARCH   The U.S. Justice Department announced a plan to scuttle its policy of asking prospective prosecutors whether they are gay. ❑ A bill designed to control the spread of AIDS by providing for contact tracing, reporting of antibody status, and possible quarantine became law in Colorado; soon after, it was overturned in court. ❑ A gay firefighter was awarded $57,000 by a Spokane, Washington, jury that agreed that his privacy was invaded when coworkers played back a telephone conversation revealing his homosexuality. ❑ Gay San Franciscans called for a boycott of the Public Broadcasting Service after it paid a gay black street hustler to discuss his plight as a prostitute with AIDS for the television show "Frontline." ❑ The Beluga Swim Club of Minneapolis, made up of fourteen lesbian and gay male swimmers, was evicted from the pool it used after a club member left a copy of *The Advocate* in the locker room.

APRIL   Gay leaders met with Surgeon General C. Everett Koop for the first time in order to brief him on AIDS issues. ❑ Dean Ludwig Bee, a West Virginia man, was acquitted of murder in the Ritchie County Court after he testified that he had gone home with a gay man, fallen asleep, and awakened to find the gay man licking condiments off his body; apparently, Bee was so disgusted that he stabbed him to death.

MAY   AIDS officially became the leading killer in New York City of men aged thirty to forty-four and of women aged twenty-five to twenty-nine. ❑ "Human immunodeficiency virus" (HIV) was selected by the International Committee for the Taxonomy of Viruses as the new name for the retrovirus believed to cause AIDS. ❑ The mayor of Anchorage withdrew his support for legal employment protection for gays, saying that AIDS had turned gay rights into a health issue. ❑ A California insurance firm that sought to identify applicants who might have AIDS was hit with an $11 million lawsuit filed by the National Gay Rights Advocates; the company later settled out of court. ❑ Two British men who kissed each other good night at a bus stop were arrested for "shocking public behaviour" and fined $150 each. ❑ A Catholic priest in Turin, Italy, who refused to conduct a church service for a dead gay man was dragged from his office by more than two hundred angry mourners and forced to say a blessing over the man's coffin.

JUNE   The federal government announced awards of $100 million in a five-year program to evaluate promising AIDS drugs. ❏ Citing his own antigay bias, a Cook County, Illinois, judge removed himself from hearing a custody case involving a gay father. ❏ A sailor who refused to take the HIV antibody test was court-martialed. ❏ The attorney general of Arkansas chastised a telephone manufacturer who offered to sell disposable phones to hospitals as a way to reduce the spread of AIDS. ❏ Death squads rampaged through Cali, Colombia, killing more than 450 beggars and homosexuals.

JULY   Closeted homosexual Manhattan lawyer Roy Cohn, infamous as an anti-communist and antigay crusader, died of AIDS. ❏ Gay Californians again faced legislative attack when political extremist Lyndon LaRouche introduced a voter initiative designed to quarantine people with AIDS and bar from certain jobs even those suspected of carrying HIV; Proposition 64, the so-called LaRouche Initiative, was defeated by a wide margin in November. ❏ The police department of Atlanta decided to allow openly gay people to join the force. ❏ Vandals tossed bricks through the windows of Giovanni's Room, a lesbian and gay bookstore in Philadelphia. ❏ Survivors of Dachau, the infamous Nazi concentration camp, rejected a marble marker commemorating gay victims of the Holocaust.

AUGUST   Monnie Callan, a New York social worker, conducted the first study on AIDS and women, examining sixty-four HIV-positive women with children to determine the psychological effects of seropositivity on the women's emotional well-being. ❏ Professional football player Jerry Smith, a retired tight end for the Washington Redskins, disclosed that he had AIDS; he died two months

Actress Elizabeth Taylor, testifying before a Senate appropriations subcommittee in May, called for a "tenfold expansion" in AIDS funding.

Heshy Friedman, along with other foes of gay rights, demonstrated outside New York City Hall during the City Council's vote in March on the gay-rights bill. After fifteen years of failure, the bill, which banned discrimination against lesbians and gays in employment and housing, passed by a large margin.

later. ❏ In a case arising from the arrests of forty-two men at a highway rest stop near Lansing, a Michigan state judge upheld the constitutionality of using video surveillance cameras. ❏ An animal-rights group accused the University of Mississippi Medical Center of conducting experiments in which cats were administered electric shocks in an attempt to find a "cure" for homosexuality.

SEPTEMBER   The U.S. Supreme Court rejected a petition to rehear *Bowers v. Hardwick*. ❏ Hoping to demonstrate the economic clout of the gay community, several businesses in the Midwest launched a campaign to stamp the words "Gay Money" on bills spent by their customers. ❏ A new study published in the *Archives of General Psychiatry* found that gay men are five times more likely than straight men to have a gay brother. ❏ California state police arrested eight

GOD Sent AIDS TO PUNISH GAYS. DUMP THE SODOMITE RIGHTS

POLICE LINE POLICE

AIDS WATCH

Researchers conducting a study of more than seven hundred gay men in Vancouver, British Columbia, revealed in January that oral sex appears to play an insignificant role in the transmission of the AIDS virus....The researchers based their conclusions on a selection of twenty-one men who had met the following criteria at the onset of the study: They had not engaged in receptive anal intercourse or receptive fisting for the previous year and had tested negative for the AIDS antibody. The men did engage in varying frequencies of oral sex: sucking; being sucked; swallowing semen; and rimming. Fifteen men reported having more than five partners in the previous year; eight reported having more than twenty partners during the same period. Several of the men made sexual contacts in bathhouses.

Only one of the twenty-one men seroconverted—that is, tested positive for the AIDS antibody after originally testing negative. He reported only rare occasions of being fucked. Thus, all the other men did not have evidence of being infected with the AIDS virus after somewhat frequent oral sexual contacts, some of them in bathhouses. In a comparison study, thirty-six of ninety-nine seronegative men who practiced anal sex in more than 25 percent of their sexual contacts seroconverted during the same period of time.

The study confirms what was already known: Receptive anal sex (without the use of condoms) with many partners presents the highest risk for sexual transmission of the AIDS virus. The data strongly suggest that oral sex presents a lower risk for exposure.

—MICHAEL HELQUIST

protesters, three of whom had AIDS, when they blocked the office of Governor George Deukmejian over his veto of a bill protecting people with AIDS from discrimination. ❏ British Education Secretary Kenneth Baker denounced a sex education book as "homosexual propaganda" and asked a London school board to ban it from school libraries. ❏ New Zealand decriminalized homosexual activity and set the age of consent for gays at sixteen, the same as for heterosexuals.

OCTOBER Pope John Paul II issued a letter calling gay people "intrinsically disordered" and maintaining that homosexuality can never be reconciled with church doctrine. ❏ In a move thought to specifically target gays, U.S. Attorney General Edwin Meese announced a redoubling of federal efforts to "pursue and prosecute with a vengeance" those selling material deemed obscene. ❏ About a hundred demonstrators protested New York City's failure to deal with the growing number of homeless persons with AIDS. ❏ Coretta Scott King, the widow of Dr. Martin Luther King, Jr., publicly proclaimed her "solidarity with the gay and lesbian community," and blasted the U.S. Supreme Court decision in *Bowers v. Hardwick.*❏ A Montreal health department study showed that being bitten or scratched by a person infected with HIV poses little risk of contracting the virus. ❏ Prostitutes at the second International Whores Convention in Brussels, Belgium, called for worldwide AIDS education programs that encourage the use of condoms.

NOVEMBER *The Wall Street Journal* began using the word "gay" instead of "homosexual" in its headlines and articles. ❏ Attorneys for Delta Airlines argued that the company should be allowed to pay less in damages for the life of a gay man than for that of a heterosexual killed in a crash the previous August; the lawyers claimed that the gay man might have contracted AIDS and thus lived a shorter life than a straight man. The airline later dropped this argument and apologized. ❏ A pink triangle with the message "Homophobia Served Here" was affixed to the front of a gay-unfriendly restaurant in Minneapolis by a militant gay group called CHRIST (Concerned Homosexuals Rising in Strength and Tenacity). ❏ The director of a Reading, Pennsylvania, center purporting to help gays go heterosexual resigned amid charges that he had had sex with many of the men and boys who came to the center.

DECEMBER In the largest settlement in gay litigation history, the Pacific Bell Telephone Company established a $3 million fund to compensate individuals against whom the phone company had discriminated solely because of their sexual orientation. ❏ Three gay men filed a discrimination suit against a grocery store—the Boys Market in Marina del Rey, California—after a voice on the store's broadcast system called out, "Faggots, get out of the market and don't come back"; the market apologized the following June. ❏ An Episcopal church in Colorado announced that it would open the first housing complex exclusively for people with AIDS. ❏ The Roman Catholic Archdiocese of Los Angeles withdrew from an AIDS education program targeted at Latino parishioners because the program discussed condoms as an effective method for prevention of the disease. ❏ Fred Schoonmaker, a gay restaurateur, gained brief attention with his plan to locate a gay commune, "Stonewall Park," in the ghost town of Rhyolite, Nevada.

JAMES BALDWIN

He sits in the bar drinking Johnnie Walker Black Label Scotch whiskey on the rocks, his hands moving to shape the air as he speaks—a habit both in public lectures and in private conversation—and his large eyes open wide, cutting from left to right, serving almost to punctuate his speech.

James Baldwin, author of the controversial *The Fire Next Time*, one of the 1960s' more troubling books for American society, as well as a host of books about the black experience in America (*Go Tell It on the Mountain, Notes of a Native Son, Tell Me How Long the Train's Been Gone, Nobody Knows My Name*) and several works about homosexual love (*Giovanni's Room, Another Country*), is tired: He has just negotiated his way through several commuter flights to give a lecture at a small Virginia college. He faces several more such flights early the next morning and then the long haul to Paris, his home—where he will be awarded the Legion of Honor.

A short time before, he discussed his views on contemporary issues before an audience of five hundred, bringing the house to laughter and applause at one point when a young woman asked, "Is there a difference between black literature and white literature, or is literature just literature?"

"Well, it's not *just* literature!" Baldwin fired back with a grin. "Literature forces one to see that he is related—by various ways—to many other human beings."

For Baldwin at sixty-one, an insistence that America reread and truly comprehend its own history is a recurring theme—whether he is talking about politics, economics, religion, race, or sex. To him, the problems—and probably their solutions—are all interwoven, irrevocably linked.

"We are living," he says, "through the end of a language, we are living through the end of a myth, we are living through the end of a legend. Now, I know that while we sense that, we don't quite know what to do about it. In short, we are living through the end of the concept of color—as far as I'm concerned, not a moment too soon."

"The concept of color," in Baldwin's view, is the myth of white, European-based supremacy; that this myth is coming to an end in our time is also, for him, linked to America's obsession with the perceived threat of homosexuality.

"Americans' concern with homosexuality is all a great waste of time," he points out. "It won't change anything. It can't change *you*." The "threat" posed by the homosexual, he feels, is similar to that posed by the black man to a culture based on what Baldwin terms the myth of white supremacy: "It's the idea of heroes. Certainly, it's all bound up in the idea of eliminating other races' sexual threat—the Indian brave, the Negro stud or buck. The myth of the stud is what it's all about—the frontiersman, the pathfinder. When the others are suppressed, it lends to the myth of white supremacy."

There's more than just the hero myth at stake, notes Baldwin. The idea of perceived sexual threats from a minority is a challenge to the masculine image, the "myths" American culture has about manliness. "Let's face it," says Baldwin, "I never represented much of a sexual threat to anyone. Yet I was with this

white girl one time in New York years ago, and this white sailor came in and started laying shit on me because I had a white girlfriend—or he thought I did, anyway. And you see, I wasn't even a threat, but he perceived it that way, anyway."

One of Baldwin's least-known works is a small volume of film criticism published in 1976, *The Devil Finds Work*. In it, he details his reactions to a wide variety of Hollywood films, some with racial themes, others because of their personal meaning for him. In that book, Baldwin discussed at some length two actresses many consider "gay icons"—Joan Crawford and Bette Davis. But Baldwin's reaction to those screen figures was quite different from that of the many gays who see hard but glamorous, strong-willed women.

"With Joan Crawford, seeing her as I did when I was just a child, she was this white lady…or at least she was supposed to be this glamorous white lady," states Baldwin. "But Joan Crawford's air was one of total hostility; so, even as a child, I sensed she was a fake. She didn't fool me a bit!

"Yet with Bette Davis—I said in my book that she moved like a nigger. For me to explain my reaction to her and what I meant, I'd have to go back to New York City when I was ten. And I have to explain that my father resented my looks, particularly my eyes, which are large and froglike, and I had a complex about that, and she [Bette Davis] made me think of myself. I used to go to the movies in those days at Lenox and Seventh Avenue, and I saw this movie, *Marked Woman,* with Bette Davis, and she moved—both her hand movements and the way she walked—like any black chick. And she had these large, bulging eyes, and I'd never seen that before in a movie.

"There was another factor too," he continues. "She made me see in that film—she was being prosecuted in a courtroom in the film—what it was to be a whore. She defined what it was to be a whore. She had a sense of having suffered that came across to me, and so much of it was simply by her mannerisms and gestures."

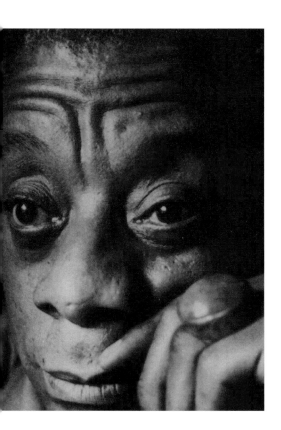

Baldwin turns again to the subject of America's obsession with homosexuality: "I think Americans are more uptight about homosexuality than about any other subject." AIDS fears have grown out of that greater obsession, he noted. And, he adds, "being open about homosexuality destroys the possibility of being furtive about sexuality in general. And sexuality in America always has to be furtive." Does he feel, then, that the inability to love is central to the American condition?

"I think," Baldwin replies, after pausing for a moment to consider the question, "that the inability to love *is* the central problem, because that inability masks a certain terror, and that terror is the terror of being touched. And if you can't be touched, you can't be changed. And if you can't be changed, you can't be alive. I don't mean to imply that Europeans are more loving and less afraid than Americans, but there's something in the structure of this country and something in the nostalgia that's at the basis of the American personality, it seems to me, that prohibits a certain kind of maturity and entraps the person, or the people, in a kind of dream love that can never stand the weight of reality."

Finally, late in the evening, the Scotch in the glasses having been drained, I ask Baldwin: What is the most important issue facing gay people today?

"It's not important to be gay…or important to be white…or important to be black," he replies. "What's important is to be *you.*"   —JERE REAL

THE ROYAL COURTS:
TRUE GRIT BENEATH THE GLITTER

In fealty and homage, gay royalty from courts all over the western United States and Canada convened in San Francisco over a weekend in late February for the Last Walk of the Imperial Butterfly Galactica Court of Empress Sissy Spaceout and the coronation of their successors.

As gorgeous as they were, the guests in no way outdid the queens. The San Francisco Spaceout Court has already taken what I believe they call at NASA the Next Big Step. The imperial theme was "Spaceship Nashville," and in a show of unity that was inspiring, more than thirty royal courts responded to this outer-space hoedown in duds that gave the term "drag" an entirely new dimension.

My dear, there was Milan Mylar and haute couture Glad Bags. The atmosphere was up and the tone was regal. The only thing grander than the four yards of material in their skirts was the four yards of real, artificial, and simulated human hair in every hue of the punk rainbow on their heads. The only things grander than their wigs were their names and titles: Crown Princess VIII of the Imperial Gem Court de Idaho Lapis; the Current Reigning Empress of Portland Dora Jar; the Firebird Queen; the Serpent Queen; Czar Ultima of the Dominion of Canada in Her Majesty's Province of Alberta; the Keepers of the Royal Crisco; the Lady in Waiting to the Current Miss Gay; and Gingerbread Princess—I mean, I hadn't heard language like this since Genet's *The Maids*.

Of course, not everyone takes the same delight as I in the gay-essencefulness of the Royal Courts. For some gay men and lesbians, the excess and exaggeration of the courtly queens is camp and confusing, their often up-front sexuality embarrassing, and the gender-bending offensive. It's a matter of image, I suppose: For some, maybe the queens are *too* gay, maybe they're not *upscale* enough. One group that has not courted the court, Empress Sissy told me, are "the hard-core political club people," even though the straight politicos have shown that they consider the Court an important entrance to a major political power base. As Eagle Empress XIV Nicole of San Diego said, "Among gay organizations, we continue to be the most controversial, the most misunderstood, and the most disliked."

Nicole and her fellow queens had congregated in San Francisco not only to celebrate the coronation but also to discuss the future of the Court System at the Third International Court Conference of the Americas. The major thrust of the meeting was on gaining credibility within the gay

José Sarria, Empress of San Francisco

community. "Don't tell them how many trophies you've won," exhorted Empress Nicole, "tell them how much money you've raised."

The money and involvement with the San Diego community shown by Nicole Ramirez Murray and his court demonstrate clearly why Nicole's epithet is "The Great." The range of recipients of monies raised by the San Diego Court is impressive: Gay and lesbian students have received scholarships and the Lesbian and Gay Men's Center has received sizable contributions, as have an impressive number of other community organizations. "One can compare the gay Court System to the Shriners, Elks, or any such similar service organization," Nicole said. "No one associated with our organization personally receives any monetary gain from any money raised at our functions. The money goes directly back into the community."

Everyone I interviewed said that of course the glamour and glitter were fun, but the real excitement of being a court member is in making a contribution to the community. Lapis of Boise told me, "In August 1985 the court decided that Idaho had to do something about AIDS, and we got together and raised $3,000 overnight. As a result, we now have the Idaho AIDS Foundation, but it was the court that got the whole thing off the ground." Empress Jovann of Hawaii organizes a yearly holiday food drive for the elderly and needy that last Christmas brought in 3,500 items. "What's rewarding," Jovann said, "is that you do something for the community. Sometime in your life you are able to say, 'I did this for someone.'"

The tradition of royal courts in the gay community was started twenty-one years ago when José Sarria put a crown on his head and proclaimed himself—by his own powers—the Dowager Widow of the Emperor Norton, Empress of San Francisco, and Protectress of Mexico. Sarria had been a local legend for some time. During the fifties, he entertained in drag at a North Beach gay café called the Black Cat. At the finish of every performance, the audience joined José in a rousing rendition of "God Save Us Nellie Queens." In 1961, José announced his candidacy for city supervisor. "I made a threat to the city," claimed the first openly gay person to run for political office in San Francisco. "I said there were more than ten thousand voting queens in this city." José made good his threat by winning more than six thousand votes.

These days, Sarria has taken on his role as Imperial Dowager with equal relish. At the conclusion of the coronation weekend, Sarria assembled the courts and their guests for a graveside tribute to his "late husband," the Emperor Joshua Norton, an eccentric but beloved figure from San Francisco's colorful past who made and lost a fortune during the Gold Rush. "Joshua Norton was a believer in individuality, freedom, uniqueness, fun, and the gay/lesbian/bisexual community," the Widow said, addressing the assembled devout. "He taught us to be whole, free, fun-loving human beings. Why not?...God had a sense of humor. I can tell that just by looking at this crowd." Then the chaplain to the Widow called the group to prayer and, my dear, when the new Empress of San Francisco Sable prays, she *prays*. The Widow then presented a marching drum with three separately tuned snare skins to the accompanying band of musicians. In the heat of the day, the Empress José, Sissy Spaceout, Sable the Clown, several Emperors, Dorothy Duster, Bubbles of Colorado Springs, and their cohorts trudged up a hill as a Chinese family watched in amazement, not expecting such a gay parade in a Colma cemetery on a Sunday afternoon, and not understanding that "California, Here I Come" is José Sarria's idea of a religious recessional.

—RON BLUESTEIN

"YOU KNOW WHAT I MISS? I MISS 'OH, MARY THIS,' AND 'OH, MARY THAT.' THAT'S WHAT I MISS."

GAY GAMES II

In early August, over three thousand athletes, plus thousands of other sports enthusiasts and spectators, traveled to San Francisco from eighteen countries to participate in Gay Games II. Washington, D.C.–based photographer and journalist Jim Marks was among the visiting crowd. Here are the concluding remarks of his report on the event for The Advocate.

You can't be in San Francisco long without knowing that this city is going through a terrible ordeal. The signs are everywhere: in the San Franciscans, who repeat a litany of lost and dying friends in a continuing service of remembrance; in the local gay newspaper's page of treacly obituaries, which would seem kitschy were they not so utterly sincere and so unutterably sad; in Randy Shilts's elegiac mid-week *Chronicle* story comparing Castro Street now with Castro Street then; in the emotion that swept the physique contest audience for competitor Christian Heren, who'd fought off AIDS paralysis through an improbable regimen of bodybuilding. In faces in the crowd.

Such an intertwining of love, death, and gayness made me recall the Mary Renault novel that begins with lovers dying of the plague that swept the ancient city of Athens during the Peloponnesian War. And when I reflected further on what it took for San Franciscans to stage the games in the midst of such struggle and sorrow, I was led to compare their spirit to those long-ago Athenians, who still produced their truth-telling tragedies and raucous comedies even though the enemy lay encamped outside the city walls and pestilence raged within. It was a great gift of faith in the future in the midst of a terrible present, and I think justified games founder Tom Waddell's closing ceremony remarks that gay people have much to teach the world.

But I also think that we—the athletes and friends and writers and tourists—gave the city something back. The Castro district that week was packed with swaggering athletes, young men and women sure they could set a goal, work hard, and attain it. Natives talked about how the street was "like it used to be." Physique judge and Detour bartender James Hamrick looked around his Market Street barroom and, in the manner of publicans quick to scent a mood, summed it up: "This has been a good season; our spirits needed a lift."

1

FRIENDS GONE WITH THE WIND

I am in a strange apartment in the Bronx, stretched out on a double chaise longue, waiting for Hitler's funeral to begin. My dear friend Vito appears in the doorway and makes his way toward me through the crowd. He lies down next to me, but when I turn to kiss him hello, I discover that he has been transformed into a withered old woman. She smiles. The funeral begins.

With tears in my eyes, I wake up. The horror of AIDS has finally penetrated my unconscious, and I know that now there is no escape from reality, not even in sleep.

Fantasy has always been an escape valve for me. When I was at my lowest ebbs or when I just needed a rest from it all, I could always go to the movies. If I was especially lucky, *Gone With the Wind* would be showing somewhere in town, and I could struggle along with Scarlett O'Hara through love and loss and sweeping change and, mustering my fortitude and determination, declare along with her, "As God is my witness, I'll never go hungry again," while stuffing buttered popcorn in my mouth.

In the urban gay ghetto of the seventies, I found an even better escape. If an evening threatened to be empty or unpleasant, I could retreat to the phantasmagoria of the baths and backroom bars, wandering through an endless maze of rooms and corridors to act out my erotic dreams with partner after partner, imagining that the likes of Rhett Butler was waiting behind each zipper or under each towel. What a fabulous party it was! All the pent-up yearnings of our represssed youths were abandoned along with our clothes. We were inexhaustibly creative and more sophisticated than everyone else, or so we fancied, unaware of our perilous innocence. We explored our dreams and our bodies as if we had invented sex for the very first time, helping countless unnamed men to orgasm, privileged to live in the generation when freedom had at last arrived. We had no idea how swiftly history can repossess its gifts, how suddenly the enemy attacks.

Most of us don't face the worst of life because we want to. We do it because we have to. So many of our people have proven to be heroic throughout this tribulation. In New York alone there is a waiting list to join the eleven hundred volunteers who visit people with AIDS—to offer comfort, shop for food, wash their floors, clean their vomit, and hold them while they cry.

These are not stereotypical, flighty, sex-addicted faggots. These are humanity at its finest. Do our critics know how often we are society's servants, its comforters and nurturers? While they excoriate us for being frivolous fun-seekers, we work as nurses and therapists and teachers beyond our proportions in the populace. There is more to the gay lifestyle than Sunday brunch. It takes nobility and perseverance and dignity and courage to be gay and proud in the face of condemnation and injustice, violence and death. I have never been so proud of our people as I am today.

I stopped partying as soon as I realized that my survival was at stake, and I settled down in a relationship. I gave money to Gay Men's Health Crisis. I talked about the epidemic in my writing. I went to benefits and rallies and candlelight marches. But I didn't become a buddy and look after the sick. I didn't look the horror in the eye, so the horror came to me.

It burst upon the nation with Rock Hudson's trip to Paris, and suddenly it was everywhere. I couldn't pick up a newspaper or turn on the TV without learning more than I wanted to know. Hysteria swept the nation, and parents took to the streets to keep children with AIDS out of school. And so I began to feel the fear. Like every gay man who participated in the party of the seventies, I check my skin for lesions after each shower, and worry about every unexplained cough.

We are not the carefree Peter Pans we once were. We are aging before our time. When we meet old friends in the street, we remember to be glad they are still with us. Our conversation sounds like my grandfather's did when he was in his eighties. "Did you hear that Charles died?" (We all read the obituary pages.) "Terrible, he was a good man." "I remember how he loved to dance." "It was a nice funeral." "George is ill." "Oh, no. When will it end?" "And you? How are you feeling?" "I'm okay. The doctor says it's just a cold." "Keep well." "You, too."

Sometimes in the midst of pain the mind wanders back to a happier time. The moon hung low over Fire Island as we wound down our hours of disco. On mescaline, everything was more than real, and magic was in the air under a sky brilliant with stars. Wiping the dance sweat from our brows, we headed into the woods, guided by white-

painted tree stumps and the sound of the surf beyond the dunes. There we met as shadows, kissing flesh to flesh, mouth to cock and cock to ass, laughing like the pixies we were, sharing our orgiastic joy, shooting great jets of semen into the night with glee, drinking one another's essence in. We were all one man there—one body, one spirit—until the majestic sun arose, and we dwindled our way to sleep, resting for the next night's frolic.

If you wait long enough, things seem to come full circle. The AIDS crisis has brought homophobes of every stripe out of the woodwork, and their fulminations against us have inadvertently helped to make some decent people aware of the real

threats faced by the gay community and of the need for legislation to protect us.

When New York City's gay-rights bill, Intro 2, surfaced once again in the City Council, our enemies called us abominations and sinners, negative role models and child molesters, trying to impose their primitive values on our lives. While Pope John Paul II counsels his priests to refrain from involvement in secular affairs, Cardinal O'Connor shamelessly lobbies with legislators and politicizes his pulpit.

Waiting near the radio for the City Council's vote to be broadcast, I thought of how some survivor of the Holocaust might have felt waiting for the results of the United Nations vote on the partition of Israel as an independent state. There was a mixture of gladness and guilt that I had lived to see it while others I knew had not. Before I left the closet in 1970, I was so intimidated by ignorance and hatred that I tried to kill myself twice, but I survived to see the

best years of my life. Once again the ignorance and hatred surround me, but Intro 2 gives me some hope that if I can endure through this dark time, something better may follow.

Who knows? If we work at it, we might win still more: perhaps even the right to marry and the legal, social, and economic advantages that come with it. Whatever we achieve, we must not let the next generation become complacent and take these treasures for granted, or they will be lost to us again.

As I stood with Vito and my lover, Larry Mass, amidst the throng in Sheridan Square, surrounded by friends celebrating the passage of the law we had all fought so long and hard for, I felt a quiet pride. (I did some leaping and whooping too.) We have made it the hard way, and we will have to fight to preserve what little we have gained. Some of us will not survive to see the future, but those of us who do must learn the infinite value of human life. Our enemies foolishly turn their backs on us and fail to appreciate how much we have to give, but their rejection only makes us stronger and more self-reliant.

In the words of Scarlett O'Hara: "After all, tomorrow is another day!"

—ARNIE KANTROWITZ

CHRISTOPHER ISHERWOOD REMEMBERED

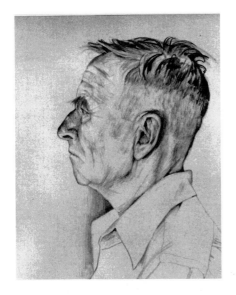

I first met Christopher Isherwood in the spring of 1980, when he was autographing copies of *My Guru and His Disciple* at the Walt Whitman Bookshop in San Francisco. I was instantly struck by his openness. He was a compact, solid little man whose quizzical eyes, staring boldly from behind bushy eyebrows, expressed a grandfatherly concern tinged with the scrappiness of a welterweight prizefighter. Immediately, at his insistence, he became not Mr. Isherwood, but simply Chris. The informality suited him.

As I knew him for only a few years before his death from cancer on January 4, at age eighty-one, I cannot supply firsthand accounts of the majority of his accomplishments. I know that he invented what we think of as "Berlin in the thirties" with his 1935 novel, *The Last of Mr. Norris,* and his 1939 collection of stories titled *Goodbye to Berlin.* The subsequent dramatizations of these stories—the John Van Druten play *I Am a Camera* and the stage and film hit *Cabaret*—immortalized Isherwood's "take" on the fall of the Weimar Republic, while adding some glossy touches of their own.

He did regret, in later life, not assigning a specific sexuality to the narrator of those stories—"Herr Issyvoo," as he had the landlady, Fraulein Schroeder, refer to him in her German dialect. He corrected this omission in *Christopher and His Kind,* his 1976 autobiography, explaining that while he had feared, in those early days, writing of his homosexual romances, he had also refused to portray himself as heterosexual. It was in this book that he first used the term "tribe" to represent the fraternal order of homosexuals. His concern for his tribe sometimes expressed itself in a cozy conspiracy: an "us against the world" position that was half joking, half serious.

Chris was accessible to everyone who wished to approach him. He kept his telephone number listed in the Santa Monica directory, and he and Don Bachardy, his lover of thirty-three years, made their home an open salon to all the interesting people who happened to come their way. Certainly he and Don were the most successful, the most "right for each other" couple I've ever met. I often glimpsed Don's loving eye watching protectively over Chris in a group function, when neither of them was aware he was being watched.

Chris could be feisty and stubborn, rebellious and unyielding. But coexisting with his scrappiness was a deep-seated serenity, an awareness of "the cosmic giggle," which surely came from his years of studying Hindu Vedanta with his spiritual mentor, Swami Prabhavananda. Chris never preached; he taught by example.

The most important lesson we can all learn from Chris's example is the necessity of openly proclaiming our homosexual natures to the world—to present oneself as gay every time the opportunity arises. The rewards—easy laughter, self-esteem, the acceptance of others, and the love of one's family and friends—seemed to lie brightly all around him, more precious than life itself.

I like to think that Chris's meditative serenity, the detachment that enabled him to look back on himself as a callow youth in Berlin, helped to ease him peacefully over the final hurdle. I doubt that there was a traditional Heaven embodied in his Vedanta beliefs, but I hope that somewhere he's being welcomed by a legion of fresh-faced, handsome young blond men in crewcuts and lederhosen. Chris was the keeper of the tribe. He will be sorely missed.

—STEVE BEERY

ART: GRAFFITIST KEITH HARING

Rich and happy, perhaps, but horribly misunderstood: That sums up Keith Haring, New York City's—let's make that the *world's*—premier celebrity graffiti artist, whose canvases now go for as much as $60,000 each. By day he draws funny three-eyed faces on blank billboards on the street and then markets the designs on T-shirts or transistor radios—which he sells in his own SoHo boutique, the Pop Shop. And by night he runs with such Manhattan stars as Andy Warhol, Brooke Shields, Richard Avedon, Madonna, and Grace Jones—the latter two whose bodies he has painted.

Haring designed this year's logo for New York City's Gay Pride Parade, depicting two same-sex dancing couples, with the partners in each linked by male or female sex symbols—like interlocking wedding bands—that are their heads.

The logo looked a lot like all the subway sketches Haring started whipping off—fleetly, to avoid the transit cops—in 1981, just three years after moving to New York from Pittsburgh. Ed McCormack, writing in New York's *Daily News* in August 1985, surmised that these stark renderings derived from Amish hex signs Haring saw when he was a kid near his hometown of Kutztown, Pennsylvania. This was quaint fantasy: Haring scoffed that he always liked to draw cartoons.

But Haring would rather talk about politics, which he got fascinated by— "Just 'cause. I mean from growing. I was born in 'fifty-eight," he says, "and I grew up in a really small town, but being American I had access to television and to *Life* and *Look* magazines....So you could see the world—at a time when America was going through political change, upheaval, sexual revolution....I couldn't be a part of it, but I was watching, and so I had some sort of consciousness. The older I got, the more I wanted to participate."

Few are seeing things the way Haring sees them now. You'll find none of his real perspective in all those volumes of light features or critiques on Haring that have run in *The New York Times, Newsday,* the New York *Daily News,* the *New York Post*—all of which have crusaded to keep Haring, who is popular in spite of them, *cute* and, well, if not heterosexual, not homosexual either: a graffiti eunuch. "In America they're very, very conservative," he states. "But in Europe, *in Europe* I've had things published in Sunday newspapers of Mickey Mouse fucking ET, a guy fucking another guy."

The Lower East Side kids who hang around his studio don't seem to have a problem seeing the real Haring. They mimic his graffiti drawings on the sides of buildings and in subways. And they swarm him everywhere he goes. "They're still basically unaffected by these other things that have ruined us," the artist says about his young groupies. "It's really satisfying to get that give-and-take with the most honest and sincere human beings I've met." Still, what do they think of him being gay? Do they see Haring as a role model?

"As a role model, but not as a gay role model," Haring explains. "I know a lot of hardcore street kids who would say they hate faggots, but they would never say that they hated me. Right? 'Cause they don't know me as a faggot. They respect me as a person, which is the most important thing. So it never really becomes an issue. I mean, there's a lot of kids I know who hang out here who know it, but they don't care 'cause it's like I'm not doing anything to them to invade their space or to try to threaten them. I don't make an issue out of it."   —DARRELL YATES RIST

Keith Haring covered the walls of the second-floor men's room of New York's Gay and Lesbian Community Services Center with this erotic mural, not long before he died of complications due to AIDS.

FILM: DEITCH'S *DESERT HEARTS*

It took seven years for Canadian author Jane Rule's classic lesbian novel, *Desert of the Heart,* to find its way into print. It would take nearly that long for San Francisco–born filmmaker Donna Deitch to complete her film version of this love story about an uptight thirty-five-year-old college professor and a free-spirited, twenty-five-year-old sculptor who earns her keep making change at a Reno gambling casino.

But if the enthusiasm that greeted *Desert Hearts* (as the movie version has been titled) at recent film festivals is any indication of the movie's impending success, both novelist Rule and filmmaker Deitch will not have shed their respective blood, sweat, and tears in vain.

At first, Rule said that she "really had to fight with Donna to start looking at this book as raw material. Donna was worried as the film changed, but the more I heard it had changed, the more comfortable I got. A lot of films have failed that have tried to be faithful to the original book. They've been too literary, scattered, and confused. This film was beautifully simplified."

Once the script for *Desert Hearts* was set, director Deitch began to focus her attention on casting the two leads. Newcomer Patricia Charbonneau, who plays the young Cay Rivvers, was the first to be selected. Then Deitch began searching for the actress to play Vivien Bell, the English-literature professor who arrives in Reno seeking a divorce. The director finally decided on Canadian-born Helen Shaver, a veteran of some twenty films. "When Patricia and Helen read together it was obvious to me that the right chemistry was happening," says Deitch.

The proof of that chemistry is on film. The two actresses make a dynamic on-screen couple, and their love scene, which could melt an igloo, is the screen's most revealing lesbian erotic duet to date.

Deitch, who always said she wanted to make the first commercial film focusing on a love story between two women, is elated over the positive response from the film festivals. Perhaps one of the most encouraging signs of the times is that the Samuel Goldwyn Company bought *Desert Hearts* intact, with no changes or cuts demanded—which was Deitch's up-front stipulation.

"It's very important to me that this picture reach out and be seen by a broad audience," says Deitch. "I also think that, especially at this time, it's very important for gay men to see the picture. There has been so much emphasis on the gay male point of view in the gay liberation movement…the male struggle. Not enough focus has been given to women and women's issues. Now, this is not a film about issues; it's a film about emotions and feelings and the kind of internal struggle that all gay men and lesbians go through at some point when they're coming out—whether it's 1985 in New York or 1959 in Reno, Nevada. So I think it's important for men to see it in order to expand and heighten their own awareness of women.

"And really, guys," concludes Deitch, "it's painless!"   —KIM GARFIELD

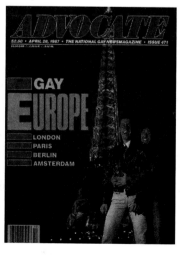

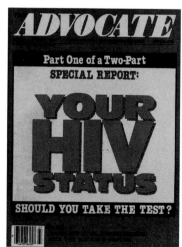

ACTING UP

In Washington, D.C., Marc Geller caught the furious energy of protesters from the direct-action group AIDS Coalition to Unleash Power (ACT UP), targeting the Food and Drug Administration and President Reagan for their failure to deal adequately with AIDS.

1987 Paradoxically, while 1987 was the year that gays and lesbians moved more heavily *into* the mainstream, it was also the year that heavy protest action *against* mainstream enterprises was launched.

"The sheer dollar amount of the settlement sends a clear message to employers—if you discriminate, it will hurt you on the bottom line!" With this, Leonard Graf of National Gay Rights Advocates announced the largest single financial settlement in the history of gay-rights litigation. In *Gay Law Students v. Pacific Tel. & Tel.*, a $3 million fund was mandated to compensate individuals the company had discriminated against solely because of their homosexuality. The legal precedent set by this case signaled the growing ability of gay and lesbian litigators to take on the establishment and win.

Working quietly behind the scenes, the Alliance for Gay and Lesbian Artists (AGLA) was taking on another Goliath—the entertainment industry. AGLA's mission was to improve the way gays and lesbians were depicted on the large and small screens of America. AGLA's groundbreaking work paved the way for the creation of the Gay and Lesbian Alliance Against Defamation (GLAAD).

A sign of the times in the Reagan years was the American public's love affair with money and what it could buy. A business boom in the gay and lesbian community reflected not only this theme, but also the changing social patterns of gay and lesbian life. AIDS-wary (and weary) gay men were doling out fewer dollars in bars and sex venues, spending their money on the trappings of domestic life instead. Lesbians were traveling more, opening new businesses, and emerging as a significant consumer group. The flow of gay dollars enabled new gay- and lesbian-owned businesses to flourish. Major national corporations began to court the new economy evolving around gay consumers.

While many in the gay and lesbian community were becoming more establishment-oriented, there also arose a movement to confront the establishment's failure to respond to the AIDS crisis. The newly formed direct-action group

AIDS Coalition to Unleash Power (ACT UP) began staging media-attracting demonstrations to raise public awareness about AIDS. By the end of the year ACT UP chapters had popped up all over the country.

In May, Ronald Reagan broke his thunderous silence on the topic, and gave his first speech entirely devoted to the AIDS crisis, but somehow he just couldn't choke out the word "gay." Reagan's speech, delivered in conjunction with the Third International Conference on AIDS in Washington, D.C., and the fervor of the protesters at that conference, produced widespread media attention. ACT UP's slogan, SILENCE=DEATH, was a cry from the heart that would inform the activist agenda for years to come.

As a psychotherapist working in the gay and lesbian community for many years, I began to see the effects of these developments in the new ways my clients talked about being gay. I was hearing more pride of ownership in a community feeling its strength, speaking out, acting up, demanding attention to its needs. Clearly this transition, at any level, from a victim's mentality to an activist mindset was having a positive impact on the self-esteem of many gays.

Other signs of gays feeling good about ourselves were seen in the emergence of black gays and lesbians organizing to build a leadership base, and more gay men and lesbians choosing to become parents. Prerogatives in gay life were increasing. The old myths about what you could or couldn't do because you were gay were being dispelled. But whatever breakthroughs there were in this year were preliminary to the defining event of 1987—the National March on Washington for Lesbian and Gay Rights.

Saturday afternoon, October 10, on a blocked-off street in front of the IRS Building, jammed into a crowd of several thousand people attending The Wedding, my lover of fourteen years and I got married. We didn't really need a ceremony to seal our commitment, but I was in the midst of writing a book about gay and lesbian partnerships and I felt compelled to take part in this historic celebration of the relationships that are, after all, ground zero for our being gay.

Sunday morning, at sunrise, we stood silently at the site of the Names Project AIDS Memorial Quilt, watching the unfolding of the last of the three and a half tons of panels volunteers had worked all night to unload. When the slow reading of the names began, I was struck by the care each name was given, as though to make sure we knew that each belonged to an individual whose life was unique and deserving of our undivided attention. It was almost unbearably solemn and it went on for three hours.

In the afternoon the sadness of the quilt experience gave way to exhilaration as, under gray and overcast skies, the marchers stepped off in an explosion of energy, shouting, singing, and chanting the rallying cries of gay pride. From our vantage point on the Mall, watching the giant mass of humanity slowly moving over the horizon toward us was an extraordinary experience. They seemed to be spilling out of the sky and there was no end to that mass—which, in a sense, was true because beyond the body of marchers lay the entire country, the millions of gays and lesbians who were in spiritual unity with those who were physically present in Washington, D.C.

The National March on Washington for Lesbian and Gay Rights was a turning point for many of the participants, who left for home ready as never before to mobilize and organize—to make a difference in the shaping of public policy that would directly affect their lives. A new cycle of gay and lesbian advocacy was emerging, born of anger about AIDS and of the sense of historical relevance that activism bestows. —BETTY BERZON

"When they put you in the lions' den, you have to learn how to deal with lions. My life for the last seven years has been learning how to deal with power as a gay person. We are not taught how…we're taught that power is bad because the power we experience growing up is bullying and macho, and we rebel against that sort of power."
—SAN FRANCISCO SUPERVISOR
HARRY BRITT

"In the sixties, many of us—myself included—stood on the outside and shouted epithets. It was easy to criticize.…But one of the really important lessons of the eighties is that gay and lesbian people have to run for office and get elected."
—WEST HOLLYWOOD MAYOR
STEVE SCHULTE

T I M E L I N E

Andy Warhol, pop artist superstar, died in February at age fifty-eight of medical complications not related to AIDS.

In a March out-of-court settlement, the Reagan Administration admitted that it had discriminated against Killian Swift, a gay transcriber fired by the White House in 1984.

JANUARY The first televised condom advertisement in the nation aired on KRON, an NBC affiliate in San Francisco; to protect themselves from protests by religious groups and the New Right, other stations steadfastly refused to run condom ads. ❏ A conservative faction tried unsuccessfully to oust members of the Log Cabin Club, a gay Republican group, from the GOP. ❏ Arizona passed a law requiring health-care providers to report the names of their HIV-positive patients. ❏ A California jury awarded $111,000 to a Garden Grove gay-bar owner who claimed police harassment drove him out of business. ❏ The Georgia State Board of Pardons and Paroles announced that HIV-positive inmates would not be paroled unless they agreed to participate in an AIDS prevention program. ❏ In what Italian authorities described as a case of "AIDS psychosis," a Verona man who mistakenly thought he had AIDS killed his pregnant wife, their two-year-old daughter, and himself. ❏ In its first such appropriation, the British government committed $30 million to public AIDS education. ❏ Beleaguered by obscenity charges, *The Body Politic*, Canada's leading gay magazine, folded after fifteen years.

FEBRUARY A Brooklyn bishop's eviction of a chapter of Dignity, a national organization of gay Catholics, capped a series of purges of gay groups from church facilities around the United States following the Pope's letter condemning homosexuality from the previous October. ❏ A three-day International Conference on AIDS in Children, Adolescents, and Heterosexual Adults was held in Atlanta, Georgia. ❏ Mentor Corporation began marketing a condom with a new adhesive feature to prevent "drop-off."

MARCH The AIDS Coalition to Unleash Power (ACT UP) formed in New York; in its first major action, 250 activists blocked morning rush-hour traffic on Wall Street. ❏ Surgeon General C. Everett Koop surprised Republicans by endorsing sex education among schoolchildren as part of the fight against AIDS. ❏ Dallas police, like more and more police departments across the country, began carrying masks, gloves, and insecticide for fear of contracting AIDS. ❏ The Reagan Administration's long-delayed AIDS education plan was released to immediate condemnation by gay and Congressional leaders as being framed in moral rather than medical terms. ❏ The Soviet Union opened its first HIV testing site.

APRIL U.S. Naval Academy midshipman Joseph Steffan, at the top of his class and decorated with honors, was discharged six weeks before graduation because of his homosexuality; he went on to fight the decision in court. ❏ The brokerage firm handling Rock Hudson's house reported that potential buyers' fear of AIDS caused a price slash from $7 million to $2.9 million. ❏ Answering tabloid reports, British Prime Minister Margaret Thatcher announced to Parliament that the late Sir Maurice Oldfield, former head of Britain's MI-6 intelligence service and believed to be the model for the fictional master spy George Smiley, was gay and regularly visited male prostitutes.

MAY Representative Barney Frank (D-Mass.) came out of the closet, becoming the second openly gay member of Congress. ❏ Paul Popham, a founder of New York's Gay Men's Health Crisis, died of an AIDS-related illness. ❏ Representative Stewart McKinney (R-Conn.) became the first member of Congress to die of AIDS. ❏ Two Boston firefighters were convicted of assaulting two lesbians while off duty. ❏ Gay former Air Force sergeant and *Time* cover man Leonard Matlovich revealed that he had AIDS. ❏ Governor John Sununu signed legislation making New Hampshire the first state to prohibit gays from becoming foster or adoptive parents. ❏ The Oregon Health Division reported that new syphilis cases reported among gay men in the state halved while the total number of cases doubled.

JUNE   *The New York Times* agreed for the first time to use the word "gay." ❏ Sixty-four people, including Leonard Matlovich and Carter aide Dan Bradley, were arrested at a Washington, D.C., protest of federal inaction on AIDS. ❏ In *SF Arts and Athletics, Inc. v. U.S. Olympic Committee* the U.S. Supreme Court ruled that the word "Olympic" could not be used in association with the "Gay Olympics" athletic competitions. The Gay Olympics were permanently renamed the Gay Games, the name used in 1982 during the first such event. ❏ President Reagan nominated notorious reactionary Robert Bork to the Supreme Court, uniting lesbians, gays, feminists, and other progressives in a campaign that ultimately defeated the nomination. ❏ An HIV-positive Arizona soldier was court-martialed for having unsafe sex with two enlisted women and one enlisted man. ❏ Canadian customs seized shipments of books and magazines destined for Toronto's gay Glad Day Bookshop.

JULY   Allegedly under pressure from his wife, Ronald Reagan appointed an openly gay person, Dr. Frank Lilly, to the Presidential Commission on AIDS. ❏ Alabama health officials criticized Scientific International, Inc., for marketing an "anti-AIDS" soap as a household cleaner in a $49.95 family-size package; the company stopped advertising the product. ❏ A top-ranking executive at Shell Oil was fired after his secretary accidentally discovered an invitation to "Premiere Jacks," a safe-sex party, and gave it to company officials. ❏ The head of the Southern Christian Leadership Conference said that "AIDS may very well be a voice from glory calling us back to one-on-one relationships." ❏ Fallen televangelist Jim Bakker said that church leaders had cleared him of charges of bisexuality, but his general superintendent countered that no such determination had been made. ❏ A Williamson, West Virginia, man with AIDS was refused admittance to the jail he was sentenced to for drunk driving; the local municipal swimming pool closed due to decreased attendance and revenues after rumors spread that the man had swum in it.

AUGUST   While testifying at Congressional hearings on AIDS, representatives of gay organizations—including the National Gay and Lesbian Task Force and the Human Rights Campaign Fund—conditionally endorsed voluntary HIV testing and backed away from their previous opposition to all testing. ❏ The National Institute of Allergy and Infectious Diseases announced that the first experimental AIDS vaccine was ready for human tests. ❏ According to the New York Telephone Company, "976" phone sex lines were so popular in New York State that the $15 million in extra revenue enabled a 6.9 percent cut in basic service rates. ❏ Hippocampe, a gay Washington, D.C., ballroom dance group, was awarded a $5,000 settlement from an apartment building that refused to rent it space.

SEPTEMBER   A two-hour television special on AIDS was broadcast, sponsored by the Metropolitan Life Insurance Company and anchored by actress Morgan Fairchild. ❏ The *San Francisco Chronicle* reported that some life insur-

In April, the Federal Communication Commissions recommended a criminal prosecution of Southern California radio station KPFK over its broadcast of *Jerker,* Robert Chesley's play about AIDS. The Justice Department dropped the case several months later.

Cal Culver, who appeared in *Boys in the Sand* and other gay porn films under the name of Casey Donovan, died in August of an AIDS-related illness at age forty-three.

ance companies had begun denying coverage to people with low T-cell counts. ❏ In what was believed to be the first gay palimony award granted by a jury, James Short of San Francisco won a whopping $2.28 million. ❏ The family of three hemophiliac boys who tested HIV-positive left Arcadia, Florida, after their house there was fire-bombed. ❏ The Minority AIDS Project in Los Angeles was granted a federally funded contract.

OCTOBER More than half a million lesbian and gay protesters, the largest gay gathering ever, converged on the nation's capital for the country's biggest civil rights march to date. ❏ More than six hundred people were taken into custody during a protest on the steps of the U.S. Supreme Court; they were the largest group of people to participate in any act of civil disobedience since the anti–Vietnam War demonstrations. ❏ The House and Senate overwhelmingly passed the Helms Amendment, which forbade federal funding for AIDS education material that "promotes or encourages homosexuality." ❏ Attendants on a Delta Airlines flight departing from Washington wore rubber gloves following the meal service. ❏ A highway billboard outside of Chehalis, Washington, showed a large Uncle Sam with his arms stretched over the words "AIDS is a miracle disease. It turns fruits into vegetables." ❏ Virginia ACT UP protesters disrupted televangelist Pat Robertson's announcement of his candidacy for President. ❏ Supporters of Lyndon LaRouche gathered more than 100,000 signatures in California, qualifying for a ballot reprise of Proposition 64, the 1986 AIDS quarantine measure. ❏ The U.N. General Assembly held its first debate on AIDS. ❏ The chairman and vice chairman of the President's Commission on AIDS resigned, citing lack of support for the commission on the part of the White House. ❏ Fifteen hundred people demonstrated in Munich against Bavaria's policy mandating HIV antibody testing for civil servants.

NOVEMBER Vincent Chalk, an Orange County, California, teacher who had been laid off because he had AIDS, won reinstatement in a landmark ruling by a panel of three judges. ❏ Luz Maria Umpierre, a lesbian poet and assistant professor at Rutgers University in New Jersey, filed a complaint with the Equal Employment Opportunity Commission, accusing the school of discriminating against her because of her gender, national origin, and sexual orientation. ❏ Officials of Baptist Bible College in Missouri vowed to prevent their school's name from being used by a proposed gay and lesbian alum association; they failed. ❏ After a bitter five-year legal battle, a San Diego Superior Court allowed a sixteen-year-old youth to be remanded to the custody of his late father's gay lover.

DECEMBER Community-based AIDS groups nationwide, working with a pharmaceutical company, began clinical trials of aerosolized pentamadine, a drug that eventually proved effective in preventing Pneumocystis pneumonia. ❏ Under threat of subpoena, officials of Burroughs Wellcome agreed to meet with New York state legislator Gerrold Nadler regarding the pricing of the company's drug AZT. ❏ Among nearly seven thousand gay men studied by the San Francisco Department of Public Health, not one who was antibody-negative seroconverted during the study's one-year term. ❏ New York AIDS activist Andy Humm filed assault charges against right-wing TV host Morton Downey, Jr., alleging that Downey struck him in the face during a talk-show taping; Downey was later acquitted. ❏ In Houston, the nation's first private hospital devoted entirely to AIDS treatment closed its doors after only a year of service.

In September, gay and feminist groups all over the nation protested Pope John Paul II's visit to American cities.

ROBERT BAUMAN

Robert Bauman lied, got caught. Lost his job, his wife and kids, his house, his friends, his credibility. What he gained—along with brutal honesty—was self-respect. At least that's the way I see it after only recently having made his acquaintance.

Honesty and self-respect don't necessarily gain friends. And so, he's very much alone. Maybe now more than ever, since he told his story in *The Gentleman from Maryland: The Conscience of a Gay Conservative*. The narrative's all there: a three-and-a-half-term right-wing congressman from the Eastern Shore of Maryland, a rabid Reaganite who rallied against the Commies (political perverts) and abortionists (moral perverts) and the like, who signed on to the Family Protection Act (its fabric stitched with antigay provisions) while fucking teenage hustlers and drinking himself into oblivion. Until, on the eve of the elevation of his political hero, Ronald Reagan, to the White House in 1980, the FBI uncovered him.

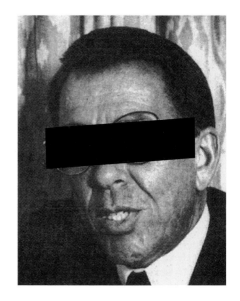

"The book is *my* account, what happened to *me*," he tells me. "I didn't attempt to be lurid. Things are different for younger gays. But people my age"—Bauman's in his forties—"are still suffering the tragedy I suffered. I suspect that my book will appeal to an audience that will either understand this intellectually or will understand it from personal experience and identify with it."

Bauman pauses, but barely, and as though to throw a gauntlet, says, "I would suspect that far greater damage is done to the gay movement by hooking up with kooky left-wing causes than anything I've said in this book." Bauman himself insisted that he wouldn't vote, were he still in Congress, to abrogate the state's right to criminalize gay sex. "Simply," he explains, "because it sets a precedent that says that Congress has a right to set your criminal laws—and that goes pretty far as a legal principle.

"I think that's the greatest failing of the liberal leadership of the gay movement—that there's this single-issue constituency. They think sexuality should color all other political judgments. And it doesn't....As far as the gay-rights movement is concerned, you've [supposedly] got to be a *liberal* to be a gay. But you *don't* have to be a liberal. Indeed, I think most gays are conservative, if only in a social sense, because most gays don't march in parades, don't come out of the closet, and don't raise their voices or sign petitions...."

Then why don't gay conservatives have a role in the gay-rights movement? "Because it's a phantom constituency in the sense of any public acknowledgment," he explains. "One of the old axioms in politics is that you put a letterhead together with names on it, whatever group you formed. You can't get gay conservatives to put their names on anything. You can call them at the White House, you can call them in the Congress, but you can't get them to come out. They're more likely to be seen in a gay bar than on a letterhead—*much* more likely, which is a sort of a commentary."

As for himself, "I've made mistakes and I've confessed them," says Bauman. "It is *society* that has a lot of atoning to do for its past, not me....You'll find out in the book that I do say something that conservatives don't say often, and that is 'I was wrong.'"

—DARRELL YATES RIST

DRAWING BLOOD

One night last October, I was standing with my puppy, Buddha—who was on his leash—in the entrance to my building, when a taxicab pulled over to the curb and deposited a well-dressed, young, but somewhat paunchy man I'd never seen before, who ran up the sidewalk in the rain.

The man didn't stop—or even slow his pace. As I bent to lift the puppy from his path, he flat-palmed me full-force against the door, halted for a second, kicked my dog, and without a demur hustled through the lobby.

I, stunned, said nothing for a moment, fearful that the puppy had been hurt—till, as I knelt, he began to wag his tail. With that assurance, I stood up and exploded. I shouted, "*Mister*, don't you *ever* kick my dog again!"

As I began to yell, he turned and rushed back at me, swinging his briefcase at my face. "Next time you see me coming in from the rain," he bellowed, puffing frantically, "you'd better get outta my way." Then he added with a snarl, "You're just a bunch of fuckin' women, *faggot*."

Was it the mothering kindness I'd shown my puppy? My too neatly fitted 501s? My earring? My slender, gym-worked build—even though the face reads late thirties? No matter. Frantic homophobia always gropes for its target.

I'd been fag-bashed in the lobby of my building just two years before—by five drugged teenage boys with a sharpened pole, which they smashed across my face, shattering my glasses and driving tiny, brittle shards into my eyes.

This time—as fast as the visions people see an instant before they think they're about to die—a lifetime of insults and assaults, of violence of one kind or another just because I'm gay, flashed across my mind. I screamed, "Take *this* from a fag!" and slammed my fist into the man's contorted face. With the fiery arc of my arm, its drive propelled by years of smoldering anger, I burned away just one more pattern of apologizing for who I am.

It is 1987, and I'm an outlaw in America—cut out of the Constitution by last summer's Supreme Court ruling, which defined the way I love as criminal. In twenty-four states and Washington, D.C., I can be punished by as little as a two-hundred-dollar fine or as much as a twenty-year prison term.

Statistics portray a virtual reign of antigay terror in the eighties. Reported assaults against gay people soared 80 percent in the first six months of 1986, while the number of men in New York City murdered just because they're gay doubled. Twenty gay men have been stabbed to death in New York City's Chelsea district alone in this past year—many of them mutilated beyond recognition. Police found all the bodies castrated. The ritual of cutting off the victim's cock and balls, according to police, is common in the murders of gay men.

My lover and I have been assaulted several times—sometimes with fists, sometimes with bottles and rocks, sometimes with sticks or bats, once with the barrel of a gun. Every attack was accompanied by shouts of "queer" or "faggot"—terrifying slurs because they resonate with the threat of violence.

They are epithets we all know well, of course—and not just from our assailants. We were raised from childhood—in our homes, at school, with friends—on their vicious sound and the hatred they convey. For, unlike "nigger" and "kike," the words "queer," "faggot," "lezzie," and "dyke" still pass in this society as acceptable comment or harmless jest. On the street, at the gym, at cocktail parties, at the office, even from some of our friends and family, we still hear the epithets and feel their hateful weight: They *always* carry warnings.   —DARRELL YATES RIST

THE SECOND MARCH ON WASHINGTON

With tears and laughter, anger and joy, several hundred thousand lesbians, gay men, and their supporters marched in Washington, D.C., on October 11 in a massive, emotion-filled demonstration to demand a federal war on AIDS and an end to homophobic discrimination. There was a disagreement on the turnout: The U.S. Park Police initially put the crowd at 50,000 but later revised the figure to 200,000, while march organizers raised their initial estimate of 500,000 to 650,000. But there was no disputing that the huge outpouring of people from all over the country made the march the largest gay-rights demonstration ever assembled, dwarfing the first gay march on Washington in 1979 and marking a new milestone in modern gay history.

"This is indeed our day," an ebullient Harvey Fierstein, the actor and playwright, called out to the vast throng assembled on the Mall near the U.S. Capitol. "We have marched out of the closets....We are gay and lesbian, and we did this."

For five hours, an array of geographical, religious, sports, political, musical, and other groups, reflecting the diversity of American gay life, marched the two miles beginning at the Ellipse, past the White House on Pennsylvania Avenue, and over to the Mall.

They chanted, "What do we want? Gay rights. When do we want it? Now," "Money for AIDS, not war," "We are everywhere; we will be free," and "Two, four, six, eight! Being gay is really great!" They sang "America the Beautiful" and "We Shall Overcome." And they angrily pointed their fingers at the White House as they shouted, "Shame! Shame! Shame!" and "Increase AIDS funding. Americans are dying."

From the stage near the Capitol, the huge throng appeared to stretch almost the dozen long blocks to the Washington Monument. The crowd held aloft a sea of pink and purple balloons, rainbow banners, placards, and signs—among them, "I Love My Gay and Lesbian Friends," "Fight AIDS, Not People With AIDS," "Thank God I'm Gay," "Get Ready for the Gay '90s," and simply "LOVE," with a pink triangle substituting for the *V*. Over and over, in speeches and interviews, marchers compared the event to the black civil rights

marches of the sixties. Many called the march, together with the planned civil disobedience action at the Supreme Court two days later, a watershed that showed how far the movement had come and how it was now prepared to move toward increased organizing and militancy.

Whether the march, huge as it was, would have any immediate political impact remains to be seen. Coverage of the demonstration was extensive, with major newspapers across the country giving it front-page play; in some cases, as with the *Philadelphia Inquirer*, it was the lead story. But gay activists maintained that the primary, immediate effect would be on the gay community itself, accelerating the sense of solidarity that has been building since the Stonewall Rebellion. —PETER FREIBERG

A Mosaic in Memoriam

They opened the package from Arizona and out tumbled a vivid tapestry of flowers in red, yellow, and purple yarn with the name "Aaron John Miller" embroidered in darker thread. His mother had made it, and it was a foot too long. "Well," Cleve Jones says with a sigh, "it's too beautiful to cut down. We'll just have to find a shorter panel to compensate."

Jones is the originator of the Names Project, a San Francisco–based volunteer organization that is assembling a huge memorial quilt with the names of people who have died of AIDS. The completed quilt will be displayed on Capitol Mall during the October March on Washington for Lesbian and Gay Rights, and it will make quite a sight. Thousands of three-by-six-foot cloth panels are being sewn, in groups of eight, into twelve-foot squares. The squares are then grommeted (bordered with metal eyelets) so that they can be laced together into ever-larger units.

When I visited the project's headquarters in early August, the office was already receiving a dozen packages a day from every part of the country: Illinois, Oregon, Texas, New Jersey. "When we get back there and lay this thing out," says Jones, "we want the person from Iowa who sent a panel to California that was transported to Washington to be able to find it and leave a flower there. So we're coding them, and there'll be a directory available."

Asked how the project began, Jones replies, "I thought of it on November 27, 1985. For almost ten years, I've been the coordinator for the annual candlelight march for Harvey Milk and George Moscone. As we were preparing for it in 1985, we learned that the death toll [from AIDS] in San Francisco had just reached one thousand. And we were so appalled by that number that we asked the marchers to bring along a piece of paper or cardboard with the name of a loved one who had died.

"Then at the end of the march, after we left the candles at City Hall, we moved down to the old Federal Building, the site of the AIDS/ARC vigil. We had ladders there, and we went up the side of the Federal Building and covered it. The whole facade was covered with these names taped to the cement. It was such a startling visual. And as I was looking at it I decided: This should be a quilt."

When Jones heard about the march on Washington, he knew he'd found a context for his quilt and took out a personal loan to bankroll it. Suddenly, a dozen people he'd never met before stepped forward and expressed interest in helping to mount the project. "What we're after is very simple," says Jones. "We want to dramatically illustrate the impact of the AIDS epidemic on American society by offering people a positive, creative way of expressing an extraordinary burden of grief."

That's why the project isn't simply accepting panels, he explains, but also furnishing the public with everything necessary for making them—a variety of fabrics, paint, glitter, and glue. "We're drawing on the American folk-art tradition of quilting and sewing bees," says Jones. "It's a symbol in itself of how this country needs to respond to the epidemic—working together in an atmosphere of compassion and trust.

—CARL MAVES

TEARS AND REVERENCE

Dawn was breaking over the Mall as an emotionally taxed, physically drawn Cleve Jones slowly traversed a walkway leading to a podium facing the U.S. Capitol. With the glare of the rising sun in his eyes, Jones, executive director of the Names Project and a veteran San Francisco street activist, looked out and surveyed the empty canvas grid that stretched for two city blocks before him.

It had taken a crew of volunteers, working steadily since two A.M. in the chilly Sunday-morning darkness, five hours to construct the enormous fabric framework that would soon contain three-by-six-foot panels bearing the names of people who have died of AIDS. Now it was finally time for the inaugural unfolding of the 1,920 memorial panels that volunteers had been able to sew together in time for the march day.

With supporters and a clutch of reporters looking on from the edge of the white fabric walkway, four eight-person teams carefully began unfurling and setting in place the twenty-four-square-foot quilts, each containing thirty-two panels.

As the unfurling proceeded, Jones, his voice cracking, finished reading his list of thirty-two names and stepped off the platform. He buried his head in his hands and sobbed.

Over the next two hours, sixty people—including actress Whoopi Goldberg, actor Robert Blake, and U.S. Representatives Gerry Studds, Barney Frank, and Nancy Pelosi—took turns reading some of the more than two thousand names emblazoned on the quilt. By nine-thirty the sixty squares were in place, securely fastened to the grid by ten thousand metal grommets.

A half-hour later, the tapestry had attracted hundreds of curious onlookers. Its effect on them was immediate and profound. Except for the somber sounds of quiet weeping, the crowd was hushed—silenced by the enormity of the quilt and the magnitude of human loss it represented.

—MARK VANDERVELDEN

CIVIL DISOBEDIENCE: A NEW MILITANT STAGE IN THE STRUGGLE FOR GAY RIGHTS?

If the mass civil disobedience demonstration set to take place on the steps of the U.S. Supreme Court October 13 lives up to the advance billing by its organizers, the protest—in which hundreds are expected to be arrested—may well be a pivotal event in the struggle by gays to win justice in this country.

Some might say that it is premature—presumptuous even—to assign historic significance to an event that has yet to occur. But never before have gay activists undertaken such an urgent, ambitious, and publicly visible act of civil disobedience. And while civil disobedience is hardly new to gay politics, the upcoming Supreme Court action underscores a deepening recognition within the gay community that a more dramatic form of moral and legal resistance is needed.

Above all else, the Supreme Court action signifies a watershed in the maturation and refinement of gay political sensibilities in America. It symbolizes a certain coming-of-age for the gay-rights movement: an emphatic declaration that gays intend to more closely align their struggle for human rights with the other great civil rights movements of this century.

Two issues—the high court's harsh antigay ruling last year in the Georgia sodomy case, and the federal government's slow and inadequate response to the AIDS epidemic—have caused even the most moderate gay leaders to call for mass civil disobedience.

Vic Basile, executive director of the Washington, D.C.–based Human Rights Campaign Fund (HRCF), describes himself as a political pragmatist. "I believe that, for the most part, the traditional mainstreaming of our issues is the thing that is going to bring results for us," Basile contends. Still, he adds, "Civil disobedience is an appropriate tool in the arsenal of weapons that gay people could use to bring about political change. Frankly, if blacks had mainstreamed all their issues, this country would still be trying to pass a civil rights act. It was the power of nonviolent civil disobedience, and the power of the media bringing that civil disobedience into millions of peoples' homes, that brought about the laws and the changes."

More and more gay people are feeling a heightened moral outrage at a government—indeed, an entire society—that denies them basic human dignity and civil rights. Many of these individuals, otherwise law-abiding citizens, now feel compelled to take public, unlawful action in response.

Witness the emergence of New York City's AIDS Coalition to Unleash Power (ACT UP), a direct-action group that has stopped traffic on Wall Street, had protesters arrested on the steps of the city's main post office, and organized a number of other actions on AIDS issues. Since it was formed last March, ACT UP has mushroomed from a handful of angry gay men to nearly six hundred members. The group's weekly meetings at the New York City Lesbian and Gay Community Services Center are spirited and emotional—and jammed.

Likewise, in Washington, D.C., Boston, Los Angeles, San Francisco, Houston, and Denver, gays either have engaged in civil disobedience or have stated their intention to do so in the near future. "People feel up against the wall," notes Susan Cavin, an editor for *Big Apple Dyke News* in New York City and the local organizer for the action at the Supreme Court.

A Piece of My Mind

MONUMENTAL DREAMS: REMEMBERING OUR GAY AND LESBIAN HEROES

Two years ago, my friend Michael and I were traveling through Europe, when he suggested that it might be interesting to visit one of the famous cemeteries of Paris. "Come on, Matt," he said, "the graves of Alice B. Toklas, Gertrude Stein, and Oscar Wilde are there. It'll be interesting." Grudgingly, I agreed. After a long walk, we stopped, and there were the graves. As I stood looking at them, an unexpected array of emotions overcame me. I was too young to have known these people during their lives, yet they somehow seemed more a part of my identity than my own family. There, in front of me, were some of the people who had given me the courage to confront the Air Force with the truth about who I really am. These were the people who made it impossible for me to live my life as a lie. I was overwhelmed with a sense of pride, history, and understanding that I'd never felt before. I knew that I wouldn't forget the experience for the rest of my life.

Even after I returned to the United States, I couldn't seem to get the image out of my mind. The knowledge that I could never have had that experience in my own country made me increasingly frustrated and angry. I knew, for example, that when Americans went to the Vietnam Memorial to remember and honor those who gave their lives fighting in that horrible war, it never even occurred to them that some of those who were the strongest, bravest, and most heroic were also gay. Why? Because even with all the advances our community has made since Stonewall, we still remain largely invisible. The public is never told that a famous figure is lesbian or gay unless an attempt is being made to discredit the individual, or the individual has been diagnosed with AIDS. There is no such thing in our culture as an American hero who is openly lesbian or gay.

It is time for us, as a community, to remedy that. Therefore, we invite you to join us at the Congressional Cemetery in Washington, D.C., on October 10 at eleven A.M. There, a portion of land will be dedicated as the final resting place of Harvey Milk. The dedication will be an official event of the National March on Washington for Lesbian and Gay Rights, and it will constitute the first project of a new national nonprofit organization called Never Forget. Never Forget intends to create additional monuments in honor of those who have advanced the positive perception of our community, and to place those monuments in highly visible sites across the United States. In doing so, we hope to help destroy the homophobic ignorance that permeates our country.

A final note: When confronted with our own mortality, it has become common in our community to have our bodies cremated and our ashes thrown to the four winds. But with the wind goes an important part of our history. And also an important part of our future. I ask you to consider the ramifications of this action on tomorrow's generation of lesbians and gays as they search for self-esteem.

As a person with AIDS, I have thought about this a great deal. I believe that we must be the same activists in our deaths that we were in our lives. I urge those of you who are facing death to find a method of leaving a lasting record of your accomplishments—including the acknowledgment that you were lesbian or gay.

If you need to summon the courage to enable you to do this, stop by the Congressional Cemetery and discuss it with Harvey. I think he'll have some advice for you.

—Leonard Matlovich

Cavin says that gays "have nothing to lose at this point" by embarking on a campaign of mass civil disobedience. "With so many gay men dying, people feel that the AIDS crisis has pushed them over the line. The urgency of winning some sort of decent treatment in this society has become apparent."

History shows that mass civil disobedience—properly executed in the spirit of nonviolent noncooperation, as expressed by Mohandas K. Gandhi and Dr. Martin Luther King, Jr.—can be an extraordinarily effective means of advancing the claims of a morally aggrieved people. Both Gandhi and King successfully used the method, not only to better the conditions of their people but also to transform the consciousness of the world in the process. But not until recently have gays drawn from the experiences of Gandhi and King, and applied that knowledge to their own forms of civil disobedience action.

There are many gay activists who, although strongly supporting the use of mass civil disobedience, openly question whether the necessary groundwork has been laid for a coordinated nationwide campaign. The gay community, they note, does not have anything remotely resembling the vast network of Southern churches where, night after night for ten years, blacks were educated about the true nature and spirit of what they were undertaking.

"I frankly don't think we've given enough thought to the use of civil disobedience," maintains Basile. "Civil disobedience should not be used lightly or frequently; it ought to be part of an overall strategy to call public attention to a serious problem. But if you just go out into the street and have a demonstration, chances are you will do more harm than good to the cause."

The most harm is done when a protest action is designed to play more to the television camera than to people's principles. When protests are carefully orchestrated, they tend to turn into media stunts—no matter how much they are cloaked in the parlance of civil disobedience.

Obviously, the benefit of this approach is that demonstrators and the police are both less likely to get hurt. The drawback, says New York City gay activist Andy Humm, is that the protests become predictable and have minimal impact. "When you don't face a jail sentence, when you don't face any real penalties other than a little loss of time, I don't think it translates into raising public consciousness as much as you'd like to. Most gay people aren't interested in taking chances getting arrested unless they can get back before lunch is over."

But no matter how well rehearsed a protest is, the stakes involved in launching a campaign of civil disobedience nevertheless remain high. The risks—both to individuals and to the cause of equal and fair treatment for gays in this society—are considerable, unpredictable, and real. For example, the potential for injury always exists when people are being arrested—particularly if they are not well grounded in the principles and practice of nonviolent resistance. Still, many gay leaders believe that the potential gains are worth the risk.

"Civil disobedience is a necessary part of any movement that takes itself seriously," says gay historian John D'Emilio. "If some part of a movement is not willing to endorse and pursue civil disobedience, I think the movement is, in effect, saying that the law is a higher authority than the justice the movement is seeking. If you are unwilling to break the law, you are saying that the process of creating law is more important than the injustice you are fighting."

Says Michele Krone, the lead organizer of the Supreme Court action, "I hope our protest will make everyone feel empowered to the point that they understand that it really is no big thing to look authority in the eye and say, 'You are wrong.' " —MARK VANDERVELDEN

VESSELS OF LIFE AND DEATH

My friend Karen is an artist. I've known her for fourteen years, loving—and learning from—her work. Karen's enormous, bold, and brilliantly colored figurative pieces, celebrating women's power and mythic history, stand against the walls of the small basement apartment that doubles as her art studio.

On a recent visit the new work that captured my attention was quite simple—a black-and-white still-life drawing of a pitcher. But instead of standing upright in the usual position, this pitcher is tipped oddly on its side, balanced by nothing, its sensual wide mouth facing the viewer dead-on. Inside, the compelling belly is half-filled with liquid, which hangs in a dark mass at the lip in that peculiar tension of water, neither spilling out nor settling into its container.

I knew immediately that Karen's picture centered on death, the major theme for gay people these days. Specifically, I knew the death was a particular one, of our mutual friend Anita, a lesbian who had recently died of cancer. Karen was one of three women chosen by Anita to nurse her at home during her difficult last days.

Weeks after her experience with helping her friend die, and still emotionally devastated, Karen attended one of Stephen Levine's death-and-dying retreats, held in Britenbush, Oregon. There she was attracted to a gay man named Doug, in one of those instant magnetic friendships that happen once or twice in a lifetime. During the ten-day retreat they became fast friends, but Karen came home with mixed feelings, for Doug had gone to the retreat because he had been diagnosed with AIDS.

Unable to sleep easily during the months of June and July, by August Karen was overwhelmingly compelled to make a trip to Oregon to visit Doug. She arrived the day he was discharged from the hospital. Once again, the choice was between home care and dying among professional strangers. Doug's friends were unsure of how to take care of him at home, and his brave lover, Tom, was prepared to take the entire passage on himself, when Karen arrived. As she quietly undertook doing the shopping, cleaning, and cooking, Tom found he had more quality time with his lover—instead of rushing frantically from chore to chore. Doug's friends—straight and gay, men and women—had gathered around, and Karen talked to them about what to expect from a dying person in chronic pain.

When she was leaving to return to her home in Northern California, Doug's friends told Karen, "You gave us Doug, you gave him to us." Three weeks later, the night of September 4, someone called to tell her Doug had died, with dignity, among his friends.

Strong, bold, and sensitive minds are needed to thread us across the lip of this fragile container, "life as we know it." And agonizing, even embarrassing though it be, we gay people are, by circumstance and habit, having our heads turned to stare directly into the maw of hard choices. As we so often have been this century, we are people who display our lives publicly, acting out the American libido in public sex, encouraging male beauty, getting women into the work force, criticizing the underpinnings of our entire culture, and now, engaging directly with death and transition. I expect we will add some gay humor and idiosyncrasy to the understanding that life has meaning whether it goes on inside or outside a container.

—JUDY GRAHN

BOOKS: *AND THE BAND PLAYED ON*

There is finally some good news for the international gay community. AIDS has not been conquered, but the fatal disease has at last been demystified, its history clarified, and its tolls tallied in a book that has had the publishing world buzzing a month before its official release.

Randy Shilts's *And the Band Played On* is the whole story of AIDS—told with a stunning breadth of vision and an economy of prose. It begins during the bicentennial celebration in New York on July 4, 1976 (the weekend Shilts highlights as the probable moment of the entry of AIDS into the United States), and continues through mid-1987, when the President made his first public address on the disease—six years and twenty thousand deaths into the epidemic. In major cities on every continent, in slums and mansions, down the corridors of hospitals and bathhouses, Shilts traces the data, the issues, the people, and most effectively, the AIDS patients, with a precision and an exactness that only words like "amazing," "staggering," and "breathtaking" can convey.

"I felt it was very important to name everyone," Shilts tells me in his San Francisco apartment. "I used as extensive identification as I possibly could. I feel that the problem with the epidemic now—and a reason for the hysteria—is that so much about AIDS has remained so mysterious. The medical literature will talk about an individual as Case A or Patient Zero, and it doesn't give that person the dimension of being really human. I felt that by saying these are flesh-and-blood people with real names, I would bring home the reality of the epidemic and make it far less frightening."

Shilts's soft voice gets loud and impassioned as he says, "It's ridiculous that in 1987 a book is coming out that for the first time is telling the story of how the Reagan Administration has dealt with AIDS. In a sane world, this stuff would have been written about and rehashed in the daily newspapers a hundred times over by now. We're six years into this epidemic! Major news organizations have literally let the Reagan Administration get away with murder and by their shallow coverage have contributed to a government that has stood by and done as little as possible while tens of thousands of Americans were dying.

"AIDS would never make it into the newspapers if it weren't for the hemophiliacs and kids," Shilts continues. "The process in the last years has been to 'heterosexualize' the disease to the extent that the news coverage is totally dishonest and distorted....The cliché of 'AIDSspeak' is that AIDS is not a gay disease. Well, that's simply not true. It is a gay disease inasmuch as most of the people who get AIDS are gay, and it's going to continue that way everywhere in the world except Africa. The fact that AIDS struck gay people has everything to do with how it's been dealt with by government, media, and science."

What effects does Shilts see as a result of the book? "This is a book that straight people are obsessed with, and they're completely getting the point that a horrible injustice has been done to the gay community. What we've seen with AIDS is what happens when you have a government that does not want to spend money on domestic interests. If my book recasts the national debate on AIDS, it will be serving the truth."   —RON BLUESTEIN

THEATER: ALAN TURING'S *SECRET WAR*

Among the pantheon of unwilling gay martyrs, Alan Turing remains the saddest waste of all. Although he helped vanquish Hitler, Turing was himself crushed six years later when he was charged with twelve counts of "gross indecency," resulting in his probable suicide at the age of forty-one. The chilling story of how one man was hounded to death by a homophobic legal system—an institutional intolerance that was exacerbated by the scientist's own closeted clumsiness—is the subject of Kevin Patterson's *Alan Turing: The Most Secret War,* recently given a staged reading by Chicago's Lionheart Gay Theater.

The tragic story of the British mathematician's life was first brought to wide public attention in 1983 when Andrew Hodges's critically acclaimed biography, *Alan Turing: The Enigma,* was published. The book has served as the source not only for Patterson's work, but also for another new play, *Breaking the Code,* by Hugh Whitemore.

Turing's finest hour came when he joined the top-secret British intelligence project at Bletchley Castle. There the thirty-year-old numbers wizard—moving from theory to practice—masterminded the cracking of the Enigma, the supposedly unbreakable German secret code, thereby shortening the war and saving countless lives.

"*Once you put on makeup, you don't need any other drug.*"
—DRAG STAR DORIS FISH

British mathematician Alan Turing

Like Wilde, Turing helped to destroy himself, when he reported a petty burglary he thought his boyfriend had committed. In the course of talking to the police, Turing naively revealed the sexual relationship. Astonished to find *himself* suddenly on trial, Turing refused to admit to any wrongdoing. Because of its continued secret status, his wartime service was deemed inadmissible evidence, and Turing's intransigence (or courage) resulted in his being forced to choose between prison and "organotherapy." To continue his work he tragically opted for the latter—barbaric hormone treatments that caused him to grow breasts and undergo a chemical depression, which partially explains the "asphyxia due to cyanide poisoning" that killed him in 1954.

Patterson's fascinating treatment uses the coroner's inquest as the basis for flashbacks to Turing's troubled life. They feelingly demonstrate Turing's penchant for putting numbers over people—and his disillusionment at the latter's maddening lack of predictability. Still, having been caned by a headmaster who, it's implied, went on to "bugger" him, abandoned in death by the boy he most loved, and literally mutilated by the country he helped to save, Turing probably had good reason to wish he *could* become a machine like his beloved computers.
—LAWRENCE BOMMER

FILM: E. M. FORSTER'S *MAURICE*

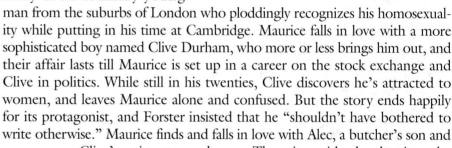

"We all construct private lives in the midst of public policies and politics and laws. In England, the state intrudes quite a lot and people spend whole lives creating privacy. My Beautiful Laundrette *and* Prick Up Your Ears *are about people disregarding the law and living out their lives anyway."* —DIRECTOR STEPHEN FREARS

It took nearly sixty years for E. M. Forster's book *Maurice,* written in 1913, to be published—long enough for all those who might have been troubled by the homosexual novel, including the author, to have died, and long enough for England to drop its laws against the "unspeakable crime of sodomy." It took another sixteen years for director James Ivory and producer Ismail Merchant, makers of last year's Edwardian hit, *A Room with a View,* to give *Maurice* a popular treatment in the movies.

Forster's novel tells the story of an ordinary young man from the suburbs of London who ploddingly recognizes his homosexuality while putting in his time at Cambridge. Maurice falls in love with a more sophisticated boy named Clive Durham, who more or less brings him out, and their affair lasts till Maurice is set up in a career on the stock exchange and Clive in politics. While still in his twenties, Clive discovers he's attracted to women, and leaves Maurice alone and confused. But the story ends happily for its protagonist, and Forster insisted that he "shouldn't have bothered to write otherwise." Maurice finds and falls in love with Alec, a butcher's son and Clive's assistant gamekeeper. Throwing aside class barriers, the two swear eternal love.

With its homosexual hero, *Maurice* becomes more than just a period piece. It describes the need we all have for a physical, sexual life, and the private horror of having to go without it. It describes the release we feel when we are finally touched, and the touch is right.

"I wanted to present these relationships in the most comfortable, natural way," says Ivory, in the Manhattan apartment he shares with Merchant. "These are very ordinary people with their tidy economic situations and conventional families. For them, their homosexual attractions are normal and natural. That's simply the way they are. It's not the result of being special in any way.

"Though the laws about sodomy have changed since Forster's day, people's basic attitudes haven't," the director continues. "When people of an ordinary cast of mind, like Maurice and Clive, discover their sexual feelings, they're faced with a dilemma. How are they going to accept their unconventional sexuality when everything around them is perfectly conventional?...Still, you can now make a movie about *Maurice,* which you certainly couldn't do when the book was first published. Younger readers today aren't so leery, and they've grown up in a slightly freer atmosphere. That is a tiny bit of progress." —MARCIA PALLY

On both sides of the Atlantic, Canadian director Patricia Rozema charmed audiences with her imaginative romantic comedy *I've Heard the Mermaids Singing.* The lesbian film was awarded the 1987 Prix de la Jeunesse at the Cannes Film Festival.

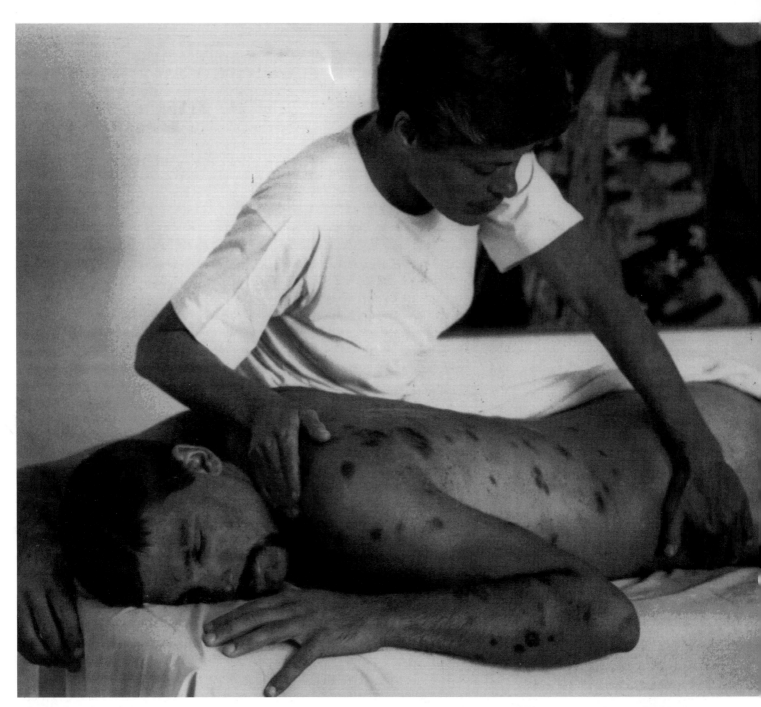

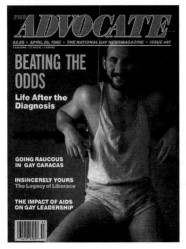

SERIOUS BUSINESS

1988 After several years of work, *Living the Spirit: A Gay American Indian Anthology* was published. It marked the first book-length work by queer Native America about itself, and demonstrated the ability of native peoples and their ancient traditions to endure despite the concerted efforts of the greater part of the non-native world to preside over the death of the entire native world, queer or not.

When I first held this small precious volume in my hand, I wept. For while I knew I held a profoundly significant symbol of endurance in my hands, I also knew that the latest in the series of white man's plagues that had decimated native populations over the centuries since contact was again threatening our survival.

From measles, chicken pox, tuberculosis, syphilis, and smallpox—as well as from more direct assaults upon us—native people had lost some 96 percent of our population. Much evidence amassed over the five hundred years of conquest and colonization strongly suggests that we did not possess the kind of immune system that Anglo-Europeans had. By the mid-eighties, native people's life expectancy had improved from a median of forty-five years to around fifty-four years, but it seemed clear to me that a dramatic drop in that newly realized gain was about to occur from the spread of AIDS, cancer, lupus, and Chronic Fatigue Syndrome.

By 1988, the types of opportunistic infections that had decimated native populations were now cutting a deadly swath through gay, African, African-American, Hispanic, Asian, and Native peoples. The reality of the plague was unavoidable. It was a year when even the Soviet Union acknowledged its first AIDS death.

Yet, in gay and lesbian Indian country, as in the rest of the queer world, not all was devastation: Native American gays and lesbians were meeting, not in militance or AIDS activism alone (though we were certainly doing both), but in an annual gathering that combined various traditional religious practices and teachings with an equally traditional and ancient respect for Indians who were of the other genders.

By the late eighties, gay people had learned to take care of each other in unprecedented ways: Irene Smith, whose Service Through Touch program is supported by the AIDS Emergency Fund, massages a person with AIDS in her San Francisco Bay Area home.

Two-Spirited peoples from all over the Americas headed to the Pacific Northwest to pray together and remember who we have always been. The traditional place of gays, lesbians, and true hermaphrodites in the Americas goes way back; long before the Christian patriarchs came and decimated us, First Nations peoples included Two-Spirited people among their numbers, valuing us for our special talents and gifts, as each individual was valued since "time immemorial." In that sense, the appearance of *Living the Spirit* was as much a reiteration of those ancient values as it was a renewed sign of hope and continuance.

Elsewhere in the United States, the general population was caught up in the Presidential election, a matter of real concern to the gay and lesbian community for a number of reasons, including the need for serious governmental commitment to halting the spread of AIDS and providing medical support services for those who were already HIV-positive. The conservative/liberal argument was contextualized in the frame of "family values"—and, perhaps, before many began to notice that "family values" was a code for a major fundamentalist Christian right power-grab on a national scale.

Who remembers Jerry Falwell? I am delighted at the memory of Sister Boom-Boom, one of the Sisters of Perpetual Indulgence, confronting Falwell at the Democratic National Convention, and of the sight of Jesse Jackson addressing the nation backed by representatives from every one of the communities to which I belong by blood and by choice. With him on the podium were Arab-Americans, Native Americans, White Americans (in my case it's Scottish), women, queers, and African-Americans. I have never seen anything like it, and I imagine I will never see its like again.

Nineteen eighty-eight: A small bit of hope, then four more years of "family values." Four more years of too many deaths from engineered causes. Four more years of the rich getting richer, the poor getting homeless, and "all of us soldiers must die," as the old warriors once sang. Indeed. But all was not grim loss. We elected gay and lesbian people to office all over the country, including two openly gay men in the House of Representatives, and passed local and state legislation protecting lesbians and gays from some of the more invidious forms of discrimination.

Outside the nation's borders, the European Court ruled that Ireland's sodomy law violated human rights, while Holland saw active recruitment of gays for military and police services. Canadian activists were forming a national gay-rights organization and returned Svend Robinson, an openly gay MP, to Parliament. And in England, Ian McKellen, the first openly gay man to be knighted, emerged as a leading spokesman for gay rights.

Other positive events occupied our attention during the year: One was the film version of Harvey Fierstein's Tony Award–winning play, *Torch Song Trilogy;* another the growing attention the literary world was paying to the inimitable Gertrude Stein. Finding her name on the list of canonical American writers at the University of California, Los Angeles, was especially pleasing to me. I had been reading her since high school—a very long time ago!

Like every other year of human history, 1988 was, on balance, mixed: some good, some very bad. It was clear that in spite of all kinds of destructive forces arrayed against us, queer visibility in society throughout the Western democracies was increasing. With it the commitment to protecting our rights was improving dramatically. In spite of seemingly growing antigay and antilesbian sentiment, it was increasingly clear that, as we say in the Indian country of the Southwest, "Nos vamos." That is, we kept on keepin' on.

—PAULA GUNN ALLEN

Members of the group Gay American Indians marched down Market Street during San Francisco's Gay Pride Parade.

T I M E L I N E

At school districts across the nation, controversy over HIV/AIDS education and discussions of homsexuality resulted in gag rules in Idaho and Utah and an increased focus on the rights and responsibilities of teachers when addressing controversial subjects. Discrimination against lesbian and gay educators also became increasingly prevalent. In January, a hate letter, penned by the "Parents Against Homos in Teaching," charging two Glencoe, Illinois, teachers with lesbianism was sent to hundreds of local residents.

In February, a federal appeals court ruled against the exclusion of homosexuals from the Army. The decision, issued in a suit filed by Perry Watkins, a former staff sergeant denied reenlistment after fifteen years of service because he was gay, marked the first time an appeals court rejected the Pentagon ban as unconstitutional.

JANUARY   The number of known U.S. AIDS cases passed fifty thousand, with nearly four hundred new cases reported each week. ❑ Joan Kroc, the major stockholder in the McDonald's fast-food chain, gave $1 million to the American Foundation for AIDS Research. ❑ Arsonists destroyed the offices of Womanspace, a lesbian organization in Philadelphia. ❑ Pacific Inter Coast Yachting Association, California's major yachting association, denied membership to the Barbary Coast Boating Club, a gay yachting club. ❑ Police arrested nineteen ACT UP activists protesting price-gouging at the Burlingame, California, offices of Burroughs Wellcome, manufacturers of AZT. ❑ A Dallas judge ordered rock star David Bowie to take an HIV antibody test after a woman testified that he had assaulted her and exposed her to the virus; in Switzerland, he tested negative and the case was thrown out.

FEBRUARY   In a follow-up to the March on Washington one hundred and seventy-five invited gay leaders gathered at a Virginia plantation for a weekend "War Conference" and raised the tactic of exposing closeted conservative politicians. ❑ The nation's first lesbian sorority, Lambda Delta Lambda, formed at the University of California, Los Angeles. ❑ Twenty-three gay Catholics, banned from standing in silent protest inside St. Patrick's Cathedral, were arrested for sitting on the sidewalk across from the Manhattan church. ❑ The U.S. Army pulled a full-page ad from the February issue of *Student Lawyer* because of the magazine's cover story, "The Legal Closet," about homophobia in law school. ❑ A government survey revealed that insurance companies attempt to screen out new applicants who have AIDS or who are likely to come down with the disease. ❑ Britain's House of Lords provisionally passed a ban on promoting homosexuality. The measure, known as Clause 28, would later become law in one of themost bitter defeats for the modern gay movement worldwide.

MARCH   A dozen gay activists were ejected from the Presidential Commission on AIDS hearing after disrupting the testimony of William Dannemeyer (R-Calif.), who told the panel that AIDS was God's punishment for homosexuals. ❑ Divine, the three-hundred-pound transvestite star of *Pink Flamingos, Female Trouble, Hairspray,* and other cult movies, died of asphyxiation at age forty-two. ❑ After the increasing popularity of "Macho Night" and all-male fashion shows at various nightclubs brought the "problem" to the government's attention, Singapore officials, citing "moral considerations," threatened to pull the licenses of bars that catered to gays, according to the Singapore daily, *The Straits Times.*

APRIL   Hollywood-based artist David Hockney threatened to cancel a major show at London's Tate Gallery in protest of antigay legislation pending in Parliament. ❑ Los Angeles District Attorney Ira Reiner announced a series of civil lawsuits designed to close the city's gay bathhouses; the bathhouses remained open. ❑ A Philadelphia restaurant whose manager allegedly told two patrons that he didn't want any "fucking queers" as customers promised in response to a protest to refrain from "practices which may be construed as being discriminatory." ❑ A North Carolina woman asked local library officials to ban Nancy Gardner's *Annie on My Mind,* an American Library Association–endorsed novel that portrays a lesbian relationship between two seventeen-year-old girls.

1988

❑ The Philippine government ordered all foreigners, including American troops, to prove they were free from HIV before being allowed to live in the island nation.

MAY The Saint, Manhattan's legendary disco, closed its doors. ❑ The *Boston Herald* revealed that the Massachusetts State Police infiltrated and spied on gay organizations. ❑ Mother Teresa announced plans to open a hospice for people with AIDS in Memphis, Tennessee. ❑ A Texas jury awarded $1.5 million to a man who claimed his marriage was destroyed by a lesbian nun who seduced his wife. ❑ Tony Award–winning actor George Rose was robbed and clubbed to death in the Dominican Republic by his adopted eighteen-year-old lover.

JUNE Representatives Jim Burning (R-Ky.), Richard Baker (D-La.), and Jim McCrery (D-La.; he was outed by *The Advocate* in 1992) sent 200,000 post-cards warning constituents against the forthcoming U.S. Public Health Service brochure "Understanding AIDS." ❑ Fear of contracting AIDS matched fears about financing college in the minds of American teenagers, according to a Chesebrough-Ponds/Lever Brothers survey of 510 high schoolers. ❑ Animal-rights activists in Maryland protested federal researchers' use of chimpanzees to test AIDS drugs. ❑ Proposition 69, an AIDS quarantine ballot proposal initiated by Lyndon LaRouche, was defeated by California voters a second time. ❑ Chanting "Praise God for AIDS," eight robed Ku Klux Klan members demonstrated at a Gay Pride rally in Florida. ❑ Leonard Matlovich died from AIDS complications. ❑ Ten ACT UP members were arrested for blocking a Philadelphia highway to protest the governor's slashing of the state AIDS budget.

JULY *The Arizona Republic* reported that Phoenix police maintained files on people believed to be HIV-positive or to have AIDS. ❑ A right-wing group asked the governor of Vermont to designate "Straight Pride Day"; the request was ignored. ❑ The lover of a man who died of AIDS bought a half-page ad in *Daily Variety* to protest the entertainment trade paper's obituary policy of listing only blood relatives and not same-sex partners as survivors. ❑ Members of a gay Alcoholics Anonymous group in Boston said they were harassed by police for hugging at the end of their weekly meetings.

AUGUST Under pressure from gay activists, Circle K, a large firm that operates convenience stores, retracted a policy denying medical benefits to employees with AIDS. ❑ The American Federation of Teachers and the National Education Association each approved gay-rights resolutions at their conventions. ❑ Activists in twenty-one American cities rallied on Free Sharon Kowalski Day, in support of the disabled woman and her lover, Karen Thompson, who was fighting to gain guardianship of her. ❑ In a pre-convention statement, Presidential nominee George Bush endorsed protection against AIDS-related discrimination, while at the same time referring to children as "innocent victims" of the disease and its social repercussions.

SEPTEMBER A one-year federal program to subsidize AZT ended, leaving thousands of HIV-infected poor scrambling to raise the $800-a-month cost for the only approved AIDS therapy, and many states attempting to fill the gaps with their own funding. ❑ Mitch Grobeson, drummed out of the Los Angeles Police Department for homosexuality, sued the department for $5 million. ❑ Honolulu lesbian activist Dianne Holmes was left comatose after a machete attack. ❑ At a Republican fund-raiser, Utah Senator Orrin Hatch referred to the Democratic

AIDS WATCH

A survey of sexually active teenagers found that most did not use condoms even though they knew condoms could prevent sexually transmitted diseases, including AIDS. The teenagers surveyed lived in a city with a high incidence of AIDS, high public awareness of the disease, and extensive public education programs. Yet only 2 percent of sexually active teenage girls and 8 percent of the boys surveyed said they used condoms every time they had intercourse.

AIDS remains relatively rare among teenagers—six hundred cases among the total number in the United States, or about 1 percent of the total—although many of the young adults in their twenties who have AIDS most likely contracted the disease while still teenagers. Currently, 21 percent of the cases in the United States are among people in their twenties. Despite a lack of HIV statistics for this group, the high rate of STDs among teens may indicate their risk for HIV infection.

Studies conducted in New York City found that teenagers are more likely to contract AIDS from heterosexual intercourse than from homosexual sex or I.V. drug use. And female teenagers get AIDS in much greater proportion than do adult women.

Effective AIDS prevention messages must emphasize the personal vulnerability of teenagers. Gay men and lesbians must develop extra measures to reach out to gay and lesbian teens whose interests will likely be ignored by the moralistic education programs now mandated by legislators across the country.

—MICHAEL HELQUIST

328

In October, more than a thousand AIDS activists stormed the Maryland offices of the Food and Drug Administration, closing offices for the day and chanting, "Test drugs, not people."

Fifty ACT UP members disrupted a September speech by Dan Quayle, who already had been criticized by gay leaders for his poor record on AIDS-related issues. The startled vice presidential candidate asked, "Who are these people?" as police led them away.

Party as "the party of homosexuals." ❑ Inspired by the hunger-relief project Hands Across America, gay Ohioans protesting state sodomy laws held "Kiss Across Ohio Day." ❑ A twenty-year-old Texan who claimed to have assaulted up to seventy gay men was sentenced to death for murdering a gay telephone repairman by stabbing him fifteen times and hitting him with a hammer seventeen times. ❑ The University of South Florida installed condom machines in its Tampa campus restrooms. ❑ Princess Diana was present at the opening of England's first outpatient center for people with AIDS.

OCTOBER The Metropolitan Community Church turned twenty. ❑ Congress passed a major AIDS package that included $800 million in research funding, but a filibuster threat by Jesse Helms forced testing-confidentiality measures to be dropped. ❑ A University of Southern California study revealed that smog can damage condoms. ❑ The Wisconsin Equal Rights Department upheld the refusal by *Wisconsin Trooper,* a law-enforcement magazine, to include the words "gay owned and operated" in a display ad submitted by the owner of a gay bar. ❑ Texas Rural Legal Aid filed a class-action suit against the Texas Commission for Human Rights on behalf of people with AIDS whose complaints regarding employment benefits had been delayed or refused by the agency. ❑ One hundred gay couples exchanged symbolic marriage vows in San Francisco in a public appeal for legal recognition of their relationships. ❑ Four hundred and fifty Dallas lesbians and gay men bought a full-page ad in *The Dallas Morning News* to disclose their names on the first National Coming Out Day; the paper altered the ad and ran it late.

NOVEMBER George Bush was elected President. ❑ Arson was suspected in blazes that gutted two AIDS hospices, in Dallas and Austin. ❑ Oregon voters repealed a year-old executive order that barred antigay discrimination by state agencies. ❑ Former Marlboro man Christian Haren, a person with AIDS, completed a five-day speaking tour of Utah, urging teenagers there to develop self-esteem as a way to avoid HIV infection. ❑ Hundreds of stores refused to sell November's issue of *Spin* magazine because it contained a useable condom. ❑ Four men who tested positive for HIV sued Louisiana state corrections officials for making them wear pink prison uniforms. ❑ The International Symposium on Education and Communication About AIDS revealed that AIDS had spread to most of the world's populations, including Khartoum and northern Thailand. ❑ Australian health authorities began a program of offering free heroin to addicts as a strategy to prevent the spread of HIV.

DECEMBER The U.S. Supreme Court ruled that the National Security Agency acted within its rights when it fired a gay employee. ❑ Three Alabama state judges asked HIV-positive defendants to make their pleas via telephone rather than in the courtroom. ❑ An increase of violence against gays in Lincoln, Nebraska, prompted a series of self-defense workshops for gay men. ❑ A West Hollywood renter sued his landlord for forbidding him to fly a Gay Pride flag from his apartment balcony; they reached an agreement the next month. ❑ Chicago broke a fifteen-year deadlock and passed a gay-rights ordinance. ❑ In a state-run radio broadcast, the government of China admitted that gays do exist in that country.

THE NEW GAY ACTIVISM

They picketed, protested, chanted, and rallied. They held sit-ins, "kiss-ins," and "die-ins." All across the United States in 1988, gays and lesbians—fed up with the ineffectiveness of traditional lobbying tactics—took their case to the streets. New groups formed in unexpected places like Kansas, Maine, Minnesota, Missouri, and Vermont. In the South, often regarded as politically inactive, groups sprang up in Georgia, Tennessee, and seven cities in North Carolina alone. Even places such as Boston, New York, and Washington, D.C., longtime strongholds of gay activism, saw the creation of new, more militant groups.

In almost every case, the new organizations were dedicated to direct political action. High visibility was the goal, and radical demonstrations more often than not ended up on the front page of newspapers and on the local news. The new era in gay activism reached a high point the week of April 29, when more than thirty new and established gay and lesbian groups across the county staged a series of direct actions, including rallies and acts of civil disobedience. Sponsored by a coalition called ACT NOW (AIDS Coalition to Network, Organize and Win), the week's actions culminated in a National Day of Protest May 7.

Eight thousand protesters braved rain for California's March on Sacramento on May 7, the National Day of Protest, making it the largest march on the capital in the state's history. Other actions included five hundred members of ACT UP blocking rush-hour traffic in New York's financial district.

National Coming Out Day

It had never been tried before, but organizers hoped that thousands of gay men and lesbians across the country would participate in the first-ever National Coming Out Day on October 11. "Coming out is critically important to our community and to our movement," said Jean O'Leary, executive director of National Gay Rights Advocates, a public-interest law firm. "Our invisibility is the essence of our oppression. And until we eliminate that invisibility, people are going to be able to perpetuate the lies and myths about gay people and, in essence, force us into a closet not of our choosing."

Rob Eichberg helped create the event with O'Leary because "the biggest resistance to having gay people out of the closet is our own personal and internalized homophobia. It's not the world out there." The well-known psychologist and founder of The Experience Weekend, a consciousness-raising workshop for gays, explained that "I have been coming out for years, as has Jean, and I have not found it unsafe out there; I have found it quite safe and quite loving. And people's fear that it will not be that way keeps them in the closet."

NATIONAL COMING OUT DAY...

OCTOBER 11

COMING OUT: A REMINISCENCE

It was Saturday, December 30, 1974. Gerald R. Ford was President. "Lucy in the Sky with Diamonds" by Elton John was number one with a bullet on the *Billboard* pop charts. It was the best of times. It was the worst of times. I was just another eighteen-year-old black gay college freshman at UCLA, helping to meet the high cost of my higher education by working part-time at the McDonald's in Westwood Village.

I suppose now is as good a point as any to mention that as of the afternoon of my eighteenth birthday, I was a virgin. Purer than Ivory soap; untouched as the parsley garnish on a T-bone steak.

Which is not to say I hadn't known what I wanted for years. Because, believe me, I'd known. I'd acknowledged myself as gay at around the age of thirteen. I read the chapter on homosexuality in *Everything You've Always Wanted to Know About Sex* and thought: *Yep, that's me alrighty.* And I'd been falling madly, passionately, head-over-tuchus in love with a veritable parade of boys. But as of that Saturday afternoon—not counting masturbation (and let's just say I jerked off quite a lot and leave it at that)—I had never had sex.

Shortly after I'd announced my birthday to our district manager, Robert, he came walking back through the grill area. Robert was thirty years old, had butch-cut blond hair and pale blue eyes and an infectiously boyish grin that never failed to make me want to bite my lip. He stopped directly behind me where I stood shooting Big Mac sauce onto buns with a big sauce gun.

"Eighteen, huh?" Robert whispered into the nape of my neck, making every hair on my body stand at attention. "How about I give you a ride home after work today?"

For the remainder of my shift, I was largely incapable of work. I would have been hard pressed to recognize a hamburger in a room full of objects. A ride home. This, I thought to myself, was it.

I remember Robert steering me out the back door of the store, calling "Lunch!" over his shoulder to whomever, and my heart pounding like a jackhammer. I remember he drove me home in a white Corvette with red leather upholstery. I remember he stopped at a liquor store and bought a bottle of crème de cassis and a large bag of Doritos. I remember he grabbed my thigh between gear-shiftings, and my dick got so hard so fast I nearly blacked out.

We sat in the minuscule living area of the single apartment I shared with the sort of nonentity roommate that college life seems to inflict upon the best of us. Needless to say, you could have sliced, diced, crinkle-cut, and julienned the sexual tension in the room.

At one point, I got up to refill our glasses in the kitchen. I was standing at the kitchen counter, pouring the stuff, and when I turned around, a full glass in each hand, there was Robert. Right there where I'd turned, so we were practically nose to nose. And I went to hand Robert his glass, but he didn't take it. So I'm just standing there like a schmuck, holding a cassis on the rocks in each hand, and just barely breathing, when Robert kissed me. Sweetly. On my lips.

As to what happened next, let's just say that of the milestones in a young man's life—his first car, his first date, that sort of thing—few things, perhaps nothing, compares with a boy's first blowjob. Robert left me feeling about as good as California law will allow, touching my body where he had touched it, and singing softly to myself, "Happy birthday to me...." —LARRY DUPLECHAN

JESSE JACKSON

The Rev. Jesse Jackson's quest for the Democratic Presidential nomination—a race in which he rose from being a sure loser only six months ago to being the near front-runner at the midway point of the race—has put gay loyalties to the test and has unexpectedly upped the political ante for gay voters in 1988.

Consider: It was Jackson, alone among the Democratic contenders, who stood with the hundreds of thousands of people gathered for last October's March on Washington for Lesbian and Gay Rights and who called for more AIDS funding, sweeping civil rights protection for gays, and an end to antigay violence. "There are those who isolate differences, desecrate our humanity, and then justify their inhumanity, just as the Nazis did with yellow stars and pink triangles," Jackson told the rally. "It was not right in Nazi Germany, and it's not right in America."

Jackson also issued that day an impassioned appeal for gay support in his bid for the Democratic Presidential nomination. "Today I stand with you," he declared. "Election time you stand with me. Together we will make a difference." Since then, no other candidate in the field—Republican or Democrat—has staked out a clearer or more comprehensive set of positions on gay civil rights and AIDS issues.

Jackson has appeared in other gay contexts. For example, he addressed a predominately gay Metropolitan Community Church congregation in Minneapolis, visited a home for AIDS patients in Dallas, and spoke at New York City's gay community center. He has drawn gays into his campaign inner circle and has set up a full-time liaison between the campaign and grassroots gay activists. During a March flight between campaign stops in California, *The Advocate* talked with Jackson about his support for gay concerns.

As you were standing on the stage in Washington last October 11, looking out over that sea of faces, what struck you most about the political statement gays were making that day?

Well, the political statement is not what struck me the most. It was the humanity of the people, in unison, reaching out for human understanding; reaching out for that most basic right, the right to be who one is. When you look at 600,000 people reaching out in that way, you cannot see them by sexual preference or by race or by sex or by religion; you just see people.

And the other thing that struck me acutely—I think this is where I almost choked up—was when I saw the people in front of me who had contracted AIDS, who were dying but reaching out in their dying moments to make a statement—trying to make a statement to their families and friends, the U.S. Congress, and the President.

How would you describe your own personal growth on the issue of gay and lesbian rights in the past decade or so?

Well, as we fought for basic civil rights in the South—if you were black, no matter what your religion was, your sex was, or your sexual orientation was,

"As children we carry a strong sense of guilt, and this feeling carries itself into your adult life...unless you address it," said Cheryl Crane (*right*), seen here with her mother, Hollywood legend Lana Turner, and her longtime companion, Josh LeRoy (*left*). In her best-selling book, *Detour: A Hollywood Story,* Crane wrote movingly of her harrowing experiences as a celebrity offspring and of coming to grips with being a lesbian.

"Last year, after I went on the march on Washington, people said to me, 'What are you doing? They're gonna think you're gay.' People think that already, because I hang out with a lot of women. There hasn't been a studio head I've worked for who hasn't come out and asked me if I'm a lesbian. It's possible. I'm not practicing at the moment, but I will not say it will never happen or hasn't happened in my past."

—ACTRESS WHOOPI GOLDBERG

you were certainly denied equal protection [because of] race. The constitutional definition of blacks as three-fifths human was based upon race. To that extent, all black people had the same struggle to gain equal protection under the law, which applied, of course, to Hispanic people and Indian peoples as well. And some of the people who were leaders, who were teachers, who were professionals, were gay or lesbian, and no one denied them their role in leading a demonstration, their right to go to jail, their right to risk their lives.

And so I grew up. I knew professionals, teachers, and musicians who were gay, and there was no witch-hunting on the matter. Though there was always a certain reluctance to promote one's gay or lesbian status, there was no witch-hunt on the question.

I take a fairly constructionist view of the Constitution, in the sense that citizens—civilians—should never be denied their civilian rights, and there is no room for one to be denied those rights based upon race, sex, or religion. On a more human level, I've known gay and lesbian people all of my life—people with whom my family and I developed good human relations. Some of my most brilliant teachers and some of my classmates were gay. They were just a part of the community of people. I think that is what is important to understand.

Have you ever imagined what your reaction might be if you discovered that one of your own children might be gay?

Well, yeah. But my position has always been with my children that whatever of life's circumstances greet them, I still love them....I can't be a part-time father or love them only when they give me gratification. Real love comes out in the low moments. You really must love people the most when they need it the most. People don't need much love when they've got a tail wind blowing. They need love when they are facing headwinds and crosswinds.

Back in the fifties and sixties, blacks were largely dependent on their white liberal friends to take care of them, politically speaking. Gays in the eighties are in a similar predicament, in the sense that they also have to depend on others—liberal friends—to take care of them. What advice would you give to gays now seeking political empowerment, drawing from the lessons that you learned from the civil rights campaigns of the past?

Well, I'm not sure that we were dependent upon liberals to take care of us. I don't think that's accurate. Rosa Parks and Martin Luther King did not depend on liberals to initiate the bus boycott.

We have a sense of self-respect and a sense of self-determination. Some liberals joined it, which was welcomed, but it was not initiated by them. The students sitting down in Greensboro for public accommodations did not depend upon liberals to initiate it or carry it on.

Blacks...led the march to vote. But we had the good judgment to reach out for alliances. Now, whether it is family farmers reaching out or abandoned workers or gays and lesbians, people who want their full rights must reach out for coalition and must have enough sensitivity in coalition to make sure [not only] that their interests are affirmed but that their interests converge with other people's interests. When you reach out bigger than yourself, you get bigger than yourself.

I know that I have done the right, constitutional, and moral thing by affirming a role for everybody in the quilt of humanity. So now the obligation is on gay and lesbian activists to be consistent. —MARK VANDERVELDEN

PROJECT INFORM: THROWING A LIFELINE

"If the government was doing its job," says Martin Delaney, cofounder of Project Inform, the AIDS treatment information organization, "there never would have been a need for Project Inform or the buyers' clubs or any of the alternative groups that have had to form. Until [it does], we're going to stay in business."

In 1985 Delaney, along with San Francisco psychotherapist Joseph Brewer, founded Project Inform. With an advisory board of local physicians and a volunteer staff of hotline operators, the pair has taken on the task of educating the AIDS/ARC/HIV-positive public about the realm of non-FDA-sanctioned AIDS treatments.

What began as an effort to chart and evaluate the "Mexican phenomenon"—individuals traveling across the border to obtain experimental AIDS drugs that were illegal in the United States—has become the country's foremost clearinghouse for information on alternative treatments for AIDS.

"The FDA insists that all AIDS-related drugs be proven by their old existing standards, which takes anywhere from five to seven years," says Delaney. "That kind of standard is fine when you're talking about a new cold remedy, but when you're talking about a fatal…epidemic, you have to change the standards and get treatments out there earlier—even if there is some risk involved. That's a choice the patient should have, as opposed to the bureaucrat in Washington. The biggest crime involved with AIDS has been the failure to get drugs tested quickly. It's inexcusable."

Behind Project Inform's plywood sign, all vestiges of a storefront operation vanish. A computer data base hums with over fifteen thousand names, including those of several hundred doctors who have requested information for treating their own AIDS patients. "You'd like to think that physicians have some formal mechanism for learning about available therapies and treatments, but they don't," continues Delaney. "There is no established mechanism for that in the country. So we're one of the ways they get that information." Four volunteers staff what Delaney says is the only AIDS alternate-treatment hotline in the country, handling over four thousand calls a month. On the wall across from the phone bank is a huge chalkboard listing the most requested drugs, treatments, prices, and related information.

Delaney insists that the key to optimism is knowing one's antibody status. "Coming down with opportunistic infections is preventable," he says, gesturing to the room. The San Francisco skyline is visible through the window. The sweep of his hand takes it all in: the city, the stacks of information packets, the computer data base, and the AIDS-treatment chalkboard. "If we get in a position where the government does have a mechanism for allowing access to these [experimental] drugs, there might come a day when there's no need for any of this. And that would be fine with me." —DAVID PERRY

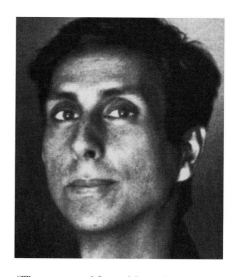

"The one word I would say is common to all long-term survivors is 'grit'… and the love of one good man."
—ACTIVIST AND SIX-YEAR AIDS SURVIVOR MICHAEL CALLEN

"I just got my HIV diagnosis a few months ago. This morning, I'm watching the 'Today Show' and there's this reporter grilling a doctor, 'Isn't it true that a positive diagnosis is a death sentence? The doctor is squirming around, but the reporter won't let up: 'It's a death sentence, right?' Meanwhile, I'm thinking, 'Jesus, I don't need this at eight in the morning.'"
—EROTIC FILMMAKER CHRISTOPHER RAGE

GAY UNDER THE COLLAR

Some years ago, a task force set up by the Archdiocese of San Francisco issued a report estimating that 30 percent of Roman Catholic religious—priests, nuns, brothers—are homosexual. Kevin Gordon, the lay Catholic theologian who headed the task force, now says that the figure was too conservative.

"Priests and nuns tell me that forty to sixty percent is more like it," he says. "Although there obviously isn't any hard data, I tend to agree." Gordon stresses, however, that the percentages pertain to sexual orientation, not necessarily behavior. "I'm not saying that all those people are sexually active."

While all Catholic religious are obliged to lead celibate lives, the distinction between orientation and behavior has special significance for gay people. Official Church teaching maintains that *being* homosexual is morally neutral, but that homosexual *behavior* is inherently sinful. Reality, however, tends to defy orthodoxy. Just as there are many homosexual Catholic laypersons who refuse to accept chastity as the condition for remaining within the Church, there are many gay people in religious life who share Gordon's belief that the orientation/behavior distinction is "pastorally useless and practically meaningless." Some go further in their dissent, rejecting both the Church's proscription against homosexual behavior and its demand that they be celibate.

"I see it [celibacy] as a valid way of living for some," says a New York–based priest who describes himself as gay and sexually active. "But as a universally demanded criterion for ordination, celibacy is hard to justify on scriptural grounds. You have to see it historically—it was introduced and enforced as a way for the institutional Church to control its workers and protect its property rights."

"I think it's somewhat easier for gay priests [than heterosexuals] to reject celibacy," says a cleric assigned to a diocese in a major Middle Atlantic state. "Many of us have decided, after much study, soul-searching, and personal experience, that what the Church teaches about homosexuality is wrong and irrelevant. Once you've rejected a moral teaching, it's easier to throw off a discipline, which is what celibacy is."

Although there are gay clergy who enjoy considerable freedom, Gordon claims many others "are on pins and needles that they might be found out. If you're gay, there's a very real possibility that you're going to be out on your ass. The hierarchy can be ruthless. The gay religious who is really devoted to his or her vocation has a lot at stake if his or her sexuality surfaces."

Some gay clergy, however, have found the "crazy stuff" sufficient reason to leave the Church altogether. Peter Carey, a former Dominican priest, entered the order in 1959 and left eleven years later when, on assignment in Rome, he met the man who became his lover. Carey now works as an editor in New York. "Many gay men are attracted to the religious life," he says. For him, as a young man disturbed by his sexual feelings, the priesthood provided "the perfect solution to this unresolved, mysterious, and terrifying inclination.

"I'm sympathetic to gay people who feel that the only way to change the Church is to work from within," he comments, "but my choice was to get out." Carey believes that Roman Catholicism "needs a clean sweep. It isn't only homosexuality—it's women's issues, it's the lack of any democracy in the Church. I didn't want to wait for the Catholic Church to come to its senses. I decided to vote with my feet." —GEORGE DE STEFANO

"AREN'T THEY NICE...A GIFT FROM MY CONGREGATION...FULL LEATHER VESTMENTS."

© 1988 by Alison Bechdel

CARTOONIST ALISON BECHDEL

Throughout the eighties, gay and lesbian cartoonists reflected the ups and downs of gay life with all the goodwill and insight they could tap in the face of hatred, bigotry, and disease. Howard Cruse, the creator of Wendell, is perhaps the best-known of the first wave of gay cartoonists. Now a second wave has crested with Alison Bechdel.

"Dykes to Watch Out For," Bechdel's intelligent, nationally syndicated comic strip about lesbian life and love, could easily serve as the text for an Introduction to Lesbianism course. Confining herself to writing about the lesbian experience used to worry Bechdel until she realized that "the subculture is not a limitation. Everyday life is my source. I can't run out of material."

Bechdel knew at age seven that she wanted to be a cartoonist, although she didn't start drawing lesbians—or, for that matter, women of any kind—until she came out at nineteen. "I think that cultural misogyny translates into how kids learn to draw," she explains. In college art classes, Bechdel had no problem drawing the women models, but "if I drew out of my head, I drew men. When I finally came out, I worried about why I couldn't draw women. Finally, I realized I could draw them if I drew lesbians."

Here is Bechdel's astute take on the ever-shifting relations between gay men and lesbians.

Parting Words from a Divine Legend

The phones were ringing. Divine was dead. The three-hundred-pound actor, whose portrayals of outrageous women in camp movies like *Pink Flamingos* brought laughter to audiences over the past two decades, was found March 7 in his room at the Regency Plaza Hotel in Los Angeles. Harris Glenn Milstead, forty-two, died of a heart attack and asphyxiation brought on by obesity.

Just a month before he had explained to the *Washington Post,* "I hate that when they call me a transvetite. If I were a transvestite, I'd be sitting here with a little crocodile handbag and a polka-dot bow. Those are my work clothes. That's how I make people laugh."

Ironically, the cult-film heroine—and gay cultural icon—died just as he was experiencing his greatest success. Divine's latest film, *Hairspray,* had quickly become a major critical and box office hit. Divine's first role came in 1968, portraying Jackie Kennedy in *Eat Your Makeup,* a bizarre low-budget film directed by his high school buddy John Waters. It was Waters, Divine once said, who gave him the name that later would even go on his passport "because he always thought that inside me was a divine person."

Many other collaborations with the filmmaker followed. Among the actor's colorful roles were Babs Johnson, "the filthiest person alive," in *Pink Flamingos* (1972); Dawn Davenport, career criminal and professional beauty, in *Female Trouble* (1974); and Francine Fishpaw, a victimized housewife, in *Polyester* (1981).

I talked with Divine in his new West 90th Street penthouse in Manhattan shortly before his death. He was the perfect host, a bit weary from promoting his new film but full of gracious good humor. I wanted to know if the actor's mainstream acceptance had changed his attitude toward his gay fans. "Of course not," he replied. "Without the gay fans I wouldn't be sitting here right now. They are the ones who gave me my start in show business. They're the ones who supported me from the very beginning. No matter what happens I will always play to them. That's just plain and simple."

His rise from a cult oddity to a serious actor in growing demand for nondrag parts had come as a surprise to some, but not to Divine. "I think every actor grows with every project he's done," he said. "If you don't, it's time to quit and put it aside because you're not an actor. I am a comedian. A comic actor. I'm still not Sarah Bernhardt, but I'm up there with Helen Hayes."

Divine's fans did not realize that he was actually a very subdued soul. Often wearing caftans that flowed about his ample frame, the quiet actor was the antithesis of his on-screen persona of sex-mad, evil-loving, big-bosomed sex goddess. He revealed this side of himself when I asked if he'd pose for a photograph mugging in character. "That's just not me, honey," he laughed. "That's just a character I do. I'd look like a big fruit. I'm actually a serious person. I'm shy."

Our interview had come to a close. "I knock on wood every day that I'm still healthy and alive," he said, walking me to the door. "I'd like to live to be into my eighties."

Two weeks later Divine was dead, his passing announced with a flurry of media coverage befitting a major star. It was a celebrity status never doubted by Divine's loyal gay fans over the years, who had followed him from his early days of dubious notoriety to the recent and hard-won celebration of a genuine and original talent.

—Brandon Judell

Authors: Edmund White on Gay Writing

Edmund White folds his hands, leans forward across the café table, and speaks in a voice that is intense yet surprisingly gentle and unassuming. "I think there is something intrinsically exciting and interesting to the straight public about gay writing, and I can't quite figure it out. And it has seemed to me ever since I was a kid to be that way."

At forty-eight, White is "America's foremost gay writer," or so says *Newsweek* magazine in its recent article on the crossover of gay fiction into the mainstream. Wearing preppy glasses, blue jeans, and a loose white sweatshirt, the writer looks more the puzzled undergrad than the gay guru. The recent spate of gay authors being "discovered" by a straight mainstream public does not surprise him. "Many of the people I have met who are gay all seem to have a philosophical attitude, even if they weren't educated, toward their lives," he says. "And I think that is perfect training for a writer. So it seems to me no accident that we have such a high proportion of good writers who are gay."

The aura of "gay sensibility" hangs heavily over this writer. White brushes off notions of some "mystical gay entity that crosses national and time barriers [linking] us to the ancient Greeks or with the gay courtiers of Elizabeth the First," yet he does believe that there is something, often indefinable, about gay art. "I think Tennessee Williams must have been one of the first gay writers I was aware of," he says. "There was something about the immediacy of the language and a love for the wounded of the world that resonated with me."

The author's newest novel is *The Beautiful Room Is Empty*. "I wanted to tell a story about what gay life was like before gay liberation," says White. "That is, under a different type of oppression than the one we're threatened with now, but still similar." White should know: Like his fictitious creations, White was present at the Stonewall Inn the June night in 1969 when modern gay liberation was born. "Who knew that we were making history?" he asks, smiling.

Beautiful Room is his "most militant book" yet, says White. "In the old days of early gay liberation, people were always calling on me to write positive role models, and I was never very interested in doing that. It seemed to me a very primitive and Stalinist view of gay fiction. But now, when all of gay culture is in danger of being wiped out and, certainly, gay rights are in danger of being suppressed, it's important to raise these books as sort of bulwarks.

"I feel that the real function of art is to unsettle people," he continues. "Most of the so-called art that we see is not really art at all. It's entertainment, and its function is to settle, to make people feel that they are at home in the world. I think a real artist makes you feel that he is a stranger and we're all strangers on the earth."

—David Perry

"Imagine trying to have safe sex if you weren't gay. Outside the gay community, safe sex means only using a rubber. Nothing more imaginative. We're light-years ahead of heterosexuals." —Author John Preston

BOOKS: OSCAR WILDE REVISITED

RICHARD HALL

From its very first issue, *The Advocate* paid attention to what was being published— good and bad—about homosexuality. But it was not until Richard Hall's tenure as *The Advocate*'s book editor from 1976 to 1982 that the magazine established a consistently high standard for covering authors and books dealing with the gay experience. Hall was a distinguished author himself—a novelist, short-story writer, and widely produced playwright—and was also a keen observer of the publishing world.

In 1978, he noted that "editors and publishers, suddenly aware that both cash and reputation were to be made from once-forbidden subjects, have—with a heady American mix of conscience and capitalism— turned homosexuality into a minor industry, rivaled only by books on meditation, Swiss banks, and how to get a cheap divorce while jogging. Naturally there has been wild jubilation in the gay community over this turn of events, particularly among those old enough to remember the fifties, when books on gay themes were so rare they had to be loaned as cautiously as the keys to the family Studebaker."

Hall was the first openly gay critic to be elected to the National Book Critics Circle. His landmark essay, "Gay Fiction Comes Home," was a front-page article in *The New York Times Book Review* in June 1988. "Richard Hall's survey of gay literature in *The New York Times Book Review* asserted that gay writing, influenced by AIDS and the slow growth of critical attention gay works have received through the eighties, has moved past the trauma of coming out," wrote Richard Labonte, who succeeded the visionary Hall as *The Advocate*'s book columnist in mid-decade. "The sharp essay's corollary is that gays are no longer the villainous stereotypes of yore, the 'heretics, witches, radicals, Nazis— you name it,' but rather, plain folk in fine books, which 'accept the right of others to be gay.'

One of Hall's last pieces for *The Advocate,* a review of Richard Ellmann's biography of Oscar Wilde, appears here.

There is something in every gay heart that responds to Oscar Wilde, something that goes deeper than thought or words, that waits in the blood, surfacing when the time is right.

Along with countless other gay men, I have made it my business to learn the details of Wilde's life. It has sorted itself into large, capitalized episodes in my mind: Oxford, Aesthete, American Tour, Marriage, Playwright, Bosie, Trials, Prison, and Exile. You know them all. Various epigrams, images, and impressions stand out, culled from biographies, movies, plays, one-man shows, and photo collections. From time to time, I have refreshed my memory by rereading *De Profundis, The Importance of Being Earnest, The Picture of Dorian Gray,* and "The Decay of Lying." The subject has never, never palled.

In due course, I realized that Wilde had become an ever-changing myth for me, ready to fill any emotional need. He was the martyr, killed for being gay. He was the artist who had punctured lies and hypocrisy. He was the supreme literary stylist, impaling the world on a word. He was also a dandy, cynic, wit, camp, lover, and victim. He was available at all times, ready to fill any role I required. And behind all this—an arching rainbow—was the great parabola of his life, the catharsis of rise, triumph, trial, agony, and execution.

As the years passed, I came to realize that Wilde's power over my imagination stemmed not from these dramatic events or usable myths, vital as they were, but from something even more remarkable. He had been the first to perform, in public and at great cost, the rite essential to my survival as a homosexual: He had created himself. For his other attributes, I admired him; for the bravery of his self-invention, I loved him.

I was, therefore, very excited to hear about a new biography, *Oscar Wilde,* by Richard Ellmann, well-known for his studies of Irish literature. It took Ellmann twenty years, and the work shows. I cannot imagine the need for another biography for a generation, if then. Ellmann discusses the life and the works. His canvas is large; his psychology acute; his literary analysis searching. Best of all, he avoids the old simplifications.

From the Ellmann book, a far more varied portrait emerges than any we have seen before. Wilde was a huge set of contraries crammed into one package. Kind but arrogant. Vain but generous. A snob but gentle toward his inferiors. Loving his children but deserting them for male prostitutes. A moralist with a taste for crime. A lover of beauty with an urge toward sleaze.

Eventually the paradoxes became too heavy—unsustainable. The words ran out, and Wilde had to act the parts that mattered more: lover, seducer. His collapse via Lord Alfred Douglas can be taken as a sign that language had failed him, that the exquisite balance of anger and wit had been overborne.

It is another of Ellmann's virtues that he regards Wilde with admiration and affection. There is no safe distance between author and subject, no impression that Wilde was a fabulous freak. I believe the gay movement and our literary efforts are partly responsible for this. In the past dozen years we have detoxified the private lives of many authors—Henry James, John Cheever, E. M. Forster, Lord Byron, and Willa Cather, to name a few—making them available for honest inspection and making closeted biography or even authorial ambivalence about their homosexuality unfashionable. Wilde, at last, has been released into respectability—which is to say, into his own life. —RICHARD HALL

NEVER AGAIN
6 JULY 1943

NEVER FORGET
22 JUNE 1988

A GAY VIETNAM VETERAN

WHEN I WAS IN THE MILITARY
THEY GAVE ME A MEDAL FOR KILLING TWO MEN
AND A DISCHARGE FOR LOVING ONE.

Gay Pride
1989

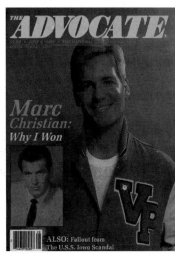

Marc Christian: Why I Won

ALSO: Fallout from The U.S.S. Iowa Scandal

Gay Images

Jeff Stryker and the Men Who Made Him

MINISTER'S GAY-BASHING TALE:
Was It a Hoax?

REBEL WITH A CAUSE?

HAPPY CAMPER

Suicide Ends Sex Probe for D.C. Lobbyist

TRIBULATIONS

1989 Two decades after the Stonewall Riots, the nation's gay political landscape was still in turmoil. ACT UP demonstrations culminated in nationwide Days of Rage, the National Endowment for the Arts controversy erupted over a Robert Mapplethorpe exhibit, and Massachusetts finally passed a gay-rights law. But this was most notably the year when the struggle to lift the military's antigay ban reached a turning point. Forty-five years after the military first adopted its antigay policies in World War II, the fight against the ban had reached a momentum that neither the gay community nor the military could stop.

When *The Advocate* covered the military events of 1989, it continued a long tradition in the lesbian and gay press. I learned about the origins of this tradition while writing *Coming Out Under Fire*, a book about lesbian and gay soldiers in World War II. A group of gay veterans contacted me to tell me how, as airmen stationed at Myrtle Beach, South Carolina, in 1943, they had put out a newsletter which they called *The Myrtle Beach Bitch*—a campy attempt to keep gay GIs in touch with each other and boost their morale. When their publication got into the hands of hostile officers, these young pioneers of the gay preess were arrested, convicted of sending obscene material through the mail, and sentenced to a year in a federal penitentiary.

In the fifties and sixties, the emerging homophile movement carved out a more legal space for an ongoing lesbian and gay press which in part documented the shifts in military policy and defended the rights of lesbian and gay military personnel. Cover stories and feature articles appeared with headlines such as UNDESIRABLE DISCHARGE (*Mattachine Review*), HOMOSEXUAL SERVICE-MEN (*ONE* magazine), and HOMOSEXUALS IN UNIFORM (*Ladder*). In the seventies, the underground press—including *The Advocate*—began to publish articles on lesbian and gay antiwar protests and followed the cases of the first wave of veterans—including Leonard Matlovich, Perry Watkins, and Miriam Ben-Shalom—who appealed their bad discharges as open homosexuals. By the eighties, the gay press broadened its coverage of the fight to lift the military's ban on homosexuals, and to a lesser degree the conflict within the gay movement between those who wanted to end military discrimination and those who were antimilitary.

The long struggle to overturn the ban, despite the ongoing appeals and protests, had few successes. At first, events in 1989 seemed to be more of the same. When *The Advocate* polled activists on their predictions for the "Gay '90s," Nan Hunter, director of the ACLU Project on Lesbian and Gay Rights, described little progress on fighting the policy. It was hard to predict, she said, when "the critical mass will be reached so that kind of irrational policy will finally be jettisoned."

In the courts there were more setbacks. A panel of the Seventh Circuit U.S. Court of Appeals rejected Ben-Shalom's appeal to reenlist in the Army. In vicious antilesbian purges, women were now being charged with sodomy for the first time. In March, following a witch-hunt at the Parris Island Marine Corps base, Barbara Baum was released from prison after serving six months on sodomy charges. And in April, the Navy reached a new low when it blamed an explosion aboard the U.S.S. *Iowa*—which killed forty-seven crew members— on a gay relationship turned sour. Discouraged activists described this serious political setback as a field day for those who wanted gays out of the military.

Depressing as these events were, the seeds of change they had germinated were growing. At the beginning of the year, Joe Steffan, who had been expelled from Annapolis months before graduation because he acknowleged he was gay, sued the government. In May, the Ninth Circuit U.S. Court of Appeals ruled that the Army had to readmit Perry Watkins—a victory that was later upheld by the Supreme Court. By the end of the year, the Navy's scapegoating of allegedly gay sailors for the *Iowa* blast was exposed for what it was—a cynical coverup of the Navy's own incompetence.

Activists opened new fronts in their battle to lift the ban. In January they formed the Gay and Lesbian Military Freedom Project (GLMFP), a loose coalition of civil rights groups. In April, GLMFP organized a group of four women who testified at Defense Department hearings that the antigay policy was used as a form of sexual harassment against all women, and that women were discharged as homosexuals at rates many times higher than were men. And during the fall, students held rallies and sit-ins on college campuses protesting the stepped-up ROTC war on lesbian, gay, and bisexual cadets.

In October, a story broke that put the military on the defensive once again. Someone had leaked to Representative Gerry Studds's office two secret "PERSEREC" reports commissioned by the Pentagon. These concluded that the military had no evidence for supporting its gay ban and that it should integrate openly homosexual personnel into the ranks. In response to the leak, the Pentagon discredited the reports and prohibited military officials from participating in the public debate over the policy that was now spreading from the campuses to professional organizations and the mainstream media.

By the end of the year, as the contours of a national political conflict were taking shape, I kept thinking back on the airmen who started their little newsletter at Myrtle Beach. Their imprisonment during World War II had made them feel so ashamed of what they had done that they were afraid to tell anyone until decades later. Now, not only had they felt enough pride to tell their story, but the nation was on the brink of addressing the injustices that had been done to them and the thousands of other veterans who had been discharged as homosexuals since World War II.   —ALLAN BÉRUBÉ

342

"My basic message is that the government is lying about nearly every aspect of the epidemic. I want to challenge gay people who go along with the government about HIV to start thinking more."
—NEW YORK NATIVE PUBLISHER
CHARLES ORTLEB

> "ACT UP has gotten me in a lot of doors. If government officials don't deal with us, well fine. We'll let Larry Kramer kick down your door and pee on your desk."
> —LOBBYIST/ACTIVIST
> MARTIN DELANEY

ACT UP demonstrators put forth a conspiracy theory about AIDS.

T I M E L I N E

In February, Karen Thompson won a court victory allowing her to visit her disabled lover, Sharon Kowalski, for the first time in three and a half years.

In January, activists, some wearing George Bush masks, pasted AIDS-awareness handbills along the Washington, D.C., parade route for Bush's inauguration.

JANUARY   Zakk Wylde, a guitarist for rocker Ozzy Osbourne, apologized for urging New Year's Eve concertgoers to beat up "faggots and queers." ❏ The nation's first full-scale, government-sponsored needle-exchange program was approved by the Tacoma, Washington, County Board of Health. ❏ The World Health Organization announced a reported total of 132,976 AIDS cases in 177 countries, with the highest number in the United States, followed by Uganda.

FEBRUARY   Nevada legislators proposed prison terms for gays or bisexuals who, regardless of their HIV status, donate blood or organs. ❏ Despite his AIDS diagnosis, Buddhist leader Ösel Tendzin announced that he would not step down from his post as the Vajra Regent at Colorado's Naropa Institute. ❏ A New York group made plans for the country's first lesbian and gay museum; it was later tabled due to lack of support.

MARCH   Three thousand protesters staged the largest AIDS demonstration yet in New York City in an attempt to "take over" City Hall to draw attention to the collapse of the city's hospital system; two hundred were arrested. ❏ Well-come-Burroughs, the British manufacturers of AZT, said that some strains of HIV had become resistant to the drug. ❏ West Hollywood began offering medical insurance coverage of up to $20,000 to domestic partners of gay and lesbian city workers. ❏ A Maryland woman with AIDS died in her county hospital bed during a fire because she was restrained. ❏ Olympic diving champion Greg Louganis got a court order to keep his former male housemate at least five hundred feet away from him. ❏ The Los Angeles County Sheriff's Department agreed to recruit gay men and lesbians. ❏ An El Paso cafeteria worker was placed on paid leave from her job at an elementary school because her son had died from AIDS complications. ❏ Nearly one hundred new AIDS cases were being reported every day in the United States.

APRIL   Pittsburgh Mayor Sophie Masloff issued an executive order banning antigay discrimination in city hiring after a three-year campaign by the lesbian and gay community culminating in a one-hundred-strong City Hall protest at which activists carried signs that read, "Sophie's Choice—Bigotry!" ❏ The Washington State attorney general ruled that needle-exchange programs designed to stem the spread of AIDS were illegal. ❏ Hecklers taunting George Bush for his inaction on AIDS interrupted the President's nationally televised speech in honor of the bicentennial of George Washington's inauguration.

MAY   "Bloody" handprints of red paint appeared on six Los Angeles county buildings, capping a year-long protest over the city's lack of a public AIDS clinic. ❏ C. Everett Koop, the U.S. surgeon general who defied the right wing (which installed him) by calling for condom use and sex education, announced that he would leave his post in July. ❏ A North Carolina jury acquitted a white supremacist of the hate-motivated slayings of three gay men. ❏ A Centers for Disease Control/American College Health Association study of seventeen thousand students from nineteen colleges and universities found that two out of every thousand college students tested HIV-positive. ❏ A South Carolina theater staging *Bent,* a play about gays in Nazi Germany, was defaced. ❏ Seven thousand marchers converged in Madison, Wisconsin, to demonstrate for gay rights. ❏ An autopsy of K. C. McClatchy, publisher of the *Sacramento Bee,* revealed the prominent newspaperman to have been HIV-positive; McClatchy, who was not symptomatic, died of a heart attack while jogging. ❏ Princeton University banned the CIA from on-campus recruiting because of the agency's antigay hiring practices. ❏ The only gay bar in the state of North Dakota closed after repeated vandalism and harassment.

JUNE   Compound Q was hailed as a possible cure for AIDS in reports at the International AIDS Conference in Montreal, refuting earlier criticisms of underground tests run on this derivative of a Chinese cucumber root. ❏ In a press conference, members of ACT UP–Los Angeles accused the County Sheriff's Department of conducting illegal searches as part of an intimidation campaign. ❏ A former Dover, Delaware, Baptist minister was arrested for responding to a government-planted ad seeking traders for child pornography pictures. ❏ A woman whose infant son was adopted by jazz pianist Billy Tipton in 1963 sued Tipton's estate for fraud after Tipton's postmortem revealed him to have been a woman posing as a man; the son expressed continuing loyalty to "my dad," and the case was thrown out. ❏ Conservative Congressman William Dannemeyer submitted to the *Congressional Record* a graphic account of what he said were the sex acts of the average gay man.

JULY   After being sued by a gay legal group, TWA agreed to reverse a three-year-old company policy and let its frequent-flier credits be used by companions who are not blood relatives or spouses of frequent fliers. ❏ More than ninety thousand employees of the Internal Revenue Service received a new contract protecting them from on-the-job discrimination based on sexual orientation. ❏ New York State's highest court ruled that two gay people could constitute a family, granting the lover of a deceased gay man the lease to their rent-controlled apartment. ❏ A lesbian-battering intervention project in Minnesota refused to accept a donation from a cogender S&M group.

AUGUST   Openly gay U.S. Representative Barney Frank (D-Mass.) was the subject of a scandal when Steve Gobie, a former hustler whom Frank hired as a chauffeur and personal aide, told the *Washington Times* that he used the congressman's home as a base for prostitution; in November, Frank easily won re-election. ❏ Gay social-services worker Jeff Gould filed suit against the Washington, D.C., chapter of Big Brothers of America for antigay discrimination; two months later, Big Brothers reversed its policy prohibiting gays from volunteering. ❏ San Francisco County Jail made condoms available to prisoners, but because sex in prison is punishable, there were no takers. ❏ The Oklahoma Court of Criminal Appeals overturned the conviction of a man for raping his nine-year-old nephew because state law did not recognize homosexual rape. ❏ Illinois state police and Chicago city police agreed to pay $226,500 to customers of a Chicago gay bar who filed a federal lawsuit charging that their constitutional rights were violated during a 1985 raid. ❏ Texas enacted a law requiring real-estate agents to tell buyers or renters if property was previously occupied by someone who had AIDS.

SEPTEMBER   Opening night of the San Francisco Opera season was disrupted by AIDS activists who blew whistles and threw leaflets from the balconies to demand increased attention to AIDS. ❏ After militant ACT UP members began shouting at fundamentalists who were protesting Orange County's first Gay Pride festival, police responded with what gay activists termed a "police riot." ❏ Eighteen Kentucky men were arrested in a Lexington

The Corcoran Gallery in Washington, D.C., brought Robert Mapplethorpe into the headlines by canceling a traveling exhibit of his photographs, many of which were homoerotic, in June. Senator Jesse Helms's championing of the censorship effort eventually resulted in restrictions on the freedom of artists funded by the National Endowment for the Arts.

Mainstream newspapers, including the *Dallas Voice,* which published this cartoon, joined gay leaders to condemn Dallas judge Jack Hampton, who in February said that he gave a lighter-than-usual sentence to a murderer because his two victims were "queers."

Black lesbian activist Mabel Hampton, a founder of the Lesbian Herstory Archives and the subject of several film and television documentaries, died in October at age eighty-seven.

The United States Postal Service commemorated the origins of gay liberation with Keith Haring's donated logo. Predictably, Jesse Helms objected.

city park as part of an undercover operation by local police. ❑ The publisher of the yellow pages for the Chicago area agreed to add the heading "Gay and Lesbian Organizations" to its 1990 directory. ❑ Community health officials in Montana warned that Native Americans had the highest rate of sexually transmitted disease of any minority group in the country, and that they might be wiped out by AIDS. ❑ A Quebec human-rights commission criticized a Montreal paper for calling homosexuality "a real killer." ❑ Denmark passed a law granting registered same-sex couples all the same rights as heterosexual married couples, with the exception of the right to adopt children.

OCTOBER Two reports commissioned by the Pentagon said that gays are at least as qualified as, and sometimes more qualified than, heterosexuals to serve in the military; copies of both reports, which Pentagon officials never released, were leaked to Representative Gerry Studds (D-Mass.), who made them public. ❑ Police arrested more than 130 demonstrators in Los Angeles and San Francisco, as gays around the country protested federal inaction on AIDS. ❑ Robert McQueen, former *Advocate* editor and chairman of the board of its parent company, died of AIDS-related illnesses. ❑ An Illinois woman was convicted of murder for helping her husband shoot and decapitate a man because they believed he was gay. ❑ Officials at the International Balloon Festival in Albuquerque refused entry to a condom-shaped balloon intended to generate donations to AIDS groups.

NOVEMBER David Dinkins, the first African-American to be elected mayor of New York, publicly thanked his lesbian and gay supporters for their role in the campaign. ❑ The American Foundation for AIDS Research launched a grants program for assistance to developing countries. ❑ The Minneapolis Civil Rights Department ruled that the local Roman Catholic archdiocese discriminated against Dignity, a group of gay Catholics, when it refused to renew the organization's lease for a religious facility on the University of Minnesota campus. ❑ North Carolina health officials suspended distribution of a safe-sex poster showing a pair of empty, unzipped jeans with the slogan "If you can't keep it zipped, keep it covered." ❑ An HIV-positive Texas inmate was sentenced to life in prison after being convicted of spitting in a prison guard's face. ❑ Craig Spence, a lobbyist for foreign businesses who had created a scandal by taking male prostitutes on a late-night tour of the White House, committed suicide in a Boston hotel room. ❑ The nation's Roman Catholic bishops reversed their 1987 support of condom education as a way to prevent AIDS.

DECEMBER Chanting "You say don't fuck, we say fuck you!" nearly five thousand New York activists demonstrated outside St. Patrick's Cathedral while several dozen disrupted services inside; 111 were arrested. ❑ Lesbian activist Jean O'Leary, under fire for her management style and alleged financial improprieties, resigned as executive director of the National Gay Rights Advocates, a public-interest law firm; just over a year later, NGRA would shut its doors. ❑ Russian activist and journalist Masha Gessen, a native of Russia, became the first openly lesbian refugee to be granted U.S. citizenship. ❑ Ron Webek of St. Petersburg, Florida, became a medical mystery when doctors could find no trace of HIV in his system after he had suffered an AIDS-related brain disease that had nearly killed him four years earlier. ❑ ACT UP–London launched a campaign to tie up the phone lines of Texaco's British branch, which required new employees to be tested for HIV.

EDWARD ALBEE

"When I write a play, I'm interested in changing the way people look at themselves and their lives. When I go to a play, I consider it an absolute waste of time unless I can start to think about something differently—or get to reexamine my own values. I mean, I write plays about certain behaviors so that people will stop behaving that way! That's what serious writing is all about." The speaker is, indeed, a serious writer, although many of his award-winning plays are laced with humor, mostly of the barbed kind. When his first full-length play opened on Broadway in 1962, theater critics lauded him as "the successor to Tennessee Williams and Arthur Miller." He would subsequently receive two Pulitzer prizes for drama during an illustrious career that has spawned twenty-six plays produced all over the world. He is Edward Albee.

Albee himself looks much younger than his sixty-one years. He was thirty-three when *Who's Afraid of Virginia Woolf?* premiered on Broadway in 1962, establishing its creator as a dramatist second to none in the United States.

Albee's first play, *The Zoo Story,* received its world premiere in Berlin in 1959; Broadway, it seems, had flatly turned it down. But the one-act play, a tragic study of two men trapped in modern alienation and the inability to communicate, was produced off-Broadway later that year. The acclaim it received was reinforced when three more plays, *The American Dream, The Death of Bessie Smith,* and *The Sandbox,* soon followed. By the time *Virginia Woolf* made its mark on Broadway, Albee was being touted as "the virtual savior of serious American theater." The Pulitzer prizes were awarded in 1966 for *A Delicate Balance* and in 1975 for *Seascape.*

As for the famous allegation that the two straight couples in *Virginia Woolf* are really surrogates for four gay men, Albee flashes an amused grin and relates how the theory took root. "Somebody who was the film critic for *Newsweek* magazine wrote in his review that he couldn't accept the piece as an accurate portrayal of heterosexual couples; therefore, they must be gay couples in disguise. Well, that's *his* problem—but he made it mine!

"And shortly after that, a very dreadful man who was drama critic for *The New York Times* for a brief time wrote a very famous article—not naming names—but attacking gay playwrights in the United States, saying that all of them were really writing about gay situations and disguising them as straight situations, which I take is for commercial reasons or out of guilt or some shit."

Albee leans back in his chair, clearly annoyed at the recollection. "I think I'm a reasonably competent playwright, and if I had wanted to write a play about two gay couples, I would have done it. There *is* a difference, although not as much as people might think—because of the fiction perpetuated by the Harvey Fiersteins of this world, [in whose plays] gays are, indeed, laughable parodies of human beings....

"It's just too preposterous to think that George and Martha would be a gay couple. And yet, I think one reason why people have to think that is because it would let them off the hook; they don't have to think that the play is about themselves."

Albee, in fact, *has* written a play that includes a gay couple. "It's called *Finding the Sun,* and I wrote it in 1982," he says. "The gay couple in the play

Bob Paris, the world-champion bodybuilder whose symmetry was called the most perfect since Steve Reeves's, came out in *Ironman* magazine. "I guess there will be people who won't like my physique anymore because I'm gay," said Paris (*right*), pictured here with his life partner, Rod Jackson. "That makes me laugh."

are no longer living together; because of societal pressures, they've both gotten into terribly unhappy [straight] marriages. [And] you know, there are gay characters running through my plays, and nobody's paid attention to them." (According to Albee, they include Butler in *Tiny Alice*, Jack in *Everything in the Garden*, and Henry in *The Ballad of the Sad Café*.) The playwright leans forward now, choosing his words carefully. "I have very complex feelings about whether a gay playwright must write about gay subjects on the theory that he or she is incapable of comprehending heterosexual responses to life. I don't think that's true.

"Another thing I don't like is ghettoization of any kind of literature. I find that too much of what is called gay literature, gay theater, and gay playwriting is turning out to be a kind of limitation. No matter how well-intentioned it is, it's ghettoization. Some of the characters in my plays are gay, and some are straight. And that's fine because that's the way life is. But gay is not a subject; societal pressure on gay people is a subject.

"AIDS, in a way, is a subject," he continues. "It's a very useful agitprop for trying to raise more money for AIDS research, treatment, and support—and as an attempt to try to make our society a little more tolerant. But I've seen so much gay writing that's not as good as it could be because it's trying so hard to be gay writing!"

Does Albee see a value in the rise of gay regional theater? The playwright ponders the question with apparent mixed feelings. "Everything that can attempt to turn straight minds into seeing gays as human beings is great. But in the commercialization of gay writing, there's a separatism that's beginning to happen that I don't like. I remember back in the fifties and sixties, during the civil rights movement, certain black writers were integrating themselves very nicely into the mainstream. Then black separatism began to happen, and it began to isolate blacks from whites. I would hate to see gay political activism and gay rights produce that kind of separatism."

We talk about National Coming Out Day, which recently celebrated its second anniversary. "I was in the Village around [the time of the Stonewall Rebellion], and I was delighted to see that happen, along with the emergence of self-respect. Most gay people that I've been around all my life have that particular kind of self-respect, and they didn't need a coming-out day. But for people who do—wonderful." For the past ten years, Albee has been touring the country, working with aspiring playwrights, and teaching master classes at universities. He seems generally pleased with the way his career—and his life—have taken shape, though there are the inevitable peaks and valleys.

"I get a little disappointed sometimes that so many of my plays have been intentionally and conscientiously misunderstood by the critics," he admits. "At the same time, I think that I'm probably writing now as well as I ever did—perfecting my craft."

And his personal life? Albee folds his hands against his chest and smiles contentedly. "I'm a reasonably, if not idiotically, happy person. I've been in a twenty-year relationship, which has made me very happy. I've always been given to long relationships: My first was eight years, and my second was five and a half years.

"I would love to live forever, because life is really wonderful," Albee concludes. "There's so much to discover all the time and to learn. I want to go on forever."
—KIM GARFIELD

THE SAGA OF MARC CHRISTIAN

Rock Hudson's 1985 death from AIDS-related illness shook the world. But an even bigger shake-up rumbled out of Los Angeles County Court when Marc Christian, self-described bartender, musicologist, and ex-lover of the late actor, sued the estate, claiming that Hudson had not informed him of his illness. A jury awarded Christian $21.75 million.

The public reaped a lurid bounty of allegations about Hudson's penis size, preferred sexual positions, and movie-star selfishness. But critics expressed alarm that Christian, who repeatedly tested negative for HIV, won sympathy for "emotional distress" and inflamed the social intolerance that drives AIDS underground.

"The verdict sends a dangerous message," said Ben Schatz, a lawyer for National Gay Rights Advocates. "It tells people that if they continue to bury their heads in the sand by engaging in unsafe sex and become infected, it's entirely their partners' fault and they don't bear any responsibility." Even the *Los Angeles Times* proposed that the ruling might force all gays to sign preliaison liability releases.

"Rock Hudson's Ex's Ex," personal body trainer Gunther Fraulob, contradicted Christian's claim of post-Rock, pre-lawsuit chastity. Fraulob, who passed two lie-detector tests, told *The Advocate* that Christian "lay back on my bed and threw his legs up in the air. I put on a condom; we didn't really discuss it."

In a long cover story entitled "Why I Won," Christian attempted to have the final word. "I almost felt sorry that I didn't go into court with Kaposi's sarcoma all over my face, because we had to sue under the tort of emotional distress"—a remark he apologized for later in a letter to the editor.

His word, however, was not the last. One infuriated reader lashed out that *The Advocate*'s coverage "offended gay men everywhere." Another wrote, "If Christian didn't consider protecting himself, he has only himself to blame. It takes two gay men in denial to have unsafe sex, not just one."

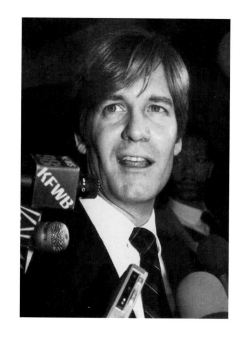

> "The dildo people came to me. From what they say, it's the best-selling dildo in the history of dildos. They added nothing in width from the mold of my dick, but they added an inch in length. It insults me that they did that."
> —EROTIC ICON JEFF STRYKER

ANOTHER EPIDEMIC: THE GULF BETWEEN "POSITIVE" AND "NEGATIVE"

Eight years ago I was diagnosed as having AIDS. I'm one of the fortunate ones: Since my diagnosis, I have managed to maintain almost constant good health with no serious or debilitating infections. But I haven't escaped one AIDS-related epidemic that has nothing to do with medicine. It has to do with relationships, and it's poisoning the gay world.

Let me give an example. I recently got a call from a man whom I'd been happily dating for some time; we had a sexual relationship. His exact words were "I don't want to have dinner with you tonight, and I don't want to see you anymore. I want to get as much distance as possible from this disease."

I was speechless. After all, the man is a teacher and psychotherapist. He should know better.

In recent years, before I met that man, I had dated at least three others. I was open with all of them about my diagnosis. One man is an editor who publishes books on AIDS; another is a psychologist who has conducted AIDS studies and sees clients (some with AIDS) in private practice; the third is a research psychologist who designed a large study for a local university investigating the psychological effects of AIDS on gay men. As for their HIV status, the three men either are negative or have not taken the test.

All four men are intelligent and educated about AIDS. Yet all of them backed away from an intimate relationship with me even though the other ingredients for romance were present. "I know it's crazy, but I don't want to get your semen on my skin," one of the shrinks told me.

Until I had undergone several of these experiences, I was aware of—but remained unclear about—the rejection of HIV-positives by HIV-negatives. Maybe a part of me bought into the leper mentality, expecting and accepting rejection because I had AIDS. But, by the fourth encounter, I was enraged. It shocked me to recognize, as I put my "data" together, that some men on the front lines of the AIDS war are just as guilty of AIDS discrimination as is the worst uneducated bigot. Their personal approach to people with AIDS makes their public work ring hollow. As I began to talk to friends who have AIDS or ARC or who are HIV-positive but asymptomatic, I discovered that all of them had experienced a similar alienation.

Evidence is piling up that many of us—on *both* sides of the diagnostic fence—are contributing to a dangerously divided gay community. This is not peculiar to romantic attachments; gay men are fleeing from all kinds of relationships. A few of my diagnosed acquaintances have been so badly burned by rejection that they now refuse to have anything to do with the uninfected.

Some will say that everyone has a right to react and behave in any way they like; after all, we're talking about life and death. True, but some of these choices are not only irrational, they hurt others. And no matter what you call these choices, it boils down to discrimination. What's doubly painful is that is is coming from gay brothers; it is exile by one's own people.

To HIV-negatives and the untested, I have just one thing to say: We who are positive remain vital, functioning people with the same needs as you. Don't deny us, don't dismiss us. You are creating a dangerous division within a community that needs all the cohesion it can muster.

—CRAIG ROWLAND

FIRE ISLAND IN THE FIFTIES

It was a perfect summer's day, and the beach was awash with glistening, suntanned bodies reclining on canvas chairs or spread out on blankets and towels. Sunday was the traditional day for making an ostentatious entrance, and this Sunday was no exception, as the wispy owner of a string of highly successful Manhattan beauty salons arrived on a golden litter, supported shoulder-high by four muscular black men in turbans and well-packed loincloths. As this parade passed near two young men sharing a brightly colored beach towel, one of them nudged his friend in the ribs and, in a bitchy sotto voce, commented, "Miss Livingstone, I presume?"

This was Fire Island in the fifties—specifically, the gay community of Cherry Grove, which many inhabitants fondly remember as the only place in the world where *we* were in the majority. It didn't matter if you were a runner on Wall Street, a chic fashion model, or the vice president of an important Madison Avenue advertising agency; while you were at the Grove, you could let your hair down or put it up, say whatever was on your mind, pursue your sexual preferences, and relax one hundred percent

A little over twenty-two miles long and a skimpy two miles wide, Fire Island, off the south shore of New York's Long Island, supported half a dozen summer colonies, of which Ocean Beach, Cherry Grove, and the rapidly growing Fire Island Pines were the best-known. In the fifties, since there were no roads, there were no cars, and beach buggies offered the only transportation between such straight settlements as Ocean Beach and both the Grove and the Pines.

If you were a typical renter, you dashed home from the office on Friday, grabbed your suitcase plus a bag of gourmet goodies and booze, then hailed a cab to Pennsylvania Station. Utterly ignoring any baleful stares, you followed a familiar trail of sequins and bits of feathers to the suburban train, which took you to Sayville, Long Island.

Then came another mad scramble for another taxi to the dock and a brief ride across the Great South Bay. Your wooden wagon was parked at the post office. After quickly loading up, you followed a maze of walks until you finally collapsed at your own front door. The entire trip averaged three hours; naturally, you reversed the journey on Sunday evening.

Most of the cottages were constructed of wood that was floated over from the mainland during the winter months. Many of them had no telephones or electricity—consequently, no television sets. Candles and kerosene supplied the lighting, and you pumped water from a well in the yard into a small metal tank on the roof. Drinking water was stored in bottles under the sink.

Traditionally, a new renter was allowed to name his or her cottage for the summer, and there were such distinctly descriptive names as the Tulle Shed, Bull Run, Get Hur, Boot Camp, and the Pit Stop.

Summer activities included many memorable moments, one of the most popular being a rough-and-tumble softball game between the gays and lesbians on the beach. One all-star lesbian player drew cheers from the assembled crowd when she belted the ball into the ocean. She was headed for a homer, but the

A sense of fun and extended family permeated Fire Island during the summer season.

halter snapped on her bathing suit, so she dived protectively for second base. She was extremely well stacked, but this posed no problem for her. She merely dug two holes in the sand, buried her attractive attributes, and sprawled there, facedown, until the game was over.

An amiable blend of straight folk and the gay life was represented by the Cherry Grove Arts Project, where, in addition to such activities as an annual exhibition of paintings and sculpture, the attractions that drew the most enthusiastic audiences were the musical revues that talented members of the colony would stage in the wooden fire station, which had been converted into a meeting hall and theater.

Off-color parodies of the latest Broadway songs plus less-than-subtle sketches constituted most of the material in the shows, augmented by a gay array of handmade costumes to lend the proper *improper* atmosphere. The audience was beside itself with delight when a dozen lesbians in full Navy drag sang "There Is Nothing Like a Dame," and a bewitching leading lady with noticeably hairy legs seductively chanted "I Enjoy Being a Girl."

Perhaps the most lavish events at the Grove were the myriad cocktail parties that crowded the weekend social schedule. Each was a theme affair, and every guest was requested to arrive in an appropriate costume. (This explains the trail of sequins, feathers, and other decorative tidbits that dribbled out of bags and suitcases across the floor of Penn Station on a Friday night.) Whether the theme was Roman Orgy, the Roaring Twenties, the Song of the White Swallow, or A Night at the Baths, someone would undoubtedly celebrate it in high style.

During the week in town, the main topic of conversation was usually that all-important Friday-night or Saturday-night excursion to the Sunken Forest, or the less romantically named Meat Rack.

Situated after the last boardwalk on the northern end of the Grove, it was laced with small winding paths leading into sandy clearings. The nightly cruising was generally punctuated by such pointed remarks as "Will you please take that gum out of your mouth?" or, shortly after *Gypsy* opened on Broadway, the siren call of "Sing out, Louise."

On one occasion, cops from the mainland were doing a guest shot at the Rack when, by accident, a burly sergeant fired his pistol into the air. The sound scared a nervous participant so much that he fainted at his trick's feet. The trick furiously screamed at the officer, "Listen, Mary, I know you don't like us, but you didn't have to shoot her!" Toward the end of one season, a house caught on fire at the Pines, and literally swarms of Cherry Grove volunteers raced up the beach to help put it out. Later, as they straggled back home, soot-stained and weary, someone asked one of the valiant firefighters whether anyone had been hurt.

"No one, dear boy," came the reply, "but fifteen cashmere sweaters disappeared in smoke."

And by the early 1960s, that carefree summer existence at Cherry Grove slowly disappeared, too. Ahead lay the sexual revolution, assassinations, the Beatles, Vietnam, and eventually, the deadly spread of a new disease. Today, many gays and lesbians would probably regard Fire Island in the fifties as slightly ridiculous and careless about many social responsibilities. But perhaps there are just as many who would see it for what it was—the perfect gay escape—and wish they had been able to go there, too.   —DRAPER LEWIS

VOICES FROM OTHER COUNTRIES

The cover of *Other Countries* shows two partially clothed black men reclining, spoon fashion, on a bed. It is morning. Strewn about them is evidence not of passionate lovemaking but of passionate reading: copies of *Gay Community News* and *Black Out*, the journal of the National Coalition of Black Gays and Lesbians.

This wedding of love and literature, amply documented in the essays, poems, short stories, and illustrations in *Other Countries*, is the product of a New York literary collective sharing the same name. This doesn't mean, however, that the two are identical. The anthology includes contributors from up and down the East Coast, while many of those who attend the group's weekly meetings in New York's gay community center are not involved in the publication. The group's name alone celebrates "not only the difference we share but our own internal diversity as a community," explains one member.

Indeed, efforts to produce a journal were so controversial that at one time the collective formally disassociated itself from the publication. But if the two have diverged at times, they have always shared a vision of an autonomous, self-conscious, black gay male sensibility.

Literary movements do not spring from nothing. *Other Countries* follows a burst of writing by young black gay men over the past few years. This ferment in black gay male letters is broadly based, as evidenced by two recent anthologies, *In the Life* and *Tongues Untied*.

Other Countries marks an important stage in this development. In the past, black writers got into print either through the efforts of a single, determined individual or through the patronage of white-run publishing houses. In contrast, as *Other Countries* editor Cary Alan Johnson says, "We did this ourselves."

With thirty-two contributors, *Other Countries* establishes a benchmark in defining a black gay male sensibility which, in this case, seems to be inspired in large part by the women's community. This feminist awareness results in a maleness that delights in sensuality without becoming mere macho preening. "I want to love you like a lesbian," Colin Robinson begins a poem that revels in the tastes and smells of man-to-man sex.

In "An Open Letter," Arthur Wilson movingly writes about the dispelling of other stereotypes: "i don't want to be/an all-day, all-night superman endurance/or a black exotic object in a sea/of senseless secrets"

Other Countries knows its definition of black gay sensibility is by no means the last word. The realization that much remains to be said keeps the group alive and evolving. The night I attended, the group was considering "Stations," a long, complex series of poems by Assoto Saint, one of *Other Countries'* best-known members, which traces an interracial gay couple's relationship. One poem in particular appeared to accept without question the white man's right to restrict his black lover's personal and sexual life. Yet no one in the group challenged the sexual politics.

African-American poet Assoto Saint.

"We're here to help each other write better, not to tell each other what to say," explains Robinson. The group's sense of a high calling is especially evident in Donald Woods's poem "In the Upper Room," dedicated to the men of *Other Countries*:

"Nail down the moment/the deliberate embrace/the smelly new/act of love," Woods urges his fellow writers. It is a proclamation that being black and gay is worth all the struggle it takes to convert the burdens of racism and homophobia into a source of joyful pride.

—JIM MARKS

Maud's Last Stand

Rikki Streicher says good-bye to Maud's and the whole era of lesbian culture it represents (*above*). Patrons celebrating the opening in 1966 of the well-known lesbian bar (*below*).

That day in 1966 when Rikki Streicher opened Maud's in San Francisco, she was certain of only one thing: The new bar would either last forever or fail to make it through the next day. "I never knew which it would be," Streicher admits with a laugh. "It was not all smooth sailing, I can tell you that. It never was."

Maud's did make it through a second day; indeed, it survived to become "the world's oldest lesbian bar." After twenty-three years, Streicher can accurately describe Maud's as "the little neighborhood bar with an international reputation." But not for much longer. In mid-September, Streicher will turn her keys over to the new owner (who plans to keep the space open, but under a different name) and bid fond farewell to Maud's and its loyal clientele. "I didn't want Maud's to go on and on until it *wasn't* anymore," says Streicher. "I wanted it to end while it was still a viable place. You know, the old neighborhood bar doesn't exist nowadays on a broad social scale. Time marches on, and Maud's has had its day."

And what a day it was. Bridging three of America's most dramatic decades, Maud's was around to watch as the revolutionary promise of the sixties grew to include the liberation of women and gay people. But it was not always thus. When Maud's opened in 1966, for example, homosexual sex was still illegal in California and so were female bartenders. Maud's first barkeeps were a quartet borrowed from Bradley's Corner, a gay men's bar half a block away.

Raids on lesbian and gay bars were a popular police pastime back then, even in San Francisco. The ever-cooperative *San Francisco Chronicle* was pleased to proclaim each new "sex raid" the biggest ever. Bar patrons were commonly booked on the charge of "visiting a bawdy house" or for "lewd and lascivious acts" (such as touch dancing). If male arrestees were "heavily mascaraed" or were "fluttering young things," as newspaper reports described them, they would be charged with the crime of female impersonation.

Looking back on those years, Streicher only shrugs. "You had to be very careful," she admits. But she was no quitter, and besides, by the time she opened Maud's, Streicher had been around the block a time or two.

Raised in darkest Ohio, Streicher fled the Midwest as soon as she graduated from college. Arriving in San Francisco on Easter Sunday, 1944, she discovered a wartime scene that included literally scores of lesbian and gay hangouts. She wasted no time inaugurating what she calls her "wild and woolly days." After some successes and "any number of failures" in the food business, Streicher heard that The Study—a homey, old-style bar in the city's Cole Valley neighborhood—was for sale. The timing was right, and Streicher jumped at the chance to create a place for lesbians.

In the grand tradition of the neighborhood pub, tribal lines and territories were soon established. The sign of a regular was knowing which group of customers held down which end of the bar. The one pool table, Streicher says, was the "center of all controversy."

As she contemplates the end of an era, Streicher remains mostly philosophical. "There aren't just bad memories and good memories at Maud's," she acknowledges, "only human memories—which are always a little bit of both. Maud's was a safe place. It was a living room. It was home."

—Wendell Ricketts

1989

FILM: AIDS AND HOLLYWOOD

Recently a segment of "Entertainment Tonight" rather superficially examined the lack of explicit sexuality in this year's summer movies. Mass-audience films, especially during the summer, have traditionally been known for their high sexual content and frequent use of gratuitous nudity.

With the advent of AIDS, however, the party seems to be over. While independent films with daring or controversial themes are enjoying something of a renaissance, mainstream films seem to be reflecting a definite conservative backlash in the face of the epidemic.

The American screen has always been squeamish and therefore schizophrenic about sex. We're all acquainted with the more celebrated examples of how sexuality in general and homosexuality in particular have been avoided in the movies. Truman Capote's Holly Golightly was turned from a worldly call girl into a cuddly, innocent eccentric for the film version of *Breakfast at Tiffany's*. Patrick Dennis's *Auntie Mame* was sanitized of its more political references to anti-Semitism as well as to Mame's "queer friends on Fire Island." Famous lesbians and gay men of history were (and still are) routinely portrayed as heterosexual.

AIDS has complicated the issue of sexuality onscreen by affecting movies indirectly, creating a climate in which old-fashioned values are promoted as some sort of solution to what's perceived to be wrong in the world. Rather than dealing with the reality of today, Hollywood has chosen to fall backward, as though a "return" to so-called family values will solve the problem.

Hollywood's "response" to AIDS is, in fact, an inability to respond. On and off the screen, the movie industry is paralyzed by AIDS. The disease is so inextricably bound up with homosexuality in the minds of the public that any film about gays must necessarily have an AIDS angle. Since nobody wants to do that, there are no mainstream films about gays. Filmmakers don't seem to be able to conceive of any way of dealing with the health crisis except by promoting monogamy and delivering stern warnings about the dangers of promiscuity.

AIDS has become the bogeyman of American film, an unseen but nevertheless ubiquitous monster lurking in the wings of every production. From *Someone to Watch Over Me* to *When Harry Met Sally*, romance has become innocent again. At the other end of the spectrum, films like *Fatal Attraction* and David Cronenberg's remake of *The Fly* have served up subtextual warnings about what can happen if people engage in "unnatural" pursuits, be they homosexual or heterosexual. Consider the dialogue in reference to Goldblum's progressive transformation:

"It seems to manifest itself as some rare form of cancer. I won't become some tumorous bore crying about his lost lymph nodes." "Stay away from him. It could be contagious. It could turn into an epidemic." "I'm sure that Typhoid Mary was a very nice person when you met her socially."

The danger here is not so much that the advent of AIDS will produce new bigots but that AIDS is becoming the excuse for old bigots to reassert themselves. AIDS is the catalyst that will enable conservatives to seize the moment and push us back to the morality of the fifties. In such a climate, homosexuality will once again be defined as unspeakable and the phrase "AIDS victim" will take on a new and more ominous meaning.
—VITO RUSSO

> "Talking about black gay identity is very difficult historically. The censorship exists within our own [black] community. The cultural gatekeepers around black history can't stand the context of Looking for Langston. In effect, they're saying, 'What you're trying to do is construct Langston Hughes as a gay icon, and he's a black icon.' It's not like whites are doing this."
> —FILMMAKER ISAAC JULIEN, exlaining why Langston Hughes's literary executors tried to prohibit his film on black gay life from being shown

354

ART: ANDY WARHOL GOES STRAIGHT

Andy in Aspen

"Andy Warhol: A Retrospective" is the first large-scale show of Warhol's work, ranging from his output as a commercial artist in the fashion industry, through pop art and celebrity portraits, to the many paintings that were done just before his death in 1987.

Following on the heels of this mammoth exhibition are biographies, reminiscences, diaries, a promised Hollywood movie, and a museum to house Warhol's work in his hometown of Pittsburgh.

"I liked the swish," Warhol wrote about his homosexuality in his autobiography, *Popism,* in 1967. "I liked the way people react." Yet the booming Warhol industry and the critical reassessment that places him in the first rank of twentieth-century art also succeed in stripping away Warhol's identity as a gay man. His image is rapidly being sanitized for public consumption.

In the retrospective catalog, a biographical videotape, and sundry reviews and books, Warhol's Catholic upbringing is credited with profoundly influencing his aesthetic. A gay sensibility is never mentioned. Warhol's public image was always enigmatic, partly because of the way he invented himself and partly because that's how a raving queen filters through the media's star machine. To go beyond that, we are forced to read between the lines.

According to *Smithsonian* magazine, Andy and his brother, John, took drawing lessons when they were boys. John quit because he'd "rather play ball." But Andy "stuck it out." John protected Andy because he was, "you know, blond, blue eyes…a target for bullies." This is code for the fact that Andy was a gay child and a sissy.

Warhol's early career moves were scripted straight out of a Susan Hayward movie. In 1949 he moved to New York, where his first commercial assignment was for *Glamour* magazine, illustrating an article called "Success Is a Job in New York." As a freelance illustrator for department stores, he acquired a reputation for drawing shoes. His window displays at Bonwit Teller are famous.

Then pop art happened. In 1962, when abstract expressionism prevailed, Warhol introduced images familiar to blue-collar America. Some—soup cans and soap boxes—were taken from his mother's kitchen. Others came from his own lexicon of desire: bodybuilding advertisements and movie-star icons, painted in two dimensions like the airbrushed covers of Tinseltown fanzines.

The paintings in "Andy Warhol: A Retrospective" include so many familiar images of the late twentieth century that the show seemed funereal, a fin-de-siècle wrap-up on modern art. Unfortunately, the show is noteworthy for what's missing. Warhol devoted six years to making sixty films mostly about gay men and sex, which was brazenly audacious in the years before the Stonewall Riots. Only twelve were shown. Examples of his *Torso* silk screens of male bodies made it into the telephone-book-sized catalog, but the *Sex Parts* series, in which he silk-screened and traced images of cocks and assholes in proximity, is nowhere to be found.

These omissions diminish our understanding of the way Warhol's art—be it his 1962 Marilyn Monroe silk screen or *Sex Parts* and piss paintings, which were inspired by New York club life in the seventies—documented our environment, including sexuality and the gay milieu. A society that eagerly reduces Robert Mapplethorpe's renown to celebrity portraits and floral arrangements now portrays Warhol as an asexual pixie who went to church. —ROBIN HARDY

YEAR OF THE QUEER

1990 "If it ain't on the six o'clock news, it ain't news," an editor at one of the Hearst newspapers once told me. In 1990, NBC, CBS, and ABC couldn't avoid us anymore. Week after week, we were six o'clock news. We had always made news, but the networks and mainstream newspapers had been able to ignore us with impunity.

Twenty years of gonzo gay activism paid off handsomely in the "year of the queer." Self-proclaimed queers, disempowering the old slur by reclaiming it as an affirmation, upstaged the more traditional approaches to activism pioneered by national organizations and gay activists in the decades after Stonewall. With the assistance of seasoned media-savvy activists like Larry Kramer and Michelangelo Signorile, queer street fighters shrewdly positioned themselves to refocus the world's televised view of homosexuality.

At the Sixth International Conference on AIDS in San Francisco, ACT UP's Peter Staley took to the stage in the opening session, made mincemeat of President Bush's simpering position on AIDS, and made international news. The divinely outrageous *OutWeek* magazine, ACT UP, Queer Nation, and Women's Health Action and Mobilization (WHAM!) publicly challenged the reporting standards of the nation's newspaper of record, *The New York Times*.

Earnest, in your face, and undaunted, queer activists forced the media, in turn, to explore the diverse struggles of the entire gay nation, issues American journalists had been ignoring for decades: gay parenting, domestic violence, living with AIDS, employment discrimination, being a minority within a minority, gay conservatism, and on and on. (The media couldn't, and still can't, tell the difference between a queer activist and a gay activist. Ralph Lauren polo shirts are a significant clue.) Hell-bent on scooping each other, print and broadcast journalists flocked to the new controversies like moths to a flame, charring their own prejudices in the process. Straight journalists got gayed up, and began questioning their own attitudes toward gays. Once again, American journalism at work demonstrated that prejudice revealed is prejudice reviled. At least partially and, of course, publicly.

The Advocate changed dramatically in 1990. Aggressive investigative reporting was initiated by the editorial staff. Cover stories attacked corporate giants like AT&T and Bank of America for employment discrimination, unveiled AIDS-phobia and homophobia in Hollywood, on Madison Avenue, and on Seventh Avenue, and explored the gay revolution on American college campuses. The staff also instituted the annual Sissy Awards for America's worst homophobes. The winner that year was cover boy Jesse Helms, whose lips were smeared with a very unflattering shade of red lipstick. *Advocate* news reports and feature stories were picked up by mainstream media around the world. *The Advocate,* like the gay nation it reflected, entered the gay nineties with a roar.

Amidst the hotly debated controversies like outing and gays in the military, another challenge to American media quietly emerged. Leroy Aarons, the gay executive editor of the *Oakland Tribune,* a highly respected California daily, conducted a survey of more than two hundred self-identified gay and lesbian journalists from mainstream publications across the country. The results—the majority of reporters maintained that their papers were doing a mediocre job covering gay issues—were presented to the all-powerful American Society of Newspaper Editors (ASNE) by Aarons. ASNE directors subsequently asked editors to prohibit antigay discrimination at their papers.

Unfortunately for United Press International (UPI) reporter Julie Brienza, ASNE's request went unheeded. Brienza, an excellent staffer at the international wire service, was fired for writing a freelance article for the *Washington Blade,* a gay newspaper. UPI reporters, many of whom freelanced, were usually only reprimanded for such behavior. Brienza's union filed a complaint, but UPI refused to budge.

A little more than a year later, when *Houston Post* columnist Juan Palomo attempted to come out in his column and was censored by his editors, Aarons was there, this time with a small but burgeoning coalition of reporters and editors, the core group of what has become the eight-hundred-strong National Lesbian and Gay Journalists Association. The *Post* caved in to the ensuing bad-mouthing they received. Palomo kept his job.

Operating on two fronts in 1990—inside the newsrooms and outside on the streets—the gay nation changed forever the anachronistic ways in which we had been portrayed by the American media: neurotic, tragic, and morally perverse. Reporters and editors came out in droves, not to advocate but to mediate. The gay and lesbian caucuses at the nation's largest dailies, *The New York Times* and the *Los Angeles Times,* began to convince their straight editors that newsworthy stories existed in the gay community, justifiably newsworthy by any paper's *objective* standards. They argued that the media could no longer ignore the facts of our existence. And they were heard.

Even that conservative nemesis of gays, *National Review* publisher William F. Buckley, was cornered into acknowledging the fabulous pink menace at his doorstep. When Marvin Liebman, Buckley's old buddy and a cofounder of the American conservative movement, came out simultaneously in the *National Review* and *The Advocate,* Buckley asked Liebman whether "it is reasonable to expect the larger community to cease to think of the activity of homosexuals as unnatural…?"

To which Liebman responded: "Now the times are changing."

—RICHARD ROUILARD

This broadsheet and others like it were widely posted in New York by queer guerrillas, further stimulating the debate over the moral implications of outing.

T I M E L I N E

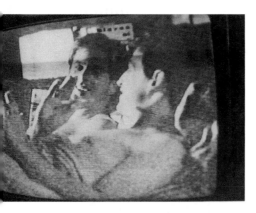

In a television first, a January episode of the yuppie hit series "thirtysomething" showed two gay men in bed together. After a roaring Christian boycott, ABC scrapped a rerun of the program.

Protesters interrupted President Bush twice during his March speech on AIDS; it was the first comment he had made on the epidemic since taking office.

JANUARY   Fourteen AIDS activists brought the Rose Parade in Pasadena, California, to a momentary halt with a banner reading, EMERGENCY STOP THE PARADE 70,000 DEAD OF AIDS. ❑ One month after his stormy ordination as an openly gay Episcopal priest, the church forced Hoboken, New Jersey, Robert Williams to resign over his statements that "monogamy is as unnatural as celibacy" and that Mother Teresa ought to "get laid." ❑ Activists targeting Georgia's sodomy law set up a brass bed with inflatable same-sex dolls in provocative poses in front of the state capitol. ❑ For the second consecutive year, the group Stop AIDS Now or Else backed up nearly fourteen thousand cars during rush hour on the Golden Gate Bridge. ❑ The British Broadcasting Corporation reported that Iran had executed twenty-eight men for homosexuality.

FEBRUARY   In one of the first federal gay-rights victories, the U.S. Senate approved a hate-crimes bill that included crimes based on sexual orientation; President Bush later signed it into law. ❑ Father Bruce Ritter stepped down as executive director of Covenant House, a shelter for homeless teenagers in Manhattan, after a self-described hustler accused him of trading financial favors for sex. ❑ At a service for a Staten Island victim of gay-bashers, three hundred supporters rallied against antigay violence. ❑ After the City Council of Pomona, California, voted to create a gay-rights commemorative week, a local NAACP official denounced the action as an example of "Satan's destructive mechanisms." ❑ Artist Keith Haring, whose graffiti-style work made him internationally known, died of an AIDS-related illness at age thirty-one. ❑ Chinese physicians told *The New York Times* that they use electroshock and herbally induced vomiting to "cure" homosexuality.

MARCH   Citing American policy barring HIV-infected travelers, French officials announced they would boycott the sixth International AIDS Conference, to be held in San Francisco in June. ❑ James Holobaugh, a 1988 ROTC poster boy, was ordered to repay his $25,000 scholarship after coming out to his superiors; under threat of a lawsuit, the Pentagon retracted its demand. ❑ Mention of the killing of homosexuals under the Nazis was censored from educational materials for a Holocaust exhibit in Utah. ❑ A plaque to honor gay people who died of AIDS planned for a Dallas park faced opponents who wanted the words "gay," "lesbian," and "AIDS" removed from its inscription. ❑ The editor of the *NAMBLA Bulletin,* the newsletter of the North American Man-Boy Love Association, was arrested and charged with paying four teenage boys for sex.

APRIL   Hypodermic needles allegedly containing HIV were used as weapons in several assaults and robberies around the nation. ❑ Federal Drug Administration–approved trials began for Compound Q, a controversial AIDS drug extracted from the roots of a cucumber found in China. ❑ Arson was ruled the cause of a fire that closed an Iowa AIDS hospice. ❑ Officials in Douglas County, Georgia, forced a resident to cut down a tree in his yard that he had carved to resemble a penis. ❑ A federal District Court prevented prison officials from barring a Pennsylvania inmate from receiving visits from her lesbian lover. ❑ A "pro-heterosexual" rally at the University of Massachusetts, Amherst, attracted nearly one hundred students, half of them counterdemonstrators. ❑ A weekly Spanish-language broadcast on lesbian and gay issues began on WBAI-FM in

New York City. ❑ Ryan White, whose 1985 legal battle to enroll in public school focused national attention on AIDS discrimination, died in Indianapolis.

MAY Chanting "Ten years, a billion dollars, one drug, big deal," more than one thousand AIDS activists stormed the National Institutes of Health in Bethesda, Maryland. ❑ Angela Bowie, ex-wife of musician David Bowie, said she repeatedly caught the pop star in bed with other men—including, once, Mick Jagger. ❑ Julie Brienza, a reporter for UPI, claimed that the news agency's decision to fire her for writing a freelance article for a gay paper on company time was based on homophobia rather than policy.

JUNE The Department of Justice dropped a two-month refusal to accept calls about antigay crimes on its new hate-crimes hotline. ❑ A National Task Force on AIDS Prevention survey indicated that while 97 percent of gay black men knew about HIV and high-risk activities, 46 percent engaged in them anyway. ❑ Two Baltimore men put their home up for sale after repeated attacks by antigay vandals. ❑ Colorado health officials said funding shortfalls prevented the opening of the state's first anonymous HIV-testing clinic. ❑ Goat cheese produced by Dancing Wind Farms, a lesbian-owned dairy in Kenyon, Minnesota, was among the foods selected by state officials to be served at a reception for Soviet President Mikhail Gorbachev.

JULY In a mostly symbolic action, the House of Representatives voted to reprimand Representative Barney Frank (D-Mass.) for his relationship with male prostitute Steve Gobie. ❑ Hundreds of gay activists demonstrated outside a Marine Corps barracks in Washington, D.C., to protest an earlier attack on three gays by Marines. ❑ Father Luis Olivares, well-known for his work with Central American refugees in Los Angeles, announced that he had AIDS. ❑ The City Council of Oshkosh, Wisconsin, approved an ordinance requiring owners of adult bookstores to fill holes in the walls of video booths. ❑ Officials of Columbia University granted subsidized married-student housing to a gay couple.

AUGUST Massachusetts Governor Michael Dukakis vetoed a bill that would have prohibited gays from becoming foster parents. ❑ The Third Gay Games were held in Vancouver, British Columbia. ❑ Hundreds of Seattle gay activists overwhelmed Christian fundamentalists picnicking in a gay neighborhood park by kissing, chanting, and pelting them with condoms. ❑ A report by the National Commission on AIDS said the federal government's drug-development efforts "fell far short of the mark" and a "shocking number of medical practitioners refuse to treat people with AIDS." ❑ ACT UP–New York staged a series of demonstrations in San Juan, Puerto Rico.

SEPTEMBER AIDS "breaks my heart," President Bush claimed at a news conference, but he disagreed that allocating more federal money would alter the course of the disease. ❑ A Navy memo leaked to the media termed lesbians "among the command's top professionals," but nevertheless called for a step-up in discharges of gay women officers. ❑ Officials at the Cheekwood Museum, a Nashville art museum, canceled a children's slide show called "Hippies, Fairies, and Trolls" because the show contained too much gay imagery. ❑ A born-again Christian nurse was sentenced to sixty days in prison for disconnecting the respirator of a New York AIDS patient; "I was sure Jesus had healed him," she said of the patient, who survived the incident. ❑ *The Advocate* reported that nearly nine hundred cases of AIDS were diagnosed in Romania fol-

Rumors about the use of rodents—in this case gerbils—in certain gay male sex acts were so pestiferous that *The Advocate* ran a feature about the persistent urban legend. Despite tabloid hints to the contrary, no movie stars (or any other people, for that matter) were found with gerbil-stuffed bottoms—only the homophobia underlying the gossip was exposed.

In July, gay activists took to the streets, calling for a nationwide boycott of Miller beer and Marlboro cigarettes to protest donations made to antigay North Carolina Senator Jesse Helms; the outspoken politician had received donations by the products' maker, the Philip Morris Corporation. The boycott lasted barely a year and was called off after the company agreed to establish a fund supporting gay and lesbian causes.

"AND NOW, A FEW MINUTES WITH A HOMOPHOBE"

Andy Rooney, famous for his folksy televised essays on such topics as airline food and cabdrivers, found himself enmeshed in the heavy issues of race, gays, and AIDS-baiting. In this anything-but-charming national controversy, The Advocate *played a key part.*

The "60 Minutes" commentator was already under fire from activists for remarks he made the previous month, in a year-end wrap-up: "There was some recognition in 1989 of the fact that many of the ills which kill us are self-induced: too much alcohol, too much food, drugs, homosexual unions, cigarettes."

Criticism intensified when Rooney told Advocate *reporter Chris Bull, "I generally feel sorry for you guys. I've been around long enough to know about homosexuality, but I still don't think it's normal....I realize that gays face a lot of prejudice, and if I have added to that, I'm sorry, but I have to say what I think, and I think that homosexuality is inherently dangerous."*

Bull reported that Rooney next went after blacks. "I've believed all along that most people are born with equal intelligence," he said. "But blacks have watered down their genes because the less intelligent ones are the ones that have the most children. They drop out of school early, do drugs, and get pregnant." Rooney later denied making the comments, and much was made of the fact that Bull had not tape-recorded the interview, but CBS executives suspended their commentator for three months without pay.

This roused the gay rabble once again. The homophobia and AIDS misinformation, which had been broadcast for all to hear, provoked nary a peep from the network brass. Once racism became a factor, however, the bigotry became unburiable.

lowing the ouster of dictator Nicolae Ceausescu, who had denied the existence of HIV in his country. ❑ Two-thirds of all donations to the central blood bank of Uganda tested positive for HIV.

OCTOBER The Fund for Human Dignity, one of the nation's largest gay education groups, closed its doors after a bitter schism over the appointment of a heterosexual executive director. ❑ Colonel Edward Modesto, a seventeen-year Army veteran, served nine months in prison for nine counts of "conduct unbecoming" after performing in drag at a gay bar. ❑ Public officials in San Francisco and Detroit threatened to cancel contracts with General Motors unless the firm apologized for a promotional video that compared GM pickups to Japanese-made "little faggot trucks."

NOVEMBER President Bush vetoed a bill that would force pharmaceutical manufacturers to lower the price of AIDS drugs. ❑ Ads that made up a $400,000 campaign by AZT patent-holder Burroughs Wellcome, which overtly promoted HIV testing, were rejected by numerous gay publications and denounced by activists as covertly advertising the controversial drug. ❑ Officials said 378 Chinese citizens tested HIV-positive.

DECEMBER A federal District Court judge in San Francisco ordered the FBI to turn over any internal documents indicating whether the federal agency based denial of security clearances on sexual orientation. ❑ Dr. Ellen Cooper, dubbed the "ice lady" by AIDS activists who criticized her obstruction of promising AIDS treatments, resigned her post as head of the FDA's AIDS drug division. ❑ Actor Ian McKellen was knighted by Queen Elizabeth in London, becoming the first openly gay man to receive the honor. ❑ Charles Haughey, Ireland's new prime minister, announced his intention to legalize homosexuality, which was still punishable by life imprisonment; at the end of his two-year term, the law would still be in place. ❑ The unified German government abolished Paragraph 175, a 118-year-old law banning homosexuality.

Women from ACT UP–D.C. demonstrated at the Health and Human Services building in October.

SIMON NKOLI

During his three years in a South African prison, Tseko Simon Nkoli often wondered if he would spend the rest of his life incarcerated. As an outspoken gay, black anti-apartheid activist, Nkoli faced prospects that did not look promising: He was to go before a government judge who had already labeled him a "revolutionary" and a "terrorist."

But overcoming even the harshest of obstacles is nothing new to Nkoli, who has led a dual battle against racism and sexual oppression in South Africa for a good part of his twenty-nine years.

"It has been very difficult to survive, but support from gay people around the world keeps me going along. I will not stop my work until the government treats black people and gay people with justice," said Nkoli during an interview in New York City, where he recently completed a twenty-six-city speaking tour.

Nkoli and twenty-one other activists were jailed in June 1984 after leading a march to protest rent hikes imposed by the white government upon the residents of Delmas, a black township near Johannesburg. They were accused of subversion, conspiracy, and treason—charges that carry the death penalty in South Africa. He was placed in solitary confinement and subjected to harassment by prison guards when they discovered that he is gay.

The Delmas treason trial became one of the country's most celebrated political trials since that of Nelson Mandela, who spent twenty-six years in prison before being released. Nearly everyone familiar with the trial believed the government's case against the Vaal 22, as they came to be known, was weak.

When Nkoli took the witness stand, he stunned the government prosecutor by coming out. He used a gay gathering he had attended as an alibi for a murder they were investigating. According to Nkoli, the prosecutor was so shocked by the sudden revelation that he was unable to continue his questioning. Eventually, charges against Nkoli and eleven of his codefendants were dropped for lack of evidence—but not before they had spent three years behind bars.

Being gay may have actually helped his cause, says Nkoli. He received thousands of letters of support from gay men and lesbians around the world. In fact, the letters became so important to him that he often cut back on necessities in order to buy postage stamps for his replies.

Several of his passionate letters from prison appeared in Boston's *Gay Community News*. In one letter Nkoli wrote, "Sometimes, like other people suffering like me, I do ask myself how long shall I go on like this. But at times I console myself and tell myself that Nelson Mandela was right when he said, 'There is no easy walk to freedom.'"

As a new era of freedom and self-government is ushered in by South African blacks, Nkoli will undoubtedly continue to advocate the rights of both blacks and gays. With some luck and his characteristic determination, the man who once thought he'd spend the rest of his life in a cage might find himself a pivotal figure in the creation of a new South Africa where being black and gay is not a crime but a cause for celebration.

—CHRIS BULL

SUSIE BRIGHT

Susie Bright is well-known in lesbian circles for her irrepressibly open, playful, and uninhibited attitude toward things sexual.

She was almost destined, then, to edit *On Our Backs,* the slick bimonthly that has been panned as degrading and hailed as "a spiritual experience." The self-described journal of "entertainment for the adventurous lesbian" reflects what Bright calls "voices and experiences that have to be authentic, because nobody could have dreamed this stuff up."

Bright remembers that "a lot of people assumed that we started *On Our Backs* because we were nymphomaniacs, or we did it for the money." But, in fact, the founders of the magazine were reacting to what Bright calls the "rigid prescriptions" of the lesbian-feminist community. As a result of feminist rhetoric, she says, "the only thing we really knew about lesbian sex was that lesbians rejected sex with men."

In the early 1980s, some women from the lesbian-feminist S&M group Samois heard Bright read her work and asked her to contribute some poems to their new magazine, *On Our Backs* (the title is a play on that of the doctrinaire feminist journal *off our backs*). When she heard the title of the infant journal, Bright says, "I just fell out of my chair laughing. I let them know I was ready and willing to do anything for this publication." The immediate reaction to the magazine was positive. Bright recalls: "We were mobbed."

But the history of *On Our Backs* has not been without a few bumps in the road, including a sometimes violent reaction from lesbians who endorse what Bright calls "the fundamentalist-feminist position on pornography."

Much of the backlash against the magazine's sexual content has come from women's studies departments at universities. Bright suggests that these virulent objections to the sassy magazine are the response of naive and impressionable young minds to their first dose of a strong antiporn philosophy.

Bright's own experiences growing up, on the other hand, were more sex-positive. "I subscribed to all the hippie ideals. I wanted to live in a commune with a big circular bed. Everybody sleeps together, everybody has sex together, everybody raises their children together."

Bright has had to face the pitfalls of being what she calls a "subcult celebrity." One way in which she copes is to slip into the persona of her alter ego, Susie Sexpert. But as she says, "I do get hot under the collar when people *expect* Susie Sexpert, Lesbian Superstar. I want to dive under the rug on many occasions. It's hard when people have stars in their eyes. It's just silly of people to think I go out on fist-fucking dates every night. I have to think about the differences between privacy and public image."

While "shy" is the last word that some would use to describe Bright, she admits: "I can't get over how many times I will sit with a lover and be tongue-tied, unable to say what I want because I'm too embarrassed. I get embarrassed about sex just like any girl. Sometimes being intellectually aware doesn't help you out in the trenches."

—KATE BRANDT

> "**W**hy would I pay $185 to go to a place that for most lesbians is a sexual candy store, but when it comes to me, they are basically telling me to check my sexuality at the door?"
> —LEATHER LESBIAN MARLA STEVENS, referring to the hotly debated ban on S&M activity at the 15th annual Michigan Womyn's Music Festival

PETER STALEY

As Peter Staley looked down on the floor of the New York Stock Exchange (NYSE), where hundreds of furious traders were shouting, "Kill the fags!" he felt no fear. He even smiled.

"Revenge was *sweet*," he recalls. "I despise Wall Street. I really enjoyed ruining their day."

A former bond trader himself, Staley returned to Wall Street last year on September 14 to perform a daring act of civil disobedience, protesting the exorbitant price of AZT, which prevents many people with AIDS from obtaining the life-prolonging therapy. AZT is produced by Burroughs Wellcome (which recorded a sizable profit last year), whose stock is traded on the NYSE floor.

Sporting business attire and forged identification, Staley and four other New York members of the AIDS Coalition to Unleash Power (ACT UP) made their way to the VIP balcony overlooking the NYSE floor, where traders were busily preparing for the market to open.

As the opening bell sounded, the activists unfurled a banner reading, SELL WELLCOME, threw counterfeit $100 bills with the inscription "Fuck your profiteering, we're dying while you play business," sounded foghorns, and chained themselves to the balcony. According to *The Wall Street Journal*, the demonstration was the first to interrupt the opening of the exchange since Abbie Hoffman accomplished a similar feat twenty years ago.

Since leaving Wall Street after he was diagnosed with AIDS-related complex in the spring of 1987, Staley has established himself as a skilled and imaginative activist in a group known for putting the disobedience back in civil disobedience.

"I just couldn't tolerate the homophobia and AIDS jokes any longer," Staley says. "So when I joined ACT UP, coming back here seemed natural."

Staley's flair for the dramatic is legendary among activists and the media, which have made him something of a darling. He has been quoted and pictured in everything from *Newsweek* to *The New York Times*, and it's not hard to see why. Besides almost single-handedly disrupting the NYSE, Staley has led several other provocative and highly charged actions.

Sitting in his apartment in Manhattan's Lower East Side, surrounded by cats, the cherub-faced twenty-eight-year-old says his transformation from upwardly mobile bond trader to flamboyant AIDS activist was easier than it might appear. He explains he had planned to make "big bucks" on the market before turning to his first love—politics.

"And that's exactly what happened, though not exactly how I had hoped," says Staley. "The pressure of my work was hard on my T-cells. It was really freaking me out. Then I came home one day and saw, ironically, ACT UP's first Wall Street demonstration on the news. I was blown away by the power of a few people. So I joined."

Now, over two years later, Staley is a veteran of civil disobedience, having been arrested eight times. So far, he's managed to avoid a criminal record. Taking issue with those who have criticized ACT UP's reliance on civil disobedience to achieve its goals, Staley says, "It's about time we upped the stakes during the epidemic. We're fighting criminal negligence on the part of the government. They're literally killing us."

—CHRIS BULL

> "*C*redited with emboldening the gay community with a new revolutionary pride, ACT UP is now going through major transitions. Throughout its ranks, there is a painful self-analysis and a rancorous split between activists who see fighting AIDS as their sole priority and others who see the organization's mission in terms of a more comprehensive social agenda."
>
> —DOUG SADOWNICK,
> reporting on the
> four-year-old militant group

NAMING NAMES

"Outing is counterproductive because it doesn't tackle homophobia. It relies on it for titillation."
—NATIONAL GAY AND LESBIAN TASK FORCE EXECUTIVE DIRECTOR URVASHI VAID (*above*)

"I think outing is nothing less than psychological rape. [Gays] have always wanted choices. Doesn't that include choosing to live in the closet?"
—DAVE PALLONE, who was forced out of the closet—and out of umpiring professional baseball—by a 1988 *New York Times* article

"Gays need to be part of the solution. If [you're] not, get the fuck out of our way, because we're coming through. And if that means we have to pull you down, well…have a nice fall."
—JOURNALIST/ACTIVIST MICHELANGELO SIGNORILE

"Outing is taking the final freedom away, the freedom of silence."
—CONSERVATIVE SPOKESMAN MARVIN LIEBMAN (*below*) in an *Advocate* interview in which he publicly came out

Gays and straights alike—especially the journalists and politicos among them—had done it and argued about it for years. But in 1990 it was named and thus became nothing less than the phenomenon of the year: outing.

In August 1989, a two-month-old New York gay and lesbian magazine called *OutWeek* published a playful prelude to the controversy that would follow. In a box bearing the title "Peek-A-Boo," the magazine's editors collected sixty-six names of famous people known, rumored, or wished to be gay. No explanation of the title or origin of the list was given. In a subsequent interview, the magazine's features editor, Michelangelo Signorile, impishly challenged any celebrity to sue *OutWeek* for including him or her in a feature called "Peek-A-Boo." The original list was followed a month later by "Peek-A-Boo II," a supplement of thirty-one familiar names.

The game picked up a few months later, with the publication, on one of the magazine's feature pages, of a faux classified ad hinting none-too-subtly that the much-ballyhooed relationship between flamboyant publishing magnate Malcolm Forbes and Hollywood star Elizabeth Taylor was one of a closeted homosexual and his beard. This teaser was to be followed, in a subsequent issue, by an investigative piece by Signorile exposing Forbes's homosexuality. In an unpredictable turn of events, the issue of the magazine, with a cover featuring Forbes on his famed purple Harley, came on the heels of Forbes's sudden death—a coincidence that both indemnified the magazine (dead people cannot sue for invasion of privacy) and endowed the story with unanticipated news value.

Overnight, *OutWeek* became the most famous gay publication in America—the only one to grab and hold mainstream-media attention. Publications from the *New York Post* to *Time* magazine reported on the alleged new gay tactic, calling it variously "outage" and "outing." By May, William Safire had included *outing* in his *New York Times Sunday Magazine* "On Language" column, giving the new term unassailable legitimacy.

Several publications and television programs reported that *OutWeek* was so named because it outed a person a week. In reality, throughout the magazine's two-year existence, its four editors never reached consensus on the rightness and value of exposing closeted homosexuals. A spring issue of the magazine gave editors the opportunity to debate one another and other community activists on the issue.

Prominent national gay and lesbian organizations, forced by the media controversy to take a stand, spoke out publicly against outing, though privately many gay leaders continued the long-standing practice of feeding gay and lesbian journalists the names of closeted politicians. Some proponents of outing, including Signorile, argued that the practice would give young gays role models among the rich and famous—though they never addressed the question of why young gays should be inspired by celebrities who had to be dragged out of the closet kicking and screaming.

Opponents, including another *OutWeek* editor, Sarah Pettit, countered that all people, including celebrities, should be spared the pain of unwanted exposure and should be allowed their secrets—though this camp never addressed the fact that if someone's sexuality were truly a secret, then the press would simply not know to expose it.

"The trade-off you make if you want to be a celebrity is that you give up your privacy," said *OutWeek* editor-in-chief Gabriel Rotello in an interview with

The Advocate's media critic, Stuart Byron. "Why is it okay to bring out Roseanne Barr as a woman who had an abortion in her youth and okay to bring out Gary Hart as an adulterer and not okay to bring out gays? Why is it acceptable to open heterosexual closets but not homosexual [ones]?"

The answer was tradition, a secret honor code between lesbian and gay journalists and powerful inhabitants of the closet. "Since the birth of the gay liberation movement twenty years ago, we gay journalists have had a fairly rigid code of conduct on the matter of bringing people unwillingly out of the closet," Byron wrote in The Advocate. "With the possible exception of closeted political figures who were actively working against the movement (such as the late Terry Dolan and Roy Cohn), it was strictly verboten, an absolute no-no."

Almost everyone had subscribed to this tradition—but not everyone. San Francisco writer

"INSTEAD OF 'OUTING' CELEBRITIES, I THINK WE SHOULD JUST STOP DATING THEM."

Armistead Maupin had been exposing homosexuals in his popular *Tales of the City* books, whose portrayals of Rock Hudson and a famous fashion designer were disguised only enough to avoid litigation. "I don't believe in the age-old code that one doesn't bring another person out of the closet without their consent," Maupin told *Lambda Book Report*. "Career and money are no longer sufficient arguments when thousands of people are dying from neglect and hatred and outright abuse."

After years of being the voice of dissent in the gay community, this argument was starting to find sympathetic ears in unlikely places. "When people like me or the editors of *The Advocate* took the old-fashioned line, it was because we thought that people in the positions that really matter in the celebrity-driven culture—big movie stars, big politicians, big business executives—would come out one by one until the floodgates opened," wrote Byron. "After twenty years, almost none of them have come out. The bottleneck remains stopped up. Only death brings celebrities out of the closet."

Byron admitted to moving "somewhat to the left"—to the side of Maupin and *OutWeek*—on the outing issue. Over the next few years, *The Advocate* itself would move in that direction.

Composer-conductor Leonard Bernstein (*right*) with pianist Krystian Zimerman at a 1988 concert celebrating the forty-fifth anniversary of his triumphant conducting debut with the New York Philharmonic.

Outing After Death

"Over and over, Leonard Bernstein gave the appearance of a profoundly troubled man desperately trying to come out. But if he never came out in the customary sense, he did everything just short of it. Those of us with nobody to hide from anymore know that if he had, it would have made him a far less unhappy man."

"Aaron Copland never came out of the closet very far, but in his memoirs, in his own hesitant, reticent fashion, he did in fact finally come out. Toward the end of his long life, he wrote that the arts 'are the only place one can express in public the feelings ordinarily regarded as private; where we never need to hide from ourselves or from others.'"

—JOURNALIST PAUL MOOR, writing on the lives, loves, and homosexuality of two American musical icons who died within six weeks of each other late in the year

BIRTH OF A QUEER NATION

In New York, Philadelphia, Los Angeles, Boston, and who knows where else by now, the word is out: Queer Nation intends to be to homophobia and heterosexism what the AIDS Coalition to Unleash Power (ACT UP) is to AIDS. In recent months, chapters of Queer Nation have sprung up around the country as a grassroots, direct-action response to "compulsory heterosexuality" and the invisibility of gays and lesbians. Militant and uncompromising, Queer Nation has the gay nation talking.

The group was founded in New York City this spring by four gay men, all under thirty, two of whom had recently been gay-bashed. They called a one-shot community meeting to discuss the problem of hate crimes and found themselves part of a new organization, one that was established that night. Meetings now draw hundreds of people. "Queer Nation was formed as a clearinghouse," explains member Laura Morrison. "There is no ideology, no statement of purpose. It's a place to bring ideas for action and find other people to work with you."

Queer Nation member Kerwin Alexander says he attended that first meeting because he often experiences "verbal harassment" on Greenwich Village streets for being both black and gay. He has friends who have also been beaten, Alexander says. When he was handed a flier advertising a meeting to deal with hate crimes, he was "already upset, pissed off. I just needed someplace to go and talk about it." The Philadelphia chapter was born when several local gay men were arrested for having sex in a park, explains member Ted Faigle. The

park was a commonly known cruising area for years but had come under police attention because "the area is being gentrified," according to Faigle. The group's first action in Philadelphia was a "kiss-in" in July, involving a hundred people. As in New York, Queer Nation's Philadelphia founders were ACT UP members who also wanted to focus on gay issues that were not directly AIDS-related.

By the time Queer Nation had formed in Los Angeles, says founder Richard Iosti, its militant reputation preceded it. The group's first action, a "queer-in" held this August in a shopping mall, was met by eighty police officers wearing riot helmets. There were more police than demonstrators, who chanted, "We're here, we're queer, we're fabulous, get used to it."

Many see in Queer Nation a rebirth of the raw militancy that fueled the Stonewall Rebellion and echoes of ACT UP's "move it or lose it" advocacy. The group's members hope that Queer Nation will become a magnet for the kind of progressive consciousness that informed early lesbian and gay liberation, linking it to other movements against sexual, racial, and class inequality.

"A lot of people could benefit if they would simply say, 'Gay is good. Be gay; be proud.' There's too much happening at the moment—too many heavy things—to get excuses from privileged people [in the closet]. I'm adamant and quite militant about this. People always scream that I'm really flaunting who I am. I think that is really outrageous when straight people are doing it every day. And they don't have to think about it."

—BRITISH POP STAR
JIMMY SOMERVILLE

A broadside apparently distributed by the group during New York's Gay Pride Parade in June urged, "Queers Read This," and proclaimed, "I Hate Straights." The sheet asserted that lesbians and gay men need to discharge their anger at heterosexist abuses. Furthermore, if heterosexuals are serious about dealing with homophobia, the sheet said, "they'll shut up and listen."

Although the strident wording of the sheet was criticized as being "too separatist" by some, many Queer Nationals agree with taking a tough approach. "By being visible, we're helping people to think a little more," says one. "However, if they don't listen in terms of tolerance, they should know that gays and lesbians are fed up with being beaten and are going to fight back."

—ROBIN PODOLSKY

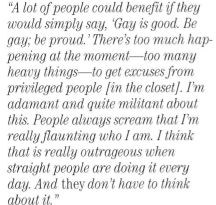

HITTING THE STREETS WITH FURIOUS ART

ART IS NOT ENOUGH. TAKE COLLECTIVE DIRECT ACTION TO END THE AIDS CRISIS. So reads a poster by the New York activist group Gran Fury, and that confrontational message has been taken to heart by gay and lesbian artists all across the country. Following the example set by Gran Fury, other groups of gay and lesbian image-makers—such as New York's Art Positive and GANG, San Francisco's Boy With Arms Akimbo, Chicago's Helms's Angels, and Los Angeles's Stiff Sheets—are now turning their creative talents into weapons of change.

READ MY HIPS:
Mr. President, Jesse Helms loves your position on AIDS. Get off your knees, George.

ACT UP DC
AIDS Coalition To Unleash Power

BLACK ON BLACK LOVE
QUEER NATION

ABSOLUTELY QUEER
JODIE FOSTER
OSCAR WINNER. YALE GRADUATE. EX-DISNEY MOPPET. DYKE.

"I really trust communal interaction," says Gran Fury's Avram Finklestein, "especially in times of crisis." Finklestein has been working collectively around AIDS since the fall of 1986, when he and five other gay men began meeting informally to share their personal experiences during the crisis. But what started as a rap group soon took another turn.

"It seemed every time we discussed our emotional issues, politics came up," says Finklestein. "At that time there was a lot of discussion in the media and the community about fear, grief, and dying, but very little about the political context surrounding AIDS." To combat this, Finklestein, who had earned his activist stripes in the sixties, suggested that the group try one of the tactics of that era—a poster campaign.

"There wasn't any way you could communicate issues via the press, so it seemed like the perfect place to speak to each other was on the street," he explains. The idea soon became the group's focus, and after weeks of strategizing, the first SILENCE = DEATH poster was born.

That powerful visual equation, coupled with the symbolic pink triangle (inverted from its concentration-camp origins, says Finklestein, as a "disavowal of the victim role"), hit the streets of New York at the same time that the first meetings of ACT UP were taking place.

The slogan SILENCE = DEATH was an activist rallying cry perfectly packaged for the media-conscious eighties. With its glossy look and sound-bite slogan, the poster provided many nonpolitical queers an accessible introduction to direct action. It also became a model for collectively produced art, a tool for grassroots mobilization, and an example of how to manipulate a culture that communicates best through graphics, advertising, and fashion.

Gran Fury, which grew out of the New York chapter of ACT UP in the fall of 1987, often lands its radical messages in very mainstream places in New York City—on subway ads, park fences, and the outer window of the Whitney Museum. But the flip side of public exposure is public protest. Recently in Chicago, Gran Fury's KISSING DOESN'T KILL posters (which show three interracial couples kissing, one straight, one gay male, and one lesbian) created a stir when they were slated to run on the sides of city-owned buses.

Chicago officials and "concerned citizens" denounced the ads in blatantly homophobic language. One poster was even tarred and feathered. Notes Chicago activist Roly Chang-Barrero: "The posters have exposed a lot of racists and homophobes to us that we didn't know about. In a way, the controversy has worked in our favor."

—KARL SOEHNLEIN

FILM: REAL TO REEL

The liveliest art got quite queer in 1990 with the release of what became three gay classics. *Tongues Untied,* a documentary on black gay life, was hailed as a rare combination of political and aesthetic brilliance; Marlon Riggs, its young director, was proclaimed the "discovery" of the year at gay film festivals from coast to coast.

A glittering and hitherto invisible segment of the minority gay and lesbian community found wide exposure in another independent release, *Paris Is Burning.* Jennie Livingston, a white Yale student, captured seventy hours of footage at the mock fashion balls that have been a staple of New York's black and Puerto Rican gay scene for years.

Livingston got busy on her project years before Madonna brought the word "vogue" into popular parlance. The director recalled, "I met these guys in Washington Square Park doing this wonderful dance and saying things like 'Saks Fifth Avenue mannequin' and 'Butch queen in drag.' I found out about the balls and knew right off that I *had* to make a film."

A movie with an even more mainstream release, *Longtime Companion,* followed the relentless progression of AIDS in a circle of affluent gay New Yorkers. *Advocate* critic Vito Russo called it "the first major movie to deal with gay men and AIDS" and praised the film's refusal to overly explain gay life to a middle-America audience.

Russo also had sharp words for those bad-mouthing the film from within the gay community. "Virtually all the characters in *Longtime Companion* are white, handsome, and upscale professionals—and rightly so, because this is exactly the population first identified with this disease in exactly the setting in which it happened….That's the way it happened, and it's insulting to tell these people that their experience is somehow not valid because they're white."

The greatest official recognition, however, was not for any of these three films, but for *Common Threads,* a film about the creation of the AIDS memorial quilt. Its director, openly gay filmmaker Rob Epstein, received the Academy Award for Best Documentary, tying him for number of Oscars, noted Russo, with Bette Davis.

One of the voguing drag queens in Jennie Livingston's documentary *Paris Is Burning.*

> "*N*ow it's up to the audience to show up and support a film that, by any standards, is a difficult experience. If you can get your ass out of the house to see Batman, you can damn well support work like this. They don't make movies that don't make money."
>
> —VITO RUSSO, on *Longtime Companion*

Filmmaker Marlon Riggs (*left*) and poet Essex Hemphill in *Tongues Untied.*

THE NEA FOUR TALK TOUGH

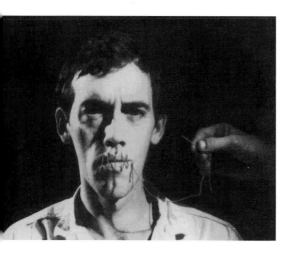

"The controversy has forced me to articulate who I am in terms of the defense of my work. I was very isolated before. I'll never go back. If the intent of people like Dannemeyer and Helms is to intimidate people like me, then they've lost."
—NEW YORK ARTIST DAVID WOJNAROWICZ (*above*), who successfully sued the American Family Association of Tupelo, Mississippi, for libel and copyright infringement after they excerpted allegedly offensive portions of his paintings in a pamphlet

"The critics of the NEA should stay away from things they know nothing about. People must express themselves the way they want to. If these men want to get busy, why don't they hit the porno magazines and see what they're doing to women? Deal with that for an education. But Robert Mapplethorpe? I think that's fabulous art. Some people consider it rude, but I do not."
—BEST-SELLING HOLLYWOOD NOVELIST JACKIE COLLINS

"Freedom of expression is tied in to the way you live. The narrow, imprisoned kind of thinking is fascistic. If they win, it will diminish the concept of democracy in this country. The idea of individuality should be the cornerstone of our society."
—THEATRICAL PRODUCER JOSEPH PAPP, on why he turned down a $50,000 NEA grant that came with a Helms-authored obscenity clause attached

In an unprecedented attack on artists dealing with gay themes, National Endowment for the Arts (NEA) chairman John E. Frohnmayer barred grants totaling $23,000 to four of eighteen performance artists in July after they had been selected by the endowment's own panel of peers. Each of the rejected "Gang of Four"—Karen Finley and Holly Hughes of New York and John Fleck and Tim Miller of Los Angeles—deals frankly with gender politics. Three of the artists (Fleck, Hughes, and Miller) are leading figures in gay culture.

"Gays are the scapegoats du jour," said Hughes. "The homophobes in the United States government don't feel that we're dying quite fast enough. They want to shove us all into the closet, where they hope that we will suffocate and die in silence."

Conservative legislators are insisting that NEA grants come with obscenity guidelines dictating what can—and cannot—be represented. Representative Dana Rohrabacher (R–Cal.) and Senator Jesse Helms (R–N.C.) have become the nation's chief art critics, using homosexuality as a political football to dictate moral standards for Americans.

According to Miller, "An analogy to McCarthyism is useful. There's a rich history of gay people being the most vulnerable link in this society to use to begin a bigoted attack on the entire society." In his grant application, "I told Jesse Helms to keep his Porky Pig face out of the NEA and out of my asshole," the artist explained. "The only way I felt I could apply to the NEA was if I was accurate about the themes in my work: gay cultural identity, sex, issues of AIDS activism, and an aggressive critique of the government's response to AIDS."

National arts groups have soft-pedaled allegations of homophobia in an attempt to save the NEA, which is facing Congressional reauthorization. But the four artists have called on the gay community to see the controversy, which has been widely covered in the nation's press, as part of a larger trend toward silencing homosexuals.

"I'm turning to the gay community for support," said Fleck, "because the art world is nervous about all this now. The NEA rejection is an attack on me as a gay person dealing with sexual politics. Just by looking at the nature of the four who got axed here, we're dealing with a repression of sexuality."

Even though Finley is not gay, "I think it would be wrong to say that the attack on me isn't about homophobia," she said. "My work is pro-gay, and I believe the foremost issue here is dread of homosexuality." Finley is particularly concerned that the straight press is focusing its attention on her as a way to avoid dealing with homophobia. "Fat chance," the artist stated. "I am saying that homosexuality is natural and should be legal in the eyes of God and society."
—DOUG SADOWNICK

The NEA Four (*from left to right*): John Fleck, Holly Hughes, Tim Miller, and Karen Finley.

THE **ADVOCATE**

THE
POLITICS
OF DRAG

A New Generation
Dresses Up Gay Activism

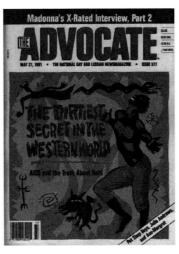

THE **ADVOCATE**

THE DIRTIEST
SECRET IN THE
WESTERN WORLD

AIDS and the Truth About Haiti

THE **ADVOCATE**

LOCKER
LOCKOUT

Dyke Bashing
In American Sports

Activist Susan Sarandon on ACT UP,
Antigay Violence, and Queer Fans

THE **ADVOCATE**

THE SECOND
ANNUAL

Starring Mike Deitz, Nancy
Reagan, the New Kids on the
Block, David Geffen, AIDA,
the U.S.S. Enterprise, the
Boy Scouts of America,
Daryl Gates, William Dan-
nemeyer, Lech Walesa,
Burger King, General
Motors, and More

THE THIRD WAVE

The first international gay and lesbian conference and film festival in Moscow and St. Petersburg in July drew over seventy Western- ers and thousands of Soviet citizens. Marc Geller photographed a kiss-in across the street from the Moscow City Council; the event attracted an instant crowd and made the front pages of newspapers all over the U.S.S.R.

1991 It was the year I went home. A lot of us did. For over twenty years, we proclaimed ourselves to be everywhere— but, with few exceptions, this statement was made from the relative safety of North America's gay and lesbian urban enclaves. We seemed to see ourselves as messengers from this mythical "every- where"—the places we had left, leaving behind gays and lesbians who could not speak for themselves. Home may have been another country or a small town or the big-city neighborhood in which we had grown up and where we no longer felt safe. Yet in 1991, we returned to assert our right to be visible and safe right where we came from.

I went home to coordinate the first gay and lesbian conference and film fes- tival in Russia. The week-long event in Moscow and St. Petersburg drew over twenty thousand people and splashed the words "gay" and "lesbian" and pho- tographs of Moscow kiss-ins across newspaper front pages. This happened in a country where the first gay group had formed just a year earlier and the first newspaper article about homosexuals had been published not long before that.

Just two weeks after the groundbreaking conference, a right-wing coup attempt threatened the early gains of the gay-rights movement. And so gay and lesbian activists took their place on the barricades with other resistance fighters. For his actions during the coup attempt—and for the risks he took coming out in the media, starting the first gay group and newspaper, *Tema,* and declaring his candidacy for president of Russia—Russian organizer Roman Kalinin earned the title of *Advocate*'s "Man of the Year," the first non-American to be so honored.

The Advocate had launched an international section that year. This was one of the many signs that the international gay and lesbian movement, until then largely limited to Western Europe, was expanding. Now it would include the countries of the collapsing Eastern bloc and the Americas. The year saw the first conference of the International Lesbian and Gay Association held in Latin America. Originally planned for Guadalajara, Mexico, the gathering was moved to Acapulco at the eleventh hour, after Guadalajara authorities threatened the gay activists with violence. This was a far cry from the Western European cities where authorities had traditionally greeted the association with open arms. But the lesbian and gay movement would no longer confine itself to the places where we were liked or tolerated.

Back in the United States, a handful of activists fired the opening salvo in a battle for the right to be where we are not wanted. A new group called the Irish Lesbian and Gay Organization applied for a permit to march in New York City's St. Patrick's Day parade. Negotiations following the parade organizers' rejection of the request pulled the mayor, the governor, and a number of other city officials into the controversy. "We won't be pushed out," gay organizer Paul O'Dwyer, an Irish émigré, told *The Advocate*. "This is where we belong."

We'd had it with acting as though we belonged only in the communities— political, spiritual, residential—we had constructed for ourselves. We would no longer accept the idea that stepping off our own gay turf would require that we be closeted or at least discreet. We reclaimed our place and our right to be vocal in countries, ethnic communities, and political movements we had once called home.

Barriers were coming down on many fronts. Gay and lesbian members and employees of Amnesty International, a sacred cow of liberal homophobia, banded together to join a seventeen-year struggle to get Amnesty to work on behalf of jailed homosexuals around the world. When Amnesty members from all over the world arrived in Yokohama, Japan, for their world conference in September, they were greeted by demonstrators from Tokyo's young gay group, OCCUR, clad in ACT UP T-shirts. A few days later, Amnesty voted to begin adopting gay and lesbian prisoners.

Perhaps no political movement has influenced gay activists more than the antiwar movement: The Stonewall generation had come of age along with this movement, while the queer generation had been born into it. In 1991, we reclaimed our place in this movement—and in America's political discourse outside strictly gay and lesbian concerns.

When the Gulf War began in January, Queer Nationals from New York to San Francisco came out with antiwar protests. Thousands of gays and lesbians joined the two-hundred-thousand-strong antiwar march on Washington, D.C., coordinated by Leslie Cagan, a lesbian who had been working in the peace movement since 1968, and one of many gay activists who saw their involvement in the nineties antiwar movement as a way of returning to their political roots.

The gay community was far from unanimous in opposing the war, however. When the National Gay and Lesbian Task Force took a public stand against the military action, it was rebuked by former members of the armed services, leaders of gay Republican groups, and the World Congress of Gay and Lesbian Jewish Organizations both for its position and for overstepping the boundaries of specifically gay issues. Ultimately, though, the Persian Gulf War demonstrated more clearly than any other event that no action by the United States government, domestic or foreign, is irrelevant to the lesbian and gay movement—and that every issue is an issue of life and death. Posters made by the Chicago chapter of ACT UP proclaimed that the $658 million spent in the Gulf each day could fund the complete research and development of one hundred and nine AIDS drugs. In the end, even the disagreements in the gay and lesbian community over the Gulf War, like other events of 1991, showed that ours was now a movement with global interests and global presence—that we are everywhere, and that everywhere is where we belong.　　　　　　　　—MASHA GESSEN

"The difference between old-line drag and new drag is that the old-liners take themselves seriously. That's tedious in any form of self-expression."
—DRAG ACTIVIST/PERFORMER LURLEEN, speaking on the new, more politicized generation of genderfuckers

After founding the first Russian lesbian and gay organization, editing *Tema,* **his country's first gay newspaper, and running for president, twenty-five-year-old Muscovite Roman Kalinin was named** *The Advocate*'s **"Man of the Year."**

T I M E L I N E

A CRIME AGAINST MAN
On the British Isle of Man, twelve men were found guilty of buggery and gross indecency in a group trial. Five of the men received suspended sentences of one-year prison terms, and the remaining seven were sentenced to two hundred hours of community service. British gays and lesbians protested the decision, demanding legislative reform.

Sherry Harris was elected to the Seattle City Council; she was believed to be the first openly lesbian elected official in Washington State and the first publicly elected African-American lesbian in the United States.

JANUARY   The Centers for Disease Control annouced that AIDS was the second leading cause of death among men between the ages of twenty-five and forty-four. ❑ Openly lesbian Gail Shibley was elected to the Oregon House of Representatives. ❑ In an article she wrote for the *Journal of the American Medical Association,* Surgeon General Antonia Novello said fighting AIDS in the Latino community would require stopping IV drug use and "overcoming a traditional resistance to acknowledging homosexuality in Hispanic communities." ❑ The Minneapolis City Council approved two domestic-partnership measures, allowing lesbians and gays to register their relationships at City Hall and take sick and bereavement leave to care for or make funeral arrangements for their lovers. ❑ The United Nations Economic and Social Council suspended the International Lesbian and Gay Association's application for official consultative status. The group's application would be granted a year and a half later, only to have the United States cave in to right-wing pressure and withdraw its support of the application after the fact.

FEBRUARY   On Valentine's Day, 275 gay and lesbian couples registered their relationships at San Francisco's City Hall as the city's domestic-partnership law went into effect. ❑ The Fenway Community Health Center in Boston reported a 75 percent rise in gay-bashings from the previous year. ❑ Bruce Davison was nominated for a Best Supporting Actor Oscar for his performance in the AIDS-themed movie *Longtime Companion.* ❑ The Cracker Barrel restaurant chain rescinded a policy forbidding employment of gays and lesbians, only to replace it with another which forbade employing people "whose sexual preferences fail to demonstrate normal heterosexual values." ❑ The Washington State Supreme Court ruled that Steve Farmer of Seattle could be given a longer-than-average prison sentence for having sex with underage male prostitutes because he was HIV-positive. Farmer had been sentenced in 1988 to eight years in prison, more than twice the usual maximum sentence of forty-one months.

MARCH   Two weeks of furious debate between the Irish Gay and Lesbian Organization and the organizers of New York City's annual St. Patrick's Day parade, who wanted to ban the group from marching, culminated with New York Mayor David Dinkins giving up his honorary spot at the front of the parade and joining the gay and lesbian marchers in a show of solidarity. ❑ Hawaii became the third state to enact a gay-rights law. ❑ President Bush called ACT UP protests "an excess of free speech," and told reporters his administration has tried "to be very sensitive to the question of babies suffering from AIDS, innocent people that are hurt by the disease." ❑ Austin gay activist Glen Maxey was elected to the Texas House of Representatives. ❑ Florida State Circuit Judge M. Ignatius Lester ruled that the state was violating its own constitution by officially prohibiting gays and lesbians from adopting children. ❑ The conservative American Family Association complained that television's "The Simpsons," "L.A. Law," "thirtysomething," and "Golden Girls" were "pro-homosexual" programs.

APRIL   The Lambda Legal Defense and Education Fund's use of the controversial musical *Miss Saigon* as a benefit fund-raiser caused a split within the organization and drew three hundred lesbian and gay demonstrators to the Broadway performance to protest the play's racist stereotypes. ❑ Washington, D.C., District Court Judge Oliver Gasch refused to disqualify himself from the case of naval cadet Joseph Steffan even though he used the term "homo" three times during a hearing; Steffan was forced to leave the cadet program because he is gay. ❑ After more than two years of organizing, the National Lesbian Conference attracted over 2,500 participants to Atlanta, but proceeded to collapse under the weight of its own political correctness and lack of structure.

MAY   The first Black Lesbian and Gay Pride Day in Washington, D.C., drew hundreds of participants. ❑ In San Francisco, spousal health insurance benefits were granted to domestic partners of unmarried municipal workers by unanimous consent of the Board of Supervisors. ❑ Los Angeles Superior Court Judge Sally Disco ruled that the Boy Scouts of America could discriminate against gay men. ❑ In a surprise reversal of policy, the National Institute of Health (NIH) issued a statement opposing Burroughs Wellcome Company's monopoly on AZT, the only federally approved anti-HIV drug. ❑ During a speech at Claremont McKenna College in Claremont, California, Supreme Court Justice Harry Blackmun admitted that in *Bowers v. Hardwick*, the infamous 1986 sodomy ruling, the court "decided on the result [it] wanted and then went after it." ❑ Richard Mitch, who cofounded *The Advocate* under the name Dick Michaels, died of cancer in Syracuse, New York.

JUNE   After Air Force Captain Greg Greeley led the Washington, D.C., Lesbian and Gay Pride Parade, Air Force officials briefly suspended Greeley's scheduled honorable discharge to interrogate him for three hours in a vain attempt to squeeze the names of other gay Air Force officers out of him. ❑ *OutWeek*, a New York gay newsmagazine famous for its outing of closeted celebrities, folded after two years of publication. ❑ San Diego Municipal Court Judge Larry Stirling ordered his courtroom cleaned and disinfected after a man with HIV appeared before the court. ❑ Well-intentioned Cincinnati, Ohio, Mayor David Mann declared an official "Gay Tolerance Day" to mixed response. ❑ In the Netherlands, Janna Van de Hoef and Pauly Van der Wildt had their lesbian relationship officially registered at Deventer's City Hall, becoming the first legally married same-sex couple in the country.

JULY   At Dodger Stadium in Los Angeles, sixty-five Queer Nationals watched a ballgame, saw WELCOME QUEER NATION flashed on the scoreboard, and took to the field to address allegations that Dodger team manager Tommy Lasorda's son was gay and had died of AIDS. ❑ The first annual Colorado Outdoor Leather Dykes (COLD) festival attracted over one hundred lesbians. ❑ The first Russian lesbian and gay conference was held in St. Petersburg and Moscow, bringing together hundreds of Soviets and seventy Americans in a historic meeting. ❑ Due to local authorities' threats of violence, the International Lesbian and Gay Association conference was moved at the last minute from Guadalajara, Mexico, to Acapulco. ❑ After years of blaming the spread of AIDS solely on blood transfusions, Japan's health ministry finally acknowledged that HIV was sexually transmissible. ❑ In Montevideo, Uruguay's capital city, two thousand gay and leftist activists waving inflated condoms marched to protest a Roman Catholic government official's cancellation of a television anti-AIDS program.

AUGUST   The airing of Marlon Riggs's *Tongues Untied* on public broadcasting stations brought thirteen formal complaints of obscenity to the Federal

An *Advocate* cartoon chastising society's treatment of PWAs as "diseased pariahs," inspired HIV-positive 'zine wizard Tom Shearer to create *D.P.N.—Diseased Pariah News.*

A Month of Hate

To illustrate America's rising tide of antigay violence, Advocate editors highlighted August as "A Month of Hate," chronicling the 127 known hate crimes committed in the nation against lesbians and gay men during that period. Among the incidents were three murders. The following is one day's account from the month:

Friday, August 23: A number of gay men leaving a bar in Austin, Texas, are attacked by a group of seven men with baseball bats.... A lesbian in New York City is harassed by two men who tell her, "You look like a man, you should take it like a man." The victim runs into a store, followed by the attackers, who grab her by the throat. The store owner refuses to call the police.... A group of gay men in New York are taunted by a dozen teenagers, some with bats, saying, "Take this bat up your ass, fags".... A gay man in Richmond, Virginia, is beaten in a cruising area by two men who originally pretend to be gay.... A lesbian in Washington, D.C., is threatened outside a lesbian bar by a man who offers her a ride. When she refuses, he tells her, "I know where you are. Next time I'll bring a knife and make you suck my dick."

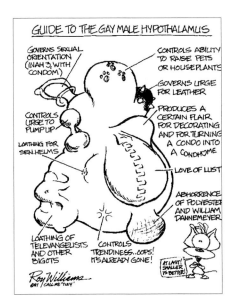

GUIDE TO THE GAY MALE HYPOTHALAMUS

Simon LeVay, a researcher at the Salk Institute for Biological Studies in La Jolla, California, advanced the theory that homosexual men possess larger hypothalamus glands than heterosexuals, invigorating the debate over whether there is a biological root to sexual orientation.

Earvin "Magic" Johnson, point guard for the Los Angeles Lakers, announced he was HIV-positive in a live press conference on ESPN and Cable News Network, creating a flood where there had previously been a drought of AIDS-related media attention. Johnson drew criticism from some gay activists, however, for adamantly asserting his heterosexuality. "I'm far from being homosexual," he said on the "Arsenio Hall Show." "To think AIDS only happens to gays is wrong." His remarks were resoundingly applauded by the studio audience. Days after his announcement, the well-loved basketball star retired from the Lakers, and President Bush appointed him to the National Commission on AIDS.

Communications Commission. ❑ In Boston, twenty queer couples and five hundred supporters celebrated a mass wedding outside the Catholic Holy Cross Cathedral. ❑ A study done by Oxford University found that AIDS was spreading so rapidly in Africa that Malawi, Rwanda, Uganda, Tanzania, and Zambia could show net population losses within a few decades. ❑ In London, queer protesters staged a mock exorcism outside the ancestral home of the Archbishop of Canterbury to rid the Church of England of the "demon of homophobia."

SEPTEMBER Actor Brad Davis died of complications due to AIDS, leaving behind a letter blasting AIDS-based discrimination in Hollywood. ❑ AIDS activists from Treatment Action Guerrillas (TAG), an ACT UP–New York spin-off, covered the Arlington, Virginia, home of Senator Jesse Helms with a giant prophylactic dropped from a helicopter. ❑ Hundreds of AIDS activists from around the nation came to Washington, D.C., for five days of protests and meetings about the future course of ACT UP. ❑ Malaysian Health Minister Lee Kim Sai said the government would distribute nearly five million leaflets and broadcast television messages calling for safe sex in the predominantly Muslim country.

OCTOBER Representative Gerry Studds of Massachusetts exposed an official Pentagon internal study concluding that gay and lesbian civilian employees at the Department of Defense pose no special security risk. ❑ A measure requiring HIV-positive health-care workers to notify patients of their condition if they perform surgical procedures was signed into law by Illinois Governor Jim Edgar. ❑ Presidential candidate Bill Clinton declared that, if elected, he would drop the ban on gays in the military. ❑ The *Sacramento Union* misquoted gays and lesbians in a protest march as saying "We're here, we're queer, we're fags, but let's get used to it." ❑ The World Health Organization estimated that 1.5 million people, a third of whom were children, had developed full-blown AIDS, 9 million had been infected with HIV, and between 30 and 40 million will have been infected by the year 2000.

NOVEMBER Two days after disclosing he had AIDS, Freddie Mercury, the lead singer of British rock group Queen, died at age forty-five. ❑ Tom of Finland, a world-renowned male erotic artist, died in Helsinki, Finland, at age seventy-one. ❑ The Argentine Supreme Court denied Comunidad Homosexual Argentina (CHA), the country's principal gay-rights organization, its nine-year-old petition for legal status. Six months later, after extensive international protests, CHA would gain legal recognition. ❑ In Moscow, the Names Project AIDS Memorial Quilt displayed 128 panels.

DECEMBER Patricia Ireland, the married new president of the National Organization for Women, said in an *Advocate* interview that she had a female lover. ❑ Mary "Dusty" Pruitt, openly lesbian ex-servicewoman and MCC pastor in Long Beach, California, was named *Advocate* "Woman of the Year" for her determination in the fight to lift the military ban on lesbians and gays. ❑ The New Orleans City Council resisted a concerted effort by religious fundamentalists by voting to prohibit antigay discrimination in housing, employment, and public accommodations. ❑ Erin Healy, a Chugiak, Alaska, high school student, wore a condom pinned to her blouse in support of on-campus condom distribution, ignoring the protests of school administrators and the taunts of classmates. ❑ The San Francisco chapter of Queer Nation closed its doors, citing division over issues of race, gender, bisexuality, and religion.

THE REVOLUTION NOBODY NOTICED

"It had to happen in Los Angeles, the city that had never had a queer rebellion," wrote Richard Goldstein in the year-end issue of *The Advocate*, proclaiming the emergence of a "third wave" of queer activism. What happened in Los Angeles and in cities and towns around California was a month-long explosion of gay rage and activism in response to Governor Pete Wilson's veto of a gay employment-rights bill. Wrote Goldstein: "A broadside pasted up along Santa Monica Boulevard at the height of the disturbances said everything about the new queer consciousness in Los Angeles and across America: "We're even angrier than we're fabulous."

The fight for passage of a ban on antigay discrimination in California had been long and grueling. A bill prohibiting discrimination had passed once before, in 1984, only to be vetoed by then-Governor George Deukmejian. Running against former San Francisco Mayor Dianne Feinstein in the 1990 election, Wilson, a moderate Republican, had pledged to sign an antidiscrimination measure if it was passed by the legislature. But by the time the employment-discrimination bill, known as AB 101, reached his desk on September 13, Wilson had waffled in public statements on signing the bill. For the next sixteen days, as more conservative Republicans pressured Wilson to veto the measure, lesbian and gay activists waited for the governor's decision, speculating that he might let the bill become law without his signature, by refusing to act on it.

On Sunday evening, September 29, the phrase "He vetoed it!" rolled down California's gay avenues—Castro Street in San Francisco and Santa Monica Boulevard in West Hollywood—as gays and lesbians poured out into the streets in a spontaneous show of protest. The following day, anger reached a boiling point as protesters descended on city downtowns, damaging government buildings in both San Francisco and Los Angeles. In San Francisco, a march of about seven thousand protesters ended with a small group of demonstrators storming a state office building, throwing newspaper vending racks through windows and setting fires to the tune of $250,000 in damages. Among those injured in the protest was mayoral candidate and former police chief Frank Jordan, attacked when he attempted to speak against the veto. That night in Los Angeles, two thousand people marched from West Hollywood to the Los Angeles County Museum of Art, where Wilson was attending a reception. The next day, about three hundred demonstrators disrupted Wilson's speech at Stanford University's centennial celebration, pelting the governor with eggs, papers, and oranges.

In the ensuing week, protest occurred in San Diego, Sacramento, and Garden Grove. Activists in Los Angeles maintained the highest pitch, organizing daily protests for over a month. Torie Osborn, then executive director of the Los Angeles Gay and Lesbian Community Services Center, called the events "Stonewall II." But while the numerous gay and lesbian publications in California struggled to keep up with the activist storm, mainstream media outlets in the state and nationally quickly lost interest in the story, causing *Advocate* senior editor G. Luther Wittington to refer to the protests as "the shot *not* heard around the world."

California Governor Pete Wilson's vetoing of gay-rights bill AB 101 made hundreds of previously apathetic gays and lesbians into activists. Some dubbed the weeks of nightly protests "Stonewall II."

Controversial queer activist Michael Petrelis lampooned the closeted Pentagon spokesman with this in-your-face poster.

THE OUTING OF PETE WILLIAMS

One of the most controversial and widely commented-on articles The Advocate *ever published was Michelangelo Signorile's outing of Pete Williams, the Assistant Secretary of Defense for Public Affairs. During the previous two years Signorile had relentlessly poked into the closets of the rich and famous in the pages of* Out-Week, *a short-lived New York–based gay and lesbian newsmagazine. Now the enterprising journalist was faced with an even bigger subject than reticent Hollywood moguls or media kingpins with double lives—his target was the inner workings of the United States government. The brief excerpt below encapsulates the rationale for Signorile's decision to go with the story.*

The first phone call came over eighteen months ago. "You must reveal the disgusting hypocrisy of the Pentagon and President Bush," the man's voice whispered.

"Sure, no problem," I responded. "What's it about?"

"Pete Williams—the PR guy for the Pentagon—is gay, and they all know it. They have a policy against gays serving in the armed forces, but their spokesman is gay, and it's all right with them. That's scandalous!" Then he hung up.

Then the Persian Gulf war broke out. Williams was on television every night. Suddenly I got many more calls and letters about the topic, as well as a lot of pressure from colleagues urging me to expose the truth.

The U.S. government's policies regarding lesbians and gay men who serve in the armed forces are infamous and atrocious. The Pentagon relentlessly conducts witch-hunts year after year and has netted almost thirteen thousand queers since 1982, all of whom have been discharged because they're "incompatible" with military service. People are interrogated and tormented after their homosexuality is revealed, their superiors demanding to know who else in the service may be gay. They're threatened with their children being taken away, their families being informed of their sexuality, and their lives being ruined. While a handful of lesbians and gay men have fought back and gone public with their stories, most slink into obscurity, humiliated and afraid.

In the face of such horrors, the fact that a top Pentagon official is gay and is accepted as such by his superiors presents an enormous double standard. Certainly this information had to be made public.

How does it get to the point where everyone in the nation's capital is whispering about the homosexuality of a top official? Better yet, how does a homosexual get to the top in Republican Washington? Actually, the same way any heterosexual does: by possessing a picture-perfect background, making all the right connections, and keeping very quiet regarding those things about oneself that simply can't be discussed in mixed company.

It's highly unlikely that Secretary of Defense Dick Cheney *doesn't* know about Williams's personal life. After all, they have worked closely together since 1986. "Williams is a policymaker, he's not just a mouthpiece," states one gay Congressional staffer. "He's closer to the President and the Secretary of Defense than any other civilian in the government. He's in on many key decisions."

"This is Mike Signorile. I'd like to speak to Dick Cheney about a story I'm working on."

"I don't think Mr. Cheney's going to be able to fit you into his schedule. He's just so busy right now."

No doubt he's up to his neck censoring a war of an entirely different kind.

MADONNA

In her eight-year rise from disco-pop contender to international multimedia legend, Madonna has never failed to elicit fascination and excite controversy with one hit record, one sensational video, one mediocre movie after another. One of the first pop stars made by and for MTV, she titillated viewers with her bare belly button and her "Boy Toy" belt buckle. During her Blonde Ambition tour, she was threatened with arrest in Toronto for masturbating onstage. When MTV banned her "Justify My Love" video, depicting a pansexual orgy in a Paris hotel room, she went on ABC's "Nightline" to, well, justify her love of provocation.

Hollywood doesn't really get Madonna. She doesn't fit any past models of Hollywood stardom. The gay world, of course, gets Madonna in a big way. Among Madonnaholics, the intensity of engagement is sometimes breathtaking. The love affair is mutual. "Effeminate men intrigue me more than anything in the world," she told *Vanity Fair*. "I see them as alter egos." She has lost many friends to AIDS—including her first dance teacher—and has done numerous AIDS fund-raisers.

This interview took place at her house in the Hollywood Hills one afternoon in March. She answered every question without hesitation. And in true Madonna fashion, what she said was often—well, see for yourself.

Tell me your whole history of working with gay people.

I'd say that after my father, the most powerful, important relationship of my life was with Christopher Flynn, who was my ballet teacher, who was gay. I didn't understand the concept of "gay" at that time. I was probably twelve or thirteen years old. All I knew was that my ballet teacher was different from everybody else. He was so alive. He had a certain theatricality about him. He made you proud of yourself, just the way he came up to me and put my face in his hand and said, "You are beautiful." No one had woken up that part of me yet. I was too busy being repressed by my Catholic father.

By the time I was sixteen, he took me to my first gay club to go dancing. I'd never been to a club. I'd only been to high school dances, and no guys would ever ask me to dance, because they thought I was insane, so I'd just go out and dance by myself....I started spending a lot of time with dancers, and almost every male dancer that I knew was gay. Then I went through another kind of feeling inadequate because I was constantly falling in love with gay men. Of course, I was so miserable that I wasn't a man.

You have a huge gay following, as I'm sure you know. What do you think you say to gay people? What message do they get?

I am a high-visibility person, and I know that they know that I'm completely compassionate about their choice in life, their lifestyle, and I support it. To have a person like me saying that is helpful to them. They appreciate that. But maybe there are other things. I don't really know. A lot of the issues I deal with are sexual, and I'm constantly trying to challenge the accepted ways of behaving sexually. Maybe they appreciate that.

There's a long tradition of singer-goddesses with gay followings: Judy Garland, Barbra Streisand, Diana Ross. You're now part of that. What do you think makes that type of woman attractive to gay men?

A lot of people saw Marilyn Monroe and Judy Garland as persecuted and

"We must bust the myth that audiences won't accept gay material. We have no evidence of people running screaming from the theater because somebody is playing a homosexual."
—BARRY DILLER, CHAIRMAN OF 20TH CENTURY–FOX

"Today I'm fish, but at a later date I may be fowl, you know? My preference? Yeah, I have a preference. But I'm also open to things. I don't put barriers on my sexuality."

—ACTRESS AND COMIC
SANDRA BERNHARD

"A female lover would have to look exactly like me to turn me on....I just think you're born gay. I don't think it's unnatural. Some are and some ain't. But I understand the pain of coming out."

—DOMESTIC GODDESS
ROSEANNE ARNOLD

tragic and vulnerable, and I think a lot of gay men feel that way because of their particular predicament in society and not being accepted completely.

What do famous people really have to lose by being known as gay?

I'm not really sure. Maybe they think, if they're the head of a big corporation or the head of a studio or the head of a record label, that people will boycott them or try to get them fired from their positions. I'm not sure. Maybe all these queens who are running this town should come right out, and maybe they'd all see that it wasn't such a horrible thing. Certainly everybody in the Hollywood community knows who the gay people are and who aren't. I think the gay community has come a long way, but AIDS has set everybody back. It gave everyone a reason to point their finger at the gay community and say, "See, you are horrible, dirty things." Maybe it pushed everybody back in their closet.

Why is the music industry so homophobic?

They're not going to be when I get finished with them.

Are you as kinky personally as your image makes you seem?

Well, what do you mean by "kinky"? I mean, I am aroused by two men kissing. Is that kinky? I am aroused by the idea of a woman making love to me while either a man or another woman watches. Is that kinky? Also, just because I'm presenting life in a certain way doesn't mean I do all these things. It's just something I choose to express.

Tell me about Sandra Bernhard.

What do you want to know?

How big is her dick?

Huge. It's the biggest dick I've ever seen....The fact is, she's a great friend of mine. Whether I'm gay or not is irrelevant. Whether I slept with her or not is irrelevant. If it makes people feel better to think that I slept with her, then they can think it. And if it makes them feel safer to think that I didn't, then that's fine, too.

You know, I'd almost rather they thought that I did. Just so they could know that here was this girl that everyone was buying records of, and she was eating someone's pussy. So there.

How do you feel about pornography?

I'm not even sure I know what pornography is—*Playboy* magazine? I look at *Playboy* magazine sometimes 'cause there are some really beautiful girls from the neck down. For some reason they're awful-looking in the face. I don't know why that is. To me, those traditional things that are supposed to turn people on—porno movies and porno magazines—are not half as exciting as other things.

You said you draw the line in terms of obscenity on TV at violence and degradation of women.

Not just of women, of anybody. To me, the vibe that I get from a lot of those videos is that men are being really cruel to women. It's an image that I've grown up with that I think is unfair. I don't think I'm being unfair to anybody....The sexuality in my videos is all consented to. No one's taking advantage of each other.

Maybe what I'm saying is hypocritical. I suppose people would say, "You emasculate men in what you do." Well, straight men need to be emasculated. I'm sorry. They all need to be slapped around. Women have been kept down for too long. Every straight guy should have a man's tongue in his mouth at least once.

—DON SHEWEY

MARTINA NAVRATILOVA

Martina Navratilova, one of the world's top-ranked women tennis players and probably the most famous lesbian in the United States, has made headlines for over ten years. She once again garnered media attention across the country when she told the *New York Post,* in characteristically candid fashion, that if she had contracted HIV, the suspected AIDS virus, instead of basketball player Earvin "Magic" Johnson, "They'd say I'm gay—I had it coming."

When Johnson was on the "Arsenio Hall Show," he got a rousing ovation for saying he is heterosexual.

It's like it's okay if you get AIDS if you're straight, but it's not okay when you're gay. Some people are saying it's God's curse on homosexuals, which is the most ridiculous thing I've ever heard: You're getting what you deserve because it's a sin to be gay, but is it okay to be with hundreds and thousands of women out of wedlock? What I find is that people are just too judgmental, and if I sound like I'm judging Magic, I'm not.

Will Johnson's announcement have a positive effect for other athletes with AIDS and for gay and lesbian athletes?

I have no idea. The tags that are there are incredible. If you're a gay man, then you must be a hairdresser or an artist. If you're a gay woman, then you must be an athlete. By the same token, everyone is pretending that no male athletes are gay, because they're macho. There are no gay football players. People [who believe this] have blinders on, and they're deaf, dumb, blind, or everything, because certainly there are gay male football players, baseball players, and basketball players, but they hide it very well.

I would love to see more gay athletes speak out. Yes, I have lost endorsements, and I'm not going to get any endorsements because [I am openly lesbian], so it has cost me money, but I can still do my job; I can still play tennis. I'm still in individual sports, so a coach can't yank me out. I can't be blackballed out of the game, so to speak. Whereas it would happen for most other professional athletes, and it probably would happen for a lot of entertainers, singers, and actors. They wouldn't be able to get a job, and that's pretty sad.

So homophobia is alive and well in the United States as far as athletes are concerned. That's why I'm hoping to make a difference. There are a lot of myths out there that need to be dispelled, and the only way they will be dispelled is if people see those gay people and gay athletes out there who look normal to them, whatever the norm is supposed to be. Phobias and prejudices start because people don't know any better.

What do you think made it possible for you to be one of the first athletes to be so open about your sexuality?

I was sort of forced into it. I don't think anyone should have to talk about their private life, whether you're a private person or a public person. The only thing I owe to the public is to give my 100 percent when I'm playing tennis. But I don't lie very well. If you really want to know, I'm going to tell you—but don't be shocked or crucify me for the answer I give you.   —CHRIS BULL

> "*I try to discourage lesbians from my teams. It isn't that I'm against lesbians. I'm a lesbian myself. But people feel lesbians have an unfair advantage in terms of their physical ability and think they intimidate other players.... In my experience, too many lesbians in women's sports make for a lot of problems that create bad teams and have a detrimental effect on the sports themselves.*"
> —AN ANONYMOUS BASKETBALL COACH OF A WELL-KNOWN SOUTHERN UNIVERSITY, quoted in an *Advocate* exposé on hostility toward lesbians in women's sports

GAY TEEN SUICIDE

Homophobes such as these create a difficult social climate for young gays and lesbians. "When you hear all the negative messages from your friends, your parents, and TV, you begin to think, What is wrong with me? It builds up," says one gay teenager.

Gay and lesbian teenagers are killing themselves in staggering numbers. They are hanging themselves in high-school classrooms, jumping from bridges, shooting themselves on church altars, cutting themselves with razor blades, and downing lethal numbers of pills.

A conservatively estimated fifteen hundred young gay and lesbian lives are terminated every year because these troubled youths have nowhere to turn. They are scared and alone. They face a government bureaucracy that could help but has instead fallen under the influence of right-wing fundamentalists. The gay and lesbian community—always wary of child-abuse accusations—offers little assistance. School boards, parents, and teacher associations all dance around the issue, putting public image above human lives. According to a 1989 study first commissioned and then squelched by the Department of Health and Human Services, gay youth are two to three times more likely to attempt suicide than heterosexual youth, and up to 30 percent of those teenagers who do commit suicide are gay or lesbian.

"The government does not have the best interest of children at heart," says Virginia Uribe, founder of Project 10, a Los Angeles Unified School District program that provides on-campus counseling for gay and lesbian youth. "Many school systems across the country have suicide-prevention units, but 99.9 percent of them make no mention of the heightened risk of being gay."

"These kids have been ignored not only by the straight community but also by the gay community," says Teresa DeCrescenzo, director of Gay and Lesbian Adolescent Social Services, a Los Angeles–based agency that is the only organization in the United States licensed to provide long-term residential treatment for gay and lesbian youth. "It's long since past time that the gay community stepped up and said, 'We'll take care of our own.'"

The Harvey Milk High School, a public school for gay and lesbian youth in New York, opened in 1985, but there are no comparable schools in the rest of the nation. On-campus support groups, like Project 10 in Los Angeles, do exist but are rare and are constantly being attacked by conservative politicians.

Many gay and lesbian youths would welcome some understanding in the school system. Leonard Jenkins, an Ohio teen, came out to his teachers when he was fourteen. "His teachers told him he had nothing to live for," recalls his mother, Rada. "The kid was just coming out, and he was scared to death." Leonard, a straight-A student, found a rope and tried to hang himself. Although unsuccessful, he was then hospitalized for nearly three months.

Society's negative messages also take a heavy toll on gay and lesbian youth. "Every day I had to deal with some type of abuse," says Scott, who grew up in Ohio. "I was trying to define who I was, and there were absolutely no role models. When you hear all the negative messages from your friends, your parents, and TV, you begin to think, What is wrong with me? It builds up. At one point, everything just climaxed. I was standing on a bridge, about to jump off."

Stacey Yother, now twenty-four, who is studying to be a clinical psychologist, remembers being suicidal at the age of thirteen. At fifteen she began carrying razor blades in her shoe, and she was hospitalized at sixteen following an unsuccessful suicide attempt. "Society told me that as a lesbian I was expendable," she says. "I was at the point where even a public-service announcement would have given me the right to live. One person coming out would have really helped."

—SHIRA MAGUEN

Amazing Grace

Life is hard. There are mornings when it is an effort to get up; days filled with numerous affronts to our humanity; nights when anxieties steal sleep or make it unrestful. Too many of our friends and families are being lost to the ravages of alcohol, drugs, low self-esteem, poverty, racism and other forms of bigotry, AIDS, cancer, murder—the list is endless.

How we manage to go on—taking time to uncover reasons to be joyful and reasonably happy, appreciate beauty, fall in love, celebrate successes—is something of a miracle and worthy of reflection.

I am of multiheritage—Cherokee as well as African-American. From each of my cultures arises a philosophy that seeks to integrate all aspects of the self as opposed to compartmentalizing the self. In African-American culture, we are raised with an innate understanding of the importance of spirit, often referred to as soul. Soul is the essence of the self as expressed through the artistry of life. Each of us possesses soul/spirit.

White culture in the United States tends to sanitize soul/spirit and passion out of people. Those in its midst refusing to cooperate with this sanitization are called artists; they are often tolerated and rarely appreciated. Spirit is not something to be honored as an external force out of a sense of obligation once a week or before meals. This is a false separation of our spirit from the rest of our lives, which often leaves us feeling empty, bereft. All is sacred. All is precious.

—Sabrina Sojourner

Black Panthers and Gay Liberation

I really wanted to be a member of the Black Panther Party when I was younger. In spite of their "baaad black man" attitudes, it never occurred to me to feel intimidated by the Panthers, for they never failed to greet me with love. I didn't know about the Panther sisters. I wish I had. Their names would have been important for me to speak as I became a woman.

In my research into African-American gay and lesbian history, I stumbled upon a letter published in August 1970 in the party's newspaper, *The Black Panther*. Addressing "the revolutionary brothers and sisters about the women's liberation and gay liberation movements," Huey Newton, cofounder of the Panthers, asserts that "whatever your personal opinions and your insecurities about homosexuality and the various liberation movements among homosexuals and women (and I speak of the homosexuals and women as oppressed groups), we should try to unite with them in a revolutionary fashion....There's nothing to say that a homosexual cannot also be a revolutionary. Quite on the contrary, maybe a homosexual could be the most revolutionary." The letter is fraught with the tension between Newton's own homophobia and sexism and his commitment to revolution. It also reveals his inability to recognize *black* lesbians and gays.

But the letter gives me hope that I can be myself in my own community without fear or betrayal. I know that Newton and the party were plagued with much of the bullshit that tears apart so many organizations and coalitions. But I'll celebrate Newton and the Panthers and think of my eight-year-old self strutting down the street in my imaginary Panther uniform, lifting my fist high and saying to any sister or brother walking by, "Power to the People!"

—Alycee Lane

VOX POPULI

WHERE IS THE INTERNATIONAL GAY MOVEMENT GOING?

Where we're going is everywhere. There should be no country in this world where we are afraid to love or to speak the truth about our lives. That's a tall order, so I guess I'll settle in my lifetime for there being no country that has five different approved forms of judicial execution for us, as is done in Iran, or where thay can cast us off a rock, as is allegedly done in Libya, or where we get put in mental hospitals, as Russians are, or where we are seen as deserving victims of semiofficial death squads, as in half a dozen Latin American countries.

What it all adds up to is listening and learning and working together across the immense boundaries of language, race, and culture. For Western, northern movements, it also means ditching some of our dogma. One of the most distressing aspects of the U.S. and British movements is the narrow-mindedness and political puritanism we have fostered, which has alienated many people who are an integral part of the movement elsewhere—bisexuals, non-feminist lesbians, drag queens, and many more. Working internationally means that we will have to accept that we don't have the last word on what it is to be lesbian or gay or bisexual.

If we are to go where we need to, we have to learn to deal with our own issues at home. If we don't learn, racism, sexism, and ageism will move with us around the world. We need to put time and money into the emerging movements in Asia, Africa, Latin America, and Eastern Europe without expecting that they will become mirrors of us. We need to support international work just as much as we support federal or state work, because the world is becoming increasingly small—and because we have just as much to gain from it.

—Lisa Power, Secretary-General of the International Lesbian and Gay Association

IS THERE A PLACE FOR GAYS IN THE REPUBLICAN PARTY?

One of our community's most important slogans, I believe, is "We are everywhere." We *are* everywhere—except as an active presence in the Republican Party. Although many of us vote Republican, are active in the party, and are even elected Republican officials, other Republicans don't know it..

I would guess that most openly gay and lesbian people fall into the liberal category, i.e., the Democratic Party. I would also guess that the vast number of closeted and uncounted gays and lesbians in our society are equally, if not more, Republican and conservative. But the few open and many hidden conservatives in this vast group remain in the political closet.

They may vote Republican, but they are fearful of taking any political action. This is a sad waste of human resources. It prevents the realization of legislation that would provide gay and lesbian Americans with the same rights and privileges as every other American. It is vital for the conservative members of our community to get involved in Republican politics in the same numbers as others do in Democratic politics.

To be gay, conservative, and Republican is not necessarily a contradiction. I'm proud to be all three. The Republican-conservative view, based as it is on the inherent rights of the individual over the state, should be the logical political home of gays and lesbians. It is up to us to help the overwhelming majority of decent Republicans reject the bigots and hypocrites who are attempting to control the party—just as the John Birch Society tried in the sixties. The Birchers failed, and the bigots will ultimately fail. The Republican Party will provide a base for gays as well as all others. The future of the party rests on the politics of inclusion; it is the duty of gays and lesbians to lead the way.

—Marvin Liebman, founder and fund-raiser for conservative political groups

IS THE GAY MOVEMENT MISSING ITS MARK?

The main agenda for the Human Rights Campaign Fund in Congress this year is the federal gay civil rights bill. It has about as much chance of passage as a federal holiday celebrating the birth of Divine, but it is the thought that counts. Ultimately, gay lobbyists assure us, something like it will get passed. The current strategy—in alliance with the Rainbow Coalition and other proponents of minority privileges—will eventually get us where we want.

I do not want to be a party pooper, but I am not so sure. The truth is, our position is far worse than that of any ethnic minority or heterosexual women. We are not allowed to marry—a right granted to American blacks even under slavery and never denied to heterosexuals. We are not permitted to enroll in the armed services—a right granted decades ago to blacks and to heterosexual women.

Our civil rights agenda, then, should have less to do with the often-superfluous minority politics of the 1991 Civil Rights Act and more to do with the vital moral fervor of the Civil Rights Act of 1964.

A better strategy to bring about a society more tolerant of gay men and women would involve dropping our alliance with the current Rainbow Coalition lobby and recapturing the clarity of the original civil rights movement.

We should focus on two powerful demands: the right to marry and the right to serve our country.

Unlike quotas or antidiscrimination laws, these demands ask for no sacrifice from any heterosexual. Both affirm values of social responsibility and patriotism that few Americans can oppose.

Above all, they hold out not privileges but opportunities. Gay men and lesbians do not want to take anything from society. We want the chance to give something back—and not disguise our sexuality in the process. That was what the civil rights movement originally stood for. It is in danger of being lost in the special-interest gay politics of today.

—ANDREW SULLIVAN, DEPUTY EDITOR OF *THE NEW REPUBLIC*

DO BISEXUALS HAVE A PLACE IN THE GAY MOVEMENT?

Bisexuals are here, we're queer, get used to it. Bisexuals are part of the gay movement. We always have been, and we always will be. In fact, many gay men and lesbians behave bisexually. Many bisexuals behave and/or identify as lesbian or gay. Some are also transgender or transsexual people. Some identify primarily with the straight community. We all share the experience of bisexuality.

The real question is: Why do some gays and lesbians have trouble admitting bisexuals are part of the movement? The truth is that bisexuality, or for that matter heterosexuality, is not the enemy. The enemy is sexual intolerance. The enemy is any cultural or political worldview that defines a certain group as "other," inferior, sick, or criminal. Those who invent an other are the real enemy.

The gay movement has been diminishing its own strength and breadth by acting exclusively. Whenever people refuse to add the word *bisexual* to titles of gay organizations (as happened a decade before when lesbians demanded that the word *lesbian* be included), whenever AIDS educators include *bisexual* in the title but not in the body of a brochure or workshop, whenever a truly bisexual hero or heroine is appropriated as supposedly really gay, whenever we ape straight expectations rather than standing tall for sexual diversity as a whole, we betray the larger goals of sexual and human liberation. This not only ostracizes a whole class of supporters and members but also perpetuates the illusion that we can appease the larger society and win concessions from it without radically transforming how it deals with sex.

Do bisexuals have a legitimate place in the gay movement? You bet your sweet ass we do.

—LANI KAAHUMANU AND LORAINE HUTCHINS, COEDITORS OF *BI ANY OTHER NAME: BISEXUAL PEOPLE SPEAK*

JUSTIFYING OUR LOVE?

It is a Saturday night in mid-December at GirlBar, a Los Angeles club that attracts an eclectic but mostly white mix of lipstick, granola, and leather lesbians. Nobody pays much attention to the video screens until Madonna's "Justify My Love" appears. At that moment everybody stops dancing and talking and even drinking, their attention riveted.

It was Alisa Solomon, in last year's "Gay Life" issue of *The Village Voice*, who first wrote of younger lesbians' affinity with Madonna. The question is: Does Madonna's status as a cultural heroine among younger lesbians signal the beginning of a generation gap among us?

In the seventies, the relationship between feminism and lesbianism was uncontested. The latter was assumed to grow out of the former in a fairly uncomplicated fashion. I suspect that sexuality carries fewer political burdens for young lesbians today. Enjoying the benefits of feminism and often oblivious both to feminism's role in achieving change and the need for continued struggle, young women remain aloof from the movement.

In the eighties, lesbianism became more politically encumbered as antiporn feminists extended the parameters of politically incorrect sex to include virtually everything of interest sexually. This sexual orthodoxy made feminism a less attractive movement, especially to younger lesbians, who have often responded by thumbing their noses at organized feminism.

As lust has increasingly become the basis of lesbianism for younger women, they have turned for role models not only to Madonna but also to gay men, who have rarely felt compelled to justify their desires in political terms. Controversial sexual practices such as S&M, jack-offs (renamed jill-offs by dykes), and daddy-boy relationships have their roots in the gay male community. But younger lesbians are not just appropriating gay male sexual styles; many of them are also working politically with gay men.

Then there is Queer Nation. The group's enthusiasm for action is remarkable. But equally remarkable (and depressingly familiar) is that with few exceptions, the white men who make up the majority of the group seem oblivious to the ways in which their race and gender affect their political formulations.

The reality is that we are not the same, and if we are going to build a nation, the standard should be inclusiveness, not sameness. Just as the rhetoric of sisterhood failed to make it a reality in the feminist movement (and often functioned instead as a way of obscuring differences arising from class, race, and sexual preference), talk of nationhood will fail as well unless queerness is broadly defined.

Feminism is still reeling from its debilitating love affair with "woman-identified" thought, sex, and behavior. It would be a shame to see Queer Nation follow in feminism's footsteps. Struggle around difference does not have to lead to the guilt that many of us sixties veterans remember. However, acknowledging that "our place [is] the very house of difference rather than the security of any particular difference," as Audre Lorde writes, will sometimes entail struggle and pain. No one group—blacks, women, lesbians and gays, Latinos, or Asians—can do it alone.

—ALICE ECHOLS

FILM: *MY OWN PRIVATE IDAHO*

My Own Private Idaho centers on a young street hustler named Mike (River Phoenix), his best friend, Scott (Keanu Reeves), and their streetwise circle, whose unofficial leader, Bob (William Richert), is an aging, drunken derelict. Revolving around Mike's search for the mother who abandoned him when he was a child and Scott's decision to leave the hustler life, *My Own Private Idaho* sounds like a conventional melodrama. But director Gus Van Sant's dryly cynical wit, quirky visual style, and intense emphasis on character keep the film well away from conventions of any sort.

Van Sant uses many different techniques to tell his story. Scenes that begin in a style that recalls Italian neo-realism suddenly shift into fantasy, as when a rack of gay magazine covers come to life and begin to speak. By contrast, a scene in which actual street hustlers talk about their lives is shot like a straightforward documentary.

Midway through *Idaho*, as Mike and Scott take off on the first leg of their search for Mike's mother, Mike sits by a campfire and tells Scott that he is deeply in love with him. It is a love, we soon learn, that will remain unrequited, since Scott intends the trip to be his hail and farewell to the hustler life. But while he loses Scott, Mike gains a sense of self-esteem that Scott will never know. And in the process, Van Sant establishes for queer moviegoers a beachhead in their ongoing struggle for cinematic representation. Hustlers may exist in the margins of the gay world, but the love that Mike feels for Scott is central to us all.

Van Sant isn't just an exception among independent filmmakers; he's an exception among gay filmmakers as well. Though he has been out of the closet from the beginning of his career, his feelings about his sexuality are in many ways still unresolved. For that reason, he doesn't relish being thrust into the position of being America's premier gay filmmaker.

Though Van Sant might not see himself as a political player, the fact of his being, in his words, a "casually" gay filmmaker is of no small political consequence. It isn't that he's the only gay filmmaker in the commercial arena, it's just that the others are so deeply closeted; they wouldn't make films about gays or lesbians even if they were guaranteed an Oscar for doing so. Whether Van Sant likes it or not, *My Own Private Idaho* is a challenge to the homophobia of mainstream filmmaking. Here's hoping he has no plans to join this mainstream. It's up to the mainstream to join him. —DAVID EHRENSTEIN

"I'm not the kind of person who wants to see 'good' examples of gays and lesbians in films, because I don't believe film is a correctional or educational device."
— TODD HAYES, CREATOR OF THE AWARD-WINNING *POISON*, one of the most talked-about gay films of the year

"As a person, by nature, unwilling to conform, I identify much more with queer punks. I always fight against anything that suggests conformity....I'm still not really comfortable with the terms 'gay' and 'straight.' I think it's good to have the terms, but then there is a lot of importance put on them—like it's either one or the other. You have to decide right now, or they're gonna blow your head off. There is no graciousness on either side. See, the thing is, you say what you like, and everyone assumes you're joining something. And I'd rather not join. But people think that if you don't join, you're lying or something."
—DIRECTOR GUS VAN SANT, on being an insider-outsider

Books: Adrienne Rich's *Difficult World*

Adrienne Rich's literary career began in 1951, when W. H. Auden selected her first book of poems, *A Change of World,* as the winner of the Yale Younger Poets competition. Rich, who had just graduated from Radcliffe College, said at the time that she felt the book was published "by a fluke." Her amazing record over the last four decades proves otherwise.

One of the few openly lesbian poets ever to win the prestigious National Book Award, Rich has produced over a dozen volumes of poems, among them *Necessities of Life, The Will to Change, Time's Power,* and, most recently, *An Atlas of the Difficult World.* In her work, Rich has followed her personal and political vision and come to grips with some of the most crucial issues of our time: the suppression of women in a male-dominated society, homophobia, and the responsibilities of the individual in an afflicted culture.

Do you think that this country will ever come to grips with homosexuality or with difference of any kind?

If it doesn't, I think that we're in for one of the most terrible, terrifying periods of repression, of brutal, vicious repression of large numbers of people that can possibly be imagined—something on a par with Nazi Germany. I feel as if all the monsters of American history are coming home to roost now, and they're monsters of privilege and monsters of repression and monsters of denial. And unless as a society we can face those monsters and look at them and give them names—describe them—they're going to take us over.

Should poets be political?

It's very hard to imagine words that aren't in some way political, and the concept that only words that are dissenting in some way from the status quo are political seems to me very false. There are words that uphold the status quo either by what they don't say or by what they do say. And any status quo is political. So I think that writing is inevitably a political act, and it's a question of "Where are you placing your energies, where are you placing your talents?"

Recently, we've seen a new community of activists forming among gays and lesbians. Can these groups recapture the energy and hope of the movement politics of the sixties and seventies?

Some of that hope was very naive—the belief in instant revolution—because Americans tend to believe in instant everything. A lot of what went sour was when the long haul began to present itself. But most of the people I've known from that period have continued to hope and fight in various ways.

Enormous amounts of activism have sprung up around the AIDS issue, certainly, and also about planetary issues. I guess I have some hope that, driven to the brink, we are making some connections that have never been made. I have a very stubborn faith in the unpredictable. I think we have to make it happen.

—David Trinidad

THE GHOSTS OF VERSAILLES

The classical music world took note when New York's staid Metropolitan Opera Company commissioned two openly gay men to create a new work to celebrate its centenary. The project took a decade for composer John Corigliano (*left*) and librettist William M. Hoffman (*right*) to complete, but in mid-December *The Ghosts of Versailles,* an eerie opera buffa populated by the specters of the French Revolution, premiered to critical and popular acclaim.

Both men have been identified in recent years with AIDS-related works—Corigliano with his Symphony No. 1 (1990) and Hoffman with his play *As Is* (1985). In writing *The Ghosts of Versailles,* the longtime friends drew upon the lessons of courage and resilience of human spirit witnessed during the epidemic. "This opera is about love and how love can transcend even death," said Hoffman. "Every time people with AIDS function and live with AIDS, that's triumphing spiritually over death. That's heroic....The message of this opera is that you can live forever in the spirit."

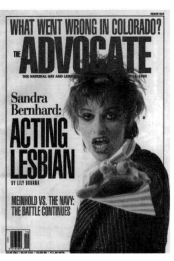

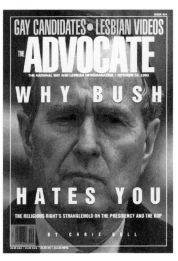

TO DARE TO DREAM

Artist and photographer Steven Arnold, long known for his phantasmagorical images of myths and archetypes, here evokes the dark, uncertain mood of the nineties.

1992 Gay, lesbian, and AIDS activists made 1992 a pivotal year for two reasons. First, because we mounted the most effective national political effort of our movement's history and helped to defeat a President; and second, because the straight media and candidates took notice. A year that began in despair at our political prospects ended in great, if misguided, hope at our progress.

Decades of hard work by gay activists within the Democratic ranks bore fruit this year. The party's candidates and platform endorsed federal civil rights protections and aggressive AIDS action. The Democratic Convention in New York City marked the most inclusive mainstream political gathering in American history. It saw large floor demonstrations of straight and gay people waving signs that said LESBIAN AND GAY RIGHTS NOW and it brought the country historic speeches by out lesbian leader Roberta Achtenberg and Clinton adviser Bob Hattoy. Speaking as a gay man with AIDS, Hattoy praised the gay community's response to the epidemic, and eloquently condemned the Bush Administration. Gay political fund-raising achieved a historic milestone, raising at least $3.4 million in gay money toward the Democratic victory.

Gay Republican organizing also peaked as Log Cabin Clubs were organized nationwide. Gay and nongay Republicans spoke out against the homophobic statements of David Duke, Patrick Buchanan, and Dan Quayle. The first openly gay delegates to the Republican convention won broad media attention, and gay conservative patriarch Marvin Liebman played an effective role as a national spokesperson for a "big-tent" vision of the GOP.

ACT UP's Presidential Project dogged candidates in the primary season on AIDS policy and gay and lesbian issues. From New Hampshire to the state of Washington, from Georgia to Michigan, activists seized media visibility and forced candidates of all parties to confront AIDS. ACT UP chapters around the nation organized local actions and sent members to demonstrations at both national conventions.

I was too young to be at the Democratic Convention in Chicago in 1968, when cops brutally attacked protesters, but I was part of the far less reported riot at the 1992 Republican Convention. At a march organized by ACT UP protesting Bush AIDS policies, some fifteen hundred people demonstrated peacefully. Without warning or reason, Houston riot police on horseback and foot charged into the crowd, hitting scores of people and seriously injuring several. I will never forget running across parking lots as fully armed cops chased me, swinging at anyone they reached. And I cannot forgive the cover-up by the straight press or the silence of the gay press, both of which were more intent on securing interviews with celebrities than in covering difficult issues.

The efforts of mainstream gay and AIDS organizations were also critical to the coordination and media coverage given to our issues during this year. Gay Men's Health Crisis, the Human Rights Campaign Fund, and the National Gay and Lesbian Task Force all dedicated significant resources to the election, linking party activists, the direct action movement, and the broader gay community, with the media and the campaigns. The United for AIDS Action Rally in New York in July was one of the largest AIDS protests ever in this country.

While a tremendous amount of attention was focused on the national election, the real drama of the year unfolded in the many battles waged by the religious right, which loaded, fired, and reloaded on a wide spectrum of cultural issues. They pressed to defund the National Endowment for the Arts for its support of gay and lesbian artists. They blocked a change in immigration policies to allow HIV-positive visitors to enter this country. And, in a sign of things to come, the right wing led antigay ballot campaigns to thwart laws expanding gay and lesbian civil rights by labeling them "special rights" measures.

But in spite of these chilling efforts, we persevered and advanced. Gay and lesbian artists continued the cultural revolution we have always led. Hollywood seemed on the verge of a breakthrough as more gay and AIDS movies got the green light, and gay activists from GLAAD, Out in Film, and Hollywood Supports kept up the pressure. Critical local victories boosted our morale as three new states (California, Minnesota, Vermont) passed gay-rights bills, and state courts struck down a sodomy law in Kentucky, an antigay police recruitment policy in Dallas, and antigay St. Patrick's Day parade policies in Boston.

At their best, Presidential election years hold the promise of something new. Competing ideologies are debated, unusual and hopeful alliances are made, and candidates seem to speak to real people's real-life problems. At worst, these are demogogic times, which spawn cynicism. It is clear that the aftermath of 1992 has been renewed cynicism among gay people. Our communities helped defeat an insensitive and deadly conservative administration, only to replace it with a more sensitive but equally deadly liberal ally.

Political promises gay and lesbian leaders thought so important evaporated. We lost badly on the effort to end the military's antigay ban, as the new President and key Democratic leaders abandoned us; and we faced a growing backlash in public opinion polls. Across the country, AIDS took more people from us every day, while scant progress was made in research, treatment, prevention, access to care, or even discrimination.

But at the end of 1992, none of this was clear. We were so elated, so hopeful that our long domestic nightmare of the last twelve years had finally ended. We liked Bill's new-age manhood, and applauded Hillary's feminism. We planned fabulous parties at the Inaugural. And we dared to dream that freedom could be ours in our lifetime.

—Urvashi Vaid

"I'm running purely for queer visibility. We're puttin' the camp back in campaign—and takin' out the pain. I'm the only candidate who can successfully skirt all the issues."
—Queer Nation Presidential candidate Joan Jett Blakk

"If elected, I would reverse the ban on gays and lesbians serving in the United States Armed Forces. Every patriotic American should be allowed to serve their country, regardless of sexual orientation."
—Democratic Party Presidential candidate William Jefferson Clinton

T I M E L I N E

During the 64th Annual Academy Awards ceremony in March, hundreds of Queer Nation demonstrators protested derogatory portrayals of lesbians and gays in the movies. The protests were discussed by major media for weeks before the action, and brought out the Los Angeles Police Department, who made ten arrests during an otherwise peaceful demonstration.

Following the success of a previous AIDS benefit album, *Red, Hot + Dance* was released to brisk sales, providing increased safer sex awareness through its provocative promotional campaign.

JANUARY   New York City Surrogate Court Judge Eve Preminger approved adoption of a six-year-old boy by the lesbian lover of the boy's biological mother. ❑ The Los Angeles School Board approved an AIDS prevention program which authorized the distribution of condoms in public high schools. ❑ In an unprecedented decision, a Canadian immigration panel granted political asylum to Argentine national Jorge Inaudi, ruling that, as a gay man, he suffered political persecution in his country. ❑ Dr. Brian Sando, senior medical director of the Australian Olympic basketball team, warned players not to compete against the U.S. team if it included HIV-positive Magic Johnson. ❑ Ukraine became the first former Soviet republic to repeal its ban on consensual gay male sex.

FEBRUARY   Louisiana Governor Edwin Edwards signed an executive order banning antigay bias in state agencies, making Louisiana the first state in the Southeast to have such a policy. ❑ Texas state judge Lawrence Fuller voided the Dallas Police Department's ban on employment of gay and lesbian officers as unconstitutional. ❑ In Florida, Aileen Wuornos, a prostitute who killed six men she alleged had raped and assulted her, was sentenced to the electric chair after prosecutors labeled her a "man hater" in connection with her lesbianism. ❑ University of Colorado, Boulder, football coach Bill McCartney sparked controversy by lending public support to the antigay conservative group Colorado for Family Values. ❑ Levi Strauss and Co., the world's largest clothing manufacturer, announced it would offer spousal health benefits to gay and lesbian domestic partners. ❑ The school board in Coeur d'Alene, Idaho, voted to bar teachers from discussing contraceptives or homosexuality with students.

MARCH   A Texas state appeals court ruled that the state's 113-year-old sodomy statute was unconstitutional. ❑ Alan Amos, a Conservative minister of the British Parliament known for his opposition to gay and women's rights, resigned his seat three days after being arrested for having sex with another man in a London park. ❑ In Buenos Aires, Argentina, nearly one hundred lesbians and gay men protested the murders of gay men in the province of Mendoza. ❑ Former Soviet republic Latvia abolished its sodomy law. ❑ The lower house of Parliament on the United Kingdom's Isle of Man voted to decriminalize gay male sex, ensuring that the infamous Manx sodomy law would be repealed; the law had made gay male sex punishable by up to life imprisonment.

APRIL   The March for Women's Lives in Washington, D.C., responding to the growing threat to women's reproductive rights, drew over 500,000 demonstrators, including a large contingent of lesbians and gay men. ❑ Retired professional tennis player Arthur Ashe disclosed he had AIDS, but said he would not use his position on the board of directors at Aetna Life and Casualty Insurance Company to push for reform in AIDS coverage by insurance companies. ❑ To prevent the spread of AIDS, officials in Myanmar (formerly Burma) allegedly killed twenty-five HIV-positive prostitutes who had been deported from neighboring Thailand. ❑ Openly gay Communist Party member Niki Vendola was elected to the Italian parliament.

MAY   In Springfield, Oregon, a citywide ballot measure outlawing bans on antigay bias passed while a similar measure was rejected in nearby Corvallis. ❑ President Bush named Anne-Imelda Radice, a conservative lesbian, to the post of acting chair of the embattled National Endowment for the Arts. ❑ Independent Presidential candidate billionare Ross Perot announced on "20/20" that he would not appoint a known homosexual to a Cabinet-level post because it didn't have "anything to do with fixing problems." ❑ Dan Quayle, while visiting a New York hospital, asked if AIDS patients there were "taking DDT"; staffers gently suggested that perhaps the Vice President of the country with the highest reported total of AIDS-related deaths meant ddI or AZT. ❑ Bisexual screen diva Marlene Dietrich died in Paris. ❑ Over 170 lesbians from thirteen countries attended the Asian Lesbian Network Conference in Tokyo, Japan.

JUNE The congressional General Accounting Office estimated that over the past decade the Pentagon had spent almost $500 million on purging the military of lesbians and gays. ❑ A Washington, D.C., ordinance extending spousal benefits to lesbians and gays took effect. ❑ The Bank of America and Wells Fargo Bank announced they would stop making donations to the Boy Scouts of America to protest the Boy Scouts' exclusion of gays and atheists; the Bank of America later reversed its decision, prompting San Francisco Supervisor Roberta Achtenberg to introduce a resolution to transfer several municipal accounts away from the bank. ❑ Nicaragua passed a sodomy statute written broadly enough to outlaw meetings by gay-rights activists. ❑ In the Netherlands, where prostitution is legal, 81 percent of male prostitutes reported using condoms.

JULY The Democratic National Convention, held in New York City, witnessed a twenty-thousand-strong AIDS protest that included speeches by the Rev. Jesse Jackson, New York Mayor David Dinkins, and actors Jessica Lange and Gregory Hines. ❑ Measure 9, an anti-gay-rights initiative sponsored by the Oregon Citizens Alliance, received enough signatures to qualify for a November ballot. ❑ Rebecca Sevilla of Lima, Peru, became the first secretary-general of color of the International Lesbian and Gay Association. ❑ In Mexico City, six gay activists, including Francisco Estrada Valle, an internationally known physician and AIDS educator, were found gagged and murdered; police investagators maintained the crimes were committed by other gays, while activists blamed right-wing extremists.

AUGUST At the Republican National Convention in Houston, Texas, over forty Pat Buchanan supporters waved signs reading FAMILY RIGHTS FOREVER, GAY RIGHTS NEVER. ❑ President Bush said on "Dateline NBC" that if he found out a grandchild was gay he would "love the child" but tell him that homosexuality is not normal and discourage him from working for gay rights. ❑ Sharon McCracken of Fort Lauderdale, Florida, became the first openly lesbian foster parent licensed by the state. ❑ HIV-positive Shelia Epps McKeller died of suffocation after police in Winston-Salem, North Carolina, arrested her on drug charges, handcuffed her, wrapped a piece of gauze around her mouth, and placed her facedown in a holding cell; the police had been afraid she might bite someone. ❑ The Ontario, Canada, Court of Appeals ruled unanimously to void the Canadian military's ban on gay and lesbian personnel; the government chose to lift the ban rather than appeal the decision.

SEPTEMBER The Kentucky Supreme Court struck down the state sodomy law. ❑ John Schlafly, the eldest son of conservative activist Phyllis Schlafly, came out in the *San Francisco Examiner.* ❑ Closeted Louisiana Congressman Jim McCrery, a "family-values" politician, was outed by *The Advocate* for his public

On orders from San Francisco Police Chief Richard Hongisto, police officers removed from vending boxes and threw out over two thousand copies of the San Francisco *Bay Times,* a gay newspaper, featuring a suggestive caricature of him on the cover. Within several weeks, Hongisto was fired.

The Presbyterian Church reaffirmed its ban on gay and lesbian clergy, voiding the previous year's selection of openly lesbian minister Jane Spahr as copastor of a Rochester, New York, church.

THE GRAY LADY GOES PINK

In the late spring, The Advocate published a two-part article on the unprecedented changes in the coverage of gay, lesbian, and AIDS issues in The New York Times. Throughout the seventies and eighties, the Times, under the iron hand of editor A. M. "Abe" Rosenthal, refused to use the term "gay," opting instead for the archaic and clinical "homosexual"—when it covered gay issues at all. But thanks to the courage of veteran gay Times staffers like HIV-positive Assistant National Editor Jeff Schmaltz and the new publisher, Arthur Ochs Sulzberger, who constantly pushed for diversity on all fronts, the cloud of homophobia was finally lifted from the venerable newspaper's pages. The new era was dubbed by some reporters and editors the "Lavender Enlightenment."

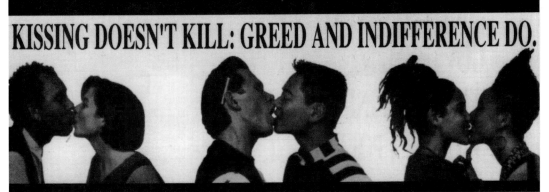

A New Hampshire ACT UP advertising campaign featuring a poster by art activist group Gran Fury was pulled from ABC affiliate WMUR-TV at the last moment. The station cited problems with the ad's "visual content."

antigay stance. He later denied he was gay and won reelection in November. ❑ Mongolia announced the discovery of the country's first confirmed case of AIDS.

OCTOBER Spanning over fifteen acres and 22,000 panels, the Names Project AIDS Memorial Quilt was shown in its entirety on the Mall in Washington, D.C.; nearly 300,000 people viewed the exhibit. ❑ The Centers for Disease Control expanded the definition of AIDS to include more conditions that affect women and IV-drug users with AIDS. ❑ The Canadian Defense Department issued a statement ending a ban on gays and lesbians in the military. ❑ Jean-Pierre Allain, Michel Garretta, and Jacques Roux, three former health officials in France who knowingly allowed HIV-contaminated blood to be used in blood transfusions, were sentenced to four years in prison. ❑ The Canadian Immigration Department granted immigrant status to Bridget Coll, an Irish lesbian who was sponsored by her Canadian lover, Christine Morissey.

NOVEMBER In an election generally considered to be a victory for lesbians and gays nationwide, William Jefferson Clinton was elected President of the United States. ❑ Measure 9, an Oregon proposal to ban gay-rights laws, was rejected by voters. ❑ Lesbian and gay organizations across the country called for a boycott of Colorado and Colorado-based businesses in protest of the passage of Amendment 2, a ban on laws against antigay discrimination. ❑ The National Cancer Institute released a study finding that up to one-third of lesbians develop breast cancer, as compared to one in eight women in general. ❑ A municipal ban on antigay bias was repealed by voters in Tampa, Florida, while a similar repeal was rejected in Portland, Maine. ❑ San Francisco federal District Court Judge Terry Hatter ordered the Navy to reinstate openly gay Petty Officer Keith Meinhold. ❑ The Navy Reserve Officers' Training Corps (ROTC) program created a policy requiring midshipmen to sign an affidavit stating that they agree with the military's gay ban and will refund scholarship money if they are found to be homosexual. ❑ Australian Prime Minister Paul Keating dropped his country's military ban on lesbians and gays. ❑ Two thousand participants attended the second International Congress on AIDS in Asia and the Pacific in New Delhi, India.

DECEMBER Hundreds of international observances of World AIDS Day took place; George and Barbara Bush burned candles in the windows of the White House. ❑ A goodwill trip by Denver Mayor Wellington Webb to fight the Colorado boycott ended in defeat after he failed to convince New York City Mayor David Dinkins not to participate in the boycott. ❑ The Food and Drug Administration finally received Bush Administration approval to fast-track experimental drugs to fight AIDS. ❑ Stanford University in California decided to extend spousal employee benefits to the domestic partners of lesbians and gays. ❑ At the U.S. naval base in Guantanamo Bay, Cuba, more than two hundred HIV-positive Haitian refugees were held in quarantine despite Centers for Disease Control recommendations to the contrary; President-elect Clinton pledged to release the Haitians once in office.

N E W S   F O C U S

THE RISE OF FASCISM IN AMERICA

Every day for well over a year, gays and lesbians in Oregon have heard themselves characterized as abnormal, perverse, and unnatural. They have endured stories detailing how gay men ingest pounds of feces during their lifetimes and pour urine on each other during parties. They have heard their sexual orientation linked to pedophilia, bestiality, and necrophilia, and they have heard their work for civil liberties characterized as a bid for special privileges.

The rhetoric may be all too familiar, but its context is not: In Oregon, arguments that were once confined to pulpits or soapboxes have moved into political debate. Because of the efforts of the Oregon Citizens Alliance (OCA), a right-wing group, the state's voters will be asked through a ballot initiative November 3 to transform hatred into law.

Activists say that if the initiative, Measure 9, is approved, it could forbid lawmakers to protect gays and lesbians from antigay discrimination, amend the state constitution to declare homosexuality abnormal, reduce state funding for AIDS services, prevent the licensure of openly gay or lesbian professionals, mandate the removal of pro-gay books from libraries, and require schoolteachers to describe homosexuality as wrong. A local version of the measure has already been enacted in Springfield, Oregon

The initiative has taught Oregon's gays and lesbians all too well the power of words, says Donna Red Wing, director of the Lesbian Community Project in Portland. "You're having an entire state discussing whether your humanity is as high as someone else's," she says. "It really grinds you down, whether you're way out there or locked in your closet. Win or lose, the OCA has done a good job of putting out extraordinary, false stuff about gay and lesbian folks that is not going to go away." Adds Gary Wilson, pastor of the predominately gay Metropolitan Community Church in Portland: "We're exhausted and stressed out. We're in an emotional Sarajevo."

On September 26, a gay man and a lesbian were killed in Salem when a Molotov cocktail was thrown into the apartment they shared. Four youths, two of whom were described by police as skinheads, were arrested. Police said that the youths had fought with the victims before the fire and were shouting epithets when they left. Less than a month previously, the man who died in the blast had been gay-bashed.

Reports of antigay violence across the state have increased 22 percent since January, and the severity of the crimes has increased, Red Wing says. The Portland and Eugene offices of groups battling the initiative have been vandalized. Even Portland Police Chief Tom Potter has received death threats because he marches in his city's Gay Pride parades.

Portland, Oregon, lesbian activist Donna Red Wing was chosen *The Advocate*'s "Woman of the Year" for her tireless fight to defeat conservative political forces in her state.

At first, few people took the OCA seriously. "If some of us had begun to speak out and called attention to the OCA's agenda six years ago, maybe we would not be where we are today," says Ellen Lowe, a spokeswoman for the No on 9 Campaign.

From its beginnings, the OCA has been involved in a series of issues, often with little success. But on one issue—gay rights—the OCA has acquired an impressive track record. In 1988 the OCA sponsored a ballot referendum seeking to overturn an executive order issued by Democratic Governor Neil Goldschmidt that prohibited antigay employment discrimination in state government. For many gays and lesbians, the initiative, known as Measure 8, seemed like a throwback to another era, one that had little chance of returning. But to the surprise of practically everyone, Measure 8 was approved, and the state's gays and lesbians were "caught flat-footed," Wilson says.

In the religious right, OCA head Lon Mabon found an audience that was receptive to his message and, more important, willing to act upon it. "The OCA has a core of supporters that is discrete, well-organized and well-disciplined," says Oregon State University political science professor Bill Lunch. "That's a function of the grassroots work that Mabon has done, and it's a very important component of his success. These folks have a core of supporters who, with a few exceptions, march to the polls and vote as instructed."

Among the religious groups that have expressed opposition to Measure 9 are the Roman Catholic archdiocese of Portland, the Episcopal diocese of Oregon, the United Church of Christ, the Oregon synod of the Evangelical Lutheran Church, and the Jewish Federation of Portland. Most of the state's politicians oppose the measure, as do business leaders, who fear that if the initiative passes, corporations will think twice before relocating or expanding in Oregon.

Despite the opposition, the OCA has been able to put together a high-profile, well-funded campaign. Peter Steinberger, a political scientist at Reed College in Portland, says that part of the reason for the OCA's success is the decline of the political party system across the nation. "The party system in the United States has been substantially weakened," he says. "That allows for more factional politics. In turn, that encourages the use of initiatives and referendums. There's no party structure to go through, so they go directly to voters."

"The OCA is not going away," says Kathleen Saadat, a former state affirmative-action director who is a member of the No on 9 Campaign's steering committee. Even if Measure 9 is defeated, she says, the OCA "will lie low for a while and come back in another form. We'd better be doing something to build a community and coalitions regardless of whether this passes or fails."

But Red Wing is not optimistic. "I hope people will understand that we need to create a permanent coalition, but they probably won't," she says. Many gays and lesbians are already involved with other civil rights and activist groups, she says, but they are not open about their sexual orientation. "They may be players, but they're not playing on the lavender team," she says.

Younger activists, who Red Wing and others say have found their voice in the campaign against Measure 9, may break out of that pattern. "Measure 9 has galvanized a whole new generation that will be unrelenting in the protection of the rights of gay and lesbian people," says the MCC's Wilson.

But it is a commitment that was dearly purchased. "We have young people in the community who had no idea what life was like before Stonewall," Wilson says. "Now they know. But it grieves me that they had to learn the lesson."

—JOHN GALLAGHER

A HEAVY TOLL ON COLORADO

Like their counterparts in Oregon, gay and lesbian activists in Colorado also fought an initiative designed to prevent lawmakers from banning antigay discrimination. Like the OCA, Colorado for Family Values (CFV), the right-wing group that sponsored the initiative, argued that bias bans are actually undeserved special privileges. And like the OCA, CFV repeatedly linked homosexuality to child abuse and other social ills.

As in the case in Oregon, the fight against Amendment 2 took a toll on Colorado's gay and lesbian community. Despite their best efforts to fight the reactionary measure, on November 3 voters approved the initiative by 53 percent. Furthermore, political analysts warned that similar measures could be on the ballot in more than thirty-five states in the next few years.

LARRY KRAMER

Larry Kramer is as famous for his wrath as for his writing. Kramer, author of the hit plays *The Destiny of Me* and *The Normal Heart,* the novel *Faggots,* and the Academy Award–nominated screenplay of *Women in Love,* has, since the early eighties, been the voice of articulate rage, railing against government indifference to the AIDS epidemic and what he saw as apathy in the gay community. Moreover, Kramer channeled his anger into action, helping to found two AIDS organizations that would eventually become among the most important in the country, Gay Men's Health Crisis (GMHC) and the AIDS Coalition to Unleash Power (ACT UP).

Kramer had been hedging on whether he'd sit for an *Advocate* interview. Finally consenting, he spoke from his antique-filled five-thousand-square-foot home in East Hampton, New York, accompanied by Molly, his wheaten terrier.

Why haven't our representatives in Washington, D.C., been able to get the powers that be to start a Manhattan Project for AIDS?

One reason—and it literally made me ill when I was living in Washington last year—was the inordinate number of gay people, men and women, who live and work for the government and who are utterly and totally useless to us as brothers and sisters looking after our interests. The one thing I have been preaching longer than AIDS activism has been our representation in Washington—25 million of us are represented in Washington by no one. We are represented by an invisible leadership, by a group of people who are all incompetent. It makes you wonder where gay identity is, where the gay community is, where gay anything in this country is. We have a death wish, and it's being rapidly acted out.

Of course, you've been saying that since you wrote *Faggots* in 1979. Has nothing changed?

I don't think things have changed much at all.

Is this death wish based on internalized homophobia—the message we get from day one that we are less than others?

That's part of it, but you can't use it as an excuse. Or if you continue to use it as an excuse, then you are indeed going to die. Everybody is unhappy one way or another, every human being on the face of the Earth. There is discrimination of all kinds. It's much easier to be a gay person in America than a black person. We have more money at our disposal probably than any population.

Only some of us are rich.

Every society has a royalty, the rich people everybody looks up to. We have the only society where the royalty we have refuses to be royalty.... *Faggots* is about people who should have been leaders but refused to be leaders.

What is required is that the really rich gays have to plunk down a million dollars apiece and form another organization, with a headquarters in Washing-

Eating our own

"I have lost patience with this community's determined descent into a cannibalistic frenzy which rips its leaders to shreds in the name of 'holding each other accountable.'"
—Cynthia Scott, editor of *Equal Time,* the largest-circulation lesbian and gay newspaper in Minneapolis–St. Paul

"I think the community's ambivalence and distrust and trashing and cannibalizing of leaders are, I would go so far as to say, our most shameful attribute."
—Torie Osborn, former executive director of the Los Angeles Gay and Lesbian Community Services Center

"We need to bring together the broken bones of our own body politic. We need to celebrate our differences, hold on to what is common to our experience, and fight together on many fronts. We have no choice. As individuals and a movement, we coalesce and heal the fracture or we die."
—Carmen Vazquez, coordinator of lesbian and gay health services for the San Francisco Department of Public Health

ton, D.C., to be staffed by the best full-time professionals, both lobbyists and executive directors, that money can buy.

Not everybody is Larry Kramer. Can't you have compassion for others?

You're making me angry. It's not about compassion. It's about standards and responsibility. I hold myself to high standards, and if you want my respect, you have to hold yourself to high standards, too. And you're right. There aren't many people I respect.

The high standards come if you realize the increasingly large number of people who are facing death. We simply don't have any minutes to waste. And again, I come back to this question of urgency. There simply is no urgency at any—repeat *any,* repeat *any*—of our AIDS or gay organizations. I don't think I'm being angry enough. I look upon the last twelve years of my life as almost wasted. We are nowhere in this fight against AIDS.

Granted, but again: Why must you be so personal in your criticism?

I simply have no tolerance for mediocrity or the second-rate or the tenth-rate. Quite frankly, I think gay people are better than other people, and we should have better representation.

But these comments of yours seem almost calculated to hurt.

Why should we have special rules of politeness for gay people? When the head of the United Way or General Motors gets caught doing a shitty job, he's replaced. And you try to choose better people next time. We never seem to get those better people.

But gay people are winning unparalleled acceptance today.

But again I say that these are all small incremental things that historically would have happened anyway. The plague should make things happen faster, bigger, better....There is not a gay organization in this country that has ever been able to get a membership list of more than 20,000 to 25,000 paid members out of 25 million people.

I have tried every trick in my arsenal, from inspiration to doom, and I have not found that any of them works particularly better than any other to get our precious community off its respected lazy asses. I've tried them all, but I still am hopeful. You couldn't live today if you weren't hopeful.

You criticize others so easily. But in *The Destiny of Me,* you also blame Larry Kramer: his childhood, his upbringing, the way his father mistreated him, his difficulty in loving and receiving love.

I've spent most of my life wanting very much to be in love and not being successful at it. And in *Faggots* and *The Destiny of Me* and even *The Normal Heart,* I've tried to find answers to why that might be. But I also hope, as every writer hopes, that the story is more universal....I think it's hard for everybody to find love, but I think that for gay people it's harder than anybody.

Why is it so hard for us to find love?

Well, there's a speech in the play where Ned lists all the things in our lives that conspire against us: "Your parents, your religion, your city, your state, your federal government, your newspaper, your television, your radio, your friends, your family, your neighbors tell you over and over and over again that what we feel and think and do is sick." It's pretty hard to rise above that and say, "I'm worthy of love." But then, I'm fifty-seven years old and HIV-positive. And I just hope that the younger generation of kids now coming out will not be so physically damaged. Once you have not received the essential love that is required in your formative years, I don't think you can ever find it. And that's sad and perhaps even tragic.

—Victor Zonana

IN THE DARK ABOUT AIDS

As Larry Kramer and other activists on the front lines of the health crisis continued to point out, few significant advances in the battle against AIDS were made during the decade since the deadly virus became first known. If anything, the social problems and personal pain brought on by the epidemic grew to almost unmanageable proportions. In regular alternating columns written by Dr. Larry Waites and Project Inform's Martin Delaney, The Advocate kept its readers informed about HIV treatment and promising new therapies. Elsewhere in its pages, the magazine ran extensive feature articles dealing with the plague's far-ranging toll—from the decimation of America's creative community to the fear and loathing faced at home and around the world.

A prison where inmates who have been infected with HIV have specially colored plates and cutlery.

Censorship of safer-sex educational materials for being too explicit or for "promoting" homosexuality.

Forced isolation of people who test positive for antibodies to HIV.

Sound like a roundup of the worst policies toward AIDS in the developing world? It is not. The prison is in Great Britain, the safer-sex materials are in Australia and Finland, and the quarantine is in Sweden and the United States.

Accustomed to equating human rights violations with Third World nations, the media have focused their attention on developing countries with reprehensible policies toward people with HIV, the virus believed to lead to AIDS. Disappearances of HIV-infected people in Latin America, quarantine camps in Cuba, the imprisonment of people with AIDS in India—these are stories we have sadly come to expect.

But developing nations do not have a corner on the discrimination market. Throughout the industrialized world, government officials and corporations have implemented policies that allow or even encourage breaches of confidentiality, inadequate health care, and other violations of the rights of people with HIV.

Since the first publicity about AIDS, activists and experts throughout the industrialized world have looked to the United States for clues to the future of the epidemic in their own countries. In the United States "there are more cases, and they started earlier," explains Aart Hendriks, a Dutch activist and author of the book *AIDS and Human Rights: An International Perspective*.

In theory, then, by studying the U.S. epidemic, other nations would have a chance to stem the tide of AIDS by instituting a massive prevention effort. But in practice many countries throw up roadblocks to effective AIDS education. Whether prevented from designing such campaigns by insidious homophobia or by homophobic laws, these countries are following the sad example of the United States: All the AIDS education literature produced by the federal Centers for Disease Control since the beginning of the epidemic fits in a large manila envelope—and none of it contains explicit safer-sex information.

If the world community is ever going to stop AIDS, the industrialized world, including the United States, will have to put its own house in order. "We are living in the era of the global community, where countries have moved beyond borders," says Robin Gorna, a British activist who works as an AIDS policy consultant to the European Community. "The developed nations have to realize that what hurts people with HIV in their own country fouls the environment for people with HIV all over the world." —JOHN GALLAGHER

LIVES ON THE EDGE

Today's economic recession has resulted in deep cuts in subsidized health-care, housing, and drug treatment programs, to the point where homelessness and HIV have become inextricably linked. Nationally, an estimated three million Americans are homeless, according to a recent study by the National Coalition for the Homeless (NCH). In New York the estimate is ninety thousand people homeless, of whom ten thousand to twenty thousand are HIV-positive.

The majority of homeless people with AIDS are African-American or Hispanic, including a "disproportionate number of gay men and lesbians," according to Charles King, a principal author of the NCH study. Among homeless people with AIDS and HIV, an increasing number are youths and orphaned children of parents who died of AIDS-related complications.

"If you come into the shelter and you're gay and you're black and you're cute, that's three strikes against you already," says thirty-year-old Wayne, who is all three and living with HIV. "You tell them you're HIV-positive—and you're definitely out of the game. That's four strikes. You're really going to have a rough time. They're going to be wearing rubber gloves and whispering and trying to do everything they can to make your life uncomfortable."

Wayne witnessed beatings and stabbings and a gang rape in a shelter bathroom and was constantly threatened. "It's very violent," he says. "It's a terrible situation." Wayne hooked up with the NCH, which filed a lawsuit against the city and won him both services and a room in one of New York's infamous single-room-occupancy (SRO) hotels.

But for twenty-year-old Michael Links, who's HIV-positive and white, life in an SRO hotel is still difficult. "Even though I'm living in a welfare hotel now, I'm still living on the streets. I'm still homeless," he says, spreading his hands out to touch both walls of his tiny room on West 95th Street. "I see a lot of people out there who don't know they have HIV—people who I know are dying."

In the SROs, Links says, "it's like, everybody's gay—really, it's all homosexual or bisexual." On the streets, among prostitutes, he adds, "I know a lot of lesbians who are homeless. They may have sex with men, for the drugs or whatever, but they're lesbians." Links says that condoms were hard to find in the shelters, while among gay and lesbian prostitutes, "the condoms are out there, but people will pay you not to use one." Links and Wayne are slowly pulling themselves out of homelessness and dealing with their HIV status. But many people, like Su Pastrana, are still caught in the cycle. A forty-five-year-old heterosexual woman, Pastrana has been living on the edge for years. An IV-drug user, she is HIV-positive, as is her current partner. Living under the Manhattan Bridge in a tiny hut made of scraps "really sucks," Pastrana says. "Nobody talks about AIDS. I don't really like to think about it. I got it, he's got it. What am I going to do?"

What Pastrana does want to talk about is the needle-exchange committee of ACT UP, which visits her shanty every Saturday. "They're the only ones who care," she says. Gripping a thin housecoat around her, her slippers stepping between the refuse, Pastrana drops a half-dozen used needles into a bucket and gets the same number of fresh ones. "I could use twice that many," she admits, shivering badly. For her, having a place in the shanty and helping others use clean needles is a step. "One day at a time," she says. "That's all I can do to survive." She shrugs, then slips back inside the darkened hut, seeking refuge from the subzero winds.

—ANNE-CHRISTINE D'ADESKY

THE GREAT AMERICAN INSURANCE SCAM

Many Americans are living in fear, and the wolf howling at the door is the insurance industry. AIDS claims are being denied, policies are being canceled, and whole industries are being redlined.

The crisis is clearly deepening. Thirty-seven million people nationwide are now without health insurance, and thousands of homeless people with AIDS are on the streets of New York City, not to mention those in equally dire straits in other American cities. Gay men are obviously not alone in the midst of this health crisis, but they are being singled out by a monstrously rich industry whose gross revenues were a whopping $217 billion in 1990. And although AIDS health-care claims account for a mere 4 percent of private health-care claims in America, the industry is running scared.

"When it comes to providing health insurance, discrimination against people with AIDS is widespread," says Representative Henry Waxman (D–Calif.), Congress's most prominent AIDS health-care advocate. "Private insurers routinely screen AIDS cases and routinely put profits before health care."

"The anti-AIDS and antigay behavior on the part of private insurance companies is contributing to unnecessary suffering and unnecessary costs," says Representative Martin Russo (D–Ill.), author of a national health care plan that abolishes private insurance. "It's time for reform."

—DOUG SADOWNICK

K. D. LANG

It's a cool, threateningly damp May day in London, the kind that forces sensible visitors into museums, theaters, and department stores. But k. d. lang, who in a gesture of pure country-bred gallantry has just fetched me from my hotel room, wants to walk, likes to walk in fact, so we detour off the diesel-fumed clog of the hotel's high street and look for a place to talk. The neighborhood that greets us is redolent with culinary aromas—Indian, Italian, French. Outside a window packed with pastries, lang says that it is just such signs of cultural diversity that she so likes about the city. More and more, a cross-section of London likes her back.

On our side of the Atlantic, it's difficult to fathom anyone not liking the thirty-year-old singer, from the start. To be sure, she has had detractors, mostly country-radio kingpins who were confused by her richly androgynous appearance, and beef-industry big shots who were outraged by her forthright vegetarianism. But for the rest of us, one encounter with her generous alto—which matched Roy Orbison's on "Crying," when she crooned mightily on "Constant Craving," her new single from the album *Ingenue*—was sufficient to instill belief. The girl who grew up in tiny Consort, Canada, in the province of Alberta, and who now keeps a farm near Vancouver and a house in the Hollywood Hills, has always sung out proudly.

Offstage, it's been a somewhat different matter. Consistently, lang has been reticent about certain subjects, her sexuality in particular. She just assumed that we all got it, and when she was asked questions about it, her responses ranged from deflective firmness to deflective irony. She became considerably more revealing when we sat down at a nondescript café for our interview.

What about your androgyny?

It's just my natural response to how I fit in society—how I feel comfortable, how I feel confident. If I had to wear high heels and a dress, I would be a mental case.

Do you get tired of people pointing up the fact that your concerts attract a lot of women?

What can I say about that? I'm offering women something they don't have a lot of: a strong example, something that's geared more to women's feelings. But no one ever says, "Why, at football games, is it ninety percent men?" It's another example of how women are constantly scrutinized for having any sort of bond. I mean, who cares if they're lesbians? There's a lot of straight women at my show. I am a feminist. I don't care if the women I reach are lesbians or not. I don't even care if men come. Music transcends. But women have to realize that we're different, and we have to find some way of making that difference known inside ourselves.

What differences are important to bring out?

Let's go to the anatomy here, the basic differences in orgasms: Men's seem to be very local, very about "out"—you know. Women's are very internal, very all-encompassing. A woman's is more oriented toward birth and about the cycle. It's two different—real different—functions. Which is great I mean, obviously, it's the way of nature. But I just think that women have a different spirituality than men. We share the same emotions basically, but social structures always have been set up by men. Almost always. Even Tampax is made by men.

What about the political part of it?

Well, the fact that anyone could say that AIDS is God's way of paying back homosexuals is really disturbing. If that's true, then lesbians are angels.

I'm always pleased to see the degree to which you play with your sexuality onstage. The other night, for example, the way you made fun of speculation in the press about your sexual orientation.

Well, I do use that onstage. It's really a hard thing to talk about. I don't want to be out like Phranc is out.

Why not?

Because that's not *the* thing to me. I don't feel political about my preference. I just don't. I'm sorry! I'm sorry to disappoint you hardcores, but I don't! I think as a human being we all feel discrimination at some time, we all feel oppression. There should be strong examples in the subculture, and I think there should be people fighting for our rights. But I don't feel like it's my passion. I feel like it's a part of my life, my sexuality, but it's not—it certainly isn't my cause. But I also have never denied it. I don't try to hide it like some people in the industry do.

I think the danger for you is that there's going to be a point at which you just don't want to hedge anymore and you say, "Let me come out and then go on with my life as an artist."

Well, I think I'm at that point.

You are?

I don't want it to be a big deal. I don't because I agree with you totally—there's a point where you just go, "Okay, enough." I think everyone knows. The people who like me, like me for my music. And that's the way I want to keep it. I have to say something else. I don't want to say the wrong things to the gay culture. Because there are so many different opinions on how to gain acceptance and how to just live normal lives. And we're fighting amongst ourselves. I struggle, too, with all the answers and all the questions. And I don't want to hurt my mother by coming out in the press. But at the same time I don't want to hurt my culture, and it's like—what do you do?

But your mother must know that you're a lesbian.

Oh, yeah, she does. I came out to her thirteen years ago.

Has your mother ever said to you, "Please, k.d., don't come out…"?

Yes.

Success has to have made some of this mother stuff easier.

Success has alleviated a lot of judgmental pressure. There's no question.

It sounds like your mother must be pretty proud of the success that you have achieved.

She is. Yeah. And I think my mother's proud of me for being an individual and being brave enough to talk about it. —BRENDAN LEMON

"It is not enough to tell us that one was a brilliant poet, scientist, educator, or rebel. Whom did he love? I can't become a whole man on watered-down versions of Black life in America. I need the ass-splitting truth to be told."
—ESSEX HEMPHILL, AFRICAN-AMERICAN GAY POET, talking about the thrust of his new book, *Ceremonies*

"It's all right to be whoever and whatever you are. If you're a screaming queen, then so be it. You could never get me to imitate those big old butch boys. It's too bizarre to even consider. Take me as I am or simply move on."
—ALEXANDER BARD, OF THE SWEDISH TECHNO-DANCE BAND ARMY OF LOVERS

Some kisses rouse sleeping beauties from a dreamlike slumber. Such a kiss is what happened for David Drake, who dramatized his political awakening in a hit off-Broadway show, *The Night Larry Kramer Kissed Me*. The actor-singer-dancer wove pivotal moments from his life into tales of a gay everyman. Drake used the slap-in-the-face experience of seeing Kramer's AIDS drama *The Normal Heart* as the galvanizing force to wake up from denial. "Larry gave us the permission to be angry," says Drake, whose one-man show spoke well for the newly politicized queer generation.

Theatergoers eagerly turned out for Tony Kushner's *Angels in America,* which opened in Los Angeles in late 1992 prior to its Broadway run. Subtitled *A Gay Fantasia on National Themes,* the epic-scaled work mixed gay relationships, AIDS, Roy Cohn, Mormonism, and the Reagan-damaged eighties into an evening that enthralled critics and audiences alike. "It's certainly about being gay, and it's certainly about the epidemic, but it's about a lot more than that," said Kushner about his play, which went on the following spring to win the Tony Award for Best Play and the Pulitzer Prize for Drama.

Director Gregg Araki emerged as the bad boy of gay film with *The Living End,* a stark tale of two HIV-positive lovers on the run. The widely distributed independent feature was dedicated to "the hundreds of thousands who've died and the hundreds of thousands more who will die because of a big white house full of Republican fuckheads," said Araki.

BOOKS: *BECOMING A MAN*

The word "fluid" is so often applied by literary critics with nothing in particular to say that the term is a cliché even when aptly applied, as it is to the writings of Paul Monette. Not that his prose isn't mellifluous; it is elegant, eloquent, even mercurial, flowing at its best on a narrative drive as subtle as a tide.

Paul Monette (*left*) and his life partner Winston Wilde enjoying a tender moment.

And now there is *Becoming a Man*, a deep, clear lake of recollection as tranquil on its surface as it is intensely passionate in the subterranean rills that feed it. Subtitled "Half a Life Story," it is an autobiography saturated with ironies. The title itself refers to what would clearly be a cheeky mid-career look back in self-anger were it not that Monette, at forty-six, is likely well past his halfway point. His T-cell count was one hundred when he wrote the book; it's twenty now. The poet, novelist, memoirist, screenwriter, and activist received his AIDS diagnosis on December 13, 1991, while writing out his Christmas cards.

Becoming a Man has captured the interest of readers and critics alike. The book has been at the top of gay best-seller lists for months; in November, it earned the National Book Award. Acknowledging that AIDS has fueled his creative juices, Monette is nevertheless acidly sanguine: "I'd rather be writing glib novels than going through the holocaust."

The spine of *Becoming a Man* is simple: It's a coming-out story, in essence, although it is better called a "having-come-out story." Tellingly, Monette "becomes a man" by jettisoning half-truths—and downright lies—about masculinity and homosexuality. In short, by claiming himself. "You do see a self being born," Monette allows, "even if it can't do gay right."

These days Monette is clearly "doing gay" right, although "doing queer" is closer to it. "My writing is inextricably bound up with my being gay," says the writer. "That's what I wanted to explore. I know that *Becoming a Man* goes over the years in which I was paralyzed, but thank God I'm gay. I wouldn't be much of a writer otherwise."

Surprisingly, *Becoming a Man* betrays almost no panic, no hysteria. It does not appear to have been written in the shadow of an executioner's noose. "That may be one of the good kinds of denial," Monette says thoughtfully. "I remember saying to Stephen [Kolzak, a lover] a few months before he died of AIDS that I can be as angry as I am at this pig-shit country and all the things that are done to us...and yet I'm happy," he adds. "I was happy with Stephen, and now I'm happy with Winston [Wilde]. I don't want to put out the message that the *only* way to live happily is to live in love, but that's how it's been for me, and it all starts with coming out." —MICHAEL LASSELL

CONTRIBUTORS

Paula Gunn Allen, a widely published poet, writer, and anthologist, is a professor of English at the University of California, Los Angeles. Her most recent work is *The Voice of the Turtle: American Indian Narratives, 1900–1970.*

Allan Bérubé is the author of the award-winning book *Coming Out Under Fire: The History of Gay Men and Women in World War Two.* A community-based historian, he is currently working on a documentary film for television based on his book.

Betty Berzon is a Los Angeles activist and psychotherapist, specializing in work with lesbians and gay men since 1972. She is the author of *Permanent Partners: Building Gay and Lesbian Relationships That Last* and the editor of *Positively Gay.*

Malcolm Boyd, author, activist, and Episcopal priest, has written twenty-five books, including *Take Off the Masks, Gay Priest, Look Back in Joy, Rich with Years,* and the national best-seller *Are You Running with Me, Jesus?* He is chaplain of the AIDS Commission of the Episcopal Diocese of Los Angeles.

Michael Bronski is the author of *Culture Clash: The Making of a Gay Sensibility.* His essays have appeared in over fifteen anthologies, including *Hometowns, A Member of the Family, Gay Spirit,* and *Flesh and the Word II.* He has written about culture and sexuality for *The Village Voice, Fag Rag, Gay Community News,* and *Radical America,* as well as many other periodicals. He has been a gay activist for twenty-five years.

Pat Califia's advice column has appeared in the classifieds section of *The Advocate* for more than ten years. Her most recent book is the erotic short-story collection *Melting Point.* A compilation of her essays, *Demonology: The Politics of Radical Sex,* is forthcoming.

Cheryl Clarke is the author of four books of poetry: *Narratives: Poems in the Tradition of Black Women, Living as a Lesbian, Humid Pitch,* and *Experimental Love.* She was an editor of *Conditions,* a magazine of writing by women, from 1981 to 1990. Her poetry has most recently appeared in *A Piece of My Heart: A Lesbians of Color Anthology, Inversions: Writing by Dykes, Queers, and Lesbians,* and *Persistent Desire: A Femme-Butch Reader.*

Robert Dawidoff is the author of *The Genteel Tradition and the Sacred Rage: High Culture vs. Democracy in Adams, James and Santayana,* and, with Michael Nava, *Created Equal: Why Gay Rights Matter to America.* He has written extensively on lesbian and gay civil rights, culture, and history. He is a professor of history at the Claremont Graduate School and lives in West Hollywood.

Martin Duberman, historian and playwright, is the author of fifteen books, including *Paul Robeson, Cures: A Gay Man's Odyssey, Stonewall,* and (as co-editor) the Lambda Award–winning *Hidden from History.* He is currently Distinguished Professor of History at Lehman College and the City University of New York Graduate Center, and founder and director of the Center for Lesbian and Gay Studies (CLAGS) at CUNY.

Lillian Faderman is the author of *Surpassing the Love of Men: Romantic Friendship and Love Between Women from the Renaissance to the Present* and *Odd Girls and Twilight Lovers: A History of Lesbian Life in 20th-Century America.* Her book *Scotch Verdict,* a study of the trial on which Lillian Hellman based *The Children's Hour,* has just been reissued by Columbia University Press.

Masha Gessen (contributing editor), who grew up in Moscow, is a journalist and activist who served as *The Advocate*'s associate editor for national and international news features in 1991 and 1992. She has written for a variety of newspapers and magazines in both the United States and Russia.

Karla Jay teaches English and women's studies at Pace University. She has written, edited, or translated seven books, the most recent of which is *Lesbian Texts and Contexts: Radical Revisions*. Her first anthology, *Out of the Closets: Voices of Gay Liberation* (coedited with Allen Young), was reissued in 1992 for its twentieth anniversary by New York University Press.

Arnie Kantrowitz is an associate professor of English at the College of Staten Island, City University of New York. He is the author of *Under the Rainbow: Growing Up Gay*, an autobiography. His essays, poems, and stories have appeared in *The New York Times*, *The Village Voice*, and numerous gay publications and anthologies. He lives in New York City with his lover, Lawrence Mass.

Jim Kepner, a Los Angeles gay activist for fifty years who has worked with scores of organizations and publications, has taught gay studies since 1956. His collection of gay materials, begun in San Francisco in 1942, grew into the International Gay and Lesbian Archives. The archives are now housed in Los Angeles and Kepner remains their curator. He has completed two books, *Loves of a Long-time Activist* and *Gay Spirit Rising*.

Sasha Lewis, a former associate editor of *The Advocate*, continues her writing career and is currently expanding it into the field of multimedia productions. Having authored five published nonfiction books, including *Sunday's Woman* and *Lesbian Life Today*, she recently completed her first novel, *The Motherland*.

Lawrence D. Mass, M.D., is a cofounder of Gay Men's Health Crisis and the author of *Dialogues of the Sexual Revolution*, volumes I and II. He is a medical director of the Greenwich House substance-abuse treatment programs in New York City.

Joan Nestle is cofounder of the Lesbian Herstory Archives, author of *A Restricted Country,* coeditor of the *Women on Women* series, and editor of *The Persistent Desire: A Femme-Butch Reader.* She is currently working on an anthology with John Preston, *Sisters/Brothers,* exploring the relationships between lesbians and gay men. For the last twenty-four years, she has been a teacher of writing in the SEEK Program, Queens College, City University of New York, where she taught the first course in gay and lesbian literature.

Felice Picano is a poet, playwright, and screenwriter, and the author of fourteen books, including novels, short stories, and the memoirs *Ambidextrous* and *Men Who Loved Me.* Coauthor with Charles Silverstein, M.D., of *The New Joy of Gay Sex,* he's a member of the legendary Violet Quill Club. Picano founded SeaHorse Press, and cofounded Gay Presses of New York and the Publishing Triangle.

John Preston has pursued a career as a writer and editor since he was the editor of *The Advocate* in 1975. He is best known for his erotica and an award-winning series of anthologies on gay male life. He lives in Portland, Maine.

Richard Rouilard is senior editorial consultant at the *Los Angeles Times.* He is the former editor-in-chief of *The Advocate,* and a former senior editor of the *Los Angeles Herald Examiner.* Rouilard was nominated for a Pulitzer Prize for his coverage of the 1988 Democratic and Republican national conventions.

Jack Nichols, currently vice president of the Brevard County chapter of the ACLU, lives on the ocean in Cocoa Beach, Florida. He is the author of *Men's Liberation* and *Welcome to Fire Island,* and is now completing his memoirs, which look back on a long lifetime of activism and romance.

Torie Osborn, former executive director of the National Gay and Lesbian Task Force and the Los Angeles Gay and Lesbian Community Services Center, is a writer and "movement management consultant" with an M.B.A. in finance and marketing and over twenty-five years' experience in the gay and lesbian, women's, civil rights, and anti–Vietnam War movements. She is a regular columnist for *The Advocate* and is currently working on her first book, *Coming Home to America: A Manifesto for the Gay 90s.*

James M. Saslow is an associate professor of art at Queens College, City University of New York, and the author of *The Poetry of Michelangelo: An Annotated Translation* and *Ganymede in the Renaissance: Homosexuality in Art and Society.* A veteran of gay journalism since the founding days of Boston's *Gay Community News,* he served as New York editor of *The Advocate* from 1978 to 1985.

Randy Shilts was the national correspondent for the *San Francisco Chronicle,* and the author of three books that have won international acclaim: *The Mayor of Castro Street: The Life and Times of Harvey Milk, And the Band Played On: Politics, People, and the AIDS Epidemic,* and *Conduct Unbecoming: Lesbians and Gay Men in the U.S. Military.* His commentaries have appeared in *The New York Times, Los Angeles Times, Newsweek, Sports Illustrated, Esquire, The Washington Post,* and other publications. He died of complications due to AIDS February 17, 1994.

Mark Thompson (editor) was a cofounder of the Gay Students Coalition at San Francisco State University in 1973 and has worked for gay and feminist causes since that time. He began his career with *The Advocate* in 1975, writing about gay culture and politics in Europe, and has served the newsmagazine during the past two decades in various capacities—as a journalist, photographer, contributing editor, art director, and, currently, as senior editor. His 1987 book, *Gay Spirit: Myth and Meaning,* has been widely acclaimed. Thompson has also edited *Leatherfolk: Radical Sex, People, Politics, and Practice* and has contributed essays to *Hometowns, Positively Gay,* and other publications about gay life.

Stuart Timmons has written about gay culture, past and present, for more than a decade. His 1990 biography, *The Trouble with Harry Hay: Founder of the Modern Gay Movement,* traces eighty years of American radicalism. He also writes fiction.

Urvashi Vaid is a community organizer and writer based in Provincetown, Massachusetts. She is author of a forthcoming book on gay and lesbian politics, *Margin to Center: The Mainstreaming of Gay and Lesbian Liberation.* Vaid is former executive director and public information director of the National Gay and Lesbian Task Force (1986–1992), and was a staff attorney with the ACLU's National Prison Project.

Index

Holobaugh, James, 359
Holy Cross Cathedral (Boston), protest at, 379
Homeless people with AIDS, 401
Homophile Action League, 18, 19
Homophile League of Holyoke (Mass), 69 Homophile Stu dents League (Columbia), 2, 103
Homophobia, 85, 104, 147, **176,** 199, 263, 311, 361
  and AIDS, 289, 292, 327, 329, 343, 378, 393, 400
  and education, 327
  and the radical left, 67
  and the radical right, 83, 100, 116, 163, 171
  as a term, 66
  See also Discrimination; Fundamentalist Christians
"Homosapien" (Shelley), 230
Homosexual: Oppression and Libera- tion (Altman), 49-50
Homosexual Bill of Rights (NACHO), 3
Homosexual Freedom, Committee for (S.F.), 22, 63
Homosexual Information Center (HIC/L.A.), 22, 56
Homosexual Liberation Front of Andalusia (Spain), 214
Homosexualities (Kinsey Institute), 164
Homosexuality and the Law (Knut- son), 212
Homosexuality Test, 10
"Homosexuals in New York: The Gay World" *(New York Times),* 99
"Homosexuals in Revolt" *(Life),* 68
Homosexuals Intransigent (NYC), 37
Hongisto, Richard, 53, 394
Hooker, Dr. Evelyn, 22, 51, **69**
Hoover, J. Edgar, 66, 67
Hope, Bob, 164
Hopewell, Fred Holub, 381
Horanzy, Don, 167
Hosmer, Harriet, 239
Hougen, Rev. Edward T., 117
Household Finance Corporation, GAA zap at, 50
Houston (Tex.), gay and lesbian community, 277, 278, 358
Houston KS/AIDS foundation, 278
Houston Post and gays, 358
"How Gay Is Gay?" *(Time* maga- zine), 197
Howard Brown Clinic (Chicago), 138
HTLV-3, 263, 277, 278, 279, 289
Hudson, John Paul. *See* Hunter, John Francis
Hudson, Rock, 153, **153,** 274, **274,** 279, 280, 287, 309, 348, 366
Hughes, Holly, 373
Hughes, Langston, 354
Human Rights Campaign Fund (PAC/Wash.,D.C.), *xxiv,* 196, 199, 310, 318, 387, 392
Humanistic Psychology, Association for, 148
Humm, Andy, 276, 311, 319
Humphrey, Hubert H., 75
Humphreys, Laud, 43
Hunter, John Francis, 66

Hunter, Tab, 154
Hurt, John, 191
Hustlers and callboys, 44, 69, 84, 197, 215, 291, 309, 344, 345, 359, 388, 394
Huston, John, 45
Hutchins, Loraine, 387
Hypothalamus glands and homosex- uality, 378

I Am a Camera (Van Druten), 303
I Have More Fun with You Than Anybody (Clarke/Nichols), 66
Ice Palace disco (Fire Island), 66
Idaho, gay & lesbian community, 50
Illinois, gay & lesbian community, 21, 147
  See also Champaign; Chicago; Urbana
Imagine My Surprise (Near), 133
Immigration and gays, 2, 51, 101, 117, 132, 180, 197, 199, 215, 261, 291, 345
Importance of Being Earnest, The (Wilde), 339
In God We Trust, 213
In the Life (anthology), 352
"In the Upper Room" (Woods), 352
Inaudi, Jorge, 393
Independence Hall (Philadelphia), demonstrations at, 18, 21
Indiana, gay & lesbian community, 117
Individual Rights, Association for the Protection of (Israel), 131
Ingenue (lang), 402
Inner Circle/Hilton Hotel, GAA zap at, 68
Inouye, Daniel, 215
Integrity, Inc. (gay Episcopalians), 117, 207
Internal Revenue Service (IRS), 20, 21, 148, 344
International AIDS Conference, 344, 357, 359, **360**
International Balloon Festival, 345
International Congress on AIDS, 395
International Gay Association (IGA), 164, 231, 279
International Lesbian and Gay Association, 375-76, 377, 378, 394
International Symposium on Educa- tion and Communication About AIDS, 329
International Union of Gay Athletes, 148
International Whores Convention (Brussels), 293
International Women's Year, 149, 171
Iosti, Richard, 367
Iran, execution of gays, 359
Ireland, Doug, 181
Ireland, Patricia, 379
Irish Lesbian and Gay Organization, 376, 377
Ironman magazine, 347
Irons, Jeremy, 228
Isaacson, Madeline, 122
Isherwood, Christopher, *xvii, xxiii,* 15, 34, 36, 120-21, **120, 121,** 303
Isle of Man, antigay laws of, 377, 393
Israel, gay & lesbian community, 99,

131
It Is Not the Homosexual Who Is Perverse, but the Society in Which He Lives (Praunheim), 49
Italy, gay & lesbian community, 67- 68
I've Heard the Mermaids Singing (film), 323, **323**
Ivory, James, 323

Jabara, Paul, 178
Jacks, George L., 9
Jackson, Don, 40, 59
Jackson, Ed, 26, 36, 42
Jackson, Henry, 132, **132**
Jackson, Jesse, 246, 261, 326, 332- 33, **332,** 394
Jackson, Michael, 244, 262
Jagger, Mick, **240,** 241, 360
James, Henry, 178, 339
Janov, Dr. Arthur, 55
Japan, gay & lesbian community, 376, 394
Jardin, Le (disco/NYC), 126
Jarvis, Howard, 165
Java, Sir Lady, 5
Jay, Karla, 81-82
JEB, 129
Jefferson, Mildred, **213**
Jenkins, Leonard, 385
Jerker (Chesley), 310, **310**
Jewett, Sarah Orne, 239
Jewish Federation (Portland, Ore.), 397
Jews (lesbian and gay male), 197, 207, 214, 376
JH Press, 228
Joachim, Jerry, **4**
John Paul II, 181, 222, 293, 311
"Johnny, Are You Queer?" (Cotton), 229
Johnson, Cary Alan, 352
Johnson, Don, 30
Johnson, Earvin "Magic," 379, **379,** 384, 393
Johnson, Joe (Miss Thing), **43, 60, 78**
Johnson, William, 67
Johnston, Jill, 93, 103
Jones, Cleve, 182, 315, 316
Jones, Dan, 163
Jones, Grace, 165
Jones, Randy, 191
Jones, Stephen L., 214
Jordan, Jamie, 59-60
Jorgensen, Christine, 200
Jovann, Empress of Hawaii, 297
Joy of Gay Sex, The (White/ Silver- stein), 234
Judell, Brandon, 269, 337
Judgment of Paris, The (Vidal), 152
Julien, Isaac, 354

Kaahuman, Lani, 387
Kalinin, Roman, 375, 376, **376**
Kamel, Rachel, 107
Kameny, Franklin E., 9, **53,** 82, 88, 104, 105-06, **105,** 107
Kansas, gay & lesbian community, 21
Kansas, University of, 52
Kantrowitz, Arnie, 49-50, **50,** 114, 130, 171, 255
Kaposi Foundation (S.F.), 235
Kaposi's sarcoma. *See under* AIDS

Katz, Jonathan Ned, 82, 130, **140,** 140-41
Kaye-Kantrowitz, Melanie, 290
Keating, Paul, 395
Kellems, Vivien, 21
Kellogg, Stuart, *xxvi*
Kempton, Murray, 66
Kennedy, Edward "Ted," 196, 215
Kennedy, Hubert, 208, **208**
Kentucky, gay & lesbian community, 392, 394
Kepner, Jim, *xviii, xviii, xx, xxi,* 3, 7, 23, 34, 42, 95
Kerns, Michael, 286-87
Kerry, Terry, 289
Kight, Morris, 34, 38, 55, **55,** 86, **87**
Kilhefner, Don, 38-39, 40, 87, 87
Killing of Sister George, The (film), 15
King, Billie Jean, 214, **214**
King, Charles, 401
King, Coretta Scott, 293
King, Dr. Martin Luther, Jr., 319, 333
Kinsey, Alfred, 102
Kinsey Institute for Sex Research, 22, 59-60, 102, 164, 204, 212
Klepfitz, Irena, 290
Knutson, Don, 212
Koch, Ed, 97, 100, 149, 181, 269, 275, 277
Koehl, Matt, 116
Kolzah, Stephen, 405
Koop, C. Everett, 291, 309, **343**
Kopay, Dave, 159
Kosinski, Jerzy, 175
Kotlowitz, Robert, 38
Kowalski, Sharon, 278, 328, 343, **343**
Kozachenko, Kathy, 99
KPFK (Calif.), Justice Department prosecution of, 310
Kramer, Larry, 45, 211, 212, 214, 228, 234, 286, 287, 342, 357, 360, 398-99, **398,** 400, 404
Kreis, Der (Zurich, Switzerland), 4
Kreuter, Dr. Marshall, 286
Kroc, Joan, 327
Krone, Michele, 319
Ku Klux Klan, 163, 171, 199, 215, 328
Kunstler, William, 52
Kushner, Tony, 404

Labelle, Patti, 126
Labonte, Richard, 339
Lachs, Stephen, 181
Ladder (lesbian magazine), 18, 69, 95, 141, 341
Lahusen, Kay, 18
Laird, John, 247
Lambda Book Report, 366
Lambda Delta Lambda (lesbian sorority), 327
Lambda Legal Defense and Educa- tion Fund, 82, 85, 377-78
Lambert, William J., III, 58
Lamble, David, 270
Lamport, Paul, 21
Lancet, The, 279
Landers, Ann, 51, 83
Lane, Alycee, 386
Lane, Bettye, photographs of, **172-73**
lang, k. d., 402-03
Langdon, Scott, 111